Behind Caesar's Back

Behind Caesar's Back

RUMOR, GOSSIP, AND THE MAKING OF THE ROMAN EMPERORS

Caillan Davenport

Yale UNIVERSITY PRESS

New Haven & London

Published with assistance from the Mary Cady Tew Memorial Fund.

Yale University Press books may be purchased in quantity for educational, business, or promotional use. For information, please e-mail sales.press@yale.edu (U.S. office) or sales@yaleup.co.uk (U.K. office).

Set in Garamond Premier Pro type by IDS Infotech, Ltd.
Printed in the United States of America.

Library of Congress Control Number: 2025938173
ISBN 978-0-300-27645-9 (hardcover)

A catalogue record for this book is available from the British Library.

Authorized Representative in the EU: Easy Access System Europe, Mustamäe tee 50, 10621 Tallinn, Estonia, gpsr.requests@easproject.com

10 9 8 7 6 5 4 3 2 1

For Meaghan

Contents

Acknowledgments

I began working on this project in early 2013, when teaching a course on the Roman empire at the University of Queensland. Engaging with both Fergus Millar's magisterial *The Emperor in the Roman World* and Keith Hopkins's review of that book, "Rules of Evidence," prompted me to start thinking about how to write a different history of Roman emperorship. I apologize to my Queensland students (and to those who took later incarnations of the course at Macquarie University and the Australian National University [ANU]) for my constant refrain: "But did it matter who the emperor was?" The original manuscript was completed in December 2021, after which I assumed a new leadership role at the ANU. This meant the process of revision slowed considerably, but it also gave me valuable time to refine and rethink ideas and arguments. During this book's long gestation period, I have benefited from the support of numerous institutions and individuals. I am grateful to the Australian Research Council for a Discovery Early Career Researcher Award (DE150101110), and to the research assistance provided by Nicola Linton and Charlotte Mann. The Alexander von Humboldt Foundation awarded me an Experienced Researcher Fellowship, which I held at the Goethe-Universität, Frankfurt am Main, generously supported by Hartmut Leppin. These funding bodies gave me precious reading and thinking time to engage with both the range of ancient sources (spanning some eight centuries) and the modern scholarship necessary to construct this book and its arguments. I would like to thank colleagues at the University of

Queensland and Macquarie University for enabling these grant applications and for allowing me to derive the full benefit from them, including spending two and a half years in Germany.

There are many people to thank for supporting funding applications, discussing my ideas, providing sparks of inspiration, and commenting on draft chapters, related articles, and the full manuscript. They are, in alphabetical order: Rhiannon Ash, Lea Beness, Alastair Blanshard, Simon Corcoran ("But what was specifically *Roman* about these stories?"), Andrew Gillett, Olivier Hekster, Tom Hillard, Ray Laurence, Hartmut Leppin, Shushma Malik, Christopher Mallan, the members of the "Social Dynamics of Imperial Imagery" project (Amy Russell, Monica Hellström, and team), and Tom Stevenson. I am very grateful to the members of the Abteilung für Alte Geschichte at Frankfurt for providing a collegial working environment during the pandemic, especially my office-mates Muriel Moser-Gerber and Marius Kalfelis, Simone Mehr, Sebastian Weinert, Alexander Weiss, and Philip Forness, who kindly advised on the translations of John of Ephesus from Syriac to English. Audiences at Macquarie University, the University of Western Australia, Warwick University, Roehampton University, Cardiff University, and the ANU offered helpful feedback and healthy skepticism in equal measure.

I owe a great debt to three referees for Yale University Press (one of whom subsequently revealed himself to be the ever-generous Noel Lenski), for writing such thoughtful and helpful reports that engaged with my ideas critically and productively. The final book is much stronger on account of their feedback. At Yale University Press, I can't thank Heather Gold enough for embracing the project so enthusiastically, providing helpful advice on its framing and argumentation, and guiding me through the publication process. I am very grateful to my copy editor, Laura Hensley, and to Elizabeth Sylvia, Chelsea Connelly, Erica Hanson, and the Yale team for their work in making this book a reality. I am likewise very appreciative of the hard work of Stefania Peterlini at the British School at Rome, who facilitated permissions that enabled access to numerous sites in Rome and Italy, including large sections of the Palatine, a visit that certainly fired my imagination. For assistance with obtaining images, I am grateful to Harriet Haugvik (Reading Museum), Markus Cottin (Domstiftsbibliothek Merseburg), Nathan Pendlebury (Liverpool World Museum), Marco Pedicini (Pedicini Fotografi), Vincenzo Saitta (Biblioteca Nazionale Vittorio Emanuele III, Naples), Johannes Wienand and Hubert Lanz (coin of Maximinus), and Georgia Pike-Rowney and Charlotte Forbes (ANU Classics Museum). I would also like to thank Ed Armstrong for proofreading the manuscript and checking references.

I would like to thank the Centre for Classical Studies team at the ANU (Tatiana Bur, Tom Geue, Simona Martorana, Meaghan McEvoy, Elizabeth Minchin, Georgia Pike-Rowney, Estelle Strazdins) for being such wonderful colleagues and enduring my leadership style without staging abusive protests in a nearby sporting venue. My parents and parents-in-law, Tony and Narelle Davenport, and Anne and Francis McEvoy, provided crucial childcare support, interest, and encouragement, and have always shown great pride in my achievements.

My greatest debt, however, is to Meaghan McEvoy, who as friend, fellow historian, traveling companion, girlfriend, fiancée, wife, and co-parent of our precious twins, Alaric and Hamish, has been a joyful presence in my life ever since she was bustled into the dining room of the British School at Rome for lunch on October 1, 2008, and made the mistake of sitting at the same table as me. It was Meaghan who taught me about the world of Late Antiquity—previously I was a Roman historian "who went up to the fourth century"—as we embarked on journeys to Santa Costanza and countless other churches and mausolea, crossed from the Villa of the Gordiani to Helena's mausoleum in the searing sun, escaped the overzealous tour guide at San Vittore in Milan, tried out Croatian auto-translation on the bus to Salona, annoyed would-be Vatican tour guides ("You won't know what you're looking at in there!"), and tested the patience of numerous museum docents (who would have thought a pregnant woman taking a sip of water would be such a problem?). Every page of this book has been influenced by conversations with Meaghan, and it has been made possible both by her historical expertise and by her endless patience, kindness, and love. This book is for you, darling.

Caillan Davenport
December 2024

Behind Caesar's Back

Introduction

TELLING TALES

Pompeii, June 64 CE. A group of boys play as they run down the Via dell'Abbondanza, barging through the crowds, hopping from stone to stone in the searing summer heat. They sing as they play. "Do the right thing, you'll be a king. If you don't, then you won't!" We follow the boys as they make their way down the street, passing the House of Aulus Trebius Valens. There, among the many painted graffiti that cover the wall in striking cursive script, is one that says, "Good fortune to the judgments of Augustus Caesar!" These acclamations are to be found all over Pompeii, especially at busy street intersections. Another, on the outside wall of an apartment building in the Ninth Region, proclaims: "Good fortune to the judgments of the Augustus, father of the fatherland, and Poppaea Augusta." The Augustus in question is the emperor Nero, who, together with his wife, Poppaea, had recently passed through Pompeii on their way to Naples. The acclamations articulated the popular sentiment that Nero was a king who had indeed done the right thing. He had granted the people of Pompeii the right to hold gladiatorial games, a privilege that had been suspended after a particularly turbulent riot a few years before.[1]

But not everyone had been happy to see Nero during his Pompeian sojourn. On the outside wall of the House of Publius Paquius Proculus (a wealthy town councilor), someone has written "Poison" and "Nero's Poison." Inside, in the vestibule of the residence, is an even more pointed graffito: "Poison is Nero's financial secretary." This scurrilous line not only associates the emperor with a murderous substance but also implies that he is guilty of arranging the deaths of the wealthy to ensure that their estates flowed to his purse. Whispers of suspicious happenings in Rome—Nero's fabulously wealthy freedman Pallas, his aunt Domitia, and his mother, Agrippina, had all died and had their property confiscated—had evidently reached Pompeii, as people talked about the emperor behind his back. "Rumor: no other evil travels more swiftly," wrote the poet Vergil. Quite what the graffiti were doing in Proculus's house is uncertain. Were they scrawled by Proculus's own political opponents as a way of criticizing the dubious, murderous types with whom he associated? Or did they allude to particularly nasty happenings during Nero's recent visit to Pompeii: perhaps he had turned his attention to the fortunes of its most prosperous residents? The idea that a king could exploit his subjects in this way would have come as no surprise to Romans who knew the fable of "The Kite and the Doves." In search of a protector, the hapless doves chose a kite as their ruler, only for him to start eating them one by one. A king could be just and generous, but, as the fable makes clear, he could also be a rapacious murderer.[2]

Four years later, Nero was dead. He committed suicide rather than fall into the hands of the praetorian guard. There were no armies marching through the Italian countryside, no battles at Rome's gates, only an emperor whose support had gradually trickled away, each new dispatch bringing the ill-tidings that senior military commanders in Gaul, Spain, and Africa had deserted his regime. As the historian Cornelius Tacitus would write several decades later, "Nero was dislodged by reports and rumors rather than by warfare." The emperor's demise was met with mixed reactions in Rome. Some ran around brandishing liberty caps as a sign of their new freedom, and within a year, a new play, *Octavia,* which purported to tell the true story of the sex and scandal in Nero's household, was being performed in the city. But others mourned the loss of their emperor, laying flowers at his tomb or placing his statues, dressed in fresh togas, on the speaker's platform. In Pompeii, there appears to have been little attempt to expunge Nero's memory by removing his name from the public record. Romans knew that regime change could be a dangerous business, as Aesop's fable "The Frogs Asked for a King" taught them: be careful if you ask for a new ruler, because you might end up with someone even worse. In subsequent decades, rumors would have Nero rising from the dead not once, but three times, foretelling his later transformation into a mysterious savior figure. These vignettes about Nero's life and afterlife in Pompeii and Rome illuminate the relationship between the Roman emperor and his subjects and, in particular, how the Roman people thought, spoke, and wrote about their rulers.[3]

Roman emperors existed from the late first century BCE to the fifteenth century CE, and many contemporary and later Eurasian leaders modeled themselves on them by taking names and titles such as "Augustus," "Imperator," "Caesar," "Kaysar," "Kaiser," or "Czar." This book covers the first eight centuries of imperial rule, from the dictatorship of Julius Caesar and the establishment of the Roman imperial monarchy under his adopted son and heir, Augustus (27 BCE–14 CE), to the reign of the emperor Heraclius (610–641 CE), which is commonly regarded as marking the end of Antiquity. The Roman world underwent several significant changes across this period. In the fourth century CE, Christianity became the imperial religion, espoused by all emperors from Constantine (306–337 CE) onward, with the exception of his recalcitrant pagan nephew, Julian (361–363 CE). The shape of Roman territory likewise changed. Expansionist conquests reached their height in the second century CE, after which defensive wars became the norm. The fifth century CE witnessed the collapse of the western empire as a coherent political unit and the refocusing of imperial rule around the eastern capital of Constantinople.[4]

At its height in the second century CE, the Roman empire was home to some sixty million people, but only a tiny fraction of the population would have seen the emperor in person (Nero was the only emperor to grace Pompeii with his presence). Still fewer would have had regular contact with the emperor, and the number of Romans who knew him personally would have been infinitesimal. But his face was everywhere, on coins, tokens, banners, standards, weights, and dessert molds, and featured in statuary, reliefs, and paintings. A soldier would march into war under the emperor's image, an enslaved person would grasp his statue in hope of gaining asylum, a judge would pronounce verdicts next to his portrait, and everyone would enjoy eating desserts bearing his face at victory celebrations (fig. 1). These images reminded Romans of the emperor's power and his function as a guarantor of peace and stability, safety and protection, law and order. But there was another, more fearsome side to the emperor: he disciplined and punished, he demanded taxes and tribute, he needed to be worshipped and propitiated—and, as the graffiti from Pompeii remind us, he could poison and pillage.[5]

The emperor was relevant to the lives of his subjects in different ways. A courtier might agonize about his most recent audience in the palace; a councilor in an earthquake-ravaged town in Asia Minor might write to the emperor in hope of obtaining financial aid; a Gallic merchant might worry about the imposition of new taxes; a woman from Thrace might petition him for a ruling on an inheritance. And all these people talked about the emperor's impact on

Fig. 1. Cake or dessert mold from Silchester, Britain, showing members of the Severan imperial family performing a sacrifice, third century CE. Reading Museum 1995.87.

their plans, hopes, and dreams. Aristocrats gathered in small groups outside the imperial palace, at their literary salons and evening dinner parties, exchanging tidbits of speculation. In taverns, barbershops, marketplaces, churches, and theaters—in short, anywhere people congregated, drank, did business, or passed the time—you could find soldiers, laborers, prostitutes, enslaved people, merchants, bakers, and money changers talking about emperors, their policies, their wars, and their taxes.

As they talked, Romans spread rumors about what the emperor had done or might do in the future, considering how whispers of an illness or a new military campaign would affect their lives. Inhabitants of the major cities swapped gossip about the emperor's sexual misadventures or his receding hairline, relieving the stresses of their day-to-day lives by puncturing the vanities of power. The dinnertime and marketplace conversations themselves are lost today, but we can still encounter them through the written record, in the form of letters, biographies, graffiti, fables, histories, songs, plays, sermons, and poems (some examples of which I have used above to illustrate popular views of Nero). This book will harvest this rich oral discourse to write a new history of Roman emperors from the perspective of their subjects. Talking about the Caesars—whether it took the form of exchanging rumors of murderous plots or swapping ribald sex stories—represented a form of political engagement beyond the world of institutional decision-making in the imperial council, courtroom, or senate house. This "everyday politics" not only reveals how Romans imagined the emperor's person and power, but also how they used speech to endorse, support, resist, or subvert imperial authority as they went about their lives.[6]

WAYS OF TALKING

Oral discourse is a fundamental part of the human social experience. It is one of the important ways in which we communicate and bond. There are a myriad of different forms of talking—speech, dialogue, chatter, discourse, conversation, debate, banter, discussion—each governed by its own social rules and expectations. I am particularly concerned with two main categories of oral discourse, rumor and gossip, because of the important role they play in revealing human mentalities and relationships. We all engage in rumor and gossip: they are the lifeblood of communities large and small, from bustling urban conurbations and corporate workplaces to small hamlets and local church groups. "Rumor" and "gossip" are often confused or used as synonyms, and although they do interact in various ways, they are distinct phenomena that arise for different reasons and often serve different social purposes.[7]

First, picture a work environment familiar to you: a law firm, a government department, a university faculty, or similar. Cast your mind back to a particular moment of stress and anxiety: the arrival of a new boss. You might have seen the manager's CV or social media profile, but this would probably not have told you anything concrete about their plans and intentions. You probably would have engaged in speculation with your colleagues about their previous employment, what plans they might have for budget and staffing, and what their vision for the company might look like: "I heard that current departments will be restructured, and spending cut in half"; "Will my project be scrapped?"; "I think she'll want to bring in new people: she only hires Ivy League, you know." In talking in this manner, you would have engaged in the generation and circulation of rumor.[8]

"Rumor" is defined as unverified or unofficial information. It emerges as a way of making sense of ambiguous situations about which there is no reliable information or when the information that is received is not considered trustworthy. Rumor is driven by a desire for risk-management, as people attempt to understand what is happening or what will happen, and consider how they will respond to it. The arrival of a new boss is a classic everyday event that leads to rumor generation, since managers not only influence many aspects of our professional lives, but also our happiness and mental health. We rarely have all the facts about why a new boss has been chosen, their previous employment, or their intentions for the company, and so we engage in generating and spreading rumors to compensate for the lack of information. This process has been aptly described by the sociologist Tamotsu Shibutani as "a form of collective problem-solving." The collective element is particularly important, since rumor rarely has a verifiable author, and this anonymity adds to its ability to act as a vehicle for common or widely shared views, concerns, and fears.[9]

We listen to and spread rumors about a whole range of events and circumstances that have the capacity to affect our lives, from the location of a new supermarket to the imposition of higher taxes. Some rumors offer positive and reassuring explanations and hope for the future, but many do not, and only end up increasing fear and speculation. Rumors about political decisions are particularly virulent, not only in their capacity to spread across whole countries, but also because of the anxiety they generate. The installation of a new president or prime minister is essentially the same phenomenon as the arrival of a new manager, but on a much larger scale. It is in times of crisis—wars, natural disasters, pandemics, assassinations of public figures—that rumor generation reaches its peak. We have seen this vividly in the recent COVID-19 pandemic, in which rumors emerged to explain everything from its origin (Wet markets or biological experimentation?) to the responses of our government (Will it impose a hard lockdown?).[10]

Despite rumors' negative reputation, it must be kept in mind that they are not actually wild and unbelievable to those who circulate them. As the historian Luise White has remarked, "rumor" "is a very poor term with which to discuss stories that the storytellers think of as true." The content of rumors shows what the people who spread them—the "rumor public"—believe to be plausible based on their own cultural and social worldview. The ability of rumor to reflect what people think, believe, and imagine means that they are, in the words of Tamotsu Shibutani, "a better index of the preoccupations of a public than most other forms of verbalization." Indeed, plausibility is the only way that rumor thrives and spreads. Rumors that are not believed simply die out. The suspicion that COVID-19 began in a Chinese laboratory—although it might seem implausible to many—has continued to circulate because it appeals to popular prejudices about China, its government, and its political agenda. Rumors often continue to circulate until official, verifiable news is received either confirming or disproving them. In the modern world, this often comes in the form of scientific evidence, such as the DNA results proving that Anna Anderson was not the long-lost grand duchess Anastasia of Russia, the daughter of Tsar Nicholas II and Tsarina Alexandra. But many rumors never receive formal refutation, which means that they continue to subsist, long after the moment or crisis that generated them has passed (and even some rumors that have been officially disproved still circulate if the confirmation is itself distrusted). Some rumors transform into traditions or historical myths, while others find their way into written texts such as histories and biographies.[11]

Let us return now to the workplace, where the arrival of the new manager caused such consternation. Think about the range of conversations you have had with your colleagues over the years, walking down the hallway, using the photocopier, and making tea in the kitchen. A good many of those conversations would have concerned work colleagues, their characters and habits, and perhaps even aspects of their personal lives, both good and bad. "Ahmed got that promotion: isn't that great news?" "Why does Jenny always use other people's milk?" "Do you think Matt has put on weight?" All these potential snippets of conversation are different forms of gossip. Gossip is evaluative social talk about individuals that circulates among specific social groups. It serves two principal purposes. First, it builds and consolidates group cohesion, as it is fun, exciting, and pleasurable to swap stories with friends and colleagues, whether in the ancient world or today. (The Greek author Lucian memorably noted that some men enjoyed having their ears tickled with gossip as much as others did with feathers!) Gossip is valuable information that can be exchanged and bartered to enhance an individual's reputation within a group, even though it might damage the reputation of another group member. This leads to the second major purpose of gossip. It demarcates the values and prejudices of groups, defining what is and what is not considered socially and morally acceptable behavior by its members. This can take the form of positive gossip, which reveals how individuals conform to the group's norms, as well as negative gossip, which details transgressions and polices conduct. Although often regarded as a stereotypically female habit, the exchange of gossip is performed by both men and women, albeit in different ways. Recent sociological research has shown that men most frequently exchange gossip with their partners, whereas women share more widely with their female friends; when men gossip with other men (who are not their romantic partners), the discussion tends to focus on themselves, their work, and achievements, whereas women talk about other female friends and relatives.[12]

The meaning and impact of gossip differ according to the values of individual communities and their religious, cultural, and gender dynamics. Banter about one-night stands might enhance social standing among a men's football team, whereas hushed whispers about similar behavior by young women in a conservative religious community would have exactly the opposite effect. Indeed, the fact that gossip delineates moral values means it is not frivolous talk. Recent research by sociologists has shown how women exchange gossip about sexual predators in order to warn others when they are prevented from doing so through formal institutional channels. Gossip can also be deliberately deployed as a weapon both among peers, as a way of damaging potential or actual rivals, and against higher authorities, as a form of resistance or rebellion. When gossip moves outside a specific social group and becomes of interest to a wider public —the whispers about the school principal's marital infidelity moving beyond hushed exchanges in living rooms, for example—it turns into scandal. If such revelations subsequently become widely known and are perceived to be shocking, they can transform into *a* scandal, or more precisely, a scandal event, marked by a series of revelations, denials, cover-ups, and apologies. Gossip does not, therefore, emerge as a way of explaining and making sense of the world like rumor does, though some rumors can spread *as* gossip if they concern private behavior and character.[13]

The type of gossip that circulates within specific social circles (workplaces, university faculty, churches, friendship groups) about other members of the same group is known as "proximate gossip." But there is also a second type, called "distal gossip," that concerns prominent individuals, such as actors, sports stars, royalty, and politicians. These people and their lives are familiar even to those who do not know them personally. Gossip about the private lives of celebrities and politicians fills the same roles as proximate gossip in social circles, assisting with group bonding and demarcating moral values. The latest news about the antics of a pop singer or a scandal involving a politician is able to bring people together in the same way as Jenny's penny-pinching use of other people's milk in the tearoom. The difference is one of scale. While gossip about employees at a law firm, residents of a village, or members of a soccer team is usually only of concern to those specific communities, gossip about public figures is relevant to the wider population. The way in which celebrities and politicians are talked about expresses the morals and values of society at large, binding small groups together into a larger community of censure. Indeed, gossip about political figures, both elected representatives and dynastic rulers, frequently passes judgment on the state and its operation. The effects of proximate and distal gossip are various. Gossip can be toothless chatter between two people, but when spread far and wide, it can become a powerful statement of communal discontent. This is especially the case if the gossip is made public and transforms into scandal or is leveraged into formal resistance and protest movements.[14]

In short, rumor helps us to make sense of what is happening in the world, whereas gossip evaluates the character and behaviors of individuals. The value of examining them together is that they collectively shed light on the full workings of the human imagination, from our hopes and fears to our values and morals. They allow us to understand how people process, mediate, and respond to information about their world at both an individual and collective level. These theoretical conclusions can be applied to the Roman world, its rulers, and their subjects as much as to the contemporary workplace and the interactions between managers and employees. The historians Lynette Mitchell and Charles Melville have emphasized that kingship is essentially "relational," the product of negotiation between ruler and ruled. Negotiation is also used by the sociologist Stuart Hall to illustrate how we receive and process messages from government, media, and other sources. The sense-making nature of rumor and the evaluative purpose of gossip mean that they are vital to understanding how the negotiation of monarchy plays out. They reveal when people wholeheartedly choose to believe and endorse the information provided by their leaders or when they act with suspicion and resistance, not to mention the numerous other permutations of understanding, confusion, or interpretation that lie between these extremes. Let's take a hypothetical scenario in which a young prince dies unexpectedly, and the government officially announces that he has passed away from natural causes. The emergence of rumors that the prince was poisoned can be interpreted as people processing the official information, rejecting it, and coming up with a better explanation based on their own ideas and preconceptions. In another scenario, if people gossip about a king's adulterous affairs beyond palace walls, then this talk constitutes a form of negotiation, as the gossipers decide whether or not these actions constitute appropriate monarchical behavior. Therefore, by collecting and analyzing rumor and gossip about Roman emperors, we open up a window into the Roman imagination that allows us to explore how the construction and negotiation of kingship played out. For, as the historian Alan

Strathern has memorably written, "It is in the imagination of their subjects that rulers live and die."[15]

BEHIND CAESAR'S BACK

The Roman emperor wanted his decisions and policies to be communicated throughout the empire. His subjects, in turn, craved such official information because of the emperor's capacity to affect their lives for better or worse. When a new imperial decree or letter arrived in a city, people gathered together to hear it read out, anxious about the news it contained. Would it be a joyful announcement of the arrival of a child or the proclamation of a new foreign conflict (or, worse, a civil war), complete with conscription and requisitions? Would the emperor be announcing new prohibitions against a specific religion or theological creed, his voice fulminating with the wrath to be visited upon the nonbelievers? After the initial reading, the emperor's words would be publicly displayed on whitened wooden boards or other impermanent media to allow Romans to check and consult them. Imperial rescripts, the emperor's replies to legal petitions from his subjects, were usually exhibited in the same manner. Sometimes the senate or the emperor took special care to inscribe their words in permanent form on bronze, even mandating that they should be displayed "in the most frequented location," to ensure the contents would be read and remembered. If people could not read, there were official criers to make announcements, as well as amateurs who would willingly read out edicts, or at least give others the gist. All these texts, as the historian Clifford Ando has written, functioned "as the guarantor of the truth," namely that the emperor and the state's version of history was correct.[16]

Yet there were numerous problems with efficient communication in the Roman world. A certain Syrus, son of Syrion, who lived in Egypt, thought Commodus was still the emperor on June 2, 193, some 154 days after he had been strangled by a wrestler in Rome. Some less scrupulous emperors deliberately obfuscated what they wanted to announce. When Caligula displayed details of his new taxes using very small letters in a location too high for anyone to read, he was greeted with serious protest from the residents of Rome. They felt they had a right to know what they were being asked to pay. Even when people did acquire official information, they were very suspicious that it did not tell them the full story. Cassius Dio, a senator and historian who lived in the third century, wrote that a climate of such secrecy surrounded the Roman imperial monarchy that even information that was made public "was not trusted because its accuracy could not be ascertained."[17]

It is at this moment of speculation, distrust, and confusion that the negotiation of Roman imperial power began, as rumor emerged to make sense of, or to compensate for, failures in the communicative process. In all pre-modern civilizations, there was no "dominant state or commercial communications sector" through which news and rumor could be mediated, as the historian Christopher Bayly has observed. Romans speculated about the reasons for their emperors' decisions, attempted to ascertain what had been left unsaid, and tried to anticipate future changes and upheavals. This argument that rumors played a crucial role in the negotiation of kingship contributes a new perspective to our understanding of the relationship between the Roman government and its subjects. In his important and influential book *Imperial Ideology and Provincial Loyalty in the Roman Empire,* Clifford Ando has argued that the Roman state engaged in "communicative action" with its subjects in an effort to build consensus about the functioning of government and the roles and responsibilities of emperor, officials, and subjects. The concept of communicative action was formulated by the sociologist Jürgen Habermas to characterize interactions in which the communicator and the receiver reach a common understanding. Ando effectively deployed the wealth of documents written both by emperors and subjects as evidence for this successful communicative action. And yet the fact that Ando's Roman world is primarily a textual one opens the possibility for a different type of approach. For it was in the oral realm, or more precisely, in the interaction between the oral and textual, that assent, evaluation, doubt, or suspicion emerged, and the idea of what it meant to be a Roman emperor, or a subject of an emperor, was truly negotiated.[18]

In contrast to the image of consensus, stability, and confidence constructed in Ando's work, Romans actively sought out and circulated information in an attempt to find out what lay behind the official missives of the state and the truth they presented. Rumor very often began at home—and for the emperor, that was the court. Major centers such as Rome and Constantinople, and sometimes other cities where the emperor was resident, played a prominent role in the generation and distribution of rumors, as well as the gossip that would be of interest outside the palace. Some imperial courtiers thrived off the "news business," selling information about the emperors and their families that could prove useful or titillating. Others just had loose lips, letting tidbits slip to friends and family or leaking political news from meetings of the emperor's council. Prominent individuals—town councilors, bishops, military officers, and so forth—wrote letters to high-placed contacts at court to obtain information or press the concerns of their communities. Not everyone, of course, had a personal relationship with a courtier. But they might know someone who knew someone, whom they could press for confirmation about a current rumor, flattering them that they would have all the right information. At court, one is "right within reach of the gods," as the poet Horace put it. Such connections are what sociologists call "weak ties"—not close, intimate relationships, but those with acquaintances and contacts—that act as conduits for the transmission of rumor and gossip both within and between social groups. These are the sort of people who, in Horace's poetic vignettes, Romans asked for news about the emperor's wars or land distributions. Dinner parties were the perfect opportunity to swap rumors about the grain supply or the movement of foreign kings—or if there was nothing to share, you could just make something up—though, as one of Martial's epigrams suggests, your friends might not believe you.[19]

News and rumor flowed in and out of the imperial capitals to other towns and cities throughout the empire. Settlements on the imperial postal routes were the most fortunate, as they could find out the latest news direct from official messengers (a roadside encounter with a courier is exactly how the reclusive Theodore of Sykeon heard that the emperor Phocas had been deposed). Beyond this, the great and the good wrote and exchanged letters and often picked up accompanying oral information from their bearers. But sometimes rumor traveled much faster than an official courier. Merchants, travelers, sailors, envoys, and pilgrims crisscrossed land and sea, bringing tidings of the emperor's health or the latest news on imperial campaigns from Rome or Constantinople to the provinces and vice-versa. Times of warfare, bad weather, and rough seas often hindered such networks, which gave rise to further panicked speculation. Information and rumor were picked up at the city gates or the docks and then disseminated among professional, social, and religious networks. Farmers and small holders from the countryside journeyed to towns and cities for trading and selling, festivals and pilgrimages, enabling them to hear the latest news and rumors.[20]

In the cities themselves, the streets, taverns, marketplaces, apothecaries, and barbershops were bustling with people, talking about everything from the high price of goods to the emperor who had failed to do anything about it, as the emperor Julian experienced during his disastrous stay in Antioch in 362–363. The late Roman bishop Ambrose of Milan wryly observed in one of his Lenten sermons that you could see men, so impoverished that they lacked both tunics and money, lounging outside taverns engaging in such discussions. As he described, "They sit in judgment on emperors and the powerful, indeed one could say that they think that they themselves rule and command armies"—or at least until the drink wore off and they crashed down to Earth. Many imperial regimes tried to put limits on the types of food or drink that could be sold in taverns and cookshops in order to limit their attractiveness as gathering places, perhaps because of the sentiments that could be expressed there. Being Christian did not mean that one was above such earthly interests, hence Ambrose's exhortations to his congregation to curb their drinking and chatter, and the lamentations of the bishop John Chrysostom about the political discussions of his own flock. Emperors and their decisions were of such pivotal importance to the structure of the Roman world that when the ascetic Mary of Egypt broke her forty-two years of solitude by talking to a monk, one of her first questions was about news of the emperor.[21]

Romans from all walks of life were engaged in the generation and spreading of rumor to feed their desire for accurate and trustworthy political information, a need that was not met by the state's official communications. Of course, across distances large and small, there was the possibility of change, distortion, and misunderstanding; routes of travel were often slowed or blocked by weather and warfare, both foreign and domestic. In the late fifth century, during the dying days of the western Roman empire, Hydatius, who was bishop of Aquae Flaviae in northwest Spain (more than two thousand kilometers from Rome), had his information about happenings in Constantinople (almost four thousand kilometers distant) filtered through messengers and contacts from Rome and Gaul. This gave rise to several significant misunderstandings, including a false rumor that the leading eastern general, Aspar, had been executed due to the failure of a naval expedition. Penetrating the opacity of the emperor and his imperial court, and actually understanding complex political happenings, could be very difficult indeed. In the late fourth century, the eastern Roman historian Eunapius complained that he could not gain good information about what was taking place in the western empire because travelers gave so many different versions (including many that were simply invented).[22]

Many rumors began with people drawing conclusions from events that they observed and then hypothesizing about the circumstances that led to them. These conjectures were not flights of fancy but extrapolated from the Romans' own understanding about the world. This is what the sociologist Stuart Hall has termed the "frameworks of knowledge" that people use to make sense of—or "decode"—the information received from multiple sources and media. An example of a rumor that emerged in the third century following the melting of public statues shows this principle at work. The emperor Septimius Severus reportedly became jealous when he discovered that large numbers of bronze statues depicting Gaius Fulvius Plautianus, his praetorian prefect, had been erected throughout Italy. He therefore ordered that some of these statues should be melted down. However, the reason for Severus's order was not made public: it was a decision taken by the emperor behind closed doors and not communicated formally in a letter or edict. Cassius Dio, a contemporary senator who saw or heard of these events, wrote that when people caught sight of Plautianus's statues being destroyed, they interpreted this as a sign that he had fallen from grace and been executed. This conclusion was based on their knowledge that when a disgraced Roman had his memory condemned by the state, his name and image, including all statues, were eradicated from public places. The rumor of Plautianus's downfall, Dio wrote, soon spread beyond Rome to the cities of the provinces and gained such traction that even the governor of Sardinia had the prefect's statues destroyed. When it was revealed that the rumor was incorrect, the unfortunate governor was himself condemned to death.[23]

Relatively few Romans had the opportunity to speak and interact with the emperor on a personal level, so their understanding of political events was dependent on these types of observations and interpretations. Residents of the imperial capitals were used to seeing the emperor and his family on a regular basis, presiding at the games, distributing largess, overseeing sacrifices, going to church, and embarking on and returning from campaigns. This meant that if an emperor suddenly disappeared from view for a long period, people started to suspect that something was very wrong. When the emperor Diocletian failed to appear in public for several months in the city of Nicomedia, his principal residence, a rumor spread throughout the populace that he was dead (and had even been secretly buried), according to an eyewitness source, the professor of rhetoric Lactantius. These sorts of rumors (and this is but one example) about imperial deaths are especially remarkable because news of an emperor's passing, and the accession of a new ruler, was probably the most publicized imperial event. Death rumors are marked by a curious dualism. They often show concern for the emperor's health and a recognition that there should always be an emperor wearing the purple. But at the same time, they also reveal an inherent distrust for authority and the state's own explanations for regime change. This suggests that even if the imperial government may have wanted to engage in genuine communicative action with its subjects, the people themselves did not always reciprocate.[24]

Observing the comings-and-goings of emperors and courtiers in the major cities generated rumor and speculation about how and when individuals had fallen from favor. For example, Nero's mother, Agrippina, assumed a conspicuous public role when he became emperor at the age of sixteen in 54. She held her own daily receptions, was surrounded by her own escort of praetorian guards, and, exceptionally, had her image prominently displayed on the obverse (the "heads" side) of Roman coins (fig. 2). Fevered rumors about the supposed sexual nature of the relationship between mother and son circulated as a way of explaining Agrippina's public prominence. In this way, wrote Dio, "anything that could possibly have taken place was reported as if it actually had, and anything that was regarded as plausible was believed to be the truth." Dio was not an eyewitness to these events, but his account squares with what we know of references to the incestuous relationship made in earlier, contemporary accounts. The relationship between Nero and his mother soon quickly soured, and in 55 he had her stripped of her bodyguard. Inhabitants of Rome therefore accurately surmised that Agrippina had fallen out of favor with Nero. The rise and fall of powerful figures such as Agrippina and Plautianus was of immense significance, because their fates caused a ripple effect through the social hierarchy, enveloping their clients and supporters, then *their* dependents, and so on, causing political ruin and financial misery up and down the social spectrum. The death of an emperor, as was suspected in the case of Diocletian, was even more significant, because it could lead to civil war with the potential to envelop the entire empire.[25]

Gossip circulated among and between social networks in a similar manner to rumor (indeed, rumors that concerned character and behavior could also circulate as gossip). Romans often exchanged stories that evaluated the physical attributes, social origin, moral character, personal habits, and sexual behavior of their friends and family, patrons, and clients. The second-century Greek author Plutarch observed that busybodies "make inquiries into everyone's affairs, including that of strangers and of rulers." Gossip was valuable social currency, to be exchanged, traded, and bartered. Emperors and their family members were irresistible targets for gossip, satire, and scandal among urban populations. Caligula was lampooned for his goatish hairiness, Caracalla for his small stature, and Julian for his beard, Jovian was thought to be far too good-looking to be an effective general, and the sexual perversions of Tiberius and Elagabalus took on almost legendary proportions. Even emperors with generally good reputations were not above this type of talk, with Galba, Vespasian, and Marcus Aurelius derided as stingy and grasping. Such moral judgments, large and small, formed part of the negotiation of kingship in ancient Rome, because people connected personal behavior and bodily appearance with fitness to rule. As Plutarch noted, "Small failings seem great when they are detected in the private lives of rulers and politicians."[26]

Fig. 2. Gold *aureus* featuring facing heads of Nero and Agrippina on the obverse, 54 CE. *Roman Imperial Coinage* 1^2 Nero 1. Münzkabinett der Staatlichen Museen, Berlin, 18219704. Photograph by Dirk Sonnenwald.

Gossip is often derided by our elite literary sources as the bad habit of the uneducated masses. However, gossip about emperors was both distal, conducted by Romans who had no personal relationship with them, as well as proximate, circulating among his own social circle, the aristocracy and the court. The intense interest in gossip in court circles is shown by the role it plays in the *Lives of the Caesars* written by Suetonius, who served in high office under Trajan and Hadrian, and who was not afraid to retell—and indeed, often relied upon—what he had heard from others. Court gossip could involve both male and female networks, as illustrated by a story told by Plutarch. Fulvius, a friend of the emperor Augustus, gossiped with his wife about the emperor's hatred for Tiberius and his plan to restore Postumus Agrippa from exile. His wife then relayed this gossip to Livia, Augustus's wife. After Livia rebuked Augustus, the emperor made his displeasure with Fulvius known, and Fulvius planned to kill himself. His wife insisted on committing suicide first, claiming that her own loose lips were to blame. The anecdote is particularly interesting because of the way the gendered networks mirror those identified by modern sociological studies of gossip: Fulvius gossiped with his romantic partner, who then spread the gossip through her friendship with another woman, Livia.[27]

Proximate and distal gossip about emperors often served similar purposes. Lampooning and laughing at the emperor were social experiences that brought together groups as diverse as tradesmen and soldiers in the tavern and bureaucrats toiling away in the bowels of the Palatine. But it could also be a form of criticism, a way of delineating proper imperial behavior and challenging an emperor who claimed to be beyond reproach by exposing his shameful secrets. The imperial virtues of *pudicitia* (sexual continence), *clementia* (clemency), and *virtus* (courage or manliness) promulgated by the state in its official coins, statues, and decrees could be rewritten in whispers and jokes. As the sociologist James C. Scott has remarked, "Gossip is perhaps the most familiar and elementary form of disguised popular aggression." Although the Roman emperor was supposed to be able to deal with public jests and jibes with equanimity and good humor, not all gossip was harmless, especially when deployed in political maneuvers. To quote Luise White, gossip "discloses the boundaries of attack and subversion." In short, it tells us which qualities in a ruler mattered to the Romans.[28]

Critical gossip assumed different meanings depending on one's relationship to the emperor. For a laborer at a building site in Rome, puncturing imperial pretensions could have been a way to cope with their own powerlessness in life, whereas for a freedwoman attendant at court, the same stories might have helped them deal with the pressures of living in close proximity to an emperor, his wife, and family. Epictetus, who was a slave of Nero's freedman Epaphroditus, pointed out that even consuls and senators were enslaved—just like he was—to their common master, their emperor. Indeed, the imperial courtier was a rather unfortunate creature, since their career, fortune, and access to power all depended on intimacy with an emperor whom they probably loathed. "No one actually loves Caesar himself," wrote Epictetus, but rather only the wealth and offices that he had the power to bestow. Therefore, gossip at court took on another, more aggressive dimension. Rival groups might use gossip to compete for the emperor's favor or conspire to discredit an imperial wife who was blocking their agenda. The letters of Marcus Cornelius Fronto, tutor in Latin rhetoric to Marcus Aurelius and Lucius Verus, help us to chart the contours of rivalries at court. On one occasion, when Lucius Verus did not want other courtiers to know that he had taken Fronto's advice on a particular matter, he refused to greet and kiss his former tutor in public, doing so only in his bedroom. This way, Fronto's influence with Verus would not be publicly seen and become the subject of gossip and resentment among other, presumably male, courtiers, who were also eager for the emperor's approval.[29]

Lucius Verus was not alone in his concern for what others might be whispering about him behind his back. Many emperors were alert to how they could be observed and talked about both at court and in the aristocratic households of its satellites. In a letter to his doctor, Oribasius, the Caesar Julian asked him to report back what Constantius II's eunuch, Eusebius—"that repulsive half-man"—had been saying about him. Loose tongues could potentially lead to punishment.

Gaius Cornelius Gallus, the first prefect of Egypt, "gossiped frequently and imprudently about Augustus," according to Cassius Dio, while Gallus's contemporary, the poet Ovid, wrote that he had "failed to hold his tongue under the influence of too much wine." Gallus's indiscretions may have taken place in the private sphere, but his fall was very public. Augustus's friendship was formally withdrawn, and Gallus was subsequently arraigned, probably on the grounds of treason for exceeding the limits of his command in Egypt. The emperor Caracalla was so concerned about gossip that he allegedly punished any courtier who let slip details of his private life and habits, according to our contemporary eyewitness Cassius Dio, who trembled at the margins of the court. Such punishments depended on people denouncing their fellow aristocrats and courtiers (as Julian asked Oribasius to do for him). Simplicius, the son of an illustrious praetorian prefect, was arraigned before Constantius II's crony Paul "The Chain" because "it was said," no doubt by one of his political rivals, that he had consulted an oracle about how to become emperor.[30]

Emperors were also cognizant of the potential for their actions to spark discussion and speculation among the wider public. When the eastern emperor Arcadius elevated his wife, Eudoxia, to the rank of Augusta (the female equivalent of Augustus) and circulated her images throughout the provinces, he did so without consulting his brother, Honorius, emperor of the West. Incensed, in 404, Honorius wrote to his brother and asked him to stop distributing the images, "so that, in keeping with the morals of our age, there is nothing for the common tongue to latch on to." This kind of anonymous talk was incredibly difficult to regulate. Emperors thought they might have better luck with the textual manifestations of rumor and gossip that appeared in pamphlets and poems. Senatorial decrees and laws from the age of Augustus through to Late Antiquity made such writings, termed *famosi libelli,* or "defamatory documents," punishable by treason, regardless of whether they were written about emperors or other individuals. But these texts were just as anonymous as most forms of oral discourse, since they were usually unsigned and circulated in public spaces, such as the senate house and theater, and were posted on walls and statues. Roman history is marked by emperors vacillating between trying to punish the authors of such tracts and laughing along with them. When authors could be found, as in the case of Felix, an unfortunate North African deacon who had written a defamatory letter about the emperor Maximian, they were treated to the full force of the law. Felix took refuge in the House of Mercurius, bishop of Carthage, and when the bishop refused to surrender him, the prelate was summoned before imperial authorities. Roman emperors were not above using the same sort of defamatory writing to undermine their opponents. Constantine's letters ridiculing the heretical priest Arius were published throughout all the cities of the empire, while the emperor Anastasius arranged for pamphlets accusing his enemy, the bishop Macedonius, of pederasty and impiety to circulate in Constantinople. These textual documents were explicitly designed to fan oral discourse about the clerics who had earned the emperors' ire.[31]

Roman talk, therefore, elucidates the negotiation of imperial power that played out in and beyond the world of imperial edicts and letters, appearances and performances, petitions and the dispensation of justice. The range of responses could be complex and multifaceted, revealing distrust and suspicion about the imperial state and the character and values of the emperor himself, as well as intense attachment to the security and stability the imperial office represented. Rumor and gossip thus expressed a variety of permutations of loyalty and resistance. But recent work on oral discourse by historians of a range of places and periods—medieval Europe, early modern England, colonial India, Stalinist Russia, the modern Caribbean, and contemporary Tuvalu—has demonstrated that we should not restrict the meaning and significance of rumor and gossip to these two polar opposites. Oral discourse might represent a critique of one particular imperial act, while endorsing the larger frameworks of power in which it was situated; it might represent the desperate search for reliable information in a time of civil war, while hoping for the emperor to be restored, not deposed; it might represent a provisional opinion about an emperor, not a final conclusion. These and other complex and contingent responses show how the negotiation of what it meant to be a Roman emperor took place in the minds and voices of his subjects.[32]

THINKING ABOUT KINGS

The frameworks of knowledge through which Romans interpreted the behavior of their emperors emerged from a range of traditions and contexts. Rome had its own kings, a line of monarchs stretching from its fratricidal founder, Romulus, to the tyrannical Tarquinius Superbus. The latter's expulsion in 510 BCE led to the establishment of the *res publica*—which literally means the "commonwealth"—but which we call the "Republic." Despite what is often thought, these kings were not universally reviled in Roman Republican culture; in fact, they were regarded as creating and shaping Rome's major political and religious institutions and its social structure. In both the Republican and imperial periods, the kings, their characters, and their actions could be used in histories and political treatises as examples of good leadership to imitate or cruel tyranny to avoid. This was not merely an elite discourse, as plays about the kings continued to be performed in the theater, the melting pot of all levels of Roman society. When Romans told stories about their former kings, they were depicted as popular figures, who tended to be hated by the aristocracy, but loved by the people. In Roman Republican political discourse, the idea of kingship (*regnum* in Latin) came to symbolize the removal of power away from the Roman people and its concentration in the hands of a powerful individual. Politicians used the accusation of "aiming at *regnum*" to malign their opponents who were becoming too popular, such as the tribunes Tiberius and Gaius Gracchus and the dictator Julius Caesar. Shortly before Caesar's murder in 44 BCE, there was even a rumor in circulation that Lucius Cotta, a member of the Board of Fifteen for Sacred Rites, would formally ask the senate to make Caesar king.[33]

And so it was that in 27 BCE Julius Caesar's heir was honored with the name "Augustus," meaning "revered one," rather than that of "Romulus," which had unpleasant connotations of fratricide and a king hated by the aristocracy. Augustus henceforth assumed a place of primacy, formally known as a "station" (*statio*), within the *res publica* of the Roman people. In doing so, he ushered in its transformation into a new hybrid type of state, a monarchical *res publica,* in which the people retained a sovereign role, as Anthony Kaldellis has demonstrated. The emperor's authority derived both from tradition (the Republican offices and the powers they conveyed) and from charisma (the extraordinary quality of the individual emperor). The ideology of imperial rule by which Augustus and his successors operated was marked by an insistence that the emperor was not a king, but a *civilis princeps,* which translates into English as something like "a ruler who behaves as if he were a fellow-citizen." The *civilis princeps* treated senators as peers, enjoyed watching gladiatorial games and chariot races, and—when jibes and criticism manifested themselves publicly, rather than behind his back—was prepared to take a critical joke on the chin. This emphasis on the emperor's civility was a performance, but it was not an empty and insignificant one, since it allowed the aristocracy to reconcile themselves to their new monarchical reality. Roman political thought focused predominantly on the ethical character of the individual emperor, his virtues and vices, rather than constitutional theory. This was influenced both by Republican thinking about what made a man a good citizen of the *res publica,* and by kingship theory developed by Greek philosophers and intellectuals in response to the monarchies within their about, including the Persian empire, Greek tyrannies, and the Hellenistic realms of Alexander the Great and his successors.[34]

Indeed, the Roman Republic existed in a Mediterranean world full of kings. They could be found in various incarnations in Sicily, Macedonia, Gaul, and Egypt, regions that were gradually swallowed up by the expanding Roman empire across the third to first centuries BCE. These kings made appearances in Roman comedies as fantastical symbols of wealth and luxury, which most audience members could only dream of possessing. The presence of kings throughout the ancient Mediterranean world should not surprise us, given that it was monarchy—not the republic or democracy—that was the prevalent form of government before the modern era. This meant that great swaths of Rome's empire had been accustomed to autocratic rule for thousands of years before Augustus. Many kingdoms had passed through one monarchy after another, such as Egypt, which was ruled by the pharaohs, then the Achaemenid Persians, then Alexander the Great and his successors, the Ptolemies, before the imposition of direct Roman rule in 30 BCE. Even after Rome itself became an imperial monarchy under Augustus, it continued to rule many smaller, neighboring kingdoms as client states. Over time, it incorporated other monarchies like Mauretania, Thrace, Judaea, Commagene, and Arabia into its territory. We need to be mindful that although these and other realms contributed to Roman aristocratic perceptions of—and unease regarding—monarchy during the Republican period, for the inhabitants of the lands themselves, kingship was an uncontroversial reality. Moreover, as Olivier Hekster has shown, these kingdoms had their own local traditions and expectations of rulership and monarchical behavior that could be quite separate from Rome's own views about its earliest kings.[35]

There were other monarchies that Rome never incorporated or conquered. Some of these remained friendly, like the kingdom of the Bosphorus, while others, such as Iberia and Armenia, played an ongoing role in the rivalry between the Roman empire and its largest eastern neighbors, the Parthian empire and its successors, the Sasanian Persians. In Roman elite discourse, Parthia and Persia embodied the very worst aspects of autocratic rule: degeneracy and decadence, secrecy and suspicion, luxury and lasciviousness, an endless list of despised vices. When Tacitus cast aspersions on the emperor Tiberius's sexual conduct on Capri, he wrote that his behavior was "in the manner of a king," encouraging his readers to think of eastern potentates in contrast to the more restrained behavior expected of a Roman *civilis princeps*. Yet for the peoples of the Caucasus, Osrhoene, Armenia, Mesopotamia, and eastern Syria, who passed alternately under Roman and Parthian or Sasanian Persian rule over the centuries, such differences in styles of rulership may not have been readily apparent. The sonorous bleating of Roman court poets and panegyrists, eager to praise their emperors as paragons of civility, probably had little impact on the perceptions of kingship in the caravan cities of Palmyra and Edessa. Indeed, it is important to stress the inherent strangeness of the ideology of the *civilis princeps* so cherished by elites of the early Roman empire. Kingship is usually founded on the idea that the monarch is separate and distinct, rather than an equal. As Roman imperial ideology changed over the centuries to emphasize the asymmetrical relationship between the emperor and his subjects, it brought Rome into line with other monarchical societies.[36]

Romans interpreted imperial decisions and character through all these different frameworks of knowledge, conditioned by their place of origin and regional background, as well as by common hopes and visions of good kingly behavior. These were not only shared across regions and cultures, but also through different social levels, from courtiers such as Seneca the Younger to villagers in Egypt. A path-breaking study of Roman morality by the classicist Teresa Morgan has demonstrated that elite Greek and Latin philosophical treatises shared many of the same sentiments as popular proverbs, fables, and maxims. We learn from these sources that Romans thought a monarch should deliver justice in a fair and impartial manner, that he should control his emotions and not descend into savagery or cruelty, and that he should show clemency to subjects and foreigners alike. They articulated the expectation that the emperor would not kill or punish indiscriminately, which was a concern for all Romans, no matter their birth or wealth.[37]

The celestial realm also furnished important concepts of rulership. Members of the Greek and Roman pantheon were embedded in all aspects of daily life from religious beliefs and practices to art and storytelling—painting, portraiture, epic poetry, and drama. The gods were of old and eternal origin, appearing in Indo-European mythological stories about cosmic order, the creation of the universe, and life and death, in which they were usually envisaged as fathers and kings. And so Jupiter and the Olympian dynasty, the warriors and princesses of the Trojan cycle, and Aeneas and his Julian progeny all provided the Romans with paradigms for understanding and imagining monarchical rule, both its virtues and benefits and its vices and terrors. Indeed, we should not seek to draw too fine a line between the earthly and heavenly spheres. The ethereal world of what the anthropologist Marshall Sahlins has termed "metapersons"—gods, spirits, demons, and other spirits—has provided the template for rulers on Earth throughout world history. Kings have traditionally functioned as "in-between things," forming "meeting points between persons and metapersons," to use the words of Alan Strathern. The slippage between kings and metapersons was encouraged by Roman emperors, who assimilated themselves in cult worship and court ceremonies to Jupiter, Apollo, Hercules, and countless other divine figures. Playing at myth was also a popular pastime for kings. In the second century BCE, Ptolemy VIII of Egypt emulated Medea by killing his own son in an act of revenge against his wife and sister, Cleopatra, while four hundred years later, Commodus reenacted the labors of Hercules in the Colosseum in Rome. Such behavior not only served imperial self-representation—it also led Romans to wonder what their rulers might be capable of doing. Rumors that advanced an incestuous sexual relationship as an explanation for Agrippina's prominent political position at the court of her son Nero may seem far-fetched to the modern reader, but they are far from implausible when one considers the number of incest stories about gods, heroes, and other kingship figures in Greek and Roman mythology, as Caroline Vout and Alastair Blanshard have explored.[38]

The rise of Christianity within the Roman world over the course of the first three centuries CE, and the enthusiastic adoption of the faith by Constantine and most of his successors in the fourth, furnished Romans with new, Christian models of monarchical rule, as demonstrated by Hartmut Leppin. The books of the Old Testament teemed with moralistic exempla, from Jewish kings and prophets (in particular David and Moses) to the foreign tyrants of Egypt and Babylon. One need not have been literate to know and understand such biblical stories, for they were regularly expounded orally in sermons, the most powerful transmitter of knowledge in the Christian world. To quote the historian of Islam Linda Jones, "In traditional societies where religious myths provide the template for the mundane order, preaching seeks to ensure that these archetypal morals and ethos are actualized." While their pagan predecessors often claimed to be Jupiter or Apollo incarnate (or at the very least their progeny), Christian emperors could not describe themselves as God, to whom they were very much subject during their time on Earth, but their actions could certainly be judged by the Almighty.[39]

This venture into the heavenly realms and anthropological studies of gods and kings leads us to move beyond Rome and the Mediterranean to consider the wider framework of human experience. The ideal of the just and fair monarch (expressed in popular fables) and the association between kings and gods (from mythology and propaganda) were concepts hardly restricted to Rome but feature prominently in pre-modern monarchical societies across Eurasia, Africa, and the Americas. These universal (or near-universal) ideas about kingship are often embedded in folklore. "Folklore" is defined as traditional knowledge, tales, and expressions of anonymous origin; it is therefore very difficult to trace when or how folkloric ideas first appeared in any one particular society and determine whether they emerged independently or through cross-cultural interaction. One of the features of folklore about kings is that it usually does not challenge the institution of monarchy itself, but only the failings of individual rulers—such as imposing harsh penalties on subjects. In many folktales, the king himself is regarded as fundamentally good, but led astray by poor advisors.[40]

We can see how folklore informed Roman conceptions of rulership in a tale retold by the historian Cassius Dio. The emperor Hadrian is traveling through the provinces when a woman attempts to give him a petition. He dismisses her abruptly, saying that he has no time to deal with her complaint. She replies: "Fine—but don't be an emperor then." This remark encapsulates popular frustration with a monarch who refuses to fulfill one of his core duties—administering justice on behalf of his subjects. Yet this anecdote is not unique to Hadrian, since it is also attributed to Philip of Macedon (father of Alexander the Great), Antipater (regent of Alexander's empire), and Demetrius the Besieger (a Hellenistic king). In fact, this interaction is sufficiently common for scholars of folklore to classify it as a "folk motif" entitled "Cease Being King." Motifs in folk literature often transcend regional and cultural boundaries. The fact that the motif not only appears in stories about Hadrian, but also about other Mediterranean kings, shows that it reflects deep-rooted monarchical ideals of justice and accessibility that crossed both time and space. A second famous folkloric motif, in which a king is instructed to do away with the richest and most powerful men in his land through an agricultural metaphor, has been named "Enigmatic Counsel" by scholars. In the famous version given by the Greek historian Herodotus, the Corinthian tyrant Periander sends a messenger to Thrasybulus, the ruler of Miletus, to ask him how he should govern well. Thrasybulus takes Periander's messenger through his wheat fields, and while talking with him, Thrasybulus cuts off the tallest of the stalks and throws them away, intimating that the tyrant should do likewise to the greatest men in Corinth. The king Tarquinius Superbus appears in multiple Roman variations, in which the tallest poppies are destroyed (hence "Tall Poppy Syndrome"), while in Jewish folklore the tale stars a Roman emperor called Antoninus who sees radishes plucked out of the ground. These stories, which scholars have classified as instances of the one folkloric motif, were not necessarily influenced by one another. They tell us less about the circumstances and behavior of individual kings than about common human conceptions of political leaders.[41]

Folklore must be considered alongside fables, morality tales, and myth as an important source for the frameworks of knowledge that underlie rumors. These frameworks predispose rumors to follow what the early modern historian Adam Fox has termed "recognized narrative patterns." In the early twentieth century, rumors about Tsar Nicholas II and his family circulated among the Russian peasantry. These stories, which focused on the tsar's stupidity, the moral turpitude of the imperial women, and matchmaking between the Russian imperial house and other European royal families, were regarded as plausible because they reflected ideas, characters, and narratives from popular fairy tales. We can see the same principle operating in the Roman world. A rumor that circulated in the fourth century claiming that Fausta, the second wife of the emperor Constantine, had a sexual relationship with her stepson Crispus, who then repudiated her, is a manifestation of the folkloric motif of "Potiphar's Wife." The story's most famous version, from which the motif takes its name, is found in the biblical book of Genesis. When Joseph is enslaved to the pharaoh's general Potiphar, the latter's wife accuses him of rape after he refuses her advances. But the motif is also attested in places as far afield as Africa, China, Italy, and Iceland, not to mention the ancient Greek world, in the myth of Hippolytus and Phaedra. Folklore has long been such an important basis for rumor because of the way it deals in stark archetypes such as the greedy king, the cruel stepmother, and the evil witch. Since people do not usually have the detailed insider knowledge to explain political events, they often interpret them through the lens of personalities shaped by folklore, myth, and tradition. In eighteenth-century France, this resulted in popular libels depicting the court as a place where nobles "could give full rein to the pursuit of lust and power," as shown by the historian Robert Darnton. In the same way, we will see how the Roman conceptions of their emperors expressed by oral discourse were influenced at different times, and in different regions, by Graeco-Roman myth, Christian tradition, and shared human expectations of leaders.[42]

UNCOVERING RUMOR AND GOSSIP

Any historian of rumor and gossip in the pre-modern world must confront methodological issues. In the course of researching this book, I have not been able to conduct interviews with the residents of Pompeii or eavesdrop on conversations in the streets of Antioch like contemporary sociologists and anthropologists can today. How then can we listen to the voices of Romans? The first point to emphasize is that our surviving written texts show that the Roman empire, like other pre-modern societies, had a rich and vibrant oral culture. There were performances of poetry and drama in the Forum and the theaters, abuses and acclamations that rang out in the marketplaces and arenas, and heroic tales and fables that passed from generation to generation. One example of how this oral culture intersected with Roman perceptions of their emperors concerns the emperor Galba, who assumed power after Nero's suicide in 68. When Galba was marching through Italy to take control of Rome, a farce was being performed in one of the city's theaters. One particular line—"Onesimus comes from his farm"—struck a chord with the audience, who began to sing the verse and make the gestures that accompanied it as a way of commenting on the new emperor. The exact interpretation of the line is disputed, given that the whole play does not survive, but the audience could have been assimilating Galba to a parsimonious old estate owner (he was known for his stinginess), or referencing the emperor's slave-like subordination to his advisors ("Onesimus" being a name with servile overtones). Whatever the precise aspect of the line that took the audience's fancy, the anecdote provides a glimpse into the lively oral culture at Rome and the capacity of the theater to function as a venue for political commentary. But we only know of this incident because it is preserved in, and mediated through, a written source, the *Life of Galba* by Suetonius.[43]

All pre-modern historians, unlike anthropologists, need to use written texts to reconstruct oral culture. Some historical periods offer a better range of evidence than others. Historians of early modern Europe generally have access to printed source materials, such as court transcripts, pamphlets or chapbooks, and newspapers, which can serve as a guide to contemporary songs, fables, legends, gossip, and rumor. The oral record, of course, has still gone through a process of selection, curation, and publication, which should not be ignored, but there is an immediacy to reading a trial transcript in which the accused recounts a rumor he has heard in his own words or to leafing through a cheap chapbook that records a popular song. Historians of other societies, such as those of ancient China, Greece, and Rome, and even of some more recent periods, such as Mughal India, do not have this print culture to draw upon. We depend heavily on descriptions of oral culture found in histories, biographies, chronicles, and philosophical treatises. These works were usually produced by elites for other elites. This does not make these traces of orality unusable—indeed, we need to employ them if we are to comprehend the ancient world in all its colors—but we need to be aware of their potential limitations.[44]

Our understanding of the politics of imperial Rome has traditionally depended on historical and biographical accounts, such as those written by Suetonius, Tacitus, Cassius Dio, Ammianus Marcellinus, and Procopius, to name only the most recognizable authors. Some of these writers were contemporary with the events they described, and thus constitute important eyewitnesses, but many were not, living decades or even centuries later. Scholars have often lamented that these writers primarily deal with elite concerns, such as imperial behavior, court politics, and warfare. But this means that they are useful for our purposes, since they were interested in recording rumor and gossip about emperors. Our historians and biographers often quote nicknames, witty verses, songs, and chants about emperors verbatim. At other times, these authors record the reception of innuendo and double meanings in performances of plays (like the Galba example quoted above). Regardless of the precise meaning, the line would not have gotten this reaction if there had not already been conversations happening about Galba. The audience's response represents the public manifestation of rumor and gossip, in the same way that chants about U.S. president Donald Trump sung by the women's resistance movement drew on popular discourse about the size of his hands, his orange complexion, and his predatory behavior toward women. What we cannot track in the instance of Galba is *who* was having those conversations. Was it only senators, who knew Galba's reputation, and their response then set off the rest of the audience, like some sort of wave in a stadium? But even if this were the case, the fact that everyone joined in made the reaction a communal experience and may have stimulated further gossip about Galba's parsimony.[45]

The authenticity of fragments of verses, songs, and acclamations quoted by our literary sources has not generally been doubted by scholars. Indeed, their style and meter are generally taken as evidence of their authenticity. The chants often appear in a meter known as trochaic *septenarii* or the *versus quadratus* (literally "square verse"), used for soldiers' triumphal songs and nursery rhymes, such as the lines about kingship that I put into the mouths of Pompeian children at the beginning of this book. Some verses and songs were made up extemporaneously by crowds in the *versus quadratus* or other popular meters. But there were also satirical poems that betrayed insider knowledge of court politics or a refined literary style. These were probably written by intellectual elites, either aristocrats themselves or the poets who depended on their patronage. Even though these poems may have come from the pen of the educated, the fact that they circulated in textual and oral form in Rome or Constantinople shows that they came to form part of a wider popular discourse. They are usually short, only a few lines long, the sort that could be easily memorized and passed on by individuals and crowds. Our ancient authors also quoted now-lost ephemeral written texts such as graffiti, pamphlets, and placards. These could have an oral dimension to them, because they were often phrased as exhortations or abuses directed at the emperor and, indeed, may have circulated orally before or after being written down. Nineteenth-century India was similar to ancient Rome in not having a developed print media, but an information culture that relied on letter-writing, public meetings, marketplace discussions, and placards. In this world, as Christopher Bayly has shown, "pinning up critical poems in a mordant style, as well as passing them by word of mouth through the bazaar" was a traditional form of political engagement. It is therefore plausible that verses circulated orally and in written form in the public fora of ancient Rome in a similar fashion.[46]

But what about the cases in which there is no quoted text, and the authors only refer to rumor and gossip? All Roman historians made choices in the presentation of their material. They decided which anecdotes to include and which to omit in order to fit with their interpretation of individual emperors and their reign, a practice of curation that certainly has had an impact on the range of material available to us. However, we should not always regard anecdotes with suspicion, especially when they derive from the world of the imperial court, where proximate gossip about the emperor flourished. Niko Besnier's anthropological study of gossip among the inhabitants of Nukulaelae Atoll in Tuvalu has shown that gossip about figures or events from the past is often deployed as jokes and anecdotes in present-day conversations on the islands. This suggests that anecdotes are a form of "fossilized" gossip. Beyond the world of the imperial court, we have to be more careful. Historians such as Tacitus and Cassius Dio were certainly acute and perceptive observers of how rumor functioned in society. Dio's description of channels of communication under the Roman imperial monarchy is very similar to the model of rumor generation proposed by sociologists. However, sometimes Roman historians describe rumors spreading among "the people" (usually the residents of the city of Rome) several centuries before their own time. A classic example is the reactions to the death of Augustus in Book 1 of Tacitus's *Annals,* in which the historian claims to present the detailed thoughts of different groups of Romans. It is methodologically problematic to automatically assume that these descriptions reflect genuine popular discussions.[47]

In order to ensure that my arguments are placed on the firmest foundations possible, my approach to these histories and biographies is to give priority to direct quotations and cases of rumor and gossip attested in a chain of oral and/or textual transmission. For example, the narrative of the murder of Caligula in Josephus's *Jewish Antiquities* (a work written decades after the emperor's reign) relies on the written account of a senator who was present on the Palatine on the day of the murder and who heard the rumors himself. Our historians also occasionally mention how they had heard particular stories, often from their own relatives—Cassius Dio's father and Suetonius's grandfather both passed on tales of emperors that found their way into the works written by their descendants. Suetonius's account is clearly distinguished by Latin verbs of telling and hearing. Tom Geue has astutely noted how, as one moves throughout the *Lives,* there is a shift from documents as sources "towards unofficial, anonymous, largely oral ways of knowing." As well as helping us to understand the literary fabric of the *Lives* themselves, these moments of orality enable us to reconstruct who talked about the emperor and how. In addition to his grandfather, Suetonius had conversations with other men of prior generations. Discussing Claudius's conduct as a judge, Suetonius wrote: "I myself used to hear older men say that the pleaders took such advantage of his good nature." In Rome, the exchange of stories about emperors between older and younger relatives and acquaintances played a vital role in setting boundaries and expectations of imperial behavior. By writing down these conversations, Suetonius endorsed the implications of the tales for past emperors and for current wearers of the purple.[48]

In other cases, when authors are writing decades or centuries after events, they sometimes note the persistence of rumors up to their own time. This occurs in Tacitus's account of a tale circulating about the death of Drusus the Younger, the son of the emperor Tiberius. The conniving praetorian prefect Sejanus had warned Tiberius that Drusus intended to poison him and that he should avoid the first glass of wine offered. The emperor complied, passing it to Drusus, without knowing that Sejanus had actually poisoned the wine—thus unwittingly causing his own son's demise. Tacitus characterized the story as "a rumor of those days which has retained such force that it has not yet dissipated." Despite Tacitus's statement, this does not necessarily mean that the rumor remained unchanged across the century between Drusus's death and the publication of the *Annals.* But the version that has come down to us is still the result of oral transmission and reflects the ways Romans thought and talked about imperial conduct.[49]

There are also historical accounts that describe events the authors themselves experienced. Contemporary history was widely written and performed in Rome, harvesting current gossip and rumor for future preservation. Pliny the Younger notes a case in which family and friends of a prominent individual pleaded for public readings of a history to be stopped in order to protect the man's reputation. Two of our most important authors of contemporary history are Cassius Dio, a senator of the late second and early third century who relates what he saw and experienced in Rome during this period, and Ammianus Marcellinus, a late fourth-century military officer who served on the Persian campaign of the emperor Julian. When Dio writes of gossip about emperors spreading through Rome, or Ammianus of rumors among the ranks of his own army, we should take their testimony seriously.[50]

No analysis of rumor and gossip about emperors can be written based on histories and biographies alone. I therefore employ a wide range of other contemporary texts whose authors provide firsthand accounts of discussions in which they participated or that they heard from others. These include Philo's *Embassy to Gaius,* an eyewitness narrative of a Jewish embassy to the emperor Caligula in Rome; Seneca the Younger's *Apocolocyntosis* (traditionally translated as "Pumpkinification"), a satire performed at the court of Nero that lampooned the deification of his predecessor, Claudius; and numerous works by the Jewish historian Josephus, who fought in the rebellion against the Roman empire before offering his services to Vespasian. Letters are an important and abundant font of information about contemporary discussions, especially in the period of Late Antiquity. We have extensive collections of letters belonging to the emperor Julian, the rhetorician Libanius, the senators Symmachus and Sidonius Apollinaris, and numerous churchmen, such as Gregory of Nazianzus, Basil of Caesarea, and Ambrose of Milan. There are also letters of provincial officials and petitioners preserved on papyrus from Egypt, which reveal attempts to contact the imperial court, as well as the news and rumors that traveled from the court to Egypt.

Many sermons that were delivered by priests and bishops in the fourth and fifth centuries survive. These have been under-exploited by historians as sources for the dissemination of political news, rumor, and gossip. For example, in a sermon given on January 6, 400, in Bithynia, which lay nearly seven hundred kilometers to the east of Constantinople, Asterius, bishop of Amasea, referenced the fall and death of the consul Rufinus in 395 and the eunuch Eutropius in 399. The individuals themselves are not named, but Asterius used the information he had heard to expound on the rise and fall of great men for the benefit of his congregation. Sermons could also introduce speculation about the lives of the emperors themselves. In his sixteenth *Homily on Philippians,* John Chrysostom provided his congregation with a series of grisly stories of imperial deaths in order to illustrate the fearful lives led by emperors. Several years later, when he was bishop of Constantinople, John Chrysostom delivered a sermon in which he criticized the faults of women, making several references to Jezebel (the Phoenician princess who married King Ahab of Israel and who became a paradigm of sexual immorality). Members of the congregation automatically assumed he was launching an attack on the empress Eudoxia, wife of Arcadius. Talk soon spread throughout the city to this effect, even reaching the ears of the imperial court. We must remember, as Lucy Grig has pointed out, that church sermons were shaped by "ecclesiastical and pastoral priorities," but the deployment of political examples—some of which were very recent—in the service of religious arguments communicated important ideas about imperial behavior to Christian communities. Indeed, sermons were intended for oral delivery and aural reception, and they still retain these vivid dimensions, even if preserved today in manuscripts and critical editions.[51]

My argument, therefore, is that written texts, far from being separate and removed from the world of Roman talk, are intimately associated with it. Conversations might turn into placards and poems, which were recited and then written down in histories, while rumors could be quoted in letters, and then passed on again in conversation. To quote the early modern historian Adam Fox, there is "an essential reciprocity between the substance of the oral and literate realms." Some limitations do remain and should be acknowledged. Most of the time we do not have a record of the actual conversation in which rumor or gossip was spread. This is the bread and butter of anthropologists who can present transcripts of oral discourse and then engage in a detailed analysis of its meaning. This technique is known as "thick description," which has entered the academic mainstream thanks to the influential work of the anthropologist Clifford Geertz. Letters are useful evidence in that they attest one aspect of rumor or gossip transmission, but often the letter bearers passed on additional oral messages that are now lost to us. To add to these problems, our sources are almost exclusively elite males from the ranks of the aristocracy, court, government, military, and the Church. They describe rumor and gossip among their own social groups or talk they heard circulating in the cities in which they lived. For example, we are exceptionally well-informed about the political climate of late fourth-century Antioch through the letters and orations of the rhetorician Libanius, the letters of the emperor Julian and his treatise the *Misopogon* ("Beard-Hater"), and the sermons of the priest John Chrysostom. Libanius, Julian, and Chrysostom all tried to influence public opinion in their own ways, which shows that the views of the population of Antioch mattered to them. At the same time, however, we do not hear the people complaining about Julian through their own voices, but through Julian's own cutting reply in his *Misopogon.* This is a limitation that we must work with, because it is better to try and reconstruct the opinions of the urban populations using the sources we do have rather than to write them out of history.[52]

The testimony for oral discourse within the larger urban communities in the Roman world, particularly Rome, Antioch, Alexandria, and Constantinople, is nevertheless much more extensive when compared to evidence for small towns and rural communities. We can occasionally get a glimpse at how imperial news spread throughout the provinces. For example, in 258, Cyprian, the bishop of Carthage, had heard rumors that the emperor Valerian intended to intensify his persecution of the Christians. After sending an embassy to Rome to confirm the rumors were accurate, Cyprian discovered that Christians had already been executed in the capital. He then dispatched a letter to Successus, bishop of Abbir Germaniciana, in the interior of Africa (its precise location is unknown), to ask him to help circulate the information throughout the province. We can never recover these provincial voices completely, but we can sometimes read what others have to say about them. For example, Philo and Josephus provide important records of the sentiments of the Jewish populace in Egypt, Judaea, and Syria during the first century. Moreover, fables and folktales, which were originally performed and exchanged orally, play important roles in reconstructing how people at lower social levels, including enslaved people, thought about kingship. Sometimes such folkloric formulations of power form the bedrock of stories about emperors told in elite sources, showing that there were common ways of thinking about Roman rulers that crossed the social strata.[53]

We are therefore dealing with what the historian Abhishek Kaicker, in his study of popular politics of Mughal India, has called a "fragmented archive," an imperfect patchwork of (mostly elite) sources and perspectives that was not necessarily meant to be read and interpreted in the particular way that I or my fellow historians of political publics wish to approach it. And yet that is our task as historians, to read and interpret against the grain in order to bring to life narratives that are lost to us. Throughout the book, I aim to draw the reader's attention to the types of sources, the date of composition, chains of evidence, and the dynamics of social status in order to explore what our evidence can and cannot tell us about the circulation of rumor and gossip in different contexts. I will also employ evidence of rumor and gossip in other monarchical societies, especially in ancient, medieval, and early modern Europe, the Near East, and Asia. The purpose of this material is not to "fill in the gaps," importing material from other better-attested periods to compensate for deficiencies in the Roman evidence, which would pose significant methodological problems. Rather, this evidence enables an approach that historians call "soft" comparative history. This looks to other time periods and cultures for possible models and ways of thinking. Comparison allows us to tease out the universal from the specific, and thereby chart the similarities and differences between Rome and other societies. One important point that will become clear is that the typology of rumor and gossip about Roman emperors is very similar to that attested for kings and rulers in other monarchical states. This suggests that our evidence, despite its scattered and somewhat piecemeal nature and the methodological issues highlighted here, does actually provide an accurate record of oral discourse about Roman emperors. But this comparative methodology raises other important questions. What, if anything, is specifically *Roman* about the stories told about Roman emperors? How do perceptions of them differ, if at all, from other kings and rulers?[54]

"POPULAR" AND "ELITE"

Words such as "popular" and "elite" are difficult to avoid and offer a certain cozy familiarity. But what do they actually mean? Definitions of "popular" and "elite" have usually been discussed and debated in terms of status, education, or culture. One possible reading, based on wealth and social status, is as follows. The elite in the Roman world constituted the very top of the status pyramid: the emperor and his family, the senatorial and equestrian orders, the city councilors, and, in Late Antiquity, the ecclesiastical establishment. All in all, we are talking about roughly two hundred thousand people out of a population of approximately sixty million. Popular culture and ideas therefore form the world of the non-elite, the other 59.8 million Romans. But history is messier than this. There is contact, blurring, and slippage along all the boundaries we erect for ourselves, as shown by Peter Burke's seminal research on popular culture in early modern Europe. Education is a crucial factor that calls into question a strict division between popular and elite solely on the basis of status. A poet might not be an aristocrat in any sense of the word—neither a senator, an equestrian, nor a member of the curial class whose members staffed town councils—but their literacy, education, and talent would mark them out as elite when compared to a tradesperson.[55]

Any approach carries a risk of simplifying a complex world (as all models and definitions do), but Burke's work helps us to see greater shades of nuance. Burke has argued for two principal paradigms of understanding, which Lucy Grig has proposed should be applied to the ancient world. The first is diversity, in the sense that even among elite and popular cultures, we must account for geographical, linguistic, and social variation. The second is unity, since elite and popular cultures were never entirely separate: their worlds interacted and collided in manifold ways. In ancient Rome, there was certainly an intellectual elite culture, the world of Seneca and Plutarch, Ambrose and John Chrysostom. This was founded on formal education in, and serious engagement with, literature, philosophy, history, religion, and rhetoric. In terms of education, literacy, and life experience, there was a gulf between these sorts of men (and they were mostly men) and the tradespeople, laborers, bakers, carpenters, farmers, enslaved laborers, and countless others who made up the bulk of the Roman population. The culture of the elite was both oral and literate, whereas the world of the other ninety-nine percent was primarily an oral one.[56]

Following Burke's arguments on diversity and unity, it is important to highlight the areas of interaction and overlap between these two groups. Firstly, the fundamental ideas and values expressed by elite culture and popular culture were often very similar, even though they were articulated in different forms and exhibited different levels of complexity. The popular moral and philosophical ideas about kingship found in fables, proverbs, and sayings share many similarities with the values of leaders articulated in elite philosophical works such as Seneca's *On Clemency*. Likewise, there were stories about Roman emperors that circulated orally among Jewish communities, but they have come down to us today because they were written down by members of the literate elite, rabbinic scholars, who regarded these tales as valuable and appropriate testimony about monarchical behavior.[57]

Secondly, although most of the population of the Roman empire could never partake in the educated elite culture, because they lacked the necessary literacy, education, or wealth, there were many cultural experiences, ideas, and frames of reference shared up and down the social hierarchy. To give but one example: witticisms and cruel observations about emperors' bodies and sexual habits occurred in the theater, where the crowd—a mixture of all elements of society—laughed about Tiberius's fondness for cunnilingus. Augustus wrote crude sexual epigrams about his opponents, the senator Cassius Dio rejoiced in retelling the lascivious sexual antics of Elagabalus, and Seneca's *Apocolocyntosis,* a work written and performed for a court audience, features the emperor Claudius announcing on his deathbed: "Oh dear me, I think I've just shat myself!" Mikhail Bakhtin, whose work on Carnival has proved enormously influential, would describe this type of humor as "low" in the sense that it deals with the lower part of the body, "the genital organs, the belly, and the buttocks." Such humor is based around "degradation," or "the lowering of all that is high, spiritual, ideal, abstract." The literary critics Peter Stallybrass and Allon White have argued that the high/low bodily dynamic has influenced European conceptions of culture and social order—we often speak of "highbrow" and "lowbrow" humor, for instance—but these supposedly popular opposites are actually deeply interconnected. And so, these Roman sexual and scatological jokes might be a form of "low" humor because they emanated from the bottom half of the body, but this humor was certainly embraced by people from all walks of life.[58]

Thirdly, both elites and non-elites engaged in the spreading of rumor and gossip. Talk about the emperors manifested itself publicly in a range of oral and written discourse such as poems, graffiti, exhortations, and chants, which moved among and between different social levels in various ways. Pamphlets, as texts that were probably longer than epigrams and graffiti, were usually a mode of communication preferred by the elites. But they could also be read aloud to a broader audience, which could ensure that their messages circulated more widely. Graffiti that were short acclamations of praise (such as those for Nero with which we began this book) or exhortations and criticisms can conceivably have been the work of literate or semiliterate citizens who ranked below the senatorial and equestrian orders (sometimes referred to collectively as the *plebs media,* or "the middling sort"). Poems could be circulated in the form of graffiti scrawled on buildings or statues, written pamphlets, or chanted aloud. As we have already observed above, some poems about the emperors show detailed knowledge of court life, and thus probably emerged from this aristocratic context, written either by courtiers or the poets they patronized. Others may well have been the work of those authors classified by scholars as "popular poets" (after a passage in Cicero's defense speech *For Archias*). These were men (or women) with literary talent and panache who had yet to attain the equestrian dignity of a Martial. No matter the identity of the original authors, the ideas in these poems entered wider public knowledge when they were displayed or read out and sung aloud.[59]

Songs could be specially composed for wide circulation. In the fourth century, the priest Arius wrote songs promoting his particular theological views on the nature of Christ in a well-known meter that could be sung while sailing, traveling, and working. But we should also not discount the creative role of the wider population or their capacity to invent ditties on the spot, for which there is excellent comparative evidence from the medieval and early modern worlds. Chants and shouts of protests were often set to the same memorable and easily recitable rhythms as the acclamations in favor of the emperor. Sometimes it was just a manner of twisting the usual words, as when the acclamations designed to herald the arrival of a new governor in Antioch were turned into insults against the child emperor Arcadius. Where did the initiative for these cries and chants come from? We know that factions and claques often had leaders who mouthed words for their members to recite. The emperor Julian wrote that the insults leveled against him in the marketplace at Antioch were the product "of those citizens with the talents to craft jests of this sort," which suggests a small group of subversive song-composers. Libanius, who was highly critical of the attacks on Julian, ascribed them to tanners, blacksmiths, and criminals. The reference to criminal elements seems like snobbery on Libanius's part (the "high" looking down on the "low"), but the role of tradespeople in the mocking of Julian should not be dismissed. Not only did the emperor fail to take proper action over the inflation of grain prices that affected the entire population of Antioch, but workers' guilds commonly functioned as political pressure groups. Perhaps the most important point is that the chanting created a collective performance. For, as Julian himself reminded the people of Antioch, they were *all* responsible for abusing him: the authors of the jibes, those who joined in and chanted the lines, and even those who listened appreciatively. This united yet anonymous oral attack on the emperor meant that its agents could not be sharply demarcated according to gender, social status, or profession. The "elite" and "popular" collapsed into one.[60]

A POLITICAL PUBLIC

I opened this book by proposing that rumor and gossip about Roman emperors represented a form of political engagement. But what do I mean by "political"? Politics has two principal definitions. The first is the institutional meaning: the exercise of government in terms of appointing or electing officials, setting policies, making laws, declaring war and peace, and other decisions within the remit of the ruler and/or the state. The second, much broader, definition characterizes politics as deliberation, argument, and negotiation about the distribution of resources and power within and between groups, usually with the aim of reaching a consensus view on the matter. That is why we can talk about "the politics of gender," concerning issues of equality between men and women in society, as well as, on a much more mundane level, "the politics of the office tearoom," about who should pay for, and who is entitled to use, the communal milk. Oral discourse about Roman emperors can be considered political in both senses. Although not necessarily always taking place within institutions, such as the senate house, it certainly dealt with institutional matters, notably the emperor's exercise of power. It was also political in the sense that it reveals that Roman individuals and communities engaged in discussion and debate about what sort of person an emperor should be, why he ruled the way he did, what his plans for the future might be, and his relationship with his subjects. Sometimes this discussion could result in support for the emperor's decisions, at other times in outright rejection, but more often it teetered in between. All this talk was a manifestation of the negotiation of Roman imperial power.[61]

But could people from all walks of life engage in genuine, meaningful political debate in the Roman world? The sociologist Jürgen Habermas proposed that a "public sphere" in which political issues were seriously discussed only emerged in Europe from the late seventeenth century onward. This was a world of coffeehouses, salons, and table societies in which an intelligent, educated "bourgeois public sphere" not only debated political issues, but also formed opinions on them that were taken seriously by the government. Habermas argued that the creation of "public opinion" contrasted with most earlier periods of European history, such as the medieval age, which was marked by a "staging" of rulership before the king's subjects, rather than genuine political engagement. The ancient world is largely excluded from his work apart from a glancing and problematic reference to the Athenian democracy. Over the past thirty years, historians of the pre-modern world have taken significant issue with Habermas's argument, both for the way in which he characterized earlier periods of history and for the manner in which he constructed one monolithic "public sphere" as opposed to multiple, overlapping spheres and publics. Moreover, his work placed an emphasis on the textual world of educated elites, rather than more widespread oral discourse. Habermas did briefly acknowledge the existence of a "plebeian public sphere," in contrast to the bourgeois focus of his argument, but he did not pursue it in any detail.[62]

This is a profitable tension to explore further. Habermas's sociological model—which largely eschewed the presentation of empirical evidence—is intimately tied to the specific world of the eighteenth-century intellectual revolution and the emergence of modern representative government. But historians of ancient, medieval, and early modern worlds have argued that people in all these periods certainly had the capacity to express *an* opinion, and more importantly, that this opinion mattered. Tom Johnson and Claire Judde de Larivière, two historians of medieval Europe, have proposed that "to speak, and especially to speak out in public in the later Middle Ages, was to participate in politics." In his study of information transmission in colonial India, Christopher Bayly has powerfully demonstrated that political discussion could, and did, exist in a society "dominated by fable" (a similarity India shared with the Roman world). Debate in eighteenth- and nineteenth-century India was conducted through placards, protests, cultural performances such as festivals, and, of course, rumor and gossip. Bayly argued that scholars need to pay attention to the dialogue between elite and popular culture in the circulation and expression of political ideas, which draws us back to the pivotal ideas of Peter Burke on unity and diversity.[63]

I would argue that most Romans probably had an opinion on a political matter such as a new, exorbitant tax, but their capability to engage with and critically assess the full dynamics would vary. Relatively small, elite groups might be able to appreciate the nuances of fiscal policy. These would be people like the anonymous fourth-century author of *On Military Matters,* a treatise that offered unsolicited advice to the emperors on topics such as taxation, the military budget, and abuses at the mint. Other reactions might be relatively simplistic and take the form of chanting or demonstrations in opposition to the tax, motivated by one factor—they could not afford to feed their families. Sociological studies have shown that crowd actions, such as protests and riots, are one of the tangible and recognizable ways in which people, especially those on the lower levels of the status pyramid, can articulate public opinion. Such open challenges are often dangerous, given that they make manifest discontent hitherto restricted to private or small group conversations, but the risk reflects the importance of the views they express. As Wayne te Brake has written, riots and protests are "an integral part of an interactive political process—as statements within an ongoing conversation." These oral expressions should be considered political actions just as much as debates among the aristocratic elites.[64]

I would therefore like to emphasize the complex and multifaceted manifestations of both "politics" and "public opinion." Habermas was correct to argue that in the pre-modern world, kings and queens presented and "staged" themselves before a public through appearances, proclamations, laws, and artistic media. But this does not preclude responses and reactions to this staging that might be considered political. Even in the Roman Republic, all politicians were supposed to present themselves before the people and, more importantly, persuade them of their case when standing for election, proposing a law, or advocating for war. The political culture of the *res publica* thus combined both "theatrical" elements (to quote the historian Tom Hillard), as well as a real sense that the decisions—or at least the persuasion—of the electorate could direct decision-making. Under the emperors of the monarchical *res publica,* the theatrical and performative elements of staging continued, while the so-called democratic elements gradually faded away or transformed into new forms, which dramatically altered the institutional political framework. In the imperial period, all Romans, from senators to members of the general population, legitimated the position of their rulers through the performance of ritualized acclamations. "These are the prayers of the people!" proclaimed the assembled crowd at the acclamation of

Leo I in the Hebdomon at Constantinople in 457. "Roman emperors, pious and fortunate, may you rule for many years!" (repeated twenty-two times) and "We ask that the codices kept in the bureaux be completed at public expense!" (repeated sixteen times), shouted the senators gathered in Rome at the acceptance of the Theodosian Code in 438 (the entire list of acclamations would have gone on for approximately an hour). "The power of the Romans for all time! The Augusti, our lords! For the fortune of the prefect!" cried the people of Oxyrhynchus in a ceremony during the visit of the prefect of Egypt.[65]

It is my contention that "politics" and the formation of public opinion(s) about the Roman emperor went beyond such ritualized oral performances. Even the emperors themselves knew this, though their reactions to what was being said could be very different. Diocletian reportedly despised the "people's empty voices," whereas Constantine decreed that all "voices of complaint" against his governors and "the voices of our provincials" should be reported to him so that he could take action. These cries of protest represented the public manifestation of rumor, gossip, and other forms of oral discourse through which rulership was negotiated in response to the emperor's own edicts, letters, monuments, and personal appearances. I characterize this engagement as "everyday politics," a phrase taken from the title of Niko Besnier's important book, *Gossip and the Everyday Production of Politics.* This is not intended to downplay the importance of oral discourse, as "everyday" sometimes implies, but to magnify it and emphasize its fundamental role in the Roman world. Moreover, the notion of the everyday helps to counteract some of the problems caused by the "elite" and "popular" dichotomy. By emphasizing its ongoing, daily existence, rather than concentrating exclusively on markers of literacy, education, and social status (which still have an important place), politics becomes something in which all Romans could—and did—participate beyond the world of government institutions and choreographed performances.[66]

Let us open our ears and begin to listen.

CHAPTER 1

The Possibilities of Power

Constantius Gallus had a short and tragic life. His mother, Galla, died when he was less than five years old. His father and elder brother were murdered when he was only twelve, victims of the bloody purge orchestrated by his cousins Constantine II, Constantius II, and Constans, following the death of their father, Constantine, in 337. All potential male rivals to the throne were murdered, with the exception of Gallus and his six-year-old half-brother, Julian. They were spared on the grounds that Gallus was so ill he was expected to die soon and that Julian was very young, though it is perhaps more likely they were saved by the intercession of the bishop Eusebius of Nicomedia. The brothers were subsequently confined to house arrest at the mountainside estate of Macellum in Cappadocia. Gallus and Julian could have lived out the rest of their days in Macellum, nervously waiting for the sound of couriers arriving with orders for their execution.

But everything changed in 350. Constans, the emperor of the West, was murdered by his officer Magnentius, who claimed the purple for himself. Constans's brother Constantius II, the emperor of the East, had to travel to Gaul posthaste to suppress the revolt. But he needed an imperial colleague to oversee the eastern provinces and ensure the security of the volatile frontier with the Persian empire. Lacking any children of his own, Constantius II turned to the now-twenty-six-year-old Gallus. In 351, Gallus was plucked from house arrest, given the title of "Caesar" (junior emperor), and married to the emperor's sister,

Constantina. The new imperial couple was sent to Antioch in Syria, the principal imperial city in the East. The next three years proved to be disastrous, mainly due to Gallus's antagonistic relationship with the local leadership of Antioch and imperial officials. When the news that Gallus had executed many of his opponents reached Constantius in the West, he summoned his cousin to Italy. In late 354, not yet thirty, Gallus was executed at Pola on the Istrian peninsula.

The savagery of Gallus's behavior in Antioch is vividly brought to life in Book 14 of the history written by Ammianus Marcellinus, a native of the city and a military officer. The book opens in 353 with stories of numerous prominent men being executed and having their property confiscated at Gallus's orders. Private conversations were produced as evidence of treason by unscrupulous informers, allegedly encouraged by Gallus's wife, Constantina (whom Ammianus portrayed as a particularly devious figure). Several years later, Julian offered an explanation for his brother's conduct. He wrote that Gallus had been treated like a prisoner by Constantius and that his natural tendency to cruelty was likely exacerbated by the long years of mountain exile at Macellum. Ammianus described Gallus in similar (although far less sympathetic) terms, arguing that the "unexpected leap" from confinement to Caesar had fueled Gallus's pride and arrogance.[1]

Ammianus painted a vivid portrait of one particularly unsavory aspect of Gallus's time in Antioch:

> Finally, Gallus set a new and ruinous standard when he dared to embark on a seriously disgraceful act, which, so it is said, the emperor Gallienus once dishonorably attempted at Rome. Gallus was accustomed to wander around at night, going to all the taverns and crossroads, with only a few companions who were secretly armed. Speaking in Greek (which he knew very well), he asked people what their feelings were concerning the Caesar. He was brash to do this in a city where the illumination of the nighttime lamps usually shines as bright as day. And so, since Gallus was often recognized and he realized that everyone would know what he was up to if he continued, he henceforth only went out in daylight to deal with matters which he thought were most pressing. There were many people who deeply lamented the things that he had done.[2]

Gallus's undercover mission to discover what the citizens of Antioch really thought of him encompassed the taverns and crossroads, both of which were known urban havens for rumor and gossip. Ammianus did not reveal how he found out about Gallus's nocturnal wanderings, but he almost certainly heard the stories circulating in Antioch, since he was stationed in the city during the

Caesar's reign of terror. He could even have seen Gallus out and about himself and made assumptions about his activities, perhaps in conversations with his fellow military officers.[3]

Whether Gallus really did embark on such surreptitious nighttime antics with the intent ascribed to him by Ammianus is open to question. The Caesar's evening walks with a small retinue could have been misinterpreted as underhand attempts to spy on his subjects. There are many anecdotes in our literary sources, such as Cassius Dio, Suetonius, and Tacitus, about other young and reckless emperors engaging in similar exploits. The teenaged Elagabalus allegedly donned a wig to play the part of a female prostitute, while Caligula reportedly frequented whorehouses and cookshops in his twenties disguised in a wig and a long cloak. Nero, who was sixteen when he received the purple, haunted bars and brothels at night, either concealing his true identity by means of a wig or a freedman's cap or by dressing as a slave. He engaged in fights and burgled shops so often that he required protection from the imperial guard, by which time his secret had been revealed. There is good evidence that the stories about Nero were also contemporary, like those told of Gallus. Pliny the Elder, a military officer who lived through Nero's reign and whose *Natural History* predates the accounts of Suetonius and Tacitus, wrote that Nero mixed the juice of thapsia plants with frankincense and wax to conceal the welts on his face from his nighttime punch-ups, "going about with unblemished skin as evidence to disprove the rumors." Not every author needs to derive their information from another written source (an assumption made time and again by modern Roman historians); it is eminently plausible that Pliny the Elder, a well-connected Roman aristocrat, *heard* the tales of Nero's antics and his cosmetic cover-up.[4]

Many aristocratic Roman youths are said to have engaged in all sorts of reckless and dangerous nighttime escapades. However, the stories about these young emperors are very similar to the common folkloric motif of the "King in Disguise," which appears in Icelandic, Indian, and Jewish traditions, among countless others. The tale about Gallus reflects several famous variations of this motif identified by scholars, who have given them titles such as "King in Disguise to Spy out His Kingdom," "King Goes in Disguise at Night to Observe His Subjects," and "King in Disguise to Learn Secrets of His Subjects." The main motif also appears in Book 2 of Tacitus's *Annals,* in which the general Germanicus, adopted son of the emperor Tiberius, moves unrecognized among his troops on the night before battle with the German leader Arminius. However, there is a crucial difference in the way the motif plays out. Germanicus is depicted as a valiant general who receives praise and affirmation from his troops while disguised. Germanicus's behavior echoes the most common forms of the "King in Disguise" motif that speak to the intrinsic goodness of the monarch, such as "Incognito King Helped by Humble Man; Gives Reward" and "Incognito King Rewards Farmer for Gift." But Gallus's motive is primarily a wicked one, as he wanted to receive affirmation from his subjects or to catch unwilling suspects talking critically about him.[5]

The stories that Roman emperors walked the streets in disguise at night, sometimes drinking, whoring, and fighting, while at other times hoping to eavesdrop on conversations about themselves, exemplify the interaction between oral discourse, popular ideas of kingship, and elite literary texts. Traditional, folkloric motifs formed the frameworks of knowledge that shaped the rumors about Gallus and Nero heard by Ammianus and Pliny the Younger; these same ideas—whether transmitted orally or through writing—certainly influenced the textual representation of imperial behavior in histories and biographies penned by Suetonius, Tacitus, and Cassius Dio. In the case of Ammianus, who was present on the scene in Antioch, we can reasonably suppose that he not only heard the stories about Gallus but also drew inspiration from Tacitus's portrayal of the young, tyrannical Nero for his presentation of these stories. The oral tales and their textual manifestations suggest that there was a deep-rooted anxiety about what an emperor—especially a youthful and headstrong ruler with minimal checks on his authority or passions—could do. This uncertainty was fueled by the fact that most Romans (even those who spent their lives at his door) could never really know the emperor's mind. This did not stop them from imagining—often in contradictory ways—what he might be doing and thinking. In a letter to a widow whose husband had died in battle, the bishop John Chrysostom conjured up an image of the emperor and his wife being terrified by foreign armies at their door, while in one sermon he told his congregation (either in Antioch or Constantinople) that the current emperor had been constantly assailed by danger and conspiracies since his coronation. By contrast, a collection of oral sayings of the monks of Egypt, collected and written down in the fifth and sixth centuries, features a poor man celebrating his freedom through an imperial allusion. Although his blanket only covered half his body, the pauper said he could stretch out his feet all the way just like an emperor (presumably imagining him as a man without a care in the world), while rich men (the emperor's victims) were kept in chains and stocks in jail. Even if much of the subject matter seems fantastical, when Romans talked about their emperors, they engaged in "everyday politics" that probed and delineated the expectations of their leaders. The surviving examples of rumor and gossip reveal that the most popular topic of conversation was what the emperor was capable of doing to his subjects.[6]

AWAITING JUSTICE

The Roman emperor was expected to deliver justice in a fair and considered manner. Posturing panegyrists and smooth-tongued sophists alike composed suitable paeans to the just and clement monarch, their florid words echoing the values and concerns of the political and intellectual elite. What mattered, however, was whether emperors actually lived up to this ideal. As Carlos Noreña has aptly put it, "It was ultimately the practical benefits of monarchy and empire . . . that had the greatest ideological resonance." For people lower on the social spectrum, their only encounter with the emperor may have been to gaze at his portrait alongside the local magistrate, but they trusted that this representative would apply imperial law in the correct manner (fig. 3). "Our savior [i.e., the emperor] has ordered that those who have been judged unfairly should come before you without fear to obtain justice," wrote an Egyptian petitioner to a minor bureaucrat to remind him of this obligation. When the apostle Paul was arrested by the Jews for his Christian preaching, he insisted that as a Roman citizen, he should be brought before the Roman governor's tribunal rather than a Jewish court. All trials were supposed to be held in public, so that justice and its enforcement would be visible to all; this idea entered the Roman consciousness to such a degree that scenes of these hearings were even found in school exercises.[7]

Popular interest in the correct application of the law is a prominent theme of Roman maxims and fables. "A judge's verdict reflects on himself as much as it does on the accused," was one of the many *Sayings* compiled in the first century BCE by an enslaved man who later won his freedom, called Publilius Syrus, whose work is one of our best sources for popular morality in the Roman world. Preoccupation with the outcome of judicial appeals can be found in other forms of popular literature. An oracular handbook known as the *Oracles of Astrampsychus,* dated to the second century, included the question: "Will I obtain the petition?" If the application of the law failed at the local level, there was a principle that all Romans, no matter their social status, were able to petition the emperor for his judgment. "We ask you, most sacred emperor, to come to our aid," wrote tenants on an imperial estate in North Africa who were suffering from abuse by imperial officials, while peasants working imperial land in Lydia appealed to the emperor's "heavenly right hand" to protect them from unjust exactions. We can see the hope embodied in these petitions in action in the case of a Thracian smallholder named Sisola. She appealed to the emperor Diocletian when a cow she had leased was subsequently killed in a "hostile incursion"

Fig. 3. Rossano Gospels, showing Pontius Pilate sitting in judgment on Christ, sixth century CE. Museum Diocescano e del Codex, Rossano. Images of Roman emperors can be found on his tribunal and on the standards behind him. Recall Pictures/Alamy Stock Photo.

(presumably a raid by a foreign people). The emperor ruled that the man who had leased the cow should pay recompense to Sisola, since he had agreed to be responsible for any loss. Even a humble farmer could potentially feel the warmth of the just ruler.[8]

Yet there was only a fine line that separated the firm and evenhanded emperor from the maddened, unrestrained tyrant. Rome's elite philosophers, such as Seneca the Younger, argued that an emperor could be severe—kings, like fathers and their children, were entitled to punish their errant subjects—but he should not degenerate into vengeful cruelty. This idea was echoed by one of the popular maxims written down by Publilius Syrus: "Anger is accustomed to forget the law." The hope that the emperor and his representatives would be fair and merciful coexisted with the fear that there was almost nothing one could do in the face of such overwhelming power. "Against powerful men no one has enough protection," opened one of the *Fables* of the former slave Phaedrus, while the dream interpreter Artemidorus wrote that it was a sure sign of death if a sick man dreamed of being a ruler, "for a king alone is subject to no one—in that, he is like the dead." The same ambivalence permeated Christian thought. The fifth-century Christian monk Shenoute proclaimed that punishing wrongdoers "is the province of the righteous emperors, into whose hand God has given the sword." But much like the Old Testament God, an emperor's wrath could be terrible, as the priest John Chrysostom often reminded his congregations. Chrysostom and other Christian preachers, such as Gregory of Nyssa, urged members of their flock to place their faith in God as a way of overcoming their innate powerlessness against secular authority.[9]

These everyday preconceptions, values, and fears about monarchical behavior that transcended the "elite" and "popular" divide provided the frameworks of knowledge that shaped the rumors that consumed the city of Antioch in early 387. The crisis began on the morning of Thursday, February 25, or Friday, February 26, when a letter from Theodosius I was read out publicly at the governor's courthouse. It contained the very unwelcome news that the emperor was asking for two taxes to be paid. The first was the "crown gold" that had to be met by city councilors in honor of Theodosius's tenth anniversary as emperor. The second obligation was known as the "five-year collection," a tax that fell on all those who engaged in commercial activities. These were not new taxes, but they were now being imposed simultaneously on Antioch, probably at a higher level than was usual, in order to meet the cost of paying and maintaining the Roman army. The assembled audience of councilors, lawyers, former soldiers, and local notables in the courtroom protested to Celsus, the governor of Syria, some even invoking the name of the Christian God to save them from this imposition. They soon moved to the colonnade outside, where they tore off their cloaks and openly lamented the emperor's impositions in front of other residents of Antioch. A group marched to the residence of the bishop Flavianus to ask him to intercede with the emperor, but he could not be found, so they returned to the governor's courtroom. By this time quite a crowd had gathered and—perhaps spurred on by the theater-claques, who were well-versed in the art of protest—the mob marched to the public baths, cutting down streetlamps and sending them smashing to the ground. Rioters launched themselves at the railings surrounding the governor's house with the hope of breaking in and sacking it.[10]

The mob soon found a new target: the images of the emperor Theodosius I and his family, including his recently deceased wife, Flaccilla, his young children, Arcadius and Honorius, and his father, the general Theodosius. People shouted abuse at these painted portraits of the imperial house and began to throw stones at them, breaking the wooden images into pieces. They then turned their attention to bronze imperial statues, which they lassoed with ropes, pulled from their pedestals, and dragged along the street. Boys jumped from statue to statue or played with the detached limbs and heads, formerly symbols of imperial majesty, now merely broken bronze. They could be heard crying out, "Gold!" time and again. This repetition of one word can be found in other acts of popular protest in fifteenth-century England ("Fire") and in nineteenth-century India ("Darkness"). These shouts of frenzied crowds, which occurred in different times and places, all functioned as significant manifestations of public opinion, furnishing the people with a potent political voice that had been denied to them through institutional channels.[11]

The riot in Antioch, despite its collective nature, actually reveals different facets and levels of political engagement. The "crown gold" was only levied on the councilors, while the "five-year collection" was to be paid by those engaged in commercial enterprises. Yet both these groups managed to stir up a much wider segment of the population of Antioch to protest higher taxes. While taxes levied on merchants and traders would have resulted in higher prices for consumers, not all the rioters may have been aware of such nuances—they may simply have thought they would be required to pay more to Theodosius's own coffers to support the army. One other possibility is that they were motivated by a dislike for the military, to whom they had already contributed so much. Although the Roman army helped to secure the frontiers and protect cities like Antioch, the actual presence of Roman soldiers was often resented, since they made indiscriminate use of private resources, including farmlands, in the region.

The chants of "Gold!" reflect this wider opposition against the emperor and his military forces. Whatever Theodosius had written in his letter (and its contents are unknown to us), this event represented a profound failure of communication between the Roman state and its subjects.[12]

The riot was only finally subdued by the troops dispatched by the count of the East, the senior imperial administrator in Antioch. They rounded up as many of the culprits as possible, who were then summarily tried and put to death. By the middle of the day, it was all over, only a few hours after the emperor's letter had been read in the courthouse. The enormity of what had taken place in Antioch struck home almost immediately. If riots can be conceptualized as part of a political "conversation," as Wayne te Brake has argued, they are nevertheless inherently risky acts because governments might respond with reprisals. This was what the Antiochenes feared. Imperial images were sacred representations, which were required to be venerated as if they actually were the emperor. An attack on the emperor's portraits and statues was nothing less than an insult to his majesty, a treasonous offense. Mistreatment of imperial images could be allowed under certain ritualized or Carnivalesque circumstances, such as on the occasion of a festival held in the Syrian city of Emesa, where the people pulled down a statue of the reigning emperor and gave his backside a damn good thrashing, like a naughty schoolboy. But the type of wanton desecration meted out to the portraits and statues of the Theodosian dynasty could only otherwise take place in an authorized fashion when an emperor or a member of his family had fallen from power and been officially disgraced (fig. 4).[13]

Even while the riot was still in progress, messengers had set out for Constantinople to inform Theodosius. The inhabitants of Antioch began to panic at the thought of how he would react, an anxiety that generated rumors. Could the emperor even appear in person? In 342, when his general Hermogenes was killed in a riot in Constantinople, Constantius II had indeed immediately rushed from the eastern front to visit the city. On that occasion, he decided to be clement and spare Constantinople's inhabitants. But the people of Antioch feared the worst of Theodosius, spreading rumors that he would be enraged and vent his wrath on the city. According to the rhetorician Libanius, an eyewitness to the events of that day, some people thought that the emperor would send his army to kill the entire population indiscriminately, others that he would murder the councilors before their eyes, still more that the city and its people would be burned in an apocalyptic conflagration. There was precedent for such horrific action. In 215, the emperor Caracalla had massacred a significant portion of the population of Alexandria after they abused and pilloried him. Even though the

Fig. 4. Relief from the "Arch of the Moneychangers" in the Forum Boarium, Rome, early third century CE. The emperor Caracalla stands next to an empty space, from which the representation of his condemned wife, Plautilla, had been removed. Photograph by Caillan Davenport.

people of Antioch probably had no knowledge of this event, which had occurred some 150 years before in a completely different city, they were certainly aware that rulers could be vengeful. There survive a variety of statues, monuments, and coins that depict emperors in military dress, often maiming, trampling, and abusing the bodies of foreign peoples (figs. 5 and 6). These

Fig. 5. Marble sculpture (50 centimeters tall) of a Roman emperor holding a captive by the hair, from Egypt, third century CE. Liverpool World Museum 1971.180. © National Museums Liverpool.

Fig. 6. Marble statue of the emperor Hadrian crushing a defeated foreigner underfoot, originally from Hierapytna in Crete, second century CE. Istanbul Archaeological Museums. Gokhan Dogan/ Alamy Stock Photo.

representations were certainly more common than images of the emperor as a peaceful judge, which were relatively rare. Although the violent images were designed to project the idea of the emperor as a defender of Rome against its enemies, they also reminded his people that such fearsome power could be directed at them. As Michel Foucault has shown, violence done to the bodies of subjects was nothing less than a "political ritual" that manifested the ruler's power in ugly, brutal, and bloody fashion. The public execution of criminals by a sovereign equated them with foreigners slain on the battlefield in a way that was designed to be memorable.[14]

Consumed by fear and anxiety over Theodosius's bloody revenge on their bodies, Antioch's citizens and their families, including city councilors, distinguished former imperial officer holders, and Libanius's students, fled to the countryside. In *Oration* 23, a speech written a few weeks after the riot while the crisis was still ongoing, Libanius said that he had tried to talk sense into those who were leaving Antioch. His contacts, men with knowledge of the imperial court, had informed him that a city would never be sacked when an emperor was not personally present. Moreover, he asked, why would an emperor—not least one as benevolent as Theodosius—want to destroy one of his greatest cities? This had never happened previously, Libanius observed (though he did not mention the Alexandrian precedent). But the city was alive with rumors, and in the absence of reliable news from Constantinople, Libanius's view of what could happen was just one of many predictions circulating in Antioch.[15]

On Saturday, February 27, John Chrysostom, at that time a newly ordained priest, took his place in the Old Church at Antioch to address his terrified flock. In Christian societies of the pre-modern and early modern period, sermons could be a powerful conduit not only for spiritual guidance, but also for the transmission of political information and ideas. Priests likewise played an important role in articulating notions of human and divine justice to their congregations. Chrysostom spoke passionately about the events of the previous days and the precarious situation in which Antioch now found itself. In particular, he admonished the behavior of the rioters. "Now I mourn and lament," the congregation heard him say, "not because of the magnitude of the punishment we are expecting, but because of the excessiveness of the madness that took place." The other citizens of Antioch, who did not personally participate, were not spared the force of Chrysostom's reprimand, for they had stood by and failed to check the sacrilege of the mob. "In order to survive the impending danger"—the emperor's wrath—he exhorted his congregation to pray fervently and piously to God and to act virtuously in all ways.[16]

That very weekend, God's earthly representative in Antioch, Bishop Flavianus, set out to Constantinople to ask Theodosius for clemency on behalf of the city's population. On Sunday, February 28, the day before the beginning of Lent, it was up to Chrysostom to deliver the sermon in the Great Church of Antioch. Standing under the mighty dome of the cathedral, Chrysostom sought to offer comfort that Flavianus would succeed in his mission. As soon as Flavianus appeared in the imperial presence, the priest told his flock, "He will at once calm the emperor's anger." Flavianus, Chrysostom continued, would remind Theodosius that this was the season of Easter, in which Jesus Christ had died to absolve the world of its sins, and he would urge the emperor to follow in Christ's path. Chrysostom then addressed the rumors that Theodosius would destroy the city and its population. Many Antiochenes were apparently turning to biblical texts in their terror and quoting a verse from the Book of Proverbs: "A king's threats are like a lion's wrath." The congregation listened to Chrysostom as he urged them to consider instead the story of the wolves and the lambs from Isaiah, arguing that God—through his emissary, the bishop Flavianus—could convert the imperial lion into a lamb.[17]

The generation of rumors about Theodosius's vengeance was a particularly urgent form of everyday politics that reflected how the Antiochenes feared for their lives. Chrysostom seized the opportunity. In the days and weeks of Lent that followed, Chrysostom used his sermons to encourage his flock to seek solace in the arms of the Church. "Our rulers make threats, and so the Church must provide reassurance," the congregation heard him proclaim on Wednesday, March 3. Theodosius then decided to send commissioners to Antioch to investigate. About ten days later, a new rumor swept through the city that it would be sacked by the emperor's troops. On Saturday, March 13, or Sunday, March 14, the governor of Syria entered the Great Church to reassure the Christian congregation that no such sack was imminent. Chrysostom's sermon, delivered immediately afterward, while ostensibly magnanimous toward the governor, could not hide his displeasure at having his authority usurped in this fashion. He instructed his flock that it was they who should teach the other people of Antioch to be brave and not give in to the fear engendered by such rumors. It is apparent, however, that Libanius's pragmatic assessments of imperial conduct, the governor's reassurance, and Chrysostom's offering of strength through Christian belief could not prevent the people of Antioch from endlessly speculating that they would meet a gruesome fate at the emperor's hands. Anyone with knowledge of Theodosius's court at Constantinople who arrived in the city was questioned for new information. But the circulation of rumors would only be quelled by the arrival of trusted and reliable news.[18]

Theodosius's representatives, the master of the offices, Caesarius, and the master of the soldiers, Ellebichus, finally arrived in Antioch on Monday, March 15. As soon as these officials reached the city, rumors about the actions they would take emerged. Libanius later recalled that the Antiochenes spent a sleepless night. Over the next two days, Caesarius and Ellebichus sat in judgment on the city councilors, and on Wednesday, March 17, they announced the penalties to be imposed. Antioch was to be deprived of its status as a metropolis, and the circus, theater, and baths were all to be closed. The distribution of bread to the poor would cease, and imperial troops would be quartered in the city to enforce law and order. Many of the city councilors would be banished, while others would face the death penalty—although the final decision about execution lay in the hands of Theodosius I himself. This possibility of leniency was secured by the intervention of monks who lived in the hills around Antioch, as John Chrysostom recalled in a sermon delivered a few weeks later.[19]

Caesarius embarked on the journey back to Constantinople on March 18, and the nervous wait for the emperor's response to the request for clemency began. It would last for several weeks. In the meantime, Antioch did not return to its former state: many of the councilors remained in prison, and the news that the emperor had not actually razed the city did not even tempt those who had fled to return. With gatherings in most public places now prevented by their closure, the Church assumed an even greater importance. Chrysostom, addressing his anxious congregation on Saturday, March 27, reminded them that all the calamities that had been rumored—that the emperor would order houses to be burned with residents still inside and the city to be razed to the ground—had been averted through prayer and intercession with God. The entreaties of Bishop Flavianus and the monks now provided a reason to hope that bloodshed would be avoided. The audience listened as Chrysostom declared that all the other punishments, such as the closure of entertainment venues, were a welcome rebuke for a city that had sinned: "His chastisement has turned out to be a correction, his punishment guidance, and his anger instruction."[20]

Forty-four days after the riot, on Saturday, April 10 (the day before Palm Sunday), the news reached Antioch that Theodosius had exercised clemency toward the city and the councilors, commuting the death sentences and restoring all its privileges. Bishop Flavianus made his well-timed return the following week on Easter Sunday, the choice of date underlining that the challenges of Lent were now over through the return of Antioch's own savior. Chrysostom's sermon that day was suitably triumphant, as he reminded his congregation that rumors of the emperor's wrath did not terrify those who had placed their faith in God. While Libanius's *Orations* were never publicly delivered, and all of those concerning the riot except *Oration* 23 were written after the arrival of Theodosius's announcement of clemency, Chrysostom had delivered his *Homilies on the Statues* as the crisis unfolded and the city was gripped by terrifying rumors. (The sermons were of course later revised, almost certainly to emphasize his own role in events, but that does not reduce their value as contemporary documents.) The priest's irritation at the governor's entrance into the Great Church to quash rumors about an imminent sack by the emperor's army reflects the fact that Chrysostom wanted to situate himself as the sole source of information, and by extension, of reassurance, to his congregation. The terror felt by the Antiochenes at the thought of what Theodosius might do was real and palpable, but it was almost certainly further stoked by Chrysostom to enhance his own position, as Hartmut Leppin has shown.[21]

This was not the end of the turbulent relationship between Theodosius and cities of the empire. In early 390, a riot broke out in the Hippodrome at Thessalonica in response to the imprisonment of a popular charioteer by the general Buthericus. In the course of the riot, Buthericus was killed. Since we depend on much later sources, in contrast with the contemporary writings that illuminate the situation at Antioch, the manner in which Theodosius's response was decided upon and communicated is unclear. There was a massacre of the inhabitants of Thessalonica in April 390, in which perhaps as many as seven thousand were slaughtered. This was almost certainly not Theodosius's intention—he probably only intended for the ringleaders to be executed. He may even have decided to send imperial investigators to examine the situation first, as occurred in Antioch in 387, and as his son, the emperor Honorius, would do later in the case of disturbances in Carthage in 419. Buthericus's troops nevertheless engaged in a full-scale bloodbath. The massacre was still interpreted as Theodosius's decision both at the time and in subsequent Christian mythologizing of the emperor's public act of repentance. Rumor and mythmaking alike were fueled by the same frameworks of knowledge, found in philosophical theories of kingship, theory, popular sayings, and biblical texts—kings were wrathful individuals who needed to be placated.[22]

THE BUSINESS OF GOVERNMENT

The riot in Antioch was sparked by anger at Theodosius I's simultaneous imposition of two burdensome taxes to support the army and his military campaigns. When Romans thought and talked about their emperors as policymakers, the issue of taxation loomed large. In his thirty-second *Homily on the Acts of the Apostles,* delivered after he had been promoted from Antioch to the see of Constantinople, John Chrysostom told his congregation that emperors were primarily preoccupied by two things: defeating their enemies and then securing taxes and tribute from the peoples under their sway. Chrysostom's picture of the imperial mind would have resonated with his urban congregation, from the artisans, craftsmen, traders, and other business owners who had to pay the "five-year collection," to the senators who were subject to a special tax on their landholding and expected to provide the "crown gold" on accessions and anniversaries. Similar views emerge from texts offering a provincial perspective. In the books that make up the New Testament, the emperor appears primarily as an agent of regulation and taxation, given the prominence of Augustus's ordination of the census and the famous "Render under Caesar the things that are Caesar's" anecdote. The Jewish community of the Levant often talked about the emperor's financial impositions. The first-century Jewish rabbi Rabban Gamaliel II pronounced: "By four things does the empire exist: by its tolls, bathhouses, theaters, and crop taxes." One of the harshest exactions was the hated "Jewish tax" instituted by Vespasian after the destruction of the Temple in Jerusalem; this was described by Rabbi Johanan as a payment to "the government of your enemies." Such talk about the emperor's taxes could certainly transform into provincial insurgency. When an imperial procurator stationed in North Africa exacted taxes too zealously in 238, the aristocratic landowners not only rose in revolt, but also managed to rally poorer tenant farmers to their cause. They murdered the procurator and proclaimed the governor Gordian as emperor in opposition to Maximinus, who was campaigning far off on the German frontier.[23]

The perennial pressure of taxation meant that Romans frequently talked about how emperors handled their finances, as well as their generosity or lack thereof in sharing the rewards of empire with their subjects. Generosity to the people (*liberalitas*) was trumpeted as an imperial virtue in edicts and on coinage alike. Tokens (*tesserae*) bearing images of emperors and their family were associated with distributions of money or grain in early imperial Rome, connecting dynastic rule and stability with the daily necessities of life. This emphasis on openhandedness meant that avarice had to be condemned. In 491, when the Augusta Ariadne addressed the people of Constantinople in the Hippodrome regarding her selection of the next emperor (and husband), she publicly promised not to choose a man ruled by passion for money or other human failings. Christian preachers likewise declaimed the image of the generous king to their flocks. Peter Chrysologus, bishop of Ravenna in the fifth century, remarked that those who ascended to the highest place of honor should be generous to their family, neighbors, and the people at large. Since Peter often delivered sermons with the Theodosian imperial family present, the message was clearly aimed both at emperors and their subjects. We can see how these ideals manifested themselves in provincial society in a petition written by an Egyptian monk asking the emperor to render assistance to the poor in his locality. The surviving corpus of petitions from Egypt suggests that the most impoverished did not often avail themselves of the justice system in the Roman world, so they depended on intermediaries such as this monk to plead their case for them.[24]

Improper imperial behavior was often met with hostile talk among different levels of society. Symmachus, urban prefect of Rome, urged the teenaged emperor Valentinian II not to follow through with his plan to requisition horses from the guild of businessmen and merchants in Rome, lest it provoke "public complaints" about the emperor throughout the city, especially among the mercantile classes. The prefect's concern shows that he did not regard such potential conversations as mere harmless chatter, but as a real sign of political discontent with Valentinian. Shortly after the murder of Julius Caesar, his adopted son and heir, the young Caesar (later Augustus), was criticized for his love of furniture and tableware in the expensive "Corinthian" style, which was made up of a combination of gold, silver, and bronze to produce a glittering effect. There was even a story that during the proscriptions of 43 to 42 BCE he had ordered the deaths of some wealthy men simply because he wanted their Corinthian finery for himself. A graffito was scrawled on a statue of the young Caesar in Rome that simultaneously impugned his heritage and his expensive tastes: "My father was a money changer, but I'm a Corinthian-dealer." The social origin of this talk and the graffito itself is difficult to pinpoint exactly, but we can say that it was broadly elite, given that the proscriptions targeted the wealthiest members of society. But the public nature of the writing could certainly have prompted further talk that circulated more broadly throughout Rome.[25]

The practice of defacing statues as a form of political protest continued into the Byzantine period. Talk about the covetousness of the emperor Anastasius—ironically, Ariadne's chosen second husband, whom she professed would not be ruled by this vice—underlies a poem that was affixed to one of the emperor's statues in the Hippodrome. The bitter epigram lamented the murder, poverty, hunger, and anger "through which you destroy everything as a result of your greed." Analysis of the poem's style shows that this was no impromptu composition by the mob, but the clever work of a member of the literate, educated elite (to use Peter Burke's terminology). The verse may have been prompted by court gossip about the emperor's stinginess, but it was made manifest in a place that would do the most public damage, since the Hippodrome was the venue in which the wider populace of Constantinople issued their verbal complaints to the emperor. The capacity of such ditties to cross the "elite" and "popular" divide is demonstrated by comparative study of political poetry in other societies. Richard Cust has argued that verses lampooning the court of the British king James I "operated on at least two levels," entertaining the aristocracy as well as providing "a means of disseminating news and opinion to the illiterate and semi-literate." The particular practice of posting poems to trigger political dialogue is attested in nineteenth-century India. Christopher Bayly has demonstrated that verses pinned in public places such as mosques or temples moved effortlessly between written and oral forms, as people read them (or had them read out to them) and then turned to chanting the lines aloud. By choosing to post the ditty about Anastasius anonymously in the Hippodrome, the author ensured that all voices and audiences, regardless of their social status, literacy, or education, would be merged together into one critical public, condemning the emperor's grasping nature.[26]

Talk about an emperor's fiscal situation could potentially have serious consequences. After the death of Julian, his relative Procopius went into hiding and began to gather intelligence for a tilt at the imperial purple by harvesting "little rumors" that the new emperor, Valens, was seizing the property of aristocrats. Now it was true that Valens did stringently enforce the collection of back taxes to repair the treasury, as attested in segments of a law preserved in the *Theodosian Code*. The "little rumors" might therefore refer to the whispers of suspicion that leaked out of the court about Valens's intention, or perhaps they had their origin in panicked stories from aristocrats who had begun to have their property seized. Procopius did manage to win enough military support to pose a threat to Valens, even though he was ultimately defeated on the field of battle. Sometimes stories of financial stringency could play a role in undermining confidence in an emperor's regime, as when rumors spread through the fifth-century Gallic elite that the western emperor Anthemius had no resources left at his disposal. Negative talk not only had immediate ramifications, but it also lived long in historical memory. "I am amazed that even now there are those who accuse him of not being generous," wrote the senator Cassius Dio about the emperor Marcus Aurelius, attesting to continued gossip about his generosity (or lack thereof) among the senatorial order thirty to forty years after his death.[27]

One of the reasons why an official like Symmachus cautioned Valentinian II against taking action that would cause hostile talk is that disgruntled feelings could move up and down the social spectrum, regardless of the level of society from which they had originally emanated. Popular proverbs and sayings frequently condemned the avaricious and miserly. "The greedy man is the cause of his own misery" and "The grasping do not live, but die slowly" were two choice offerings from the freedman Publilius Syrus. These ideals manifested themselves openly in abusive chants by members of the urban population, when they were unable to have their voices heard in other ways. The people of Alexandria protested against the harshness of Vespasian's taxes, calling him "Cybiosactes," a Greek word that meant "salt-fish dealer." This witty moniker had previously been applied to Seleucus, who had married the Ptolemaic queen Berenike IV in 56 BCE, only to be murdered a few days later. The greed and stinginess of the Byzantine emperor Maurice was the subject of contemporary talk in Constantinople. It found expression in chants at the Hippodrome abusing him as a "Marcianite," referring to a heretical belief that did not subscribe to charitable giving. In both these outbursts, we see how the content of verbal attacks on the Caesars were shaped by regional and religious contexts. But they were all underpinned by the shared expectation that an emperor should be generous to his subjects. Emperors who did not live up to these virtuous ideals would find the narratives of their reign and personality being rewritten through these many different forms of political talk. In the case of Maurice, the chants formed part of a wave of protests that created the conditions for the centurion Phocas to stage a successful revolt.[28]

Emperors could choose whether to stay silent in response to these accusations or engage in a dialogue with their subjects. The emperor Vespasian, who was forced to take drastic measures to restore the treasury after the depredations of Nero, declined to answer the people of Alexandria. But during the rest of his reign, spent in Rome, he used humor to defuse criticism that he was stingy and grasping, even posting public replies to these accusations. The most famous Vespasianic joke concerns his tax on the use of urine by fullers to bleach cloth. When his son Titus criticized him for this new imposition, Vespasian is said to have brandished a coin in front of his son's nose and asked him whether it smelled bad. Titus replied that it did not, to which the emperor is said to have replied: "And yet it comes from urine." While the authenticity of many imperial sayings has often been doubted, the preservation of this and numerous other unique Vespasianic witticisms in Suetonius and Cassius Dio suggest that they had become well known in court circles. But Vespasian's alleged avarice certainly circulated beyond the walls of the palace, since it was mocked by the mime actor who imitated the emperor at his public funeral. Vespasian's fiscal stringency was evidently thought worthy of criticism. But it was also forgivable to a certain extent, given that the emperor himself engaged elites and the wider population of Rome in joking about and defending his actions (presumably having learned his lesson in Alexandria).[29]

In the cities of Rome and Constantinople, the emperor's care for feeding his populace assumed a preeminence in the public mindset on par with taxation. In his *Res Gestae* ("Achievements"), a formal, public account of his reign, Augustus boasted of his provision of grain to the citizens of Rome (or more, accurately, a subset of them known as the *plebs frumentaria,* "the grain-receiving populace"). Early in his political career, the young Caesar had committed a serious *faux pas* that had brought home the seriousness of feeding the population. In 39 BCE, while Rome was suffering from a grain shortage, he had hosted a decadent dinner party in which all the aristocratic guests dressed up as gods. When news of the banquet spread through Rome, young Caesar, who had imitated Apollo, was publicly mocked as "Apollo Tortor"—Apollo the Torturer. People cried out: "The gods have gobbled up all our grain!" Unlike some anonymous witty epigrams attacking emperors that may have had elite authors, this chant can be identified as a genuinely popular form of criticism emerging organically from the populace. The complaint was only four words in the original Latin, and it was very easy to twist short, positive acclamations such as names and epithets into negative ones.[30]

After this false start, Augustus assumed permanent responsibility for the grain supply to Rome. This responsibility was taken up by his successors, and in the fourth century, the privilege was extended to Constantinople. Rumors of the grain fleet being late or unable to reach the capitals appear in contemporary documents (such as the *Letters* of the fourth-century senator Symmachus). These whispers were always tinged with trepidation at the resulting panic, protests, or riots. It is not surprising that there would be some form of public demonstration in response to a food shortage, given that this was one of the few avenues available to a starving population to have their voices heard. Food protests and riots are well documented throughout the pre-modern world, but their motivations and manifestations were often quite divergent—sometimes they were directed at merchants, suppliers, or inspectors, while at other times they were symptomatic of deeper political discontent and a desire for constitutional change. In the Roman world, these demonstrations were usually aimed squarely at the emperor and his representatives, because the "beneficial ideology" envisioned the *princeps* as a father figure who would provide for his children (the residents of Rome and Constantinople). Many emperors were accosted by an angry mob during a food shortage, from Claudius, who had bread hurled at him in the Forum Romanum, to Theodosius II, who was stoned by the people of Constantinople when he went to inspect the city's granaries. Both rulers and subjects could therefore easily be caught up in the eddies of rumor about food shortages. When a rumor reached the ears of the emperor Leo I that the Vandal king Geiseric intended to attack Alexandria, a move that would cut off the grain supply to Constantinople, the emperor was so concerned that he sent an envoy to consult the holy man Daniel the Stylite about whether this would actually come to pass. The emperor's presence was regarded as a comforting guarantee that the grain supply would continue to arrive. Caligula's extensive preparations for a journey to Egypt in 41 sparked a nervous rumor that he wished to make Alexandria the capital of the empire, which would have meant that Rome would have been deprived of its special status. In the Roman urban mindset, imperial rule was inextricably connected with the provision of the necessities of life, and the people were entitled to express their discontent when their needs were not met. If we consider "politics" as a battle for control over power and resources, food—one of the most precious resources that sustained life—certainly constitutes a political issue that engaged Romans from all walks of life.[31]

When emperors visited major provincial cities, local economic problems that would usually have been the responsibility of governors suddenly became an imperial concern. Upon Julian's arrival in Antioch in July 362, the people appealed to him to do something about the shortage of grain, which had driven up local food prices. "We've everything here, but everything's dear!" they shouted at him in the theater. Julian initially left the problem to the city councilors, but when they failed to do anything, he issued an edict that imposed the maximum prices at which grain and other food could be sold. The impact of this was disastrous. Julian was hated by the shop owners, because he had limited their ability to turn a profit. But he also aroused the ire of the wider population, since the rich had hoarded grain and then sold it for higher prices in the rural communities outside the city. The country people got wind of what was happening and flooded into Antioch, where the food was now cheaper (as decreed by Julian's edict), and so the city population had to compete with them for basic necessities. Popular discontent boiled over. During the New Year's celebrations in January 363, Julian was greeted with abusive chants in both the Hippodrome and the marketplace. The people criticized his beard, dislike of horse-racing and the theater, and numerous other items deriving from gossip about his appearance and personality. Although the abuse of Julian took place within an urban environment, its perpetrators likely included members of the rural population, who had come to participate in the Kalends of January celebrations. Julian was furious. Not long after, he abandoned the city for his Persian campaign, writing his *Misopogon* as a parting shot to the people of Antioch and leaving the economic crisis unresolved. This was an attempt by Julian to answer his critics like Vespasian had done, but it backfired spectacularly because of the bitter, satirical tone of the *Misopogon*. The difference between the two emperors was that the witty Vespasian successfully took control of public discussion about his financial management, while Julian ensured that people would continue to speak in a hostile fashion about his Antiochene edict long after his death. This negotiation of kingship was as much a contest over an individual emperor's memory as it was about the present moment.[32]

How often did protests actually result in any change of imperial policy? Emperors often turned a deaf ear to petitions and protests, no matter how loudly they were uttered. The best example of mockery that is thought to have persuaded an emperor to change his mind concerns Domitian's vine edict of the early 90s. When Domitian noticed that the city of Rome was short on grain but blessed with a surplus of wine, he took measures to free up precious agricultural space for the production of grain, decreeing that no more vineyards should be planted in Italy, and that half the vineyards in the provinces should be removed. This was not popular with regional landowners. The province of Asia sent an embassy led by the sophist Scopelianus to Domitian to ask for its repeal. Scopelianus was successful, which the Greek intellectual Philostratus attributed to the sophist's persuasive rhetoric. However, according to the biographer Suetonius, "it was believed" that Domitian actually abandoned the policy because of the impact of pamphlets that were distributed throughout Rome. These featured a Greek epigram by the poet Evenus:

> Goat, even if you chew me right down to the root,
> There'll still be enough for your sacrificial wine from my fruit.

The pamphlets were probably written or commissioned by those most affected by the emperor's restrictions—wealthy Roman winegrowers. But their anonymous authorship meant that they gained a multi-vocal plurality that enabled them to represent wider public opinion, regardless of their origin. The verse speaks as if it is the grapevine personified, while the goat can be none other than Domitian himself. Goats were regarded as sexually promiscuous, deviant, hairy, and smelly animals by the Romans. This epigram also charged Domitian with lack of sexual continence, undermining his assumption of the office of "censor for life" (*censor perpetuus*), a position that made him the arbiter of Roman morality. Even though it was very rare for public complaints to result in the reversal of imperial policies, this example shows that there was always the possibility that it could happen—or the *hope* that it could happen (after all, Suetonius said "it was believed" that Domitian caved because of the pamphlets: no one knew his intention definitively). It was this glimmer of hope that drove Romans to exercise their political voice through public demonstrations.[33]

Protests could sometimes have delayed consequences. In his *Jewish Antiquities,* Josephus included a story about Caligula drawn from an earlier Roman author, the senator Cluvius Rufus, who experienced the emperor's reign firsthand. When the people petitioned Caligula at the chariot races to grant a tax remission, he refused. Their chants gradually grew louder, and so the emperor sent soldiers into the crowd to kill anyone shouting, which quelled the discontent. The protest itself failed, but it did, so Josephus wrote, increase the determination of the praetorian tribune Cassius Chaerea to plot Caligula's removal. Almost two centuries later, Elagabalus's financial official Aurelius Eubulus was so hated that the people of Rome called for him to be handed over to them, according to the contemporary senator Cassius Dio. Such criticism could only have manifested itself in a public arena if Eubulus had already been the topic of discussion. These demands went nowhere at the time, but when Elagabalus fell from favor, Eubulus was "torn into pieces by the people and by the soldiers." Everyday politics had real impact.[34]

REGULATING BELIEF

Taxes, the food supply, and economic policies had the potential to affect Romans of different social status and background. Regardless of their individual place in the social hierarchy, everyone needed to eat, buy essential goods, and pay taxes to the imperial government. A third issue of imperial policy that became more significant and widespread in its impact over time was religion. The Roman government usually tolerated the Jewish monotheistic belief, though when there were revolts in Judaea, as occurred under Nero and Vespasian in the first century and Trajan and Hadrian in the second, the reprisals were swift and bloody. In the middle of the third century, empire-wide persecutions of followers of Christianity were instituted for the first time. The scale of the persecution varied from edict to edict and the severity of the punishments levied depended on social status. Christian communities were therefore thrust into a continuous state of high anxiety. In the summer of 258, rumors circulated in North Africa that the emperor Valerian planned to issue orders to his provincial governors regarding a new phase of anti-Christian measures. Anxious to confirm the veracity of what he had heard, Cyprian, the bishop of Carthage, sent a delegation to Rome. The embassy reported back that they had gained access to the emperor's letter to the senate, which confirmed the rumor that directives would soon be sent to provincial governors, including those in Africa. Although this was not good news for Cyprian and his fellow Christians, at least they now had some certainty, which allowed them to make plans for the future.[35]

These fears did not dissipate in the fourth century and beyond once emperors became Christian. This is because the Church was divided by long-running Christological disputes, such as whether God the Father and God the Son were composed of the same substance (the "Nicene" or orthodox view, laid down at the Council of Nicaea in 325) or were rather made up of similar substances (the "Homoean" position). In the late fourth century, the city of Milan was a particular flashpoint for conflict between the two Christological beliefs. The bishop Ambrose was a Nicene Christian, but the teenaged emperor Valentinian II, who resided in the city between 375 and 387, subscribed to the Homoean view. Whispers of the conflict in Milan soon reached the ears of Valentinian's Nicene imperial colleague Magnus Maximus, who was based in Gaul. "For," Maximus wrote in a letter to Valentinian, "rumor is never content to lay hidden, especially when it is circulated among the people." This was actually an open letter that was designed to inform the Nicene community that Maximus would change ecclesiastical policy if he controlled Italy, which he promptly invaded the following year. Maximus's missive shows that he was alert to the political potency of talk. Maximus intended to harness the opinions of the Nicene Christians to support his regime and exercise supremacy over Valentinian II.[36]

Rumors of an emperor's Christological beliefs were taken so seriously that they came to assume a preeminent position in public discourse in Constantinople, particularly from the fifth century onward. Following the death of the emperor Zeno in 491, his widow, the Augusta Ariadne, was permitted to choose the next ruler. When she appeared in the Hippodrome, the people implored her to choose wisely. "An orthodox emperor for the world!" they cried out repeatedly. Ariadne promised to choose a man with orthodox beliefs, but it was rumored that her nominee and soon-to-be husband, Anastasius (he of the greedy reputation), had Monophysite leanings. This was a belief that God the Father and God the Son were of one nature, as opposed to the orthodox position decreed by the recent Council of Chalcedon, held in 451, that God and Christ were one being with two natures. The bishop of Constantinople, Euphemius, made Anastasius sign a document professing his orthodoxy. This is an example of how different forms of oral discourse—rumor (an unauthorized, anonymous mode of speaking) and acclamations (highly ritualized acts performed by a group)—coalesced to put pressure on the imperial regime. These whispers did not disappear, however, showing how the everyday politics of oral discourse could fester over many years. Over time, it turned out that the rumors were true, and that Anastasius did actually support Monophysitism, despite his official statement. This prompted some inhabitants of Constantinople to turn to the streets in public protest. On one occasion, several decades after Anastasius's accession, a Monophysite verse was sung in the "Hymn of the Trinity" in Hagia Sophia. In protest, a crowd gathered and overturned the emperor's statues and called for the aristocrat Areobindus to be acclaimed emperor instead. The last years of Anastasius's reign were dominated by a revolt of his leading general in Thrace, Vitalianus, who upheld the theological decisions of the Council of Chalcedon. Widespread disbelief in Anastasius's professed orthodoxy therefore manifested itself in crowd responses, encompassing a large cross section of the Constantinopolitan population, and an elite rebellion, in the form of Vitalianus's insurgency. These were political acts that demonstrated how debate about Anastasius's fitness to rule consumed Constantinople for decades.[37]

We see similar issues at work in 578, when Tiberius II was serving as Caesar to the incapacitated Augustus, Justin II. Tiberius's provision of a church for Constantinople's community of Homoean Goths gave rise to a rumor, which "buzzed" throughout the city, that the Caesar was himself a Homoean, according to John of Ephesus, writing from prison across the Bosphorus. When Tiberius II was crowned Augustus later that same year, he was met with hostile chants from the populace, and he was forced to issue an anti-Homoean edict, which he posted publicly, in order to dispel the rumor. This is an excellent example of how observation of an emperor's actions could lead to incorrect suppositions about his true intentions. The political impact of the rumors was so serious that Tiberius II could not afford to dismiss them as "empty voices" (to quote the dismissive remark of his predecessor, Diocletian). Doctrinal issues were important because Christians dreaded that an emperor's heterodoxy would lead to the wrath of God punishing his people. When the Muslims captured the Egyptian city of Alexandria in 641, shortly after the death of the emperor Heraclius, the Christian community believed this was a direct result of his "persecution of the Orthodox," according to the contemporary Egyptian bishop John of Nikiu. Romans knew—and feared—that an emperor's decisions had far-reaching implications on both Earth and in heaven.[38]

THE CIRCLES OF POWER

The anxious talk that these issues of taxes, food, and belief could inspire among the empire's inhabitants reveal the realities of everyday politics in the Roman world. It meant that there was always a need for reliable official news regarding the emperor and his policy decisions. We have already observed how this news came in the form of imperial edicts, laws, and letters, which the state represented as emanating directly from the emperor and representing his own judgments. Although Clifford Ando has argued that this constituted "communicative action," through which the state and its subjects reached a consensus about the workings of Roman imperial power, rumors show that considerable ambiguity remained. Anastasius's public profession of orthodoxy did not put a stop to talk about his theological beliefs, and hostility toward the emperor only intensified, eventually resulting in the revolt of the orthodox general Vitalianus. In this case, popular talk had it that Anastasius was a liar.

On other occasions, we can detect a widespread anxiety that the emperor's decisions and words were not actually his own. As Christopher Kelly has astutely observed, all emperors had to delegate, for they could not do everything, but at the same time delegation strengthened the powers of the emperor's bureaucrats. It was the gap between the myth of supreme imperial oversight and the everyday reality of administration that allowed rumor to flourish. There were, for example, countless rumors about forgery and malfeasance at the imperial court. In the second century, the senator Cassius Apronianus told his son, the historian Cassius Dio, that the empress Plotina had really been the one to sign her husband, Trajan's, final letters to the senate, because he was already dead. The biographer Suetonius reported suspicions from various informants that the emperor Titus had been a master forger. This led to speculation about the validity of documents issued during the reign of his father, Vespasian, and Titus's brother Domitian allegedly claimed that even their father's will had been forged. Such misgivings were sometimes shared by the recipients of imperial letters. Theodoret, bishop of the Syrian city of Cyrrhus in the fifth century, refused to believe that an order from Theodosius II confining him to his diocese under pain of punishment was genuine, despite the fact that the letter was supposedly written in the emperor's own hand. Theodoret promptly wrote to several contacts at court, including a patrician, a prefect, and a consul, to ask whether the order really did come from the emperor and represent his authentic view. In this case, the answer for the unfortunate bishop was "yes."[39]

These suspicions about the authorship of imperial decisions were nourished by the belief that emperors could be manipulated by other powerful figures.

Claudius's absentmindedness was a topic of conversation during his reign both inside and outside the court. Seneca's *Apocolocyntosis* suggested that the emperor forgot that he had ordered the execution of his wife, Messalina; in a later version told by Suetonius, Claudius asks why Messalina has not joined him for dinner. The people who were really in charge of the empire, so the rumors went, were his enslaved and freedmen secretaries. I propose that these stories were even familiar to audience members in Rome's entertainment venues. When, in the course of performing a play by the Greek playwright Menander, an actor delivered the line "A successful, whip-able slave is unendurable," the audience turned to look at Claudius's petitions secretary, Polybius, who was sitting in the theater that day. In staring at the freedman, the theatrical audience transformed the original line, which was "unintentionally ambiguous," into a statement that was "politically allusive" (to quote Shadi Bartsch). This action gained its potency and safety as a political act not by being a poem or pamphlet directly attacking Claudius and Polybius, but as the anonymous, collective movement of the crowd.[40]

A century and a half later, the Roman crowd knew exactly what it was doing when it made an allusion to the power of Septimius Severus's powerful praetorian prefect, Gaius Fulvius Plautianus. According to the senator Cassius Dio, an eyewitness to these events, the crowd in the Circus Maximus addressed the prefect directly: "Why are you trembling? Why are you pale? You hold greater power than the Three." The cries implied that Plautianus exercised greater authority than the imperial college of Septimius Severus, Caracalla, and Geta. "They said that this was not directed at him [i.e., Plautianus] but was meant differently," Dio wrote in his history. Quite who "they" were is uncertain from the narrative. Perhaps there was some kind of response on the day by Plautianus or the emperors that forced the crowd to shout out denials. In contrast with the Claudian incident, when the crowd took a line out of context as a reference to Polybius, the Severan audience—or more probably, a group of ringleaders within the audience—created a chant to criticize Plautianus, but then denied that it actually pertained to him. These two events show how knowledge about powerful courtiers could manifest itself in different forms of oral protest. These not only harnessed preexisting rumor and gossip, but also very probably generated further talk after the event.[41]

Outside of Rome and Constantinople, far from the imperial court and the rumors and gossip that flowed between palace and city, the transmission of oral discourse depended on one's connections. Prosper of Aquitaine, a Christian chronicler who lived in southern Gaul, relied on his ecclesiastical networks for news from Rome. Speculation reached him about the downfall of Aetius, senior general of the emperor Valentinian III, whom the emperor had suddenly murdered in 454. In his *Chronicle,* written in 455, Prosper noted that the murder had occurred even though the two men had recently exchanged oaths, and that there had even been a marriage pact between the emperor's daughter Placidia and the general's son Gaudentius. Prosper writes that the relationship soured because—"as it was believed"—the eunuch Heraclius had plotted against Aetius. Our chronicler relied, like everyone else who did not witness the events of that fateful day, on rumors that were shaped by popular conceptions of court politics. Sometimes such stories could be fomented by local encounters with an emperor. One Jewish tale related how the Jews of Caesarea Philippi had petitioned Diocletian to reduce their taxes because the financial imposition was so heavy that they would be forced to leave their homes. But the emperor's (unnamed) advisor urged him to reject the petition on the grounds that if they did flee, they would come back anyway, because there was nowhere else to go. These rumors about Valentinian III and Diocletian were shaped by the folkloric idea that good kings were manipulated by evil counselors.[42]

The same point can also be made about women, who were regarded as especially untrustworthy influences, since they exercised authority that depended on intimacy rather than official laws or institutions. One Jewish story, which circulated orally before being written down by the rabbis in Late Antiquity, focused on the wrath of Plotina, the wife of the emperor Trajan. Plotina thought that when the Jews lit candles during Hannukah, they were actually celebrating her recent miscarriage. She promptly ordered her husband to end his campaign against a foreign enemy and crush the Jews instead. This tale probably emerged among the eastern Jewish diaspora as an explanation for why, during Trajan's Parthian campaign, he engaged in the suppression of Jewish rebels in Egypt, Cyrene, Crete, and Mesopotamia. Women were even suspected of making monumental political decisions on their own authority. Hydatius, a bishop in northwestern Spain, wrote of hearing "a wicked tale spread by rumor" about the Augusta Licinia Eudoxia. This story had it that the recent Vandal sack of Rome in 455 came about because Eudoxia had entreated the Vandal king Geiseric to come and rescue her after the murder of her husband, Valentinian III. Hydatius got his news from travelers and embassies traveling between Spain, Gaul, and Rome, suggesting that this rumor originated somewhere along this network as an explanation for why the Vandals were able to sack Rome so easily. What was originally a fifth-century rumor was later enshrined as fact in historical works of the sixth century and beyond. The responses and acclamations in the theater and circus in Rome, stories told by Christian chroniclers in Spain and Gaul, and Jewish legends all share the same anxiety about the power that courtiers and family members could have over emperors.[43]

Such anxieties about who was running the government were especially acute if the emperor was a child or teenager. Even when delivering a panegyric in honor of the boy Augustus Gratian at the imperial court in Trier in 367–368, Quintus Aurelius Symmachus relayed the senate's view of his elevation at eight years old: "We thought he had been chosen when the time was not quite right." Such elite concerns could be broadcast beyond senate or palace walls through sermons delivered by bishops. Members of the congregation did not need to possess full or even partial literacy to absorb the arguments of these homilies. In 387, the Nicene bishop of Milan, Ambrose, gave a sermon in which he attacked the influence of the Homoean bishop Auxentius over the teenaged emperor Valentinian II and his court. This was not designed to be preached to a silent crowd: the written version that survives today is clearly marked by a train of thought and pauses designed to accommodate applause and cheering. The congregation heard Ambrose claim that the recent law issued by the emperor in favor of Homoean Christians was actually "written by the hand and spoken by the mouth of the bishop [Auxentius]." Auxentius, the bishop claimed, wanted "to arouse the emperor's ill-will" and ensure that Ambrose's case would be heard only in the palace. In the course of his sermon, Ambrose strategically deployed the day's reading about Naboth, who had been executed by King Ahab after he had been "deceived by womanly counsel"—that of his wife, Jezebel. There could be no doubt that this was a not-so-veiled allusion to the influence of Valentinian II's mother, Justina. If his congregation had not already suspected that Valentinian II was not in complete control of his court, they would certainly have done so by the time they had finished listening to Ambrose's homily. John Chrysostom's preaching in Antioch following the riot of the statues, which we examined earlier, was designed to reassure the congregation about the power of the Church to mollify a Christian emperor and was therefore full of predictions and possibilities. Ambrose's sermon, on the other hand, expounded an alleged insider's view of court politics, and thus masqueraded as the dissemination of news and information to the Nicene community of Milan.[44]

These widespread beliefs about the incapacity of child emperors constituted the frameworks of knowledge behind rumors circulating in North Africa during the early fifth century. In August 408, Stilicho, the most senior general in the West, fell from power and was executed. He had been the de facto head of government since January of 395, when the emperor Theodosius I died and was succeeded by his ten-year-old son, Honorius. Even as Honorius grew to adulthood, Stilicho maintained effective control over the imperial administration until the conspiracy that toppled him. His death was greeted by several dispossessed groups in North Africa as an opportunity for change. One of these was the Christian sect known as the "Donatists," whose beliefs were regarded as unorthodox and heretical both by the Church and by the imperial administration. In 399, Honorius had issued an edict in which financial penalties were imposed on, and privileges withdrawn from, the Donatists, who had allegedly colluded in a recent revolt against his government in Africa. This was followed by another edict in 405, which outlawed Donatism and another belief known as "Manichaeism" as heretical. Honorius had also targeted pagans, sending imperial officials to Carthage to close the pagan temples and destroy their statues.[45]

And so, when news that Stilicho had fallen reached Africa late in 408, these "enemies of the Church"—as they were described by Augustine, bishop of Hippo—seized the moment. They concocted rumors that cast doubt on "those laws concerning the destruction of idols and the correction of heretics" issued by the imperial administration during Stilicho's period of preeminence. "For they deceitfully spread it about—and perhaps even really think—that these acts were done without Honorius's knowledge or without his consent," Augustine wrote in a letter to Olympius, who was now the leading official at the imperial court. All "sacred letters" that emanated from the administration were delegated to chancellery officials, as Augustine well knew, but they were presumed to have the emperor's personal stamp of approval. He implored Olympius to issue a letter confirming that the "the laws that were sent on behalf of the Church of Christ were dispatched under the authority of the son of Theodosius, not of Stilicho." The idea that Honorius's government was run (successfully, it must be said) by Stilicho was accurate, but it was exploited by the pagans and Christians estranged from the Church to sow dissent in North Africa. This could only be quelled, so Augustine thought, by a new official missive from the court stating that Honorius was really in charge, given the scale of the belief that he was a mere puppet. The problem here was that if the Africans did not believe Honorius was the author of earlier edicts, why should they trust this new confirmation? The Donatists' rumor played on the expectation that the people of Africa might willingly reject (or at least doubt) the state's efforts at communicative action. As father, benefactor, and judge, the emperor was expected to rule with a firm but munificent hand—how could this happen if he was not really in charge?[46]

NEAR AND FAR

The power of the emperor was felt regardless of where he was physically located, with statues, edicts, officials, and soldiers serving as representatives of his authority throughout the empire. Theodosius never set foot in Antioch during the uneasy Lent of 387, but his absence did not lessen the people's fears about the cruel punishments he could inflict upon them—indeed, it may have actually increased them. As Rhiannon Ash has shown, neither the presence nor the absence of the emperor reduced Roman anxieties about imperial behaviors but only caused them to manifest in different ways. When an emperor traveled to a new province or city, he could grant privileges, build much-needed amenities, and notice local injustices that needed remedying, all while citizens were literally dazzled by his glory, according to eulogistic panegyrists. But he could also make burdensome requisitions to support his traveling court, enforce controversial policies, or make punitive decisions. The emperor Constantine often made threatening promises to visit provinces in order to sort out theological disputes himself. This duality of the imperial presence is captured by a remark made by the fourth-century author of the *Explanation of the Whole World,* who said the emperor's presence in Gaul not only brought abundance but also caused prices to rise.[47]

We can get an indication of the fears caused by an imperial journey in a flurry of letters exchanged between ecclesiastical officials in 365. The Nicene church communities of Asia Minor were terrified by the news that the Homoean emperor Valens would soon leave Constantinople and travel through their region on his way to Syria. Gregory, a priest based at Nazianzus in Cappadocia, wrote to Basil, a priest at Caesarea (about a four- to five-day journey eastward), regarding his fears about the arrival of the "contingent of heretics." Gregory also sent a letter to Basil's superior, Bishop Eusebius of Caesarea, describing the emperor's court as "wild beasts laying waste to the Church." On this occasion, the fears of the Nicene clergy did not come to pass, since Valens was distracted by the revolt of Procopius and had to return to Constantinople. But the emperor did set out on another journey through Asia Minor five years later. This meant countless requisitions and exactions to support the traveling army and court, which was about "to eat its way through Cappadocia" (in the memorable words of Peter Brown). For some, then, the presence of an imperial retinue would mean economic hardship. For the Nicenes, this represented the potential threat of an assault on their faith. Gregory of Nyssa, Basil's brother, described "the emperor bearing down on the Church from the Propontis [i.e., Constantinople] like an angry storm cloud." Contemporary letters written by Basil, who by this time was bishop of Caesarea, show his mood frequently changing depending on the rumors he received from Constantinople about Valens's interference in ecclesiastical affairs.[48]

The emperor did not always need to arrive in physical form to cause consternation. This is dramatically demonstrated by the incidents that unfolded in 40, during the reign of Caligula. Philo of Alexandria recalled that when he and other ambassadors were waiting at Puteoli for an audience with Caligula, a fellow Jew rushed up to them with terrible news: the emperor wanted to set up a statue of himself in the Temple at Jerusalem! Publius Petronius, the governor of Syria, then marched to Jerusalem with his army to install the statue, sparking new rumors that Caligula intended to make war on the Jewish people. Petronius, as it turned out, was determined to avoid bloodshed and actually wanted to negotiate with the Jews. During a meeting of Jewish leaders at Tiberias, the governor pointed out that if he did not obey and install the statue, he would be put to death—and Caligula would send an army to punish them regardless. Caligula might have been far away in Rome, but his presence—and his potential to exert his power through the armies—still resonated in Judaea.[49]

Members of the imperial court could never escape the emperor, since they were forced to live constantly in his presence. Family members, friends, advisors, doctors, officials, freed and enslaved workers, and guards usually followed him wherever he traveled, whether that was for summers spent in Campania or harsh winters on the Danubian frontiers. The court was a place of privilege, offering opportunities for social advancement and intimacy with the emperor, but it could also be an environment of fear, intimidation, and anxiety. Julian, who was summoned to be installed as Constantius II's new Caesar after his brother Gallus's execution, described his time there as "the most bitter and painful slavery," while the senator Ausonius, who served at the court of Gratian in Trier, aptly characterized it as a place that "shows men's faces, but cloaks their intentions." Nor was this view restricted to members of the imperial family and the senatorial aristocracy. The freedman Epictetus, who had been an enslaved worker toiling away at the Julio-Claudian court, lamented the influence and control of the palace functionaries—themselves enslaved or freed people—whose menial duties put them in intimate proximity with the emperor. "How is it that a fellow is suddenly made wise when Caesar appoints him overseer of the chamber pot?" he wrote, frustrated at the need to kowtow to this menial nobody. Yet all honors and perquisites, from the right to preside over imperial bowel movements to the glory of the ordinary consulship, were only granted at the emperor's whim. This is encapsulated in one of the *Fables* of the freedman Phaedrus, in which an enslaved worker stationed at the imperial villa of Misenum goes to great lengths to prepare Tiberius's path by pouring water over hot earth or settling the dust in front of the emperor's feet. Tiberius's response? You need to do much more than that to earn your freedom, lad. Phaedrus insisted the anecdote was a "true story"; regardless of whether or not we believe this, it imparted a truthful message about the dynamics of imperial power, which applied equally to senators as it did to slaves.[50]

Imperial words and deeds at court were rarely secret. When serving as Caesar in Gaul, Julian said he specifically criticized the praetorian prefect Florentius in front of many people—"whom I knew would carry the news back to him"—as an alternative to confronting the prefect directly. While it is rare to be able to get an emperor's own perspective on court networks like this, the number of anecdotes and apophthegmata—pithy or witty statements—that are set at the imperial court testify to the centrality of orality to this community, as its members spread rumors and exchanged gossip about what the emperor had done, was thought to have done, or might do. Philo, who trailed Caligula around Italy for months in hope of securing an audience at which he could lobby the emperor on behalf of the Jewish community of Alexandria, wrote that Caligula's "dreadful deeds, which lay beyond atonement, were on everyone's lips, but because of fear, they were not spoken openly, but in hushed tones." The writings of Seneca the Younger, a senatorial member of Caligula's court, give us an indication of the topics of such whispers: an equestrian invited to dinner by Caligula after the emperor had just executed his sons; victims beheaded during the emperor's evening stroll in the gardens; and sponges shoved into the mouths of victims so they would not cry out. Similar stories are associated with the western court of the late fourth-century emperor Valentinian I. The military officer Ammianus, who was based in the East at the time, relates information he had "heard" or to which "various reliable pieces of information bear witness," including the cruel execution of debtors, an attendant bashed to death because he let the emperor's hunting dog loose too early, and a groom stoned for choosing inadequate horses. When a provincial governor was executed for asking to administer a second province, Valentinian reportedly said to his master of the horse: "Go now, general, and change his head, since he wants his province changed." Many of these tales show Caligula and Valentinian exhibiting a sadistic wit, which is mirrored in the folkloric image of other fierce monarchs, such as the sixteenth-century Russian tsar Ivan the Terrible. Emperors who simply ordered executions were par for the course, but those who did so in cruel, vicious ways with a hint of black humor were talked about and remembered.

Their deeds were so terrible that they were not limited to the oral realm but had to be committed to text, so that they would be preserved for the future as warnings about monarchical whims.[51]

While an emperor was alive, talking about his cruel deeds (real or imagined) functioned as one way to cope with the terrors of his rule. But after his death, this talk transformed into a celebration of collective survival. On the occasion of the first Saturnalia (a Carnivalesque religious festival held every December) after Claudius's demise, the court staged a performance of Seneca's *Apocolocyntosis,* a rambunctious and rude satire on the emperor's reign and his deification. Claudius is presented as a stumbling, stuttering mess who shakes his head threateningly, gets hot and mumbles incoherently when angered, and orders executions with a gesture of his hand—a movement well known to the audience (and presumably acted out) at the Saturnalia recital. Courtiers would have remembered the shaking of the emperor's head and the movement of his hand as their friends and peers were dispatched to execution, with Claudius notching up a gruesome tally of thirty-five dead senators and 321 equestrians across his fourteen-year reign. In the giddy atmosphere of that first Saturnalia, the transformation of these terrifying moments into mocking satire enabled the court to let off steam, take stock, and regroup under a new emperor (unfortunately that was Nero, but hope springs eternal).[52]

Even though living in close proximity to a cruel impresario like Claudius was unbearable, Romans could be equally paranoid about an emperor who shunned company and deliberately secluded himself. Tiberius spent the last ten years of his reign on Capri, an island in the Bay of Naples, surrounded only by his closest associates. This caused much heated speculation back in Rome, both among the senatorial aristocracy and the population at large. There were lurid tales that he engaged in pedophilic activities in the woods with children dressed up as Pans and nymphs. According to Suetonius, the grove where the alleged sexual abuse took place was so famous that "at the time people constantly referred to it openly in conversation as the 'The Goat's Lair' (*Caprineum*)." The Latin word was both a pun on the name of the island and a reference to the sexual deviancy of goats. Another sensational tale described a new form of torture created by the emperor on Capri. Tiberius would ply men with copious quantities of wine in order to expand their bladders to the limit, then have their penises tied with cords so they could not urinate. This tale, again retold by Suetonius, probably derives from the pen of the contemporary senator Servilius Nonianus, who visited Tiberius on Capri and returned to Rome with all sorts of sordid stories. But Suetonius was not content to rely on written sources—his account suggests a personal visit to the island. "On Capri, people point out the site of his executions," Suetonius wrote, "from where Tiberius was accustomed to order the condemned—who had already suffered drawn-out, excruciating tortures—to be flung headlong into the sea as he looked on." This was not the end of the tale: Tiberius's soldiers would allegedly retrieve the bodies from the sea and beat them with oars to make sure they were dead. The idea that the inhabitants of Capri were talking about the cliff-top murder spot at least half a century after Tiberius's own demise suggests that the everyday politics of negotiating imperial power was sustained long beyond an individual emperor's lifetime.[53]

All this talk about Tiberius revealed that Romans, both at the time and in subsequent decades, imagined that the emperor's absence enabled him to indulge his baser instincts, both sexual and sadistic. Woe betide anyone who interrupted his seclusion uninvited! A fisherman is said to have found this out the hard way when he approached Tiberius to offer him a mullet as a gift. Tiberius, Suetonius's story went, was so alarmed by the man's sudden appearance that he ordered his face to be scrubbed with the fish. When the fisherman remarked he was grateful he had not offered the emperor the lobster he had caught, Tiberius ordered his face to be torn up with that as well. As Edward Champlin has shown, the memorable anecdote is actually a version of an international folkloric tale, "Thank God They Weren't Peaches." In the tale type, a low-status character presents an offering to a ruler, who rejects the offering and then throws it at them. The unfortunate individual then remarks how they are relieved not to have presented the king with something that would have caused more damage (peaches in the original version, hence the name). There was also a Jewish adaptation featuring the emperor Hadrian and an offering of ripe figs. "Praise your Creator that they were figs rather than citrons, and that they were ripe rather than unripe," says the victim's family of his lucky escape from having hard lemons rubbed on him. The folktale reflects the popular understanding of how rulers treat their subjects: a king has the capacity to turn even a generous offering against his subjects, who must nevertheless cheerfully accept their injuries. The existence of the Hadrianic variant, which circulated orally among Jewish communities before being written down, suggests that the Tiberian version recorded by Suetonius likewise had an oral origin, as people imagined what it would be like to encounter him on Capri. What is particularly striking about these court stories is that they focus on the emperor's ability to harm his subjects' bodies, not only by killing them, but also by damaging their mouths, faces, and genitals. Michel Foucault and Maud Gleason have demonstrated how acts of punishment and torture were inherently political. I would argue that the circulation of such gruesome stories was likewise political, as Romans delineated the bounds of acceptable imperial behavior and warned each other about how they should behave around their rulers. One needed to be close to the emperor to receive honors and favors—but never too close.[54]

MURDER MOST FOUL

If emperors were thought capable of executing the whole population of a city or spending their days in sadistic perversions, then it required little stretch of the imagination to consider that they might themselves be murderers. "I have plainly heard," wrote the senator Cassius Dio, that Marcus Aurelius's life was ended by his doctors at the orders of his son Commodus. By committing this oral rumor to the text of his *Roman History,* Dio ensured that all future readers would talk about this possibility. He was not the only Roman aristocrat to use the power of the written word to shape imperial memories. Hadrian, who knew better than most what emperors could do, since he was one himself, wrote in his autobiography that he thought that Vespasian had been poisoned by his son Titus at a banquet. These rumors share a common folkloric motif, "Parricide to Obtain Kingship," which brings together stories from different cultures, all of which envision princes as ambitious and impatient for the throne. Emperors were also supposed to have done away with their wives. Libanius heard such a rumor about the emperor Julian from his friend Polycles, a former provincial governor, when he made one of his regular afternoon visits to his house in Antioch. Polycles told Libanius that Julian had bribed one of his doctors with a jewel to poison his wife, Helena. Libanius refused to believe the rumor, since, he said, the other doctors at court would surely have noticed that Helena had been poisoned. Moreover, the emperor Constantius II would have declared war against Julian for doing away with Helena, who was his sister. Libanius's reasoned skepticism was not shared by Polycles and the other courtiers who had spread the rumor, which was generated and sustained by their shared belief that emperors were indeed capable of such murderous acts.[55]

A love affair and a mysterious death formed an especially potent combination when it came to rumor generation. And so it was that when Antinous, the teenaged male lover of the emperor Hadrian, tragically drowned in the Nile during a sightseeing tour of Egypt, tongues began to wag. In his autobiography, Hadrian wrote that it was all a dreadful accident, since Antinous had inadvertently fallen into the river. This official version was endorsed by sycophantic courtiers who claimed that Antinous had ascended to heaven, and by court poets who wrote simpering verses in the youth's honor. Hadrian himself commissioned countless memorials, founded a new city (Antinoopolis), and deified his lover as Osiris-Antinous. Such an outpouring of monumental grief for an imperial lover, and a male one at that, was not only unprecedented—it was more than a little suspicious. We have no contemporary source that firmly attests to rumors distrusting the official version, but the fact that Hadrian issued such a stern denial in his autobiography suggests that there had been considerable speculation at the time. Histories and biographies written after Hadrian's death report that Antinous's death was indeed no accident. The young man had voluntarily sacrificed himself as part of a magical ceremony designed to ensure that Hadrian would live longer. This tale would have been given credence by the presence of the sinister Egyptian magician Pancrates in Hadrian's entourage. According to second-century sources, Pancrates had impressed the emperor by using his sorcery to render a man bedridden within two hours and killing him within seven. After such a display, who would not have suspected that Antinous had been sacrificed in a magical rite gone wrong?[56]

One death that was not believed to be accidental was the demise of Nero's mother, Agrippina. She survived countless attempts on her life—including a journey on an ingenious collapsible boat devised especially for sinking—before Nero eventually sent soldiers to kill her. In his official letter to the senate, Nero charged Agrippina with treason for fomenting a conspiracy. But not everyone was convinced. Darkly humorous ripostes in both Greek and Latin were posted publicly in Rome and also circulated orally throughout the city:

Nero Orestes Alcmaeon Motherkiller.

A new formula: Nero = killed his own mother.

Who denies that Nero is from the noble stock of Aeneas?
He carried off his father, now this one has carried off his mother.

The first of these, written in Greek, parodies Nero's own official nomenclature—"Nero Claudius Caesar Augustus Germanicus"—by giving him the names of two matricides from Greek mythology, Orestes and Alcmaeon (whom Nero had also played onstage), and then a new title, "Motherkiller." The second text, likewise in Greek, hinges on understanding that all Greek letters also function as numbers, with alpha meaning "one," beta "two," and so forth. In Greek, the letters in "Nero" add up to 1,005, as do those in the words "killed his own mother." The final one, written in Latin, is a rather clever joke that alludes to the great hero Aeneas, ancestor of the Julio-Claudian dynasty, famously hoisting his elderly father, Anchises, on his shoulders as they escaped the burning ruins of Troy. But the Latin word for "carried off" also functioned metaphorically, as does the English equivalent, to mean "killed." We do not know who composed these witticisms—they could have derived from aristocrats at court or the poets they patronized—but regardless of their authors' identities, their oral circulation shows that they entered wider discourse in Rome. The verdict was that Agrippina's death was not a justified punishment of a conspirator, but a cold-blooded murder. Nero had joined the lines of famous Greek matricides and betrayed the values of Aeneas, the paradigmatic symbol of Roman parental dutifulness.[57]

Nero was not only suspected of having his mother murdered. He also boasted an impressive list of poisoning victims, which was relatively rare for a man, since poison was traditionally regarded as a woman's weapon. These included his brother Britannicus, the freedmen Doryphorus and Pallas, the praetorian prefect Burrus (who thought he was drinking cough syrup), and his aunt Domitia (given poison in one version of the tale, a quick-acting laxative in another). Many of these victims were not only rivals or opponents—they were also very wealthy. At the start of this book, we saw how rumors about Nero's murderous capabilities spread beyond Rome all the way to Pompeii, where they manifested themselves in graffiti. Rumor even flew as far as the Greek island of Euboea, where a local resident told the orator Dio Chrysostom a story about one of their major landowners. "They say that he was put to death by the emperor who wanted his money," was the explanation for the magnate's sudden end.[58]

The Euboea story takes us into the realm of local traditions about the emperor and his victims. These tend to be more timeless than the graffiti and poems that circulated in Rome, referring to "an emperor" rather than a specific individual (we only know that Euboean legend refers to Nero because we can establish the chronology from Dio Chrysostom's life and career). One story that circulated among the Christian community of Antioch in Late Antiquity concerned a murderous emperor and his interaction with the bishop Babylas, which took place at some time in the third century. The most extensive version, which appears in John Chrysostom's *Discourse on Saint Babylas,* tells how, in the course of negotiating a peace treaty between the Roman emperor and the king of a foreign nation, the emperor took the king's young son as a hostage and promised to rear him as his own. However, the Roman emperor went back on his word, taking a sword and running it through the boy's neck. The emperor then tried to enter a church, but he was removed from the building for his impious deeds by the bishop Babylas. In some versions, the emperor is explicitly identified as Philip (whom many believed to be a Christian, though good evidence is lacking) or Numerian, both of whom spent time in the East. There are also differences in the precise details of the murder: a version attributed to Bishop Leontius of Antioch had it that Philip's crime was murdering the son of his predecessor, Gordian III (who in reality died as a teenager without issue). The story of the emperor and Babylas is what we call a "floating anecdote," which could be attributed to different rulers or have its details changed to fit the context of its telling. But the core message remained the same, revealing that Christians in Antioch believed that emperors were capable of murdering children, and for that they needed to be humbled before God.[59]

Constantine's conversion to Christianity in the early fourth century, and the adoption of the faith by all subsequent emperors (except the short-lived Julian), did not put an end to discussion about their homicidal capabilities. In the fifth century, Valentinian III hacked his general Aetius to death with a meat cleaver in the palace at Rome, while the eastern emperor Leo ordered the murder of the general Aspar and his two sons, for which he earned the nickname "The Butcher" (Makelles). In subsequent centuries, it became Constantinopolitan folklore that Leo had plied his trade as a meat butcher before becoming emperor. The idea of emperors as killers was fueled by the sermons of priests and bishops, for whom they functioned as excellent examples of powerful figures whose significance was understood by their congregations. In his sixteenth *Homily on Philippians,* delivered either in Antioch or in Constantinople, John Chrysostom told the assembled flock that emperors commonly murdered their own relatives for fear that they were plotting against them. "Of course, the floors of the imperial palace are always covered in the blood of the emperor's kinsmen," the assembled churchgoers heard Chrysostom say. The bishop then proceeded to offer a grisly catalogue of recent murders, deaths, and executions. (If the homily was delivered in Constantinople, one can imagine the congregation giving the imperial palace a wide berth as they walked home from the service.) One unnamed emperor, Chrysostom said, did away with both his son and his wife, the latter even being exposed on the mountainside to be eaten by wild animals. We can identify the emperor as Constantine, who had his son Crispus and his own wife, Fausta, executed, though the predominant rumor was that she had been poached alive in an overheated bath. Chrysostom's story indicates that there was a completely different oral tradition in circulation, which bore little resemblance to the facts but conjured up the idea of the emperor as a barbaric murderer. Through his preaching, Chrysostom himself formed a vital link in the oral transmission of such tales, circulating them beyond the world of the imperial court to the illiterate or partially literate members of Christian society who relied on and believed his words. We are not sure in what terms Constantine announced the death of Fausta, since the state's official version does not survive, but whatever the emperor proclaimed, it was clearly not trusted, since Romans came up with a variety of stories describing her death at the hands of baths or bears.[60]

WONDROUS AND TERRIBLE DEEDS

To be a Roman emperor was to equal or surpass the achievements of kings and gods—"to crave the truly incredible," as Tacitus memorably wrote of Nero. Emperors extended Roman territory beyond "Ocean," razed mighty mountains, bent stone obelisks to their will, gathered hippocentaurs and other strange beings to display in their palace, and commanded animals to revere them as gods in the Colosseum. Jewish tales imagined Rome as a city of 365 marketplaces, where emperors distributed endless supplies of food to their privileged citizens and dined on cucumbers all year round (a sign they had conquered the natural agricultural cycle). Caligula once engaged in the truly outrageous act of commandeering grain ships to build a seven-kilometer-long bridge across the Bay of Baiae, which he proceeded to ride across accompanied by armed soldiers and a Parthian child hostage. The contemporary senator Seneca the Younger wrote that this action was "in imitation of a king, who was mad, foreign, and full of ill-judged arrogance," a reference to the Persian Xerxes, who famously bridged the Hellespont as part of his invasion of Greece in 480 BCE. But this was only one of multiple rumors circulating about Caligula's actions. "When I was a boy, I used to hear my grandfather telling the story, which came to him from courtiers very close to the emperor, about the motivations for the bridge," recalled the imperial biographer Suetonius. His grandfather's version was that Tiberius's astrologer, Thrasyllus, had apparently declared that it was no more likely that Caligula would become emperor than he would ride over the Bay of Baiae on horseback—and so he did. Both explanations reflect the belief among Caligula's courtiers that he needed to prove himself as emperor with an extravagant display marshaling both human and material resources.[61]

There was always a disturbing undercurrent to the imperial lust for the marvelous. Roman emperors not only staged fantastical beast hunts in which beautiful animals were killed for pleasure, they also executed criminals by forcing them to reenact mythological scenes. These included the mating of Pasiphae and the bull and the fateful flight of Icarus, scenarios that ended in the condemned being raped to death or smashing dramatically to the ground (Nero himself got splattered with blood as a result of one flight attempt). Such horrific executions are rich in layers of meaning. Not only were they a "political ritual" of execution, but, as Ari Bryen has pointed out, they also equated the emperor's human subjects with the fauna frequently dispatched in a similarly brutal manner. These grotesque performances cast the emperor in the role of impresario, bringing myth to life, to the horror and amazement of the Roman crowd, as Kathleen Coleman has argued. The public nature of such spectacles also nurtured rumor and speculation about what other wondrous and horrifying things the emperor could do. When Commodus decided to stage a magnificent fourteen-day festival with games and fighting in the Colosseum, which was normally an occasion for popular rejoicing, most of the population of Rome decided to stay away. Some turned up and had a look around before scurrying off, while others did not dare venture near the Colosseum at all. The senator Cassius Dio, a contemporary observer of these events, wrote that a terrifying rumor had spread through Rome that Commodus intended to fire arrows at the spectators while reenacting the myth of Hercules and the Stymphalian birds (with the emperor as the hero, of course). Imperial love for bringing myths to life in spectacular and destructive fashion created the frameworks of knowledge that made this rumor very plausible to the people of Rome. The rumor was given further believability by Commodus's own Hercules-mania. By this point in his reign, he was frequently dressing up as the hero, having a club and lion skin carried before him in public processions, and being depicted as Hercules on coins and in sculpture. There had already been rumors that Commodus had rounded up a group of Romans who had lost their feet as a result of disease or accidents, attached costumes resembling serpents' bodies to their knees, and then beat them to death with clubs, in imitation of Hercules and the giants. It would be safer for people to stay away from the festival, lest they be forced to star in Commodus's next Herculean performance.[62]

The trauma of religious persecution and punishment by the Roman state gave rise to stories of the emperor's hideous actions among Christian and Jewish communities. In the early 260s, Dionysius, bishop of Alexandria, wrote a letter to Hermammon, bishop of another (unknown) town in Egypt, in which he informed his colleague what he had heard about the origin of the emperor Valerian's persecution, which lasted for three long years between 257 and 260. The letter survives because it is quoted in the early fourth-century *Church History* by Bishop Eusebius of Caesarea, who collected and cited many original documents.

The principal agent, Dionysius wrote, was the emperor's financial secretary, Macrianus, who was nothing less than a sorcerer! He allegedly persuaded Valerian to engage in unspeakable acts, such as cutting children's throats and sacrificing newborn babies, so that he could search through their entrails for divine signs. Through this letter, rumors of Valerian's alleged sacrifices were able to pass through the network of Egyptian bishops, confirming their belief that persecution was the work of a heinous emperor and his odious advisor. Human sacrifice was a standard charge attributed to tyrants; the slaughter of infants was a particularly horrific variation. Eusebius himself ascribes the examination of babies' innards to the later, fourth-century emperor Maxentius in both his *Church History* and his *Life of Constantine.* Was Eusebius inspired by Dionysius's letter about Valerian that he had read and quoted? Or were separate stories about Maxentius circulating orally during Eusebius's lifetime, which he then committed to writing? We cannot be certain, but what this does suggest is that ideas of cruel behavior derived from traditional frameworks of knowledge could spread through different forms of oral and textual discourse.[63]

The tales of imperial retribution that circulated orally among Jewish communities in the eastern provinces even credited emperors with slaughter of biblical proportions. These stories survive because they were written down in Late Antiquity by rabbis commenting on the Talmud, demonstrating the strong interaction between oral and textual realms of storytelling. There was a significant revolt throughout the Jewish diaspora in Egypt, Cyrene, Cyprus, and Mesopotamia in the last years of Trajan's reign (115–117). An anecdote attributed to Rabbi Simeon ben Yohai, who lived under Trajan, said that the emperor had had all the Jewish men in Alexandria killed, but promised he would spare the women if they obeyed his soldiers; when the women refused, Trajan had them massacred as well. Such an act was supposedly outdone by his successor, Hadrian, who was said to have killed eighty thousand myriads—eight hundred million Jews—in the siege of Bethar, which took place during the Bar Kohkba revolt (132–135). A rabbi from this period, Rabbi Simeon ben Gamliel, claimed that Hadrian enclosed his vineyard, which stretched from Tiberias to Sepphoris, with deceased Jews, who were positioned upright with their arms stretched out. These tales reflect the experiences of countless Jewish men, women, and children who perished in the revolt, many of whom were forced to eat the flesh of their own relatives to survive, while countless others lay unburied across the land. The people of Rome, Egypt, and Judaea were united across time and space in the way they talked about the emperor not only as a worker of marvelous wonders, but also as a perpetrator of great terrors.[64]

In the case of the Jewish people, there is a real sense that their discontent was not only with the individual emperor, but also with the imperial system of Roman rule. In 130, Hadrian refounded Jerusalem as a Roman colony, Aelia Capitolina, a move that was designed to eradicate the city's religious and cultural identity. The Jewish reaction was to fight for the removal of Roman rule. Simeon bar Kosiba (later known as "bar Kokhba," or "Son of a Star"), who led the Jewish revolt against Hadrian, minted coins with Hebrew legends on which he styled himself "prince of Israel" and that carried slogans such as "Freedom of Jerusalem" and "Redemption of Israel" (fig. 7). As two Jewish brothers put it in a story that was later incorporated into the *midrash* (commentaries on the Hebrew Bible): "The conclusion of the whole matter is that we must take Hadrian's crown and set it upon our own head."[65]

There was little sympathy for the Jewish people in histories written by Roman senators and equestrians. They were more concerned with the idea that an emperor could have committed such a heinous crime of setting fire to Rome itself. According to three ancient authorities—Tacitus, Suetonius, and Cassius Dio—when the city was consumed by a nine-day-long conflagration in July of 64, the finger of suspicion was pointed squarely at the emperor Nero. They describe arresting scenes of frenzied and terrified Romans wondering how the fire had started, some reporting that they had seen men throwing firebrands to get it going. None of our authors was alive during these events—the earliest, Tacitus, wrote about sixty years after the fire—but their description of panic and rumor is certainly very plausible. Romans did not think about fires in the rational sense as being sparked by poor urban conditions, instead blaming them on human or divine causes. Comparative testimony from early modern Europe shows that rumors of arson or fears of divine punishment flourished after major fires, such as that which ravaged the French city of Troyes in 1524, or London in 1666, for which even King Charles II and his brother, the duke of York, were blamed. Whether or not the Roman people pointed the finger at Nero is difficult to determine, since the sources do not cite verses, chants, or graffiti to illuminate the popular sentiment. But we can be fairly certain this was the view of some members of the imperial court. In August of 64, the young senator Marcus Annaeus Lucanus (better known as "Lucan") composed a poem entitled *On the Burning of the City,* which blamed Nero for the fire. The emperor was enraged and banned all readings of Lucan's poetry. The following year, Lucan participated in a failed conspiracy to remove Nero from power. One of the praetorian officers who joined the conspiracy, Subrius Flavus, told Nero to his face: "I began to hate you, after you showed yourself to be a murderer of your mother and

Fig. 7. Top: Silver tetradrachm of Simeon bar Kokhba, 134–135 CE. American Numismatic Society, New York, 2010.76.107. Bottom: Bronze coin of Simeon bar Kokhba, 132–133 CE. American Numismatic Society, New York, 2010.76.19.

your wife, a charioteer, an actor, and an arsonist." The anecdote comes from Tacitus, who assured his readers that he had provided them with Flavus's exact words, suggesting that the historian here depended on an oral tradition.[66]

Not long after Nero's suicide—possibly in 68 itself, when the ideas of liberty and freedom were in the air—the emperor's alleged crimes were brought to life onstage in the *Octavia,* a dramatization of his relationship with his first wife.

The author of this work is unfortunately unknown, but they were familiar with details of imperial politics. The dramatic date of the play was 62, but it offered premonitions of the emperor's future evils, so that Nero, enraged at the people of Rome and their support for his estranged wife, could be heard wishing that "the city's buildings may soon fall under my flames." The theater was *the* place for political commentary in Rome, attended by a widespread cross section of society. The *Octavia* therefore had the capacity to generate widespread debate and discussion about Nero's culpability for the fire, either confirming what the theatrical audience already suspected or planting new possibilities in their minds.[67]

The fire provided Nero with space in the center of Rome to embark on the construction of the magnificent Golden House (lending credence to a later explanation that Nero wanted to burn the city down to build the new palace). This Golden House was intended to connect the imperial complexes on the Palatine and the Esquiline hills. There was a vestibule with a bronze colossal statue of Nero himself (120 Roman feet high), a magnificent lake, gardens, and a dining room with an ingenious revolving ceiling to allow flowers to rain down on guests. While modern historians have often been at pains to stress the limited amount of space the Golden House occupied in Rome, this was hardly the perception at the time. Suetonius quotes the following contemporary verse mocking its huge size:

> Rome is going to become one house: head for Veii, Romans,
> Unless that house consumes Veii as well.

These lines allude to the sack of Rome by the Gauls in 390 BCE, when the inhabitants were forced to flee north to Veii in search of safety, deploying this moment of past disaster to criticize Nero's massive palace driving out citizens once again. Since the Golden House was never finished, the poem reflects the anxieties of a city that resembled a construction site. The author's identity is anonymous, and as with other such epigrams, they are likely to be found among the literary elite, aristocrats and the poets they patronized. However, as with the *Octavia*'s accusations about Nero starting the fire, such a poem, even if it does not reflect wider popular discourse, certainly had the potential to generate it.[68]

Christianity ushered in new ways of conceptualizing the wondrous and terrible deeds of emperors. The most famous account is probably that of Procopius's *Secret History,* a lurid and sensationalistic account of the alleged crimes of the sixth-century emperor Justinian and his wife, Theodora. The *Secret History* is a difficult work to assess, since it could be a collection of contemporary gossip harvested by Procopius, but it could equally be composed of imaginative invective. Procopius certainly claims to depend on oral sources in his depiction of Justinian as a demonic figure, such as when he writes that the emperor's mother had told her closest friends that her son was conceived through intercourse with a demon. He also offers the testimony of priests and courtiers who worked long into the night with the emperor, one of whom swore he saw Justinian walking around headless. Even if one believes that Procopius invented the tales about Justinian's demonic behavior, it is surely the case that his inclusion of such stories in the *Secret History* and the circulation of the work, possibly among a small group of fellow dissidents, was itself a form of gossip-mongering. This would have provided an outlet for elite intellectuals and officials to demonize the emperor (quite literally, in this case). Justinian was an emperor who, in Procopius's eyes, embodied the many different facets of imperial wonder-working. In the panegyrical *Buildings*, Procopius wrote that he was motivated to record the emperor's many magnificent constructions because otherwise people would not believe they were the work of a single man, while in the *Secret History*, Justinian appears as a corrupt embezzler and a murderer on a massive scale, responsible for the death of a trillion people.[69]

The descent into madness of Justinian's nephew and successor, Justin II, was described by his hostile contemporary John of Ephesus as the result of demonic possession, reflecting the entrenchment of this Christian idea. John reported talk circulating in Constantinople that the emperor had eaten two of his officials, a story sparked by the fact that he had bitten the men on the head when they were trying to restrain him. Justin II was also famed for building projects on a Neronian scale. He bulldozed houses in northwest Constantinople to make way for a new palace, hippodrome, and gardens. He then decided to construct a mighty lighthouse, to which a mocking poem was soon attached, urging Justin to climb up and take in the view himself:

> Build your column! Build and raise it as much as you can! Ascend and stand above it!
> Perceive, look, and see: the East, West, North, and South have been devasted and destroyed in your days!

Constantinople was a city full of columns, which had been commissioned across the preceding centuries by emperors including Constantine, Theodosius I, Arcadius, Theodosius II, Marcian, Leo I, and Justinian; there were even some erected to honor empresses, notably Helena, mother of Constantine, and Eudoxia, wife of Arcadius. All the columns were topped by a statue of the respective imperial figure, either standing or on horseback. This anonymous witty poem played on the idea of emperors presiding over the city skyline—only Justin II was not looking on a wondrous view from atop his lighthouse, but on an empire he had ruined.[70]

Imperial ambitions were driven by a desire to be regarded as superhuman into the Byzantine period, with the idea that these wondrous feats were only completed with God's blessing (which Justin II manifestly did not possess, in the opinion of the anonymous poet). As a sample of this later discourse, I shall cite the example of the eleventh-century emperor Constantine IX Monomachus (1042–55), who constructed an extravagant pleasure park in Constantinople. As his contemporary Michael Psellos described it, the process of constructing the gardens was no ordinary feat: luscious green turf was dug up from the mountains, and fruit-bearing trees were excavated from other locations and transplanted wholesale to the pleasure park to satisfy the emperor's desires. An epigram inscribed on one of the pavilions in the complex described how the visitor would marvel at all the beauty that the emperor had gathered in one place—with God's help, of course. The gardens were the subject of contemporary discussion and criticism, according to Psellos. He narrated one story that the emperor had part of the gardens hollowed out and filled with water exactly level with the ground, so that unwary visitors would accidentally plunge into the lake while enjoying their promenades. There was a certain poetic justice to Constantine IX enticing his guests to fall into the lake: on one occasion, after bathing in the water himself, he fell ill and died—an emperor who was undone by his own amazing wonder.[71]

MIRACLE WORKERS?

The Roman emperor was clearly thought capable of many extraordinary and terrible things. But did people talk about him performing miracles? The reverence and sacrosanctity attached to emperors is undoubted: their birthplaces were turned into shrines, portents presaged their rise to power, their images offered the right of asylum, and petitioners left their appeals at the feet of their statues. However, the one concrete example of an emperor performing (alleged) miracles was a staged propaganda performance. In 69, when the newly acclaimed emperor Vespasian was staying in Alexandria, he allegedly cured a blind man by rubbing his spit on his eyes and cheeks. Vespasian then restored another man's lame leg or damaged hand (the precise limb depends on the version) by touching or stepping on it. Tacitus, writing in his *Histories* about fifty years later, said that "those who were present still tell of both these cures today, when they could not be expected to gain a reward for lying." While we should not doubt that some people believed and talked about what they saw, Vespasian is never reported to have performed healing miracles again in his lifetime. This suggests that these miracles were concocted by his advisors to transform Vespasian from an avuncular Italian senator into the living embodiment of the Egyptian healing god Serapis. Here we find the imperial regime seeking to encourage and drive public discussion about Vespasian, aware that this was just as important a component in the construction of his power as edicts, statues, and coins.[72]

The limitations on the emperor's power are encapsulated in the views of the former imperial slave Epictetus, who taught philosophy about the same time as Tacitus was writing his *Histories.* The emperor's rule, he said, could secure peace and stability on land and sea—but he could not bring relief from fevers, shipwrecks, fires, earthquakes, and lightning. Indeed, miraculous events tended to happen around the emperor, rather than being the result of his own intervention. We see this in the accounts of Romans who tried to heal Hadrian and were rewarded by the gods by having their own ailments cured. Nor did Christian rulers have the capacity to perform miracles: they only benefited from the actions of holy individuals or the curative power of relics. Justinian is reported to have had painful knees cured by the bones of the Forty Martyrs of Sebaste that were found during the construction of the Church of the Martyr Eirene. When the chest containing the bones was placed on Justinian's knee, oil flowed out and covered the emperor's clothes and feet. Justinian did try to harness the miracle to emphasize his sacrality by displaying his cloak in the palace, where it became a contact relic. But the emperor did not perform the miracle himself, nor are there stories about people making pilgrimages to be healed by him. There was no expectation in the Roman world that all emperors possessed the healing powers of the "the royal touch," as later developed in medieval France and England, nor that they were capable of performing other miracles, like the Mughal ruler Akbar or Japanese emperors. Indeed, it is only with the gradual transition of Constantine and his mother, Helena, to sainthood, and the even later veneration of their remains, which is not securely attested until the ninth century, that the relics of an emperor or a member of his family were regarded as possessing intercessory power. In the fourteenth century, an anonymous Russian visitor to Constantinople reported seeing Christians venerating Constantine's tomb in the Church of the Holy Apostles and being healed. This type of imperial miracle was, therefore, a very medieval phenomenon.[73]

This historical background explains why there were no sense-making rumors in the Roman world that explained acts of healing or salvation as miracles being performed by the emperors. Indeed, the emperors themselves depended on the intervention of the gods or God to save them from desperate situations. The "rain miracle," which saved Marcus Aurelius's army from being slaughtered in the Marcomannic Wars, was either the result of the prayers of the Egyptian *magus* Arnuphis, the emperor himself, or, in a later Christian tradition, the Christian soldiers. It was the emperor Theodosius I's prayer to God that earned him victory in the Battle of the River Frigidus in 394, as the Almighty summoned up fierce winds that forced the enemies' arrows back into their faces. The end of a pandemic or pestilence could likewise only be achieved by intervention from the heavens. Titus sought all human and divine remedies to stop a plague, but to no avail, while the Byzantine empress Sophia dedicated a church to the physician martyrs Cosmas and Damian in order to secure her husband's victories over diseases and his enemies. When placed in this wider context, it is clear that Vespasian's miraculous deeds in Alexandria were staged performances, and that most Romans did not usually think or talk about the emperor in this fashion. It was only in Byzantine apocalyptic literature of the seventh century and beyond that there developed the idea of the "last Roman emperor" who would one day return as a savior of Christians, but this idea was divorced from the earthly man who wore the purple.[74]

THE LIMITS OF THE POSSIBLE

The Life of Secundus the Silent Philosopher is a work most people have never heard of outside certain scholarly circles. Yet between the second and seventh centuries, it was one of the most popular stories in the eastern Roman empire, appearing in Greek, Armenian, and Syriac versions. It later enjoyed a successful afterlife in the medieval world in both Arabic and Latin translations. *The Life of Secundus* opens with a tragic series of events in which the eponymous hero decides to test the proposition that all women are unchaste, and therefore offers himself, in disguise, to his widowed mother. When Secundus decides he cannot go through with the sexual act, the pair spend a chaste night together. The next morning, Secundus reveals his true identity to his mother, who kills herself because she nearly had sexual relations with her son. The grief-stricken young man takes a vow of silence because his talking had driven his mother to end her own life. The emperor Hadrian hears of Secundus's vow and summons him to Athens, where he orders him to speak. When the sage continually refuses to do so, Hadrian has him led off to execution. Still Secundus does not speak. The impressed emperor relents and decrees that they can converse in writing, which leads to an extended dialogue between sage and ruler on philosophical topics such as friendship, poverty, beauty, death, and the nature of the universe. At the beginning of their exchange, Secundus writes that he has no fear of the emperor. Hadrian, he says, has the right to put him to death, "but you have no power over my voice and the words I utter."[75]

Like other examples of popular literature that circulated in the Graeco-Roman world, such as *The Life of Aesop* and *The Alexander Romance, The Life of Secundus the Silent Philosopher* is a work that features numerous signs that it circulated orally before being written down. The prologue, in which Secundus plans to sleep with his mother to test her chastity, is both an international folkloric motif and a defined tale type ("A Mother Dies of Fright When She Learns That She Was About to Commit Incest with Her Son"). The philosophical question and answer session between Hadrian and Secundus resembles the dialogues attributed to Alexander the Great and the Gymnosophists of India. Secundus's heroic pronouncement that Hadrian does not have the power to control his voice not only shares similarities with Near Eastern tales of forthright advisors, but also the stories crafted by Greeks, Christians, and Jews about their champions who exercised *parrhesia* ("frank speech") before the emperors. These tales all gave voice to the ideal (or fantasy?) that true philosophers or the religiously righteous could confront the emperor with home truths even within the rarified atmosphere of the imperial court. The sentiment that an emperor's power was somehow transient or limited is also found in the *Sentences* of Sextus, a Christian collection of maxims from the second century: "The lion and tyrant both have power over the body of a wise man—but only that." This is a statement that John Chrysostom would have agreed with, and encouraged his congregation in Antioch to believe, as he reminded them of how the bishop Babylas had humbled a murderous emperor before God, and when he urged them to have faith as they waited nervously for news of Theodosius's response to the riot of the statues. Pagans, Christians, and Jews all sought reassurance in the face of the power of the Roman emperor by reminding themselves that this power had some limits.[76]

This small comfort was necessary because of all the terrible things the emperor could do, or was thought capable of doing. Romans across the social spectrum talked about the emperor's capacity for killing, both the courtiers who lived in his shadow day in and day out and the people who only saw him from a distance (or not at all). Killing could take many forms: a lover drowned in the Nile, a child hostage slain, or the inhabitants of an entire city wiped out in an act of imperial justice. With an added twist of grotesque monarchical whimsy, an emperor might dress up as Hercules and dispatch his subjects in bloody reenactments. Other forms of malfeasance were no less terrifying in their own ways: the emperor who stalked streets at night in disguise searching for whispers of resistance, the Christian heretic whose unorthodox beliefs brought ruin to the empire, the old pervert who assaulted children in the woods. Since it was impossible to know what it was like to be an emperor or to ascertain what he was really thinking, this void was filled by rumor. These rumors were not wild flights of fancy, but were completely plausible to those who spread them, rooted as they were in shared frameworks of knowledge: observations and memories of previous imperial behavior, or what people had learned from folklore, fable, and the Bible about how kings behaved.

Imperial letters and edicts, the voice of the ruler himself propelled across the empire on the wings of horseback messengers, offered the possibility of certainty and consensus. Those close to the center of power knew such missives were the product of the imperial chancellery, a carefully negotiated product of imperial initiative and bureaucratic verbiage. But nevertheless, in both the elite and the popular imagination, politics was always conceived in personal terms. Deep down, people wanted to believe that the emperor had really crafted these words himself as he worked long into the night answering petitions and formulating edicts. Yet they also feared that wily wives and conniving counselors were able to exert influence on their rulers, especially those who were children or easily misled, turning them away from their natural instincts and enacting harsh policies. This had the potential to undermine the official pronouncements of the imperial state and the acceptance of the truth that they offered.[77]

The emperor provided reassurance to the people of the empire. Taxes went to pay the armies that defended the frontiers, the state oversaw the transport of grain to feed the people of Rome and Constantinople, and economic measures could be taken to help other cities in need. This was the message of imperial rule that was reinforced on a daily basis through various forms of iconography on coins, statues, and public buildings, as Olivier Hekster has most recently emphasized. Yet time and again, Romans did not simply accept the version of imperial government provided in the emperor's own letters, edicts, and laws. They lamented the emperor's failures, his corruption, his misuse of funds, and his stinginess, for this meant that the emperor had not lived up to his principal functions as the father of his people. By speaking in pairs, small groups, and en masse, Romans were able to respond to such disappointments and thereby play a role in the negotiation of imperial power. A funny epigram about the Golden House or a witty acclamation of the emperor as "Torturer," chanting at the games and in the marketplaces, pamphlets posted up in the city—these acts all functioned as political statements about how the current wearer of the purple failed to live up to his subjects' expectations. The precise nature of the protest depended on the social status of those affected: the general population was more likely to lament high prices or a cessation in the grain supply than the wealthy who had their private food hoards, whereas complaints about the emperor's law affecting businessmen in the wine trade probably came from higher up the social pyramid.[78]

This broad picture of Roman views of "the emperor" can be further nuanced with reference to individual rulers, which shows how problematic it is to group all such talk under the heading of "resistance." The gossip about Marcus Aurelius's stingy behavior heard by Cassius Dio does not form part of an extensive litany of complaints directed at the philosopher prince, but appears to be a relatively rare moment in which we see some elite Romans rebuking a particular failing. The same might be said about Theodosius II, pelted with rocks by the people of Constantinople when he went to visit a granary as they made their feelings about a food shortage known. Normally Theodosius II was held in high regard by the people of Constantinople, whom he ruled like a pious, Christian father, but hungry stomachs have a way of fomenting discontent against even the most just rulers. We can set these examples of limited criticism against groups of tales that indicate wider misgivings about specific emperors. The stories of Tiberius's predatory and sadistic conduct are sufficiently pervasive to suggest that many in the city of Rome felt fear and anxiety toward him, while the issue of Anastasius's unorthodox beliefs haunted his entire reign and caused several outbreaks of public protest in Constantinople and beyond (not to mention the grumbling about his avarice). In these circumstances, we can interpret Roman talk as representative of more extensive concerns about how Tiberius and Anastasius lived up to imperial ideals.

The everyday act of exchanging rumors and swapping gossip, usually in private or in small groups, could manifest openly in poems, pamphlets, and the amorphous shouts of the crowd. Talking directly *to* Caesar, rather than behind his back, was a dangerous business, but these anonymous or collective ditties and outbursts effectively shrouded individual culpability. It was the sort of criticism that a good emperor was supposed to be able to endure with equanimity. Indeed, all this discourse that circulated in overlapping oral and textual forms—even the most terrible stories of imperial cruelty—enabled Romans to articulate their views on how the emperor should exercise his power. When they expressed disappointment, fear, hope, frustration, and anger, their voices were largely directed at the individual emperor and his decisions, rather than at the imperial system itself. However, there is evidence that even this was challenged by some forms of talk, especially if we view the Jewish tales about Trajan and Hadrian in the context of wider independence movements and revolts in the first and second centuries. The negotiation of Roman kingship certainly took on a different character when whispers and rumors transformed into more explicit protests, whether by the Jews who wished to replace Hadrian with the rebel Simeon bar Kosiba as prince of Israel, or by the people of Antioch, who merely wanted to challenge Theodosius's new taxes rather than dismantle the foundations of Roman imperial rule. In both cases, the potential limits of bargaining with the emperor were laid bare. The people might speak, but the emperor could still choose to exercise power over their bodies, and Romans knew it.

CHAPTER 2

Sex, Scandal, and Satire

At the age of eighteen, when his contemporaries were engaged in all manner of sybaritic pleasures, Gaius Octavius (the future emperor Augustus) resolved to abstain from sex for a year. According to his contemporary biographer, Nicolaus of Damascus, Octavius made the decision "in order to safeguard his voice and vigor." Romans believed that the excessive release of semen sapped the body of strength and made the voice effeminate (one famous orator even put lead plates on his chest at night to prevent involuntary ejaculation). The vow made by Octavius, the great-nephew and soon-to-be adopted son of Julius Caesar, demonstrated his determination to be regarded as a serious political player. However, after Caesar's assassination in 44 BCE, Octavius—whom we should now properly describe as the "young Julius Caesar"—was subject to attacks on his sexual continence. Marcus Antonius declared that the adoption had only come about because the youth had allowed his great-uncle to anally penetrate him. Marcus's brother, Lucius Antonius, went further by claiming that the young Caesar had prostituted himself to the general Aulus Hirtius in return for 300,000 sesterces (the rough equivalent of millions of U.S. dollars). These smears were designed to rob the young Caesar of his virility—and by extension his fitness as a political leader—by claiming that he enjoyed being the passive sexual partner, the penetrated plaything of real Roman men.[1]

Such accusations were part and parcel of the cutthroat political culture of the Roman Republic. Senators targeted the bodies, morals, and habits of their rivals in speeches delivered in the law courts, the senate house, and on the speaker's platform. Bodily imperfections and sexual deviancies marked an individual out as an unfit man, citizen, and politician. In 142 BCE, the censor Scipio Aemilianus, whose office gave him the power to regulate public and private morality, publicly lambasted the senator Publius Sulpicius Gallus for his effeminate habits. After describing Gallus's fondness for dousing himself in perfume, his penchant for depilating his thighs, and his questionable taste in long-sleeved tunics, Scipio reached his crescendo: "Is there anyone who doubts that he practices what *cinaedi* usually get up to?" The Latin word *cinaedus* has no direct equivalent in English. One of its meanings was a man who gained pleasure in being anally penetrated by others; it has also been suggested that it signified a "gender deviant" in Roman thought. When Marcus and Lucius Antonius slandered the young Caesar, they were marking him out publicly as a *cinaedus.* The sexual invective found in speeches, edicts, and pamphlets did not necessarily draw on current gossip (the accusations could simply have been invented as part of political invective), but it certainly had the potential to generate talk. The scurrilous tale that Julius Caesar had, as a young man, prostituted himself to the aging king Nicomedes of Bithynia was first aired in a courtroom as early as 77 or 76 BCE, but was still talked about thirty years later when his soldiers mocked him for the affair in his triumph of 46 BCE.[2]

Sexual invective about the young Caesar circulated in both written and oral discourse in the years after his adoptive father's murder. Lead sling-bullets recovered from the Italian city of Perusia, where his army besieged Lucius Antonius in the winter of 41/40 BCE, are inscribed with crude and aggressive sexual jokes directed at the young man (who is called Octavius, to undermine the legitimacy of his adoption by Caesar). "You suck cock, Octavius," reads one. Another orders: "Sit your gaping asshole on this, Octavius" (accompanied by a crude drawing of a penis to drive the message home). These particular insults survive as written abuse, but we can imagine that they had an oral dimension as Antonius's soldiers joked and shouted the slurs while they let their ammunition fly.[3]

In the decades that followed, the young Caesar defeated Lucius and Marcus Antoninus and assumed his station at the head of the developing monarchical state as Augustus. But his alleged sexual past was not forgotten. On one occasion, during a theatrical performance in Rome, the audience broke out into thunderous applause at the line "Do you see how the *cinaedus* beats the tambourine with his finger?" In the original text of the play, the *cinaedus* referred to a lascivious dancer, but the double meaning of the Latin led the audience to interpret the line as "Do you see how the *cinaedus* [i.e., man who enjoys being penetrated] rules the world with his finger?" They obviously took this as a reference to the sexual past of their present lord and master Augustus. The double entendre would only have generated this reaction if the people in Rome had already been gossiping, laughing, and bantering about the emperor being sexually penetrated by other men. All this talk, like the line in the play, had a dual nature. There was something funny and humanizing about imagining Augustus engaging in sexual intercourse, particularly in positions that the Romans regarded as unmanly (as the merry prostitutes sing in *Les Misérables:* "See them with their trousers off, they're never quite as grand!"). But rumor and gossip about an emperor's personal life—his sexual behavior, his body, and beliefs—could also function as commentary on his fitness to rule.[4]

THE POLITICS OF THE PERSONAL

> Great honor is distinguished above all by the fact that it allows nothing to be hidden, nothing to remain secret. This is especially the case with rulers, for not only their residences, but even their bedrooms and most private sanctuaries are thrown open, and all their secrets known to the goddess Rumor are revealed and displayed.

This was how Pliny the Younger described the abiding interest in the private lives of the great and the good in his panegyric for Trajan, delivered in 100. The reigning emperor and his family had nothing to fear from such intrusive public scrutiny, for they, so Pliny claimed, were distinguished by a panoply of virtues and not a single vice. This sentiment had its roots in the Republican idea that the words, deeds, and characters of politicians should be judged openly before all citizens of the state. Not all emperors would have agreed. In 409, Honorius and Theodosius II ordered that any houses that came close to the palace walls in Constantinople should be demolished, "for the great matters of imperial rule ought to be kept secret from the world." In reality, no emperor escaped unscathed from the prying eyes or speculation of the inhabitants of the cities in which they lived. However, the mechanics of talking about the powerful had undergone a significant shift from the days of the Republic. It became effectively impossible for senators to criticize the emperor in word or speech like a peer, ending the tradition of open invective to which the young Caesar had been subjected during the civil wars. Defamatory writing and speech about the emperor by elites could potentially lead to a charge of *maiestas* ("high treason"). This meant that anonymous verses and lampoons about the emperor's sex life, his drinking, or his receding hairline came to form an important vehicle of criticism for aristocrats and the people alike. Behind such public outbursts lay the circulation of gossip and rumor, driven by discussions in taverns, on street corners, and in palace courtyards.[5]

Where did this rumor and gossip come from? Much talk was generated by what people could read, observe, and hear. When an anonymous individual ripped down Diocletian's edict ordering Christian persecution at Nicomedia in 303, he cried out "that it proclaimed the victories of Goths and Sarmatians." The joke was that far from triumphing over foreign peoples, as their victory titles that headed all edicts proclaimed—"Greatest Conqueror of the Goths," "Greatest Conqueror of the Sarmatians," and so on—Diocletian and his imperial colleagues were themselves foreigners (or more precisely, in the Roman mindset, barbarians). This witticism was given added piquancy by the public knowledge that the emperors were all of humble birth, brought up in the Danubian provinces, perilously close to the frontiers. Diocletian even changed his name when he became emperor; he was previously the humbler "Diocles," a fact that the Latin professor Lactantius exploited mercilessly in his invective about the emperor and his colleagues. Romans not only talked about imperial origins, they also closely watched what their rulers did in public. The abuses that the people of Antioch leveled at Julian were primarily based on body features and public behavior—his beard, his temper, his conduct at the games, and his coinage—none of which depended on insider knowledge. But the Antiochenes also knew of Julian's preference for sleeping military-style on a pallet, which suggests the circulation of at least some details of his private habits outside the court.[6]

We often think of court gossip being circulated solely between elites. This certainly did happen—the Christian cleric Gregory of Nazianzus cited court insiders as sources for his *Orations* on Julian—but gossip also flowed outward and downward. During the last century of the Republic, Quintus Cicero advised his brother, the more famous Cicero, to ensure he was loved by all members of his household, "for almost all gossip pertaining to your public reputation comes from domestic sources." In the sixth of his *Satires*, Juvenal conjured up the image of an elite woman who attends her husband's meetings with the emperor's generals, then goes gossiping throughout Rome at the gates and crossroads on all matter of topics, personal and political, from love affairs to comets presaging the deaths of kings. Juvenal's woman is an exaggerated stereotype, but she does illustrate the principle of news moving outward from households. Such impulses were magnified when it came to the emperors. Anyone who had the slightest connection to the court disseminated juicy stories to the members of the public who were "beguiled and bewitched" by these tales, as the historian Eunapius aptly put it (despite the vain hopes of Honorius and Theodosius II that the palace walls would act as an information barrier). The spread of gossip was fueled by "weak ties"—people who knew someone who knew someone—the casual connections, meetings, and informal discussion circles in homes and public places.[7]

The witty poems that circulated anonymously about the emperor's private life and court affairs in Rome, Constantinople, and other major cities were most probably not written by the putative man on the street. The insider knowledge and literary talent required to author these verses suggests that they came from the world of the aristocratic and literary elite; indeed, courtiers could have commissioned them from poets they patronized, revealing multiple agents involved in the process. One classic example concerns an epigram written about bed-hopping and adultery at the court of Nero. When Nero fell in love with Poppaea Sabina, the wife of his friend Marcus Salvius Otho, he ordered the pair to divorce so that he could marry Poppaea himself. Since Nero feared that subjecting Otho to some sort of public disgrace would bring the sordid affair to light, he sent him to govern a province in faraway Spain. However, the ménage à trois and the subsequent cover-up were brought to wider public attention by the circulation of the following poem:

> Why, you ask, has Otho been exiled under the pretense of promotion?
> He'd set an adulterous affair with his own wife in motion.

This model of gossip transmission from the court to the public sphere occurs in other historical periods. In sixteenth-century France, a scandalous incident at Dijon involving one of Queen Catherine de' Medici's ladies-in-waiting was transmitted back to Paris in the form of Latin poetry, while a chamberlain at the seventeenth-century Mughal court lamented that verses about his marriage circulated "among high and low" in Delhi. These channels between court and capital had even greater import during the revolutionary eras of eighteenth-century France and twentieth-century Russia. Scurrilous verses about Marie Antoinette's immorality in popular printed literature could be traced back to courtiers, while stories about Tsarina Alexandra are attested both in the writings of government bureaucrats and circulating among the peasantry. These poems and tales played a significant role in undermining the sacrality of the queens and the monarchy at large, which helped to bring down both the Bourbon and Romanov dynasties. Although the ancient world did not have the printing technology to foster and support the production of libelous literature on the scale found in France and Russia, poems and pamphlets were circulated in written form within Rome and other capitals. They were either anonymous or tried to implicate known dissidents, as in the case of Junius Novatus, who claimed his tract was actually written by Agrippa Postumus, Augustus's estranged adopted son. When senators, soldiers, tradesmen, laborers, and women sat together in the theatrical audience, their laughter at jokes alluding to the emperor's sex life, personal appearance, or character was stoked by gossip, generated either by personal observation or stories that had flowed outward from the court. Here the boundaries between "elite" and "popular" discourse dissolved into united political commentary on their emperors.[8]

Gossip about the powerful functions in multiple interconnected ways. "Proximate gossip" occurs when the leader is part of the social group, such as a line manager or department head. Gossiping about their financial incompetence or weight gain is more than just idle chatter. It delineates community values and prejudices, both justified (managers should be skilled) and misleading (fatness is an outward sign of an inner lack of restraint). But it also gives people a sense of control over their environment, and even prevents discontent from manifesting itself openly in public fora. "Distal" gossip about leaders not personally known to the community at large, such as a member of Parliament or president, has a similar function. People joke about politicians' comb-overs or criticize their predatory sexual behavior in the lounge room, coffee shop, or bar as a small act of defiance or to warn others. Depending on the topic, this can bring amusement and pleasure to the gossipers, as they are bound together by the joy of talking and laughing, or generate a sense of shared solidarity formed by mutual disgust and revulsion. It is important to note that politicians can also be the subject of proximate gossip within their own communities, such as the U.S. president's senior staff, and indeed, this is where much gossip that eventually becomes distal originates.[9]

This gossip, both in its proximate and distal forms, very often gnaws at the pretensions of the powerful but does little to effect change. In order to challenge the status quo, gossip needs to be mobilized into an overt form of protest or resistance, often by becoming public and transforming into scandal. But this only occurs when the subject of gossip is significant enough to warrant condemnation in that particular social and cultural context. In contemporary France, accusations of financial impropriety are much more likely to result in public censure and political downfall than sexual affairs. The situation is different in the United States, where attitudes toward the private lives of presidential candidates have fluctuated widely, depending on the values of the media and society at large. While whispers of an affair brought down Democratic frontrunner Gary Hart in 1988, the numerous accusations of sexual impropriety against Donald Trump have had little impact on his electability among his supporters. This reminds us that gossip, along with its meaning and impact, is always subject to negotiation: sexual gossip may actually enhance politicians' reputations among some groups.[10]

The role and function of gossip in the Roman empire shares many similarities with these modern scenarios. It could be a way of expressing discontent, letting off steam, or puncturing the vanities of power, both at court (proximate) and in the wider public sphere (distal). However, there are also significant differences between Rome and other autocratic regimes and western liberal democracies today. It was more dangerous for Roman aristocrats to gossip about an emperor than for us to talk about a modern politician, though the Roman state seemed to care less about gossip the more one moved down the social spectrum. For all Romans, there was certainly a greater risk in transforming gossip into overt acts of resistance or revolt, such as damaging imperial statues. We also need to account for differences in moral values. Some topics of gossip simply did not constitute grounds for protest. If an emperor committed adultery with multiple lovers, his courtiers would certainly have talked about it, but it was never considered grounds for calling for him to be removed from office, in the same way as an Australian cabinet minister's affair with an administrative assistant might today. Emperors could simply ignore this sort of gossip because their power was not authorized and legitimized in the same way as a democratically elected politician. Their sexual indiscretions had to go much further to destabilize their positions.[11]

The emperors, their family members, and their courtiers were also the subject of rumors about their private lives and relationships. Major events in the imperial household—an estrangement or divorce, the sudden retirement of a trusted advisor—could generate rumors if there was no official news about what had happened or if the authorized version was distrusted. As with gossip, these rumors could emerge as the result of public observations, or they could start at court and disseminate outward. Gossip likewise played a role in the generation of rumor by providing preexisting content that offered potential explanations for political change. We can see this at work in reactions to Augustus's departure from Rome in the summer of 16 BCE. Augustus's official explanation was that he was needed in Gaul after the crushing defeat suffered by his legate Quintus Lollius at the hands of the Germans. However, by this point gossip had been circulating for many years that Augustus was engaged in a long-term affair with

Terentia, the wife of his close friend Maecenas. This gave rise to the rumor that Augustus had really left Rome to continue his relationship with Terentia away from the city, which was regarded as more plausible than the official explanation of a provincial tour. In the Roman imagination, the personal and political lives of the emperors were inseparable.[12]

PILLOW TALK

The young Caesar celebrated his third marriage on January 17, 38 BCE, at the precocious age of twenty-four. He and his new wife, Livia Drusilla, had both divorced their respective spouses to allow the new union to go ahead—in fact, the betrothal had come about so swiftly that Livia was still heavily pregnant with her second son by her ex-husband, Tiberius Claudius Nero, at the time of the nuptials. When the boy, Drusus, arrived in April that same year, a mocking verse in Greek iambic trimeter began to circulate in Rome: "Only the fortunate have children after three months." This line was so well known that it soon became proverbial, Cassius Dio tells us, which attests to its wide oral circulation throughout the city of Rome and its entrance into popular discourse. The talk about Augustus's relationship with Livia and their swift marriage, not to mention his affairs with Terentia and many other women, had renewed relevance some twenty years later when he embarked on an ambitious program of social legislation. In 18 BCE, Augustus passed two laws, "The Julian Law on the marriage of the orders," designed to increase the rates of marriage and childbirth among the senatorial and equestrian elite, and "The Julian Law on repressing adultery," which imposed new penalties on extramarital relationships with the aim of promoting reproduction within legal marriages. There was a gulf between the morality that Augustus wished to impose on the Roman people and his alleged lack of sexual continence. In contrast, Drusus (the baby born with such a short gestation period) was remembered long after for only ever having sex with one woman—his wife.[13]

The transition to a monarchical state under Augustus meant that his sprawling family—wife, daughter, adopted sons, daughters-in-law, grandchildren, and countless other relatives—came to assume a preeminent place in Rome's *res publica.* Provincials erected elaborate statue groups celebrating the new imperial household, and cities sent embassies to Rome to celebrate milestones in the life of the Augustan family. Despite his own sexual reputation, Augustus took great pains to ensure that the female members of his family were beyond reproach. Women were—and still are—held to higher standards than men. In Roman law, the crime of adultery was defined as sex between a married woman and any man who was not her husband. Men only committed the crime if they had relations with married women; sex with enslaved women and low-status women did not constitute adultery. Augustus took care to raise his daughter, Julia, and his granddaughters as traditional Roman matrons, so that they even reportedly spent their time working wool and making his clothes. He kept away potential suitors whose visits to the imperial household might be seen to impugn their honor. Suetonius told his readers that he had seen a letter that was sent by Augustus to one such gentleman caller, Lucius Vinicius, ordering him to stay away. The emperor's concern for public gossip and its deleterious effects was such that he "forbade his female relatives to do or say anything unless it could also be openly recorded in the daily journal," according to Suetonius. The term "daily journal" suggests a record that would enable people to read of the activities of the imperial house, a sort of Roman "court circular."[14]

This happy domestic image was shattered in 2 BCE, when Augustus felt compelled to obey the terms of his own law. His daughter, Julia, was exiled to the windy and desolate island of Pandateria on the grounds that she had committed adultery with multiple sexual partners. Rather than trying to suppress the reason for Julia's disappearance, which would have encouraged the generation of rumors about what had happened to her, he announced his decision publicly in a letter to the senate. Augustus wanted to be seen as a *pater familias* ("father of the household") who was exercising proper control over his family. While there was gossip and speculation about the identity of Julia's lovers, the reaction to her exile was largely negative. In a spectacular failure of communicative action, Augustus's decree was met with public protests in the city of Rome (perhaps in the theater or other entertainment venues) as people entreated him to recall his daughter. On one occasion, when Augustus told the protestors that fire would be combined with water before he would recall Julia, residents of Rome hurled torches into the Tiber River. The emperor eventually gave in to public pressure, and although he never returned Julia to Rome, he did relocate her to Rhegium on the Italian mainland.[15]

There is a remarkable group of apophthegmata attributed to Julia. Some present Julia as an independent woman who can give as good as she gets. When Augustus notes that Julia is surrounded by a coterie of attractive young men at the games, while his wife, Livia, has a circle of old and important men, Julia responds: "But mine will grow old too" (the implication being that Livia was no different at her age). Another anecdote refers to Julia's adulterous behavior, but in a way that still marks her out as a witty and crafty figure. When people close to her observe how much her sons resemble their father, Marcus Agrippa, Julia remarks: "I don't take on a passenger unless the ship is already full of cargo." The joke explains how Julia got away with being adulterous for so long without resulting in a pregnancy, but it also undermines Augustus, who apparently turned a blind eye to Julia's conduct because he knew all her children looked exactly like Agrippa. The collection of Julia's jokes, which survives only in a Late Antique work, has been plausibly attributed to the Augustan poet Domitius Marsus. Whatever the identity of the original compiler, and regardless of whether or not the jokes were really spoken by Julia herself, they attest an oral tradition—or traditions—emanating from the court that reflected a fascination with the private life of Augustus and his family, who so zealously legislated on moral issues but could apparently never live up to the standards they set. Julia's clever and ready wit gives her a certain sympathy that tallies with protests for her recall at the time. Augustus's version of events was on public record—his letter to the senate is quoted by Pliny the Elder—but the witticisms restore some agency to Julia. Similar manifestations of public sympathy for royal women mistreated by rulers appear in ancient China, medieval Byzantium, and early modern Britain, revealing that public opinion could at least attempt to hold patriarchal regimes to account.[16]

Augustus's moral legislation promoted traditional Roman family values. But Rome's transformation into a monarchical state also enabled the emergence of a sexual counter-ideology, based on divine extravagance and display. Poetry written and performed under Domitian celebrated his relationship with his Greek eunuch and cupbearer, Earinus ("Springtime"). "Out of all the court, it is that boy who is most loved by our lord," wrote the poet Martial, who sycophantically compared Earinus's relationship with Domitian to that between Jupiter and his cupbearer, Ganymede. Even though Domitian was a married man, it was acceptable for poets to celebrate this pederastic association because it allowed the emperor to be publicly lauded as the equal of Jupiter. The dour Republican idea of male virility, in which sex was a means for continuing the family line, retained its force under the empire—witness the many children on the Altar of Augustan Peace or the coinage of Marcus Aurelius, on which his wife, Faustina, almost groans under the weight of her many offspring (fig. 8)—but it now competed with the allure of divine sexual performance and control, the god-like emperor whose conquests rivaled those of Jupiter himself. Sometimes the two value systems existed simultaneously in different media and contexts. Hadrian's official coinage promoted his *pudicitia* ("sexual continence"), presumably referring to his conjugal devotion to his wife, Sabina. But poetry celebrating Hadrian and his

Fig. 8. Bronze *sestertius* of Faustina the Younger, showing the empress with her children on the reverse, 161–176 CE. *Roman Imperial Coinage* III Marcus Aurelius 1674. Münzkabinett der Staatlichen Museen, Berlin, 18204293. Photograph by Reinhard Saczewski.

teenaged male lover, Antinous, continued to be read and performed in Egypt one and a half centuries after their deaths.[17]

If poetry shows us how these new divinely inspired expressions of sex and leadership could be publicly celebrated, then court gossip brings to life the discontent that it fostered. Nero reportedly castrated a boy called Sporus, who bore a striking resemblance to his wife, Poppaea Sabina, and even married him in a ceremony in Greece after Poppaea's death. No doubt some hack poet was called upon to compose some verses for the event, offering an encomiastic take on the marriage similar in theme, if not in quality, to Martial's evocation of Domitian and Earinus. Yet not everyone was taken in by Nero's new marriage. "The rather clever joke that someone made is still current today," wrote Suetonius in the early second century, "that the world would have been a better place, if Nero's father Domitius had had a wife like that."

As wisecracks go, this is a particularly funny one, and therefore all the more effective in criticizing Nero's actions. Courtiers who talked in this fashion could not lambast Nero to his face, but by making jokes and sharing them with their friends, they subtly undermined his regime, while also allowing themselves a moment of light relief by imagining a world in which Nero had not been born. The jokers also distinguished themselves from sections of the court community who supported and lavished praise on the emperor and his sexual celebrations. These were the sort of courtiers whose blandishments had driven Nero to perform onstage, according to Plutarch, an eyewitness to the emperor's flamboyant tour of Greece and its festivals. "Was it not the praise of his flatterers that did this?" he lamented. Gossip was thus a weapon that could be deployed not only against the emperor, but also against rival groups at court.[18]

Something that would never have been celebrated at court was a sexual relationship between the emperor Nero and his mother, Agrippina, for that was a taboo that offered no chance of poetic rehabilitation. Yet gossip about their incest was a successful way to undercut both Agrippina's influence and Nero's fitness to rule. Two Neronian historians, Cluvius Rufus and Fabius Rusticus, captured and retold the gossip circulating at court, Rufus attributing the initiative for the sexual relationship to Agrippina, Rusticus to Nero. The talk about Nero's sexual habits did not play a direct role in the Pisonian conspiracy that tried to depose him in 65, nor in his final downfall in 68, but it was certainly a manifestation of the discontent with his rule among sections of the court, many of whose members sat in the senate that eventually declared him a public enemy.[19]

The Roman imperial court therefore emerges as an environment distinguished by competing sexual value systems that can be mapped by following the currents of gossip. Emperors who engaged in unorthodox or deviant sexual practices did have followers who indulged in the same vices in order to win their favor. When he was a teenager, the future emperor Vitellius spent time on Capri "among Tiberius's prostitutes," according to Suetonius. Vitellius's island sojourn earned him a nickname—"Spintria"—that he carried for the rest of his life. Edward Champlin has argued this was a Tiberian neologism meaning "bracelet worker," but it was coined as a double-entendre, for just as the bracelet squeezes the arm of the wearer, so the bracelet-worker squeezes a penis with their own circular orifices. "Spintria" was quite a name for Vitellius to bear, as it marked out his intimacy with Tiberius in more ways than one. The development of sexual coteries in the open—as opposed to a secluded island—is apparent in the reign of Caracalla. Cassius Dio, a contemporary of the emperor, wrote that when Caracalla began to suffer from impotence he indulged in other (unspecified) obscene sexual acts "and in emulation of him, so did other men of similar habits." The men boasted that they did this for the well-being of the emperor (who was suffering from a range of medical ailments in addition to his impotence). This statement shocked the conservative Dio, who nevertheless deployed these and other stories of Caracalla's court in his history to undermine the emperor's claim that he was actually a self-controlled ruler. In doing so, Dio reworked oral gossip into a literary weapon not only against Caracalla, but also against court factions who supported him, thus ensuring that it was his version and that of the aristocratic group he represented that would be preserved in a textual history.[20]

Sexual gossip was never exclusively confined to the court. The stories and jokes about Augustus's performance of homosexual acts and Julia's adulteries show the overlap between elite and popular discourses, even if we cannot delineate the contours as precisely as we would like. "Only the fortunate have children after three months" may have been coined by an elite wit, but its proverbial nature attests to its wider circulation. Julia's jokes could have begun life circulating among the aristocracy, but the protests generated by Augustus's decision to exile her suggest wider discussion of Julia's life and agency within the city of Rome. Public reactions to lines in plays performed at the theater are perhaps our best guide to what people in Rome had heard about the emperors' sexual habits, as we saw in the case of Augustus the *cinaedus.* There is another famous example from the reign of Tiberius. According to Suetonius, one line in an Atellan farce, "'the old goat licks the she-goats' privates,' was greeted with great acclamation and became widespread thereafter." The implication was that Tiberius, by now in his seventies, liked performing oral sex on younger women. This was seen as the most submissive sexual act a Roman male could engage in, worse even than being penetrated by a man, for cunnilingus was the equivalent of being penetrated by a woman. Such intimate information may have come from senators who had made a visit to Capri (which serendipitously meant "Goat Island"), or perhaps from aristocrats who had never been there, but still fabricated tales of what Tiberius was getting up to, far from everyone's sight. In order for this line to generate laughter in the theater audience, this gossip must have already been circulating among other aristocrats, who sat in the front rows. The fact that the line became widespread after this performance suggests that if non-aristocratic Romans had not been gossiping about Tiberius's sexual habits before, they certainly were afterward. The chain of transmission is significant not only for understanding how gossip circulated, but also to show how its aristocratic origins could have reinforced its believability. In their study of the Russian Revolution, Orlando Figes and Boris Kolonitskii have shown that gossip about the Romanov imperial family was regarded with greater credence by the lower orders precisely because it emanated from, and was trusted by, their aristocratic betters. Courtiers could therefore establish trends and topics in public discourse.[21]

Why were Romans outside the court so interested in sexual stories about the emperor and his family? Entertainment value is certainly one reason. Roman men played games with counters describing the losers—or the winners?—as "ass-fucked," "pussy-licker," or "*cinaedus.*" At the most basic level, it would have been fun for Romans to imagine and ridicule emperors for their own alleged fondness for anal sex or cunnilingus. Since everyone in Rome knew who the emperor was, everyone could talk and laugh about him, not only within their own social group, but also with acquaintances and outsiders, at the barbershop and the tavern, at the forum and the crossroads, at dinner parties and poetry readings. This was the sort of humor that nibbled at the margins of imperial power, exploring and exposing the emperors' humanity, while simultaneously serving as an antidote to the poetry and panegyric that lavished praise on imperial chastity or lifted their sexual relationships to divine heights. A rhetorician like Menander Rhetor could advise a prospective panegyrist to credit the emperor for all blissful conjugal relationships and legitimate offspring throughout the whole empire, but gossip allowed the emperor's subjects to reject such assertions. It thus had a political role to play in the negotiation of ideas of appropriate monarchical behavior both inside and outside the court, just as much as the rumors about taxes, grain supply, and justice we examined earlier.[22]

Sexual gossip could sometimes be weaponized into more explicit forms of protest. The people of Alexandria mocked Caracalla's mother, Julia Domna, by calling her Jocasta, the name of the Theban queen who famously had two warring sons (Eteocles and Polynices) from her incestuous union with her first son, Oedipus. The insult thus not only lampooned Caracalla's murder of his brother Geta, whose memory was condemned and face and name obliterated throughout the empire, but also insinuated that Julia Domna was having a sexual relationship with Caracalla. The lampoon subverted the imperial use of mythology for political and ideological purposes—Caracalla wanted to emulate both Achilles and Alexander the Great—by offering up a new, more fitting mythological paradigm for the imperial house. Although it lies well beyond the chronological scope of this book, the story of how scurrilous residents of ninth-century Constantinople trained parrots to squawk "The whore got what she deserved!" at the empress Euphrosyne from street corners is too good not to include. This was a particularly clever lampoon, as it transferred the act of criticism from humans to animals, evading any potential identification and punishment of the real culprit.[23]

The coming of Christianity provided new paradigms for deploying sex as political commentary. The inhabitants of Antioch, furious with Julian's failure to solve their food crisis, accused him of associating with dissolute male and female companions, including prostitutes. Speaking some twenty years later, the bishop John Chrysostom recalled the emperor's coterie of degenerates in his *Discourse on Saint Babylas.* This was not mere invective: Chrysostom assured his listeners that there were people present in his audience who remembered Julian's processions and could support his own testimony. The stories about Julian also spread from Antioch to Edessa, about three hundred kilometers to the east, near the Syrian frontier. In late 363 or early 364, the hymnographer Ephrem of Edessa wrote a series of *Hymns against Julian* in which he exhibited detailed knowledge of popular responses to the emperor in Antioch. Ephrem recounted the emperor's pagan revels with his companions, his lack of modesty, and his excessive devotion to Aphrodite after the death of his wife, Helena. The gossip about Julian's behavior probably spread through the letter-writing network of Christian clergy, who were eager to find ways to condemn the pagan emperor. By the time Ephrem composed his *Hymns,* Julian was dead. But he harnessed these stories to discredit Julian's memory, by attributing the surrender of Nisibis (which was actually handed over to the Persians by the Christian Jovian) to his paganism and his dissolute behavior.[24]

Popular interest in the sexual habits of the powerful was not only about sniggering and subversion, both of which provided an emotional thrill in their own ways. It also had a more serious side. The people with whom the emperors, their sons, and their daughters had sex and procreated could affect chances for the continuance of the imperial line and the smooth transfer of power. Julia was Augustus's only child, which meant her fertility and her alleged adulteries were a matter not only for her family, but for the Roman state at large, since Augustus intended that a son or grandson would succeed to his position. This explains the story about Augustus taking comfort in the fact that her children did look like her husband, Marcus Agrippa—despite Julia's adulteries, he would have heirs, averting the potential for civil war to once again break out at his death. As Angela Hug has observed, there are many ways of bequeathing power attested in monarchical regimes. Kin-based succession was a choice made by Augustus, which was then followed by his successors in various ways. The mockery of Julia Domna and Caracalla for having an incestuous relationship, Tiberius for abusing children, and Julian for being more devoted to Aphrodite than choosing a new wife all had a serious dimension, regardless of their accuracy, since deviant sexual behaviors did not result in the production of legitimate sons and, hence, future emperors. This reflects the wider anxiety about death and the succession that generated countless rumors. In the Roman imperial monarchy, sex and politics were inseparable.[25]

SCANDAL AND DOWNFALL

When talk about the morals and behavior of the powerful becomes public, it becomes scandal and can even give rise to *a* scandal. The definition of "scandal" is a "grossly discreditable circumstance, event, or condition" involving a transgression of moral values (usually sexual, financial, and/or ethical in nature). When these are publicly disclosed, they cause reputational damage to the people involved. Scandals follow several stages, each of which is distinguished by a series of speech acts. First, there is rumor and/or gossip about the transgression, after which a revelation brings it to public attention. This results in community condemnation in oral and/or written form and, finally, the response or responses by the accused party or parties. The type of scandal that we are most familiar with today is what sociologists call a "mediated scandal." Coverage in print and electronic media allows a worldwide audience to follow the cycle of revelations, cover-ups, and denials in real time. Celebrities and politicians are the best-known subjects of modern scandals—Bill Clinton and Monica Lewinsky being the paradigmatic example—but monarchies are certainly not immune. The relationship between Prince Andrew and convicted sex trafficker Jeffrey Epstein is but one recent scandal to engulf the British royal family. On rare occasions, scandals have forced rulers from their thrones. When the British king Edward VIII declared his intention to marry the American divorcée Wallis Simpson in 1936, he was compelled to abdicate, since the relationship was regarded as incompatible with the royal office.[26]

Scandals could and did exist in pre-modern societies, but they were much more localized and did not always follow the precise series of speech acts laid out above. The scandalized public were usually the inhabitants of one city or region, and the scandalous revelations traveled by word of mouth or letter, rather than through electronic media. One famous example of an early scandal, amply attested in contemporary documents, is the attempt by the ninth-century Frankish king Lothar II to divorce his wife, Theutberga. This involved claims of adultery, incest, abortion, sterility, and magic and enveloped members of the aristocracy, the clergy, and—according to Hincmar, archbishop of Rheims—even the common people. Scandals could have real consequences for a monarch if they caused lasting reputational damage. Neither the French Revolution of 1789, which was quickly followed by the downfall of the Bourbon monarchy in 1792, nor the Russian Revolution that deposed the Romanov dynasty in 1917, was caused by rumor, gossip, and scandal. But, as noted above, they did help to create the conditions in which such revolutions could succeed by demystifying the monarchy and stripping it of its sanctity.[27]

Roman emperors were never condemned in scandals of ethics and corruption, though some were conscious to limit talk about their financial affairs. Marcus Aurelius consulted legal experts to ensure that his decision regarding a contested will did not unduly favor his wife and daughters who stood to profit from a bequest of jewelry. But these decisions depended on an emperor's own moral compass: there were no crime and misconduct commissions or investigative journalists to hold them to account (in contrast with senators, who were frequently tried for corruption and embezzlement). We might say that the Roman public could be "scandalized" by stories of imperial spending—there was considerable shock when it was revealed after Commodus's death just how much he had paid the "little shits" (*copreae*) who served as his court jesters—but there was no scandal "event" in which an emperor was required to answer for his behavior. Emperors were much more concerned about the potential for scandal caused by their female relatives, as Augustus's policing of his daughters and granddaughters shows. When Plotina, the wife of the emperor Trajan, was about to enter the imperial palace for the first time, she made a public declaration that regal splendor would not corrupt her: "I intend to be exactly the same sort of woman when I enter here as when I leave." Despite the moral strictures imposed on imperial women, it was actually the way in which Roman emperors treated their wives that tended to result in public reaction and condemnation that most closely conformed to the pattern of a scandal event. These incidents show that the Roman people did not always endorse the official version of imperial relationships promoted by the state and its administrative apparatus.[28]

Nero was embroiled in such an incident in 62, when he divorced his wife, Octavia, the daughter of his stepfather, the previous emperor, Claudius, in order to marry his new lover, Poppaea Sabina. At first, Nero alleged that Octavia was infertile, but not long afterward he accused her of adultery with an enslaved official and exiled her to Campania, which sparked a series of public protests in Rome. Soon a rumor began to circulate in Rome that Octavia was going to be recalled from Campania, leading a crowd to climb the Capitoline Hill brandishing her images in protest (an event dramatized in the near-contemporary play *Octavia,* probably written and staged in 68 or 69). The scale of the public outcry is important, because it shows that the people of Rome were not content to talk in hushed whispers about Octavia's treatment and were prepared to face the risk of reprisals. The demonstration did actually open up a political conversation with the emperor, since Nero decided to respond and defend his actions—a crucial part of any scandal scenario—by issuing an edict. Edicts were headed with the names and titles of the emperor and were addressed directly to the people of the empire. They were usually read out publicly before the text was posted on a white-washed board for consultation. For Nero to address his divorce in an edict illustrates the gravity of the matter. He condemned Octavia for adultery with the fleet prefect Anicetus, claiming that she had conceived a child with him and had an abortion, and then accused her of plotting to overthrow him. Octavia was sent to Pandateria, the same island to which Augustus's daughter, Julia, had been banished for adultery, and then forced to commit suicide.[29]

The emperor Domitian was embroiled in a similar scandal in 83 when he sent his wife, Domitia Longina, away from Rome for an extended period (some later sources even refer to it as a divorce). After popular discontent at her absence, Domitian brought Longina back, announcing in the senate that "she had been recalled to his *pulvinar*." The Latin word *pulvinar* meant both a marriage bed as well as a couch on which images of the gods were placed, which suggests that Domitian wished to celebrate her return as heralding the possibility of heirs for his own "divine house" (*domus divina*). The move was a popular one. When the imperial couple appeared in the Colosseum at a later date, the people joyfully acclaimed, "Good fortune to Our Lord and Lady!" Domitian's decision to issue a formal response in the face of protests suggests that this affair meets the definition of a scandal, even if we cannot trace all its elements in detail. Throughout his reign, there were also rumors that Domitian was having an affair with his niece, Julia, after executing her husband, Flavius Sabinus. He was so sensitive about this talk that he had the senator Helvidius Priscus executed for writing a play about the Trojan prince Paris and his wife, Oenone, whom he abandoned for Helen of Sparta. Domitian suspected that Priscus's play was a thinly veiled critique of court politics, with audiences meant to identify him with Paris, Longina with Oenone, and Julia with Helen. Unlike the creative interpretation of theatrical lines by audience members that hid under the relative anonymity of collective reactions, here Domitian could blame a specific individual for political criticism. When Julia died relatively young, soon after there emerged a rumor that she had perished in the course of an abortion. The talk about Domitian and Julia was certainly *scandalous* in nature, but it never became *a* scandal, because there was no public reckoning that forced the emperor to account. Adultery was commonplace and accepted on the Palatine, but the people of Rome could not brook the emperor setting aside his wife entirely. *That* was the scandal.[30]

Was a scandal about illicit sexual behavior ever one of the primary reasons for an emperor's demise? There is evidence that points in this direction in the case of the third-century Syrian teenager Marcus Aurellius Antoninus, better known today by his nickname, "Elagabalus." Gossip about his effeminacy and sexual liaisons with men was rife in court and literary circles. Cassius Dio, a contemporary senator, spent most of Elagabalus's reign in Asia Minor, first serving as curator of the cities of Pergamum and Smyrna, and then convalescing from illness in his home province of Bithynia. But this enabled him to ascertain firsthand some of the talk about one of the emperor's liaisons. Dio wrote that a Greek athlete from Smyrna, Aurelius Zoticus, was spotted by the emperor's scouts, who were allegedly on the lookout for men with large penises. They sent the well-endowed Zoticus to Rome to serve as Elagabalus's bed-chamber attendant. For gossip about the rest of Zoticus's life, Dio probably depended on letters from friends from Rome. He was certainly well-informed, since his *Roman History* features a large number of sayings attributed to Elagabalus, which, in the tradition of Julia's jokes, likely originally circulated within the court. When Dio described how Zoticus met Elagabalus for the first time and called him *dominus* ("master"), the anecdote is made all the more memorable by the emperor's coquettish reply: "Don't call me master, for I am your mistress." Zoticus reportedly did not last long in Rome because Elagabalus's jealous lover, Hierocles, spiked his drink to stop him from getting an erection. Whether Zoticus really did have an enormous penis is beside the point—the tale functioned as a critique of power and patronage in Elagabalus's regime. This type of sexual gossip was not restricted to the court society but was also transmitted outward to other elite groups. The Greek intellectual Aelian, who boasted that he avoided the court and all its enticements, wrote a work attacking Elagabalus, entitled *The Denouncement of a Womanly Man.* Although this invective does not survive complete, fragments show that Aelian knew of similar gossip to what Cassius Dio reported. He criticized the emperor as "the womanish thing from Syria"—the neuter "thing" is intentional—both for his lack of sexual continence and the groups of dissolute men and women who congregated around him. Unsurprisingly perhaps, Aelian's critical tract did not circulate until after Elagabalus's murder.[31]

While carrying on these same-sex liaisons, Elagabalus married and divorced three different women in turn, including the chief Vestal Virgin, Iulia Aquilia Severa. This was a major affront to Roman moral and religious sensibilities. Although we cannot trace the public reaction to the union with Severa in detail, we are justified in calling this a scandal, since it was a grossly disreputable event that required Elagabalus to publicly account for his actions. The historian Herodian wrote that Elagabalus sent a letter to the senate defending the marriage on the grounds of love, adding that it was appropriate for a priest—the emperor was both chief priest of the Roman state and a priest of the god Elagabal—to marry a priestess. Cassius Dio recorded another one of Elagabalus's sayings (perhaps a line from the letter to the senate) as his justification for the marriage: "I have done this so that children fit for my god might be born from me, the chief priest, and from this woman, the chief priestess." But the emperor divorced Severa after only a few months of marriage, which again required a public statement. A fragmentary letter preserved on papyrus from Egypt, intended for circulation throughout the province by the governor's office, has been plausibly identified as Elagabalus's announcement of the divorce. In this document, the emperor proclaimed that his wife "will no longer be in my bedchamber." Here the scandal was that Elagabalus had married a Vestal Virgin and grossly violated the religious values of the Roman state.[32]

Elagabalus's downfall came in March 222, when he, his mother, his lover, Hierocles, his financial secretary, and his two prefects were murdered in the praetorian camp by the soldiers, who then proclaimed his cousin, the Caesar Alexander Severus, as emperor. This purge represented the bloody climax of a long-simmering struggle at court between the supporters of Elagabalus and Alexander Severus. Cassius Dio and Herodian, our two sources from the third century, had no doubt that Elagabalus's sexual behavior played a role in his downfall, stating that the praetorian guard came to despise him for his licentiousness and effeminacy. Sometime in late 221, prior to the March purge, the praetorians had demanded the young emperor hand over his "licentious companions." Elagabalus agreed, though according to Dio he pleaded through tears to retain his lover, Hierocles. Elagabalus's perceived sexual misdemeanors, including his relationships with Hierocles and Zoticus and his marriage to Iulia Aquilia Severa, generated rumor and gossip among the court, the soldiers, and the wider intellectual elite (represented by Aelian). All this talk, I suggest, cannot be separated from the political maneuvers that led to his murder.[33]

Christianity brought with it new sexual mores and ways of policing them. The emperor's sexual relationships were not only discussed inside and outside the court, but were also subject to criticism and condemnation from the Church. In 613, the emperor Heraclius married his niece Martina after the death of his first wife, Eudoxia, a union that would turn out to have serious ramifications for his dynasty. (Fig. 9 features a contemporary drawing of the biblical Job modeled on Heraclius, Martina, and family.) The days of having a sycophantic senator propose a new law, as had occurred in the case of the marriage between Claudius and his niece Agrippina, were long in the past. The union of an uncle and a niece had been explicitly forbidden by Constantine, the first Christian emperor, and

Fig. 9. Coptic manuscript of the Old Testament from Egypt, c. 610–700 CE. The page features a drawing of Job and his daughters; the iconography is inspired by Heraclius and the female members of his family. Biblioteca Nazionale "Vittorio Emanuele III," Naples (MS.IB.18). Su concessione del Ministero della Cultura. © Biblioteca Nazionale di Napoli.

such marriages were regarded as incestuous by the Church. The reaction to Heraclius's union has many features of a scandal. Sergius, the bishop of Constantinople, tried to persuade Heraclius not to pursue the union, but the emperor refused to back down, telling the bishop that the decision—and responsibility—was his alone. Nevertheless, public opinion was not on Heraclius's side, and there were protests in the Hippodrome at the time of the marriage. In an unfortunate turn of events, George of Pisidia's poem *The Persian Expedition,* published shortly before the union, contained a line urging the emperor to conquer both his passions and the barbarians like the prophet Elijah. Whether or not this was an intended attack on the relationship with Martina, it was certainly interpreted that way by the emperor, and George fell from grace. According to a later history by the patriarch Nicephorus, who relied on a contemporary source, even Heraclius's own brother, Theodore, reproached his union with Martina by saying, "His sin is always before him," a reference to Psalm 51:3.[34]

This criticism was never enough to destabilize Heraclius's position as emperor. His reputation recovered because he subsequently vanquished the Persian empire and recovered the True Cross from Jerusalem, actions that transformed him into a heroic figure. But the incestuous relationship did have serious consequences for Martina and their son, Heraclonas. (We should observe that Martina, a teenager at the time of her marriage to her uncle, would have had little choice but to acquiesce.) After Heraclius's death in 641, the empire was supposed to be jointly ruled by Heraclonas and Heraclius Constantine, the emperor's son by his first wife, Eudoxia. Martina tried to subvert this arrangement by appearing in public demanding that she be accorded first place in the empire, perhaps as Augusta regnant, but she was forced to relent in the face of protests. Four months later, Heraclius Constantine died of tuberculosis, and Heraclonas became sole Augustus. The Christian Church was adamantly opposed to having Heraclonas rule alone as emperor, since he was the product of an incestuous union. The general Valentinus seized the moment to stage a coup, marshaling support from the army and the people of Constantinople, leading the senate to depose Heraclonas. The senate decreed that his nose should be cut off, Martina's tongue severed, and that both should be exiled from Constantinople. Constans II, the eleven-year-old son of Heraclius Constantine, was then installed on the throne. In his accession speech, doubtlessly written for him by courtiers, Constans attacked Martina and the illegitimacy of Heraclonas and paid tribute to the senators' pious actions in deposing them. The brutal treatment meted out to Martina and Heraclonas was a direct result of Heraclius's sacrilegious union. There can be no doubt that it was a sexual transgression that turned public and ecclesiastical sentiment against mother and son, and ultimately resulted in their removal from political power.[35]

FAMILY AFFAIRS

Augustus's announcement that he had exiled his daughter, Julia, for adultery was intended to forestall rumor and gossip about her disappearance by providing an official explanation. But on other occasions, the official version for the movement and disappearance of imperial family members was not believed. The rumors that emerged in these circumstances illustrate the failures in communication between the imperial regime and the inhabitants of the empire. One of the first examples concerns Augustus's right-hand man, Marcus Agrippa, who had commanded his fleet during the civil wars, held consulships as the emperor's colleague, and married his niece, Claudia Marcella. However, in

23 BCE, Agrippa suddenly left Augustus's side and Rome entirely. The official reason was that Agrippa had been granted a special command over all the eastern provinces for five years. This was ostensibly a great honor, which further cemented Agrippa's standing as the second man in Rome. But not everyone interpreted the commission in this manner. "Agrippa had withdrawn during this time, so the rumors declared, because of his seething resentment toward Marcellus," wrote the historian Velleius Paterculus (who was born shortly after these events and likely heard the rumors from his parents' generation). Marcus Claudius Marcellus was Augustus's nephew and son-in-law, who, at nineteen years of age, was more than two decades younger than Agrippa and was clearly being prepared for great things. The plausibility of the rumors was increased by the fact that Agrippa never made it to Syria, where he was to govern the East, only making it as far as the Greek island of Lesbos. Given Velleius Paterculus's own background as an equestrian military officer, it is probable that the rumors were circulating among elites, as they tried to figure out if Agrippa's departure was a symptom of greater troubles within the imperial family. Later generations of historians accepted the speculation that Agrippa's command was a smokescreen to cover up his political rivalry with Marcellus.[36]

Marcellus fell ill and died suddenly in the middle of 23 BCE. Two years later, Agrippa returned to Rome and married Marcellus's widow, Augustus's daughter, Julia, with whom he fathered three children: Gaius Caesar, Lucius Caesar, and Agrippa Postumus. Gaius and Lucius were adopted by Augustus as his own sons, making his intentions clear as to who would assume his station within the *res publica*. Yet these youths were not the only options available. Augustus had acquired a stepson, the talented and loyal general Tiberius, through his marriage to Livia. In 6 BCE, Tiberius was given command over the East, but he asked to withdraw from public life and removed himself to the Greek island of Rhodes, where he remained for the next nine years. Tiberius was regarded as an outcast. Two years after he decamped to Rhodes, the news was well known beyond Rome. At this point, people of Nemausus (modern Nîmes) in southern Gaul, where Tiberius had previously been governor, destroyed his statues and all other images to rid their city of any association with him. He was referred to as "The Exile" at a dinner party in Rome at which Gaius was present, and the unflattering nickname endured even after Tiberius himself became emperor in 14 CE. One verse that entered wider discourse went as follows:

> You're no equestrian. Why not? You don't have the dough.
> Want to know more? Rhodes is where exiles go.

The poem was probably a political protest on the part of wealthy Roman citizens who were not members of the equestrian order. Tiberius had tried to police the qualifications for equestrian status, which required that a man had to be a citizen of free birth and possess 400,000 sesterces. The verse implied that during his sojourn on Rhodes, Tiberius was officially an exile, which meant he lost his citizenship. He was not eligible to be an equestrian, let alone an emperor.[37]

As in the case of Agrippa's time on Lesbos, rumors began to circulate about why Tiberius had really left for Rhodes. One explanation was that his relationship with Julia, whom he had been compelled to marry after Agrippa's death, was deteriorating quickly. Other rumors concentrated on a perceived rivalry with Gaius and Lucius. Despite their precocious ages—Gaius was only fourteen and Lucius eleven—they were Augustus's adopted sons, already commemorated on coinage and monuments, and Gaius had recently been elected consul. One story had it that Tiberius feared his own rise would anger Gaius and Lucius, and he left Rome to avoid confrontation, while another less charitably said that he had been banished for plotting against the youths. These explanations all appear in later historical sources (Suetonius, Tacitus, and Cassius Dio), but there are good reasons for thinking that rumors of this sort did genuinely circulate in the late first century BCE. Julia's exile for adultery, which came to light while Tiberius was still in Rhodes, was certainly common knowledge, and it may have plausibly prompted speculation about the state of their marriage. Our strongest evidence, however, comes from a statement made by Tiberius himself, which is recorded by Velleius Paterculus and Suetonius. The real reason for his stay on Rhodes, Tiberius said, was that he did not want to be seen to be standing in the way of Gaius's and Lucius's advancement. When Gaius was himself sent out to the East, Tiberius attempted to put the rumors to rest by going out of his way to meet with the young man on Samos. As with Agrippa's withdrawal, it is likely that the rumor and speculation began in elite contexts in Rome, but soon spread beyond that, as shown by the reaction in Nemausus.[38]

The speculation about Agrippa and Tiberius reflected anxiety about who would occupy Augustus's station at a point when the imperial *res publica* was still in its infancy. Observation of, and conjecture about, the movements of members of the imperial family and their principal lieutenants continued for centuries thereafter. When Constantius II appointed his cousin Julian as Caesar and placed him in charge of Gaul and protecting the Rhine frontier, it sparked a rumor that the emperor wanted his bookish relative to perish in conflict, according to the contemporary military officer Ammianus Marcellinus. The rumor was all the more plausible given Julian's lack of experience in warfare. Julian himself commented on the ridicule he received when kitted out in the attire of the model military emperor (though he turned out to be a rather good general in the end). Julian's mission was regarded as a symbol of his weakness, whereas in other cases movements throughout the empire were taken as evidence of a plot. When the eastern emperor Arcadius died in 408, leaving his seven-year-old son, Theodosius II, as his successor, the western general Stilicho mounted a campaign to march east on behalf of the emperor Honorius. But it was rumored that Stilicho instead intended to install his own son Eucherius as emperor (either in place of Theodosius II or, less plausibly, Honorius).[39]

One of the most surprising journeys of a member of the imperial family occurred in the mid-fifth century. In 441, Aelia Eudocia, who had been married to the emperor Theodosius II for twenty years and had given him two children, left Constantinople on a pilgrimage to Jerusalem. There she devoted herself to the patronage of monasteries and the construction of the Basilica of Saint Stephen, where she installed relics of numerous saints. Eudocia never set foot in Constantinople again, remaining in Jerusalem until her death in 460, not even returning after Theodosius II fell from his horse and died in 450. Eudocia's absence in the Holy Land was promoted as a pilgrimage, casting her as a paradigm of piety, humility, and charity, all of which were key virtues of Christian imperial women. But it was believed by some that this official reason was merely a smokescreen for a sexual and political crisis that had prompted Eudocia's departure. Writing in 451, Nestorius, a former bishop of Constantinople, referred to "that demon, the chief of adultery, who cast down the empress with insult and contumely." The unnamed adulterer is Theodosius II's childhood friend Paulinus, who was executed in 440, shortly before Eudocia left for Jerusalem (and about whom we shall say more shortly). The allegation of an adulterous liaison may have been conjured up by the influential court eunuch Chrysaphius, who also masterminded the downfall of the urban prefect Cyrus of Panopolis. When Cyrus left Constantinople, he gave a public reading of a poem in which he openly criticized the "destructive drones" at court. Whatever took place in Theodosius's palace—and it must have been terrible for the empress to leave and never return, even after her husband's death—Eudocia's pious pilgrimage to Jerusalem was specifically designed to forestall rumors by providing a plausible reason for her long-term absence.[40]

Contemporary speculation about Eudocia's departure was transformed into a tale of love and misfortune that was heavily influenced by folkloric motifs. This story appears in Book 14 of John Malalas's *Chronicle,* written between 532 and 540 (and, curiously, this book has a prurient interest in court intrigues not found elsewhere in the work). In Malalas's telling, a poor man came to court to honor Theodosius II with the gift of an enormous apple (very much in keeping with the tradition of wondrous items being presented to emperors). Theodosius gave the apple to Eudocia, but she passed it on to Paulinus, the emperor's boyhood companion and by now a senior government official at court, to cheer him up because he had a sore foot. However, in a tragic misunderstanding, Paulinus then regifted the apple to Theodosius. The emperor asked Eudocia what had happened to the apple, and Eudocia swore that she had eaten it. Theodosius then revealed that he in fact now possessed the apple and accused his wife of having an affair with Paulinus, whom he executed shortly afterward. After this palace crisis, Eudocia asked her husband for permission to embark on a pilgrimage to Jerusalem. The story as relayed by John Malalas features two particular folkloric motifs, as Tommaso Braccini has shown. One is classified by scholars as "Husband's Magic Gift Returns to Him." This is found in Indian and Arabic oral traditions, as well as in this Roman version, in which the amazingly huge apple makes its way back to Theodosius II. The second is the motif of "The Calumniated Wife," who is exiled after being the subject of false accusations. The apple also had a long history in Greek and Roman culture as an erotic symbol and lover's gift, not to mention a reputation as a representation of strife and discord. Now the execution of Paulinus is a verifiable historical event, which occurred in 440. This suggests that the story of Eudocia and the apple is a tale that emerged to explain Paulinus's death and the empress's subsequent long absence from Constantinople (though this coexisted with rumors of an affair between the empress and Paulinus).[41]

Remarkably, this is only one of two versions of the apple story set at the court of Theodosius II. The *Life of Dioscorus* (a bishop of Alexandria), which was written in the late fifth century, casts Theodosius's virginal sister Pulcheria and the military officer Marcian in the role of the lovers. In this version, an apple is passed between the various parties in the same way, but instead of being executed for having an affair with Pulcheria, Marcian is sent into exile. The historical background to this story is that after Theodosius II's death in 450, Marcian was chosen as his successor, and Pulcheria married him in order to give his rule dynastic legitimacy, although she remained chaste. This was no love match, but an act of political expediency. In 451, the imperial couple presided over the Council of Chalcedon, which decreed that Christ had two natures in one, and outlawed other Christological beliefs, such as Monophysitism, whose followers believed Christ had only one nature. The *Life of Dioscorus* was a pro-Monophysite work that wished to discredit Marcian and Pulcheria's marriage by claiming it was the result of a long-standing, immoral love affair. Some scholars have suggested that the version featuring Eudocia and Paulinus found in John Malalas was invented by supporters of the Council of Chalcedon to provide a response to the discrediting of Pulcheria. The Christological factions certainly seized on these stories, but the oral nature and the folkloric architecture of the tales, together with the contemporary rumors about Eudocia's adultery, indicate that their origin lay in the realm of speculation and gossip about relationships at the imperial court, before they spiraled out into the Machiavellian world of ecclesiastical politics.[42]

BODY

Sex and reproduction required bodies—and the Roman emperor cut a striking figure indeed. Gold coins gave his profile a regal glimmer, marble sculptures made him into the model statesman, painted freezes displayed his valiant military conquests. As people went about their daily business, they exchanged his coins in the market or played dice in the shadow of his statues (fig. 10). In times of usurpation, revolt, and protest, these images bore the full brunt of popular discontent, as attested by the headless, battered, and smashed bodies of Theodosius and his family at Antioch. But the emperor's human body also functioned as a site of discussion and resistance. The body of a Roman male, just like his sexual behavior, reflected his membership in the citizen community. Not all Romans were perfect physical specimens, but there were degrees of incongruity that distinguished those who belonged from those who did not. A wart on the nose might be the subject of good-natured teasing and earn a man a funny nickname that could be worn as a badge of honor, but to be born with a twisted leg bore with it the stigma of terrible deformity inflicted by the gods. The significance of such incongruities was magnified when they belonged to an emperor. Everyone knew that the official representations of the emperors were idealized, since no one expected that a sixty-year-old was really boasting a washboard stomach and bulging biceps under his toga. But there was still something striking about the contrast between these images and the reality that the emperor's body, like all human figures, could be bumpy, mottled, leaky, and smelly. An imperfect imperial body reversed the normal power dynamic, exposing him to laughter, mockery, and ridicule, transferring superiority (even if only for a brief moment) to his subjects.[43]

In elite political thought, the emperor's body became a metaphor for the health and vitality of the state. Suetonius's *Lives of the Caesars* feature the most

Fig. 10. Raised panel of topographical border on the Mosaic of Megalopsychia, Village of Yakto, Syria, showing men playing dice next to statues in Antioch, fifth century CE. Antioch Excavation Collection, Department of Art and Archaeology, Princeton University, New Jersey, A-008558.

famous descriptions of imperial bodies, with their protruding stomachs, blotchy skin, and weak eyes, and this fascination with body types is replicated to a certain extent in Ammianus Marcellinus's history and Byzantine chronicles. But such descriptions do not tell us which aspects of the emperors' bodies were actually talked and joked about at court and in the public sphere, for which we need to turn to a wider variety of anecdotes. These show that hair—both hairlessness and hirsuteness—was always a hot topic. Hair delineated and policed the boundaries between human and animal, normality and ridiculousness. Although it is very common for most men to suffer from some form of hair loss, Romans, like the Greeks before them, regarded the baldness of virile young and middle-aged men as worthy of ridicule. The way to get away with mocking a Caesar for his baldness was to do it in a ritual context where such lampooning was not only authorized but encouraged. Julius Caesar was particularly self-conscious about his receding hairline but could not complain when his troops affectionately mocked him as a "bald adulterer" in a triumph, when it was customary for soldiers to subject the victorious general to a humorous ribbing. The Floralia, a riotous six-day festival in honor of the goddess of flowers, spring, and fertility whose attractions included a chorus line of naked dancing prostitutes, was another formal occasion that permitted such license. On one occasion during the reign of Tiberius, the praetor in charge of the Floralia, Lucius Caesianus, recruited only bald men to star in the daytime shows and staged an evening procession featuring five thousand boys with shaved heads. The aim was to tease Tiberius, who was going seriously bald. The ritual context of the lampoons meant that this was an authorized type of mockery, not intended to really challenge the existing power dynamics. In fact, the social hierarchy was reinforced through these acts, because the lampoons took place with the permission of Julius Caesar and Tiberius.[44]

Outside of these licensed festival contexts, talking about the emperors' hair loss could be riskier business. Domitian was said to have been personally affronted whenever someone else was mocked for his shiny pate, though he did at least show he had a sense of humor by writing a pamphlet on hair care (fig. 11 shows him with both a perfect body and a full head of hair). Caligula was less forgiving, according to stories circulating at his court, which said that he forced men with a full head of hair to be shaved and that he executed another man because he disliked his bouffant coiffure. The emperor even allegedly made it a crime for anyone to look down on his head from above lest they conduct a detailed examination of his scalp. Caligula may have been losing his hair on his head, but his body was reportedly covered with it. His hirsuteness was completely the wrong way round, which made him look like a goat ("Cilician goat" was a proverbial term for shaggy men). The goat was regarded as a rutting, sexually deviant animal to which no virile Roman man would have liked to be compared, least of all an emperor. But how did people know about Caligula's furry body? Unlike today, it was common for some Romans to see their leaders completely naked—and not just in heroic nude statuary. Courtiers, from lofty aristocrats to household slaves, would have encountered the emperor in the nude when they attended the morning call in his bedroom or accompanied him to the palace baths. Some emperors, such as Titus and Hadrian, are known to have frequented the public baths, letting it all hang out for everyone to see. Caligula knew that people talked about his goatiness, since he had made it a crime punishable by death to use the word "goat," regardless of the reason. He also had a writer of Atellan farce burned alive for a double entendre in one of his plays, which may have alluded to his goatish nature (just recall the mockery of Tiberius and his goatish fondness for cunnilingus). Caligula wanted to control what Romans talked and laughed about both in public and private, because discussion and mockery of his hair made him something less than a perfect imperial specimen.[45]

Julian was probably the most famous goat-like emperor. He was not only very hairy, but also had a prominent beard, which clashed with the bare chin favored by other members of the Constantinian dynasty (fig. 12). When Julian

Fig. 11. Marble statue of the emperor Domitian in heroic nudity, probably recarved from a statue of Nero, first century CE. Munich Glyptothek. Peter Horree/Alamy Stock Photo.

served as Caesar to Constantius II, his cousin's courtiers complained about his military successes in Gaul by comparing him to a goat. "It's a she-goat, not a man, who is driving us mad with his victories," they whined, using Julian's hairiness to undermine his masculinity. Julian's beard was mocked by the people of Antioch, not only during the Kalends of January festivities when such license was permitted, but throughout his stay there in 362 to 363. "You say that it should be twisted into little ropes!" Julian snarled in his *Misopogon,* claiming that his hirsute nature instead made him into a lion, the king of the animal kingdom. Julian's beard was so famous throughout the province of Syria that the Christian cleric Ephrem of Edessa incorporated mockery of the emperor's facial hair into the second of his *Hymns against Julian:*

Fig. 12. Gold *solidus* of the bearded emperor Julian minted at Antioch, 361–363 CE. *Roman Imperial Coinage* VIII Antioch 195. Münzkabinett der Staatlichen Museen, Berlin, 18233259. Photograph by Reinhard Saczewski.

He was for them he-goat and priest
and for (the thing of) shame he grew his beard long like a Nazirite
and he bowed down so that the incense of the smoke (of sacrifice)
might ascend through it. . . .
The he-goats of the breed of that yearling goat,
who let their ringlets grow and stank with their beards
surrounded the black one who did not look on a marriage.

In this Christian interpretation of Julian's hairiness, the emperor was not envisaged as a rutting sexual animal—he was actually berated for remaining chaste after the death of his wife—but as a Nazirite, or Jew. Participation in the denigration of Julian was not limited to Ephrem, the educated Christian cleric who wrote the hymn, but all those who sang it, regardless of their social status, and whether they were literate or illiterate.[46]

Hair was a popular subject for gossip and satire not only because it was such a visible physical characteristic, but also because it was imbued with a deeper significance in all the cultures that made up the Roman empire, resonating equally with a banker in Rome and a laborer in Edessa. This mockery tested and provoked the boundaries of an emperor's rule, rather than disqualifying him from the purple. The exception that proves the rule occurred in the twelfth century. John Doukas asked to be crowned emperor following the downfall of Andronicus I Komnenos, but the people of Constantinople refused to countenance this after he removed his hat and they caught a glimpse of his bald head. After the disastrous reign of Andronicus, the people said they did not wish to be ruled again by an old man, and so Isaac II Angelos was crowned emperor instead. This suggests that underneath all this hairy mockery there always lay the possibility that imperfections could—in a perfect storm such as that which enveloped John Doukas—render a man unfit to be emperor.[47]

The emperor's body was particularly noticed when it clashed with the expectations of an imperial image. The people of Alexandria mocked Caracalla's small size in comparison with his heroes Alexander and Achilles, while our perennial punching bag, Julian, was compared to a dwarf by the Antiochenes. The more humiliating the affliction, the more likely it would be noticed and talked about. Commodus suffered from a very serious condition known as an inguinal hernia. This involves the intestine or bowels descending into the scrotum and pushing against the testicles, causing both swelling and considerable pain. Sufferers find it difficult to walk, have sexual intercourse, urinate, and complete other everyday tasks. It is also very difficult to conceal. Commodus's scrotum had swollen to such an extent that it was visible under his clothes when he made public appearances. Romans seem to have found the sight of grotesquely engorged scrotums extremely funny. There are jokes about men with inguinal hernias in the poems of Martial, as well as in *The Laughter Lover,* a joke book published in the third or fourth century, in which sufferers trip over their scrotums at night and struggle with them as they get out of pools. The changing room of the Suburban Baths in Pompeii even featured a fresco with a series of couples engaged in sexual acts juxtaposed with the image of a male reading alone because his scrotum is too engorged to take part.[48]

In light of this Roman fascination with swollen scrotums, it is no surprise that many satirical poems were written about Commodus's condition, which the senator Marius Maximus collected in his now-lost *Life* of the emperor. The combination of the intestines and the testicles, representing the perfectly sordid mix of defecation and copulation upon which grotesque humor relied, had the effect of lowering Commodus from the Herculean heights to which he aspired to the level of an all-too-human caricature. After Commodus's murder on New Year's Eve 192, he was abused throughout Rome with hostile nicknames such as "Gladiator," "The Left-Handed," and "The Hernia," according to Cassius Dio, who was present in the city at the time. These negative acclamations were easily coined and shouted by the people themselves, because they reversed the positive acclamations that they were accustomed to pronounce at the games and on other public occasions. They therefore represented a genuinely popular reaction to Commodus's body.[49]

The discussion of imperial bodies is marked by interesting patterns. Claudius's disabilities were satirized mercilessly in Seneca's *Apocolocyntosis,* in which he was portrayed as a monster who dragged his lame right foot behind him, twitched his head violently, and mumbled incomprehensibly. Yet this court-based gossip about Claudius's disability was not reflected in public mockery of the emperor recorded by our sources, perhaps because its symptoms were more apparent or terrifying close-up. There is a similar dissonance between the commentary in Suetonius's *Lives* about legs, stomachs, skin, noses, and teeth and the popular discourse. There is no evidence that, for example, the mottled and stinky body of Nero was ever the topic of popular mockery. Talk about imperial bodies largely focused on features that were outrageously grotesque or had particular cultural symbolism, such as Commodus's hernia and Julian's beard. There is likewise an interesting absence of imperial nicknames that traded on bodily features or deformities, in contrast to those famously born by Republican politicians, such as Bambalio ("The Stammerer") or Verrucosus ("Mr. Warty"). But these monikers emerged from a culture of Republican aristocratic sociability and peer-to-peer mockery: imperial senators could not simply give the emperor a nickname based on his big nose or balding head in the same way. Bodily nicknames do return with the fifth-century emperor Anastasius, who was dubbed "Dikoros" ("The Two-Pupiled") because his eyes were different colors, but its precise social origin is difficult to determine, and it could have been the product of theological invective directed against his Monophysitism rather than popular mockery. All this gossip about the imperial body worked on multiple levels. For elite Romans, steeped in philosophy, physiognomy, or rhetorical theory, physical characteristics potentially opened a window into an emperor's true nature. But the grotesque idea of the emperor as a hairy, sexually deviant goat or sporting a swollen scrotum represented a form of "low" humor that resonated at all social levels.[50]

The same principle applies to vices, such as excessive drinking. Drunkenness had a moral and ethical basis in elite philosophy, but was also a fruitful source of comedy. One cannot easily forget Cicero's vivid and vituperative description of Marcus Antonius's night of heavy drinking, which culminated in him vomiting all over himself at a public meeting. Antonius, of course, was a military man, and drinking was an expected and celebrated part of Roman camp culture. When the future emperor Tiberius was an officer, fellow soldiers turned his full name, "Tiberius Claudius Nero," into "Biberius Caldius Mero," or "Mr. I-Drink-Hot-Wine-Straight-Up," a sort of Roman twist on James Bond's catchphrase, "Shaken, not stirred." But the world of politics demanded different standards, and drunkenness, like other forms of excess, was regarded by elite philosophy as a tyrant's vice. When Tiberius became emperor, army banter was transformed into political criticism in the form of the following poem, which portrayed him as a bloodthirsty ruler:

> That man scorns wine, because he now has a thirst for gore:
> He drinks that as greedily as he imbibed unmixed wine before.

Not all Romans who derided a drunk emperor would have been alert to philosophical thinking about alcohol and self-control. The seventh-century ruler Phocas was taunted by the Green faction in the Hippodrome at Constantinople with the chant: "You've drained your cups again, you're pissed out of your mind again." These lines were probably made up on the spot, as they employed the same formulas as the standard metrical acclamations in support of the emperors, which were easy to remember and recite by the crowds in the Hippodrome. Reappropriation of popular rhymes is a feature of protest movements from early modern England to contemporary Indonesia and the United States. Here we see how gossip could be repurposed into a blunt act of popular criticism.[51]

As with the emperors' bodies, there are interesting patterns in the way Romans of different social status talked about and lampooned imperial vices. Gluttony is one example of this. Stomachs and what went in and out of them had long been a feature of Roman literary satire. Excessive size had even been policed by the Roman state in the Republic (one aristocrat was memorably deprived of his equestrian rank for being too fat). Overeating rulers figure prominently in Suetonius's *Lives,* particularly Nero, Galba, and the grossly oversized Vitellius, who is depicted with a habit for vomiting up food in order to eat even more. Yet there is little evidence for popular talk of imperial size or eating habits in the form of satirical chants or reactions to lines in the theater. One rare example concerns Vitellius, who was being dragged to his death by soldiers through the Forum Romanum. According to Suetonius and Cassius Dio (both of whom depended on the same, earlier source), Romans pelted Vitellius with manure and mud and called him "Glutton" to his face. This kind of direct attack on the emperor was permitted because Vitellius had been overthrown by the forces of Vespasian and was about to die. The abuse leveled at Julian in Antioch does also seem to have included jibes about the emperor's vomiting, since he defended his continence in the *Misopogon.* Unlike other people, Julian claimed, he vomited publicly only once, and not as a result of overeating, but because he breathed in fumes from the charcoal fire in his room and was advised to purge by his physicians. Yet two examples of popular criticism across more than seven centuries of Roman history are rather slim pickings, especially given the fascination with food and vomiting in elite Roman satire. The dissonance between popular abuse and elite invective may perhaps be explained by the fact that for most Romans, extravagant banqueting and eating was actually seen as aspirational, rather than something to be condemned.[52]

The verbal abuse and humor directed at the emperors' bodies represented a form of everyday politics that used physical imperfections to comment on fitness to rule. This criticism could be tolerated and even licensed by the emperors, but it always had the potential to escape the boundaries of orality and transform into physical violence, not only against statues and images, as happened at Antioch in 387, but against the very person of the ruler. A few days before his murder in January 69, Galba had been flattered as a young and vigorous leader, to which he replied by quoting a line from Homer, "And yet my strength remains steadfast." Galba's reply circulated throughout the city, among whose inhabitants the emperor's "strength" was taken to be a boast about the seventy-year-old's continued sexual virility. After Galba had been killed in the Forum, his successor, Otho, gave his severed head to his servants; they promptly paraded it around, laughing at his bald visage with the ditty: "Galba the Lovebird, may you now enjoy your youth!" The human features, such as baldness and hair, for which Romans mocked their emperors in life became special targets on their dead—or soon-to-be dead—bodies. When the praetorian guard rebelled against the co-emperors Pupienus and Balbinus in 238, the soldiers dragged them from the imperial palace into the streets at Rome, stripped off their clothes, and pulled at their beards and eyebrows, depilating all the hair from their faces. There are numerous examples of the heads of emperors, or would-be emperors, being paraded through the empire on spikes before they came to rest in Rome, Constantinople, or other imperial capitals (fig. 13). Such processions were a grisly reversal of imperial cult ceremonies or other rituals in which bronze, silver, or gold imperial busts were solemnly paraded around, even in rural areas, to judge by a copper-alloy head of Marcus Aurelius found in the British countryside (fig. 14). Sometimes the populace even created these trophies themselves. In 455, the emperor Petronius Maximus tried to flee Rome as

Fig. 13. Manuscript of the *Consularia Marsiburgensia* previously known as the *Ravenna Annals,* showing the heads of the defeated fifth-century usurper Jovinus and brothers Sebastianus and Sallustius, sixth century CE. Cod. I, 202, Domstiftsbibliothek Merseburg. © Domstiftsbibliothek Merseburg.

Fig. 14. Copper alloy head of Marcus Aurelius (16.2 centimeters high), second century CE, discovered in Northamptonshire, United Kingdom. Ashmolean Museum, Oxford, AN2011.46. © Ashmolean Museum.

the Vandal army approached. He was recognized and struck down by a flying rock, after which the crowd tore his body limb from limb, then carried the dismembered pieces about on a pole. All these events exhibit widespread awareness of the symbols and rituals of the imperial government. They did not represent the assenting performances of successful communicative action, but a different form of dialogue with the state, in which Romans remixed the language and ceremonial of imperial power to inscribe statements about an emperor's fitness to rule on his very own body.[53]

. . . *AND SOUL*

The Romans' interest in the qualities of their emperors extended beyond their exterior visage. The virtue of *pietas* ("piety")—which meant the emperor's devotion to the gods, the fatherland, the people, and his family—was regarded as intrinsically connected to the favor shown by the gods to his rule and to the empire at large. Yet Romans could not peer into the souls of their emperors, and so had to judge their piety through external performances of religious devotion, such as their edicts on religious matters, the construction and dedication of temples and churches, and the performance of rites and sacrifices. Excessive or insufficient religiosity was not usually the subject of satire. One rare example is the mockery of Marcus Aurelius's large number of sacrifices in a Greek distich written from the perspective of the animal victims:

> We white bulls Marcus Caesar cherish,
> but should you win again, we'll all perish.

The ditty is quoted by Ammianus Marcellinus in his discussion of the emperor Julian's own zealousness for public sacrifice, to which we will turn in a moment. Yet one wonders if the context and aim of the epigram about Marcus Aurelius were actually the same as with Julian. The poem could be interpreted as a loyalist quip about the emperor's substantial military successes—he received ten imperatorial acclamations in his reign—rather than his religiosity. As for the piety of Christian emperors, this does not seem to have been satirized at all by their Christian subjects, perhaps because one could never be too devoted to God.[54]

The considerable public discussion, abuse, and mockery of the emperor Julian's piety stands out as exceptional. When he came to the throne, he was not only the first Roman ruler in some forty years not to be an avowed Christian, but he was also extremely militant in his desire to restore pagan worship in the form of bloody animal sacrifice, a zeal that he claimed was shared by his soldiers. When Julian and his army arrived in Antioch to spend the winter of 362–363, his enthusiastic performance of blood sacrifices was a shock to the new sensibilities that had taken hold, even among pagans, in the eastern provinces. Ammianus recorded that the emperor was mocked by the people of Antioch as a "sacrificial attendant" (*victimarius*), a name that carried with it negative connotations. These officials were of very low status compared with supervising priests, of which the emperor was of course the most senior. Julian received a number of other nicknames for his religious behavior, which were enthusiastically recorded by Christian writers. According to Gregory of Nazianzus, who had studied in Athens at the same time as Julian, he was chided as "Beef-Eater," an epithet of Hercules that parodied the emperor's own self-association with the hero, and "Bull-Burner." The bishop John Chrysostom, writing some twenty years later, added "Butcher" and "Meat-Dealer" to the list, prompted by the alleged size and bloodiness of the emperor's sacrifices. These hostile monikers were not only prompted by Julian's enthusiastic paganism, but also by the behavior of his soldiers, who feasted heavily on the sacrificial meat and lurched drunkenly around the city of Antioch, which, as we saw in the previous chapter, was afflicted by serious food shortages at the time. Julian's reign and his revival of imperial paganism was short-lived, but he shocked both Christians and non-Christians alike by the lengths to which he pursued his religious devotion.[55]

In contrast with the relatively sparse discussion about piety, the divine aspirations of emperors were a popular target for satire and mockery by elites and the public at large. These divine claims could take many forms, from public statements of heroic or divine ancestry to emperors expecting worship as a living god. Poets, panegyrists, and painters competed to find new ways to flatter Rome's rulers and endorse or concoct such divine associations. Ordinary people likewise honored emperors as gods at temples and in festivals. But, as we already observed, this world of flattery, image-making, and cult worship competed with more subversive views that there were limits to the emperor's power. Not everyone believed the story that the Julian family, of which Julius Caesar and Augustus were members, could actually be traced back to the Trojan prince Aeneas and his mother, Venus, the goddess of love. One wealthy Pompeian individual commissioned a frieze depicting Aeneas and Romulus as dog-headed apes, which has been persuasively interpreted as a commentary on Augustus's claims to divine ancestry (fig. 15). Even more pointed is a graffito found in the peristyle at the Villa of Boscotrecase, not too far from Pompeii, which reads, in iambic

Fig. 15. Detail from a frieze, showing Aeneas, his father, Anchises, and his son Iulus/Ascanius as dog-headed apes, discovered in the "Masseria di Cuomo," Pompeii, first century CE. Museo Archeologico Nazionale, Naples, inv. 9089. © Pedicini Fotografi.

pentameter: "The mother of Caesar Augustus was a mortal woman." This line appears to be a subversive take on the stories that Augustus's mother, Atia (the niece of Julius Caesar), was not only divine herself but had been impregnated by Apollo in the form of a snake (much like Olympias is said to have sired Alexander the Great after intercourse with Zeus in a similar form). As with the dog-headed apes, this commentary occurs in an elite context, since it is thought that the villa was owned by Marcus Agrippa before passing into the hands of the imperial family. The metrical nature of the original line in Latin suggests it may be a riff on Domitius Marsus's funerary epigram for Atia, which emphasized that she was a mortal woman, using the same Latin word (*femina*). This does not mean appreciation of the line's humor was restricted to the owners: its brevity and meter means that it could have easily been recited by enslaved or freed people at the villa.[56]

We find a more explicit example of the mingling of elite and popular criticism in the satire of Nero's musical performances and his identification with Apollo as the god of music. The following verse was among those that were "either posted up or recited publicly" in Rome during his reign, according to Suetonius:

So our lord plucks at his lyre, while the Parthian stretches his string,
We've got Apollo the singing showman, but they've got Apollo the bowman.

The context is the struggle between Rome and Parthia for the control of the kingdom of Armenia, which lay nestled between the two superpowers. Nero conducted this campaign through his generals, though not always with success. In 62, the forces of the senator Caesennius Paetus were routed by the Parthian king Vologaeses, which caused considerable embarrassment to the emperor when news of the defeat reached Rome the following year. The poem mocked Nero by claiming that he only emulated Apollo's musical qualities and not his military ones, which were embodied by Apollo Hecatebeletes, "the far-shooter" (translated here as "bowman" for the rhyming effect). This epigram likely originated among the educated elite, but the idea that a singer did not make an ideal emperor circulated widely in Roman society. When the Gallic governor Vindex staged an insurrection against Nero in 68, "scribblings on columns announced that he had even driven the Gauls to revolt by his singing," according to Suetonius.[57]

Emperors could legitimately become gods after their death, with a vote of the senate securing their eternal place in the celestial pantheon. The precedent was set by the progenitors of the imperial line, Julius Caesar and Augustus, followed more controversially by Caligula's sister, Julia Drusilla, the first Roman woman to be deified by the senate, at the insistence of her grieving brother. The idea that poor-quality humans made equally poor gods lay behind the portrayal of Claudius in Seneca's *Apocolocyntosis.* Seneca joked that only one witness could be found to say that they saw Claudius ascending to heaven—the same man who swore that he had observed Drusilla's apotheosis. This was the canny senator Livius Geminus, who was reportedly paid a million sesterces by Caligula for his "testimony." Seneca's satire cruelly illustrated Claudius's unfitness for godhood through the deficiencies in his body: the emperor limped around, talked like an animal, and exited life with an almighty shit. The gods of Olympus themselves could of course be hilarious, inappropriate, and grotesque in their own ways, but Claudius's portrayal represented a specific judgment on his conduct as emperor. A similar idea recurs in the emperor Julian's satirical work, *The Caesars,* in which all emperors, even the deified ones, are assessed by the gods at the Saturnalia and found to be unworthy of the standards expected of them. Neither the *Apocolocyntosis* nor *The Caesars* should be taken as evidence that elites were opposed to deification, but these satires show that they carefully weighed up which emperors were really worthy of becoming gods. In Seneca's satire, Claudius was condemned to a life of servitude, transforming his potentially divine body through the ultimate act of dehumanization into another's property.[58]

Christian and Jewish inhabitants of the empire did not acknowledge the divinity of kings or emperors, whether living or dead. The first-century king of Judaea, Herod Agrippa, who failed to check the flattery of gentiles who hailed him publicly as a god, was punished by being eaten inside out by worms, according to the *Acts of the Apostles* and the works of Josephus. The story of a wormy death was one often told about tyrants, because it showed that harsh rulers received their comeuppance in the end, to the satisfaction of readers and listeners. Followers of the Christian and Jewish religions delighted in reading, telling, and sharing stories in which the Roman emperor was trumped by their God. The *Acts of Peter,* written in the second century, featured the deceased apostle appearing to Nero in a dream in which he then flogged the emperor. Although the story survives today in a textual form, it is very likely that it was read out in church communities, just like the accounts of Christian martyrdoms. One very popular Jewish tale, of which multiple variations survive, concerned the emperor Titus, who was eternally reviled by the Jewish people for his burning of the Temple of Jerusalem in 70. In this story, Titus not only destroyed the temple but also committed sacrilege by having sex with a prostitute on top of the Jewish Law within the Holy of Holies. The tale grew in the telling, so that by the fourth century, Jews had begun to say that a gnat with a copper beak and iron claws had entered Titus's head while he was having sex. The gnat eventually became so large that it killed him. In one version, the huge gnat was set free from Titus's head at the same time that the emperor's soul departed, which was clearly a satirical attack on the Roman practice of deification. Titus was a terrible ruler in Jewish eyes, and to make him a god, the equivalent of their God, was the ultimate sacrilege. Although they emerged from different cultural and religious contexts, the Christian and Jewish tales, Seneca's *Apocolocyntosis,* and Julian's

Caesars shared the same belief that emperors would someday leave the mortal realm and be judged by higher powers. In criticizing the emperor's divinity—or lack thereof—these stories share a fascination with the corporeal punishment they were fated to suffer. The Jews were denied the opportunity to do violence to Titus's body like the people of Rome to the corpses of Galba and Petronius Maximus, but they hoped that God would do it for them.[59]

SACRED COWS

In the winter of 601–602, the city of Constantinople suffered a severe famine that stirred up considerable popular discontent toward the emperor Maurice and his family. When Maurice and his son Theodosius were participating in the nighttime celebration of Candelmas on February 2, they were pelted with stones and forced to flee to the Blachernai palace in the northwestern part of the city. The assembled crowd, possibly led by the chiefs of the circus factions, then found a man who looked like Maurice, sat him backward on a donkey, and crowned him with garlic bulbs. The crowd then chanted in unison:

> He found the heifer soft and tender,
> and like the young cock he mounted her,
> spawning kids like wooden wart-heads;
> no one dares speak, he's gagged all.
> Saint, my saint, terrible and mighty,
> strike his head to stop him swelling,
> then I'll bring in vow your great big bullock.

This ribald sexual verse, which envisioned Maurice as a cock and his wife, Constantina, as a cow, did not depend on intimate knowledge of court politics, but on the well-publicized fact that the fertile imperial couple had no fewer than nine children. Such a stable of heirs and spares was usually the sort of thing that would be celebrated by the imperial regime and the people alike, but on that cold February night the hungry people of Constantinople ridiculed the emperor for spending all his time rutting instead of looking after their needs. The verse is in the same meter as the acclamations in favor of the emperors shouted by the audience in the Hippodrome. This suggests that members of the circus factions came up with the lines extemporaneously, using a rhythm that could be easily chanted by the angry crowd. The concluding vow to sacrifice a bull to a saint for striking Maurice, a common folk religious practice, confirms the popular nature of the outburst.[60]

The Candelmas gathering is remarkable because it is the first known example of the emperor being impersonated in a humiliating ritual protest, often termed a *charivari,* after the medieval French rite of mockery. Such mummery was not completely unknown in the early Roman empire—the Greeks of Alexandria had dressed up an intellectually disabled man as the Jewish king Herod Agrippa in the first century—but impersonations of emperors themselves only took place at their funerals, where, like triumphs, this ridicule was authorized and encouraged. The decidedly unauthorized demonstration against Maurice was shaped by two political and social rituals that were particular to Late Antiquity. The first was the festival of the Kalends of January, which spread widely throughout the empire in the fourth century and featured mockery of both gods and emperors (as Julian found out to his chagrin in Antioch). As Lucy Grig has explored, the clergy was opposed to such Carnivalesque license, and Asterius, bishop of Amasea in northern Asia Minor, complained about soldiers who lampooned the emperor by riding on chariots with mock spear-bearers. There were also other festivals that involved ritual abuse of a substitute emperor, such as the smacking of Constantius II's bronze bottom in Emesa. The second ritual that appeared in Late Antiquity was the parade of infamy, first attested in the early fifth century, in which a defeated foreign leader or Roman usurper was humiliated by being led to his execution on a donkey. The festive license of the Kalends of January permitted making fun of the emperor, but by giving Maurice his own parade of infamy, the people of Constantinople were engaging in an unauthorized and aggressive act of opposition to his rule, transforming him from king to clown, a ritual of humiliation that became increasingly popular in the medieval world.[61]

The personal lives, habits, and bodies of the emperor and his family were a subject of continual fascination because they represented shared reference points for everyday political discourse. The imperial family was promoted as the "Augustan house" (*domus Augusta*) and the "divine household" (*domus divina*), which served as a paradigm of virtue and morality for families throughout the empire. Their exemplarity and, in some cases, their divinity was monumentalized in shimmering statues and painted portraits. Yet emperors could commit adultery, incest, and deviant sexual acts, they could be consumed by jealousy and envy, and they could punish and kill their nearest and dearest. Imperial bodies could suffer from afflictions ranging from the commonplace to the grotesque that marked them out as just as human as the men and women in the marketplace or theater. It was in this space between perfection and imperfection, ruler and subject, god and man, that rumor and gossip about the emperors and their families flourished, as Romans swapped tales about sexual positions, hairy bodies, and domestic crises. This talk is mostly lost to us today, but it manifested itself in actions recorded in our sources, such as the laughter at the theater, the chants in the marketplace, the protests in city centers, and the ditties circulated at court and beyond. Sometimes the rumors and gossip focused on topics that we would regard as inherently political—a divorce, estrangement, the disappearance of a trusted advisor—since they concerned the workings of government and the imperial succession. But I would argue that *all* this everyday talk, laughter, and chanting constituted political acts. They delineated the contours of ideal imperial bodies and behavior and evaluated whether or not the current ruler lived up to them.

In this way, gossip about the emperors teetered uneasily between the extremes of loyalty and resistance as part of an ongoing conversation between ruler and ruled. If emperors allowed such discussion and laughter to take place unpunished, their permission actually reinforced the traditional hierarchies of power. It undoubtedly gave Romans a small sense of satisfaction and control to mock the emperors in this manner, but the Caesars could take the high road and retain the upper hand. Nero, so mercilessly pilloried for his singing, understood this, never punishing anyone who wrote humorous poems about him, even when presented with their names, while Vespasian cleverly turned talk about his stinginess into a sign of his civility and jocularity. Caligula and Caracalla were far less understanding; enacting harsh edicts and reprisals, their actions transformed talk that criticized and probed specific aspects of their rule into bloody incidents that became serious indictments of their leadership. Perhaps they feared the potential for all mockery to move from oral criticism to physical attacks; laughing at an emperor's body could be simply an act of letting off steam, but it could also be a step toward attacking the real thing.

And so, it is important to explore the full gamut of responses that lie between devotion and opposition through the life stories of individual emperors. The original insults about the young Caesar's fondness for fellatio were circulated by his political rivals in the days of the civil wars, in which it was not inevitable he would emerge victorious, nor that he would ever come to rule the Roman empire as Augustus. When the Roman theatrical audience laughed at a double entendre about his preference for anal penetration some years later, it was in a world in which he now had no rivals of the likes of Marcus Antonius. Sexual gossip about Augustus would instead have taken on a quite different function at this point, representing discontent with his treatment of his daughter, Julia, or his strict moral legislation. Talk therefore transitioned from outright opposition to the young Caesar as a leader to criticism of Augustus's policies, as both emperor and subjects negotiated his role within the emerging monarchical *res publica.*

The popular support for Julia during her exile and the jokes that circulated about her sexual life reflect another facet of this negotiation: how women would fit into the public life of the new imperial state. I propose that the talk about Julia, the sexual depravity of Tiberius and his associates like Vitellius the penis-squeezer, the opposition to Nero's divorce of Octavia, and Nero's sexual relationship with Sporus reveal related, overlapping discourses at court and in the city of Rome, all of which crystallized around the importance of a central, stable conjugal relationship to the continuance of the *res publica.* The extravagant poetic celebration of the quasi-divine pederastic relationship between Domitian and Earinus reflected a new form of monarchical sexual display that could potentially coexist alongside the union of emperor and empress. But not all sexual relationships between emperors and male lovers were able to be convincingly fashioned in this way, as the denigration and downfall of Elagabalus several centuries later shows.

Indeed, gossip had real teeth when it became a vehicle for dissent and empowered the emperor's critics, such as the courtiers exasperated with Nero's excesses or the soldiers horrified by Elagabalus's sexual sacrilege. Nor was such talk restricted to elite circles, as the popular protests against Nero's treatment of Octavia or Heraclius's incestuous marriage to Martina demonstrate. In these circumstances, emperors could be embroiled in controversies that share many of the same aspects as modern sexual and political scandals, forcing them to publicly account for their actions. Although evaluative gossip rarely dethroned an emperor, it was still political debate with the potential to be mobilized into genuine protest if people cared enough about the issue at hand, as shown by the fate of the unfortunate Martina and Heraclonas. The latter's condemnation as the offspring of an incestuous, sacrilegious union rewrote the imperial government's own messaging of the prosperous Heraclian family unit, which was promoted on gold and bronze coins. The brave Christian who tore down the Edict of Persecution in Nicomedia likewise harnessed talk about the Tetrarchs' humble origins in an overt act of resistance. He paid for this action with his life, yet it shows the potential for Romans to not only disagree with the administration's attempts at communicative action, but also to oppose them.

Gossip could be deployed within a larger opposition movement, as in the case of Maurice's *charivari,* which was but one of several protests prompted by food shortages that marked the last year of the emperor's reign. Here we see how sexual talk could be activated to criticize a ruler's failure to deal with the serious issue of feeding his populace. In November of 602, Maurice was overthrown by the usurper Phocas, and he and his sons were brutally executed. On this occasion, the people of Constantinople had gotten their wish, but the death of an emperor often created more problems than it solved.[62]

CHAPTER 3

Death and Dynasty

In the summer of 117, the sixty-three-year-old emperor Trajan suffered a stroke at Antioch in Syria. He was a very successful emperor by Roman standards, having waged two triumphant wars against the Dacians and bequeathed numerous new amenities to the city of Rome, but his final campaign against the Parthian empire, Rome's greatest rival, was to prove his undoing. Seized by a reckless desire to rival Alexander the Great, Trajan had committed significant manpower and sunk Rome's financial resources into the war, only to find his new conquests being chipped away as soon as they had been won. Then came the stroke, which left Rome in a very precarious position. Trajan and his wife, Pompeia Plotina, had been married for more than thirty years without issue. There were stories of Trajan's fondness for young men, but same-sex affairs had never stopped Roman emperors from procreating before. Nor had Trajan adopted a son, despite the political ramifications of not designating an heir. His own acclamation as the adopted son and successor of Nerva back in 97 had restored confidence in the weak and elderly emperor and his equally dilapidated regime. Perhaps Trajan thought that everyone knew whom his successor should be—the general Publius Aelius Hadrianus (better known as Hadrian), his former ward, who was also married to his great-niece, Vibia Sabina. But without any formal adoption procedure or grant of the title of "Caesar," by now conventionally used to designate an heir-apparent, Hadrian's position was open to challenges from other leading senators.[1]

After the stroke, Trajan and Plotina decided to return to Rome by sea, accompanied by key members of the imperial court, including the prefect of the praetorian guard, Publius Acilius Attianus (another former guardian of Hadrian, who had lost his own father in his youth). Trajan was by this time partially paralyzed, and there must have been grave fears among his entourage that he would not make it back to Italy. The fleet was soon forced to berth at the city of Selinus in the province of Cilicia (now Gazipaşa in southern Türkiye). There, in early August, Trajan passed away, his wife by his side. On August 9, a letter reached Hadrian, who had remained at Antioch, that the emperor had adopted him. Two days later, on August 11, a second letter came with the news that Trajan was dead. Hadrian was acclaimed emperor by the troops, accepting the honor of the purple swiftly, without waiting for the customary senatorial authorization. The imperial administration was caught off guard by the announcement of Hadrian as successor, though efforts were made to remedy this as quickly as possible. New coins minted at both Rome and Antioch showed Trajan and Hadrian shaking hands, accompanied by the Latin legend *adoptio* ("adoption").[2]

This official version of Trajan's death and Hadrian's accession was not universally accepted, even decades after his death. One skeptic was the senator Cassius Apronianus, who launched his own investigation when he served as governor of Cilicia in the early 180s. Apronianus talked about his discoveries to many friends and associates, including his own son, the historian Cassius Dio, who later recorded his father's theories in his *Roman History.* The whole affair—so Apronianus claimed—was a sham. The adoption had been engineered by the praetorian prefect Attianus and Trajan's wife, Plotina, because she was in love with Hadrian. They allegedly kept the news of Trajan's death secret for many days to ensure that the announcement of Hadrian's adoption would be revealed first. Plotina even signed the letters sent by Trajan to the senate herself. This tale—despite Apronianus's claim to have researched it thoroughly—was a rumor, which reflected widespread distrust of the administration's own version, a skepticism that persisted for decades after Trajan's death. Dio believed his father's claims, minimizing Hadrian's status as Trajan's preferred successor in his *Roman History,* and he even repeated the allegation that Hadrian owed the purple to the machinations of the lovestruck Plotina. These rumors originated in the tense early years of Hadrian's reign, in which he took the suspicious step of executing four former consuls who had been trusted associates of Trajan—and potential rivals for the purple—though he tried to exonerate himself of the responsibility for the executions in his autobiography.[3]

Modern historians have indulged in considerable speculation about the events at Selinus. In the epigraphic collection of the Vatican Museums, there is an epitaph recording the career of Marcus Ulpius Phaedimus, one of Trajan's freedmen, who rose from serving at the emperor's table to become secretary for imperial grants and indulgences. The inscription reveals that the twenty-eight-year-old Phaedimus died at Selinus on August 12, 117, a mere few days after Trajan himself. Was the unfortunate Phaedimus killed because he knew too much about Plotina and Attianus's actions? Or did he perhaps have a role in advancing Trajan's death, so that Plotina's beloved Hadrian could claim the purple? The epitaph says that Phaedimus's body was only returned to Rome seventeen years later. Was this to prevent it from being carefully examined by people in Rome? The possibilities are only limited by the extent of one's imagination. The rumor recounted by Apronianus, and subsequently entertained by ancient historians and modern scholars alike, has all the ingredients of what we would expect from a palace intrigue—a suspicious death, an uncertain succession, a conniving woman—which both conformed to and reinforced Roman conceptions of court politics.[4]

THE WORLD HANGS BY A THREAD

"Rumor is always more terrifying when it concerns the deaths of the powerful," wrote the senator Cornelius Tacitus, our most acute observer of Roman imperial politics. His statement can be equally applied to monarchs and potentates, both dynastic and elected, who, by continuing to draw breath, are regarded as representing stability, continuity, and peace in their realms. Their deaths bring a combination of anxiety, tension, hope, and excitement, because they open up a world of possibilities for the future, ranging from the smooth succession of an heir to a long and bloody civil war. The potential of a ruler's death to rupture the body politic has led countless monarchical regimes to conjure up elaborate funeral and coronation ceremonies to offer the reassurance of a seamless transition from one sovereign to another. The very necessity of these rituals of continuity reflects the fact that there existed, even for a brief moment, those other terrible prospects of dissent, conflict, and war, which could threaten the fabric of the state. In the case of a disputed succession in Rome, the ideal scenario was for all politicking to take place swiftly behind closed doors—depending on the circumstances, sometimes even blood relatives were not guaranteed the purple—so that the death of an emperor and the elevation of his successor could be announced simultaneously. This was a rare occurrence that required a combination of hard-nosed diplomacy and luck to achieve. But when it did happen—as with the concurrent proclamation of Claudius's death and Nero's accession on October 13, 54, and the similar announcement of the death of Justinian and the accession of Justin II on November 14, 565—the senate, the army, and the populations of Rome and Constantinople accepted their new emperor without dissent.[5]

The fragility of this moment of transition meant that it was forbidden for astrologers, diviners, and soothsayers or their clients to make inquiries "into the health of the emperor or the situation of the *res publica,*" on pain of death. When the emperor Vitellius issued an edict ordering astrologers to leave Rome before the Kalends (the 1st) of October 69, they responded by posting a reply using the formulaic language of imperial pronouncements decreeing that Vitellius should die by the same date. This public war of words between emperors and astrologers in the city of Rome illustrates the power of these fortune tellers to destabilize the state's desire to restrict all discussion of the emperor's end. Indeed, when an emperor did pass away, the government often tried to carefully manage the flow of news and information so that it could be released at a time and manner that suited the regime. The eastern emperor Theodosius II did precisely this when his uncle, the western emperor Honorius, died without issue in August 423. He suppressed the news until he had "secretly" sent a military force to Salonae on the Adriatic coast in order to protect his territory in case of usurpations from the West (the port was 1,383 kilometers east of Constantinople, which was a twenty-three-day journey by rapid military march, so the delay was potentially quite a substantial one). Romans knew—or plausibly surmised—that the state was capable of delaying or suppressing news of an emperor's death in this manner. When Diocletian fell ill and was not seen by the residents of Nicomedia throughout the winter of 304/305, a rumor gripped the city that he had died. "There was no lack of people who suspected that his death was being concealed until the Caesar arrived, lest the soldiers should happen to try anything revolutionary," wrote Lactantius, who was living in Nicomedia at the time as professor of Latin. Given the precarious nature of Diocletian's health, the rumor may not have been too far off the mark, as officials and courtiers scrambled to anticipate what would happen if the man who had dominated the Roman world for twenty years should pass away. If it was difficult to obtain reliable news about the emperor's health in the city in which he was living, such problems were magnified the further one moved from the imperial center. The transmission of information throughout the empire depended on a range of factors, such as the sailing season, the weather, and the vicissitudes of land and sea travel. In the early empire, the pronouncement of a new emperor could travel from Rome to Egypt in as little as twenty-seven days or as many as eighty-three. The fifth-century bishop Hydatius, who lived in far-flung Gallaecia in northwest Spain, often heard of the deaths of emperors and other major events from travelers or returning envoys well before receiving any official communications.[6]

The imperial regime's efforts to manage the flow of information when emperors were diseased, dying, or dead clashed with the intense public interest in the leader's health, the circumstances of his death, and the possibilities for the succession. The gulf between the demand for reliable, official news and the availability and believability of that information could be filled by rumor. The emergence of rumor depended on various factors, such as the emperor's age, health, place of death, the number of witnesses, political circumstances, atmosphere of the court, and the nature of the succession. This is why it was generally accepted that the seventy-five-year-old Antoninus Pius died of old age after eating too much cheese and was then seamlessly succeeded by his adopted sons, Marcus Aurelius and Lucius Verus. But the passing of Tiberius at seventy-nine—to be followed, after some politicking, by Caligula—generated several different versions, as we shall see. The emergence, circulation, and typology of these rumors were driven not only by the sense-making impulse, as Romans tried to understand how or why the emperor had died, but also by the risk-management instinct, as they attempted to plan for their future. We have more surviving evidence for rumors about deaths and the succession than for any other topic concerning emperors. This is not simply a reflection of the emperor-focused narratives of our major histories, biographies, and chronicles, since the rumors can be found in a wide variety of other sources, from sermons and letters to horoscopes and hagiographies. The tenor and frenzy of talk surrounding the death of the Roman emperor is a striking example of everyday politics, for, as Tacitus observed, it had ramifications for people from all walks of life.

RISK AND REWARD

The gravest fear was that an emperor's passing would spark a civil war. The conflicts that consumed the state in the last decades of the Republic had left a deep and lasting impression of the horrors of internecine conflict and its capacity to tear the Roman community apart. The rise of Augustus and the transformation of Rome into a monarchical *res publica* were celebrated as ushering in an age of peace and prosperity. And so, when Augustus passed away at the Italian seaside town of Nola on August 19, 14, forty-four years after he had defeated Marcus

Antonius and Cleopatra at the Battle of Actium, the Roman world held its collective breath. It was "the time of our greatest fear," wrote Velleius Paterculus, then a junior senator. This was no hyperbole but reflected the fact that Augustus's death would test the limits of the monarchical *res publica.* The legions stationed on the Rhine and in Pannonia rose in revolt, demanding better pay and conditions. Some troops in Germany did not favor the smooth succession of Augustus's adopted son Tiberius, instead preferring his grandson, the dashing young general Germanicus.[7]

The anxiety that gripped Rome in the final months of 14 had the potential to repeat itself every time a Caesar passed away. People watched the stars for signs of comets or other celestial portents that might signal regime change. When Halley's Comet blazed across the sky in May and June 218, it caused consternation in Rome that Macrinus would soon die (which did actually come to pass in far-off Syria). Fear and terror likewise enveloped Rome when assassinations occurred in the city. Cassius Dio described in vivid detail the panic when Pertinax was murdered by the praetorian guard in 193 after a reign of less than three months. The new emperor, Didius Julianus, surrounded the Forum and the senate house with soldiers, forcing Dio and his colleagues to push their way through the amassed troops. Nor were such feelings limited to major cities. After the news of Maurice's murder at the hands of Phocas reached the Palestinian coastal town of Sycamina in 602, a Jewish rabbi told a crowd of merchants and townspeople that the emperor's death signaled the coming of the End Times, just as the prophet Daniel had predicted.[8]

The death of an emperor could lead to panic about continuity of food supply. When Caligula was murdered in Rome in 41, the possibility of civil war was only narrowly averted when several senatorial candidates for the purple withdrew and agreed to support the emperor's uncle Claudius. The situation had been a dangerous one, but exactly how hazardous was only made clear much later when it was discovered that the state warehouses in Rome only had a seven- or eight-day supply of grain left to feed the populace, a fact that government officials had successfully concealed at the time to prevent wide-scale rioting. Only a small, privileged group of two hundred thousand Roman citizens, chosen by lot, would receive this grain free, but everyone depended on its continued supply, regardless of whether they received a handout or paid for, begged, or stole it. Bread, as the sixth-century historian Procopius observed, was something that no laborer or poor person could do without. Nor was it only grain that flowed into the capital cities and fed their inhabitants. In Late Antiquity, privileged residents of Rome also received oil, pork, and state-subsidized wine, and those of Constantinople, oil, wine, and lard, at least until the seventh century.[9]

The connection between the imperial presence and the continuity of food supply is dramatically demonstrated by an incident that unfolded in Constantinople on September 9, 560. When Justinian returned from Thrace but did not hold audiences, a rumor swept through the city that he had died, leading people to rush to the marketplaces and buy up all the bread. Order was only restored when the senate ordered lights to be lit to show the emperor was still alive. These fears were particularly acute if there was a possibility that the succession would not be smooth and there was the potential for civil war (Justinian had no son or declared heir). Challengers for the purple knew that a surefire way to gain the upper hand was to seize control of either Africa or Egypt to prevent the grain ships from reaching Rome or Constantinople. Emperors also needed to feed their soldiers and, as the anonymous fourth-century author of the *Explanation of the Whole World* wrote, it was Egypt that supported the eastern armies that protected the empire against the Persians.[10]

Panic that an emperor might die could spread across the entire empire. When Caligula fell gravely ill in the autumn of 37, the news was swiftly carried from Rome across the Mediterranean by sailors returning to their homes for the winter. Philo, a contemporary witness from Alexandria, wrote of the terror that set in among people in the eastern provinces: "For they turned over in their minds the many terrible things which anarchy brings forth: famine, war, devastation, the destruction of properties, loss of goods and possessions, being carried off into captivity, desperate fears of enslavement and death, for which there was no physician, the only treatment being Caligula's restoration to health." Philo's account reminds us that civil war had the potential to envelop all levels of Roman society in a tragic tale of human and economic ruin: senators forced to pick sides, young men marched off to war, families divided, and women and children sold into slavery. Nor is Philo's description a unique occurrence. The records of Prosper of Aquitaine, a fifth-century Christian chronicler, show that the political event that most concerned him was civil war. Fables reveal how such conflicts were feared by the illiterate and dispossessed. "It is the little people who suffer when the powerful quarrel," was the message of Phaedrus's tale "The Frogs and the Battle of the Bulls."[11]

The worries about crops, food, and hunger in both the capital cities and the provinces remind us just how poor most inhabitants of the empire were, caught in an endless cycle of subsistence living in which the smallest change could cause malnutrition, disease, and death. These were men like the African peasant-turned-estate-owner who wrote that: "All my life, since the day I was born, I have tilled my fields; there was never rest for the fields nor for me." The presence of an emperor, and a peaceful transfer of power from Caesar to Caesar, brought reassurance of support and assistance to these people. When, in the late fifth century, the inhabitants of Syria and Mesopotamia were ravaged by a destructive locust plague that caused famine, the situation was so serious that it could not be resolved on the local level—only the emperor could provide assistance. The bishop of Edessa and the provincial governor journeyed to the emperor Anastasius in Constantinople to plead for tax relief.[12]

Dynastic succession from father to son or another male relative offered the best hope for an orderly transition. But their legitimacy still depended on their acceptance by the army, the senate, and the people, as Egon Flaig has argued. This acceptance could not always be relied upon, as demonstrated by the Rhine mutinies that followed the death of Augustus and the numerous contested successions in fifth- and sixth-century Constantinople. Some legitimate heirs were simply removed by other, more powerful forces. Claudius's natural-born son Britannicus was allegedly eliminated by Nero at a dinner party, while Varronianus, the infant son of Jovian, was blinded and sent to live in Constantinople with his mother, Charito, since the army had instead given the purple to the veteran military officer Valentinian I. The accession of an heir who was young or inexperienced was also a precarious situation, as shown by the events following Valentinian I's own death in November 375. The emperor expired suddenly after an apoplectic rage during an ambassadorial reception, leaving his sixteen-year-old son, Gratian, heir to his western throne. When the first communication from Gratian, who was based in Trier, arrived in Rome on the morning of January 1, 376, the senator Symmachus recalled that he and his fellow aristocrats rushed into the senate house in the dead of night to hear the news that it contained. Their excitement was not merely prompted by the fact that Valentinian I had died, to be succeeded by Gratian. For the senators had already received the news that a second emperor, Gratian's four-year-old brother, Valentinian II, had been proclaimed by the general Merobaudes, who sought to exercise power as a proxy for the boy ruler. The situation could have easily deteriorated into civil war between the supporters of the two imperial brothers, a fear that was no doubt percolating in the minds of Symmachus and his colleagues that fateful night.[13]

Merobaudes's masterstroke in using Valentinian II as a political pawn to advance his own agenda shows that the death of an emperor was not only a time of fear and anxiety, but also one of hope and opportunity. Senators in Rome probably did not mourn the harsh and unlikable Valentinian I, with whom they had an antagonistic relationship. The orator Symmachus praised the accession of Valentinian's son Gratian as the "longed-for hope of a new age." When the succession was uncertain, the consuls and senate sometimes assumed the lead, managing public business and convening debates about the choice of the next ruler, as occurred in 41 after the murder of Caligula, in 193 when the senate was forced to decide the fate of Didius Julianus, and in 238 after the defeat of Gordian I and II in Africa. In the case of the events of 41, the discussion was about much more than who should be the next emperor—it was about whether there should actually be one at all. This was one of the last moments that a return to the Republic was contemplated; coins minted by some generals after the death of Nero in 68 proclaiming republican values and ideas suggest that similar feelings resurged then as well. Thereafter, competition was for the imperial purple itself. This was initially waged among senatorial aristocrats, but from the mid-third century onward it was primarily a contest among military officers. To emerge victorious, potential emperors needed the support of the army, as the Jewish historian Josephus acutely observed. The accession of the elderly Galba led to the "Year of the Four Emperors" in 69, a scramble for power that was later topped by the "Year of the Five Emperors" in 193, and then again by the "Year of the Six Emperors" in 238. Even when there was no civil war, a disputed succession gave senators or courtiers opportunities to act as kingmakers. When the emperor Anastasius died without issue in 518, four officials supported by different military, popular, and aristocratic groups emerged as candidates, resulting in a volatile political situation in Constantinople, which had to be arbitrated by court officials.[14]

Regime change always had the potential to reshuffle the structures of power and patronage, as some courtiers and officials fell from office while others rose to new heights. When Constantius II died suddenly in 361 and was succeeded by his cousin Julian—conveniently avoiding a looming civil war between the two—the Antiochene rhetorician Libanius rejoiced that this would mean the removal of Constantius's unpopular henchmen from court office. Libanius had much to look forward to under Julian's regime, but many had to scramble to propitiate the new emperor. Bassianus, the son of the praetorian prefect Thalassius, who had been hostile to Julian's brother Gallus, was forced to write an open letter in praise of Julian to rid himself of any odium that had attached to his father. Usurpation likewise had benefits and drawbacks, depending on one's perspective. The murder of Gratian by the usurper Magnus Maximus in 383 meant that his powerful and much-disliked courtier, Macedonius, was removed from office and committed to stand trial before the urban prefect Symmachus in Rome. Macedonius, however, disappeared before he reached Rome, resulting in the circulation of rumors about his whereabouts. Some officials needed the intervention of higher forces to save them from punishment. For example, in 610 Domentziolus, the nephew of the deposed (and decapitated) emperor Phocas, had to have the holy man Theodore of Sykeon appeal to the new emperor, Heraclius, to spare him from the bloody reprisals being meted out to his relatives. On the positive side, new emperors required adherents to staff their government, which one might have thought would have been an enticing opportunity for ambitious climbers and sycophantic mediocrities alike. But as the number of usurpations spiraled in the late Roman world, aristocrats and bureaucrats had to weigh up the potential perils of serving a regime that might prove to be short-lived. Paulinus of Pella lamented that he was appointed head of Priscus Attalus's finances after Attalus seized the purple in Bordeaux in 414–415. When the Visigoths sacked the city, Paulinus and his mother lost their property and only just escaped with their lives.[15]

The same tension between the risk and rewards of regime change can be observed beyond the world of the aristocracy and the imperial court. Civil war did bring with it death and devastation, but contenders for the purple often spent lavishly on the soldiers who supported their claims to power. There was even a faint hope that the poor could see their fortunes changed by an emperor's murder and the rise of a better ruler, as predicted in a fragmentary astrological text from Egypt. These hopes for a change of emperor, rather than the dismantlement of the imperial system, need to be juxtaposed with the evidence of foreign peoples who wanted to use disorder to overthrow imperial rule *tout court.* During the "Year of the Four Emperors" (69), the Batavians, a Germanic people who chafed at the bit of Roman rule, took advantage of internal chaos, particularly that which followed the demise of Vitellius (emperor number three), to launch their own revolt in a bid for freedom.[16]

There is excellent evidence that urban populations in politically connected centers such as Rome, Constantinople, and Antioch watched carefully for news of regime change. In 238, the inhabitants of Rome got wind that the senators Pupienus and Balbinus had been proclaimed as co-emperors in opposition to the hated Maximinus. They protested on the Capitol, not out of any love for Maximinus, but because Pupienus had administered the city with a severe hand when he was urban prefect. They demanded instead that a member of the family of Gordian I, the elderly proconsul of Africa who had perished during a revolt against Maximinus, be acclaimed. Herodian, a contemporary historian, wrote that the people assembled with stones and sticks prompted "either by the whispers of Gordian's friends and family or because they had heard a rumor" of what was taking place in the Temple of Jupiter Optimus Maximus. This protest could not prevent Pupienus's designation as Augustus, but it did secure the appointment of the young Marcus Antonius Gordianus as Caesar. The impact of regime change was not limited to the emperors themselves. Sometimes urban communities hoped that unpopular satellites—bishops, court officials, or generals—would fall from grace. After the death of Jovian, an Antiochene mob attacked the property of the courtier Datianus, thinking that he would soon be out of favor. But Datianus was retained by the new emperor, Valentinian I, which meant that Antioch's city council was forced to make a groveling formal apology.[17]

Peaceful transitions of power still offered many opportunities and benefits. New emperors issued pardons and political amnesties and recalled exiles. "If the emperor sends letters releasing men from prison, there is celebration and joy," John Chrysostom told his Antiochene congregation in his *First Homily on Acts.* The death of an emperor could also mean his harmful policies would be abandoned. Josephus wrote that the Jews welcomed the death of Caligula because he had intended to desecrate the Temple in Jerusalem by installing a statue of himself inside, while Libanius reported that the people of Antioch rejoiced at the death of Julian, because of their opposition to his economic measures. The soldiers and the people of Rome received generous financial handouts from new Caesars, which only became more lavish over time. Emperors often canceled debts to the state, complete with magnificent public burning ceremonies of financial ledgers in the city of Rome. Hadrian commemorated his generosity with a coin proclaiming that he had remitted nine million sesterces in money owed, and the grateful senate and people of Rome erected a monument in his honor. Debt was a real and pressing financial issue for people across the empire. A second-century handbook, the *Oracles of Astrampsychus,* featured crucial everyday questions that Romans could pose to the oracle, such as "Will I be able to borrow money?" and "Will I pay back what I owe?" Potential answers included: "You'll pay back what you owe," "You'll borrow money with collateral," "You won't be able to borrow money just yet," and "No one will lend you money now, just wait." The consequences of owing money to the imperial treasury were severe: debtors could have their property seized and sold to cover the arrears. And so we can see how the accession of a new emperor, whether it occurred in a palace murder, on the battlefield, or through orderly succession, could prompt genuine hopes of debt relief that would have an impact on Romans across the Mediterranean.[18]

The tension between crisis and opportunity at an emperor's death is embodied by the issue of religious change. In Late Antiquity, the transition between emperors was closely watched because it could mean a change in religious outlook, and hence safety and preferment—or persecution and danger—for adherents of specific beliefs. There survives a letter of Dionysius, bishop of Alexandria, in which he described to his counterpart in Antioch the anxiety he felt when, in 249, he heard that the emperor Philip had fallen victim to a coup led by his general Decius, who was known not to be friendly to the Christians. Sometimes there was a rapid turnover of emperors with different religious beliefs, which only exacerbated the situation. In only a few short years in the 360s, the Roman world was rocked by the death of the Christian Constantius II, followed by the accession of his pagan cousin Julian in 361, then less than two years later by Julian's own demise in battle, and the reassertion of imperial patronage of Christianity under Jovian in 363. The pagan Libanius experienced these highs and lows firsthand, initially celebrating Julian's accession, then facing attacks from his enemies under Jovian. Julian's accession also resulted in changes for Christian officials; most despised him and his paganism, but the new emperor did restore those whose theological beliefs had been outlawed by Constantius.[19]

The late Roman and Byzantine Church was constantly divided by schisms over different Christological teachings and the adherence of emperors to one or another theological position. The Homoean emperor Valens caused considerable consternation among Nicene clerics when he ruled the eastern empire between 364 and 378, as we have already observed. His demise at the Battle of Adrianople was greeted with delight by the exiled bishop Gregory of Nyssa, who was finally able to return to his see unmolested. The same is true of Marcian's succession to the eastern throne in 450 following the death of Theodosius II. This was welcomed by Pope Leo the Great in Rome, since the new emperor promised to call an ecumenical council at Chalcedon to resolve the Christological disputes that had plagued Theodosius's last years. News of Theodosius II's demise was followed by more specific reports reaching Rome that his eunuch Chrysaphius, who had played a prominent role in his Christological policies, had been killed. Various rumors about the manner of his death appear in the literary sources, but the earliest survives in an anonymous Roman chronicle of 451, whose author had connections to the ecclesiastical establishment. He recorded that Chrysaphius "died after being beaten with cudgels," a unique testimony given nowhere else, which reflects the flow of news and rumor on ecclesiastical and political matters between Constantinople and Rome.[20]

Imperial deaths and Christological disputes not only affected bishops and other members of the ecclesiastical elite, but had the potential to envelop whole cities, whose populations were frequently divided by the question of religious doctrine. When Marcian died in 457, having successfully held his council at Chalcedon, the anti-Chalcedonian church in Alexandria took advantage of the situation. It elected its own bishop, Timothy (nicknamed "The Weasel"), as a rival to the existing incumbent, Proterius, without even waiting to find out who the new emperor would be (indeed, he had not yet been chosen). The provincial governor cracked down on the anti-Chalcedonians by marching his army into Alexandria, resulting in days of mob violence that culminated in the lynching of Proterius. The interregnum between the death of Marcian and the naming of his successor had opened up a brief, tantalizing window of freedom from imperial control. It was in these moments of transition that rumor flourished as Romans weighed up the risks and rewards that could come their way.[21]

SHOCK AND SUSPICION

Despite the Roman practice of watching for signs and portents that might predict an emperor's death, the death of a Caesar could still catch the world off guard. This was what happened when Caligula was assassinated on January 22, 41, during the final day of the Palatine Games held in honor of the deified Augustus. He had spent his final hours watching a farce (*Laureolus*) and a tragedy (*Cinyras*), both of which involved gruesome deaths and considerable amounts of stage blood. This cheery program was later interpreted as an omen of Caligula's forthcoming death, as was his morning sacrifice of a flamingo, in which the hapless bird's blood splattered all over the emperor or one of his closest associates (depending on which version of the story one follows). The most detailed account of Caligula's murder, the reaction to it, and the role of rumor in these events can be found in the *Jewish Antiquities* of Josephus, a Jewish author who found favor with the Flavians for prophesying that Vespasian would become emperor. Josephus was only born in 37, the year of Caligula's accession, so he relied on earlier Roman accounts, which were exceptionally well-informed about the events of January 22. One of these was written by a historian and senator called Cluvius Rufus. As it happens, Josephus records the presence of Cluvius in the theater that fateful day. We can therefore follow Caligula's death through an account that derives from eyewitness testimony.[22]

According to Josephus, halfway through the proceedings, Caligula decided to take a break for lunch and a bath, which gave the conspirators, led by the praetorian officer Cassius Chaerea, an opportunity to strike. When the emperor separated from his companions because he wished to greet a group of visiting performers, Chaerea and his allies stabbed him furiously in a corridor and left the bloody corpse where it had fallen. Soon after, the news reached the audience at the theater—which included members of the aristocracy as well as ordinary citizens and enslaved people—that Caligula was dead. Many were struck dumb with disbelief, according to Josephus, particularly the young people, the women, the enslaved, and the soldiers. The historian gives various reasons for the love felt by these different groups toward Caligula, many of which ring true, such as the soldiers' reliance on the emperor for their pay. A number of senators in the audience were overjoyed but were worried that the information was false. They did not want to express their happiness too readily lest the emperor soon return to the theater very much alive. Indeed, a rumor soon spread around the theater that Caligula had merely been wounded and was being treated by his doctors. Then came another rumor that Caligula had survived the assassination attempt and had made it to the Forum, where he was presently delivering a rousing speech to the people in his blood-spattered state. No one in the audience dared to leave the theater to ascertain the truth of these rumors, lest they be later accused of being involved in the plot.[23]

Their terror increased, Josephus recorded, when Caligula's German bodyguards poured into the theater, brandishing the heads of senators whom they had killed because they thought they had been involved in the assassination. The situation could easily have devolved into further bloodshed, were it not for the arrival of an auctioneer, who announced that Caligula was definitively dead. The praetorian tribunes then disarmed the German bodyguards, who gave up all hope now that their benefactor was no more. The death of Caligula, who had a baby daughter with his wife, Caesonia, but no son, left the succession uncertain. Josephus wrote that the senate intended to restore the *res publica* to its pre-monarchical state, but the people preferred the candidate of the praetorian guard—Caligula's uncle Claudius—because this transfer of power would help to avoid another civil war. For the soldiers, Claudius was a "Germanicus," just as his nephew Caligula had been, and this dynastic connection represented the continuity of pay and donatives.[24]

Josephus's thrilling account of the death of Caligula and the reaction in the theater, plausibly derived from the eyewitness testimony of Cluvius Rufus, exhibits several key tenets of rumor generation. Firstly, the lack of reliable news about the emperor's fate resulted in rumor filling the void. Rumors about what had happened then continued to circulate until the audience received reliable information in the form of the auctioneer's announcement. Secondly, the rumors, such as the suggestion that Caligula had survived and was being treated, were regarded as plausible to those who spread them. Even the rumor that a blood-soaked Caligula had made it as far as the Forum Romanum to address the people was believable, since Caligula was an emperor known for his outrageous acts and grand gestures. The fear of expressing joy too soon, lest it turn out that the emperor really had escaped, is also all-too-credible, given that an emperor who had survived an assassination event was bound to be vengeful. Writing in the early second century, Suetonius—his source unknown—says that there was even a suspicion that Caligula had manufactured the rumor to discover people's real intentions toward him.[25]

Disbelief at the news of imperial deaths is a common occurrence in Roman histories. Josephus wrote that after Tiberius passed away at Misenum in 37, contradictory reports about his death and survival arrived in Rome. This caused particular alarm to the Jewish king Herod Agrippa, who had been imprisoned in Rome by Tiberius but promised his freedom by Caligula. Herod was first released by his captors when they thought Tiberius was dead, then re-imprisoned, and then finally pardoned. The announcement of Commodus's murder on New Year's Eve 192 was similarly distrusted when it was sent to provincial governors, according to the contemporary historian Cassius Dio, who added that some governors even imprisoned the envoys who brought them the news, thinking it was some kind of test of loyalty. These stories represent more than a historiographical convention regarding the deaths of bad emperors. Josephus was exceptionally well-informed about Jewish history, and Dio personally experienced the turbulence that followed the fall of Commodus. News of imperial deaths was particularly distrusted during civil wars, when fear and paranoia reached greater heights. Libanius, orator and friend of the emperor Julian, related that when Julian was marching to meet Constantius II in battle, he received the announcement of his cousin's death, only for his supporters to claim that it was a trick to catch them off guard. Although Constantius II had indeed died, Julian's men were right to be suspicious, as some leaders did promulgate tales of this sort. Procopius, who challenged Valentinian I and Valens for the purple in 365–366, produced emissaries who had allegedly traveled from different parts of the empire bearing news (or, as the contemporary orator Themistius put it, "wicked rumors"), including that Valentinian himself had died. These stories suggest that Roman political elites regarded it as very plausible that emperors would spread false news in order to smoke out potential opponents. Romans at the highest levels distrusted the state's efforts at communicative action, even when they themselves were part of the government apparatus. Yet the belief that an emperor had not actually died as reported was not always confined to these elites. We will see in the next chapter that there was sometimes popular speculation in the provinces that an emperor had escaped death, accompanied by rumors of sightings.[26]

Emperors were regarded as being easy targets for assassination. "No one is safe at the top unless he watches his step," went one of the *Sayings* of the freedman Publilius Syrus. The Christian fathers Tertullian, John Chrysostom, and Jerome lamented the terrible fates that so often befell kings and emperors, even at the hands of their nearest and dearest. Peter Chrysologus, fifth-century bishop of Ravenna, reminded his congregation of the need for watchfulness, remarking that a king is always alert for the plots of his enemies. This view no doubt resonated with his congregation, especially the imperial family members and government officials who attended his sermons. Even an anonymous Egyptian astrological text about an unknown emperor's demise has the pertinent detail that he was murdered by his rival "in his own home." Indeed, the death of an emperor represented the perfect breeding ground for rumor since it so often took place behind closed doors, which meant that very few people knew what had really happened. According to Ammianus, when Valentinian I lay on his deathbed after an apoplectic fit, his chamberlains summoned other officials into the chamber "so that no one would suspect that he had been murdered." The consequences of not having reliable witnesses are shown by the different explanations given by historians for Tiberius's death in his villa at Misenum. Some are relatively innocuous (he refused food while suffering fever; he collapsed and cried out, but then died because no one replied), while others pointed the finger at Caligula, who either poisoned Tiberius, had him suffocated with a pillow, or strangled him with his own hands. The attribution of responsibility to Caligula fits in with the common suspicion among courtiers and other elites that emperors had been murdered by their successors.[27]

Perhaps the most tragic case of a suspicious imperial death is that of the twenty-one-year-old emperor Valentinian II, who was found hanging in the imperial palace at Vienne on May 15, 392. Valentinian had been in conflict with his general Arbogast—essentially the true wielder of power at his court—over Valentinian's desire to lead the army to defend north Italy from foreign attacks. This posed a challenge to Arbogast's authority, which depended on keeping the young emperor palace-bound and pliant, while he handled military and government affairs. Ambrose, the bishop of Milan, was faced with the difficult task of delivering the funeral oration for Valentinian. The bishop was enormously diplomatic, hinting that the emperor had killed himself to prevent a conflict with Arbogast, although he did not state this explicitly, given the negative Christian views on suicide. But not all Romans subscribed to this version. Writing four years later in 396, Jerome stated baldly that Valentinian had been murdered and his body strung up. What is remarkable about this testimony is that by this point in his life, Jerome was living in Bethlehem, which means that the rumor must have reached him all the way from southern Gaul or Italy through his network of Christian correspondents. Rufinus, who wrote his *Church History* only a few years after Jerome, said that it was common public opinion that Arbogast had murdered Valentinian. Modern historians generally agree that Valentinian committed suicide: Arbogast had little to gain from killing him, since his authority was dependent on controlling the emperor. But in the world of rumor, such nuances were lost. A young emperor had died horrifically and suddenly, and the conniving military man was the most obvious culprit.[28]

In the case of Valentinian's tragic demise, the immediate cause of death was at least readily apparent, even if the agent was not. This was not always the case. On the night of February 17, 364, the healthy thirty-two-year-old emperor Jovian suddenly died in his sleep at Dadastana in Asia Minor, where he had stopped on his journey from the Persian front to Constantinople. There was not a blemish on his body. The earliest source to comment on the reason for his death is the *Short History,* written five years later by the high-ranking court official Eutropius, who was almost certainly present at Dadastana. Eutropius gave three possible causes of Jovian's demise: he had indigestion as a result of eating too much; the room in which he slept had recently been plastered, and the smell killed him; or he asphyxiated from burning too much charcoal in the room on account of the cold. The military officer Ammianus, who was also probably on the scene, gave exactly the same reasons as Eutropius, though his account does also contain a hint that Jovian was the victim of foul play. Ammianus wrote that there was no investigation of the cause of Jovian's death, as had also been the case when the Republican politician Scipio Aemilianus expired suddenly (and equally suspiciously) in 129 BCE. There was certainly a rumor that Jovian had been murdered in circulation by the 380s, when John Chrysostom claimed in both a personal letter and a public sermon that Jovian had been poisoned by conspirators hoping to remove him from power (and the sermon would certainly have ensured that this version gained further traction). The rumors that emerged in the wake of Jovian's sudden demise show how people tried to explain it in different ways.

Some looked to the conditions of the room in which he slept, while others sought explanations in plots and poisons, which reflected the common belief that emperors were always susceptible to danger. This reveals how in these anxious moments of transition, Romans drew on the frameworks of knowledge derived from myths, histories, sermons, religious writings, and numerous other textual and oral sources to explain happenings in the world around them.[29]

THE FOG OF WAR

In January 89, the city of Rome was gripped with panic after the governor of Germania Superior, Lucius Antonius Saturninus, declared himself emperor in opposition to Domitian. The Greek biographer Plutarch—who probably was in Rome at the time, although he also said the story was widely known—related how a rumor began to spread throughout the city that Saturninus had been defeated and his army wiped out. No one knew how the rumor started, but it was quickly and hopefully believed, and magistrates even began to offer sacrifices in thanksgiving. The news nevertheless remained unconfirmed, and Domitian prepared to set out for Germany, only to receive the official dispatches announcing Saturninus's defeat when he was already on the move. This is an excellent example of how the panic of civil war could generate hopeful rumors about the demise of usurpers. The opposite case occurred in 388, when the eastern emperor Theodosius I was in the West waging a war against Magnus Maximus, formerly his imperial colleague, now in open revolt. No one knew who would win. The bishop of Alexandria, Theophilus, hedged his bets by dispatching one of his presbyters to Rome with letters congratulating both Theodosius and Maximus on their victory. Since Theodosius, unlike Domitian, was already on campaign, rumors about the emperor's fate swirled in Constantinople, where his second wife, Galla, waited nervously with her stepchildren. One story had it that Theodosius's army had been defeated and even offered casualty figures as proof of veracity; another said that Theodosius himself had nearly been captured by Magnus Maximus. The rumors were picked up, embellished, and circulated by the city's Homoean community, which had profited from Valens's patronage but disliked Theodosius's Nicene orthodoxy. The Homoeans took advantage of the unstable political environment to burn the house of Nectarius, the Nicene bishop of Constantinople. This was spur of the moment opportunism, not part of any long-term strategy, since Magnus Maximus was himself staunchly Nicene and would not have authorized any changes in religious policy, even if he had come to control Constantinople.[30]

These two crises capture the problems of information transmission from one part of the empire to another, especially in times of warfare. The rumor about Saturninus was true, and Domitian (and Rome) avoided a bloody civil war, while the speculation about Theodosius I was false, and the emperor lived to see another day. But the endemic internal and external conflicts that afflicted the empire throughout the third and fourth centuries meant that many other emperors were not so lucky and perished on the battlefield. This changed in later centuries, as most eastern emperors chose—or were forced to—remain in the city of Constantinople rather than take to the field. When Heraclius decided to campaign against the Persians in person in the seventh century, there was considerable discontent among the people and the government establishment in Constantinople, so risky was the potential loss of the emperor in battle.[31]

One of the most famous examples of an imperial death concerns the emperor Julian, who perished on June 26, 363, when he and his army were ambushed by the Persians deep in their territory. Having failed to put on any armor before joining the fighting, Julian was mortally wounded by a spear. On the face of it, this would appear to be an open-and-shut case of an emperor who was killed by an enemy combatant. But according to Ammianus, an army officer who was present as these events unfolded, rumors immediately began to circulate that Julian had actually been targeted by a Roman soldier. The army was ambushed again on June 29 as it was withdrawing from Persian territory under the new emperor, Jovian. The Persians, who had heard from Roman deserters the rumor that Julian had been slain by one of his own, proceeded to abuse their demoralized enemies as traitors and murderers. Ammianus emphasized that there was no truth to the story, but observed that no one had seen precisely who had thrown the weapon that killed the emperor. It was this uncertainty that allowed rumor to flourish.[32]

News of Julian's death reached Antioch later that summer. The grief-stricken Libanius embarked on an urgent search for information about the circumstances of his hero's demise, writing letters to courtiers and soldiers who had been present on the campaign. This correspondence shows that Libanius soon came to characterize Julian's death as a murder, and in a letter to his friend Alcimus, he intimated foul play. The gods knew who threw the spear, he wrote ominously. Libanius's changing views can also be observed in his two orations about Julian. In his *Monody,* published in the first half of 364, he wrote that the emperor perished at the hands of a Persian, but in his *Epitaphios,* which was completed by mid-365, Libanius claimed that Julian's killer was not only a Roman soldier, but a Christian one.[33]

The sudden demise of Rome's pagan emperor naturally interested the Christian community, whose members also had their ears to the ground for rumors. Ephrem the Syrian, who wrote his *Hymns against Julian* within a year of the emperor's death, painted Julian as having a suicidal death wish because he had failed to put on his armor. The number of stories soon proliferated. In his two *Orations against Julian* (dated to late 364/early 365 and late 365/early 366, respectively), Gregory of Nazianzus recorded four different culprits: a Persian; a Saracen; a foreign jester in the Roman army's train; and a Roman soldier who had heard Julian lament that he had to abandon the campaign and lead the army home. These rumors show that it was widely suspected that Julian had been killed by one of his own from a very early stage. However, the idea that the murder was the result of a specifically Christian plot was unique to Libanius. He grew more obsessed with this idea over time. In a later oration addressed to Theodosius I, Libanius claimed that the Christian Jovian had offered a Saracen a reward to kill Julian in battle, a tale that blended his own suppositions with the story of the Saracen known to Gregory of Nazianzus.[34]

At least Julian's body was recovered, and he was able to be given a proper burial at Tarsus. The corpse of the emperor Valens was never found after the bloody Roman defeat at the hands of the Goths at the Battle of Adrianople (August 9, 378). Two different versions of how Valens perished developed in subsequent years. The official story, which was reported to his widow, Domnica, in Constantinople, and was known to both Jerome and John Chrysostom, was that Valens had burned to death when the Goths set fire to a small house in which he and some soldiers were hiding. However, Libanius, writing in Antioch in 379, said that Valens had been offered a getaway horse, which he refused, and instead died fighting to the last. Ammianus, whose account written in the 390s offers the most detailed narrative of the Battle of Adrianople available to us, recorded both the burning house tale (apparently relayed by one lucky soldier who escaped) and the report in which Valens died fighting. Since the distressing tale of Valens's fiery end was the version reported to Domnica, it is the most likely to be correct, for why needlessly traumatize the grieving widow unless it was believed to be true?[35]

The heroic tale of Valens fighting to the end was a romantic idea that likely emerged on the battlefield as soldiers tried to find out what had happened to their emperor. Ammianus compared Valens's death to the story of Trajan Decius and Herennius Etruscus, who were last seen riding bravely against the Goths at the Battle of Abrittus in 251. But the unpopular Valens would not be venerated as a hero like Decius. Nicene Christians, such as Ambrose of Milan and the ecclesiastical historians Sozomen and Socrates, turned the tale of Valens being burned alive into an act of divine retribution for his Homoean beliefs, as Noel Lenski has shown. This view was not limited to the great and the good, however. A painted red graffito found in a church in Göreme, Cappadocia, declared: "You committed evil, Valens Augustus, since you gave up the church to those heretical Arians" ("Arians" being a derogatory term to describe Homoeans, named after the fourth-century Egyptian priest Arius). The patterns of rumor generation in the aftermath of an emperor's battlefield death articulated both the grief of the Romans who mourned his death and the joy of those who celebrated his passing.[36]

FALLEN STAR

Keepers of the dead, block all the ways to the underworld;
And gates, bolt your bars into their sockets;
I, Hades, command: "Germanicus belongs to the stars,
not to me; Acheron cannot hold a ship of such size."

So wrote the poet Lollius Bassus of Smyrna of the unexpected and premature death of Germanicus Iulius Caesar, the popular general and adopted son of the emperor Tiberius, on October 10, 19. He had passed away after a short and mysterious illness at Daphne, near Antioch in Syria, where he was serving as commander-in-chief of the eastern provinces, with power and authority second only to that of Tiberius himself. As he lay dying, Germanicus had accused the governor of Syria, Gnaeus Calpurnius Piso, and his wife, Munatia Plancina, of foul play. His corpse was displayed naked in the center of Antioch so that it could be publicly examined for signs of poisoning. The evidence was inconclusive, though there were stories that his body was covered in spots. Despite the lack of certainty, a notorious Syrian female poisoner, Martina—an alleged friend of Plancina—was rounded up and sent to Rome. The following year, the senator Lucius Vitellius, who was charged with prosecuting Piso and Plancina, proclaimed during the trial that Germanicus's heart did not burn during his cremation, which was clear evidence that he had been poisoned. Pliny the Elder, who had access to the speeches delivered in the trial, wrote that Piso's defense team argued in response that Germanicus's illness was natural and not the result of poisoning. The charge of murder failed to convince the senate, especially since the poisoning was alleged to have been committed by Piso himself at a banquet in full sight of others. But, as we will see, there was a difference between forensic evidence and popular belief.[37]

The news of Germanicus's demise arrived at Rome in early December of the year 19, plunging the city into grief and mourning. The inhabitants' spirits were briefly lifted when they received new information that he still lived from merchants who had recently arrived in the city from Syria. A crowd ascended the Capitoline at night in order to make sacrifices for Germanicus's safe delivery. In the *versus quadratus,* a meter common to popular chants and songs, they cried: "Rome is saved, our fatherland is saved, for Germanicus is saved!" But it was not long before Germanicus's death was officially confirmed, and a formal period of mourning was declared on December 8. The tempo of these events—the news of death, followed by a rumor of survival, then by confirmation of death—is the same as the reaction to the murder of Caligula in the theater on the Palatine two decades later. The willingness to believe that Germanicus had survived testifies to the depth of popular feeling for the young general.[38]

Our three main historical sources for these events, Tacitus, Suetonius, and Cassius Dio, all of whom were writing decades or centuries afterward, reported that a jealous Tiberius was widely suspected of having a hand in Germanicus's death, with Piso and Placina acting as his agents. Do their accounts reflect contemporary rumor in any way? There are several pieces of evidence that indeed suggest that the official version of Germanicus's demise was not believed at the time, and that all the talk about the young prince in the city of Rome was regarded as possessing serious political import. First, according to Suetonius, who avidly recorded graffiti and acclamations found in Rome, the plaintive cry "Give us back Germanicus!"—only two words in Latin, *redde Germanicum*—was written in different places throughout the city. This phrase was also frequently chanted at night after Piso's return to Rome and during the trial itself. Suetonius's testimony is supported by two contemporary senatorial decrees that still survive (at least in part) today because they were inscribed in bronze. The first was passed in late December in the year 19 and commended the people of Rome for their grief at Germanicus's passing and for their promise to erect statues in his honor. The second text, the *Senatorial Decree concerning Gnaeus Piso the Elder,* passed on December 10 in the year 20, described how the urban population managed to moderate its anger, "even though the people were inflamed by an overwhelming desire to exact punishment from Cn. Piso the elder themselves."[39]

This takes us to our second point. The *Senatorial Decree concerning Gnaeus Piso the Elder* was required to be inscribed in the most frequented place in the largest city of each province and in the winter quarters of the legions, so that it could be read by as many people throughout the empire as possible. Tiberius was also given the authority to erect an inscribed copy of the decree and of his own speech to the senate wherever he wished. The senate evidently wanted its official version of events to be available everywhere, almost certainly, I would argue, to counterbalance rumors that were currently in circulation. The decree makes clear that Piso—who committed suicide before the trial was concluded—was not convicted of murder. Instead, he was found guilty of treason, because he had incited war with Parthia and Armenia, suborned the soldiers in Syria, and fomented civil war. The charge of murder is mentioned, but in an oblique fashion—that Germanicus on his deathbed "had himself borne witness that Gnaeus Piso the elder was the cause of his death." But there was no evidence that could support this. Martina, the alleged Syrian poisoner and friend of Plancina, had suddenly (and helpfully) died at Brundisium while on her way to Rome. We do not know the precise charges laid in the senate against Plancina: they do not appear in the senatorial decree, because she was pardoned by Tiberius at the request of his mother, Livia. This left her involvement open to speculation.[40]

Thirdly, we must consider Tacitus's account in his *Annals,* which is the most extensive surviving narrative of the Germanicus affair, although it was written a century after the events. His history is full of references to rumors, their role in public discourse, and their effect on key individuals in the trial. This ambiguity and doubt contrasts with the certainty of the senatorial decree. Tacitus knew, and made use of, the *Senatorial Decree concerning Gnaeus Piso the Elder,* but he also drew on oral traditions as sources for his history. One such tale concerned a document that Piso held in his hands throughout the trial, which allegedly contained secret orders from Tiberius. At the conclusion of his narrative of Piso's downfall, Tacitus wrote that rumors about Germanicus's death circulated not only at the time, but also in subsequent generations. Since it is a tenet of rumor generation that rumors continue to thrive, and even grow, until accurate news is received and, crucially, believed, it seems that the *Senatorial Decree concerning Gnaeus Piso the Elder* failed to suppress speculation and dissent. Tacitus's narrative draws on these rumors, passed down through oral traditions, to subvert the decree's version of events.[41]

The depth of mourning for the young prince's demise is exemplified in the literary tributes paid to him, such as the poem by Lollius Bassus included above, a paean on Germanicus's last moments by Clutorius Priscus (which even received a cash prize from the emperor), and Tiberius's own lament for Germanicus, which the senate decided should be inscribed in bronze and publicly displayed wherever the emperor wanted. The mourning for one lost so prematurely has been compared to the popular reaction to the death of Diana, Princess of Wales, in 1997. But in the case of Germanicus, the rumors about the nature of his death and the grief that followed were about more than an admired royal who died too soon—it concerned the loss of an heir and the stability he would provide. Germanicus was not only Tiberius's presumed successor, but also the choice of the emperor Augustus, who had made Tiberius adopt the young prince in the first place. The *Senatorial Decree concerning Gnaeus Piso the Elder* went to great pains to emphasize that Tiberius did actually have another son, Drusus the Younger, who was the product of his first marriage to Vipsania. In the decree, the senate moved "that Tiberius direct all his care, which he had once divided between his two sons, to the one who remained," and furthermore expressed the hope that the gods would care for Drusus even more in the future, because "in him alone is preserved all the future hope for his father's position of care for the state." Despite what might seem rather tortured rhetoric to the modern reader, the message of the decree is clear: Germanicus may have died, but the imperial succession has not been affected. The decree stressed family continuity. The entire Augustan house appeared in the text—not only Tiberius and Drusus, but also Augustus's widow, Livia, Germanicus's widow, Agrippina, his mother, Antonia, his sister Livilla, his three sons, and his brother Claudius. Nor would attempts to foment rebellion as Piso had attempted be tolerated, for "all the evils of civil war had long since been buried through the divine will of the deified Augustus and by the virtues of Tiberius Caesar Augustus." This promise of stability was the news that Rome needed after the death of her cherished Germanicus—but the continued circulation of rumors about the causes of his death showed that not all Romans believed the senate's story.[42]

SONS AND LOVERS

The thirty-year marriage of Marcus Aurelius and Faustina the Younger offers a different tale of hope and tragedy within the imperial house, one that foregrounds the relationship between imperial mothers and their children. Marcus and Faustina had no fewer than fourteen children (including two sets of twins), but only six survived to adulthood, five daughters and a son—Commodus. After decades of adoptive—but often still familial—succession dating back to Nerva, the arrival and survival of a purple-born heir was greeted with great rejoicing by people throughout the empire. But events took a nasty turn when Marcus fell seriously ill in 175. Commodus was thirteen years old and held the rank of Caesar, or junior emperor, which meant that he was primed to succeed his father should the worst come to pass. The story of what may have happened next is told by Cassius Dio. He was only a teenager when the events transpired, but he was someone who, as we have seen, developed many contacts in the imperial administration over the course of his long career, not least his gossipy father, Cassius Apronianus. Faustina, so Dio reported, considered that Commodus was too young and foolish to succeed Marcus and became worried that his death would result in a struggle for power. She therefore wrote to the governor of Syria, Avidius Cassius, a decorated general with three legions at his command, to ask him to be ready to assume the purple in the event that Marcus passed away. Faustina also promised Avidius Cassius her hand in marriage, since her status as the daughter of Antoninus Pius and widow of Marcus Aurelius would confer dynastic legitimacy on his regime. But the situation soon took a turn for the worse when Avidius Cassius received a false report that Marcus had died. Without waiting for confirmation of the report's accuracy, he launched his bid for the throne in April 175. Cassius refused to back down even after the news reached him that the emperor was still alive.[43]

This tale has many puzzling elements, not the least of which is that it would have been unprecedented at this point in Roman history for an imperial woman to overlook her own flesh and blood when it came to the succession. The choice of Avidius Cassius is also surprising, given that four of Faustina's own daughters were married to prominent senators who would have made excellent emperors. The tale's origins must lie in rumors that developed in the aftermath of the revolt. These stories cleaved to traditional expectations of how power worked, particularly regarding the culpability of imperial women. Avidius Cassius's brief usurpation ended with his murder at the hands of one of his own men in July 175, and Faustina herself passed away less than a year later, either from gout or—as Dio hinted—by suicide, so that she would not be convicted of being involved in the revolt. Marcus Aurelius, stricken with grief at the terrible turn of events, forbade investigation into Cassius's supporters and ordered no trials be held. This act of imperial mercy may have prompted contemporary speculation about why the emperor was so compassionate toward treasonous senators, which gave rise to the idea that Faustina had been involved. But Dio's version actually seems to be a combination of several different rumors. Faustina's repudiation of Commodus reads as a tale that developed during or after his reign, when Romans realized what a disastrous ruler he had turned out to be.[44]

Faustina's siring of Commodus later gave rise to fanciful stories in our historical accounts—none of which can be shown to be contemporary rumors that people actually exchanged—that he was the product of an affair with a gladiator. Indeed, the attitude to Commodus ascribed to Faustina in Dio's *Roman*

History is exceptional, because such stories usually clustered around imperial stepmothers, rather than mothers. This tallied with the popular folkloric belief, also present in the Roman historiographical tradition, that stepmothers were naturally cruel and conniving. Agrippina's sidelining of Claudius's son, Britannicus, in favor of her own child, Nero, is perhaps the most famous example. The near-contemporary play *Octavia,* performed not long after the end of the Neronian age, attributes responsibility for Britannicus's poisoning both to Agrippina and Nero. A less well-known, but particularly potent, example of how Romans conceived of the relationships between imperial sons and stepmothers is the case of Constantine's eldest son, the Caesar Crispus, and Constantine's second wife, and mother of his other five children, Fausta. Both perished within a few months of each other in 326, Crispus after being tried and executed by his father at Pola, and Fausta after being suffocated to death in a hot bath. Our major historical accounts, all of which date from the late fourth century or beyond, explain the deaths by suggesting either that Crispus and Fausta were having an affair, or that Fausta had claimed Crispus tried to rape her. There are several folkloric motifs behind these tales: the cruel stepmother, suffocation in a hot bath, and most famously, "Potiphar's Wife," in which a woman seduces a man only to accuse him of rape. This motif was well-known to Romans in the form of the myth of Phaedra and Hippolytus, and the comparison between this mythological couple and the ill-fated Fausta and Crispus is explicitly made by the later ecclesiastical historian Philostorgius. However, there is a difference: the story of Crispus and Fausta cleaves to the traditional folkloric climax in which the stepmother is executed, as opposed to the mythic tale, as in the Phaedra story, in which the woman commits suicide.[45]

These rumors attested in later histories emanated from genuine contemporary speculation about the fates of Crispus and Fausta. A satirical poem—anonymous, though it was thought to have emanated from the pen of Constantine's praetorian prefect Flavius Ablabius—was posted on the palace doors after their deaths:

> Who would now want the golden age of Saturn?
> Ours is a diamond age—of Nero's pattern.

We owe the preservation of this verse to the fifth-century bishop Sidonius Apollinaris, who quoted it in the context of a discussion about Crispus and Fausta. The ditty implied that just like Nero and Agrippina, Crispus and Fausta were engaged in an incestuous affair. There were efforts to correct such rumors in subsequent generations. In his panegyric of Constantius II (Fausta's son) written in 355, Julian lauded Fausta as the sister, mother, wife, and daughter of kings. He wrote that the only other royal woman with such an illustrious lineage was the Persian queen Parysatis. But she had married her brother, whereas Fausta "ensured that those family relationships were undefiled and pure in accordance with our laws." This statement cannot help but be interpreted as Julian's riposte to those who had recently claimed otherwise.[46]

There were also different stories about the manner of Fausta's death. Although the bath tale is by far the most prevalent in our written sources, in his sixteenth *Homily on Philippians,* John Chrysostom publicly proclaimed to his congregation that an emperor's wife (identifiable as Fausta by the context) had been tied up on the mountainside to be eaten by wild animals. This radically different version recalls both the myth of Andromeda as well as the Roman criminal punishment of condemnation to the beasts. This shows that when Romans tried to explain how Constantine had lost both his eldest son and wife in the space of a few months, their imaginations cleaved to traditional folkloric and mythological models that had long been used to comprehend the power relations of royalty. What is particularly telling about the stories of Faustina, Fausta, and their children is that they all circulated among the political and ecclesiastical elite. Even the educated and well-connected aristocrats, writers, and preachers, many of whom had experience and knowledge of court life, still imagined its upheavals and tragedies in these traditional terms.[47]

THE FRAGILITY OF HOPE

In the years prior to her untimely demise, Fausta had been depicted on imperial coins cradling two of her children in her arms, an image that was accompanied by the Latin legend *spes rei publicae* ("the hope of the state") (fig. 16). Imperial children, and especially male heirs, had been associated with the idea of hope and the future security of the empire since the emergence of the monarchical state under Augustus. Coins featuring the goddess Spes, the divine personification of Hope, and the legends *spes* or *spes rei publicae* were minted either for the birth of children, such as Claudius's son Britannicus, or their elevation to the rank of Augustus, as in the case of Gratian, son of Valentinian I. In Late Antiquity, Christian iconography emphasized God's divine blessing for the regime and its continuance under the emperor's progeny. Gold coinage minted by Heraclius after his restoration of the True Cross to Jerusalem in 630 showed the splendidly mustachioed emperor flanked by his sons Heraclius Constantine and Heraclonas, all holding orbs topped with a cross (fig. 17).

Fig. 16. Gold *solidus* showing Fausta holding two of her children, 324–325 CE. *Roman Imperial Coinage* VII Sirmium 61. Münzkabinett der Staatlichen Museen, Berlin, 18217899. Photograph by Reinhard Saczewski.

Fig. 17. Gold *solidus* depicting the emperor Heraclius (center), flanked by his sons Heraclonas (left) and Heraclius Constantine (right), 638–641 CE. Dumbarton Oaks Coin Catalogue Heraclius 43c. Australian National University Classics Museum, Canberra, 2024.01. Photograph by Charlotte Forbes, Collections Officer, Australian National University. © Australian National University Classics Museum.

The message of these images and legends was clear: dynasties with male children had a future.[48]

The fragility of this vision was exposed by the brutal reality of imperial politics, which saw Britannicus poisoned, Fausta executed, Gratian murdered, and Heraclonas mutilated. Yet at least these imperial regimes had been able to anticipate a future for a time, something that could not be said about emperors who remained childless or who lacked a male heir. The pressure to continue the family weighed heavily on emperors. Marcus Aurelius reflected in his *Meditations* on the demise of Roman imperial and aristocratic families when there were no heirs to carry on the line. "Consider how much their ancestors had been consumed by anxiety to leave behind a successor," he pondered to himself. Despite the high infertility rates in the Roman world, which affected emperors and aristocrats just as much as traders and farmers, the number of rumors that proliferated about imperial childlessness suggests that it was not only a source of anxiety, but also a situation that required explanation. Romans had a limited understanding of reproductive processes, which meant that infertility was usually regarded as a female problem. It was generally thought that emperors who became impotent or failed to father children had either offended the gods or had been secretly given potions by women. Constantius II allegedly considered both his childlessness and his inconclusive campaigns against the Persians to be divine punishment for his role in the brutal massacre of most of his living male relatives in 337. Or at least, according to Julian, "those were the things that people around the court and my recently deceased brother Gallus kept on saying." In this febrile court environment in which the emperor's childlessness was the subject of such hostile talk, Julian particularly sympathized with Constantius II's wife, Eusebia, and sent her his best wishes for the much hoped-for pregnancy.[49]

The pressure on Eusebia to bear a child must have been enormous. After the murder of his brother Constans in 350, Constantius II was the sole surviving son of Constantine, and if the couple were to have no children, the direct male line would die out. This would increase the possibility of yet another civil war, to add to the many that had consumed the empire in recent decades (there were also problems with the female line descending from Constantine's daughters, which we will address in a moment). In 360, Eusebia took the step of receiving treatment for her perceived infertility, which in the Graeco-Roman world could involve diet and medication or more invasive treatments. In this case, pessaries (and perhaps other medications) were inserted into the empress's vagina, causing Eusebia's death. At least, this is the version that John Chrysostom—with less precise medical detail, and once again not naming the specific empress—told his assembled congregation in his sixteenth *Homily on Philippians.* Even though Chrysostom did not identify the emperors and empresses in his sermon, the examples were sufficiently vivid to fire the imaginations of his flock as they listened to the bishop. There was also another story, found in Ammianus Marcellinus, that it was actually Eusebia who prevented the successful childbearing of her sister-in-law Helena, Julian's wife. She allegedly bribed a midwife to cause the death of a boy born to Helena and Julian in Gaul, and later on, when both women were in Rome, gave Helena a poison to ensure that she only had miscarriages thereafter. This suggests either that Chrysostom—or the person who had told him the story—had confused Eusebia and Helena, or there were rumors circulating about the infertility of both women, which is plausible, since neither ever bore children. As people talked at court, in churches, and among the officer corps about these unfortunate women, their identities and personal stories were lost, instead contributing to a more general widespread idea of "the empress," her life, character, and behavior.[50]

Once he succeeded Constantius II as Augustus in 361, Julian's own childlessness became a source of serious concern. Although Constantine himself had fathered six children, there was only one living grandchild descended from him. This was Constantia, the posthumous baby daughter of the emperor Constantius II and his third wife, Faustina. Helena was also a daughter of Constantine, but she and Julian never had another child after they lost their baby boy, and Helena herself passed away in 360. Julian refused to remarry and instead embraced a life of chastity, despite the pleas of his advisors to take care for the succession. In his *Monody for Julian,* Libanius, wracked with grief at his hero's death in Persia, lamented that Julian had died so young and without heirs to carry on his religious program. Later, in 365, when Julian's relative Procopius staged a usurpation, there was a rumor—probably manufactured and circulated by Procopius and his followers—that Julian had named him his heir, but this was not generally believed. In the years after Julian's death, another rumor began to circulate among imperial officials (including a former provincial governor and praetorian prefect) that the emperor had bribed one of his doctors to kill Helena. This tale, which many (though not Libanius) regarded as plausible, has its origins in the tense political atmosphere created by the tragically human conditions of infertility, miscarriage, and stillbirth.[51]

The elevation of elderly and childless emperors likewise gave rise to rumor and speculation about the succession, and more precisely, who would be adopted or otherwise marked out as the next Caesar. When Galba came to power in June 68, after Nero's suicide, he was sixty-nine years old, and his two sons had predeceased him. Galba's age and childlessness were common talk at the time, according to our main historical accounts written by Plutarch, Suetonius, and Tacitus. Although they wrote several decades after the events, they did rely on an earlier, common source familiar with events in Rome (perhaps our old friend Cluvius Rufus, from Caligula's assassination). When Vespasian, then governor of Syria, sent his son Titus to pay homage to Galba, rumors began to circulate that he was a potential candidate for adoption by the new emperor. The same problem reared its head almost thirty years later, when the sexagenarian Nerva came to the throne in September 96 after the murder of Domitian. Nerva did not have children, though Cassius Dio said that he still had (presumably distant) relatives alive. In the first half of 97, Rome was gripped by panic that the governor of Syria, who had three legions at his disposal, would make a play for the throne. We can get a glimpse into these events through the testimony of the contemporary senator Pliny the Younger. He was warned by one of his friends not to undertake the prosecution of the senator Publicius Certus, since it might make him prominent enemies, "naming a certain someone who at that time commanded a mighty army in the East and was the subject of serious unconfirmed rumors." It was in response to these rumors, and a plot by the praetorian prefect, that Nerva chose Trajan, then governor of Germania Superior, as his heir in October 97. This measure was designed to secure the succession and forestall the looming civil war (a turn of events that makes Trajan's own reluctance to name a successor even more perplexing).[52]

The issue of the succession consumed the eastern Roman empire in the second half of the fifth century, which saw the accession of a series of older emperors. These rulers either had no children or only daughters: Marcian (who gained the purple at age fifty-eight), Leo I (fifty-six), Zeno (around fifty; his son died within the first year of his reign), and Anastasius (sixty-one). Leo I asked the holy man Daniel the Stylite to pray that he and his wife, Verina (who already had two daughters together), would soon have a son; this came to pass, but despite holy intercession, the poor child lived only a few months. The Isaurian general Zeno, who reportedly had designs on the throne himself, had an interest in the baby not surviving. He asked his astrologer to cast a horoscope (remarkably, still preserved on papyrus today) that predicted the boy's untimely demise. The conniving Zeno was soon married to Leo's daughter Ariadne, but Leo resisted elevating Zeno to the rank of Caesar because he, and Isaurians in general, were unpopular with the people of Constantinople. Instead, he chose to make Zeno's five-year-old son, Leo II, Caesar in 472. This was the same year that Mount Vesuvius erupted, sending ash as far as Constantinople, where the arrival of darkened skies was taken by the populace as a bad omen for the future. In November the following year, the seventy-three-year-old Leo appeared in the Hippodrome—where his infirmity was recognized by the crowd, who chanted that he should sit down—to acclaim the boy as Augustus. Yet a mere three weeks after Leo passed away, the young Leo II was compelled by factions at court to make his father, Zeno, an Augustus as well. Ten months later the child died, leaving Zeno as sole ruler. It is interesting that contemporaries do not seem to have regarded Leo II's premature death as suspicious, perhaps because the child was known to be ill. But a few decades later, an African cleric based in Constantinople, Victor of Tunnuna, wrote that he had heard a rumor about the boy's fate. The story went that Leo II's mother, Ariadne, was so afraid that Zeno would kill him that she found a boy of similar appearance and substituted him for her son, whom she hid in a church in Constantinople. Victor wrote that the boy was still alive in his own time.[53]

The story features the folkloric motif of the "Substituted Child," in which one child is swapped with another. In the Leo II version, the exchange is an act of deception carried out to save the imperial heir. However, it actually confuses the fate of Leo II with another of Zeno's later Caesars, for, in the desperate search for an heir during a turbulent reign, he entered into a number of short-lived dynastic arrangements. One of these saw Leo Basiliscus, the young son of his general Armatus, elevated to the rank of Caesar. But Zeno soon repented the arrangement, killed Armatus, and had Leo inducted into holy orders as a reader at the Church of Blachernae in Constantinople. As people in Constantinople remembered and talked about the—frankly bewildering—dynastic politics of the reign of Zeno, they had clearly confused the fates of the two Leos. They were primed to believe that the unpopular Zeno, who finally died in 491 without any heir to follow him, had wanted to kill his own son to claim the throne. The elevation of Leo II had been celebrated with coins trumpeting the *salus rei publicae* ("the safety of the state"), but the people of Constantinople were right to interpret the arrival of the ashes from Vesuvius as an omen of the boy's, and the empire's, fragility. The births, anniversaries, and elevations of imperial sons were greeted with an outpouring of joy in the Roman world because they offered a small measure of hope for a stable succession, despite the conspiracies of family members, generals, and courtiers who tried to murder them—or stop them from being born in the first place.[54]

THE DYNASTIC IMPULSE

One day a hungry and emaciated wolf encountered a healthy and well-fed dog. The wolf asked the dog how he came to be in such a fortunate position, when he himself was the stronger animal. The dog said that he was lucky to serve a master, since in exchange for guarding the master's house, he was given bread and scraps. The wolf replied he would also be happy to serve such a master if it meant an easy and well-fed life. But then he noticed the mark of a chain on the dog's neck and asked what had happened. The dog said his master tied him up during the daytime but gave him freedom at night, so long as he remained in his service. The wolf decided against entering the master's service, for his food and protection were not worth the price of freedom.

This classic Aesopic fable, which circulated in archaic Greece before being written down by Phaedrus and Babrius in the Roman period, encapsulated the everyday reality of kingship in the ancient world. The ruler—tyrant, king, emperor, or governor—looked after his people's everyday needs, and in turn they acknowledged his mastery over them. The wolf's preference for hunger and liberty was a lofty sentiment, but one that few people could really afford to share, certainly not the residents of Rome and Constantinople, for whom rumors of an emperor's passing could spark panic about the food supply, or Philo's eastern provincials, who feared the devastation of their lands, famine, and enslavement if Caligula died and the Roman world was divided by civil war. These rumors emerged from the widespread attachment to the emperor as an important benefactor and father figure. Despite the potential for Rome's rulers to be irrational and wrathful beings, at the moment of crisis, people still wanted there to be a new emperor to secure the everyday necessities of life.[55]

There are more rumors dealing with death and the succession than any other subject concerning Roman emperors and their families. This underlines the importance of that moment of transition between rulers, which was full of endless perils and possibilities for all inhabitants of the empire, from ambitious senators and politicking bishops to soldiers, farmers, merchants, and enslaved people (particularly those at court). The imperial government was aware of the widespread interest in regime change and tried to control news of an emperor's poor health or final passing as long as possible, so that it could be released in a way that did not cause panic or revolt. Very often Romans, like the well-fed dog in our fable, just wanted a smooth transfer of power to ensure that their basic needs continued to be met. But these imperial transitions also brought with them the tantalizing potential of religious changes, financial rewards, benefactions, and pardons for people up and down the social spectrum. Some deaths, like the heretic Valens burned alive on the battlefield, were even regarded as divine judgment, a welcome sign that higher powers were looking out for Rome. The way Romans talked about the passing (or potential passing) of emperors provides us with an insight into their thought processes as they weighed up the risks and benefits of change, both for the state itself and for their own personal circumstances. Rumors were manifestations of hope or panic, depending on the character of the individual emperor and his relationship with different status groups and communities, as illustrated by the stories that circulated in the immediate aftermath of Caligula's assassination. Sometimes the news of an imperial death was met with outright disbelief and rejection, a sign that Romans (even—or especially—in high circles) thought it was eminently plausible that the state would deliberately promulgate misinformation.

Rumors could only emerge if there was this element of doubt, suspicion, or confusion regarding an emperor's health and death (including the outcome of battles) that required confirmation or refutation. The content of the stories was shaped by an emperor's individual circumstances and the prejudices of those who circulated rumors. Libanius's attachment to Julian meant he was predisposed to regard his hero's death as a form of foul play, amplifying and developing the preexisting uncertainty in the army attested by Ammianus. The tales about the death of his successor, Jovian, emerge from a quite different set of circumstances: his youthful vigor meant a natural death was unlikely. The rumor that he had been murdered, which was promulgated by John Chrysostom, cleaved to established frameworks of knowledge about the behavior of kings, aristocrats, servants, and the dangers of court life. Both inside and outside the court, discussions of imperial deaths dealt in traditional mythological and folkloric paradigms that reduced complex situations to personalities and archetypes. This is why Fausta and Crispus were thought to be having an affair, and the lack of male heirs produced by Constantius II and Julian could be ascribed to female rivalries. In a world in which infertility and reproductive complications were poorly understood, even Constantius II engaged in the search for explanations about his lack of an heir, his personal uncertainty probably fueling the rumors about sons and the succession that bedeviled his household.

The dynastic impulse drove a large proportion of these rumors. In the first century, there was enthusiasm in some elite circles for removing the emperors and restoring the *res publica* to its pre-monarchical form, a sentiment that almost became a reality following the murder of Caligula in 41 and again after the suicide of Nero in 68. But this coexisted with, and was largely overshadowed by, a much more widespread popular investment in the imperial system. The grief and mourning that resulted from the premature deaths of imperial heirs, such as Germanicus, and the rumors that circulated as people tried to make sense of the tragic events reveal a widespread attachment to dynastic continuity and the stability it could provide from the very beginning of the monarchical *res publica.* The events that followed the sudden death of Germanicus show how various individuals and groups responded to and negotiated such a situation, which was distinguished by a stunning breakdown in communication and understanding between the imperial state (the emperor and the senators) and the population of Rome.

Imperial names could become a focus for loyalty and hope. Claudius may have been a political nobody, treated as the butt of jokes at Caligula's court, but he was, as the soldiers who elevated him that fateful January day put it, a "Germanicus," a name and a symbol that all was right with the world. This is why members of current or former imperial dynasties were frequently intended to play a role in usurpations. The Pisonian conspirators who wanted to unseat Nero planned to have Claudius's daughter Antonia accompany them to the praetorian camp in order to gather public sympathy for their revolt. Several centuries later, the usurper Procopius had Constantia, the posthumous daughter of Constantius II, paraded in a litter before his army to show the soldiers that he was a true Constantinian and the rightful emperor, unlike his upstart rival, Valens. The dynastic messages of coins, portraits, and statuary were not bland and routine, the product of administrative or artistic inertia, but were genuinely designed to appeal to the minds and hearts of the Roman people by offering them hope and stability.[56]

This offers the opportunity to tease out different reactions to the government's efforts to engage the inhabitants of the Roman empire in communicative action. The topics and themes of rumors reveal a profound sense of attachment to emperors and to dynastic continuity, which illustrates an alignment between the messages and beliefs of state and subjects. But at the same time, the emergence of these rumors in the first place was generated by suspicion about the truthfulness of the Roman government's own version of these events. These polarities, and the many manifestations of loyalty, assent, confusion, and opposition that flourished between them, illustrate how Roman emperorship was discussed and negotiated at the crucial moment of transition. This was truly everyday politics, in the sense that an imperial death could affect the provision of basic amenities such as grain, but also because Romans were alert to how the daily appearances of Roman emperors signified stability. When Diocletian was not seen in Nicomedia for an extended period or Justinian disappeared in Constantinople, these were signs that sparked serious concerns.

Roman dynasties were not especially long-lasting: between fifty and ninety years was a respectable showing in the period covered by this book, and none made the magic hundred. Imperial families were constantly afflicted by infertility, mortality, and warfare and often brought to brutal and sudden ends by rivals for the purple. The dynastic impulse was a strong one, but it coexisted with, and could be overridden by, other considerations: Christians certainly did not mourn the passing of Julian, the last Constantinian emperor, nor did Nicene communities regret that Valens had gone up in flames on the field of Adrianople, his only son having predeceased him. In this tug-of-war between the stability of the current ruling family and the hope that a new, unrelated ruler might offer a better future, every claimant to the purple dreamed that he would be the one to found the dynasty that would endure. And so, when the emperor Maurice and his wife, Constantina, welcomed a son in 584, they named him Theodosius, in honor of Theodosius II, the last Roman emperor who had been born in the purple and survived long enough to rule (unlike the short-lived son of Leo I). The cleric John of Ephesus described the rejoicing of the people of Constantinople as they celebrated this miracle. They gathered in the Hippodrome to welcome Theodosius's birth, shouting out that he had rescued them from the "servitude of the many," that is, the scourge of competition for the purple among courtiers and generals. This young Theodosius would, many years later, do something else truly remarkable that also got the people of Constantinople talking—he would cheat death.[57]

CHAPTER 4

Rumored Returns

On September 13, 45 BCE, Gaius Julius Caesar sat down to write his will at his estate in central Italy. Caesar was by this time the acknowledged master of Rome. He had recently defeated the sons of Pompey the Great in Spain and been voted the office of dictator for ten years. But Caesar lacked a legitimate son to carry on his legacy, his only offspring being the two-year-old Caesarion, born from his dalliance with Cleopatra VII of Egypt. Therefore, he named as heirs to his estate his three great-nephews, Gaius Octavius, Lucius Pinarius, and Quintus Pedius. To the seventeen-year-old Octavius he bequeathed the lion's share (three-quarters) and adopted him as his son, though the young man was not yet aware of this extraordinary benefaction. The will made provisions for the possibility that a son would still be born to Caesar, naming guardians for any future offspring. Having put his affairs in order, Caesar set off for Rome, where he was due to celebrate a triumph for his victories.[1]

An unwelcome surprise awaited Caesar in Rome. This was a man who claimed to be Gaius Marius, the grandson and namesake of the famous general Gaius Marius, victor over the Cimbri and Teutones and seven-time consul. If this were true, the man would be Caesar's cousin, since the dictator's aunt Julia had been Marius's wife. This Marius was not the first man to claim to be the long-lost relative of a high-profile senator, but his arrival was particularly unsettling to Caesar, because he had long positioned himself as the political successor to the great general. There were good reasons to doubt the authenticity of

Marius's claim, since the general's son, Gaius Marius the Younger, had been childless when he died in his twenties. But the impostor had been extraordinarily successful in gathering support. Using the Marian name, he had become the patron of numerous towns, veteran colonies, and trade guilds throughout Italy. He had even managed to persuade some unnamed female relatives of Julius Caesar to testify to his status and lineage. Together with these women and a not insubstantial crowd of supporters, Marius had presented himself to the young Gaius Octavius in search of recognition. However, Octavius, his mother, and his aunt rejected Marius's claim; the impostor represented a challenge to Octavius's position within the family.[2]

Marius needed to petition Caesar in order to gain the formal recognition he so desired. Sometime in late September 45 BCE, the dictator threw open the gates of his Roman estate to the people to celebrate his victory over the Pompeians. Showing a considerable amount of nerve, Marius turned up to the public reception and was thronged by almost as many well-wishers as Caesar himself. We do not know if the two men came face-to-face at this event, and if they did so, what was said, but Caesar soon made his views on Marius's claim clear. The dictator passed a decree banishing him from Italy, and Marius's support soon dissipated. Our ancient sources do not agree on the man's real identity. They give him different names—Hierophilus, Amatius, or Chamates—and variously claim he was a slave, a low-born individual, a horse doctor, or an eye doctor. Cicero offered no firm opinion on the genuineness of Marius's claim in his contemporary letters, but condemned him as a servile impostor after his death. Whatever Marius's background, he was certainly wealthy enough to become a patron of communities and organizations in Italy, and convincing enough to win over veterans and some female relatives of Caesar. Some modern scholars have even entertained the possibility that he was the real deal.[3]

This uncertainty goes to the heart of issues surrounding imposture and identity in the pre-modern period, a world without passports, identity cards, government surveillance, and electronic databases. For the most part, the acknowledgment that impostors were precisely whom they said they were depended on community acceptance. When Arnaud de Tilh famously appeared in the French village of Artigat in 1556 claiming to be Martin Guerre, a man who had abandoned his family and property some eight years before, his imposture succeeded because he was acknowledged as Martin by many of the villagers, Martin's relatives, and, most crucially, his wife, Bertrande de Rols. As Natalie Zemon Davis has masterfully shown, the sheer weight of this recognition counted against the naysayers (many of whom made excellent points, such as

Martin's mysteriously shrunken shoe size). In that case, however, Martin Guerre was a real person who was known to have existed, whereas the news that Gaius Marius had a grandson came as a revelation for all concerned. Any offspring of Gaius Marius the Younger should have been officially registered during the census, held every five years, which specifically mandated the declaration of all dependents. There is no evidence that anyone involved in the Marius affair checked the records. Even if they had done so, and found no entry for a son, a cunning trickster could have come up with a plausible story. Whether this man was a real Marian or an impostor, the best proof of his identity remained the same: acceptance as a member of the family by Caesar. This, as we have seen, the dictator was not willing to bestow.[4]

Caesar's murder on the Ides of March, 44 BCE, provided Marius with a new opportunity for recognition. By early April, he had returned to Rome, where he stoked the volatile political situation by gathering together crowds of supporters. Marius led them in the construction of an altar and column in the Forum Romanum on the site of Caesar's funeral pyre. His popularity and his readiness to capitalize on his alleged relationship with the dictator was a concern to two other men with an interest in being seen as the defender of Caesar's memory: his henchman, Marcus Antonius, and his adopted son and heir, the young Julius Caesar (the new name of Gaius Octavius). Cicero, who was not in Rome at the time, received letters from his friend Atticus, who told him that Antonius had executed Marius without a trial. This prompted Marius's supporters to riot in the Forum until Antonius sent in troops to execute them. The young Caesar tried to distance himself from Antonius's actions, but he was surely happy to have this particular rival removed from the scene once and for all.[5]

The backing that Marius gained after his return shows that Caesar's earlier repudiation had had little impact on his ability to muster considerable popular support in volatile circumstances. When he first appeared on the scene, Marius may only have wanted recognition for his purported lineage and the wealth that came with it, but upon his return in 44 BCE he had a greater agenda. The people wanted a champion to honor Caesar's memory and to hunt down his murderers, Brutus and Cassius. This situation reminds us that people who fit into the broad category of political impostors—individuals who masqueraded as kings, queens, emperors, aristocrats, and their relatives—are quite different from individuals of the Martin Guerre type, who usually have more limited and personal aims. Political impostors can sometimes be sufferers of mental illness, but most often they—or their backers—have exploited dynastic instability, discontent with the current ruler, or a wider economic and social crisis in order to accumulate money, status, and power. Some, such as the Persian impostor Smerdis of the sixth century BCE, the Hellenistic kings Alexander Balas and Andriscus in the second century BCE, and the Russian first false Dmitry of the seventeenth century CE, have even succeeded in ruling in their own right. Between his two appearances, Marius made the transition from the Martin Guerre type into a political impostor. These individuals used their assumed identities to marshal large groups of followers, with their popular support representing the triumph of belief over any official proof of identity.[6]

Caesar's legacy was contested because it was inextricably connected with the future of the Roman *res publica* itself. Even though there was as yet no imperial monarchy, Caesar's dominance had been so all-encompassing that people looked for a man to fill his place. And so it was that his illegitimate son, Caesarion—now joint ruler of Egypt as Ptolemy XV—also came to play an important political role. As the uneasy alliance between Marcus Antonius and the young Caesar gave way to undisguised hatred, Antonius publicly announced that Caesarion was a legitimate son because Julius Caesar had lawfully married Cleopatra. The boy represented a threat to the young Caesar's legitimacy: as the philosopher Areius remarked at the time, "It is not good to have too many Caesars." After defeating Antonius and Cleopatra at the Battle of Actium and capturing the city of Alexandria in 30 BCE, the young Julius Caesar had Caesarion put to death, simultaneously extinguishing both Caesar's own blood lineage and the male line of the Ptolemaic rulers of Egypt in one brutal act.[7]

STUDYING IMPOSTURE

The problem raised by the philosopher Areius recurred every time an impostor materialized claiming to be a Caesar or one of his relatives. These appearances were never benign but posed an explicit challenge to the current emperor. In contrast with the false Marius, who maintained he was somebody most people did not even know existed, Rome's imperial impostors all assumed the identities of known individuals who were thought to be dead or imprisoned. The foundations for their imposture were laid by rumors, which said that these figures had not really died or had managed to escape confinement. Deaths that were somehow ambiguous—for example, if there had been no proper funeral in public or people did not trust the official version provided by the imperial administration—were always the subject of rumor and speculation. But in order for an impostor to gain supporters, he had to offer something that the reigning emperor could not.[8]

Rumors of a royal cheating death or escaping prison lie behind numerous other monarchical impostors, from the English boy Perkin Warbeck, who claimed to be Richard of York, one of the so-called Princes in the Tower, to the monk Grisha Otrep'ev, the first of many false Dmitrys who plagued Russia during the "Time of Troubles." Nor was this an exclusively western phenomenon—after the demise of the Chinese Ming dynasty, two impostors appeared claiming to be the eldest son of the last Ming emperor, to take but one example. But the specific reasons for impostors lie in the social, political, and cultural context in which they emerge. As Natalie Zemon Davis has remarked, impostor stories resonate precisely because of their universal themes, but "if the tension between the universal and the historically specific is relaxed too much, the account loses in richness and resonance." As we will see, the appearance of Roman impostors and the support they attracted are closely tied to the evolutionary course of the imperial *res publica*.[9]

This is perhaps the most speculative chapter of the book. Although we do have contemporary evidence for some of our impostors, there is certainly nothing like the trial records that Natalie Zemon Davis was able to draw upon in her study of Martin Guerre. Roman historians who wrote about rumors of returning Caesars faced problems of evidence collection, especially since events often unfolded in provincial contexts. "I have not been able to discover anything more about the beginnings or conclusion of the affair," wrote Tacitus of the false Drusus. Our elite sources are also less interested in the people who supported the pretenders, instead using the impostor stories as a way of exposing the illegitimacy of the reigning emperor. But the preoccupations of elite historians do not mean that we should dismiss the significance of popular movements. The revolt of the Boukoloi ("Herdsmen") under the priest Isidorus in second-century Egypt is an excellent example of a similar incident, which received a cursory treatment by the historian Cassius Dio. However, contemporary papyri reveal that the Boukoloi were a real group of disaffected provincials driven to rebel because they were suffering from excessive taxation. This means that we need to take popular movements, especially those that occurred in the countryside, seriously as historical phenomena.[10]

CON ARTISTS AND CHARLATANS

Impersonations of a Roman emperor or a member of his family were not isolated acts of pretense. They occurred in a world in which amateurism, imposture, and charlatanism existed and flourished in a range of guises. Some claimed to be professional doctors or barbers—too many flashy utensils and huge mirrors gave away the frauds—or masqueraded as intellectuals and teachers, butchering lines of Vergil by the quayside to potential students. Rome's lands teemed with purveyors of supernatural reassurance: holy men, soothsayers, and exorcists who preyed on the lovelorn, hopeful, and desperate in equal measure. Rich widowers and widows had to be on the lookout for charismatic young con artists with winning smiles and smooth lines in search of a patron(ness) to leave them a bequest. City streets were full of individuals who claimed to be philosophers, growing their hair long and wearing shaggy clothes, dispensing faux wisdom on street corners and at the gates of temples. One could see sophists in flashy clothes, waving books and escorted by waves of attendants, showing off their alleged intellectual or rhetorical prowess. Jews and Christians needed to watch for men and women who claimed to be the mouthpieces of their God, and followers of different religions cast aspersions on each other as false believers plying their deceptive trade in the marketplace. Christian impostors pretended to be deacons and bishops, with one Cappadocian upstart even successfully gathering a coterie of virgins around him. Workers of wonders and miracles—both pagan and Christian—claimed divine inspiration (or even to be divine themselves) while roaming the countryside in search of fresh victims for their sorcery. No doubt many of these men hoped to replicate the success of Jesus Christ himself, who gathered large crowds of followers as he moved throughout the Levant.[11]

The ultimate goal of many of these fraudsters was money. The sixth-century alchemist John Isthmeos conned numerous money-dealers in Antioch and Constantinople before his good luck ended when he failed to fool the emperor Anastasius. There were many other tales like this. Philosophers passed around hats during their street-side performances, astrologers foretold the future and lapped up "donations," and wandering Syrian priests clawed in coins and food as they danced with their idols. Christians were advised that a traveling prophet who wanted lodging for more than two days, or who asked for money, was an impostor. Such fears were justified, as shown by the case of the second-century charlatan Peregrinus Proteus, who managed to set himself up as the head of a Christian community. He continued to rake in considerable amounts of money from his flock even after the Roman authorities had thrown him in prison. The consequences of such charlatanism were usually local—an old woman fleeced here; golden ornaments stolen from a temple there—but occasionally they had greater impact. Alexander of Abonuteichos in northern Anatolia invented the cult of a snake-god called Glycon, whose oracular utterances were produced with the aid of a puppet snake, tubes, and ventriloquism. Glycon's prophecies deceived Marcus

Sedatius Severianus, the governor of Cappadocia, who followed the snake's advice and invaded the kingdom of Armenia, destroying both himself and his army.[12]

One of the issues that encouraged such acts of fraud and imposture was the lack of proper regulation of personal identity and professional competency. When the emperor Caracalla decreed that ordinary Egyptians should be expelled from the city of Alexandria (whose citizens had a more exalted status), he proclaimed they could be detected by their speech and lack of manners, qualities that could not be officially documented and were open to abuse and prejudice. The prize of Roman citizenship was jealously guarded by the state, and it was supposed to be formally recorded and regulated. But it could certainly be usurped through fake birth registration, even unwittingly so, as in the case of a group of Alpine tribes who had to be retroactively given citizenship that they thought they had possessed all along. This was a world in which men could pretend to be equestrians by wearing a gold ring or usurping reserved seats at the theater. Some of these were cook-shop owners using their supposed rank to avoid fines, while others were members of the nouveau-riche who craved the social respectability to match their wealth. Impersonating an aristocrat could be surprisingly easy, as in the case of the school master Numerianus, who claimed to be a senator when raising forces for Septimius Severus's armies. Even Severus believed him—there were six hundred members of the senate, and an emperor could not be expected to remember all those names.[13]

Everyday interactions also depended on external markers to assist people in recognizing precisely whom they were dealing with. An armed man in an alleyway might brandish his sword and claim to be a soldier, but he could actually be a mugger, confident that his prey would acquiesce rather than challenge him. Local bureaucrats could usurp the official dress of higher-ranked military officers or officials. Faux philosophers only had to adopt the stereotypical dress and habit to convince a crowd. Put on the right costume and a bandit could transform himself into a magistrate; appear with a troop of horsemen and he could claim to be a military tribune and even kiss the emperor; have a herald announce him as a treasury official and he could fleece a rich aristocrat for all he was worth. In Petronius's novel *The Satyricon,* the trickster Eumolpus laments that he and his cronies lacked the right sort of clothing and props that would assist them in conning the inhabitants of the south Italian town of Croton. Personal and professional identity relied on external markers such as clothes, hairstyles, and accessories, but it also depended on community recognition—a doctor, teacher, or philosopher needed the assent of his peers or his customers to have his expertise confirmed.[14]

For those Romans who wished to impersonate a known individual, living or dead, it certainly helped if they bore more than a passing resemblance to them. Valerius Maximus's *Memorable Deeds and Sayings,* written in the early first century, featured an entire section devoted to dead ringers for famous individuals. Among these he included the citizen Vibius and the freedman Publicius, who looked so much like Pompey that people would do double-takes wherever they went. Even Augustus is said to have had a lookalike, who caused a great stir when he arrived in Rome from the provinces. Some men could be convinced that they resembled the great and the good. Lucian poked fun at a Syrian whose sycophantic friends persuaded him that he looked identical to an (unnamed) king and paraded about the streets imitating the king's dress and bearing, just like those men who fancied they were Alexander the Great or Nero. As we have seen with the case of Marius under Julius Caesar, public recognition and acceptance were crucial. When a woman from Milan said she was a certain Rubria, who had died in a fire, in order to claim the deceased's property, she was able to marshal a number of witnesses to support her identity. Many impersonators of famous individuals depended on their followers to vouch for them, such as the slave Geta who said he was Scribonius Camerinus, the son of the consul Marcus Licinius Crassus Frugi. In sixth-century Gaul, a citizen of Bourges maintained that he was Jesus Christ and proceeded to parade about the region gathering followers with a woman claiming to be his "Mary."[15]

The primary motivation for masquerading as a specific individual was the acquisition of wealth, property, and status, just like the small-time charlatans and con artists who said they could tell the future or promised a quick return on an investment. There was much that united Marius, who claimed to be Julius Caesar's long-lost relation, the slave Geta, who wanted to be a Crassus, and Rubria, who saw a woman's tragic death as a way to gain property in Milan. Perhaps those who claimed to be famous individuals wanted to be bribed to simply disappear. (Augustus famously paid off the Spanish bandit-leader Corocotta with one million sesterces.) But imitators of senatorial and imperial relatives played a much more dangerous game than charismatic robber chiefs, for such imposture flew much closer to the sun, threatening aristocratic sensibilities and imperial stability. One young man pretended to be Marcellus, son of Augustus's sister Octavia, by claiming that he had been switched at birth with the real child. The emperor had him attached to the oar of a trireme, and he was rowed to death.[16]

In other cases of impersonation, the acquisition of material goods appears to have been tied up with a desire for fame, adulation, and even personal worship. In the reign of Elagabalus, an individual reportedly traveled throughout the

Balkans, accompanied by a retinue of four hundred men with thyrsi and fawn skins, claiming to be Alexander the Great. The false Alexander was provided with food and lodging at public expense with the acquiescence of (or at least no resistance from) the Roman authorities. Cassius Dio, who heard about the pseudo-Alexander's progress when he was living in nearby Asia Minor, wrote that the impostor journeyed to Byzantium and thence to Chalcedon, where he made sacrifices, buried a wooden horse, and disappeared. The most plausible explanation is that the impostor was mimicking Caracalla's own progress through the region several years before, since Caracalla had modeled himself on Alexander the Great. Without venturing too far into the realm of psychoanalysis—always dangerous territory where the ancient world is concerned—the false Alexander was probably seized by some desire for personal enrichment, combined with self-aggrandizement or narcissistic tendencies. The same point can be made about the false Christ described by Gregory of Tours who went around fraudulently claiming to heal the sick, and in doing so amassed more than three thousand followers. The Alexander and Christ impostors are different from other examples, such as Marius and Rubria, because they claimed to be gods or god-like individuals returning from the dead. (Cassius Dio even called the false Alexander a "divine being.") Pretending to be a magician or prophet was a good way to con people out of money, but there was probably some psychological element behind these types of divine deceptions. There also had to be a public willing to believe in them and vouch for them. Even after Peregrinus Proteus had publicly committed suicide on his own funeral pyre at Olympia, an enthusiastic devotee swore that he had seen him, clad in white, walking through the city.[17]

LES MISÉRABLES

If impostors depended on supporters to give them legitimacy, what sort of people believed in them? Rural populations, particularly in Italy, Anatolia, and Syria, figure prominently in the rumors about false Caesars. Although Roman political impostors sometimes traveled to cities, they rarely emerged there fully formed. The picture of the rural environment and its inhabitants that features in our literary sources is not a positive one. Elite Romans conceived of the countryside beyond their estates as a turbulent no-man's land occupied by bandits, robbers, and criminals avoiding detection while plotting their next raid on a fattened farm or a criminal venture in a nearby city. The wealthy urbanites who dared embark on journeys between cities and villas faced the risks of this dark and dank netherworld. Aristocrats and military officers were known to disappear without a trace in the peaks and troughs of Italian hills, suspected of being murdered by enslaved people or sinister forces. This is not to say that towns were necessarily themselves any safer: pickpockets lurked at every corner, and bands of young men could roam the streets after dark, their tomfoolery turning ugly and leaving dead bodies in their wake. But the rural environment was regarded as a particularly fertile source of recruits who would be eager to follow charismatic and rebellious leaders.[18]

Behind these aristocratic fears and prejudices lay the reality of rural destitution, depression, and discontent. Indeed, the picture painted by our elite literary sources was not entirely incorrect. "Killed by bandits" was a commonplace lament on funerary inscriptions, family members sometimes disappeared while out hunting, never to be heard from again, and merchants were robbed while traveling. Daily life was hard. Farmers, pastoralists, and laborers all tried to do an honest day's work, their daily concerns centering on crop yields and their animals. These were men and women who prayed to "crop-giving nymphs" to give them a good harvest. But their prayers were not always answered. Their subsistence-level existence meant they could be easily turned in other directions for money or better opportunities, being mobilized as an ersatz force by landowners or turning into armed bandits of their own volition. Straightened circumstances, such as a grain shortage, might encourage such desperation. Moneylenders sent their henchmen to villages to "convince" debtors to pay up; leaving the village altogether was a realistic option to escape such pressure. Often those who engaged in raiding were branded as criminals by the Roman state, but they were actually overburdened by taxes and threatened by environmental change. Enslaved people could be roused to revolt when pamphlets promising them freedom were spread throughout the land. The impoverished fled their homes to avoid paying taxes, army deserters were unable to return to a world they had forsaken, and the enslaved sought freedom anywhere and everywhere—all these people could be enticed to a life of crime. This was their way of taking back control in a world that offered them few remedies for their ills.[19]

This picture means that we need to take seriously the idea that charismatic individuals could muster supporters from among the provincial population, especially the rural poor and dispossessed—subsistence farmers, itinerant laborers, bandits and robbers, military deserters, and runaway slaves—and that these itinerant groups and their leaders could give rise to rumors about their identities, as well as panic and concern for the Roman and local authorities. When Jesus Christ moved through the Levant, crowds gathered to meet him wherever he went, and rumors reached the Tetrarch Herod Antipas that this man was either the resurrected form of John the Baptist, the prophet Elijah, or another holy man of former times. Brent Shaw has persuasively argued that stories about bandits and other popular leaders reflected a wider desire for "a savior from the present networks of power in which they were enmeshed, a man who could rescue them from their oppression." Throughout history, peasants and other dispossessed groups have looked to soldiers, landowners, and aristocrats—men of higher social status—to act as their leaders and saviors.[20]

There was a close connection between criminality and imposture. Sometimes these were small-time thieves or rebels, such as the group in Apuleius's *Metamorphoses* who dressed up as ghosts to frighten nighttime travelers, or the Egyptian Boukoloi who donned women's clothes to dupe a Roman centurion. But leaders of criminal bands very often took on other identities, from Mariccus, who plundered the regions of the Aedui in central Gaul while telling his eight thousand supporters he had godly powers, to the robber Bulla Felix, who terrorized Italy with six hundred men, often assuming other guises in pursuit of his crimes. The imperial impostors whom we will discuss in this chapter all emerged from this world of pretense and charlatanism. Like rebel outlaws and false prophets, their masquerades transcended the ordinary flimflammery of medical quacks and literary hacks, transforming them into charismatic leaders who offered hope to the disenfranchised residents of the empire. And it all began with rumors that a Caesar still lived.[21]

POSTUMUS RETURNS TO LIFE

When Augustus lost Gaius and Lucius Caesar—his grandsons and adopted sons—within a few short years of each other, he was forced to redraw his dynastic plans. In the year 4, he adopted their fifteen-year-old brother, Agrippa Postumus, as well as Tiberius, his forty-five-year-old stepson. Tiberius already had a son, Drusus the Younger, but Augustus ordered him to adopt his nephew, the promising young general Germanicus. Augustus, who had been remarkably unlucky with his potential successors up to this point, with Marcellus, Agrippa, Gaius, and Lucius dying over a period of twenty years, now had multiple contingency plans in place. He was wise to have such foresight. In 6, Postumus was suddenly banished to Surrentum, and then the next year he was formally exiled by senatorial decree to the island of Planasia (modern-day Pianosa) in the Tyrrhenian Sea. The reasons given in the ancient sources—Postumus's temper and inclination to vice—probably represented the official version that concealed more sinister, but ultimately unknowable, machinations. And so it was that after Augustus's death in 14, Tiberius became head of the Julian family and assumed his adoptive father's station in the monarchical *res publica*.[22]

The first crime of the new regime, as the historian Tacitus memorably described it, was the murder of Agrippa Postumus by a centurion on the orders of Tiberius. The new emperor had wasted no time in removing his closest rival. Even while Augustus was still alive, Postumus's lineage had meant that his continued existence served as a flashpoint for dissenters. In 11, two men had allegedly hatched a plan to rescue Postumus and his mother, Julia, from the islands to which they had been exiled, intending to spirit them away to the legions. The men were caught, but their attempt signaled discontent with Tiberius as Augustus's successor. Tiberius would probably have been further disquieted by the story that shortly before his death, Augustus and his close friend Fabius Maximus had visited the island of Planasia, where he had been reconciled with Postumus. Whatever the truth of this tale, Augustus did not change his will, or perhaps he did not have time to do so before he passed away. The execution of Postumus was soon followed by the demise of his mother, Julia, who starved to death, and her lover, Sempronius Gracchus, who was killed on the order of Tiberius (though he tried to blame the proconsul of Africa).[23]

Not everyone had hoped for such a smooth transfer of power from Augustus to Tiberius. Clemens, an imperial slave who had previously been attached to Agrippa Postumus, and who was about the same age as his master, hatched a bold plan when he heard of Augustus's death. He decided that he would make for Planasia, rescue Postumus from his captors, and then take him to Germany and present him to the armies stationed there (a plan identical to the ill-fated earlier scheme of 11). The idea of presenting Postumus as an alternative to Tiberius is made plausible by the fact that there were indeed military revolts following the death of Augustus in Pannonia and Germany, which had to be suppressed by Drusus the Younger and Germanicus. But fate intervened to stop Postumus from making his miraculous appearance before the troops. Clemens was slowed down by the ponderous progress of the transport on which he had gained passage to Planasia, and Postumus was dead by the time he arrived. Clemens therefore took his former master's ashes and sailed east to Cosa on the coast of Etruria, which lay some 140 kilometers northwest of Rome. There he went into hiding in order to grow his hair and beard long, all the better to resemble an Agrippa Postumus who had escaped the executioner's sword on Planasia. An impostor needed to look the part, because, as we have seen, it was on those grounds that his identity would be judged.[24]

It is difficult to determine whether Clemens conceived of this new plan to impersonate Agrippa alone. There are no hard and fast rules of political imposture that allow us to extract certainty from comparative examples. Some political impostors, such as the boy Lambert Simnel, who was crowned Edward VI in Dublin in opposition to the Tudor monarch Henry VII, were pawns of more powerful forces from the beginning. Others, like the monk Grisha Otrep'ev, who claimed to be the Russian tsarevich Dmitry, son of Ivan the Terrible, clearly came up with their imposture alone before seeking support. Tacitus's account gives the impression of a slow and cautious approach, with Clemens initially confiding in a few well-chosen allies who proceeded to circulate the news of Agrippa Postumus's survival. He then made his way through Italy, being careful only to appear in towns at twilight—presumably to add to the mystery, as well as to avoid close scrutiny—allowing rumors of Agrippa's return to lay the groundwork for an eventual public appearance. I must emphasize that we are dependent on Tacitus's much later narrative here. But there is a plausibility to his account, given that the Italian highways and byways were full of peasants, wanderers, and robbers, just the sort of people who might have been attracted to Clemens's imposture. Less than a decade later, in 24, southern Italy was thrown into confusion when a former soldier from the praetorian guard enticed enslaved people to his cause with the promise of freedom. It is not known how long this surreptitious game actually went on, but Clemens was certainly ready to make his move in the middle of 16. By this time, Tacitus wrote, Italy was seized by the rumor that Agrippa was alive, and its truthfulness was readily believed among the population of Rome, which reveals a distrust of the state's official version of his exile and death. The spreading of rumors about Agrippa's survival was a way of articulating discontent with Tiberius and his regime without directly challenging the emperor. But people who actively supported Agrippa crossed the thin line between subversion and rebellion.[25]

By the year 16, Clemens's supporters reportedly included senators, equestrians, and members of the emperor's household, who offered him both money and advice. They did not necessarily believe in his assumed identity as Agrippa Postumus. Here comparative analysis is more helpful, since one recurring feature of political impostors is that although their identities are believed by the people at large, elite backers generally used them for cynical purposes. It is therefore likely that many of the aristocrats who financially supported Clemens did not care whether he was Agrippa, only that he functioned as an effective symbol of their unhappiness with Tiberius. The identity of these backers is unfortunately unknown. Some modern historians have argued that one illustrious supporter was the praetor Marcus Scribonius Drusus Libo. He had a formidable pedigree, being the great-grandson of Pompey the Great and the emperor Tiberius's own cousin. Libo was condemned in the senate on September 13, 16, on the charge of imperiling the safety of the state, as shown by contemporary epigraphic evidence, which provides effective support to Tacitus's much later account of his downfall. The young man had been egged on by one of his friends, Firmius Catus, who persuaded him to consult astrologers and use magical rites to accomplish his ends. To a nervous Tiberius, these were no empty charges. The connection between Libo and Clemens is far from conclusive: the ambitious young senator could simply have been inspired to take action by the rumors of Agrippa Postumus's survival. Connected or not, the near-simultaneous occurrence of these events certainly fostered a climate of fear and uncertainty in Rome.[26]

Libo committed suicide on September 13, the day of his conviction in the senate, which was henceforth declared a public holiday. At some uncertain point soon after, Clemens arrived in Ostia, the port of Rome, where he was met by huge crowds—the size of support he attracted is emphasized by all our literary sources, which suggests it should be taken seriously. From Ostia, Clemens moved to Rome itself, where his supporters had to meet him in secret, out of fear of being discovered by Tiberius. The emperor is said to have asked that his closest associate, Sallustius Crispus, take the necessary measures to suppress Clemens's insurgency. He was seized at night and taken to the Palatine to meet with Tiberius. Tacitus and Dio both report that when Tiberius and Clemens finally came face-to-face, they had a memorable conversation. Tiberius asked the slave how he had become Agrippa, to which Clemens replied: "The same way that you became Caesar."[27]

This witty exchange is apocryphal. It is a Roman version of the folkloric motif, "He Who Steals Much Called King; He Who Steals Little Called Robber," in which the convicted criminal turns the tables on their royal accuser. The scene responded to people's desire to know what really happened when the two met face-to-face, providing a dramatic closure to Clemens's story. There was no public trial in the senate, and Clemens was quietly put to death in the chambers of the Palatine. The folkloric repartee also works as an effective coda to the events because it exposed the fragile basis of Tiberius's position as emperor. Clemens had made sure that he looked the part of Agrippa Postumus by growing his hair and beard to appear like a man ravaged by years of imprisonment, but at the end of the day the success or failure of the imposture depended on people believing him. The later emergence and circulation of this exchange highlighted that Tiberius's position as Caesar likewise rested on acceptance by the people, the senate, and the armies (to return to Egon Flaig's argument). In the contemporary moment, the reappearance of Agrippa Postumus represented a moment of wonder and alchemy. As Homi Bhabha has written of the appearance of the last Mughal king, Bahadur Shah, during the Indian mutiny against the British in 1857, "The king as spectacle becomes that name that can work like magic." Bahadur Shah was the physical embodiment of the rebels' challenge to the British government of India, just as Agrippa encapsulated discontent with Tiberius, as the magical properties of his name traveled through Italy to Rome itself.[28]

THE OTHER DRUSUS CAESAR

Tiberius would be equally unfortunate in his heirs as Augustus. The death of his son Drusus the Younger followed shortly after the tragic loss of Germanicus in Syria. The emperor's powerful praetorian prefect, Aelius Sejanus, then allegedly began to connive against Germanicus's widow, Agrippina, and her two eldest sons, Nero and Drusus Caesar, who were now Tiberius's natural successors. In order to accomplish his plans, Sejanus turned Drusus against his elder brother, who was implicated as engaging in inappropriate homosexual affairs. Agrippina and Nero were exiled to islands, where they died. In 31, Sejanus reportedly achieved the demise of Drusus Caesar with the complicity of his wife, Aemilia Lepida, but rather than having him killed immediately, Drusus was instead incarcerated in the bowels of the Palatine, where he perished two years later.[29]

Later in 31 or in 34 (our sources disagree), a young man appeared in the Cyclades—a group of Greek islands some 150 kilometers to the southeast of Athens—claiming to be Drusus Caesar, who had either escaped prison or death, depending on which date we follow. When he moved to the Greek mainland soon after, a rumor that Drusus still lived spread not only throughout the province of Achaia but also across the Ionian Sea to Asia Minor. The imposture was consolidated by imperial freedmen, possibly attached to the emperor's landholdings in Greece, who vouched for his identity. (Imperial freedmen were known to support other rebellious causes, such as the third-century Italian brigand Bulla Felix.) Tacitus is our most detailed source for the false Drusus's appearance, which he placed in 31; as noted earlier, he engaged in genuine research to try and find out precisely what occurred. He wrote that the impostor claimed to have escaped from prison in Rome and intended to travel to the armies of his father, Germanicus, which he would use to invade Syria or Egypt. These could have been the eastern legions, but they are more likely to be the German armies, who remembered Germanicus with great fondness and had wanted him to succeed Augustus. The tall tale enabled the nascent insurrection to gain substantial support in Greece, particularly from other young men, who were perhaps looking for adventure, a new life, or a new purpose. The imperial freedmen—who, as Tacitus notes, did not really think this young man was Drusus—provided a sense of plausibility to the escapade, as did the derring-do of a youth intent on claiming his father, Germanicus's, inheritance, a cause enough to motivate the downtrodden and the dispossessed. Drusus's appearance was taken sufficiently seriously by the imperial government to warrant the intervention of the governor Gaius Poppaeus Sabinus.[30]

Drusus traveled westward across Greece, as one would if trying to make for Germany, and he reportedly gathered followers from both the rural and urban population as the rumor spread of his escape. He eventually came to the important port of Nicopolis, which lay on the Adriatic Sea and was the ideal place to find ships to sail to Italy. It was also where his putative father, Germanicus, had celebrated his consulship thirteen years before. But Nicopolis was where Drusus's insurrection fell apart. When the governor Poppaeus Sabinus, who had pursued his trail across Greece, arrived there, he was told that Drusus had been questioned—by whom we do not know—and confessed that he was actually a son of the consul Marcus Silanus. After many of his supporters abandoned him, Drusus decided to take a ship to Italy. Tacitus observed that Sabinus could follow Drusus's trail no further and wrote to Tiberius about what he had discovered. Cassius Dio's narrative offered a rather different ending, in which Drusus is arrested and sent to Tiberius. This suggests that there were many explanations for the imposture and its end in circulation by the time Tacitus and Dio came to write their accounts in the early second and third centuries, respectively. The escapade attests to popular attachment to the name of Drusus and the memory of his father, Germanicus.[31]

Who was this enigmatic young man in reality? The origin of the imposture in the Cycladic islands provides one clue, since this was where Roman political exiles were commonly banished in the imperial period. Some of these islands, notably Gyaros and Seriphos, were forbidding and barren places, but others, such as Andros or Amorgos, were far more congenial. Unlike members of the imperial family, senatorial and equestrian exiles were not commonly kept under guard, but could range freely across their island, receive visitors, buy property, and become local benefactors. Given his knowledge of imperial politics and of the real Drusus's disappearance into the Palatine dungeons, our man was most likely one such exile, perhaps even the son of Marcus Silanus, as he later claimed.

He may even have been in contact with more powerful forces in Rome who were discontented with Tiberius's rule. The Cyclades, and Greece as a whole, were sufficiently far away from Rome to stage an imposture based on the fact that Drusus had escaped from prison. The "escape narrative" underlies many other similar acts of royal imposture, such as the supposed reappearance of Richard II of England. As the British historian Simon Walker has written, such impostors attracted followers because they functioned as a form of opposition to the current ruler by "couching resistance in the idiom of consent to legitimate authority, while offering . . . a ready means of disavowal in the face of reprisals." The success of the false Drusus's enterprise depended on motivating Greeks to join the cause, which he evidently accomplished before the deception fell apart at Nicopolis. They then disappeared into the ether, since there is no evidence that Poppaeus Sabinus enacted any punishments or retribution. If they had been caught, they could simply have claimed they were motivated by loyalty to Germanicus's son.[32]

NERO LIVES!

On June 9, 68, the emperor Nero committed suicide in the suburbs of Rome. The dagger through his throat, driven home with the assistance of his secretary, Epaphroditus, was a desperate act to avoid being captured alive. Nero's body was cremated, and his ashes were placed in a marble sarcophagus in the family tomb on the Pincian Hill. There were no grand obsequies, merely a ceremony overseen by his nurses and his mistress, Acte. Suetonius, writing about forty years later, reported that people ran through Rome wearing liberty caps to celebrate their deliverance from Nero's tyranny. But Suetonius also observed that there were others who cherished Nero's memory, decorating his tomb with flowers, placing statues of him on the speaker's platform, and posting his edicts in public "as if he were still alive and would soon return to wreak destruction on his enemies." The memory of Nero was cultivated by two of the short-lived emperors of 69, Otho and Vitellius. Otho was hailed by the people as "Nero," and he is even said to have used the name in formal pronouncements; he also re-erected the emperor's statues or allowed people to do so themselves. Vitellius made a public display of devotion by sacrificing to Nero's shades in the Campus Martius. Such exhibitions would have been impolitic if Nero had not been popular among some of Rome's inhabitants. Indeed, in the days, months, and decades after Nero's suicide, there was a persistent rumor that he had not actually died. The continued circulation of this rumor into the late first and early second centuries is attested in the works of Tacitus, Suetonius, and the Greek intellectual Dio Chrysostom. The facts of Nero's passing were not ambiguous, since he did have a funeral and was buried in a mausoleum in the city of Rome. The rumor that he still lived must instead be ascribed to suspicion about this official version of events, and in particular, to the belief that the man buried there was not actually Nero. The appearance of men claiming to be Nero himself represents a spectacular failure of communicative action, since it shows how distrust of the state's pronouncements could not only give rise to rumor, but also to corporeal realities.[33]

By the end of 68, a rumor had started to spread throughout Greece and Asia Minor that Nero was alive. This caused terror among the provincials, according to Tacitus, who was a youth when these events took place and depended on unknown sources to write his account. Where this rumor began is a mystery, but we can imagine it circulating rapidly in the taverns and cookshops of Aegean ports and trading posts, as merchants and travelers passed the story back and forth across the Ionian Sea. A man who claimed to be Nero soon recruited Roman soldiers (from precisely where we do not know) who had deserted the army, becoming wanderers on the lookout for the next opportunity. It was all too easy for soldiers to make the transition from being enforcers of law and order to vagrants, criminals, and bandits. The impostor made grand promises (unfortunately unrecorded), probably offering the deserters riches that would liberate them from their life of penury. Only a few years before, during the Jewish revolt in Judaea, John of Gischala had successfully recruited a band of deserters and villagers to serve as his personal army before swindling his way through Galilee. Our Neronian impostor likely had similar profiteering in mind. He and his band took ship, but a storm drove them to the island of Cythnus, one of the Cycladic isles, which lay southeast of Cape Sounion.[34]

No one knew who the impostor really was, but there were plenty of stories told after the fact. One was that he was a slave from Pontus in northern Asia Minor, another that he was a freedman from Italy. Whatever his background, he looked similar to Nero (the emperor's distinctive curled hairstyle was easily affected), and he had the emperor's talent for singing and playing the cithara. He was likely someone from outside the mainstream social order, perhaps a Greek who had been exposed at birth or who had fallen on hard times and been sold into slavery (many enslaved people in the imperial period came from Asia Minor originally). Alternatively, the impostor could have been an actor from a traveling troupe, whose considerable talents had not translated into wealth or respectability (such individuals were of very low status in the Roman world). This is all, I freely admit, rather speculative, but I incline toward the latter scenario. Acting, dancing, and singing all required considerable training and physical stamina (as the rigorous demands of Nero's own exercise regime show), not to mention charisma and a talent for persuasion, all of which were excellent qualifications for potential impostors. The pretender's aims were quite different from those of the false Agrippa and false Drusus, both of whom intended to march on Rome or to the legions in order to displace Tiberius. Nor did this Nero have any connections with members of the aristocratic elite who might hope to use him as a pawn. Instead, he appears as a charismatic outlaw, looking for money, booty, and followers.[35]

The sorry charade unraveled on the island of Cynthus in the early months of 69. The false Nero terrorized the local population and tried to force Roman soldiers on leave from the army in Syria to join his cause. Those who refused were killed. His band then turned their attention to merchants in the harbor, robbing them of their goods and making off with their slaves. A Roman centurion managed to escape the impostor's grasp, leaving Cynthus in secret and spreading the rumor of Nero's return, or at least that someone was claiming to be him. Many people in the region were terrified, but others traveled to Cynthus to join the cause—"Nero" offered both a famous name and the hope of escaping the current chaos (Rome was by this time on the second of its four emperors for the year). By chance a Roman official, Nonius Calpurnius Asprenas, arrived at Cynthus. Asprenas was on his way to take up the governorship of Galatia and Pamphylia, accompanied by two triremes from the fleet based at Misenum. After a short standoff, his forces boarded the false Nero's ship and killed him. The impostor was decapitated, and his head was sent first to the mainland of Asia Minor—presumably to quash the rumor of Nero's return that had caused such anxiety—before being dispatched to Rome. The head functioned as proof either that Nero was finally dead, or that this man had never really been the emperor at all. The sight of a bloody, severed head carried a level of believability that exceeded any written pronouncement by the state.[36]

PARTHIAN POLITICS

For the next ten years or so, Nero continued to live in people's hearts and minds, as the Greek orator Dio Chrysostom observed. He reappeared in the reign of Titus (79–81). Since the relevant books of Tacitus's *Histories* are lost, we depend on much later Greek sources, Zonaras and John of Antioch, who identified the impostor as a man from Asia Minor called Terentius Maximus. Like his predecessor, Maximus possessed a resemblance to Nero in both appearance and voice, and he could play the lyre. He told potential followers that he had managed to escape the soldiers in Rome and had then gone into hiding. I would speculate that the background to Maximus's imposture places him in a similar category to the first false Nero—a talented, but unscrupulous, ne'er-do-well from the margins of society out to capitalize on the emperor's name for adventure, riches, romance, and a chance of a better life. Rather than making for Rome, Maximus marched eastward through Asia Minor, gathering some followers from the towns, villages, and countryside as he did so. These were probably the sort of people who were attracted to the causes of charlatans and outlaws, either villagers fed up with extortion from Roman soldiers or peasants who roamed the countryside attacking wealthy properties. The rural inhabitants of Asia Minor commonly made prayers to the gods for good harvests and protection, sometimes styling them the "kings" of their villages. Now they had a real-life protector, the emperor Nero, walking among them.[37]

Maximus and his band soon crossed the Taurus mountains into the lowlands of Syria, moving toward the Euphrates River. We are told by Zonaras that he then fled for protection to Artabanus III, one of the claimants to the throne of Parthia. Why Maximus needed to seek refuge in this fashion is not made clear by our sources—perhaps he had fallen foul of Roman authorities—but it suggests that he had not been aiming to seek Parthian support from the beginning. He was warmly welcomed by Artabanus. The real Nero had been on very good terms with the Parthians, since he had formally bestowed the kingdom of Armenia on Tiridates, the brother of King Vologases I. Artabanus was engaged in a civil war for the kingdom with his brother Pacorus II, who was Titus's preferred candidate, and he planned to threaten Titus by making plans to support the restoration of Nero. Zonaras's story stops there, but John of Antioch recorded that Maximus was killed when the Parthians discovered he was not actually Nero. It is unlikely that Artabanus had cared if Maximus was the real Nero or not. When the Portuguese monarch Philip IV was faced with a possible resurrected Mughal sultan, Dawar Bakhsh, he informed his viceroy in Goa that he would consider endorsing the claimant regardless of his authenticity. As Jorge Flores and Sanjay Subrahmanyam put it: "A good impostor was thus as useful as the real thing." There are valid grounds for regarding the unfortunate Maximus as a similar sort of impostor to the first false Nero, a charismatic leader in search of fame and fortune. However, when he was forced to flee to the Parthians, he became a political pawn.[38]

Suetonius himself heard the rumors of a third false Nero when he was a young man, some twenty years after the emperor's death. Although we cannot trace all the conversations that led to Suetonius picking up the rumor, they represented sustained political engagement and debate about imperial rulership and identity. The biographer knew little of the impostor's background and story, only that he had also been assisted by the Parthians, who then reluctantly surrendered him to Roman authorities. Suetonius's contemporary Tacitus wrote that "imposture of a false Nero almost drove the Parthians to warfare," but the books of his *Histories* dealing with the events are now lost. Military diplomas attesting auxiliary military units stationed in Syria in 88 suggest that there were serious tensions between the Roman emperor Domitian and the Parthian monarch Pacorus II (who had been successful against his brother Artabanus). Domitian was acclaimed *imperator* ("victorious general") for the seventeenth time that same year, almost certainly for the suppression of the false Nero. There is little else that is certain about this pretender. However, the emergence of three Neros within twenty years of the emperor's death fits into the wider historical pattern of impostors inspiring further impostors.[39]

Fascination with Nero's life and afterlife continued to play on the Roman imagination in subsequent decades. In his dialogue *On the Delays of Divine Vengeance,* the Greek philosopher Plutarch pondered the matter of Nero's reincarnation. The emperor was intended to be condemned to a life as a viper, living in and eating his pregnant mother. But the gods decreed that he should instead be transformed into "a musical animal"—either a frog or a swan, depending on the interpretation of the original Greek words—because of his munificence toward the Greek province of Achaea. Nero had granted the inhabitants of the province freedom from taxation, which was subsequently rescinded by Vespasian. The idea that Nero was reincarnated by the gods as a singing creature seems to be an allusion to the first and second false Neros, both of whom played up the performative aspects of the emperor's character. I am skeptical about attempts to link the followers of these impostors to a specifically "Greek" enthusiasm for Nero occasioned by his grant of freedom to Achaea, which was but one Greek-speaking province in the eastern Mediterranean. The first false Nero caused fear and terror as much as he inspired (or bribed) men to follow him, and the second moved eastward, gathering followers in Asia Minor, a region that was not granted privileges by Nero. Plutarch's dialogue hints at a connection between Nero's munificence and his later reincarnation, but this seems to be his own interpretation, rather than reflecting the reality of the impostures themselves.[40]

The rumors that Nero escaped to Parthia found new life in works of popular literature known as the *Sibylline Oracles,* prophecies written in hexameter verse that foretold doom and destruction. They were named after the prophetesses known as "Sibyls," though in this collection the speakers take on different guises. The collection of fourteen oracles, written in Greek, are often described as Judeo-Christian texts, since they contain elements of both religions as well as pagan themes and motifs. The transmitted text of the *Fourth Sibylline Oracle* provides valuable contemporary testimony regarding the rumors about the second false Nero, since it was assembled in the eastern provinces during the reign of Titus (in 80 or shortly thereafter). The *Oracle* foretold how "a great king will flee from Italy like a runaway slave, unseen and unheard over the channel of the Euphrates," and predicted that Nero, with Parthian help, would lay waste to the eastern provinces. This far-reaching eschatological vision of destruction has no connection with any putative Greek enthusiasm for Nero; instead, the emperor appears as a destructive avenger. The *Fifth Sibylline Oracle,* composed by Egyptian Jews in the late first or early second century, when rumors of Nero's survival were still current, envisioned the emperor as a true popular hero who would right wrongs and lift up the oppressed. These texts show that rumors of Nero's survival had made the transition to folklore and legend, as the classicist Edward Champlin has brilliantly explored. Imposture and prophecy were closely intertwined in the popular imagination. False emperors offered followers their "own" ruler, to whom they had direct access and who would look after their interests, whereas prophecy predicted that such a man could possibly emerge in the future (though in a variety of different manifestations).[41]

Historians have often looked for definite connections between the real Nero's actions, especially his tour of the Greek festival circuit in Achaea and the subsequent freedom of the province, and his transformation into a heroic, avenging figure as represented in the *Sibylline Oracles.* Peter Burke has observed the same phenomenon among scholars of medieval and early modern Europe who have tried to understand the reappearances of rulers such as Frederick Barbarossa by connecting them with real historical events. However, such transfigurations do not actually occur because of detailed familiarity with a specific king's actions or policies, but because, in Burke's words, "certain individuals conform, or are seen as conforming in certain respects, to a hero-stereotype like that of the just king or the noble outlaw." Nero's musical and performing talents, aped by the first and second imitators, may be one aspect of his character that identified him in the popular imagination as an emperor outside the mainstream. As rumors of his return circulated and intensified, other aspects of heroic kingship began to "crystallize" around Nero, so that the final legendary figure bore little resemblance to the historical person. The emergence of Nero as both an agent of destruction and a popular hero in different works of Jewish and Christian literature is a product of this complex and multifaceted transformation that evades any one particular explanation.[42]

Over the course of the centuries, Nero not only became a heroic figure, but also the ultimate villain. In the fifth century, Augustine of Hippo described how many Christians of his time held opposing views about Nero's fate and return. Some believed that Nero had actually died that fateful June day in Rome, but would one day be resurrected as the biblical Antichrist, which is known as the Nero *redivivus* ("reborn") legend. Shushma Malik has persuasively demonstrated that this idea is first attested in the third century, when it appeared in the works of Christian writers such as Commodian (a poet from Africa) and Victorinus of Pettau (author of the *Commentary on the Apocalypse*). Augustine noted that others thought Nero had not been killed but was merely hiding until it was time for him to reappear. This *rediturus* ("return") legend emerged from rumors of the emperor's survival and escape to Parthia. The competing views of Nero as Antichrist and Savior described by Augustine were developed versions of the respective reactions of terror and hope that had greeted the first rumors of the emperor's return in Greece and Asia Minor centuries before.[43]

The belief that Nero had gone into hiding conforms to the international legend of the "sleeping" or "hidden" king, who will one day return as a savior figure to help his people. Some of the most famous examples of sleeping kings include the German monarchs Frederick I Barbarossa and his grandson Frederick II (who were conflated in legend), Sebastian I of Portugal, Edward VI of England, and the last Roman emperor, Constantine XI Palaeologus, who vanished fighting against the Ottomans on the walls of Constantinople in 1453. The Roman belief that Nero would return in this fashion would have been fostered by the frameworks of knowledge that encouraged the assimilation of kings with gods. The most significant example of the hidden king was Zeus, who was secreted away as an infant by his mother, Rhea, to stop his father, Cronos, from eating him, before returning to free his siblings from their father's stomach. As with the transformation of kings into heroes, the phenomenon of the sleeping king is not necessarily connected to an individual ruler's character, but to what he represented. When the Portuguese king Sebastian I died childless in battle during an ill-advised campaign in Morocco, the crown of Portugal passed to the Spanish king, Philip II. This meant that rumors of his return were connected with ideas of Portuguese nationalism and the longing for the past in which they had their own monarch. A similar point can be made about the hope that the last Roman emperor, Constantine XI Palaeologus, would one day reappear, since it would mean the restoration of the Roman empire. Nero's own sleeping king legend did not represent the glorious return of the Julio-Claudian dynasty, but instead envisioned him as the champion of all those who needed his assistance.[44]

PRODIGAL SONS

After the false Neros, it would be four hundred years before the Roman empire was again gripped by rumors of another imperial return. In 479, the brothers Flavius Marcianus, Procopius Anthemius, and Romulus, the sons of the former western emperor Anthemius, led a revolt against Zeno, the emperor of the East. When their rebellion collapsed, Marcianus was tonsured and became a monk, but Procopius Anthemius and Romulus escaped to the West. Soon after, a man called Theosebius, who bore a resemblance to Procopius, traveled through the cities of the eastern province claiming to be him. The reasons for Theosebius's imposture are obscure: he persuaded many of his legitimacy, but for what end we do not know. But his choice of Procopius Anthemius as an identity suggests that he was trying to take advantage of the chaos of the reign of Zeno (which was marked by constant usurpation), for either political or personal gain. Procopius Anthemius had outstanding imperial lineage. Not only had his father, Anthemius, ruled the western empire between 467 and 472, but his mother, Euphemia, was the daughter of the eastern emperor Marcian (451–457). The real Procopius Anthemius was not dead, merely far away in Italy, but Theosebius depended on that knowledge not being widely circulated, so that he could masquerade as having escaped Zeno's clutches while remaining in the East.[45]

Rumors that an emperor had escaped death lay behind the final case of an imperial impostor in the period covered by this book, that of Theodosius, the son and co-ruler of the emperor Maurice. On November 27, 602, at the harbor of Eutropius in Chalcedon, the soldiers of the usurper Phocas murdered five of Maurice's sons—the youngest a mere baby—and then slew the emperor himself. This tragic event was marked, so the story goes, by an attempt at a type of imperial imposture. The baby's nurse is said to have secreted him away and provided her own child to be killed in his place, but Maurice confessed to the soldiers that the infant was not his son. This folkloric motif of the "Substituted Child," here subverted through Maurice's admission, belonged to a hagiographical tradition that developed after the emperor's death and depicted him as a saintly figure. The teenaged Theodosius escaped this massacre of his male relatives because he had been sent on a mission to the Persian empire to seek the assistance of the Persian Shahanshah ("King of Kings") Khosrow II. However, he was soon recalled to Constantinople, where he was captured and killed by Alexander, one of Phocas's officers, after taking refuge in a church.[46]

The news of Theodosius's death was not believed by the inhabitants of Constantinople, because his head had not been publicly displayed at the Hebdomon with those of his father and brothers. As with the case of the false Nero, his head functioned as a guarantor of death with a level of believability that went beyond any imperial proclamation. A rumor began to circulate that the man executed in the church had been a lookalike, and that Theodosius had actually escaped to foreign lands. The contemporary historian Theophylact Simocatta investigated the rumor and found it groundless, but said it was widely believed by others. One of these was Phocas himself. When the tale reached the new emperor's ears, he had his officer Alexander executed for being duped by a doppelgänger. A few years later, continuing rumors of Theodosius's survival were plausible enough to prompt his mother, Constantina, his wife, and his sisters to plot against Phocas, but they were discovered and executed. There was no happy ending for Theodosius either, even in the world of rumor, which had it that he eventually committed suicide.[47]

There is a parallel tradition in East Syrian, Armenian, and Islamic sources that Theodosius did survive the coup and managed to reach the court of Khosrow II. The Persian Shahanshah then crowned Theodosius as Roman emperor in Ctesiphon before invading Mesopotamia. One senior Roman general, Narses, who had remained loyal to the deceased Maurice, subsequently recognized Theodosius as the true emperor in the Mesopotamian city of Edessa. Theodosius is last attested in 607–608, when he persuaded the population of the appropriately named city of Theodosiopolis in Armenia to surrender to Persian forces. Modern historians have seriously considered the possibility that Theodosius was no impostor, but the genuine article, especially given the authority invested in him by both Khosrow II and Narses. His flight to the Persians in search of legitimacy and support not only recalls the efforts of the second and third false Neros, but also numerous other political impostors throughout world history who used foreign powers to achieve their aims, or alternatively, were manipulated by the foreign governments themselves. Whether or not Theodosius really survived being murdered in that Constantinopolitan church—and I think it is extremely unlikely—the belief that he had escaped played a significant role in internal and external politics for many years afterward.[48]

POLITICS FROM BELOW

In 1262, a poor, blind peasant boy from the highlands to the east of Nicaea in Asia Minor was unfortunate enough to be hailed as John IV Laskaris, emperor of the Romans. The real John had, at the tender age of eleven, been blinded on

Christmas Day and imprisoned in the Bithynian citadel of Dakibyze on the orders of Michael VIII Palaeologus, formerly the boy's regent, who now ruled as emperor in his place. But the Laskarid dynasty, which had governed the empire from Nicaea after the capital, Constantinople, had been captured by a Crusader army, remained very popular in Asia Minor. The Laskarids were not only native Anatolians, but had also been generous patrons to the towns, villages, and peoples in and around Nicaea, especially the border population (known as *akritai*), who formed a vital bulwark against the Turkish sultanate of Rūm. The contemporary historian George Pachymeres wrote that the rural population of the region, devastated at the blinding of the boy emperor and aroused by the rumors that he had escaped, rallied to the cause of the false John IV and vowed to fight in his name. This was a serious challenge to Michael VIII's nascent regime. His army marched into the highlands, where they eventually managed to buy off some of the rebels, while wearing down and killing others. The young impostor himself evaded capture, instead fleeing to the Turks. Two more pretenders claiming to be John IV subsequently manifested themselves, one in 1273, who sought the help of Charles of Anjou to oust Michael VIII, and another in 1305, the priest John Drimys, who tried to unseat Michael's son, Andronicus II Palaeologus. Throughout all this upheaval, the real John IV Laskaris lived a relatively quiet life as a monk. After his death in the early fourteenth century he became a saint, and his body lay in the monastery of Saint Demetrius for pilgrims to kiss and venerate.[49]

The story of the hapless blind boy and the peasant rebellion against Michael VIII Palaeologus, as told by George Pachymeres, comes from a much later period in Roman history than that covered by this book, but it is remarkable for the way it describes the motivations and hopes of the rural population who believed the rumors of John IV's escape. Our earlier Roman narratives pay far less attention to the aims and agency of supporters. This can be ascribed to a combination of factors. Sometimes impostures are attested only in fragments or summaries of earlier works (such as John of Antioch and Zonaras). But even when the account survives in its entirety, our historians often did not possess sufficient knowledge about how the imposture developed at the grass-roots level. In their narratives, rumors and pretenders alike sweep through cities and regions, with the lives and experiences of the population going largely unexplored, except in the most general terms. In his account of the false John IV Laskaris, George Pachymeres captures the deep and lasting attachment of ordinary people to a dynastic name and the hope of stability the name provided, restoring some agency to the often-voiceless rural population of the empire. We might plausibly imagine similar scenarios as "Agrippa Postumus" made his way through Italy, the second false Nero moved through Asia Minor, or the impersonator of Procopius Anthemius gathered supporters in the eastern provinces. The rumors that these men had cheated death or escaped provided the context for the impostures, but their personal presence offered the sense of hope. When Michael VIII's forces proposed to take some of the rebels to visit the real John IV, who remained imprisoned in the fortress of Dakibyze, this did not win them over. The resistance members said that the Palaeologan emperor could simply present them with a child pretending to be John. They regarded Michael VIII and his pronouncements as inherently untrustworthy, so it was better to put their fate in their own hands and those of their "own" emperor.[50]

Rumors, whispers, and conversations about the survival or return of imperial figures constituted a type of everyday politics that tapped into people's desire for a new ruler, one who might restore an unspecified idealized and romanticized past that would change their fortunes. We see evidence of such genuine popular sentiment in a fragmentary third-century astrological text from Egypt. The author's predictions, which derived from observations of the stars at the beginning of the Egyptian New Year, foretold a great reckoning in which the wealthy would have their property confiscated and the emperor would be murdered. The poor people would rise up, the rich would be humbled, and a new emperor would claim the purple. The sociologist James C. Scott has argued that "oppressed groups so often read in rumors promises of their imminent liberation." The impostor phenomenon revealed support for both the imperial monarchy and the principle of dynastic succession. Although they might have distrusted the current ruler, many Romans could not imagine a world in which they were not led by *an* emperor. The relationship between provincials and the Roman state received an unusual twist in the *Fifth Sibylline Oracle* in which it was Nero—a former emperor—who emerged as a popular avenger against Rome itself. But we must bear in mind that this sentiment, although widely attested, was not universally shared by all inhabitants of the empire. There were certainly impostors who chose other monarchical or religious identities, such as the false Alexander the Great of third-century Thrace or "Christ" and "Mary" in sixth-century Gaul, who attracted large groups of followers. The Jewish revolt against Hadrian and the acclamation of Simeon bar Kosiba as "prince of Israel" likewise imagined a different form of rulership. All these stories vacillate between polarities of loyalty and dissent, but they nevertheless provide a window into the imagination of Roman provincials, many of whom hoped that one day they would have their *own* savior.[51]

Political imposture is a historical phenomenon attested across Eurasia from Spain to China. But its dynamics are shaped by specific political, social, and cultural circumstances, to return to Natalie Zemon Davis's important methodological reminder. The frequent capture of European lords and monarchs during the Crusades saw a rash of impostors claiming to have escaped from Muslim captivity and wishing to be "restored" to power; the French Revolution and the execution of Louis XVI gave rise to some forty men who said they were the dauphin Louis, the last of the Bourbon line; and widespread peasant discontent and economic crisis resulted in no fewer than forty-four impostors plaguing Russia in the eighteenth century. Some royal impostors in other monarchical societies have offered specific political programs, even issuing decrees criticizing the high taxes and other misdemeanors of the incumbent ruler. Although our pretenders must have made some promises to their followers, they never manifested themselves in such a developed form that made it to the ears of, or was thought worth recording by, our elite literary sources. Instead, they used a name—Agrippa, Nero, Theodosius—and the promise that it held, in order to win adherents. This had been the pattern for Roman pretenders stretching back to the Republic, as we can see in the case of the false Marius, and even earlier impostors, such as Lucius Equitius, who masqueraded as the illegitimate son of Tiberius Gracchus, the great reformer of the second century BCE. Equitius's imposture, which saw him elected tribune of the plebs, was supported by the Roman people because it was hoped that his alleged bloodline meant he shared the same values as Gracchus.[52]

It is important to emphasize that imperial imposture was not a ubiquitous phenomenon in the Roman world from the first century BCE to the seventh century CE, the period covered by this book. The cases cluster in the first century (14, 31 or 34, 68/69, 79, 88) before reappearing in the late fifth (480s) and the early seventh centuries (602–607/608). Even though they are not exact parallels, since they did not claim to be emperors or an imperial contender, we could add to this list the false Marius, who masqueraded as a cousin of Julius Caesar, and the man who said he was Augustus's nephew Marcellus, both of whom are also located at the beginning of our period. All our rumored imperial returns can be connected to specific political crises, particularly discontent with the current ruler and the end of a dynasty. The false Agrippa Postumus and false Drusus Caesar, whatever the original motivations of the individuals, ultimately reflected unhappiness with Tiberius as the successor to Augustus. The Julio-Claudian family was Rome's first imperial house, and so its abrupt end with the suicide of the childless Nero represented a significant reconfiguration of the political landscape. The emergence of another Procopius Anthemius in the fifth century played on dynastic heritage, while simultaneously exploiting the antipathy toward the eastern emperor Zeno. The seventh-century Theodosius was reputed to be the sole survivor of a family massacre in which his father, Maurice, and brothers perished at the hands of the usurper Phocas. There are clear parallels to these circumstances in world history. Impostors emerged after the fracturing of the Han dynasty in first-century China, the end of the Staufer family and their stranglehold on the office of Holy Roman Emperor in thirteen-century Germany, and the death of Richard III of York and the rise of the Tudors under Henry VII in fifteenth-century England. Likewise, all our Roman pretenders were men, as is common in monarchies that do not accept queens or empresses regnant, for such masquerades would only offer female impostors the opportunity to be exploited for marriage and childbearing by ambitious men.[53]

It may at first seem surprising that Rome did not have many more impostors between the first and seventh centuries, since its imperial dynasties did not tend to be long-lasting. Imperial families that endured for more than a century did not become a feature of Roman imperial rule until the late Byzantine period, as Gilbert Dagron has observed. The longest-reigning imperial family was actually the last, the Palaeologan house, which ruled from 1259 to 1453. We cannot ascribe the lack of impostors to a downturn in charlatanism and fraud more generally, for there continued to be plenty of hucksters masquerading as aristocrats, from the man who impersonated the illustrious second-century senator Quintilius Condianus to the fifth-century decurion Valerianus, who forced his way onto the council of the governor of Syria. There could, of course, be more imperial pretenders who lurk forgotten because they did not warrant attention from our sources or because the evidence is lost to us today. Our knowledge of the Theosebius who impersonated Procopius Anthemius depends on a fragment of John of Antioch, which consists of just twenty-one Greek words.[54]

One potential explanation for the Roman pattern is the nature of imperial deaths and disappearances, which needed to be ambiguous or disbelieved in order to spark rumors that the individuals concerned had survived or escaped from prison. When we look at the sweep of Roman history, it becomes clear why certain periods saw no such rumors and, hence, no impostors. The second century, the age of the Antonine dynasty, had no suspicious imperial deaths, nor did the sixth-century eastern empire, which was ruled largely by men who grew old in office and died in their beds. But there are cases in the third, fourth, and fifth centuries that could fit the bill, including Macrinus, who fled Syria in disguise before being recognized and beheaded in 218; the teenaged Gordian III, who was either murdered by his praetorian prefect or died in battle against the Persians in 244; Trajan Decius and his son, Herennius Etruscus, who vanished heroically while fighting the Goths in 251; Valerian, captured by the Persians in 260; Constans, murdered while out hunting by the supporters of Magnentius in 350; Julian, mortally wounded in a skirmish while retreating from Persia in 363; Valens, who disappeared (presumed dead) at the catastrophic Battle of Adrianople in 378; the cloistered Valentinian II, who died by suicide or at the orders of his general Arbogast in the palace in 392; and even the boy Romulus Augustulus, who was sent into exile in 476 and never heard from again in our sources.

But an emperor also had to have some qualities that made people want to believe that he had survived. Many of the rulers mentioned above were widely disliked (Macrinus and Valens), had disgraced the empire through their capture (Valerian), or were relatively powerless and anemic figures (Valentinian II). An emperor did not have to be universally popular to inspire rumors or impersonation, as the example of Nero shows, since whispers of his return sparked terror and rejoicing in equal manner. The emperor Julian was perhaps the most promising candidate for rumors of survival and imposture in the Neronian vein: not only was he a member of a long-reigning dynasty, but he inspired loyalty and devotion among those who did support him. Ammianus reports that after Julian's death, a former army quartermaster did rouse troops stationed at Reims in Gaul by falsely claiming that the emperor was alive and that "some middle-ranker" had staged a rebellion. The soldiers responded by killing Lucillianus, the father-in-law of the middle-ranker himself, Jovian, who had been sent ahead by the new emperor to secure the region. After this unfortunate incident, there were no further attempts to resurrect Julian. Potential impersonators may have thought it was too risky to take up his mantle of zealous paganism in an empire that was becoming progressively more Christian. When there was a challenge to the next dynasty, the Valentinianic house, it came from Procopius, who was related to Julian on his mother's side. Procopius played on his connections to the Constantinian dynasty, enlisting the support of Constantius II's wife, Faustina, and his daughter, Constantia, to aid his cause. The backing that Procopius attracted does suggest that there was discontent with Valentinian I and his brother Valens, but the preferred method of challenging them was a claim to the purple based on family connections.[55]

One interesting feature of the pattern of Roman imperial impostors was that the majority were not actually reigning Caesars, but descendants and relatives. Pseudo-Marius was the cousin of Julius Caesar, and he was followed by an impersonator of Augustus's nephew Marcellus, then by Augustus's adopted son,

Agrippa, and grandson, Drusus. In Late Antiquity, Procopius Anthemius was the son of the western emperor Anthemius and grandson of the eastern emperor Marcian, while Theodosius was the eldest son of Maurice. Rumors that these men had survived death or escaped prison may have caught on precisely because they offered a certain youthful promise. Nero is the exception to this pattern, since he actually ascended the throne and ruled alone for fourteen years, although he also died young, at the age of thirty. This suggests that the Roman impostor phenomenon was not usually concerned with the return of a reigning emperor who had been assumed to be deceased, but about challenging the new ruler—Tiberius, Zeno, and Phocas, respectively, in our cases—with an alternative candidate who possessed a connection to current or past imperial dynasties. The difference between these impostors and someone like Procopius, who vaunted his connection to the Constantinian family by marriage, was perhaps not so great as we might imagine.[56]

Indeed, there were many other challengers for the purple who made dynastic claims that involved some level of pretense. In the middle of the third century, a priest from Emesa called Sampsigeranus styled himself Lucius Iulius Aurelius Sulpicius Severus Uranius Antoninus, claiming connections with both the Antonine and Severan dynasties, while the fifth-century western usurper Constantine III renamed his sons Constans and Julian to link himself to the Constantinian house. Emperors who successfully claimed the throne were not above playing the same game. Galba, the first non–Julio-Claudian emperor, minted coins associating himself with Augustus's wife, Livia, while Septimius Severus had himself adopted as the son of Marcus Aurelius and renamed his son Septimius Bassianus as Marcus Aurelius Antoninus (known to us as "Caracalla," after the cloak he wore). Elites often poked fun at these dynastic appropriations. Cassius Dio mocked the Severan emperor Elagabalus, officially Marcus Aurellius Antoninus, as the "false Antoninus." But this cynicism from those at the center of power does not negate the importance of dynasty to soldiers and other inhabitants of the empire, who valued names they remembered and trusted.[57]

Although these dynastic claims were frequently made and could be very effective, a prospective imperial candidate did not have to be related to a current or previous emperor in order to claim the purple. All but two of our imperial impostors emerged at the beginning of the empire, claiming membership in the Julio-Claudian dynasty, Rome's first ruling house. This reflects attachment to this particular family as well as a contemporary uncertainty as to whether someone who was not a Julio-Claudian could legitimately claim the purple. But the "Year of the Four Emperors" that followed Nero's demise revealed that it was the support of the army, either the praetorian guard in Rome or the provincial legions, that was the crucial factor in securing the imperial office. "The secret of empire had now been made public—it was possible for an emperor to be made elsewhere than at Rome," as Tacitus astutely observed.[58]

Indeed, the cases of the first and second false Neros (we know too little about the third) reflect the dissonance between popular expectations and the reality of power. The Neros were not controlled by powerful aristocratic forces but emerged on their own initiative in Greece and Asia Minor, where they received support from the poor, the dispossessed, and the opportunistic, the same sort of people who later supported the false John IV in the thirteenth century. This reveals that provincials had a sense that they had a political voice just as much as urban populations. In contrast, the senators who did claim imperial power in the years after Nero's demise—Galba, Otho, Vitellius, and Vespasian—did so with the backing of the army but without the Julio-Claudian name. This established the pattern that henceforth distinguished the monarchical *res publica.* Dynastic connections were desirable for prospective emperors, but they were not an imperative, because emperors could also be chosen by the army, and increasingly in Constantinople of the fifth century and beyond, by different factions at court. This meant that when poor or harassed provincial populations looked for a local leader to represent their interests and offer a change in fortunes, as happened increasingly from the third century onward, they did not necessarily need to be related to a current or past imperial family. As the anonymous author of *On Matters of War* counseled the emperors Valentinian I and Valens, the harsh economic conditions in the provinces could lead to violence and brigandage "and then, ascending up the ladder of criminal behavior, foster usurpers." This was very different from the world of medieval Europe, explored by Robert Bartlett, in which "a political claim was primarily in the person and the blood, much more than in election or divine commission." In Rome, by contrast, election—by the army, the people, or the senate—was an imperative that existed alongside, and competed with, dynastic claims.[59]

Where does this leave the charismatic individuals, charlatans, and con artists who wanted to exploit rumors of an imperial figure's survival or return? It seems that they realized that actually claiming to *be* an emperor was not the best way to do this. Moreover, it could lead to unnecessary complications, including outright civil war or international conflict (as in the case of the third false Nero and the false Theodosius). This explains the centuries of Roman history that had no imperial impostors. Times had changed since the false Marius had sought to lay hands on wealth and status by claiming to be the great general's grandson and

Caesar's cousin. The cutthroat world of Roman imperial politics, in which emperors and dynasties could fall as quickly as they had risen, was not necessarily what charismatic charlatans wanted. Instead, there were numerous other acts of religious and divine imposture that met their need, while also filling the desire for a savior figure among provincial populations. After all, one could claim to be the spirit of Alexander the Great, receive generous food and lodging all at state expense, and then disappear magically into the ether.

CHAPTER 5

Patterns of the Past

Marcus Cornelius Fronto was a man of many apologies. As tutor in Latin rhetoric to Marcus Aurelius, the adopted son and heir of the emperor Antoninus Pius, he was expected to attend events at the imperial court on a regular basis. Members of the senate greeted the emperor daily when he was in Rome, rushing from their houses all over the city to ascend the lofty Palatine Hill. There they would be divided into hierarchical groups to enter "the residence that equals heaven itself," as the poet Martial put it. The court gorged itself on a cornucopia of festivities all year round, from the special New Year's Day celebrations (to which even the common people were admitted) to the formal events marking imperial anniversaries. Yet time and again Fronto sent formal letters to Antoninus Pius and Marcus Aurelius asking that his attendance be excused. His fragile body could not endure the crowds of well-wishers thronging to the palace at New Year, his gouty feet meant that he needed to take the waters rather than join the birthday party for Marcus's children, and neck and shoulder pain kept him away from the celebrations of Pius's imperial anniversary. Some modern historians have pondered if Fronto might have been a hypochondriac, such were the excessive details of his aches and pains that he imparted to his lords and masters, but he was more likely worn out by the exhausting demands of court life.[1]

The celebrations that Fronto did his best to avoid were not restricted to the rarefied air of the imperial court. The Roman religious calendar was festooned with imperial births, accessions, victories, and deaths, many of which were commemorated empire-wide, others by particular cities or regions. The Greek city of Messene staged a three-day festival to welcome Tiberius as emperor, while the prefect of Egypt ordered ten days of compulsory garland-wearing throughout the province to inaugurate the reign of Hadrian. Perhaps the most extravagant form of recognition came from the province of Asia, whose council decreed that Augustus's birthday marked the start of an entire new era of human existence. Rich and poor, rural and urban, men and women all celebrated together, from the workmen hired to carry imperial statues into theaters to the aristocrats who donated painted portraits or held religious offices. There was no escaping these rituals, even if one lived out in the sticks. Every five years, the residents of thirty-five Anatolian villages flocked to the city of Oenoanda in Asia Minor for an agonistic festival, each village choosing a representative to travel there and to sacrifice to the emperor on behalf of their community. Such celebrations were not only enacted in honor of the current ruler and his family, but the entire line of Caesars stretching back to the deified Julius himself, providing that they were judged worthy (some, like Caligula and Elagabalus, were not). The Twentieth Palmyrene Cohort stationed at Dura Europus in eastern Syria, the veritable edge of Roman territory, still performed supplications for Germanicus Caesar two hundred years after his death. These anniversary celebrations, gradually shorn of their pagan accoutrements, continued in Late Antiquity, where they were joined by a proliferation of new Christian imperial ceremonies. Theodosius II's barefoot walk of penitence through the streets of Constantinople as expiation for a devastating earthquake that struck the city in 447 was still commemorated in the tenth century. Although the emperor himself no longer participated, members of the clergy were assigned the thankless task of replicating Theodosius's eleven-kilometer trek to the Hebdomon parade ground. The Roman world marched in step to its emperors.[2]

This beguiling picture of imperial cohesiveness, which transcends multiple boundaries—of geography, chronology, social status, and religious belief—is not inaccurate, but it is only one way of interpreting the evidence. As historians such as Peter Burke and Natalie Zemon Davis have taught us, culture, ritual, and performance are produced just as much by individuals and communities as they are by the apparatus of church and state. Diversity is therefore equally as important as unity. The way Fronto experienced the emperors and their power was different from the Anatolian villagers who flocked to Oenoanda and the soldiers sacrificing at Dura Europos, despite their shared participation in the celebrations of imperial rule. Fronto could absent himself from court through the production of simpering letters of apology written to Caesars he knew well, but no such excuses could be entertained from soldiers or provincials engaged in mandatory garland-wearing or compulsory sacrifices. The ways in which Romans across the empire talked about their rulers were likewise shaped by a variety of social, geographical, cultural, and religious factors.[3]

COURT AND CAPITAL

"Does the Roman tongue ever spare one of the Caesars?" asked Tertullian of Carthage. The theologian, who lived in the late second and early third centuries, thought it was unfair that loyal Christians should be regarded as opponents of the imperial regime, when the residents of the seven hills on the Tiber were renowned for their outspoken criticism and mockery of the emperors. The majority of our evidence for rumor and gossip about emperors comes from Rome and its successor as the heart of the empire, Constantinople. Rome, which had been the location of the major political institutions of the Republic, remained the primary imperial residence from the first to third centuries. After a hiatus in the fourth century, when most emperors resided in provincial imperial cities, Rome returned to prominence as an important seat in the fifth, alongside Ravenna in north Italy. Constantinople was founded by Constantine in 324, but it did not become the permanent residence of the eastern Roman emperor until the Theodosian dynasty made the city its home in the late fourth century. The proportion of evidence stemming from Rome and Constantinople should not surprise us, as major cities have always been hubs for the generation and circulation of rumor and gossip. This is especially the case for monarchical regimes, since rulers and their courts have a special relationship with urban centers, which serve as the principal venues for displaying themselves to, and engaging with, their subjects.[4]

Rome and Constantinople both possessed sizable populations. Rome had approximately one million inhabitants in the period from Augustus to the fourth century, though a series of wars and invasions saw it decline precipitously to about eighty thousand by the sixth. At this point, its eastern neighbor, Constantinople, boasted a population of as many as six hundred thousand people. Both cities were therefore home to a substantial political public that outstripped most other European urban centers before the nineteenth century. To give a sense of comparative scale, by 1800, London had a population of nearly one million and Paris about seven hundred thousand, while other major cities such as Vienna and St. Petersburg numbered approximately two hundred and fifty thousand. The sheer size of our two major Roman capital cities, and the way in which the emperors dominated their social, cultural, and religious fabric, from appearances at the Colosseum and Hippodrome to triumphal arrivals and relic processions, meant that these were the preeminent locations where imperial politics was performed and talked about. Naturally, Rome and Constantinople did not have the same developed print culture as these early modern conurbations, but they were still major centers where people spread and shared news, gossip, and rumor among friends and audiences (Libanius even observed that his letters from Antioch were read aloud in Constantinople). The status of Rome and Constantinople as political and intellectual hubs meant that they were also where the majority of the elites encountered in this book lived and wrote their letters, treatises, sermons, chronicles, and histories. Even more importantly, some of these writers, such as Suetonius and Theophanes, assiduously recorded verbatim samples of elite and popular opinion in poems, acclamations, songs, chants, and graffiti from the court, the street, the theater, and the Hippodrome—priceless fragments of oral discourse that allow us to reconstruct the workings of everyday politics.[5]

In the fourth century, emperors resided in a range of major cities throughout the provinces, especially Antioch in Syria, Nicomedia in Asia Minor, Sirmium in the Balkans, Milan in north Italy, and Trier in Gaul. In the early fifth century, western emperors elevated Ravenna, a swampy military base close to the Adriatic Sea, into an important residence. The imperial presence had an impact on the cities themselves and the wider regions in which they were located, as the emperor, army, and court interacted with—and imposed themselves on—local aristocrats, merchants, farmers, and laborers. Regardless of the burdens, the imperial presence was officially regarded as a privilege—Antioch was most offended when Julian wanted to relocate to Tarsus, for instance. Yet our ability to reconstruct oral discourse about the emperor, both at court and in the cities themselves, is dictated by the patterns of our evidence. None of these cities was consistently the center of intellectual culture and historical writing across the centuries in the same way that Rome and Constantinople were.[6]

We are best informed about Antioch, which served as the primary eastern headquarters of early Roman emperors during their Parthian campaigns. In the second century, Lucius Verus's Greek mistress, Panthea of Smyrna, bedazzled residents with her public processions accompanied by flocks of eunuchs and female slaves, while Caracalla berated Antioch's councilors for their laziness in the third. But the city on the Orontes most memorably blooms into view in the late fourth century, when we are blessed with a cornucopia of contemporary writing from the pens of the rhetorician Libanius, the bishop John Chrysostom, the soldier Ammianus Marcellinus, and the emperor Julian. In contrast, we are not nearly so well-informed about western imperial cities. Our knowledge of oral discourse about the emperor in Milan depends almost entirely on the letters and sermons of the bishop Ambrose, while Trier, the mighty and monumental northern center on the Moselle, remains largely opaque beneath a veneer of panegyric and poetry. Ravenna likewise lacks contemporary records of rumor and gossip, even though the city witnessed many shocking political events, such as the murder of the master of the soldiers, Felix, and his wife, Padusia, on the steps of the Basilica Ursiana, a public assassination that must have provoked frenzied discussion at the time.[7]

These patterns of evidence mean that fourth-century Antioch, and particularly the emperor Julian, have featured prominently throughout this book, but it does not mean that either the city or the emperor were different or exceptional historically. We get a sense of the capacity of the imperial court-in-residence to generate oral discourse wherever it was located from the letters of the fifth-century politician Sidonius Apollinaris. From 459 to 461, the emperor Majorian used the southern Gallic city of Arles, which had replaced Trier as the capital of the Gallic prefecture, as his primary headquarters between his Spanish campaigns. Sidonius described how an anonymous satire attacking prominent individuals, including the parvenu Paeonius, who had risen to the praetorian prefecture from a municipal background, began to circulate at court. The contents of the poem soon became well-known throughout Arles, as Paeonius stirred up his allies against the author, whom he claimed was none other than Sidonius. The news that Sidonius had become something of a pariah at court and in the city reached the ears of the emperor Majorian, who mockingly asked Sidonius to spare him his biting wit at a dinner party. For much of its history, Arles would not have been a place where rumor and gossip moved from court to city and back again, but for those few years in the late fifth century, it was the center of the world.[8]

THE SPACES OF EMPIRE

Imperial visits to all cities got people talking, regardless of whether they were the emperors' usual residences or stopping-off points on a longer journey. Acclamations of appreciation and approval were regular and expected, but the same crowds that praised emperors to the heights could also denigrate them, as Vespasian discovered in Alexandria, whose population had a particularly notorious reputation for outspokenness. The emperor's presence not only meant that he could be assailed in person for policy decisions (hence the heckling of Vespasian over his taxes), but also that people beyond Rome, Constantinople, or other capitals could see what he really looked like. And so it was that when Caracalla visited Alexandria, people noticed that he was not really as physically imposing as his heroes, Alexander and Achilles, and the people of Antioch made fun of Julian when they came face-to-face with his fabulously déclassé beard. Local traditions developed about an emperor's time in particular cities, and these passed down from generation to generation, so that Dio's father heard rumors about Trajan's death at Selinus decades later, the Jewish community of Palestine swapped stories about Diocletian's visit to Caesarea Philippi for generations, and John Chrysostom was able to relate how an emperor long ago had been refused entry to church in Antioch after murdering a child.[9]

News, rumor, and gossip flowed back and forth between the imperial court—or courts, as was often the case—and major cities through official and unofficial communications channels. Fronto, who lived in Italy throughout his years in the imperial service, knew all about the hostile talk regarding the sybaritic behavior of Lucius Verus, his former pupil, in Antioch. The stories reached Fronto through his extensive network of friends and contacts; one of his protégés, Gavius Clarus, was in Syria at the same time as Verus. The people of Alexandria were talking about Caracalla and his treatment of Geta well before he arrived in the city, since his brother's murder and all-encompassing obliteration from public records and imagery had clearly made a significant impact on the Egyptian imagination. But Caracalla also knew what the Alexandrians were saying about him, probably through advance letters sent to him by the prefect or one of his subordinates. (A century later, Constantine would officially decree that all provincial acclamations should be reported to him, as part of a wider move to monitor popular sentiment.)[10]

There was no sophisticated communications network composed of newspapers, television, and the Internet to integrate the different regions of the empire. But the spread of information and speculation did extend beyond the major centers in which emperors resided. These included Nemausus in Gaul (910 kilometers from Rome by land, slightly longer by sea), where people knew of Tiberius's self-exile on Rhodes; Caralis in Sardinia (460 kilometers from Rome by sea), where the governor Raecius Constans pulled down Plautianus's statues; and Carthage in North Africa (625 kilometers from Rome by sea), where the bishop Cyprian had heard whispers of Valerian's new persecution measures. When Jovian arrived at Nisibis on August 20, 363, the residents had already heard the terrible news that the city was to be handed over to the Persians, which had been agreed upon during negotiations that occurred between July 8 and 11 near Dura (356 kilometers to the south of Nisibis, about a twelve-day journey by road). Now, we know that when Jovian was at Ur (about 150 kilometers away from Nisibis) between August 9 and 11, he sent messengers to all governors and military commanders announcing Julian's death and his own accession. Ammianus wrote that the news of the peace treaty reached Nisibis *before* these official couriers, perhaps through travelers, traders, or camp followers who had left the army behind, though it is equally possible—since Ammianus remained with Jovian's army and did not know precisely what was said—that the messengers themselves let the news slip. We should not presume that communication on these and other occasions happened directly through one letter or interlocutor. For example, the report from Constantinople that Valens's new bishop, Demophilus, was making a show of support for Nicene orthodoxy was spread first by travelers from the city making their way to Caesarea in Cappadocia (a journey of some 920 kilometers). There they passed the news orally to Basil, before he sent the details in a letter to Eusebius, bishop of Samosata, which lay to the southeast of Caesarea, almost six hundred kilometers by road.[11]

We can get a better sense of the complexities of disseminating rumor about Roman emperors when we turn our attention from major cities to the regions. Networks very much depended on local contacts. Some provincial communities were fortunate enough to have an immediate connection in the emperor's retinue, as was the case of the villagers of Skaptopara in Thrace. Their petition was presented to the emperor Gordian III by the local landowner and praetorian soldier Aurelius Pyrrhus. Less fortunate was Lollianus, a grammarian from Oxyrhynchus in Egypt, who wanted to complain to Valerian and Gallienus that his salary was being paid in weevil-ridden grain. He tried to reach the emperors' munificent ears through many contacts, including a military officer and a man he called "brother," who reportedly knew the consuls. We have no idea if Lollianus's plea was ultimately successful, or if he was forever doomed to a diet of insect protein. But these were the types of networks along which news and rumor flowed, potentially keeping people informed of, or speculating about, happenings at court and vice-versa. They show that towns and villages in Thrace and Egypt could be recipients of political news from Rome, even if it was not on a regular basis.[12]

We do have to bear in mind the time communication took. Ammon, a lawyer from Panopolis in Egypt, lamented that a report of the death of his brother, Harpocration, a panegyrist at the court of Constantius II, had taken so long to reach him that another official with advance knowledge of his passing had already come to Alexandria to claim his brother's enslaved workers. Reports were also liable to distortion and inaccuracies over long distances. In the late fifth century, Hydatius, bishop of Aquae Flaviae in northwestern Spain, heard that in Constantinople, the powerful general Aspar had been dismissed from his position and that his son Ardaburius had been executed for conspiring with the Vandals. This report, which Hydatius had heard from ambassadors of the local Suevic king Remismund, was more rumor than accurate news. For it was actually Ardaburius who had been removed from his command, and both father and son remained very much alive for several more years. Perhaps what is even more startling is that the Spanish bishop was able to write much at all about Constantinople, which lay almost four thousand kilometers to the east. Despite being a member of the ecclesiastical hierarchy, Hydatius's writings show no evidence of knowing the outcome of the Council of Chalcedon of 451, which attempted to resolve Christological disputes within the Church. Sometimes news and rumor were only transmitted by luck.[13]

There was, of course, a vast world below the literate and educated elite where oral discourse was not merely one of several channels of communication, but the *primary* one. We should not presume that all rural communities were really as innocent as depicted in Synesius's satirical pastiche of village life in Cyrenaica, where, he claimed, people knew that there was an emperor (for they paid him taxes), but many thought he was Agamemnon, the mythical Homeric king of Mycenae. Even illiterate villagers had to swear oaths in the name of the emperor, as documented for the inhabitants of fifth-century Caranis in Egypt, who swore by Valentinian III and Theodosius II that they would not take water illegally. The peasants of Skaptopara in Thrace did certainly know that Gordian III was emperor and gave him the correct imperial titles, which was no mere feat, given he was the last of six emperors to reign in the year they wrote their petition. This was the sort of information that it was important to get right, so illiterates usually hired a scribe to ensure that their plea reached the right ears and was correctly dated. Beyond these interactions with the world of officialdom, most information derived from oral circulation of news and rumor. This could be communicated through traveling court officials, who did often stay in villages along their routes, and through local political or religious leaders. (One wonders what the Egyptian bishop Hermammon told his congregation after receiving a letter from Dionysius of Alexandria claiming that Valerian had murdered babies and examined their entrails.) Information, rumor, and gossip could spread through various forms of community networks and the casual encounters known as "weak ties," as demonstrated by the many Jewish tales about

Roman emperors, their taxes, punishments, and incredible deeds, or indeed the whispers heard throughout Italy that Agrippa Postumus had not been killed on Planasia.[14]

DISTRIBUTION PATTERNS

Even though news, rumor, and gossip about emperors could move through various networks of contacts and couriers, this did not mean that all items of information *did* travel, nor that they were all of equal concern throughout the empire. The topic with the highest level of interest, and correspondingly, the furthest reach geographically, was the death of the emperor. This was news that was officially announced throughout the empire (sometimes with a strategic delay), but the widespread possible consequences of an imperial death—the rise and fall of officials, a succession crisis, and even civil war—meant that sense-making rumors flourished in anticipation of, and in response to, the passing of a ruler or a member of his family. Speculation could potentially encompass the court (Was Jovian poisoned?), the city (We haven't seen Justinian for days—is he dead?), and the provinces (Caligula's sickness will bring ruin and civil war!). But some rumors had very local circulation and outcomes. It is telling, for example, that no false Nero arose at Rome itself, but that rumors of his survival and the impostors who pursued their deceptions appeared in the Greek islands and highlands of Asia Minor, where there was genuine enthusiasm for a returning savior. In seventh-century Egypt, according to the bishop John of Nikiu, people believed that Heraclius had perished because his coinage was filled with images of his family, leaving no room for the name of the Roman empire. Such a story may seem implausible to us, but it was generated and shaped by contemporary conceptions of power and divine justice among Egyptian Christians.[15]

The emperor's decisions about the fundamentals of life, both secular and spiritual, were of high interest throughout the Roman world. Declarations of war, imposition of taxes, matters of food supply and prices, and religious policies had equal resonance in Trier and Tarsus. Imperial edicts had general application throughout the empire, and senatorial decrees and imperial letters could likewise achieve wide circulation. The senate ordered that the *Senatorial Decree concerning Gnaeus Piso the Elder* be displayed in all cities, and Elagabalus's letter on his divorce turned up in the sands of Egypt. Decisions and proclamations were awaited with due trepidation and terror, but their distribution was not necessarily fast. In the fourth century, edicts took a median travel time of 134 days to be transmitted from the imperial court to North Africa, communication being especially slow in winter. This vacuum was filled by rumor and speculation. Few people had the resources of Cyprian, bishop of Carthage, to be able to send a delegation to Rome to discover exactly what the senate had decreed, and often, when decisions rested in the emperor's hands, as was the case with Theodosius's punishment of the people of Antioch, contacts at court were not useful, because they could not read the emperor's mind. Such rumors could also be generated by malicious forces, like the Donatists who wanted the inhabitants of North Africa to believe that Honorius had not been signing his own edicts, which invalidated his legislation. While our evidence for these rumors for the most part comes from the pens of our elite writers, Romans did not need to be literate to spread, hear, or believe these falsehoods or items of speculation.[16]

Indeed, there was significant talk about the capabilities and limits of imperial power in capitals, urban centers, and the regions. Sometimes this was spread by elites giving speeches, such as Dio Chrysostom, who declaimed about Domitian's tyrannical behavior at Athens and Prusa, or priests like Ephrem the Syrian, who had his congregation in Edessa singing hymns about Julian's malfeasances. That is not to say that all this discussion exhibits a detailed knowledge of an emperor's deeds and policies. In the *Sibylline Oracles,* Nero is portrayed as a matricide, actor, and attempted cutter of the Isthmus of Corinth, several key facts that were then spun into a larger web of imagination and prophecy. The power of folklore and myth to influence conceptions of imperial power meant that Plotina could be imagined as anti-Jewish in the Jews' own oral tales, but pro-Jewish in Greek Alexandrian texts. These stories were united by the common belief that women were unsuitable influences on emperors.[17]

Emperors' deaths, decrees, and decisions were of wide interest across urban, provincial, and rural contexts because they had real potential to affect people's lives. The same cannot be said for gossip (and sometimes rumor) that discussed the emperors' personal habits, foibles, or appearance. Gossip was certainly an important way for Romans to assess an individual emperor's fitness to rule, but it was very much concentrated in Rome, Constantinople, and other major cities that served as imperial residences. In these urban contexts, courtiers made jokes about sexual behavior and wrote witty ditties about imperial relationships, and audiences laughed at lines in the theater or chanted lewd lyrics in the Hippodrome. Caligula's hairiness and Commodus's hernia were sniggered about in Rome, but were they regularly discussed in the taverns of Gaul or the marshes along the Nile? There is no evidence that they were, nor should we automatically assume this was the case. People far away from the center could not see the real emperor and his physical imperfections, only his idealized image on coins and the statues to which they propitiated and prayed. The consistently negative gossip about Caligula and Commodus that survives is largely the product of the urban environment of Rome and the interaction between court and capital (even Philo's embassy encounters can be located in this milieu). That does not mean that such talk and banter did not take place when the real-life emperor came to town, as Caracalla found out in Alexandria, but it was probably not the general rule. Caligula was certainly hated by the Jewish population for his actions regarding their temple, but there is no evidence that critical discourse in Judaea itself focused on his body or sexual proclivities.[18]

All royal courts have their gossip and scandals, even the insular Japanese royal establishment, but their "publics" differ. Sometimes they consist of only the court and the aristocracy, while other times, as in today's mediated scandals, these stories can potentially encompass the entire nation or world. In the Roman empire, gossip about the sex lives of the emperors, and the scandal this could generate, was largely confined to the great cities. The people of Rome protested Domitian's treatment of his wife, Domitia, and the citizens of Constantinople condemned Martina's marriage with her uncle Heraclius as incestuous, but we have little evidence for such topics being talked about in regional towns, villages, and the countryside. This is perhaps surprising given the close connection between sex and the succession, which was of widespread interest because of its potential political impact. It is also a very different picture from that recorded for later European monarchical societies. Gossip in England about children supposedly born to Elizabeth I and her lover, Robert Dudley, had far reach throughout the country, and tales of depravity at the French Bourbon court made their way into printed books that circulated outside Paris. Is this absence of evidence, or evidence of absence? The Roman picture could certainly be the result of our fragmentary historical archive, since the majority of our texts come from the literate elite of the cities, who were most likely to report on events that took place there. We lack good records from more rural areas, such as the court transcripts available to scholars of early modern England. Oral traditions, fables, and proverbs, our best guide to how people perceived Roman authority beyond the centers, are mostly concerned with the workings of power rather than sexual peccadillos. The Jewish story about Titus having sex with a prostitute in the Temple of Jerusalem was not based on contemporary gossip but was a piece of invective targeting the profanation of sacrality that Titus's sordid behavior represented.[19]

There is some epigraphic and papyrological evidence that should give us pause about ruling out the wider spread of sexual gossip entirely. We turn first to

Pompeii, where graffiti in the peristyle of the House of Marcus Lucretius identify two individuals, Ianuarius and Restitutus, as "belonging to Nero" (presumably because they were enslaved or freedmen members of his household). Beneath these graffiti, an unknown individual or individuals added two more graffiti, identifying Ianuarius and Restitutus as *cinaedi*, men who liked to be penetrated anally. The accusation that Nero had *cinaedi* in his entourage might be straightforward invective, designed to criticize the emperor by association, but it could also be a response to gossip about Nero's liaisons with other men. While Nero was likely the active partner in his relationship with Sporus (whom the emperor castrated), he is also reported to have married the freedman Doryphorus, by whom the emperor himself was sexually penetrated. Nero's sexual liaisons were certainly a topic of discussion during his reign and the decades afterward. Writing in the early second century, the biographer Suetonius claimed, "I have ascertained from several individuals that Nero was of the firm belief that no man is undefiled and unstained in any part of his body." Could similar conversations have been taking place in Pompeii decades earlier, prompted by the visit of Nero and his entourage there in 64? Our second piece of evidence comes from the sands of Egypt. A horoscope cast at Oxyrhynchus in the mid-third century for a certain Apolinarius, who was born in the second year of Elagabalus's reign, describes the emperor "Antoninus the *koruf(os)*." The abusive Greek term may mean "catamite," and at the very least has a lewd connotation; it is also possible that the same word appears on two other Egyptian horoscopes, though they are very fragmentary. There is also a planetary table, which comes from late third-century Oxyrhynchus, that describes Elagabalus as "the sacrilegious little Antoninus," in contrast with his more traditionally minded successor, who is simply called Alexander. Elagabalus did announce the dissolution of his marriage to a Vestal Virgin in Egypt (and presumably the rest of the empire), which provides a context for his sexual and religious behavior catching the eye of Egyptian astrologers even in later decades.[20]

Rumors about the Roman emperor—chiefly his death, the succession, and key financial and religious policies—therefore had the potential to circulate widely across the empire, while gossip about his appearance, character, and sexual life was more restricted, largely confined to the court and the cities in which he lived before the eyes of the people. Distal gossip about Roman emperors did not regularly travel as far as chatter about the Tudors or Bourbons, let alone the Windsors or Trumps today (the Pompeii and Oxyrhynchus examples being the exceptions that prove the rule). There was, of course, no way in which a true mediated sex or relationship scandal—which, as we now conceive of it, requires print or electronic media with wide communicative capacities—could occur in the Roman world. This does not mean that rumors that had wide geographical reach were necessarily well-informed or based on a detailed knowledge of political events. Instead, they were shaped by traditional frameworks of knowledge about kings that emerged from the world of fables, proverbs, and maxims, both secular and biblical. These taught Romans that rulers always had others at their mercy.

HIGH AND LOW

When the bishop Epiphanius returned from Rome to his hometown of Ticinum (modern-day Pavia) in early 471, he received a jubilant reception from the populace. They had heard that he had successfully brokered a peace treaty between the emperor Anthemius and his general Flavius Ricimer. The precise details of the delicate political situation would not have been known to the residents of Ticinum, but the feud between the emperor and his general did matter, because it could have resulted in civil war consuming Italy, its inhabitants, their livelihoods, and their dreams. As it happened, the peace treaty was swiftly broken, and a mere five years later Ticinum itself would go up in flames in the course of another civil war, this one between the Roman general Orestes and the Germanic leader Odoacer. News of imperial politics not only spread geographically, from Rome to Ticinum, but also up and down the social spectrum, from generals and bishops to ordinary townspeople.[21]

The emperor's death, the question of the succession, and his capacity to make decisions about war, the economy, and religion, were of interest regardless of one's place in the social hierarchy, though each of these issues affected people in different ways. The unexpected death of an emperor could result in suspicions of murder and conspiracy, with the court consumed by discussion as to who the successor might be. But merchants might be concerned about a potential civil war interrupting their supply chains, and ordinary people about the continuing arrival of grain—hence the run on bread in Constantinople after its residents thought that Justinian had passed away. Landowners focused on specific policies that affected their income, such as Domitian's vine edicts, while the shopkeepers of Antioch despised Julian because he had capped the price at which they could sell their goods. Talk about these issues could result in various forms of popular unrest, as when people in Rome cried out, "Give us back Germanicus!" after the death of their favorite prince, and shouted, "The gods have gobbled up our grain!" at the young Caesar's insensitive revelry during a food shortage.

The question of the imperial succession and government policies were closely connected, which meant that the death of an emperor was often welcomed as an opportunity for change. The Nicene clerics of Asia Minor celebrated Valens's fiery demise at Adrianople, and the anti-Chalcedonian populace of Alexandria used the death of Marcian as an opportunity to unseat their bishop. Even if we need to acknowledge that leaders, both secular and ecclesiastical, very often whipped up the crowds to do their bidding, as Ambrose did in Milan when he tried to turn the populace against Valentinian II and Justina, they were appealing to, and fermenting, feelings that already existed. The same point can be made about imperial impostors who were exploited by higher powers. The false Agrippa and false Drusus were supported by aristocrats discontented with Tiberius, and two of the false Neros and the false Theodosius by the Parthian and Persian empires. But this did not change the basic fact that the existence and success of these charlatans depended on people believing the rumors that young imperial princes or emperors still lived.[22]

The Roman imperial court generated tales and anecdotes about the emperor's murders, his sexual indiscretions, and his childlessness, as courtiers fretted about their chances of promotion—or survival. Anonymous witticisms were the preferred way of criticizing the emperor; even Constantine's praetorian prefect Ablabius was thought to have lampooned his master's familial slaughter in this fashion. Much court gossip was collected, written down, and preserved for posterity, whether in the collections of Julia's jokes, the sayings of Elagabalus, or Seneca's witty account of Claudius's "Pumpkinification." Even the popular verses that circulated openly in written and oral form in Rome show enough knowledge of court politics, and were composed in a sufficiently polished literary style, to suggest that they had an elite origin, bringing the gossip of the palace to the people. Aristocratic courtiers, despite their propensity to engage in such talk, did not usually classify this gossip as proper political discussion. Seneca the Younger, who successfully lurched between the courts of Caligula, Claudius, and Nero before the latter ordered his suicide, contrasted the "best men" who attended the senate all day with those who "wasted away their time in some discussion circle." Seneca and his ilk may have despised these "circles," but they were certainly content to deploy their alleged conversations and political judgments to criticize an emperor. Tacitus, in his innuendo-laden account of the final days of his father-in-law, the illustrious senator Cn. Iulius Agricola, wrote that the people of Rome talked of his demise "in public places and in discussion circles." These venues allowed the "constant rumor" that Agricola had been poisoned by the emperor Domitian to flourish, and by committing the rumor to writing, Tacitus ensured that aspersions would continue to be cast on the emperor for centuries to come.[23]

Senators and other elites often complained about the circus and the arena, but it was through these venues that kingship was negotiated as much as in philosophical treatises and histories. In his famous digression on the habits of the populace of Rome, Ammianus mocked old men who claimed that "the *res publica* would not be able to stand firm" if their favorite charioteers failed to perform on the day. This remark not only satirized traditional state rhetoric about the continuance of the *res publica,* but also implicitly acknowledged that these circles did have wider, political importance. In the monarchical state, entertainment venues became the preeminent political arena in Rome, Constantinople, and other major cities, enabling the whispers of rumor and gossip exchanged behind the emperor's back to openly manifest in popular protests calling him to account. When Tiberius stole Lysippus's famous Apoxyomenos statue from the Baths of Agrippa and installed it in his own bedroom, enough people in Rome knew what had happened to stage a successful protest in the theater. The theatrical laughter and reactions to Augustus the *cinaedus,* Tiberius the old goat, and Galba as the villa owner Onesimus all show how talk could be transformed into other forms of popular criticism. Verses and ditties could be invented on the spot, as the supportive acclamations of the theater and Hippodrome were appropriated for new purposes. Jesting about Tiberius's fondness for oral sex or Phocas's drunkenness was not the same form of political engagement as speeches in the senate or the emperor's council, but it was still political talk through which Romans articulated their views about appropriate monarchical behavior. In Constantinople, the chants and protests of the circus factions—the "Blues" and "Greens"—arguably became the most important element of popular political discourse because the emperors themselves used the Hippodrome as a primary arena in which they were acclaimed before the people. It was entirely appropriate that it was in the Hippodrome that the Blue faction chanted that the inexperienced centurion-turned-emperor Phocas should go and find out the proper ceremonial protocols from his predecessor, Maurice.[24]

There was considerable unity in the way in which elites and non-elites envisioned the emperor in conversations at aristocratic dinner parties, church sermons, and regional stories about imperial visits. The idea that the emperor was prone to manipulation by women and advisors was shared by courtiers in the know, as well as people much lower down the social spectrum, because it conformed to their ideas, gleaned from histories, fables, myths, and the Bible, about how power worked. When Jerome repeated and endorsed the rumor that Valentinian II had been murdered by his general Arbogast, he was motivated by these preconceptions, rather than a detailed appreciation of court politics (which would have suggested that Arbogast would never have killed his own puppet). The idea of the emperor as a vicious murderer was shared by the people of Rome, who laughed (nervously) at Nero's matricidal tendencies; the courtiers of Hadrian and Julian, who suspected them of doing away with their nearest and dearest; and even John Chrysostom, who shared with his flock that an unnamed emperor had exposed his wife on the mountainside to be eaten by wild beasts. Sometimes these stories represented widespread—though not necessarily universal—discontent with a specific ruler (Nero being a prime example), whereas in other cases oral discourse was harnessed to make a point about emperors in general and did not necessarily damage an individual ruler's overall reputation. (Chrysostom tactfully did not mention to his congregation that Constantine was the unnamed emperor who committed uxoricide.)

Men and women of high and low status likewise shared fantasies of punishing the emperor, whether they were courtiers who laughed at Claudius being condemned to a life of servitude as the subordinate of Caligula's freedman, or the Jews who imagined Titus having his head gnawed incessantly by a giant gnat. The emperor's sex life and body peculiarities were popular topics of discussion, not only because they were inherently funny to people from all walks of life, but also because they functioned as an effective everyday way of critiquing, and negotiating the boundaries of, imperial power. Commodus's bloated bowel and swollen scrotum were the very embodiment of Bakhtinian "low" bodily humor, which had wide popular appeal, but the jokes and chants also had a serious element, taking the shine off the emperor's Herculean pretensions. However, as Peter Burke has reminded us, the existence of shared cultural frames of reference should not obscure variety and diversity in how ideas were expressed. There is no clear correspondence, for instance, between Suetonius's description of emperors, their appearances and their foibles, and the bodily imperfections criticized in the city of Rome in the form of verses, chants, and abusive shouts. Nor did physical characteristics all have the same meaning—many people found hirsuteness and hairlessness funny or strange, but the exact reasons for doing so depended on their own cultural or religious backgrounds.

The interpretation of jokes and barbs likewise varied according to culture and education. When the new emperor Jovian reached Antioch in early October 363, having marched his army back from Persian territory, he was greeted with songs, jests, and pamphlets because the population already knew (probably from soldiers, traders, or travelers) that he had surrendered Nisibis in a humiliating peace treaty. The pamphlets—some strewn in the streets, others posted on buildings—adapted lines from Homer's *Iliad,* comparing the young and dissolute Jovian to the Trojan prince Paris: "You returned from the war: better than you had perished there" (originally spoken by Helen to Paris), and "Unhappy Paris, so pretty to behold" (Hector to Paris). Another, slightly longer, barb adapted Odysseus's line to the old Thersites by suggesting that Jovian should be deprived of the clothes with which he had attempted to hide the shame of his defeat, after which he ought to be handed over to Persians. Such insults were authored by, and could be best appreciated by, men and women with the knowledge of the *Iliad* and Paris's handsome, yet unwarlike, character. But they also functioned in and of themselves as indictments of the cowardice of Rome's handsome new emperor, so that all who heard, shared, and shouted them could revel in the message. We should not dismiss these criticisms as empty jests. They were probably manifestations of real fears and anxieties among the people of Antioch. Jovian's treaty that had surrendered Roman territory made the city more vulnerable to Persian incursions. These emotions were the mirror image of the joy felt by the people of Ticinum after the signing of the pact between Ricimer and Anthemius.[25]

So far, we have largely remained enclosed within the walls of the major imperial cities, which emphasizes once more the important connection between emperors and the urban audience, though our evidence does at least show that in these cities, talking about the emperors occurred up and down the social hierarchy. If we move outward beyond Rome, Constantinople, Antioch, and other imperial residences, while remaining in the broad social category of the literate and educated, we can get glimpses of discussions about the emperors. Clerics such as Augustine of Hippo in North Africa and Basil of Caesarea in Cappadocia tried to stay informed, through their ecclesiastical and court networks, of the emperor's decisions and key events in Rome, Ravenna, and Constantinople. This gathering and exchanging of news and rumor about what the emperor had done, and what he might be capable of doing, should be distinguished from gossiping about the Caesars. Evaluative social talk did certainly occur. Ephrem the Syrian knew many details of Julian's private life, and it is inconceivable, for example, that Nestorius, the deposed bishop of Constantinople, did not share with his supporters the tale that Augusta Eudocia's departure for the Holy Land was the result of an adulterous affair. But it is probable that outside the major imperial residences, emperors more often had a supporting role in the gossip of elite circles, which would have focused predominantly on local affairs and personalities. Dio Chrysostom complained that he was the subject of malicious gossip circulating in his home city of Prusa, which intimated that his embassy to Trajan had not been well received. Chrysostom, who plumed himself on his intimacy with emperors, lamented that all this talk was part of a whispering campaign to discredit his building plans for the city. Trajan did feature in these conversations, but the gossip was actually about Chrysostom himself.[26]

THE RURAL PERSPECTIVE?

Only about five percent of the empire's population lived in cities. As one moved further away from urban centers into small towns, villages, and religious communities—and also down the social ladder, beyond the clerics, councilors, and judges with connections to the provincial and imperial establishments to the laborers, farmers, and monks—the Roman emperor remained relevant in different ways. He was a symbol of continuity and justice, a ruler and warrior who kept foreign invaders at bay, and who could be called upon to right local wrongs. Even an enslaved person was able to run and grasp an image of the emperor in the marketplace and protest their treatment by their master. Representatives of local communities sent petitions and embassies to the court to seek redress, often at great personal expense (both Synesius of Cyrene and Dioscorus of Aphrodito remained in Constantinople for three years while trying to press their cases). The false Agrippa Postumus gained support among the inhabitants of Italy, Drusus of Greece, the second pseudo-Nero of Asia Minor, and Procopius Anthemius of the East. Yet the provincial image of the emperor was not wholly positive. Rumors about emperors and their cruel capabilities did circulate in the regions. Jewish oral tradition represented many Caesars in a hostile fashion and mourned the brutal and barbaric punishments meted out by Trajan and Hadrian. These tales embodied a real fear that the emperor's military power could not only be directed against foreign invaders, but also against his own people.[27]

The emperor's administrative decisions had a powerful local impact. Basil, bishop of Caesarea, reacted strongly to news of Valens's plan to divide the Anatolian provinces, because it would reduce the size of his episcopal see. Smaller provinces also meant more government officials to enforce the law and to oversee the collection of taxes. This fear is memorably brought to life in Lactantius's complaints about Diocletian "cutting the provinces into morsels," and the emperor's imposition of a new census to improve the flow of income to the imperial treasury. Yet this was not mere rhetoric from a hostile Christian professor. The story about how the Jews appealed to Diocletian to reduce taxes or they would be forced to leave their homes attests to the real consequences that these decisions could have on local communities. This is vividly brought to life by rumors about military recruitment and the taxation associated with it. In mid-fourth-century Egypt, the tax collector Dorotheus wrote to his brother Papnuthis, also a collector, asking him to send money urgently, "since a rumor has emerged about the tax on recruits and everyone is looking for gold *solidi* and the price is going up every day." In Late Antiquity, landowners either had to supply men for the army from their estates or pay gold in lieu, so the suspicion that the emperor needed recruits had an impact on Egyptians from all walks of life. The potential for state intervention to generate rumors among the rural populace is supported by comparative evidence from more recent, and better documented, periods of history. In nineteenth-century India, for example, the British Raj's decision to conduct the census gave rise to different rumors in Bihar province. One claimed that new taxes were about to be introduced, another that the British intended to conscript locals. In the Roman provincial imagination, emperors were considered both guarantors of safety and stability as well as enforcers of punishment and taxation.[28]

Rumors about imperial powers and government decisions need to be separated from evaluative gossip about the emperor's character, body, and sexual habits. As we move along this geographical and social axis, outward from the major cities to villages and smallholdings, and down the social spectrum, gossip about the emperors' private lives largely recedes behind local concerns, the relationships and rivalries that mattered within communities, organizations, and families. Egyptian papyri, which provide our best insight into people's daily lives and preoccupations, contain little evidence for talk about Roman emperors (except for the horoscope featuring Elagabalus the catamite). Instead, local gossip in the regions concerned the sexual adventures of men and women, marriage preparations and the size of dowries, women who deceived their husbands, enslaved people talking about their mistresses, questions of inheritance and disinheritance, suspicions about neighbors' backgrounds, tales of social mobility, who was joining the army or priesthood, squabbles with landlords, the crimes of drunken soldiers or local vagrants, women describing beatings by their husbands, and reports of marauding outsiders who raped local women. It was a rare person who could boast on their tombstone that "harsh tongues had never injured them with a single accusation," as one African harvester claimed. When gossip on these personal topics moved beyond the private sphere into the public arena, it became local scandal, as when the small village of Azitta in Anatolia was gripped by rumors that a certain Jucundus had been poisoned by his mother-in-law. We might compare the situation with that on Nukulaelae Atoll in Tuvalu, as studied by the anthropologist Niko Besnier. Although the Tuvalu government's decisions did have an impact on the island, most of the gossip actually revolved around local issues, personalities, and relationships. In the Roman world, gossip about the emperor was likewise focused on the aristocracy, the court, and to some extent also the cities in which he lived; in other communities, especially rural and provincial ones, the emperor was likely but one topic of gossip among many, and usually not the most important one at that.[29]

POLICING TALK

The extent and circulation of imperial gossip has implications for understanding the aims and power of the Roman imperial monarchy. Roman emperors, as a rule, were not deaf to what people said about them. From the reign of Augustus onward, Romans could be prosecuted for the crime of defamation, including speaking ill of the emperor or other illustrious men and women. Political rivals deployed gossip about the emperor, or accusations of gossiping, against each other. In 15, the proconsul of Bithynia, Granius Marcellus, was accused by his quaestor Caepio Crispinus of engaging in improper discussions about Tiberius. According to Tacitus's account, Crispinus chose "from the most disgusting aspects of the emperor's behavior" and presented them to the senate as if they had come from Marcellus's own mouth. Yet the only individuals who were usually prosecuted for such seditious and defamatory talk were aristocrats and imperial officials. Evidence from lower down the social spectrum is limited. A rare example from Augustus's reign concerns a Cassius Patavinus, described by Suetonius as "one of the people," who announced at a dinner that he had both the desire and the fortitude to kill Augustus. He was promptly exiled. But the decision as to whether to prosecute seditious talk was up to the individual emperor, even in the supposedly more authoritarian world of Late Antiquity. Constantius II's notorious court weasel Paul "The Chain" earned his nickname for linking together accusations to build cases against other government officials, which appealed to the nature of the suspicious emperor. Yet in 393, the emperors Theodosius I, Arcadius, and Honorius made a quite different ruling in response to a query from the praetorian prefect Rufinus about a man who had abused the emperor while drunk. The emperors decreed that if the inebriated man had been high-spirited or insane, or had simply wanted to insult them, then his talk was not treasonable, but they asked Rufinus to refer the exact words to them for closer examination.[30]

This perhaps explains why we do not have extensive evidence for ordinary Romans denouncing each other for gossiping about or speaking ill of the emperor. The most likely source for this kind of behavior would be the records of trials and petitions preserved on papyri from Egypt. In medieval and early modern England, defamatory and seditious talk against the monarch by ordinary people—ranging from calling the king a "son of a whore" to genuine plots against his life—shows up frequently in legal records because English men and women denounced each other to the state. But our Roman papyri are silent on such matters. Our conclusion should not be that Romans did not talk about their emperors in negative terms (they plainly did), but that this talk was not the basis for accusations of treason at the local level. This stands in contrast with the denunciations of neighbors to the state for being Christians (in the early empire) or espousing heretical theological views (in Late Antiquity), which often emerged from gossip about members of the community. Despite the aims of Roman legislation on verbal defamation of the emperor, neither individuals nor the state cared enough about this issue to police it to the same extent across all regions and social levels.[31]

Such a conclusion reminds us that the world of Tiberian treason trials as depicted in Tacitus's *Annals* and other elite texts, which pondered the difficulties of free speech under the emperors, do not capture the complete Roman experience. Indeed, *delatores* ("informers") were primarily creatures of the imperial court and its satellites, in which elites accused each other of defaming the emperor as a political tactic. *Delatores* could certainly be found among the non-elites—the law codes reveal fears that enslaved people in particular could be turned against their masters—but their targets were always from the upper echelons of society. The imperial freedman Epictetus did tell an anecdote about a man who sat down in the theater, only to make uncomplimentary remarks about the emperor to his neighbor, a soldier in disguise. The hapless talker was then dragged off to meet his maker. But this strikes me as the experience of a courtier transposed to a theatrical setting, rather than reflecting universal fear of slandering the emperor or genuine surveillance of gossiping theatergoers. We should not assume that the Roman empire operated like modern authoritarian regimes, such as Stalinist Russia, Communist East Germany, or North Korea, and shared their totalitarian trappings of censorship and secret police.[32]

Individual rulers can have an impact on the exercise of free speech within a particular society. The English cycle of surveillance and denunciation intensified during the reign of Henry VIII, for instance, while in eighteenth-century Germany, liability to prosecution increased if one was a subject of Eberhard

Ludwig, duke of Württemberg, who forbade anyone to spread rumors about himself, and imposed stiff penalties on all those found contravening the law. Some monarchical states have undergone general intensification of the investigation of, or punishment for, loose speech over time. The Ottoman empire increased its surveillance of people in the mid-nineteenth century as a way of sampling public opinion, at the same time that the sultan himself was becoming more of a public figure. In early modern France, the crime of *lèse-majesté* was, as at Rome, largely focused on monitoring the aristocracy, but after an attempt on Louis XV's life in 1757, officials were commanded to monitor towns and villages for seditious talk. The Roman imperial government did show a stronger interest in popular views in Late Antiquity, but this focused on collective expressions and acclamations that had to be reported to the emperor (similar to agents in the Han Chinese empire who were entrusted with recording popular rhymes). Beyond the elite level of government and court, everyday talk about emperors remained political, in the sense that it commented on a ruler's policies and character, but it was not usually regarded as a crime worthy of denouncing friends and neighbors to the state.[33]

LACUNAE AND LIMITATIONS

There are surprising gaps and omissions in our evidence, including several topics that I would have expected to feature more prominently as subjects of rumor and gossip. One of these is military ability, such as the emperor's bravery or cowardice, talents as a general, and conduct as a leader on the battlefield. This is especially surprising given the importance of *virtus*—"manliness" and "courage"—to the imperial image. The fortitude of the young Caesar was certainly contested during the civil wars of the late Republic, as he was the subject of numerous accusations of cowardice by his opponents Marcus Antonius and Sextus Pompeius. In his first autobiography, *On His Life,* completed in the mid-20s BCE, Augustus took the opportunity to defend himself against these charges. Thereafter the evidence for contemporary discussion is less comprehensive, as we must exclude assessments of military campaigns or imperial bravery that feature only as the opinions of individual historians, unless they specifically mention eyewitness accounts or conversations. Suetonius's account of Caligula's pale body, which those with knowledge of physiognomy would have taken as a sign of cowardice, must also be set aside. There are hints of talk about imperial leadership qualities in the poem about Nero as Apollo the singer that circulated through Rome, but the pickings are generally very slim.[34]

One of the problems is recovering the voices of the soldiers, from whom rumors of an emperor's military conduct would likely emerge. Herodian wrote that shortly before his death, the teenaged emperor Alexander Severus was abused by Maximinus's recruits as a "stingy sissy" too attached to his mother, comparing him unfavorably to the brave Maximinus. This is not an implausible incident, but it is problematic to push it too far, given that Herodian was not an eyewitness to these events on the German frontier. Soldiers certainly did talk, but we cannot reconstruct their conversations with any certainty. We are better informed about the views of military officers. Suetonius Laetus, an equestrian tribune of the thirteenth legion, served under Otho during his civil war against Vitellius in 69. Laetus also happened to be the father of the imperial biographer Suetonius. In a precious piece of testimony, Suetonius said that after the war, his father "was accustomed to repeat time and again that Otho despised civil conflicts even before he became emperor." Laetus was part of the emperor's retinue during the final conflict between Othonians and Vitellians in north Italy. When a soldier appeared in Otho's camp at Brixellum and declared that their army had been defeated at the Battle of Bedriacum, he was accused of being a coward and making up the news. The soldier killed himself before the emperor's own eyes to prove the veracity of his statement. "My father used to say," wrote Suetonius, "that at this sight Otho cried out: 'I will not place such well-deserving men in further danger.' " Otho committed suicide the next morning in order to bring the war to an end. Laetus's conversations with his son played a significant part in the rehabilitation of Otho's memory.[35]

We are likewise on firmer ground when we turn to the views of the military officer Ammianus Marcellinus, who lamented Jovian's surrender of Nisibis in his history. Though Ammianus's outlook was certainly affected by his admiration for Julian, the abandonment of Nisibis was also discussed and debated by other contemporaries. These include the authors of the hostile pamphlets comparing Jovian to the cowardly Paris of Troy, and Ephrem the Syrian, who (incorrectly) blamed the pagan Julian for the surrender of Nisibis and criticized his military tactics, including burning the Roman fleet and returning home on foot. The transition from Julian to Jovian seems to have been a period in which the military qualities of emperors were contested both inside and outside military circles, and we might therefore tentatively suppose that similar conversations took place after other significant military losses. The attribution of Valens's death and catastrophic defeat at Adrianople to his Homoean beliefs would certainly fit in with this proposal.[36]

In the case of other political issues, the nature of our evidence means that we can glimpse only one side of the conversation. In reaction to Julius Caesar's decision to admit Gauls into the senate, a placard was posted publicly in Rome that mocked the new arrivals with the language of government edicts: "May it be well done. Let no one wish to point out the senate house to a new senator." The following verse was also sung by people throughout Rome:

> Caesar led the Gauls in his triumph, then into the senate,
> Dropping the trousers of their own land, they assumed the tunic with the wide band.

The hostile ditty paints all Gauls with the same trouser-wearing brush. In fact, Caesar had only elevated citizens from Gallia Narbonensis, which had long been Roman territory and whose elites had certainly not just been led in triumph, rather than the recently conquered peoples of Gallia Comata ("long-haired Gaul"). When the elites of Gallia Comata petitioned Claudius to be allowed to enter the senate about a century later, their plea was the subject of considerable discussion both publicly and within Claudius's council, according to Tacitus. Although Tacitus always did his research, and we should not discount what he has to say about the situation, good contemporary evidence of precisely how Romans talked about the admission of the Gauls is elusive. Yet the most significant lacuna is the fact that in both cases, the Gauls themselves remain voiceless. We can imagine that in Gallia Narbonensis and Comata, rumors did circulate about if, when, and on whom Caesar and Claudius would bestow these privileges, reflecting their own anticipation and excitement, in contrast with the resentment and hostile discussion in Rome itself. But this talk has not survived today. The same point can be made about voices of opposition to the Roman state: we can grasp the motivations of the Jewish rebels under Simeon bar Kosiba through their coinage heralding a new prince and the oral tales later written down by the rabbis, but we cannot reconstruct the day-to-day conversations through which they mapped out the precise currents of their opposition to Rome and its emperors.[37]

There are also significant limitations in our understanding of how rumor and gossip were generated and spread. Our sources usually describe talk in general terms, and it is rare to have specific exchanges between named individuals. This problem is not unique to the study of ancient Rome but is faced by all pre-modern historians who cannot listen to and transcribe conversations. But it certainly deserves consideration, because gossip is a transaction that "establishes and structures relationships between people" (in the words of Christopher Wickham). As the imperial freedman Epictetus opined, men who impart confidences expect similar confidences in return. Gossip about the emperor was valuable currency. When Gregory of Nazianzus pronounced in his Julianic *Orations* that his picture of the emperor was informed by sources inside the court, he was announcing to his audience that he was a man in the know. Yet this promotional use of gossip in rhetorical display was different from the everyday transactions that occurred in oral discourse between relatives, friends, and acquaintances. Our sources do provide us with some suggestive hints of these conversations. The rumors about Trajan's death and Caligula's bridge imparted to Cassius Dio and Suetonius by their father and grandfather, respectively, indicate that talking about the emperor could be a way of passing down memories from one generation to the next. But we would also benefit from knowing, for example, the identities of those who first shared Julia's jokes or Elagabalus's sexually suggestive lines, because this would enhance or challenge our existing interpretations of the function and significance of these pieces of gossip.[38]

One of the few very detailed accounts of a gossip transaction featuring named interlocutors comes from Libanius, who related how he heard the rumor that Julian had arranged for a doctor to kill his wife, Helena, and gave him a jewel as reward. This was a sense-making rumor, since it explained Julian's childlessness and reluctance to remarry, but it circulated as gossip about the emperor's character exchanged between high-ranking individuals. The story passed from Helpidius, a former praetorian prefect of the East, to Polycles, a former governor of Syria Phoenice, who shared it with Libanius during one of his daily visits to the rhetorician's house. The discussion does not come down to us in direct speech, only in Libanius's retelling in his oration *Against Polycles,* but it is nevertheless possible to engage in some "thick description" of the exchange and its significance. On that afternoon, the two men talked about Julian's reign and its merits, with Libanius championing the emperor and Polycles criticizing him for giving the ownership of whole villages to eunuchs. Polycles then delivered his trump card against Libanius by revealing the story of the doctor and the jewel, which he heard from Helpidius, who had even sworn an oath that it was true. By sharing the tale in this fashion, Polycles gained the upper hand in the conversation, not only by telling Libanius something that he did not know, but also because the rumor was hostile toward Julian and undermined the rhetorician's arguments. Libanius then parried Polycles's attack by introducing hostile gossip against the original source, Helpidius, claiming he enjoyed being the passive partner in sexual acts with other males. Here we see how gossip about emperors could be deployed within conversations between elites as a way of establishing the participants' own authority as interpreters of political events. This incident is also significant in the way it gave rise to more parochial gossip about Libanius and Polycles within Antioch. Libanius began his oration *Against Polycles* by stating that people may have started to wonder why Polycles no longer visited Libanius's house. The speech was intended to prevent tongues from wagging by setting the record straight, while at the same time defending Julian against the slanderous stories in circulation. Gossiping about the emperor operated on multiple levels: the topic of gossip itself, the context in which it was shared, and then the ramifications of that sharing.[39]

These transactions through which gossip was shared and circulated are even more difficult to trace and identify beyond the court, aristocracy, and ecclesiastical and intellectual elites. The poet Horace lamented being pressed for news of political events because he was a close friend of Maecenas, but he did so in general terms to illuminate his complaints about the busy city life. The more historically minded Eunapius complained about the unreliability of gossip-mongers who spread stories about the court to the wider public, but he did so without citing any by name. This means that we can talk in general terms about the benefits of gossiping about the emperor—the pleasure of swapping tales, the delineation of morality, the bonding experience—and how this talk manifested as political discourse about an emperor's fitness to rule, but we can say much less about the transactional nature of individual exchanges.[40]

SEARCHING FOR ROME

On April 9, 44 BCE, Cicero was at his villa in Tusculum, which lay about thirty kilometers to the southeast of Rome. He wrote a letter to his friend Atticus, who was then in the city, to ask about talk circulating on his estate. Some of Cicero's builders had recently returned from Rome, where they had gone unsuccessfully to buy grain. They reported a rumor circulating in the city that there was no grain available because Marcus Antonius had been hoarding it all. Cicero told Atticus that he knew the rumor was false, for otherwise Atticus would certainly have diligently reported it to him in their correspondence. But the very existence of the rumor conveys the anxiety that pervaded Rome in the weeks after Caesar's murder, an atmosphere in which it seemed plausible that one politician would exploit the power vacuum for his own profit. The connection between the death of a Caesar, public panic, the grain supply, and the emergence of rumor would be repeated numerous times throughout subsequent centuries. The depth of popular resentment that could fester when there was insufficient food is shown by an incident in Constantinople in 626. With the emperor Heraclius out of the capital on campaign against the Persians, there were sizable protests against one imperial official, John Seismos ("The Earthquake"). All imperial food handouts had been suspended after the loss of Egypt to the Persians. The price of bread was set at three *folles* per loaf, but John, it was rumored, wanted to increase it even further to eight. Demonstrations in Hagia Sophia resulted in John's deposition and the destruction of his images throughout the city. The author of the contemporary *Easter Chronicle* stated plainly that John's nefarious plan had been stopped by God.[41]

These anecdotes are suggestive of the two momentous changes in Roman politics and society that occurred between the first century BCE and the seventh century CE, the period covered by this book. The first was the transition from a republic in which power was invested in the people, the senate, and the magistrates to a monarchical state headed by an emperor. The second was the coming of Christianity, its adoption by all but one emperor from Constantine onward, and the attempts by the state to administer and arbitrate questions of Christian piety and orthodoxy. To what extent did these changes affect the way in which people talked about the emperors? And how does this compare with other historical cultures and periods?

There was significant continuity in how Romans discussed the emperor. Imperial deaths, heirs, and the question of the succession remained topics of perennial political discussion, connected as they were to a whole host of other issues that affected people's lives, such as the potential of civil war, the continuity of the food supply, changes to tax arrangements, religious policies, and persecutions. This mirrors the pattern of rumor generation in other monarchical societies, which likewise viewed the death of a king or queen as a moment of disruption that created potential crises and opportunities. We can observe suspicious rumors about the premature death of a young monarch in the case of Alexander the Great, trace worries about the presence and health of rulers in regimes as far apart as Assyria in the seventh century BCE and early modern Papal Rome, and note the efforts to cover up royal deaths in the Ottoman empire. People regarded the death of a king as a precarious time, which could result in crises and rebellions (attested in rumors circulating in both the Carolingian and Holy Roman empires), or the hope that the new ruler might reduce taxes, a belief that drove rumors about the demise of Henry VIII. Popular attachment to individual dynasties and the cachet of dynastic names manifested itself in excessive mourning for deceased rulers, protests against intended abdications, and, of course, rumors that monarchs had escaped death. These connections and commonalities across time and space suggest that the proposals about Roman oral discourse advanced in this book form an accurate historical reconstruction.[42]

What is interesting and distinctive about Rome's situation is that its imperial monarchy had evolved from a republican system of government, and yet rumors reveal the acceptance of the monarchical regime and its Caesars at a very early stage. In the final months of Julius Caesar's life, the suspicions that he was aiming at *regnum* ("kingship") not only caused consternation among the aristocracy, but also among some sections of the Roman people. However, the atmosphere in the aftermath of Caesar's murder, which saw rumors about the grain shortage and the reappearance of "Marius" as the people's champion, indicates that there was considerable attachment to Caesar both personally and politically. The subsequent decades witnessed conflict between Romans who favored the investment of all political power in another Caesar, and those who supported a return to the republican system of government.

In the aftermath of the civil wars of 44 to 31 BCE and the internal peace and stability ushered in by Augustus's sole rule, the former view largely won out. The anxiety at Augustus's death, the enthusiasm for the false Agrippa Postumus, the mourning of Germanicus, the panic at Caligula's illness, the acclamation of Claudius, and then the emergence of the false Nero(s), all captured in contemporary talk and speculation, reflect an attachment to the descendants of Caesar and Augustus and to their place in the monarchical *res publica,* as well as a devotion to specific members of the family who were regarded as more suitable rulers than others. One could argue that Romans had always had an attachment to dynasties in one shape or another, since in the Republic they had voted consulships to men with the names of Cornelius Scipio and Caecilius Metellus generation after generation. And yet after the Julio-Claudian dynasty fell with Nero, Rome did not settle on an entrenched pattern of long-lived imperial houses, but vacillated between dynastic names and the prospects offered by outsiders rising to the purple. The many rumors about imperial health, death, and the succession, not to mention those concerning returning emperors and princes, reflected this tension between dynastic certainty and the lure of the new in a way that was distinctly Roman. Rumor and gossip about the emperors who followed Augustus did not necessarily fall neatly into categories of resistance or opposition. The currents of talk show the reputation of some emperors improving over time: compare the reception of Vespasian's fiscal policies in Alexandria versus Rome, or contrast the sexual stories that circulated about Otho, Poppaea, and Nero with Otho's heroic final suicide, which Suetonius's father did much to publicize. The reputations of other rulers remained largely positive despite one major negative incident (such as Constantine and the deaths of Crispus and Fausta). All this discussion instead represented the negotiation of

Rome's monarchical power, and no one, not even Marcus Aurelius, emerged completely without fault.[43]

The rise of Christianity and its adoption as the imperial religion was a transformation that was just as significant as Rome's evolution from republic to monarchy. Rumor patterns show that this change resulted in the emperor's religious policies becoming a concern for a much greater proportion of Roman society. In the first to third centuries, only followers of the Jewish religion and nascent Christian communities were affected by imperial decisions about their faith, which came in the form of taxes, restrictions, punishments, wars, and persecutions. These worries manifested themselves in oral tales about imperial policies found in Jewish rabbinic literature and in the rumors about potential persecutions spread by bishops such as Cyprian. However, once the emperors themselves adopted Christianity in the fourth century, they began to issue decrees on traditional Roman or "pagan" religion, whose followers were now affected by the specter of imperial punishment in significant numbers for the first time. Christians themselves were far from immune from the consequences of imperial decisions in Late Antiquity, however, since the endless divisions over Christological beliefs and religious orthodoxy forced emperors to choose sides. They legislated, often quite vociferously, against Christian sects that were regarded as heretical, resulting in the spread of rumors about imperial religious policies in areas such as North Africa and Egypt. The adoption of Christianity meant that the emperor's religious policies were the subject of much greater discussion throughout the empire and across the social spectrum. The avenging sword of faith did not discriminate between rich and poor.

One other way of ascertaining what was specifically *Roman* about this talk is to consider the wider discourse of kingship. We began this book with boys running through Pompeii shouting the popular ditty, "Do the right thing, you'll be a king. If you don't, then you won't!" The troops who marched in Julius Caesar's Gallic triumph of 46 BCE craftily reversed the lines of the song by crying out, "If you act well, you'll be up for punishing. But if you act badly, you'll be made king!" The soldiers meant that if Caesar laid down his magisterial power, he would be open to prosecution by his peers, but if he refused to do so, he would be acting in violation of the laws and setting himself up as a sole ruler. Not only was kingship regarded as incompatible with the Roman *res publica* at this time, but monarchs were frequently suspected of behaving in a way that contravened laws and morals. Kings could be greedy and grasping, commission wasteful building projects, possess vast sexual appetites, and surround themselves with evil advisors and manipulative women. All these stereotypes are found throughout the Roman world and in many other monarchical societies, counterbalancing the ideal image of the just and benevolent ruler celebrated in the original ditty. To take but one example among many, the greed and avarice of emperors was a frequent topic of popular songs in Han China, the same qualities for which Vespasian was harangued in Alexandria and then affectionately mocked at his funeral in the city of Rome.[44]

This does not mean that there is nothing interesting or important to say about individual rumors, because they are always shaped by specific cultural contexts. Many societies tell stories about the cruelty of rulers toward children. The rumor spread by Christian bishops that Valerian sacrificed babies to examine their entrails shares similarities with tales about Chinese emperors who allegedly murdered children to use their organs for medicines. It also has parallels in the panic that enveloped Paris in 1750 when children were snatched off the street, reputedly because King Louis XV needed to bathe in their blood to cure his leprosy. The story of Valerian was influenced by Christian views about the evils of pagan magical practices, while the Chinese tales were shaped by Buddhist legends about bad kings. The Parisian rumor recalls a Late Antique tale, which appeared in the fifth-century *Acts of Sylvester* before achieving widespread popularity in the medieval work *The Golden Legend,* that Constantine had been advised by pagan priests to wash in the blood of children to rid himself of leprosy. Yet at the time, Parisians were actually thinking of the French king Louis XV as a new King Herod, based on their assumption that Herod's "Massacre of the Innocents" had been motivated by a need to gather blood for the king to bathe in.[45]

One related rumor topic, which also concerns the innocent and vulnerable, is the ruler's abuse of female virgins for his own sexual pleasure. When officials of the Chinese Zhengde emperor came to Yangzhou to prepare for his visit to the city in 1519, a rumor arose that they were there to seize virgins to serve as imperial concubines. Families throughout Yangzhou hurriedly arranged marriages for their daughters to prevent them from being captured. Although the Zhengde emperor had a special reputation for dissoluteness, he was far from the only Chinese ruler to be the subject of such rumors about snatching female virgins. This was due to the Chinese popular tradition of "divine marriage," in which girls were betrothed to gods. People thought that the emperor would act in the same way when he first came to the throne or embarked on a progress through the empire. Moving westward and several hundred years into the future, we come to eighteenth-century Paris, where there were suspicions that Louis XV was running a brothel at Versailles called the Parc aux Cerfs ("The

Deer Park"). There he not only purportedly raped young girls but also took baths in the blood of virgins (which intersected with the Herod rumor). This suspicious oral discourse was an exaggerated version of the reality that Louis XV's valet did procure women, many of whom were quite young, for the king from brothels in Paris. The French monarch's behavior, and the speculation and suspicion it engendered, shares obvious similarities with Tiberius's own secluded park, the Caprineum on the island of Capri, and the perversions in which he reportedly engaged there. Tiberius's depravities on Capri, including the sexual abuse of young aristocratic boys and girls, had their roots in Roman fears about an absent ruler who did not engage with the people, and the speculation that he was behaving in the manner of cruel tyrants from myth and history. These tales of child sacrifice and sexual abuse illuminate the themes of unity and diversity, as they reveal common fears about monarchical cruelty that emerge from, and are shaped by, specific cultural contexts.[46]

This anxiety about what Roman emperors were capable of doing did not stifle criticism or mockery. Throughout the imperial period, there was significant continuity in how people reacted to, joked about, criticized, and probed the limits of imperial power. Imperial bodies, sex lives, foibles, and characters remained fair game for satire right through to the Byzantine period. This type of discussion was not only fun to engage in, but it also acted as a vehicle for criticism that mapped the contours of appropriate imperial conduct. This was not a phenomenon unique to Rome, for royal bodies and behaviors have served as focus points of discussion and condemnation in many monarchical societies. Rulers are expected to have sex and sire children to ensure the continuance of their family lines and the realm itself, but clashes between royal sexual behavior and cultural or religious sensibilities have always prompted talk. Since the body of the ruler and the state are frequently regarded as intertwined, the perceived failings of the royal body often have political impact. During a water shortage in early fourteenth-century Cairo, popular sentiment against the sultan Baybars al-Jashnikīr was expressed in a ditty that called him "Little Stick," a play on his regnal name ("Pillar of the Earth"), which had all-too-obvious connotations about the size of his manhood.[47]

In delineating the contours of monarchical bodily discourse, it is important to realize that not all kings and queens have promoted and publicized their bodies. Images of Greek Hellenistic kings and Roman emperors appeared on coins, mosaics, paintings, and monuments, both during their lifetimes and after their deaths. The creation and circulation of these images were founded on the assumption that it mattered what the ruler looked like. But this was not the case in all monarchical regimes: images of the Chinese and Ottoman emperors were not publicly circulated before the seventeenth and nineteenth centuries, respectively. Talk about the Roman emperor's body flourished (at least in cities) in much the same way that gossip and satire about rulers circulated in later European monarchies that pursued similar strategies of publicizing the royal image. This focus on the sexual and scatological is why the political culture of early modern England and France seems so familiar to historians of ancient Rome. Robert Darnton has memorably remarked that French libels gave the impression that the monarch and his court were living in "a kind of satanic fairyland where they could give full rein to the pursuit of lust and power." It is hard not to see the similarities between ideas in circulation in early modern Europe and how Romans perceived the young Caesar's "Banquets of the Gods," Tiberius's behavior on Capri, Nero's expansive Golden House, not to mention the judgmental views on women of the imperial family.[48]

But in Rome, at least based on our surviving evidence, gossip did not easily transform into visual humor of the sort we find in later European chapbook illustrations and pamphlets with lewd cartoons. Rome did not, of course, have the same developed printing culture, but we do not even hear of the pamphlets and poems that circulated about emperors being accompanied by offensive doodles. Nor do we have trinkets like the wonderful satirical coins and medals that spoofed the genuine articles created by Louis XIV's court. One of these mocking medallions showed the pope preparing to give the king an enema while His Majesty vomited into a pot (a reminder that French elites, like their Roman counterparts, certainly enjoyed "low" humor). The visual evidence that does survive from ancient Rome evades easy interpretation. We have already encountered the portrayal of Aeneas as a dog-headed ape in a Pompeian fresco, which could be a commentary on Augustus's claims to divine ancestry. The only images of emperors in graffiti—a drawing of Nero by a soldier on the Palatine (fig. 18) and Diocletian and Maximian on a brick from Pannonia—could either be mocking cartoons or loyalist sketches, depending on one's interpretation.[49]

Visual humor in Rome focused on the modification or desecration of existing monuments and objects. Signs or poems were attached to emperors' statues, or graffiti was written on their bases; these written words were often taken up and chanted orally, revealing an interaction between art, text, and speech that is largely lost to us today. Imperial statues were often destroyed when an unpopular or condemned emperor fell from power, but we also have evidence for the smaller-scale modification of coins. An excellent example is a bronze coin of the third-century emperor Maximinus, who was killed in a mutiny outside Aquileia in 238 (fig. 19). The heads of Maximinus and his son Maximus were then

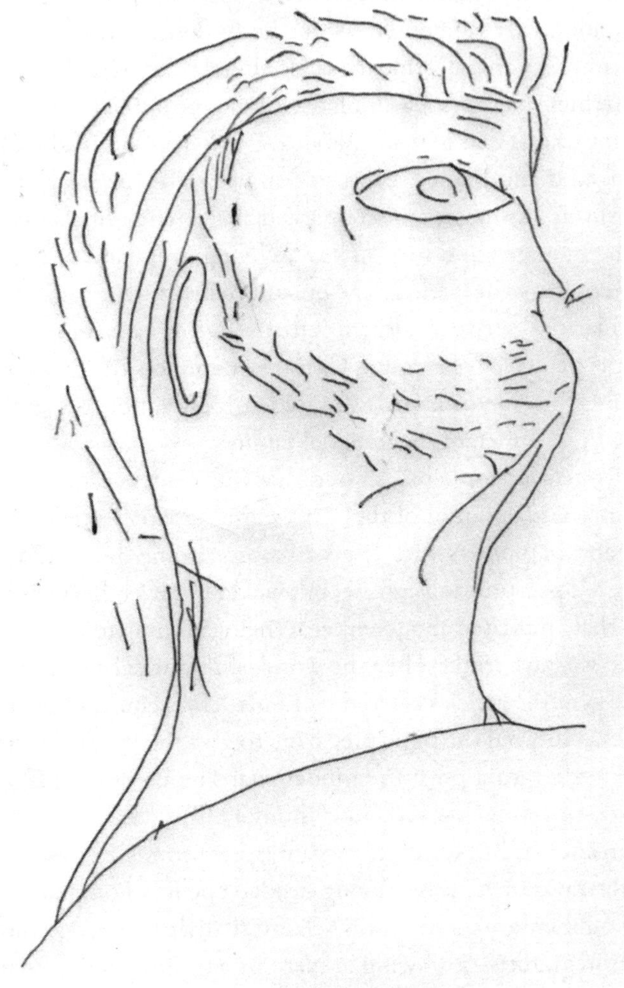

Fig. 18. Graffito of Nero from the *Domus Tiberiana,* Palatine Hill, first century CE. Art Collection 2/Alamy Stock Photo.

paraded throughout the cities of Italy all the way down to Rome itself. The obverse of this coin has been modified to depict the emperor's head on a spike, with a bird pecking at his forehead and a worm emerging from the rear; the reverse was retooled to show a head on a long spear. Unlike the ambiguous graffito portraits, this is clearly the work of a Roman triumphantly mocking the emperor's demise by transforming the "heads" side of the coin—the imperial

Fig. 19. Bronze *sestertius* of Maximinus that has been retooled on the obverse and reverse, third century CE. *Roman Imperial Coinage* IV Maximinus Thrax 90. Private collection. Image courtesy of Professor Johannes Wienand. © Dr. Hubert Lanz.

portrait guaranteeing the denomination's value and authority—into a rotting, severed head fit only to be eaten by animals. So rather than minting a series of coins parodying imperial virtues, as at Louis XIV's court, it seems Romans preferred to comment visually on their emperors by modifying preexisting artworks.[50]

Performances in the theater, though ephemeral in nature, could also have a subversive visual dimension that drew on contemporary oral discourse. When the script of an Atellan farce required the Neronian actor Datus to speak the line "Goodbye father, goodbye mother," he accompanied it by miming drinking and swimming. Since the people of Rome had been talking about Nero's murderous antics, the audience knew that it was a commentary on attempts to remove Claudius at a banquet and Agrippina by collapsible boat. But the sort of street-fair mummery and *charivari* in which emperors were impersonated, familiar from medieval and early modern festival culture, only appears very late in our period. These charades did take place at imperial funerals in the early empire (as the case of Vespasian's impersonator shows), but there is no evidence that people regularly dressed up as emperors in festivals and fairs. Only in Late Antiquity does this emerge as a more frequent practice, initially in the Kalends of January celebrations and then in the mocking "parades of infamy," like that to which Maurice's substitute was subjected in Constantinople. This did not represent a change in how people thought and talked about the emperor, but in how these ideas manifested themselves in public performance.[51]

The function and impact of bodily satire and invective likewise differed between Rome and later European states. In early modern England and France, the discussion of the body and sexuality of kings and queens played a role in desacralizing and undermining the image of kingship. Charles II of England was mocked for his drinking and whoring, which not only had an obscene and grotesque dimension—one famous ditty said his lovers could play with the king's penis in one hand while influencing the scepter (that is, rule) in the other—but also undermined his role as head of state and the Church of England. Even the seemingly harmless picture postcards of the Romanov family of Russia played an unintentional role in destabilizing the monarchy. These postcards portrayed Tsar Nicholas II and Tsarina Alexandra as ordinary mortals rowing in a lake or nursing the wounded, imagery that had recently been so successful in shaping the image of their Victorian cousins in Great Britain. In Russia, however, they had the opposite effect, portraying the Romanovs as ordinary people, rather than as rulers clothed in majesty. From there it was an easy step to pornographic picture postcards of Alexandra being groped by Rasputin. In Rome, however, the monarchy evolved from a republic, in which such ribald criticisms of politicians' bodies had been commonplace, and these practices continued throughout the imperial period. Efforts were certainly made both by the imperial regime and by flattering poets and panegyrists to mystify and sacralize the emperor and his image (the first reference to the *domus divina,* or "divine house," appears relatively early under Tiberius). The aloof and distant monarch had become the accepted norm by the Late Antique and Byzantine periods, a process aided by the Christianization of the empire and its rituals, which meant that the emperor now performed the role of God's vicegerent on Earth. But the sacred coexisted with the Carnivalesque, and so talk about imperial sex and bodies remained an accepted way to negotiate expectations of imperial behavior in the Roman world. This did not, however, lead to high-level intellectual debates about whether or not it was appropriate to have an emperor at all—the mainstream acceptance of imperial rule remained largely unaffected, unlike in early modern Europe.[52]

Emperors had to decide for themselves how to react to popular voices satirizing or criticizing their person, not only in terms of their appearance and sexual conduct, but also in other matters of character and morality. In the early empire, following the model of Julius Caesar and some other Republican politicians, emperors often decided to respond personally to jokes, jibes, and attacks, either in speeches or written edicts. This route was taken—with varying levels of success—by Augustus, Claudius, Vespasian, Marcus Aurelius, and, after a long hiatus, Julian, in the form of his *Misopogon* replying to the lampoons of the people of

Antioch. The reluctance of other emperors to answer their critics in person can either be interpreted as evidence of their "citizen-like behavior" (*civilitas*)—it was better to smile and ignore such jibes—or as a desire to adopt a remote, monarchical silence. Criticisms and abuses in the Hippodrome, the theater, and in public protests continued into the Byzantine period, but the only personal topic on which Christian emperors decided to issue responses was the question of their piety and orthodoxy, which, as we have seen, was a contested political and religious issue that went to the heart of their legitimacy as God's representative.[53]

The adoption of Christianity did not stop emperors and their flatterers from experimenting with sexual self-presentation in the style of a Nero or Domitian. In the twelfth century, we see the emergence of Eros, the god of love, as a monarchical figure ("Eros the King") in art and literature. The emperor Manuel Komnenos (1143–80) was himself compared to Eros and was portrayed like Digenes Akrites, the dashing young romantic hero of the Byzantine epic of the same name, praise that repurposed contemporary gossip about his vociferous sexual appetites. Christianity did, however, change moral dimensions and implications of sexuality, especially for women. Eudocia's departure from Constantinople after she was accused of adultery and Pulcheria's marriage to Marcian became morality plays that were deployed in Christological disputes. Emperors and their families not only had to obey the laws of the empire, but also those of God. The whispers that Domitian had engaged in an incestuous relationship with his niece never threatened the emperor's position, whereas the marriage of Heraclius and Martina did lead to significant religious and popular opposition in Constantinople. When Heraclius died, the legacy of this sacrilegious union undermined the efforts of Martina and their son Heraclonas to maintain a hold on power, eventually resulting in their downfall, mutilation, and death.[54]

WHY DOES THIS MATTER?

We cannot put a precise date on the return of monarchy to Rome. Julius Caesar's appointment as dictator for life in 44 BCE, the acclamation of the young Caesar as Augustus in 27 BCE, the succession of Tiberius to Augustus's position in 14 CE, the acclamation of Caligula as *imperator* by the praetorian guard and the passing of a law granting him imperial powers in 37 CE—these all represent important milestones in the transformation of the Roman *res publica* into a monarchical state. The Roman people remained central to the fabric of this state; over the course of the first century CE, they ceased to elect magistrates and approve or reject legislation as they had in previous centuries, but their acclamations in Rome and in provincial cities came to represent their assent to the structures of imperial power and the rule of individual emperors. The workings of the monarchical *res publica* were subsequently enshrined in the design of the city of Constantinople. The imperial palace, the seat of emperor and court, directly adjoined the Hippodrome, where the inhabitants congregated to acclaim their new rulers. Across the centuries that passed between Augustus and Heraclius, the Roman imperial state tried to engage the inhabitants of the empire in these and other acts of consensus-building through the promulgation and reception of laws and edicts, the creation and circulation of coins and images, and the staging of festivals and performances. The ideal of communicative action—in which ruler and subjects reach a level of mutual understanding about how government should operate and their respective roles within it—was a fitting ambition for a state that still regarded itself as a *res publica.*

This ambition was not always successful. When Romans talked about their emperors, they articulated doubts, concerns, suspicions, fears, and resistance alongside expressions of assent, support, hope, and loyalty. Sometimes this talk took the form of frenzied rumors about the possibility of an emperor's death or whispered gossip about imperial sex lives; at other times it transformed into public outbursts of laughter at the theater or cries of protest on the streets of Constantinople. In all these various manifestations—rumor and speculation, gossip and scandal, jokes and poetic ditties, acclamations and improvised chants—talking about the Caesars was an inherently political act, regardless of whether or not it was consciously regarded as such by those who were doing it. The emperor's position was continually being negotiated behind, betwixt, and beyond the world of institutions, edicts, and rituals.

This everyday politics manifested itself in different forms up and down the social spectrum, throughout cities and provinces, and across chronological boundaries. Ideas and ideals of imperial behavior were shaped by Greco-Roman religion and the deeds of the Olympian gods, but they were also the product of folklore, fables, and proverbs, biblical stories and parables, tales and memories of Roman and foreign kings, and shared human conceptions of how rulers should and should not behave. At different times and in different places, some people might fear Caligula's illness and death, but there could be many who wished him dead; Heraclius could be regarded as a triumphant hero who returned the True Cross or a man who engaged in a sacrilegious, incestuous union that doomed his family; emperors could be capable of wondrous things, but those deeds might be terrible and terrifying performances that brought mythic slaughter to life; some Romans might hope that a new ruler would be a member of a previous dynasty, while others might crave a local ruler who would look after their own community (and some, like the Jews who revolted against Hadrian, hoped that the ruler would not be a Roman emperor at all). All these diverse views were nevertheless united by the shared belief that the messages of Roman imperial power should not simply be accepted but considered, questioned, and debated.

No matter how far-fetched some of this oral discourse sounds—that Caligula rode across the Bay of Baiae to prove a prophecy wrong, that Domitian committed incest with his niece and forced her to have an abortion, that Commodus intended to fire arrows into the audience at the Colosseum, or that Constantine exposed his wife on a mountain to be eaten by beasts—it needs to be taken seriously as an expression of the many ways in which the Romans imagined their Caesars. For the Roman emperor was not only created by the political power bestowed on him or the statues, paintings, and coins that displayed his image, but also in the hearts, minds, and tongues of his subjects.

Did you hear what they said?

Roman Emperors

Names of emperors and dynasties reflect modern conventions, not necessarily how the emperors and their families saw themselves. Generally, only emperors who held the title of "Augustus" are listed. Caesars ("junior emperors") who never became Augustus are omitted unless they feature in the book; the same principle applies to those considered "usurpers." Periods in which there were multiple imperial rivals, such as the middle decades of the third century, or particularly complicated collegiate relationships, have been simplified. Imperial women who play a role in this book, or who help to clarify the larger dynastic context, are included, but this is not a list of all imperial marital unions. Important members of imperial families who are featured in key stories are also included in *italics*. Emperors or their relatives who were the subject of rumors about their return are underlined.

THE JULIO-CLAUDIANS

Julius Caesar — *named dictator for life in 44 BCE*

Augustus — 31 BCE–CE 14 (born Gaius Octavius; Gaius Julius Caesar/"The young Caesar" from 44 BCE to 27 BCE; thereafter known as Augustus; m. Livia)

- *Gaius* — *adopted by Augustus in 17 BCE; died in 4 CE*
- *Lucius* — *adopted by Augustus in 17 BCE; died in 2 CE*
- *Agrippa Postumus* — *adopted by Augustus in 4 CE; died in 14 CE*

Tiberius — 14–37 (m. Vipsania; m. Julia, Augustus's daughter)

- *Drusus the Younger* — *son of Tiberius; received tribunician power in 22; died in 23*

Tiberius Gemellus	*son of Drusus the Younger; adopted in Tiberius's will alongside Caligula, but died in 38*
Germanicus	*adopted by Tiberius in 4; died in 19 (m. Agrippina the Elder)*
Drusus Caesar	*son of Germanicus; imprisoned in 30*
Gaius "Caligula"	37–41 (m. Caesonia)
Claudius	41–54 (m. Aelia Paetina; m. Messalina; m. Agrippina the Younger, Germanicus's daughter, and mother of Nero)
Antonia	*daughter of Claudius and Aelia Paetina; died in 65*
Octavia	*daughter of Claudius and Messalina; died in 62*
Britannicus	*son of Claudius and Messalina; died in 55*
Nero	54–68 (m. Octavia, Claudius's daughter; m. Poppaea)

THE YEAR OF THE FOUR EMPERORS

Galba	68–69
Otho	69 (m. Poppaea)
Vitellius	69

THE FLAVIANS

Vespasian	69–79 (m. Flavia Domitilla)
Titus	79–81 (m. Arrecina)
Julia	*daughter of Titus and Arrecina; made Augusta in 79; dead by 90*
Domitian	81–96 (m. Domitia Longina)

THE ANTONINES

Nerva	96–98
Trajan	98–117 (m. Plotina)
Hadrian	117–138 (m. Sabina)
Antoninus Pius	138–161 (m. Faustina the Elder)
Faustina	*called "the Younger"; daughter of Antoninus Pius and Faustina the Elder; made Augusta in 147; died in 176*
Marcus Aurelius	161–180 (m. Faustina the Younger, Antoninus Pius's daughter)
Lucilla	*daughter of Marcus Aurelius and Faustina the Younger; made Augusta c. 163; died in 181 or 182*
Lucius Verus	161–169 (m. Lucilla, Marcus Aurelius's daughter)
Commodus	177–192 (m. Crispina)

THE YEAR OF THE FIVE EMPERORS AND CIVIL WARS

Pertinax	193
Didius Julianus	193
Pescennius Niger	193–194
Clodius Albinus	193–197

THE SEVERANS

Septimius Severus	193–211 (m. Julia Domna)
"Caracalla"	198–217 (m. Plautilla)
Geta	209–212
Macrinus	217–218 (not related to the Severans)
Diadumenianus	218 (son of Macrinus)
"Elagabalus"	218–222 (m. Cornelia Paula; m. Aquilia Severa; m. Aurelia Faustina)
Alexander Severus	222–235 (m. Orbiana)

MAXIMINUS AND THE YEAR OF THE SIX EMPERORS

Maximinus	235–238
Gordian I	238
Gordian II	238
Pupienus	238
Balbinus	238
Gordian III	238–244

THE MIDDLE DECADES OF THE THIRD CENTURY

I have omitted the so-called Gallic empire from this period, as it is not discussed in this book.

Philip I	244–249
Philip II	247–249
Trajan Decius	249–251
Herennius Etruscus	251
Hostilianus	251
Trebonianus Gallus	251–253
Volusianus	253
Aemilianus	253
Valerian	253–260
Gallienus	253–268

Claudius II Gothicus	268–270
Quintillus	270
Aurelian	270–275
Tacitus	275–276
Florianus	276
Probus	276–282
Carus	282–283
Numerian	283–284
Carinus	283–285

THE AGE OF THE TETRARCHS

Diocletian	284–305 (m. Prisca)
Maximian	285–305; 306–308 (m. Eutropia)
Fausta	*daughter of Maximian and Eutropia; made Augusta in 324; died in 326*
Constantius I	305–306 (also the first Constantinian, as father of Constantine I; m. Helena; m. Theodora, daughter of Maximian)
Galerius	305–311 (m. Galeria Valeria, Diocletian's daughter)
Severus	306–307
Maxentius	306–312 (m. Valeria Maximilla, Galerius's daughter)
Licinius	308–324 (m. Constantia, Constantine's half-sister)
Maximinus "Daza"	310–313

THE CONSTANTINIANS

Constantine I	306–337 (m. Minervina; m. Fausta, Maximian's daughter)
Crispus	*son of Constantine I and Minervina; Caesar, 317–326*
Constantina	*daughter of Constantine I and Fausta; died in 354*
Helena	*daughter of Constantine I and Fausta; died in 360*
Constantine II	337–340
Constans	337–350
Magnentius	350–353 (usurper in the West; m. Justina, a member of the Constantinian dynasty)
Constantius II	337–361 (m. Eusebia; m. Faustina)
Constantia	*daughter of Constantius and Faustina; died in 383*
Constantius Gallus	*Caesar, 351–354 (m. Constantina, Constantine's daughter)*
Julian	361–363 (previously Caesar, 355–361; m. Helena, Constantine's daughter)

INTERLUDE

Jovian	363–364 (m. Charito)
Varronianus	*son of Jovian and Charito*

THE VALENTINIANS

Valentinian I	364–375 (m. Marina Severa; m. Justina)
Valens	364–378 (m. Domnica)
Procopius	365–366 (usurper, connected to the Constantinian dynasty)
Gratian	367–383 (m. Constantia, daughter of Constantius II)
Valentinian II	375–392
Magnus Maximus	383–388 (usurper, subsequently officially recognized)

THE THEODOSIANS

Theodosius I	379–395 (m. Flaccilla; m. Galla, daughter of Valentinian I)
Arcadius	383–408 (East) (m. Eudoxia)
Pulcheria	*daughter of Arcadius and Eudoxia; Augusta from 414; died in 453*
Honorius	393–423 (West) (m. Maria; m. Thermantia)
Theodosius II	402–450 (East) (m. Eudocia)
Licinia Eudoxia	*daughter of Theodosius II and Eudocia; Augusta from 437; died sometime after 462*
Constantine III	409–411 (usurper, West)
Constantius III	421 (West; m. Galla Placidia, daughter of Theodosius I)
John	423–435 (usurper, West)
Valentinian III	425–455 (West) (m. Licinia Eudoxia, daughter of Theodosius II)
Marcian	450–457 (East) (m. Pulcheria, daughter of Arcadius, sister of Theodosius II)

THE LAST GENERATION OF WESTERN EMPERORS

Petronius Maximus	455
Avitus	455–456
Majorian	457–461
Libius Severus	461–465
Anthemius	467–472 (m. Euphemia, daughter of Marcian from his first marriage)
Procopius Anthemius	*son of Anthemius and Euphemia; consul in 515*

Olybrius	472
Glycerius	473–474
Julius Nepos	474–480 (in exile, 475–480)
Romulus "Augustulus"	475–476

From this point on, all emperors are eastern, based at Constantinople.

THE LEONIDS

Leo I	457–474 (m. Verina)
Ariadne	*daughter of Leo I and Verina; made Augusta in 474; died in 515*
Leo II	474 (son of Zeno and Ariadne)
Zeno	474–475; 476–491 (m. Ariadne, daughter of Leo I and Verina)
Basiliscus	475–476 (brother of Verina)
Leo Basiliscus	*Caesar, 476–478 (son of the general Armatus)*
Anastasius	491–518 (m. Ariadne, after Zeno's death)

THE JUSTINIANS

Justin I	518–527 (m. Euphemia)
Justinian	527–565 (m. Theodora)
Justin II	565–578 (m. Sophia)
Tiberius II Constantine	578–582 (m. Ino Anastasia)
Maurice	582–602 (m. Constantina, daughter of Tiberius II)
Theodosius	590–602 (son of Maurice and Constantina)

INTERLUDE

Phocas	602–610

THE HERACLIANS

Heraclius	610–641 (m. Eudocia; m. Martina, his niece)
Heraclius Constantine III	613–641 (son of Eudocia; m. Gregoria)
Heraclonas	638–641 (son of Martina)
Constans II	641–668 (son of Heraclius Constantine III and Gregoria)
Constantine IV	668–685
Justinian II	685–695; 705–711

Notes

All dates are CE unless BCE is specified, though CE is sometimes used to avoid potential confusion for the reader. Translations of Latin and Greek sources are my own except where noted; translations from other ancient languages (e.g., Hebrew, Syriac) are by the scholars indicated.

ABBREVIATIONS USED IN THE NOTES

Papyri are abbreviated according to the Papyri.info Checklist of Editions of Greek, Latin, Demotic, and Coptic Papyri, Ostraca, and Tablets: https://papyri.info/docs/checklist. All other abbreviations are listed below.

AE	*L'Année épigraphique*
AshLI	*Ashmolean Latin Inscriptions,* https://latininscriptions.ashmus.ox.ac.uk
ATU	Aarne-Thompson-Uther Index: Hans-Jörg Uther, ed., *The Types of International Folktales: A Classification and Bibliography: Based on the System of Antti Aarne and Stith Thompson* (Helsinki: Suomalainen Tiedeakatemia, 2004)
BNJ	*Brill's New Jacoby*
Cicero, *Letters* SB	Cicero's *Letters,* in D. R. Shackleton Bailey, ed., *Cicero's Letters,* 6 vols. (Cambridge: Cambridge University Press, 1965–80)
CIIP	*Corpus Inscriptionum Iudaeae/Palaestinae*
CIL	*Corpus Inscriptionum Latinarum*
CJ	*Codex Justinianus*
CSLA	*Cult of the Saints in Late Antiquity,* http://csla.history.ox.ac.uk

CTh.	*Codex Theodosianus*
DOC	*Dumbarton Oaks Coinage*
IG Bulg.	Georgius Milhailov, ed., *Inscriptiones Graecae in Bulgaria repertae,* 5 vols. (Sofia: Academia Litterarum Bulgarica, 1956–97)
Julian, *Letters* W	Julian, *Letters,* in Wilmer C. Wright, ed., *Julian,* vol. 3, Loeb Classical Library 157 (Cambridge, MA: Harvard University Press, 1923)
Libanius, *Letters* B	Libanius, *Letters,* in Scott Bradbury, ed., *Selected Letters of Libanius from the Age of Constantius and Julian,* Translated Texts for Historians 41 (Liverpool: Liverpool University Press, 2004)
Libanius, *Letters* N	Libanius, *Letters,* in A. F. Norman, ed., *Libanius: Autobiography and Selected Letters,* 2 vols. (Cambridge, MA: Harvard University Press, 1992)
LSJ	Henry George Liddell, Robert Scott, and Henry Stuart Jones, eds., *A Greek-English Lexicon,* 9th ed. (Oxford: Clarendon, 1940)
MGH	*Monumenta Germaniae Historica*
Nov. Theod.	*Novellae Theodosiani*
Nov. Val.	*Novellae Valentiniani*
OED	*Oxford English Dictionary*
OGIS	*Orientis Graecae Inscriptiones Selectae*
PG	*Patrologia Graeca*
PL	*Patrologia Latina*
PLRE I	A. H. M. Jones, J. R. Martindale, and J. Morris, eds., *The Prosopography of the Later Roman Empire,* vol. 1, *AD 260–395* (Cambridge: Cambridge University Press, 1971)
PLRE II	J. R. Martindale, ed., *Prosopography of the Later Roman Empire,* vol. 2, *AD 395–527* (Cambridge: Cambridge University Press, 1980)
PLRE III	J. R. Martindale, ed., *Prosopography of the Later Roman Empire,* vol. 3, *AD 527–641,* 2 vols. (Cambridge: Cambridge University Press, 1992)
RIC	*Roman Imperial Coinage*
SCPP	Werner Eck, Antonio Caballos, and Fernando Fernández, eds., *Das senatus consultum de Cn. Pisone patre* (Munich: C. H. Beck, 1996)
SEG	*Supplementum Epigraphicum Graecum*
TAM	*Tituli Asiae Minoris*
TMI	Thompson Motif Index: Stith Thompson, ed., *Motif-Index of Folk-Literature* (Copenhagen: Rosenkilde and Bagger, 1955–58)
TS	*Tabula Siarensis:* M. H. Crawford, "37: Lex Valeria Aurelia, 38: Lex for Drusus Caesar," in *Roman Statutes,* vol. 1, ed. M. H. Crawford (London: Institute of Classical Studies, 1992), 507–47

INTRODUCTION

1. Rhyme: Porphyrio on Horace, *Epistles* 1.1.59: "rex erit qui recte faciet, qui non faciet, non erit" (trans. Dilke, "Horace"). Aulus Trebius Valens: "iudici(i)s Aug(usti) C(aesaris) felic(iter)" (*CIL* IV 7625). Ninth Region: "iudici(i)s Augusti p(atris) p(atriae) et Poppaeae Aug(ustae) feliciter" (*CIL* IV 3726). Distribution: Benefiel, "Rome in Pompeii," 64–65. Nero: Franklin, Jr., *Pompeis Difficile Est,* 119–26. Privileges: Magaldi, "Echi di Roma," 82–100.
2. Publius Paquius Proculus: *CIL* IV 8065: "Cucuta"; *CIL* IV 8066: "Cu(cuta?) | Cucuta Ner(onis)"; *CIL* IV 40875: "Cucuta ab ra[t]ioni[b]us | Neronis Augusti"; Lohmann, *Graffiti,* 178–93; Malik, "*Cucuta ab rationibus.*" Rumor flies: "fama, malum qua non aliud velocius ullum" (Vergil, *Aeneid* 4.174). "Kite and the Doves": Phaedrus 1.31.
3. Nero's demise: Tacitus, *Histories* 1.89.2: "Nero nuntiis magis et rumoribus quam armis depulsus." Reactions: Suetonius, *Nero* 57; Tacitus, *Histories* 1.4. *Damnatio* in Pompeii: Mouritsen and Gradel, "Nero in Pompeian Politics," 153. Fable: Phaedrus 1.2. Rising from the dead: Chapter 4.
4. Heraclius: Howard-Johnston, *Last Great War,* 384–87.
5. Millar, *Emperor,* is a path-breaking analysis of *the* emperor as ruler, as opposed to the biographical approach that had dominated up to that point; for the government of Late Antiquity, it is difficult to better Kelly, "Emperors," and *Ruling.* The idea of the emperor as a unifying figure underlies several excellent treatments of the imperial period, notably Hopkins, *Conquerors,* 197–242; Ando, *Imperial Ideology;* Noreña, *Imperial Ideals;* Hekster, *Caesar Rules.* Mold: Boon, "Roman Pastrycook's Mould"; for other examples of imperial images on terracotta lamps and weights, see Grig, "Looking," 116–26. Enslaved woman: I retain "slave" when quoting original texts or referring to the Roman perspective; "enslaved" is used in other contexts to emphasize that these individuals were human beings who were treated as property.
6. This sketch draws on: Philo, *Embassy to Gaius* 15–18; Tacitus, *Annals* 3.54.1; Tertullian, *Apology* 35.6; Julian, *Misopogon,* esp. 364A–B, 366D; Libanius, *Letters* N 120.2; Ambrose, *On Elijah and Fasting* 12.42 (*PL* 14: 746). My approach is influenced by Hopkins, "Rules of Evidence," who, in reviewing Millar's *Emperor,* highlighted "the possibility and the attractiveness of entering the minds, beliefs, intentions and justifications of ancient actors, both emperors and subjects." Two books that also aim to present a "bottom-up" perspective (Beard, *Emperor;* Christoforou, *Imagining*) were published in 2023 when my manuscript was in its final stages. These are both excellent, stimulating works, and I have noted (pleasing!) points of agreement in the notes. I take the opportunity here to highlight two key differences: (i) Beard and Christoforou concentrate on the first three centuries prior to Christian imperial rule; (ii) my methodology emphasizes orality, contemporaneity, and chains of transmission in the generation and circulation of ideas about emperors.
7. Rumor and gossip: Shibutani, *Improvised News,* 41; White, "Between Gluckman and Foucault," 75, and *Speaking with Vampires,* 56; DiFonzo and Bordia, *Rumor Psychology,* 22.
8. Luhmann, "Der neue Chef"; DiFonzo and Bordia, *Rumor Psychology.*

9. Rumor: Allport and Postman, *Psychology of Rumor;* Shibutani, *Improvised News;* Kapferer, *Rumors;* White, *Speaking with Vampires;* DiFonzo and Bordi, *Rumor Psychology.* Problem-solving: Shibutani, *Improvised News,* 17. Anonymity: Guha, *Peasant Insurgency,* 251, 259–60.
10. Crisis: Allport and Postman, *Psychology of Rumor,* 18; Guha, *Peasant Insurgency,* 257; Aja Sánchez, "*Vox populi,*" 303–8. War: Jal, *La guerre civile,* 119–27; Shibutani, *Improvised News,* 52.
11. Truth in rumor: White, *Speaking with Vampires,* 58; Guha, *Peasant Insurgency,* 264. Rumor plausibility: Allport and Postman, *Psychology of Rumor,* 60; Shibutani, *Improvised News,* 76–86, 128; Paillard, "L'écho," 133–34; and for comparative insights: Gauvard, "Rumeur et stéréotypes"; Fargette, "Rumeurs, propaganda," 314 (medieval and early modern Europe); Guha, *Peasant Insurgency,* 220–77 (colonial India); Johnston, *Being Soviet,* xliii–xliv (Stalinist Russia). Verbalisation: Shibutani, *Improvised News,* 65. End of rumor: Bird, *Rumor as Folklore,* 97; for a Roman perspective, see Tertullian, *To the Nations* 1.7.1–4. Confirmation: the senator Symmachus (*Letters,* 9.108) wrote to a Vestal Virgin directly to ask if the rumor she intended to leave her post prematurely was true. Anastasia: Fowler, "Anastasia." Rumors to traditions and myths: Vansina, *Oral Tradition,* 20; Zongli, *Early Chinese Empires,* 275.
12. Evaluative social talk: DiFonzo and Bordia, *Rumor Psychology,* 19; see further, Gluckman, "Gossip and Scandal"; Wilson, "Filcher of Good Names"; Merry, "Rethinking Gossip"; Spacks, *Gossip;* Hunter, "Politics of Reputation" (ancient Greece); Wickham, "Gossip and Resistance" (medieval Italy). Pleasure: Lucian, *Slander Should Not Be Believed* 21; Besnier, *Gossip,* 18–19, 97–98. Group dynamics: McAndrew, "Gossip," 196: "People are most interested in gossip about individuals of the same sex as themselves who also happen to be around their own age"; Kniffen and Wilson, "Utilities of Gossip" (focusing on a college rowing team). Women and gossip: Semonides, frag. 7, ll. 12–15; Polybius 31.26.10; Plutarch, *On Being a Busybody* 519F; McAndrew, "Gossip." Gossip and men: Gottesman, *Politics and the Street,* 59–60 (ancient Greece); Horodowich, "Gossiping Tongue" (early modern Venice); McAndrew, "Gossip," 182–83.
13. Serious issues: Walquist et al., "Sexual Assault." Weapon: Paine, "What Is Gossip About?"; Merry, "Rethinking Gossip"; Besnier, *Gossip.* Scandal: Gluckman, "Gossip and Scandal"; Merry, "Rethinking Gossip," 275–76.
14. Proximate and distal: DiFonzo and Bordia, *Rumor Psychology,* 21; Gluckman, "Gossip and Scandal," 315; Bergmann, *Discreet Indiscretions,* 51–52. Effect of gossip: Scott, *Arts of Resistance,* 142–43; Wickham, "Gossip and Resistance," 18–19. Gossip and the state: White, "Between Gluckman and Foucault," 79.
15. Rumor and gossip together: White, *Speaking with Vampires,* 62. Processing and responding: Jauss, *Aesthetic of Reception,* esp. 15, 23; Hall, "Encoding/Decoding," esp. 136–38. Kingship: Mitchell and Melville, "Every Inch a King," 16–20; see also te Brake, *Shaping History,* 6, on politics as "bargaining." Live and die: Strathern, *Unearthly Powers,* 318.
16. Emperors and politics: Eunapius, fragments 66–67 (ed. Blockley); Flaig, "Wie Kaiser Nero"; Courrier, *La plèbe de Rome,* 605–736, esp. 684–97; Courrier, "Roman Plebs";

Hawkins, "Pollio's Paradox"; Kröss, *Die politische Rolle,* 233–37. Communication: Corbier "L'ecriture," and *Donner à voir;* Harris, *Ancient Literacy,* 206–18; Eck, "I sistemi"; Ando, *Imperial Ideology,* 80–130; Moatti, "La communication." Letters and edicts: Matthews, *Laying down the Law,* 187–91; Corbier, *Donner à voir,* 26; Eusebius, *Church History* 8.2.4–5; Libanius, *Orations* 17.16; John Chrysostom, *Homilies on Matthew* 19.9 (*PG* 57: 285); *The Chronicle of Pseudo-Joshua the Stylite* 31; see Shaw, *Sacred Violence,* 539–42, on the violent language of religious edicts. Reading aloud: Ando, *Imperial Ideology,* 104; Moatti, "La communication," 218, 223; Chaniotis, "Listening," 300, 302–3; Bond, *Trade and Taboo,* chap. 1, esp. 52–54. Decrees: *P. Lond.* 1912; *P. Fay.* 20; Suetonius, *Life of Caligula* 41.1. Petitions: Harris, *Ancient Literacy,* 215. Permanence: Corbier, "L'ecriture," 31, 42–43, and *Donner à voir,* 25–29. Frequented places: *SCPP* ll. 72: "i(n) celeberrimo loco." Oral reading: *Scholia* on Persius, *Satires* 1.134. Truth: Ando, *Imperial Ideology,* 130; see also Moatti, "La communication," 225, 241.

17. Desire for efficient communication: Ando, *Imperial Ideology,* 116; Moatti, "La communication," 230–32. Problems of distance: *BGU* II 515; Duncan-Jones, *Structure and Scale,* 12 (on Syrus); Kelly, *Ruling,* 115–17. Caligula's taxes: Cassius Dio 59.28.11. Accuracy: Dio 53.19.3: ἀνεξέλεγκτά γε ὄντα ἀπιστεῖται.

18. No press: Bayly, *Empire and Information,* 5. Approach to the state: Ando, *Imperial Ideology,* building on Habermas, *Communication,* and *Communicative Action,* in particular; on consensus, see also Moatti, "La communication," 242–44. Orality: Ando, *Imperial Ideology,* 199–205, discusses positive acclamations, but not negative ones.

19. Rumor at home: Cicero, *A Short Guide to Electioneering,* 17; see also *Digest* 37.14.1. Court: see the essays in Kelly and Hug, *Roman Emperor;* Davenport and McEvoy, *Roman Imperial Court.* News business: Plutarch, *On Talkativeness* 508A–B; Martial, *Epigrams* 4.5.7; *Historia Augusta, Life of Elagabalus* 10.4; Sidonius Apollinaris 3.7.3. Council leaks: Ambrose, *Letters* 72.10 (*PL* 16: 963); *Letters Outside the Collection* 11.2 ([M 51]; *PL* 16: 1160). Contacts: Basil of Caesarea, *Letters* 74; Synesius of Cyrene, *Letters* 48, 88; Horace, *Satires* 2.6.50–58: "deos quoniam propius contingis" (l. 52). Weak ties: Granovetter, "Weak Ties"; stories spreading in this fashion are illustrated in Plutarch, *On Talkativeness* 506F–507F. Sociability: O'Neill, "Going Round in Circles"; Courrier, *La plèbe de Rome,* 535–46. Speculation: Martial, *Epigrams* 9.35.

20. Letter bearers: Basil of Caesarea, *Letters* 205; Symmachus, *Letters* 3.60, 61; Moffatt, *World Both Small and Wide;* Lenski, "Moving the Mail," esp. 524–25, on oral messages. Rumor is faster: Symmachus, *Letters* 2.27, 2.38. Travelers, sailors, merchants, envoys: Ovid, *Tristia* 3.12.27–50; Philo, *Embassy to Gaius* 15, 200–201; Juvenal, *Satires* 6.408–9; Plutarch, *On Curiosity* 519A–B; Eunapius, frag. 66.2 (ed. Blockley); Theoderet, *Letters* 76; Sotinel, "L'utilisation," "How Were Bishops Informed?," and "La circulation"; Gillett, "Communication." Wars: Basil of Caesarea, *Letters* 268; Ambrose, *Letters* 15.2 (*PL* 16: 955–56); Procopius, *Vandal Wars* 1.14.3–13. Jewish networks: Philo, *Embassy to Gaius* 185–88. Postal routes: *Life of Theodore of Sykeon* 152 (ed. Festugière). Villagers: Chapter 1 (Antioch) and Chapter 5 (Oenoanda); similar patterns are attested for Greece (Larran, *Le bruit qui vole,* pt. 1, chap. 2, sec. 43); this is not to say all rural populations behaved in the same way (see the discussion in Chapter 5 on limitations to networks).

21. Apothecaries and barbers: Horace, *Satires* 1.7.1–3; Lucian, *How to Write History* 24; Plutarch, *On Talkativeness* 505A–B; Toner, "Barbers." Marketplaces: Julian, *Misopogon* 364A–B, 366D; Libanius, *Orations* 51.8. Taverns: Ambrose, *On Elijah and Fasting* 12.42 (*PL* 14: 746): "de imperatoribus et potestatibus iudicant, immo regnare sibi uidentur et exercitibus imperare"; see further Magalhães de Oliveira, *Participation populaire,* 129–30; Grig, *Popular Culture,* 10–11. Sociability, the street: Courrier, *La plèbe de Rome,* 183–85, 536 (Rome); Hartnett, *Roman Street,* 53–59 (Pompeii and Herculaneum); Magalhães de Oliveira, *Participation populaire,* 131–36 (North Africa). Politically engaged life: Patlagean, *Pauvreté économique,* 203–15. Limits: Suetonius, *Tiberius* 34.1, *Nero* 16.2; Dio 60.6.7; O'Neill, *Culture of Sociability,* 229–32. Congregations: John Chrysostom, *Homilies on Matthew* 69.4 (*PG* 58: 653); Anastasius of Sinai, *On the Holy Synaxis* (*PG* 89: 829–30). Ascetic: *Life of Saint Mary of Egypt* 14 (trans. Kouli, "St. Mary of Egypt").
22. Warfare: Basil of Caesarea, *Letter* 268; Symmachus, *Letters* 7.13, 14; Leo the Great, *Letters* 83. Aspar: Davenport and McEvoy, "Circulation of News." Limited understanding: Dio 53.19.1–5; Eunapius, *History* frag. 50, frag. 66.2 (ed. Blockley); Davenport, "Envisioning Audiences."
23. Observation: Laurence, "Rumour and Communication," 62–63; for similar habits in other societies, see, e.g., Gestrich, *Absolutismus und Öffentlichkeit,* 138, on eighteenth-century Germany. Decoding: Hall, "Encoding/Decoding." Plautianus: Dio 76(75).16.2.
24. Diocletian: Lactantius, *On the Deaths of the Persecutors* 17.4–9.
25. Nero and Agrippina: the contemporary nature of the rumors is shown by Tacitus, *Annals* 14.2, where he cites the earlier Julio-Claudian historian Cluvius Rufus. Observation: Dio 61(61).8.4–6: τά τε ἐνδεχόμενα γενέσθαι ὡς γεγονότα διεθροεῖτο καὶ τὰ πιθανότητά τινα λεχθῆναι ἔχοντα ὡς καὶ ἀληθῆ ἐπιστεύετο (quotation from 8.5).
26. Gossip and private behavior: Martial, *Epigrams* 7.62; Plutarch, *On Curiosity,* 518A–B, 519F; Augustine, *On the Ways of the Manichaeans* 68, 71; for biblical prescripts against gossip, see, for example, Proverbs 11: 13, 20: 19; Valerian of Cimiez, *Homilies* 2.4, 6.3 (*PL* 52: 698, 710). Busybody: Plutarch, *On Curiosity* 517A: πάντα πράγματα ζητεῖ, τὰ ξένων, τὰ ἡγεμόνων. Martial: Greenwood, "Language of Rumor." Imperial gossip: Suetonius, *Caligula* 27.4 (Caligula); Herodian 4.9.2 (Caracalla); Julian, *Misopogon* 364B (Julian); Eunapius, *History* 5.29.1 (Jovian); Suetonius, *Tiberius* 42–45 (Tiberius); Dio 80(79).13.1–16.7 (Elagabalus); Suetonius, *Life of Galba* 12 (Galba); Suetonius, *Vespasian* 19; Dio 66(65).8.2–6 (Vespasian); Dio 72(71).32.3 (Marcus). Politicians: Plutarch, *Precepts of Statecraft* 800D–801A: τὰ μικρὰ φαίνεται μεγάλα τῶν ἁμαρτημάτων ἐν ἡγεμονικοῖς καὶ πολιτικοῖς ὁρώμενα βίοις (quotation from 800E).
27. Elite and court gossip: Richlin, *Garden of Priapus,* chap. 4; Vout, *Power and Eroticism,* 10–17; Chong-Gossard, "Who Slept"; Blanshard, *Sex,* 79–87; Meister, "Klatsch," 110–12; on gossip in Suetonius, cf. Wallace-Hadrill, *Suetonius,* who shies away from using the term "gossip," given its many negative connotations (24, 176) (though his work was path-breaking in consideration of the court context). Gossip criticism: Tacitus, *Histories* 1.7; Plutarch, *On Curiosity* 516B–C; O'Neill, "Going Round in Circles," 157–62. Oral sources: Suetonius, *Caligula* 19.4; *Claudius* 15.11; *Otho* 10.1–3; *Titus* 3.3; Gascou, *Suéton historien,* 511–13; Geue, "Suetonius and Justin," 214–20;

Saller, "Anecdotes," 73–76. Fulvius: Plutarch, *On Talkativeness* 508A–B; Tacitus, *Annals* 1.5.1–2 for a different telling of the same story.

28. Ideal imperial behavior: Wallace-Hadrill, "*Civilis princeps*," 38; see also Edwards, *Politics of Immorality*, 4: "The political and the moral were also overlapping categories," and further, 24–28. Aggression: Scott, *Arts of Resistance*, 142. Boundaries: White, *Speaking with Vampires*, 63.

29. Slavery: Epictetus, *Discourses* 4.1.6–14, 4.1.60. Competition: Paine, "What Is Gossip About?" Verus: Fronto, *Letters to Verus as Emperor* 1.7 (ed. van den Hout); on the court and competition, see Wallace-Hadrill, "Imperial Court."

30. Oribasius: Julian, *Letters* W 4 [384D]: μιαροῦ ἀνδρογύνου. Gallus: Dio 53.23.5: πολλὰ μὲν γὰρ καὶ μάταια ἐς τὸν Αὔγουστον ἀπελήρει; see also Suetonius, *Augustus* 66.2 (with Rich, *Cassius Dio*, 157–58; Wardle, *Augustus*, 426–29); Ovid, *Tristia* 2.446: "linguam nimio non tenuisse mero"; on the charges, see Peachin, "Judicial Powers," 519; while Seneca, *On Benefits* 3.27.1, describes the encroachments of the Augustan period. Dinner gossip: Petronius, *Satyricon* 37–38, 51; Tacitus, *Annals* 3.54.1, 14.48.1; Ammianus 15.3.5–11; Saller, "Anecdotes," 70–71; O'Neill, "Going Round in Circles," 148–49. Caracalla: Cassius Dio 78(77).15.3–6. Simplicius: Ammianus 19.12.9: "dicebatur."

31. Honorius: *Collectio Avellana* 38.1: "quod in moribus temporum carpat, publica lingua non habeat." *Famosi libelli:* Suetonius, *Augustus* 55; Bauman, *Impietas in principem*, 25–31. Late Antiquity: Matthews, *Laying down the Law*, 193–95. Felix: Optatus, *Against the Donatists* 1.17; Shaw, *Sacred Violence*, 813–15. Arius: Socrates, *Ecclesiastical History* 1.9. Macedonius: Theodore Lector, *Ecclesiastical History* 490; for similar accounts, see Evagrius, *Ecclesiastical History* 3.32; Theophanes AM 6004; Meier, *Anastasios*, 264.

32. Range of responses: Wickham, "Gossip and Resistance," 18; Johnson and Judde de Larivière, "Ordinary Politics," 2–4; Coast and Fox, "Rumour and Politics," 228–29; Bayley, *Empire and Information*, 210; Besnier, *Gossip*, 8–12; Johnston, *Being Soviet*, xxi–xxxiii; Derby, "Beyond Fugitive Speech," 126; see also te Brake, *Shaping History*, 8, who advocates for the use of "popular political practice" instead of "resistance."

33. Kings: Cornell, *Beginnings of Rome*, 150; Glinister, "Kingship and Tyranny," 23–25; Smith, "*Adfectatio regni*," 61. Plays: Kragelund, *Roman Historical Drama*, 15–16. Accusations: Morstein-Marx, *Julius Caesar*, 318–19, 522–23. Caesar: Cicero, *On Divination* 2.110, shows the contemporary nature of the rumor; see also Plutarch, *Caesar* 60.2–3; Suetonius, *Caesar* 79.3; Rawson, "Caesar's Heritage," 149–50.

34. *Statio:* Velleius Paterculus 2.124. Monarchical *res publica:* Kaldellis, *Byzantine Republic*. Types of authority: Weber, *Economy and Society*, esp. 212–25, 241–48, 1122–23. Political thought: Wallace-Hadrill, "Emperor and His Virtues"; "*Civilis princeps*"; Kelly, "Emperors," 146–48; Noreña, "Ethics of Autocracy," and *Imperial Ideals*, 37–100; Hekster, *Caesar Rules*, 23–27; while Christoforou, *Imagining*, 28–61, offers a valuable analysis of the emperor's constitutional powers and how they shaped perceptions of his position. Millar, *Emperor*, is fundamental to understanding how the emperor administered the state. On *civilitas* and political culture, see Wallace-Hadrill, "*Civilis princeps*"; Meister, "Lachen und Politik," 30–32; Beard, *Emperor*, 48–50.

35. Eastern kings: Richlin, *Slave Theatre,* 434–51. Monarchy as standard: Crone, *Pre-Industrial Societies,* 50. Client kingdoms: Braund, *Friendly King.* Greek tyrants: de Lisle, *Agathokles of Syracuse,* 69–94. Hellenistic kings: Ma, "Kings," 191–92. Local traditions: Hekster, *Emperors and Ancestors,* 317–18.
36. Eastern kings: Gagé, "L'empereur romain." Capri: Tacitus, *Annals* 6.1.1; Woodman, *Annals,* 89. Separation: Quigley, "Character of Kingship," 2–4; Graeber and Sahlins, *On Kings.*
37. Popular morality: Morgan, *Popular Morality;* see also Fox, *Oral and Literate Culture,* 112–71, esp. 113, on the popular nature of proverbs from the early modern perspective. Justice: Morgan, *Popular Morality,* 37, 40, 64–66, 97, 101, 109–11, 119, 168–69; Noreña, "Ethics of Autocracy," 273–74; Hekster, *Caesar Rules,* 160–62. Fables: Christoforou, *Imagining,* 176–78.
38. Indo-European gods: West, *Indo-European Poetry,* 120–65, esp. 131. Metapersons: Graeber and Sahlins, *On Kings,* 2–3; Sahlins, "Kings before Kingship," 32. Kings and metapersons: Strathern, *Unearthly Powers,* 124; Moin and Strathern, "Sacred Kingship," 14. Gods in popular culture: Morgan, *Popular Morality,* 31–35, 55, 75, 114, 161, 216. Emperors as gods: Clauss, *Kaiser und Gott;* Vout, *Power and Eroticism,* 5, 27–31; Blanshard, *Sex,* 85–87. Myth: Diodorus Siculus, 35/34.14 (Ptolemy), Dio 73(72).20.2–3 (Commodus).
39. Bible and kingship: Isele, "Moses oder Pharao?," esp. 108–10; Leppin, "Das Alte Testament," and "Pastoral und Politik," 328. Power of sermons: Jones, "Shifting Allegiances," 66; Shaw, *Sacred Violence,* 409–11.
40. Folklore: Thompson, *Folktale,* 4; Bird, *Rumor as Folklore,* 83; Bronner, *Folklore,* 1; Garry and El-Shamy, *Archetypes and Motifs,* xv. The just king: Burke, *Popular Culture,* 204–5; Crone, *Pre-Industrial Societies,* 56–57; Duindam, *Dynasties,* 24–25; West, *Indo-European Poetry,* 420–22. Bad rulers: Scott, *Arts of Resistance,* 80–82; Duindam, *Dynasties,* 281; Röhrich, "König, Königin," 139–41.
41. Hadrian: Dio 69.6.3: καὶ μὴ βασίλευε; other versions are discussed by Welch, *Tales of Philip II,* 91–97. Motif: TMI J1284.2 "Cease Being King." "Enigmatic Counsel" stories: Felton, "Advice to Tyrants"; TMI H599.5.
42. Folklore: Bird, *Rumor as Folklore,* 76. Recognized narrative patterns: Fox, "Popular Political Opinion," 616, a study of early modern English popular politics, but generally applicable; see also Cust, "News and Politics," 68; Coast, *News and Rumour,* 84, 90. Russia: Aksenov, "Peasant Popular Consciousness." "Potiphar's Wife": TMI K2111; Genesis 39: 1–20; Hansen, *Ariadne's Thread,* 332–52; Kim, "Orality, Folktales," 317–18. Witches and stepmothers: Scobie, "Storytellers," 245–51; Anderson, *Ancient Fairy and Folk Tales,* 6; Watson, *Ancient Stepmothers,* esp. 258–66. Women: van Leeuwen, *Narratives of Kingship,* 49–50. Personalities: Darnton, *Art of Slander,* 5–6.
43. Conversations in person: Bergmann, *Discreet Indiscretions,* 39–41; see, in detail, Besnier, *Gossip,* for anthropological work conducted in Tuvalu. Oral culture of Rome: Cupaiuolo, *Le pasquinate,* esp. 7–25; Horsfall, *Roman Plebs,* esp. 11–17, 24–26, 31–47; Wiseman, "Popular Memory"; *Roman Audience,* 163–82. Comparative evidence of the marketplace: Davis, *Society and Culture* (early modern France); Bayly, *Empire and Information,* 19, 202–3 (colonial India). Heroic tales: Langlands, *Exemplary Ethics,*

and "Extratextuality." Recitation: Suetonius, *Galba* 13: "venit Onesimus a villa"; Horsfall, *Roman Plebs,* 13–14; Power, "Galba." Political commentary: Edwards, *Politics of Immorality,* 115–19; Bartsch, *Theatricality and Doublespeak,* 71.

44. European history: Gauvard, "Rumeur et stéréotypes"; Fargette, "Rumeurs, propagande" (medieval France); Wickham, "Gossip and Resistance" (medieval Italy); Hartmann, "Das Gerücht" (medieval Europe); Hunt, "Rumour, Newsletters"; Villard, "Incarnare una voce" (early modern Italy); Fox, "Popular Political Opinion," and *Oral and Literate Culture,* 335–405; Shagan, "Rumours and Popular Politics"; Coast, *News and Rumour* (early modern England). Problems: Davis, *Society and Culture,* 197–99 (on curation of peasant traditions in France); Burke, *Popular Culture,* 103–30. Han China: Zongli, *Early Chinese Empires,* 108, 113–18. Ancient Greece: Kurke, *Aesopic Conversations,* 2–15; Forsdyke, *Slaves Tell Tales,* 6–11. Mughal India: Kaicker, *King and the People,* 9–11. Textual culture: political pamphlets are attested, especially in the late Republic, but there was no mass printing process: Eich, *Politische Literatur,* 269–93; Rosillo-López, *Public Opinion,* 132–41.

45. Orality and politics: Thomas, *Literacy and Orality,* 111 (Greece); Zongli, *Early Chinese Empires,* 113–14 (China). Nicknames: Bruun, "Roman Emperors," counts almost 130 nicknames up to the third century; see also Makhlaiuk, "Emperors' Nicknames." Roman sources: Courrier, *La plèbe de Rome,* 607–9. Manifestations: Merry, "Rethinking Gossip," 285. Trump: Manabe, "Chants," 6–8.

46. Quotations: Courtney, *Latin Poets,* 473–82; Cupaiuolo, *Le pasquinate,* 61–84. Cf. the attribution of specific statements to the emperors themselves, about which there is more skepticism, because the same sayings are often ascribed to multiple individuals in our sources (Laurence and Paterson, "Power," esp. 191–94). But we should not dismiss all sayings of emperors entirely, since some derived from eyewitnesses (e.g., Suetonius, *Otho* 10.1–3). Songs and chants: Fraenkel, "Die Vorgeschichte," 364–65; Jeffreys, "Political Verse," 183–86; Aldrete, *Gestures and Acclamations,* 100–164; Montlahuc, *Le pouvoir,* chap. IV, sec. 1.B.2, esp. 15 on soldiers absorbing rumors and then generating them through their chants. Graffiti: Morstein-Marx, "Political Graffiti"; Hillard, "Graffiti's Engagement"; Lohmann, *Graffiti,* 9; Montlahuc, *Le pouvoir,* chap. IV, sec. IIA. Preservation: Gascou, *Suéton historien,* 517–18, 563–66; Slater, "Speaking Verse." Memorization: see Kaicker, *King and the People,* 136–37, for comparative evidence from Mughal India. Exhortations: Eich, *Politische Literatur,* 282–83. Interactions between oral and written: Lecuppre-Desjardin, "Des portes qui parlent," esp. 153–55, 171; Fox, *Oral and Literate Culture,* 1–5, 39–40; Butterworth, *Unbridled Tongue,* 203–4; for the ancient world, see Angius, "Graffiti e pamphlet"; Magalhães de Oliveira, "Communication," 312–13. India: Bayly, *Empire and Information,* 199–207 (quotation from 202).

47. Anecdotes: Neureuter, "Zur Theorie"; Wehrli, "Gnome, Anekdote"; Saller, "Anecdotes"; Christoforou, *Imagining,* 24–28. Ancient historians: Hardie, *Representations of Fama* (Livy, Tacitus, Pliny); Ries, *Gerücht;* Shatzman, "Tacitean Rumours"; Gibson, "Rumours"; Giua, "Tra storiografia"; Feldherr, "Poisoned Chalice" (Tacitus); Davenport, "News, Rumour" (Cassius Dio). Fossilized gossip: Besnier, *Gossip,* 115; Bird, *Rumor as Folklore,* 101. Augustus: Tacitus, *Annals* 1.9–10.

48. Use of sources: see Larran, *Le bruit qui vole,* on ancient Greece and the difficulties of employing Roman authors like Plutarch. Caligula: Josephus, *Jewish Antiquities* 19.17–211. Dio's father: Chapter 3. Suetonius's grandfather: Suetonius, *Caligula* 19.1–3: "narrantem . . . audiebam." Orality: Geue, "Suetonius and Justin," 215. Claudius as judge: Suetonius, *Claudius* 15.3: "Illud quoque a maioribus natu audiebam, adeo causidicos patientia eius solitos abuti."

49. Tacitus, *Annals* 4.10–11: "eorundem temporum rumorem validum adeo ut nondum exolescat."

50. Readings: Pliny, *Letters* 9.22. Eyewitness: this does not mean, of course, that these works lack narrative self-fashioning (e.g., Kelly, *Ammianus;* Ross, *Ammianus' Julian*).

51. Rufinus and Eutropius: Asterius of Amasea, *Sermons,* 9.1.5 (ed. Datema); Bauer, *Asterios,* 10–21. Chrysostom: Chapter 3. Eudoxia: John delivered two sermons in 403–404. In the first, the Jezebel reference was interpreted as indicating the empress; the second he delivered in response to the noisy dedication of a statue of Eudoxia, in which he compared her to Herodias: Palladius, *Dialogue on the Life of John Chrysostom* 6, 8 (written 408, only a few years after events); see also Socrates, *Church History* 6.15, 18, and *Church History* 8.16, 20; Zosimus, *New History* 5.23; Holum, *Theodosian Empresses,* 73–77; Kelly, *Golden Mouth,* 170–71, 228–29, 239–40. Pastoral priorities: Grig, *Popular Culture,* 31. Aurality: Harrison, *Art of Listening.*

52. Text and orality: Fox, *Oral and Literate Culture,* 39; see also Harrison, *Art of Listening,* 9. Thick description: Geertz, *Interpretations of Cultures,* 3–30, esp. 5–7. Antioch: Leppin, "Steuern"; Stenger, "Libanios"; Julian, *Misopogon* 349D–350A (reaction of shop owners to his policies), 364A, 366D (abuse he received in the agora).

53. Rural voices: Grig, "Introduction," 19–20. Persecution news: Cyprian, *Letters* 80.1–2; Baumkamp, *Kommunikation,* 321–23. Philo: Christoforou, *Imagining,* 190–94. Oral and performance culture behind fables: Kurke, *Aesopic Conversations,* 42; Jennings, "Divination," 190; see Horace, *Satires* 2.6.77–177, for a recitation of a fable by Horace's neighbor. Folklore: Hansen, *Ariadne's Thread,* 16.

54. Fragmented archive: Kaicker, *King and the People,* 13. Comparison and popular culture: Burke, *Popular Culture;* Forsdyke, *Slaves Tell Tales,* 4–6; Grig, "Introduction," 13. "Soft" comparison: Kolchin, *Sphinx,* 3–4; and for applications to the ancient world, see Webster, "Less Beloved," 107; Joshel and Petersen, "Introduction," 22–23; Padilla Peralta, "Slave Religiosity," 320. This is also known as "asymmetrical comparison," as in Kocka, "Asymmetrical," who weighs the drawbacks and benefits of this approach; a positive is that it "can lead to questions that cannot otherwise be posed and to answers that cannot otherwise be given" (49). Value of comparative history: Mahoney and Rueschemeyer, "Comparative Historical Analysis," 11; Baldwin, "Comparing"; Scheidel, "Introduction," 5. We can look forward to a forthcoming collection of essays on this topic edited by Dylan James and Stephen Harrison, *Theorising Comparative History for the Ancient Mediterranean.*

55. Defining elites: Matthews, "Elites," 429–30. Popular: Toner, *Popular Culture,* 1–3, who sets aside the army; cf. also Horsfall, *Roman Plebs,* 26: "the systematic application of precise terminology is best abandoned." Early modern Europe: Burke, *Popular Culture.* Education: Parker, "Toward a Definition," 161, argues that one of the features of

popular culture is that it is produced by people without "the long training and apprenticeships of *embodied* cultural capital." Education without school: Horsfall, *Roman Plebs,* 48–63. Poet: I am thinking here of the Neronian author of epigram, Lucillius, who benefited from some form of patronage by Nero, but cannot be located among the aristocracy (Nisbet, *Greek Epigram*).

56. Diversity and interaction: Burke, *Popular Culture;* from the ancient perspective, see Grig, "Introduction," who critiques the barrier between "popular" and "elite" culture (esp. 18–19); see further Courrier, " 'Une' culture populaire," who argues against one monolithic "popular culture"; and Parker, "Toward a Definition," 151–52, on diversity lying behind categories. Oral and literate elites: Wiseman, *Roman Audience,* 8–9.

57. Popular and high philosophy: Morgan, *Popular Morality,* esp. 1–5, 297–99. Oral culture and rabbinic scholarship: Kraemer, "Mishnah," 308–10; on the rich Jewish material, see Goodman, *State and Society,* 6–14.

58. Elites and popular culture: Burke, *Popular Culture,* 49–56, in which he discusses the "great" and "little" traditions in early modern Europe; see Horsfall, "Cultural Horizons," 112–14, for Rome; and Kurke, *Aesopic Interactions,* 7–8; Forsdyke, *Slaves Tell Tales,* 6–12, for Greece. Blurring of lines: Ruffell, "Beyond Satire," esp. 64; Christoforou, *Imagining,* 19: "elite voices ... were not hermetically sealed from the rest of society." Tiberius: Chapter 2. Sex and scatology: Martial, *Epigrams,* 11.20 (Augustus); Dio 80(79).13.1–16.7 (Elagabalus); Seneca, *Apocolocyntosis* 4.3: "vae me, puto, concacavi me" (Claudius); Richlin, *Garden of Priapus,* 83–104. "Low" humor: Bakhtin, *Rabelais,* 18–30 (quotations from 19, 21); Stallybrass and White, *Politics and Poetics,* 1–26, esp. 1–6.

59. Political rumors: Coast, *News and Rumour,* 105, a study of seventeenth-century England, points out that these are usually the result of interactions between elite and popular discourse; see further Coast and Fox, "Rumour and Politics," 227; Gestrich, *Absolutismus und Öffentlichkeit,* 141, on eighteenth-century Germany; and Solovyova, *National Monarchy,* 208, on rumors about Tsarina Alexandra of Russia. Epigrams and elites: Cupaiuolo, *Le pasquinate,* 134–40. Pamphlets and graffiti: Angius, "Graffiti e pamphlet," esp. 270–72; on the strategic anonymity of such texts, which conceals the identity and social status of their authors, see Geue, *Author Unknown,* 15–16. Graffiti: the Republican graffiti from 133 BCE asking Tiberius Gracchus to use public land for the poor (Hillard, "Graffiti's Engagement," 106–9), or those urging Brutus to take action in 44 BCE, may be popular in origin because they are simple formulations (Morstein-Marx, *Julius Caesar,* 526–27). Popular poets: Cicero, *For Archias* 25: "poeta de populo"; Angius, "Graffiti e pamphlet," 272–77. Reciting of verses: compare the early modern English ballads, written by one author, but often taken up and sung by all (Freist, *Governed by Opinion,* 147–64), and poems written to be read out and sung (Cust, "News and Politics," 67–69; Fox, *Oral and Literate Culture,* 318–19).

60. Arius: Philostorgius, *Ecclesiastical History* 2.2; Athanasius, *On the Decrees,* 16; West, "Metre," 105. Meter: Aldrete, *Gestures and Acclamations,* 125–27, 131–34, 138–42. Arcadius: Libanius, *Orations* 56.16; Seeck, "Libanius," 89–90. Invention: evidence from late Byzantium (Bernard, "Laughter," 51–52), medieval Cairo (Guo, "Protest Songs"), early modern Britain (Fox, "Ballads"), and early modern France (Davis, *Society and Culture,* 200) shows satirical chants being improvised on the spot. These were often

derived from the rhythmic language of the marketplace (Bakhtin, *Rabelais,* 153–54, 181–82). Songs as political engagement: Zongli, *Early Chinese Empires,* 107–68 (China); Nuyts, "Siege to Songbook" (Low Countries); Manabe, "Chants" (modern United States). Composition of verses: Julian, *Misopogon* 364A: τῶν ἱκανῶν τὰ τοιαῦτα χαριεντίζεσθαι πολιτῶν; Libanius, *Orations* 15.77, 16.32; Gleason, "Festive Satire," 110–11; Grig, "Looking," 132; see also Philo, *Against Flaccus* 35, in which the people of Alexandria take inspiration from mime writers for their insults about Herod Agrippa. Guilds and leaders: Cameron, *Circus Factions,* 85–86, 237, 331 (including one leader mouthing words for the crowd to follow). In the Byzantine period, the circus factions also had their own poets, who composed praise and criticism for chanting (Magdalino, "Political Satire," 111–13).

61. Definitions: Leftwich, "Thinking Politically," 2, 23–25, and "Political Approach," 101–3; Peters, "Politics," 25; Hague and Harrop, *Comparative Government,* 3–4; Tansey and Jackson, *Politics,* 4–7; for politics beyond the institutional level in historical analysis, see Kaicker, *King and the People,* 8–9; and for Rome, see Yavetz, *Plebs,* esp. 132; Kröss, *Die politische Rolle;* Montlahuc, *Le pouvoir,* intro., sec. 20–23; Hawkins, "Pollio's Paradox"; Christoforou, *Imagining,* 11–23.

62. Public sphere: Habermas, *Communicative Action,* esp. 3, 7–8, 25–26, 30–38, 62–67, for key programmatic statements, and 3 and 52 on Athens, with the critique of Gottesman, *Politics and the Street,* 6. Ancient world: Kuhn, "Politische Kommunikation," 12–20; Gottesman, *Politics and the Street,* 4–6; Rosillo-López, "Introduction," 9–10; Meister, "Klatsch," 112–14; for other cultures, see, e.g., Symes, *Common Stage* (medieval France), esp. 127–30; Boucheron and Offenstadt, *L'espace public* (medieval Europe); de Vivo, *Information and Communication* (Venice); Bayly, *Empire and Information,* esp. 180–83 (colonial India); Gorshkov, "Democratizing Habermas" (Russia); see also Kaicker, *King and the People,* 1–9 (Mughal India), who characterizes the people as "political subjects." Plebeian: Habermas, *Communicative Action,* xviii; for later ideas, see Habermas, "Further Reflections," 425–27, and "Concluding Remarks," 464–65.

63. Capacity to express opinions: Kaldellis, *Byzantine Republic,* 125–38. Medieval Europe: Johnson and Judde de Larivière, "Ordinary Politics," 16. India: Bayly, *Empire and Information* (quotations from 201, 210). Rumor essential to politics: Shagan, "Rumours and Popular Politics"; Kaicker, *King and the People,* 36–38. Cf. Veyne, *Bread and Circuses,* 295–96, who dismisses all notion of public political discourse outside the senatorial elite in the Roman world.

64. Taxes: *On Military Affairs,* pref. 6–7, 1.1–5.4. Group actions: Noelle-Neumann, *Spiral of Silence,* 111; Magalhães de Oliveira, "Age of Crowds?," 25–62; Yavetz, *Plebs and Princeps,* 131–32. Conversation: te Brake, *Shaping History,* 11.

65. Republican politicians: Millar, *Crowd,* esp. 224; see further Kuhn, "Politische Kommunikation," 18; Russell, *Politics of Public Space,* 53–55. Theater: Hillard, "*Res publica,*" 4–5. Monarchical *res publica:* Kaldellis, *Byzantine Republic,* chap. 1. Leo I: *Book of Ceremonies* 1.91: αὗται εὐχαὶ τοῦ λαοῦ. Senators: *CTh. Acts of the Most Distinguished Senate* 5: "Romani imperatores et pii felices, multis annis imperetis; codices in scriniis habendi sumptu publico fiant, rogamus"; Matthews, *Laying down the Law,* 46. Oxyrhynchus: *P. Oxy.* 1.41: εἰς [ἐ]ῶνα τὸ κράτος τ[ῶ]ν [Ῥ]ωμαίων, Ἄγουστοι

κύριοι, εὐτύχῃ [ἡγεμ]ών; see further Wiemer, "Akklamationen," who discusses Late Antique acclamations at different levels of society and the various agents involved.

66. Emperors: *CJ* 9.47.12: "vanae voces populi" (Diocletian); *CTh.* 1.16.6.1 (331): "querellarum vocibus; provincialium nostrorum voces" (Constantine); Dillon, *Justice of Constantine,* 126–36. "Everyday": Besnier, *Gossip,* esp. 11. I have chosen this terminology over "popular political practice" (te Brake, *Shaping History,* 8) or "popular politics" (Shagan, "Rumours and Popular Politics"), in order to emphasize the overlap and interaction between elite and popular discourses. Two late medieval scholars have recently advocated the term "ordinary politics" in order to evade similar issues caused by the term "popular" (Johnson and Judde de Larivière, "Ordinary Politics," esp. 7–9).

1. THE POSSIBILITIES OF POWER

1. Historical background: Baker-Brian, *Constantius II;* Tougher and Baker-Brian, *Sons of Constantine.* Gallus's behavior: Ammianus 14.1.1: "insperatu saltu"; Julian, *Letter to the Athenians* 271D.
2. Incognito: Ammianus 14.1.9: "novo denique perniciosoque exemplo idem Gallus ausus est inire flagitium grave, quod Romae cum ultimo dedecore temptasse aliquando dicitur Gallienus, et adhibitis paucis clam ferro succinctis vesperi per tabernas palabatur et conpita quaeritando Graeco sermone, cuius erat inpendio gnarus, quid de Caesare quisque sentiret. et haec confidenter agebat in urbe ubi pernoctantium luminum claritudo dierum solet imitari fulgorem. postremo agnitus saepe iamque, si prodisset, conspicuum se fore contemplans, non nisi luce palam egrediens ad agenda quae putabat seria cernebatur. et haec quidem medullitus multis gementibus agebantur."
3. Method: Ammianus 15.1.1 states that he had witnessed all incidents up to this point himself or he had learned of them by questioning people (this is of course a programmatic statement to give his narrative authority, but that does not mean it is untrue). Ursicinus: Ammianus 14.9.1–9; Sabbah, *La methode,* 179–80. Antioch: Matthews, *Empire of Ammianus,* 18, 34–35, 406–9, and "Origin of Ammianus"; Ross, *Ammianus' Julian,* 78–80.
4. Nocturnal antics: Dio 80(79).13.2 (Elagabalus); Suetonius, *Caligula* 11 (Caligula); Suetonius, *Nero* 26.1–2; Tacitus, *Annals* 13.25; Dio 61(61).8.1, 9.2–4 (Nero); cf. *Commodus* 3.7, in which the emperor does not adopt a disguise. Contemporary: Pliny, *Natural History,* 13.126: "contra famam cutem sinceram circumferens"; Bradley, *Nero,* 155.
5. Youth: Veyne, "Le folklore," 28–30; Laes and Strubbe, *Youth in the Roman Empire,* 57, 138–40. Folkloric motifs: Walsh, "King in Disguise"; Bercé, *Le roi caché,* 270–75; TMI K1812 ("King in Disguise"); K1812.17 ("King in Disguise to Spy out His Kingdom"); P14.19 ("King Goes in Disguise at Night to Observe His Subjects"); N467 ("King in Disguise to Learn Secrets of His Subjects"). Germanicus: Tacitus, *Annals* 2.12–13; Jasnow, "Germanicus, Nero." Early modern period: Burke, *Popular Culture,* 205 (emphasizes the goodness of the king). Other variations: TMI K1812.1 ("Incognito King Helped by Humble Man; Gives Reward"); K12812.9 ("Incognito King Rewards Farmer for Gift"), and ATU 925, "King and the Soldier" tale.

6. Ammianus and his predecessors: Ross, *Ammianus' Julian,* 66–71. Emperor's mind: Philo, *Embassy to Gaius* 339–48. Foreign armies: John Chrysostom, *Letter to a Young Widow* 4 (*PG* 48: 605). Plots: John Chrysostom, *Homilies on Philippians* 16(15).5 (*PG* 62: 295). Poor man: *Sayings of the Desert Fathers* 214 (ed. Nau); Wortley, *Anonymous Sayings,* 1–2 (the date), 4: "a tradition that was both oral and Coptic in origin." I am not claiming that this was a verbatim record of a specific old man, but rather a concept of the emperor that circulated orally among Christians in Egypt.
7. Emperor as judge: Millar, *Emperor,* esp. 228–52, 516–49; Färber, *Gerichtsorte,* chap. 3; Tuori, *Emperor of Law;* Christoforou, *Imagining,* chap. 2. Elite: Noreña, "Ethics of Autocracy," 273–74; Nasrallah, *Christian Responses,* 154–61; Tuori, *Emperor of Law,* chap. 3. Practical benefits: Noreña, *Imperial Ideals,* 101. Images: *Acts of Pionius* 4.24; Apuleius, *Apology* 85; Lendon, *Empire of Honour,* 19; Kelly, "Emperors," 143; Ando, *Imperial Ideology,* 208–9, 232–39; Hekster, *Caesar Rules,* 62–63; see further Humfress, *Orthodoxy and the Courts,* 46–51, on governors representing emperors. Egypt: σωτ̣ῆ̣ρ̣ο̣ς̣ τ̣άξαντος τοὺς [ἀδικουμένους] συ προσειέναι ἀδεῶς τῶν δικαίων τευξομένους (*P. Mich.* 6.425). Paul and Felix: Acts 25: 8–10. Christian acceptance: Hebrews 13: 17; I Peter 2: 13–17. Public consciousness: Dillon, *Justice of Constantine,* 122–52; Dickey, *Daily Life,* 51, 53 (school exercises); Davenport, "Envisioning Audiences," 305; the ubiquitous idea of the emperor as judge contrasts with the limited number of judicial images of emperors (Hekster, "Imperial Justice?").
8. Popular values: Publilius Syrus, *Sayings* 698: "tam de se iudex iudicat quam de reo," and see also 296, 673; Morgan, *Popular Morality,* 87–89, 110; *Oracles of Astrampsychus,* question 45 (trans. Stewart and Morrell, "Oracles"); for imaginations of Roman justice across a wide variety of texts and genres, see Davenport, "Dying for Justice," and "Envisioning Audiences," 284–96. Pleas for help: "rogamus, sacratissime imp(erator), subvenias" (*CIL* VIII 10570 = Hauken, *Petition and Response,* no. 1); οὐρανίου δεξιᾶς (Hauken, *Petition and Response,* no. 3). Sisola: *CJ* 4.23.1: "hostilis incursionis"; Connolly, *Lives behind the Laws,* 102–6.
9. Anger: Harris, *Restraining Rage,* 229–63; Morgan, *Popular Morality,* 104, 333; Davenport, "Dying for Justice," 275–77. Philosophical perspectives: Seneca, *On Anger* 1.19.1–8, 2.5; *On Clemency* 2.4; Publilius Syrus, *Sayings* 345: "legem solet obliviscier iracundia," with Dunkle "Greek Tyrant" on connections with the world of elite invective. Power: Phaedrus, *Fables* 2.6: "contra potentes nemo est munitus satis"; Artemidorus, *On the Interpretation of Dreams* 2.30: ἀνυπότακτος γὰρ μόνος ὁ βασιλεύς, ὥσπερ καὶ ὁ ἀποθανών; see Babrius, *Fables* 102, for the common ancient view that most kings were cruel. Christians: *Acephalous Work of Shenoute* A1 556 (ed. Layton); John Chrysostom, *Homilies on Colossians* 7.3 (*PG* 62: 347–48), *Homilies on Matthew* 43.3 (*PG* 57: 460–61); Gregory of Nyssa, *Homilies on the Beatitudes* 4 (*PG* 44: 1236).
10. Tax: Browning, "Riot of AD 387," 14–15; Petit, *Libanius,* 145–46, 238–39. Riot of the Statues: Libanius, *Orations* 19.25–37, 20.3–5, 22.4–9 (my narrative combines the evidence of the different *Orations*). I depend on van de Paverd, *Homilies on the Statues,* for the dates of events.
11. The crowd: Noelle-Neumann, *Spiral of Silence,* 112. Riots, crowds, and politics: Rudé, *Crowd in History;* Yavetz, *Plebs and Princeps,* 36; Holton, "Crowd in History," with

Magalhães de Oliveira, "An Age of Crowds?,' " 30–31, on different groups at Antioch. Chants: Cohn, *Popular Protest,* 37 (England); Bayly, *Empire and Information,* 202 (India); see also Shoshan, *Popular Culture,* 52 for slogans in medieval Cairo. Institutional channels: Aja Sánchez, "*Vox populi,*" 313, writes of "para-institutional communication."

12. Military and the land: *CTh.* 7.7.3 (398) (referring to Antioch).
13. Executions: van de Paverd, *Homilies on the Statues,* 33–38. Imperial images: Ando, *Imperial Ideology,* 232–39; Christoforou, *Imagining,* 74–78; see also Ziegler, *Die Königsgleichnisse,* 20–21, for Jewish material. Risk and reprisal: te Brake, *Shaping History,* 11. Violence to statues: *Digest* 48.4.4.1, 48.4.6; Ziegler, *Die Königsgleichnisse,* 24; Ando, *Imperial Ideology,* 223, 240–45; Stewart, *Statues,* 267–78. Emesa: Libanius, *Orations* 19.48–49, 20.27–28; Jones, "Three Temples," 864–65. Destruction: Eusebius, *Church History* 9.11.1–2.
14. Messengers: Libanius, *Orations* 20.4, 21.5, 22.10; John Chrysostom, *Homilies to the People of Antioch on the Statues* 6.2 (*PG* 49: 83) (hereafter abbreviated to *Statues*). Constantius II: Skinner, "Violence at Constantinople"; Baker-Brian, *Constantius II,* 183. Caracalla: Dio 78(77).22.1–23.4; Herodian 4.9.1–8. Images: Davenport, "Roman Emperors, Conquest"; Hekster, "Imperial Justice?"; Hekster, *Caesar Rules,* 293–309. Violence: Foucault, *Discipline and Punish,* 23–49, 57, on the similarities between executions and warfare.
15. Fears and exodus: Libanius, *Orations* 20.5, 21.5, 22.10–11, 23 *passim,* esp. 12–16; see also John Chrysostom, *Statues* 2.1 (*PG* 49: 5), 17.1–2 (*PG* 49: 172–74); van de Paverd, *Homilies on the Statues,* 43–48; Aja Sánchez, "*Vox populi,*" 305–6. Benevolence: Leppin, "Steuern," 117.
16. Sermons, news, and rumor: Davis, "English Political Sermons"; Jones, "Shifting Allegiances"; Hunt, "Succession in Sermons"; Slater, "Rumour and Reputation." Justice: Bailey, "'No Use Crying,'" 22–23. Chrysostom moved between different churches: Eltester, "Die Kirchen Antiochias," 277–78; Mayer, "Chrysostom and His Audiences," 72–73; "Liturgical Space," 111. Saturday: John Chrysostom, *Statues* 2.1 (*PG* 49: 34): Ὀδύρομαι καὶ θρηνῶ νῦν, οὐ διά τὸ μέγεθος τῆς προσδοκωμένης ἀπειλῆς, ἀλλὰ διὰ τὴν ὑπερβολὴν τῆς γεγενημένης μανίας; 2.4 (*PG* 49: 38); 2.9 (*PG* 49: 47): ἵνα καὶ τὸν ἐπικείμενον διαφύγωμεν κίνδυνον.
17. Flavianus: van de Paverd, *Homilies on the Statues,* 48–50. Sunday sermon: John Chrysostom, *Statues* 3.1 (*PG* 49: 48): εὐθέως καταστεῖλαι δυνήσεται τὸν θυμόν; 3.5 (*PG* 49: 49): Ἀπειλὴ βασιλέως ὁμοία θυμῷ λέοντος; Chrysostom references: Proverbs 20: 2; Isaiah 11: 6–9. Old Testament: Leppin, "Pastoral und Politik," 328.
18. Lenten sermons: John Chrysostom, *Statues* 6.1 (*PG* 49: 81), 6.2 (*PG* 49: 83–84) (Wednesday, March 3); 16.1–2 (*PG* 49: 161–64) (Saturday, March 13, or Sunday, March 14, with van de Paverd, *Homilies on the Statues,* 55–56, 317–24). Questioning: John Chrysostom, *Statues* 11.1 (*PG* 49: 119). Rhetoric: Leppin, "Steuern," 107–12, 121.
19. Speculation: Libanius, *Orations* 21.6; for the fear, see John Chrysostom, *Statues* 17.1 (*PG* 49: 172). Trials: Libanius, *Orations* 21.7, 23.25; van de Paverd, *Homilies on the Statues,* 59–62. Verdicts: Status of Antioch (Libanius, *Orations* 20.6, 23.7; John

Chrysostom, *Statues* 17.2 [*PG* 49: 176–78]); Circus, theater, and baths (Libanius, *Orations* 20.6, 23.6–7; John Chrysostom, *Statues* 17.2 [*PG* 49: 176]); bread distribution (Libanius, *Orations* 20.7, 20.38); troops (Libanius, *Orations* 23.6); councilors (Libanius, *Orations* 20.6–7). Monks: John Chrysostom, *Statues* 17.1–2 (*PG* 49: 172–75). Holy men: Brown, "Holy Man," 81, 92–93. Libanius's agenda: Leppin, "Steuern," 113–17.

20. Caesarius: Libanius, *Orations* 22.27. Antioch waits: Libanius, *Orations* 22.29–33, 23.25–26. Closures: Leppin, "Steuern," 107. March 27: John Chrysostom, *Statues* 17.3 (*PG* 49: 172), 17.2 (*PG* 49: 176): ἡ κόλασις αὐτοῦ διόρθωσις γέγονε, καὶ ἡ τιμωρία παιδαγωγία, καὶ ἡ ὀργὴ διδασκαλία.

21. News arrives: Libanius, *Orations* 34.6; John Chrysostom, *Statues* 21.4 (*PG* 49: 220); van de Paverd, *Homilies on the Statues,* 156–58. Rumor and faith: John Chrysostom, *Statues* 21.1 (*PG* 49: 211–12). Christian triumph: Leppin, "Steuern," 120; on Libanius's rhetoric, see also Grig, "Looking," 134–46.

22. Thessalonica: Kolb, "Der Bußakt von Mailand," 48–49; McLynn, *Ambrose of Milan,* 315–30; Leppin, *Theodosius der Große,* 153–63; Sozomen, *Church History* 7.25, has the emperor ordering only a certain number of executions. Carthage: the situation is not fully understood, but Augustine, *Letters* 15*, 16*, and 23A*, in particular, suggest a nervous wait for imperial commissioners after a revolt over taxes: Chadwick, "New Letters," 431–32; Berrouard, "Un tournant," esp. 53–61. Uncertainty: Kelly, "Emperors," 154–55.

23. Imperial preoccupations: John Chrysostom, *Homilies on Acts* 32.2 (*PG* 60: 237). Emperor's taxes: Luke 2: 1–3 (census); Matthew 22: 15–22; Mark 12: 13–17; Luke 20: 20–26 (coin). Jewish tales: Hadas, "Roman Allusions," 379–80; Hadas-Lebel, "La fiscalité romaine"; Feldman, "Some Observations," 58–59, 71–74; *The Fathers According to Rabbi Nathan* 28 (trans. Goldin, *Fathers,* 116); *Mekhilta De-Rabbi Ishmael, Tractate Bahodesh* 1 (trans. Lauterbach, *Mekhilta* II, 291); these and other stories do not necessarily represent the views of all Jews; the elites benefited from their role as intermediaries in tax-collection (see Keddie, *Class and Power,* 111–51; on tensions between these groups, see Goodman, *Ruling Class,* 51–75). Revolt: MacMullen, "Tax-Pressure"; Herodian 7.4–5.

24. *Liberalitas:* Noreña, *Imperial Ideals,* 82–92; Christoforou, *Imagining,* 120–30; Beard, *Emperor,* 245–46. Tokens: Rowan, *Tokens and Social Life,* 44–45. Ariadne: *Book of Ceremonies* 1.92. Generosity of kings: Peter Chrysologus, *Sermons* 23.4 (ed. Olivar) (imperial family present: McEvoy, *Child Emperor Rule,* 281); for preaching on the sin of avarice, see Valerian of Cimiez, *Homilies* 2.5 (*PL* 52: 699). Monk: Rea, "Österreichische Nationalbibliothek," with Kelly, *Petitions,* 125–27, on the poor. Legislation suggests that Christian emperors did at least profess an interest in poverty, e.g., *CJ* 1.2.12 (451); see further Brown, *Poverty and Leadership,* 89.

25. Valentinian II: Symmachus, *State Letters* 14.1: "querella publica." Augustus: Suetonius, *Augustus* 70.2: "pater argentarius, ego Corinthiarius," with Wardle, *Augustus,* 446–47, on the meter (an iambic *senarius*).

26. Anastasius: *Palatine Anthology* 11.270, 271: οἷς πάντα φθείρεις ἐκ φιλοχρημοσύνης (270, l. 4); the other version is in John Lydus, *On the Magistrates* 3.46; Anderson,

"Disappearing Statue," 303–5. Comparative evidence: Cust, "News and Politics," 66–68 (quotation from 67); Bayly, *Empire and Information,* 202.

27. Valens: Ammianus 26.6.6: "rumusculos," with Lenski, *Valens,* 291–92, citing *CTh.* 11.1.3 and 12.6.10 (365). Anthemius: Sidonius Apollinaris, *Letters* 2.1.4. Marcus Aurelius: Dio 72(71).32.3: καὶ νῦν θαυμάζω τῶν αἰτιωμένων αὐτὸν ὡς οὐ μεγαλόφρονα γενόμενον.
28. Proverbs and sayings: Publilius Syrus, *Sayings* 14: "avarus ipse miseriae causa est suae"; 47: "avaro non est vita, sed mors longior"; Morgan, *Popular Morality,* 47, 93. Vespasian: Suetonius, *Vespasian* 19.2; Dio 65(66).8.2–8. Maurice: Theophylact Simocatta 8.9.3, a contemporary source, with Whitby, "Defender of the Cross," 327; repeated later in Theophanes AM 6094. See further John of Ephesus, *Ecclesiastical History Part III* 5.20–22 for contemporary discussion of Maurice's failings.
29. Vespasian: Suetonius, *Vespasian* 19.2, 23.1–3; Laurence and Paterson, "Power," 185; Milns, "Vespasian's Humour"; Montlahuc, *Le pouvoir,* chap. VIII, sec. I.A.1, B.1.
30. Emperor and grain: Noreña, *Imperial Ideals,* 112–22; Augustus, *Res Gestae* 15.1, 15.4. Banquet: Suetonius, *Augustus* 70.1–2: "omne frumentum deos comedisse" (this is reported speech, but the original direct speech would also have been four words: "dei omne frumentum comederunt"); see Wardle, *Augustus,* 443, on the date. Short chants, popular tunes, adaptation: comparative evidence for the same phenomenon in Shoshan, *Popular Culture,* 53 (medieval Cairo); Davis, *Society and Culture,* 118, 199–200 (early modern France); Fox, *Oral and Literate Culture,* 26–27 (early modern England); Angkasa, "Synchronous Chanting" (modern Indonesia).
31. Comparative material: Thompson, "Moral Economy"; Cohn, *Lust for Liberty,* 70–75 (medieval Europe); Shoshan, *Popular Culture,* 58–66 (medieval Cairo); Wong, "Food Riots," and "Les émeutes de subsistances" (early modern China); Rogers, "1866 grain riots" (nineteenth-century Sri Lanka); for Roman responses, see Kelly, "Riot Control." Grain fleet: Symmachus, *State Letters* 18; *Letters* 2.4, with *CTh.* 1.15.14 (395), 14.15.3 (397), on the continuance of grain supply from Rome to Africa; see further Kohns, *Versorgungskrisen;* Ruggini, *Economia e società,* 152–76. Riots and protests: Suetonius, *Claudius* 18.2; Marcellinus *comes* s.a. 431; Garnsey, *Famine and Food Supply,* 29–31; Yavetz, *Plebs and Princeps,* 13 (Rome); Patlagean, *Pauvreté économique,* 215–16 (Constantinople); Erdkamp, "Urban Markets and Food Riots" (aimed at emperors and officials). Fathers and children: Jongman, "Beneficial Symbols"; Hillard, "Popular Reception." Leo I: *Life of Daniel the Stylite* 56. Guarantee: Tacitus, *Annals* 15.36.4. Caligula: Philo, *Embassy to Gaius* 172–73, 250–53, 338 (shows contemporary nature); Suetonius, *Life of Caligula* 49.2; Wardle, *Caligula,* 322.
32. Antioch: Julian, *Misopogon* 349D–350D, 364B–C, 365D, 366D, 368C–370D: πάντα γέμει, πάντα πολλοῦ; see also Ammianus 14.1–2; Libanius, *Orations* 18.195; Socrates 3.17; Garnsey, *Famine and Food Supply,* 22–23; Matthews, *Empire of Ammianus,* 409–13; Wiemer, *Libanios und Julian,* 269–355. Kalends celebration: Gleason, "Festive Satire"; Grig, "Looking," 131–32. Rural population: Grig, "Kalends of January," 242. Elites hoarding grain: see Dio Chrysostom, *Orations* 46, on similar suspicions in Prusa, with Jones, *Dio Chrysostom,* 19–25.
33. Turning down: *Digest* 40.9.17.1 records that Marcus Aurelius decreed slaves should not be freed "as a result of an acclamation of the people" ("ex adclamatione populi"). Vine

edict: Suetonius, *Life of Domitian* 7.2, 14.2: "creditur"; κἂν με φάγῃς ἐπὶ ῥίζαν, ὅμως ἔτι καρποφορήσω, | ὅσσον ἐπισπεῖσαι σοί, τράγε, θυομένῳ. See also Philostratus, *Life of Apollonius of Tyana* 6.42; *Lives of the Sophists* 520. Discussion in Patterson, "Rural Change and Urban Development," 116–18; Jones, *Domitian,* 77–78; Coleman, "Epigram, Society," 69. Anonymous impact: "they seem to index an opposition made to look like a tip of an iceberg" (Geue, *Author Unknown,* 17). Goats: Hoffmann, *Schimpfwörter,* 26; Keller, *Die antike Tierwelt,* 296–309, esp. 308. Censor: Suetonius, *Domitian* 7.1, 8.2–5. Rare changes: Hawkins, "Pollio's Paradox," 142–43.

34. Caligula: Josephus, *Jewish Antiquities* 19.24–27; a variation of the story appears in Dio 59.28.11; Cameron, *Circus Factions,* 162–64. Eubulus: Dio 79(80).21.1: ὑπό τε τοῦ δήμου καὶ τῶν στρατιωτῶν διεσπάσθη.

35. Jews: Goodman, "Trajan," esp. 11–12. Rumors: Cyprian, *Letters* 80.1–2; Clarke, "Prosopographical Notes," 437–39; on the wider fear of persecution, see Cyprian, *Letters* 57.1, 58.7.

36. Theological discussion in cities: Gregory of Nyssa, *On the Deity of the Son and the Holy Spirit* (*PG* 46: 557 B–C); Lim, "Religious Disputation." Imperial laws: Humfress, *Orthodoxy and the Courts,* 233–68, is fundamental; efforts to control, see, e.g., *CTh.* 16.6.2, 16.5.5. Magnus Maximus: *Collectio Avellana* 39.3: "nam fama non patitur occultari, praesertim quod agatur in populos"; McEvoy, *Child Emperor Rule,* 87–89, 124–27; see McLynn, *Ambrose of Milan,* 181–208, on the "Basilica Crisis."

37. Constantinople: Pfeilschifter, *Der Kaiser,* 313–29. Anastasius: *Book of Ceremonies* 1.92: ὀρθόδοξον βασιλέα τῇ οἰκουμένῃ; Meier, *Anastasios,* esp. 38–45, 65–75. Vitalianus: Marcellinus *comes* s.a. 512; Evagrius, *Ecclesiastical History* 3.32; Ps. Zachariah Rhetor, *Chronicle* 7.1 (ed. Greatrex et al.); Theophanes AM 5983, 5987–89, 6003–7; Haarer, *Anastasius,* 125–83; Meier, *Anastasios,* 295–319; Ruscu, "Revolt of Vitalianus."

38. Tiberius II: John of Ephesus, *Ecclesiastical History Part III* 3.13, 3.26. I thank Philip Forness for confirmation of the word "buzzed" in the Syriac text. Heraclius: John of Nikiu 121.2 (trans. Charles, *Chronicle of John*).

39. Delegation: Kelly, *Ruling,* 191. Plotina: Dio 69.1.4. Titus: Suetonius, *Titus* 3.2: "e pluribus comperi" ("I have learned from very many people"); Suetonius, *Domitian* 2.3. Theodosius II: Theodoret, *Letters* 79–81, with Millar, *Greek Roman Empire,* 182–84, on the context; Kelly, *Ruling,* 217–18, on imperial letters. Forging imperial letters: *P. Oxy.* 83.5353.

40. Advisors: Lucian, *Slander Should Not Be Believed* 10, 12. Claudius: Seneca, *Apocolocyntosis* 1.11; Suetonius, *Claudius* 39.1. Polybius: Dio 61(60).29.3: ἀφόρητός ἐστιν εὐτυχῶν μαστιγίας (the original Greek demands the translation "slave" rather than "enslaved"), with Bartsch, *Theatricality and Doublespeak,* 77–78.

41. Plautianus: Dio 77(76).2.2–3: τί τρέμεις, τί δὲ ὠχριᾷς; πλεῖον τῶν τριῶν κέκτησαι. Courtney, *Latin Poets,* 483, translates this back into the Latin *versus quadratus,* the meter of popular verses: "quid tremis? quid expallescis? possides plus tu tribus." Dio's further comment: ἔλεγον δὲ τοῦτο οὐ πρὸς ἐκεῖνον δῆθεν ἀλλ' ἄλλως.

42. Heraclius: Prosper, *Chronicle* 1373 (ed. Mommsen): "ut creditum est"; Davenport and McEvoy, "Circulation of News," 215. Diocletian: *Jerusalem Talmud, Tractate Ševiït* 9.2 (trans. Guggenheimer, *Tractates Kilaim and Ševiït,* 606), as interpreted by Lieberman,

"Palestine," 351–52; see Goodman, *State and Society,* 139–40, on the memory of Diocletian's progress in Jewish sources more broadly. Evil advisors: Burke, *Popular Culture,* 208; Hekster, *Caesar Rules,* 130–31.

43. Women: Hekster, *Caesar Rules,* 226–30. Plotina: *Midrash Rabbah, Lamentations* 1.16 (trans. M. P. Ben Zeev, *Diaspora Judaism*); for the historical context, see Gambash, *Provincial Resistance,* 167–69; Horbury, *Jewish War,* 170. Licinia Eudoxia: Hydatius, *Chronicle* 160 [167] (ed. Burgess): "malum fama dispergit"; Davenport and McEvoy, "Circulation of News," 220–22. As Kelly, *Ruling,* 222–23, points out, stories of malicious or incompetent advisors made them excellent scapegoats if required.

44. Gratian: Symmachus, *Orations* 3.23: "quem paene intempestive putabamus electum"; Sogno, *Symmachus,* 18; Cameron, *Last Pagans,* 752. Valentinian II: Ambrose, *Against Auxentius* (*Letters* 75A), 16: "episcopi manu scripta et ore dictata"; 29: "de imperatore invidiam commovere"; 17: "muliebri consilio deceptum"; McLynn, *Ambrose of Milan,* 204–7.

45. Stilicho: McEvoy, *Child Emperor Rule,* 180–86. Edicts: *CTh.* 16.2.34, 16.5.38, 16.6.3, and see also 16.6.4–5; Lenski, "Imperial Legislation," 180–84. Pagans: Augustine, *City of God* 18.54; Brown, *Augustine,* 227, 285–86.

46. Rumors: Augustine, *Letters* 97.2: "inimici ecclesiae leges illas quae de idolis confringendis et haereticis corrigendis . . . quo nesciente vel nolente factum sive dolose iactant sive libenter putant"; 97.3: "leges quae pro ecclesia Christi missae sunt, magis Theodosii filium quam Stilichonem curasse mittendas"; Magalhães de Oliveira, *Participation populaire,* 270–71; McEvoy, *Child Emperor Rule,* 190–92.

47. Imperial movement: Ash, "Tiberius in Space." Crowds and emperors: Pliny, *Panegyric* 22.1–23.6; Pacatus, *Latin Panegyrics* 2(12).47.3; Kelly, *Ruling,* 192–93. Privileges: Lehnen, *Adventus principis,* 85–97; Hekster, *Caesar Rules,* 289; Beard, *Emperor,* 299–303; for some examples, see Dio 54.9.7; Libanius, *Orations* 18.163; *Leviticus Rabbah* 26.1, with Hadas, "Roman Allusions," 384. Injustices: *AE* 2005, 1348; *AE* 2009, 1428 (letters of Hadrian regarding abuses). Constantine's threats: Pottenger, *Power and Rhetoric,* 192–93, for example, see Optatus, *Appendix* 7. Gaul: *Explanation of the Whole World* 58 (ed. Rougé).

48. First journey: Gregory of Nazianzus, *Letters* 19.5: σύστασις αρετικῶν; 18.2: οἱ καταδραμόντες θῆρες τῇ ἐκκλησίᾳ. Feeding the court: Brown, *Poverty and Leadership,* 41–42, showing that emperor and bishop did actually join forces to alleviate serious food shortages in the region. Second journey: Gregory of Nyssa, *Against Eunomius* 1.128: καθάπερ νέφους τινὸς χαλεποῦ τῆς δυναστείας ἐκ τῆς Προποντίδος κατὰ τῶν ἐκκλησιῶν κινηθείσης; Basil of Caesarea, *Letters* 48, 71; Lenski, *Valens,* 246, 253; Studer, "Der geschichtliche Hintergrund," 7–8, 15.

49. Images: Lehnen, *Adventus principis,* 307–13. Caligula's statue: Philo, *Embassy to Gaius* 184–208, 225–26, 238; Josephus, *Jewish War* 2.184–200.

50. Court composition: Kelly, "Introduction," 5–8; Davenport and McEvoy, "Introduction," 4–7, 22–23. Privilege and fear: Kelly, "Emperors," 139–40; *Ruling,* 187–90, 197–99. Court experiences: Julian, *Letter to the Athenians* 273C: πικροτάτην καὶ χαλεπωτάτην . . . δουλείαν; 277A–C; Ausonius, *Letters* 12: frontes hominum aperit, mentes tegit; Epictetus, *Discourses* 1.19.17: πῶς δὲ καὶ φρόνιμος γίνεται ἐξαίφνης ὁ ἄνθρωπος, ὅταν Καῖσαρ αὐτὸν ἐπὶ τοῦ λασάνου ποιήσῃ; Beard, *Emperor,* 172–73. Tiberius: Phaedrus, *Fables* 2.5: "vera fabella"; Henderson, *Telling Tales,* 29–31.

51. Florentius: Julian, *Letters* W 4 [385B]: οὓς ᾔδειν ἀναγγελοῦντας αὐτῷ. Caligula: Philo, *Embassy to Gaius* 66: ὡς διὰ παντὸς στόματος δυσκάθαρτα ἄγη συνηχεῖσθαι, φανερῶς μὲν οὐ διὰ δέος, ἠρεμαιοτέρᾳ δὲ τῇ φωνῇ; Seneca, *On Firmness of Purpose* 18.1–2, *On Benefits* 2.12.1–2, and *On Anger* 1.33.3–6, 3.18.4, 19.3–4. Valentinian: Ammianus 27.7.5 (officials), 27.7.8 ("audiebatur"), 29.3.2 ("indicia varia testantur et certa"), 29.3.3–6 (catalogue of cruelty), 29.3.6 ("abi . . . comes, et muta ei caput, qui sibi mutari provinciam cupit"). Ivan the Terrible: Perrie, *Image of Ivan,* 96–101.
52. *Apocolocyntosis:* Eden, *Apocolocyntosis,* 4–13, with Dio 61(60).35.3 (Seneca as author); Münscher, *Senecas Werke,* 49–50 (circulated in court society, though originally anonymous); Nauta, "Seneca's *Apocolocyntosis*" (Saturnalian recitation). Fear and letting off steam: Nauta, "Seneca's *Apocolocyntosis,*" 91–95; Geue, *Author Unknown,* 203, emphasizes the "collective relief" of the court. Imperial anger: Seneca, *Apocolocyntosis* 5.2, 6.2, 10.3–11.5, 13.4–14.1.
53. Tiberius on Capri: Ash, "Tiberius in space"; Tacitus, *Annals* 4.57.1, 4.67.1; Suetonius, *Tiberius,* 43.2 ("palam iam et uulgo . . . Caprineum dictitabant"), 62.2 (torture; death from the cliff: "carnificinae eius ostenditur locus Capreis, unde damnatos post longa et exquisita tormenta praecipitari coram se in mare iubebat"). *Caprineum:* Champlin, "Sex on Capri," 322, 330; "Tiberius and Pan," 160–61. Servilius Nonianus: Suetonius, *Tiberius* 61.6, names a consular annalist, identified by Syme, *Tacitus,* 277, as Nonianus. Everyday: the present tense Latin verb *ostenditur* shows that this was taking place in Suetonius's own lifetime. The verb is passive, literally "it is pointed out," but this can be translated as the third-person active "they point out," as occurs in several modern translations.
54. Capri: Suetonius, *Life of Tiberius* 60; Champlin, "Tiberius the Wise," 408–10. "Thank God They Weren't Peaches": TMI J2563, ATU 1689. Hadrian: *Leviticus Rabbah* 25.5, Munich manuscript; Hasan-Rokem, *Tales of the Neighbourhood,* 86–137 (translation on 87). Violence: Foucault, *Discipline and Punish,* 29, 34; Gleason, "Mutilated Messengers."
55. Murder and the tyrant: Dunkle, "Greek Tyrant," 169. Marcus Aurelius: Dio 72(71).33.4^{2}: ἐγὼ σαφῶς ἤκουσα. Vespasian: Dio 66(66).17.1. Parricide to obtain kingship: TMI S22.1; note also in Jewish stories the common idea of the emperor's "bad son" and his rebelliousness (Goodman, *State and Society,* 153–54). Poisoning as folkloric motif: TMI S111. Julian and Helena: Libanius, *Orations* 37.1–13; one of Julian's doctors, Oribasius, wrote a memoir that no longer survives (Ross, *Ammianus' Julian,* 15, 167).
56. Antinous: Dio 69.11.2–4; Victor, *On the Caesars* 14.7–9; *Historia Augusta, Life of Hadrian* 14.6–7; Tatian, *Oration to the Greeks* 10; Birley, *Hadrian,* 247–57; Brennan, *Sabina,* 110–24, with Vout, *Power and Eroticism,* 113–21, on the cult. Pancrates: *PGM* IV.2446–55; Lucian, *Lover of Lies,* 33–36; Birley, *Hadrian,* 244–45; Ogden, "Apprentice's Sorcerer." Poetry: Höschele, "Two Lovers." Afterlife: Vout, *Power and Eroticism,* 59–61.
57. Agrippina: Ginsburg, *Representing Agrippina,* 46–53; Ps.-Seneca, *Octavia* ll. 310–30, is the earliest source for the plot; Tacitus, *Annals* 14.10.2–11.2 on the letter to the senate. Suetonius, *Nero* 39.2: Νέρων Ὀρέστης Ἀλκμέων μητροκτόνος. | νεόψηφον Νέρων ἰδίαν μητέρα ἀπέκτεινε. | "Quis negat Aeneae magna de stirpe Neronem? sustulit hic matrem,

sustulit ille patrem"; Dio 62(61).16.2^{2}–3 offers a slightly different take on the first. Motherkiller: Slater, "Speaking Verse," 300; see also Bartsch, *Theatricality and Doublespeak,* 38–40, on the use of Nero's stage roles in these jokes. Calculation joke: Kierdorf, *Claudius und Nero,* 218; note also modern anagrams, which work in a similar way: "President Clinton of the USA = to copulate he finds interns" (cited by Nisbet, *Greek Epigram,* 134n2). Elites and poetry: Zadorojnyi, "Transcripts of Dissent?," 123–24; Montlahuc, *Le pouvoir,* chap. VIII, sec. I.A.3. Note also Nisbet, *Greek Epigram,* 127–30, on *Palatine Anthology,* 11.247, a poem by the writer of epigrams, Lucillius, that alludes to the watery death of Agrippina.

58. Britannicus: Ps. Seneca, *Octavia* ll. 45–46, 115–24, 166–73; Suetonius, *Nero* 33.2–3. Other deaths: Suetonius, *Life of Nero* 34.2 (Agrippina), 35.5 (Burrus, cf. Tacitus, *Annals* 14.51.1–2, giving poison as a possible cause), 35.6 (freedmen, with Tacitus, *Annals* 14.65.1), 36.2 (children); Dio 62(61).17.1–2 (Domitia), cf. Suetonius, *Nero* 34.5 (laxative). Island: Dio Chrysostom, *Orations* 7.11–12: φασὶ δὲ καὶ αὐτὸν ἀπολέσθαι διὰ τὰ χρήματα ὑπὸ τοῦ βασιλέως.

59. Babylas: John Chrysostom, *Discourse on Saint Babylas* 5–6 (*PG* 50: 539–42), cf. Eusebius, *Ecclesiastical History* 6.34; *Chronicon Paschale,* 503B–504C (ed. Dindorf) (Leontius version); John Malalas 12.35; on the source tradition, see Schatkin, "Discourse on Blessed Babylas," 46–70.

60. Late Antique murders: Priscus, frag. 30.1 (ed. Blockley); John of Antioch, frag. 224.2–3 (ed. Mariev) (Valentinian III); *Chronicon Paschale* s.a. 467; John Malalas 14.40, 45 (Leo); McEvoy, *Child Emperor Rule,* 295–97; "Becoming Roman?," 491–92. Afterlife of Leo: *Patria* 3.104; Magdalino, "Generic Subversion," 215. Imperial woes: John Chrysostom, *Homilies on Philippians* 16(15).5 (*PG* 62: 294–95): Ἀμέλει καὶ συγγενικῶν αἱμάτων ἀεὶ γέμει τὸ ἔδαφος τὸ βασιλικὸν; Allen and Mayer, "*In epistulam ad Philippenses*"; Raschle, "Jean Chrysostome," 361–64. Social composition of church congregations: MacMullen, "Preacher's Audience," argued for predominantly wealthy male elites, but this has been nuanced by Mayer, "Who Came to Hear," and Maxwell, *Christianization and Communication,* 65–87, who note evidence for tradespeople, enslaved people, and women; see also Harrison, *Art of Listening,* 3, who proposes that only 10 percent of the early Christian population possessed "functional literacy."

61. Nero: Tacitus, *Annals* 15.42.2: "incredibilium cupitor." Wondrous deeds: *CIL* XIII 1668 (Claudius conquers the Ocean); *CIL* VI 960; Dio 68.16.3 (Trajan razes mountains); *CIL* III 737 (Theodosius I raises the obelisk); Pliny, *Natural History* 7.35; Phelgon of Tralles, *On Marvels, BNJ* frag. 36 XI–XXXV: 34–35; see further Beagon, "Situating Nature's Wonders," 30–32, 37–39 (prodigies exhibited); Martial, *On the Spectacles* 20(17), with Riemer, "Wundergeschichten," 219–23; Coleman, *Liber Spectaculorum,* lxxv, 157–58 (animals in Colosseum); and see now the excellent analysis in Christoforou, *Imagining,* chap. 4. Jewish tales: Feldman, "Some Observations," 54–55; Weingarten, "Rabbi and the Emperors," 54–59. Caligula's bridge: Seneca, *On the Shortness of Life* 18.5–6: "furiosi et externi et infeliciter superbi regis imitatio"; Suetonius, *Life of Caligula* 19.1–3: "sed auum meum narrantem puer audiebam causam operis ab interioribus aulicis proditam"; Barrett, *Caligula,* 242–43. Grandfather: Suetonius, *Otho* 10.1.

62. Mythological reenactments: Suetonius, *Nero* 12.2; Martial, *On the Spectacles* 6(5), 10(8); Coleman, "Fatal Charades," esp. 70–73; Bryen, "Histories of Violence," 142, with Foucault, *Discipline and Punish,* 47–49. Commodus: Dio, *Roman History* 73(72).20.1–3; see also *Historia Augusta, Commodus* 9.6; Hekster, *Commodus,* 117–29, 135–36; Christoforou, *Imagining,* 156–58.

63. Valerian: Letter of Dionysius, quoted in Eusebius, *Church History* 7.10.4; Baumkamp, *Kommunikation,* 85–87. Maxentius: Eusebius, *Church History* 8.14.5; *Life of Constantine* 1.36.1. Sacrifice: Marasco, "Costantino"; Rives, "Human Sacrifice," 72–73; for related folkloric motifs, see TMI S260.1.1 ("Child Sacrifice as Religious Rite"), S263.2 ("Child Sacrificed to Gain Favor of Gods").

64. Written down: Goodman, *State and Society,* 136, highlights the rare historical specificity in Jewish stories about this period. Trajan: *Jerusalem Talmud, Tractate Sukkah* 5.1 (trans. Guggenheimer, *Tractates Šeqalim, Sukkah*); Stemberger, *Die römische Herrschaft,* 75–78; Goodman, "Trajan," 25–27. Hadrian: *Jerusalem Talmud, Tractate Ta'aniot* 4.8 (trans. Guggenheimer, *Tractates Ta'aniot, Megillah*); with Schäfer, *Der Bar Kokhba-Aufstand,* 161–62, 166–68, on the tradition of the eighty thousand dead; and Horbury, *Jewish War,* 395–401, on archaeological evidence and memories.

65. Aelia Capitolina: Goodman, "Trajan," 28–29. Coins: Jacobson, "Insights"; Goodman, "Coinage and Identity," discusses Hebrew legends celebrating Jerusalem, Israel, and Zion on coinage produced in the earlier revolt of 66 to 74. Removing Hadrian: *Midrash Rabbah, Lamentations* 2.2.4 (trans. Freedman and Simon, *Midrash Rabbah*).

66. Fire: Tacitus, *Annals* 15.38–41; Suetonius, *Nero* 38; Dio 62(62).16.1–18.5. Explanations: Dio 50.10.3–6 (31 BCE); Dio 55.8.6 (reign of Augustus); Tacitus, *Annals* 4.64.1 (Tiberius); Dio 66(66).24.1–3 (Titus); Eusebius, *Church History* 8.6.6 (Diocletian). Comparative evidence: Roberts, "Arson"; Allemeyer, "Profane Hazard"; Cressy, *Dangerous Talk,* 33; Barrett, *Rome Is Burning,* 117. Rumor not widespread among the people: Champlin, *Nero,* 184, 319–20. Lucan: Statius, *Silvae* 2.7.60–61, with Tacitus, *Annals* 15.49; Vacca, *Life of Lucan* (ed. Hosius); Suetonius, *On the Lives of Illustrious Men* (ed. Rostagni); and above all Ahl, "Lucan's *De Incendio Urbis,*" whose interpretation I follow here. Subrius Flavus: Tacitus, *Annals* 15.67.2–3: "odisse coepi, postquam parricida matris et uxoris, auriga et histrio et incendiarius extitisti," followed by "ipsa . . . verba" ("the actual words"), with Syme, *Tacitus,* 300–301; Champlin, *Nero,* 185–86; Ash, *Book XV,* 297, who notes that Tacitus usually paraphrases, which marks out this verbatim quotation as a significant statement. Oral tradition: Marx, "Tacitus und die Literatur," 93.

67. Nero's revenge: Ps.-Seneca, *Octavia* l. 831: "mox tecta flammis concidant urbis meis"; for the date, see Boyle, *Octavia,* xiv–xvi (early Flavian); and Kragelund, *Roman Historical Drama,* 297–360 (late 68), against the implausible attempts of Ferri, *Octavia,* 5–30, to argue for a Domitianic date. Intellectual background: Kragelund, *Roman Historical Drama,* 306–14; Geue, *Author Unknown,* 113–14, argues the play deliberately attempts to blacken the emperor's reputation and popularity with the people of Rome.

68. Golden House: Tacitus, *Annals* 15.42.1; Suetonius, *Nero* 31.1–2; Griffin, *Nero,* 133–42; Champlin, *Nero,* 200–209. Verses: Suetonius, *Nero* 39.2: "Roma domus fiet: Veios

migrate, Quirites, | si non et Veios occupat ista domus." Other criticism: Lucillius, *Palatine Anthology* 11.184, a contemporary epigram, alludes to the gardens of the Golden House and in particular Nero's "fatal charades" staged there (Nisbet, *Greek Epigram,* 123–27; Smith, "Art, Nature, Power," 339–42).

69. Demonic witnesses: Procopius, *Secret History* 12.18–23; Gantar, "Kaiser Justinian"; Procopius, *Gothic Wars* 3.32.9 has priests as the emperor's companions; on asceticism and wakefulness, see Meier, *Das andere Zeitalter,* 620–23; Leppin, *Justinian,* 287. Demons: Cameron, *Procopius,* 54–57, notes that the demonic accusations were meant seriously; see further Ruffini, *Aphrodito,* 136–38, on belief in demons in an Egyptian village. Publication: Procopius, *Secret History* 1.1–3, 30.34; Cameron, *Procopius,* 47–52, arguing that the work was unrevised at Procopius's own death, with Kaldellis, "Dissident Circles," on opposition. Faces: Procopius, *Buildings* 17; *Secret History* 8.27–33, 12.20–32, 18.1–45.

70. Justin II: John of Ephesus, *Ecclesiastical History Part III,* 3.2, 3.24 (I am grateful to Philip Forness for the translation of the poem). Columns: McEvoy, "Emperors, Aristocrats, and Columns," 444–46, esp. n76; as McEvoy notes, the other figures who presided over the Constantinopolitan skyline were the holy men who took up residence on columns within divine favor.

71. Park: Michael Psellos, *Chronography* 6.10, 14, 23–28, 161–63, 173–75, 186–87, 201–2; Maguire, "Gardens and Parks," 259–62; Spingou, "Snapshots," 61–65.

72. Augustus's house: Suetonius, *Augustus* 5–6; Donderer, "Zu den Häusern," 649–50; Riemer, "Wundergeschichten," 224. Portents: Vigourt, *Les présages impériaux;* Potter, *Prophets and Emperors,* 163–64. Images: Suetonius, *Tiberius* 53.2; Tacitus, *Annals* 3.36.1–3, 4.67.4; Hopkins, *Conquerors and Slaves,* 220–23; Price, *Rituals and Power,* 188–93. Petitions: *P. Oxy.* 17.2130; Kunderewicz, "Quelques remarques," 127–28. Vespasian's healing: Tacitus, *Histories* 4.81; Dio 66(65).8.1; cf. Suetonius, *Vespasian* 7.2–3 (who gives the version with the lame man). Eyewitnesses: Tacitus, *Histories* 4.81: "utrumque qui interfuere nunc quoque memorant, postquam nullum mendacio pretium." Belief: Leppin, "Imperial Miracles," 244. Vespasian as Serapis: *P. Fouad.* 8; Henrichs, "Vespasian's Visit," 69–72. New form of legitimacy: Engster, "Der Kaiser als Wundertäter," esp. 304–5. One-off event: compare the sick who flocked to Jesus and spread news of his healing miracles far and wide (Matthew 4: 23–25, 9: 27–31, 35, 12: 15–16; John 1: 40–45). Regime control: Potter, *Emperors and Prophets,* 173.

73. Limits: Epictetus, *Discourses* 3.13.9–10. Hadrian: *Historia Augusta, Hadrian* 25.1–3. Justinian: Procopius, *Buildings* 1.7.1–16; Leppin, *Justinian,* 287–88; "Imperial Miracles," 245–46; cf. Meier, *Das andere Zeitalter,* 622–25 (suggesting Justinian himself gained the capacity to heal because the oil covered his feet, not just his clothes). Miracles: Bloch, *Royal Touch,* 12–27, locates the beginnings of the "royal touch" in France in the reign of Robert the Pious, and under Henry I in England. Romans did not have it: Lendon, *Empire of Honour,* 9–10; Spahlinger, "Sueton-Studien II," 434–44. Mughal emperor Akbar I: Mukhia, *Mughals of India,* 167–68. Japanese emperors: Shillony, *Sacred Subservience,* 162. Sainthood of Constantine and Helena: *CSLA* S00185–86; Drijvers, "Helena Augusta," 131–35; Harbus, *Helena of Britain,* 33–34, 44–51; Hillner, *Helena,* 343–44, shows that Helena's transition to sainthood occurred

more quickly in the western empire. Constantine's chapel: Mango, "Constantine's Porphyry Column." Rites and relics: Wortley, "Sacred Remains," 357–61. Russian visitor: *Anonymous Description of Constantinople* in Majeska, *Russian Travellers,* 150–51. Nor was the ability to heal shared by all imperial saints: Talbot, "Pilgrimage," 156–57.

74. Emperors and miracles: Clauss, *Kaiser und Gott,* 113–15, 346–47; Riemer, "Wundergeschichten"; see also Fishwick, "Votive Offerings," on the lack of prayers to emperors as gods. Rain miracle: Dio 72(71).8–10; *HA Marcus Aurelius* 24.4. Prayers: Ruggini, "Ecclesiastical Histories," 109–18. River Frigidus: John Chrysostom, *Homily against the Novatians* (*PG* 63:491–92); Rufinus, *Ecclesiastical History* 11.33; Cameron, *Last Pagans,* 93–131. Plague: Suetonius, *Titus* 8.4. Sophia: *Palatine Anthology* 1.11 = *CSLA* E00554 (E. Rizos). Apocalyptic: Alexander, *Byzantine Apocalyptic;* Kraft, "Last Roman Emperor"; "Miracles." Cf. the avenging Nero in the *Sibylline Oracles,* discussed in Chapter 4.

75. Secundus and Hadrian: *Secundus the Silent Philosopher* (ed. Perry): τῆς δ' ἐμῆς φωνῆς καὶ τοῦ ἐμοῦ προφορητικοῦ λόγου οὐδεμία σοί ἐστιν ἐξουσία (quotation from ll. 19–20). Date: Perry, *Secundus,* 1–23 (on context and history of the Greek text); Overwien, "Secundus," 340–43 (on more recent discoveries).

76. Oral tradition: Kim, "Orality, Folktales," 304–7, 317–18. Incest: TMI N383.3, T412,2, ATU 823A* ("Mother Dies of Fright"), 920A*. Alexander: Stoneman, "Naked Philosophers," 114; TMI K2101. Body: Sextus, *Sentences* 363b: σοφοῦ σώματος καὶ λέων ἄρχει, τούτου δὴ μόνου καὶ τύραννος." *Parrhesia:* Davenport, "Envisioning Audiences," 284–88, on the court; Leppin, *Paradoxe der Parrhesie,* 94–147, on this phenomenon on a larger canvas.

77. Imperial workload: Millar, "Emperors at Work."

78. Images: Heskter, *Caesar Rules,* 285–92. General population: note Goodman, *State and Society,* 152, on perceptions of emperors in rabbinic sources: "The function of kings seems to be the waging of war, dynastic struggle, and the control of family and advisers."

2. *SEX, SCANDAL, AND SATIRE*

1. Abstinence: Nicolaus of Damascus, *Life of Caesar* 36: φωνῆς ἅμα καὶ ἰσχύος προνοῶν; Wardle, *Augustus,* 427; with Dugan, "Preventing Ciceronianism"; Brown, *Body and Society,* 18–19, on the medical background; Pliny, *Natural History* 34.166, on the plates. Accusations: Suetonius, *Augustus* 68; Parker, "Teratogenic Grid"; Richlin, *Garden of Priapus,* 92, notes that Romans thought effeminate men were more interested in sex.

2. Bodies: Edwards, *Politics of Immorality,* 63–97; Corbeill, *Controlling Laughter,* 14–56; Meister, "Pisos Augenbrauen"; *Der Körper des Princeps,* 21–107. Sexual invective: Richlin, *Garden of Priapus,* 86–104; Corbeill, *Controlling Laughter,* 104–27, 143–69; Rosillo-López, *Public Opinion,* 125–27, 131–34. Scipio: Aulus Gellius 6.12.5: "eumne quisquam dubitet, quin idem fecerit quod cinaedi facere solent?" *Cinaedus:* Parker, "Teratogenic Grid," 58; Williams, *Roman Homosexuality,* 175–83, 209–18. cf. Richlin, "Not before Homosexuality," 530, who argues it was "roughly the equivalent of the

English term 'queer.' " Invective as gossip: Harding, "All Pigs," a critique of Hunter, "Politics of Reputation"; but there were certainly interactions between the formal speech of orations and the informal speech of rumor and gossip, e.g., Eidinow, "Gossip, Slander" (Greece); Dufallo, "Appius' Indignation," 138–39 (Rome); Rizzi, "Violent Language," 149–50 (early modern Italy). Octavius: Antonius's criticisms were made in the form of an edict: Cicero, *Philippics* 3.5; Scott, "Political Propaganda," 11–12. Gossip: Richlin, *Garden of Priapus,* 83–86. Nicomedes: Osgood, "Caesar and Nicomedes"; Kelly, "An Unforgotten Episode"; Suetonius, *Caesar* 49.1–4; Dio 43.20.2; and see Montlahuc, *Le pouvoir,* chap. IV, sec. 1.B.2, on triumphal songs articulating current rumors while simultaneously generating new ones.

3. Lead sling bullets: e.g., *CIL* XI 6721.5, 7, 9a, 9b = *AshLI* 428: "Octavi || felas"; 6721.11: "Octavi | laxe || sede"; Hallett, "*Perusinae Glandes,*" 152–60. Aggression: Richlin, *Garden of Priapus.*
4. Augustus: Suetonius, *Augustus* 68: "uidesne ut cinaedus orbem digito temperat?"; Wardle, *Augustus,* 439–40. Already gossiping: Richlin, *Arguments with Silence,* 53.
5. Rumor: Pliny, *Panegyric* 83.1: "Habet hoc primum magna fortuna, quod nihil tectum, nihil occultum esse patitur; principum vero non domus modo sed cubicula ipsa intimosque secessus recludit, omniaque arcana noscenda Famae proponit atque explicat"; with Chong-Gossard, "Who Slept," 318–19. Republican idea: Cicero, *On Duties* 2.44; Welch, "*Lux.*" Palace: *CTh.* 15.1.47 = *CJ* 8.11.17 (409): "nam imperio magna ab uniuersis secreta debentur." Republic to Empire: Edwards, *Politics of Immorality,* 27–28; Langlands, *Sexual Morality,* 348–53 (focusing on Suetonius, but the point is generally applicable); Courrier, *La plèbe de Rome,* 650–52, 666–74; Hawkins, "Pollio's Paradox"; on the impossibility of knowing what was happening in a monarchy, see Dio 53.19.2–6; Davenport, "News, Rumour." Anonymity: Scott, *Arts of Resistance,* 140–52. Libel and *maiestas:* Suetonius, *Augustus* 55; *Digest* 47.10.5.9–10; Bauman, *Impietas in principem,* 25–51; with Harries, *Law and Crime,* 77–81; Peachin, "Judicial Powers," 537–40, on treason.
6. Edict: Lactantius, *On the Deaths of the Persecutors* 13.2: "victorias Gothorum et Sarmatarum propositas"; for a possible example of a similar pun in a satirical epigram of Palladas, see Wilkinson, "Sarmatian and the Indians." Julian's pallet: Julian, *Misopogon* 340B.
7. Invectives: Gregory of Nazianzus, *Orations* 4.52, 96. Reputation: Quintus Cicero, *A Short Guide to Electioneering* 17: "nam fere omnis sermo ad forensem famam a ticis emanat auctoribus." Elite woman: Juvenal, *Satires* 6.398–412. Neighbours: *Distichs of Cato* 3.2: "arbitrii non est nostri quid quisque loquatur." Palace gossip: Eunapius, frag. 66.1 (ed. Blockley): θελγόμενοι καὶ καταγοητευόμενοι; frag. 50. Discussion circles: O'Neill, "Going Round in Circles"; Quintilian, *Institutions of Rhetoric* 12.10.74; Tacitus *Annals* 3.54.1.
8. Otho: Suetonius, *Otho* 3.2: "cur Otho mentito sit quaeritis exul honore? | uxoris moechus coeperat esse suae"; see also Tacitus, *Histories* 1.13.2; *Annals* 13.45–46. Elite authors: Zadorojnyi, "Transcripts of Dissent?" Poets like Lucillius, who skewered Nero in his epigrams, could be the "anonymous" authors. See Nisbet, *Greek Epigram,* 113–33, for the relationship, esp. 133 for the suggestion that Lucillius may have been the one

"setting the agenda" for the anonymous poets cited by Suetonius; cf. Floridi, *Lucillio, Epigrammi,* 4–5, who unconvincingly dismisses all political meaning in Lucillius's poetry. Popular poets: Angius, "Graffiti e pamphlet," 272–77. Catherine de' Medici: McIlvenna, "Poison," 142–43, 153–54. Mughal Dehli: Kaicker, *King and the People,* 99–100. France: Hunt, "Many Bodies," 116; Darnton, *Art of Slander,* on the libel industry. Russia: Figes and Kolonitskii, *Russian Revolution,* 13–18; Aksenov, "Peasant Popular Consciousness." Pamphlets: Suetonius, *Augustus* 51.1, 55; Dio 55.27.1–3.

9. Consequences: Gluckman, "Gossip and Scandal," esp. 312; Scott, *Arts of Resistance,* 142–44; Wickham, "Gossip and Resistance," esp. 18–19; Merry, "Rethinking Gossip," esp. 296. Emotional experience: Besnier, *Gossip,* 18–19, 97–98.

10. Limits of joking: Critchley, *On Humour,* 10–11; Clarke, *Looking at Laughter,* 7–9. Sex and scandal: Sarmiento-Mirwaldt, Allen, and Birch, "No Sex Scandals" (France); Summers, "Politics and Pecadilloes"; Bai, *All the Truth Is Out* (United States). Negotiation: White, "Between Gluckman and Foucault," 78.

11. Powerful ignoring gossip: Merry, "Rethinking Gossip," 286–87. Resistance: O'Neill, "Going Round in Circles," 145.

12. Terentia: Dio 54.19.1–3, see also 55.7.5; with Rich, *Cassius Dio,* 7–8; Swan, *Augustan Succession,* 21–23, on Dio's first-century sources; the contemporary nature of the gossip is shown by Suetonius, *Augustus* 69.2, who quotes a letter from Marcus Antonius referring to Augustus's love of Terentia; Wardle, *Augustus,* 442–43.

13. Marriage to Livia: Suetonius, *Claudius* 1.1: τοῖς εὐτυχοῦσι καὶ τρίμηνα παιδία; Scott, "Political Propaganda," 31; Hurley, *Divus Claudius,* 57; Dio 48.44.5. Legislation: Suetonius, *Augustus* 34.1–2; Dio 54.16.1–7; for discussion, see Treggiari, *Roman Marriage,* 277–98; Edwards, *Politics of Immorality,* 37–42. Augustus as example: Augustus, *Res Gestae* 8.5. Drusus: Valerius Maximus 4.3.3; see Noreña, "Hadrian's Chastity," on male sexual continence.

14. Imperial house: Corbier, "La maison"; Moreau, "La *domus Augusta*"; Hug, *Fertility,* 192–94. Women: Merry, "Rethinking Gossip," 278–80. Augustus's family values: Severy, *Augustus and the Family;* Milnor, *Gender, Domesticity.* Julia: Suetonius, *Augustus* 64.2: "vetaretque loqui aut agere quicquam nisi propalam et quod in diurnos commentarios referretur"; Edwards, *Politics of Immorality,* 61–62; Milnor, *Gender, Domesticity,* 85. Clothes: *Augustus* 73.

15. Julia's exile: Velleius Paterculus 2.100.2–5; Suetonius, *Augustus* 65.2; Dio 55.10.12–16; Severy, *Augustus and the Family,* 180–84; Wardle, *Augustus,* 420–21. Lovers: Velleius Paterculus 2.100.4–5; see also Plutarch, *Sayings of Kings and Commanders* 207D–E. Augustus goes public: Seneca, *On Benefits* 6.32.1–2. Protests: Suetonius, *Augustus* 65.3; Dio 55.13.1.

16. Julia's wit: Macrobius 2.5.5–9; "et hi mecum senes fient" (6); "numquam enim nisi navi plena tollo vectorem" (9); Long, "Julia-Jokes," 25; Richlin, *Arguments with Silence,* 94. Humorous stories as gossip: Besnier, *Gossip,* 115. Augustus: Dio 55.9.13; Macrobius 2.5.3; on Augustus's personal conduct, see Chrol and Blake, "Sexuality," 366–67. Marsus and Julia: Long, "Julia-Jokes," 344; Richlin, *Arguments with Silence,* 90, 98. Augustus's letter: Pliny, *Natural History* 21.9. Sympathy: Schaberg, "Word of Mouth," 22–23 (China); Bartlett, *Blood Royal,* 127 (Byzantium); Hunt, "Morality and Monarchy" (Britain).

17. Sexual display: Langlands, *Sexual Morality,* 353–57; and on the court environment, Chrol and Blake, "Sexuality." Sex and childbearing values: Hug, *Fertility;* Brown, *Body and Society,* 19–21; for examples in Late Antiquity, see *P. Gr. Vindob.* 29788C recto, l. 16; Priscian, *In Praise of Anastasius* l. 42. Earinus: Martial, *Epigrams* 9.11–13, 16–17, 36; Statius, *Silvae* 3.4; Vout, *Power and Eroticism,* 167–204, is fundamental, esp. 170; Martial, *Epigrams* 9.16.3: "ille puer tota domino gratissimus aula." Hair: Statius, *Silvae* 3.prcf.17–20; Henriksén, "Earinus," 285–89. Emperors and gods: Vout, *Power and Eroticism,* 1–39; Blanshard, *Sex,* 85–87. Hadrian: Noreña, "Hadrian's Chastity." Antinous: *P. Oxy.* 63.4352, frag. 5, II; Vout, *Power and Eroticism,* 100–102; Livrea, "Chi e' l'autore," suggests the author was the African poet Soterichus of Oasis.

18. Sporus: Dio Chrysostom, *Orations* 21.6–8; Suetonius, *Nero* 28.1–2; Dio 62(62).28.1–3, 3a, 62(63).13.1–2; Vout, *Power and Eroticism,* 136–61. Joke: Suetonius, *Nero* 28.1: "extatque cuiusdam non inscitus iocus, bene agi potuisse cum rebus humanis si Domitius pater talem habuisset uxorem"; Richlin, *Garden of Priapus,* 91, observes that such stories "feed the hostile fantasies of those who hear them." Humor: Beard, *Laughter,* 3–6, 37, 135–36 (resistance to power); Critchley, *On Humour,* 9 (as liberation). Gossip as a weapon: Paine, "What Is Gossip About?"; Besnier, *Gossip,* 16. Flattery: Plutarch, *Moralia* 56F: οὐχ ὁ τῶν κολακευόντων ἔπαινος; Bartsch, *Theatricality and Doublespeak,* 24–25.

19. Nero and Agrippina: Tacitus, *Annals* 14.2.1–2; Levick, "Cluvius Rufus," 550–53; "Fabius Rusticus," 568–69; see *Annals* 13.20.2 for Fabius's relationship with Seneca. Other sources: Suetonius, *Nero* 28.2; Bradley, *Nero,* 163; Dio 62(61).11.4. Revolt: Dio 63(63).22.2 includes a speech of the Gallic governor Vindex in which he gives the incest and murder of Agrippina as a reason for revolt, but we cannot be sure that Vindex actually made such a claim; Dio 63(63).27.2b; Plutarch, *Galba* 7.1 (Nero declared public enemy).

20. Vitellius: Suetonius, *Vitellius* 3.2: "inter Tiberiana scorta"; Champlin, "Sex on Capri," 322–27; Woodman, *Books 5 and 6,* 91–92. Caracalla: Dio 78(77).16.2[1]: καὶ ἀπ' αὐτοῦ καὶ ἕτεροι τῶν ὁμοιοτρόπων; Davenport, "Sexual Habits," 90–96.

21. Tiberius: Suetonius, *Tiberius* 45: "adsensu maximo excepta percrebruit, 'hircum uetulum capreis naturam ligurire'"; with Champlin, "Mallonia," 225–26, on the translation, though I do not agree with him that the entire story, including the line from the farce, is invented. There are similar themes in extant plays, e.g., Plautus, *The Merchant* 575; Augoustakis, "Castrate the He-Goat!" 42; Mallan, "Tiberius the Goat," shows the link between goats and oral sex. Men performing oral sex: Parker, "Teratogenic Grid," 51–53; Clarke, *Looking at Laughter,* 198–201. Russia: Figes and Kolonitskii, *Russian Revolution,* 25–26. Mechanics of transmission: Montlahuc, *Le pouvoir,* chap. VIII, sec. I.A.3.

22. Games: Hülsen, "Miscellanea epigrafica," 228 no. 2 ("patice"), 229 no. 20 ("cunu•linge"), 230 no. 30 ("cinaidus"). Humor: Critchley, *On Humour,* 9–10; Beard, *Laughter,* 196–97, on laughter as a "marker of areas of disruption and anxiety"; Röcke and Velten, "Einleitung"; Althoff, "Vom Lächeln," shows how laughter shapes communities; on humor and the emperor, see Laurence and Paterson, "Power"; Christoforou, *Imagining,* chap. 5. Gossip and social groups: Gluckman, "Gossip and Scandal," 15; Bergmann, *Discreet Indiscretions,* 51–52. Orations: Menander Rhetor, *Treatise* 2.1.32 (376).

Gossip and politics: Scott, *Arts of Resistance,* 136–37; Beard, *Laughter,* 3; Gottesman, *Politics and the Street,* 16–19, 81–83 (on Athens, but the principle can be applied to Rome).

23. Caracalla: Herodian 4.9.3; Davenport, "Sexual Habits." Euphrosyne: Niketas Choniates, *History* (ed. van Dieten): πολιτικὴ τὸ δίκαιον.

24. Julian: John Chrysostom, *Discourse on Saint Babylas* 14 (*PG* 50: 555); see also Ammianus 22.14.3; Ephrem the Syrian, *Hymns against Julian* 2.4–9; Lieu, *Emperor Julian,* 100–101; Forness, "Faithful Rulers," 145–53; Griffith, "Ephraem the Syrian," 244, for the idea of "biblically oriented meditations." Nisibis: Drijvers, *Forgotten Reign,* 37–49.

25. Adultery: Beard, *Emperor,* 204–5. Choice: Hug, *Fertility,* 238–39, building on the work of Duindam, *Dynasties,* e.g., 88: "dynasty cannot be equated with the practice of male primogeniture alone"; note also Chrol and Blake, "Sexuality," 353–54, who point out that monogamy "limited an emperor's reproductive power" and the ensuing options for dynastic stability.

26. Scandal: *OED,* s.v. "scandal," n., 3a; Thompson, *Political Scandal,* 1–59; Clark, *Scandal,* 1–10, 208–10; Gluckman, "Gossip and Scandal," 312. Edward VIII: the scandal broke in the British press across December 1–4: Siebert, "Press," 122–24; Mort, "Love in a Cold Climate."

27. Rome: Klein and Moser, "Modern Scandal Theory." Lothar: Stone and West, *Divorce of King Lothar,* esp. 121–22. Monarchy and sex: Airlie, "Private bodies" (Lothar II); McLaughlin, "Disgusting Acts" (Henry IV of Germany); Clark, *Scandal,* 180–81 (eighteenth-century Britain). Revolutions: Hunt, "Many Bodies"; Maza, "Diamond Necklace Affair"; Darnton, *Literary Underground,* 142–47; Figes and Kolonitskii, *Russian Revolution.* There can of course also be scandal about nonpolitical figures; for Roman examples, see Shanzer, "Some Treatments" and "Augustine's *Epp.* 77–78."

28. Marcus Aurelius: Fronto, *Letters to Marcus as Emperor* 2.1, 2.2, and *Letters to His Friends* 1.14 (ed. van den Hout); Davenport and Manley, *Fronto,* 143–49. Commodus: Dio 73(73).6.1–2. Plotina: Dio 68.5.5: τοιαύτη μέντοι ἐνταῦθα ἐσέρχομαι οἵα καὶ ἐξελθεῖν βούλομαι.

29. Octavia: Tacitus, *Annals* 14.60.1–61.1 (there is a lacuna in the text, but the sense of the passage requires the circulation of a rumor); Suetonius, *Nero* 35.1–2; Pseudo-Seneca, *Octavia,* esp. ll. 183–85, 273–90, 572–80, 646–68, 780–859, 877–98 (this shows the contemporary resonance); Kragelund, *Roman Historical Drama,* 206–9, 278–80; Ginsberg, *Staging Memory,* 115–40. Edicts: Benner, *Emperor Says,* 25–30; Corbier, "L'ecriture," 33, 52. Edict, exile, murder: Suetonius, *Nero* 37.2; Tacitus, *Annals* 14.62.1–3. Knowledge of the edict likely comes from Tacitus's use of the archives, on which see Syme, *Tacitus,* 278–86, 294–96; Devillers, "L'*Octavie.*" Like Kragelund, *Roman Historical Drama,* 303–6, I think that the *Octavia* depended heavily on oral discourse, rather than written sources.

30. Domitia Longina: Suetonius, *Domitian* 13.1: "reuocatam eam in puluinar suum"; 13.1: "Domino et Dominae feliciter"; Dio 67.3.1–2. *Pulvinar:* van den Berg, "*Pulvinar,*" 256–57, 267–68. Her life: Jones, *Domitian,* 34–38; Fraser, "Domitian Longina." Julia: Suetonius, *Domitian* 22; Jones, *Domitian,* 38–40. Flavius Sabinus: Jones, *Domitian,*

44–74; Suetonius, *Domitian* 10.4. Helvidius Priscus: Suetonius, *Domitian* 10.4; Bartsch, *Theatricality and Doublespeak,* 78–79. Contemporary nature of talk: Pliny, *Panegyric* 52.3, 63.7, delivered a decade later, has offhand references to the incident that presuppose people knew what he was talking about (thus Blanshard, *Sex,* 83); for later sources, see Pliny, *Letters* 4.11.6; Juvenal, *Satires* 2.29–33 (with Braund, *Juvenal,* 16). Interpretations: Fraser, "Domitia Longina," 232–35, emphasizes rumor and gossip; Vinson, "Domitia Longina," invective.

31. Asia: Dio 79(80).7.4, 18.3, shows Dio did receive information from elsewhere in the empire. Lovers: Dio 80(79).15.1–16.6; Osgood, "Secret History." Large penises: Garland, *Eye of the Beholder,* 53–54, collects examples of other Romans with (alleged) similar desires. Sayings: Dio 80(79).9.3, 16.4: μή με λέγε κύριον· ἐγὼ γὰρ κυρία εἰμί; 18.4 (two), 19.3. Aelian: Philostratus, *Lives of the Sophists* 625: κατηγορία τοῦ Γύννιδος; *On the Nature of Animals,* Epilogue (avoidance of court): Smith, *Man and Animal,* 11–28. Fragments: Smith, *Man and Animal,* 274–79; *Suda* K82: γύναιον ἐκ Συρίας (I use Smith's translation); *Suda* E1382; Dio 80(79).13.3–4 (palace gatherings).

32. Aquilia Severa: Dio 80(79).9.3–4: ἵνα δὴ καὶ θεοπρεπεῖς παῖδες ἔκ τε ἐμοῦ τοῦ ἀρχιερέως ἔκ τε ταύτης τῆς ἀρχιερείας γεννῶνται, τοῦτ' ἐποίησα; Herodian 5.6.2; *Historia Augusta, Elagabalus* 6.6. Letter: Rea, "Letter": "in cubiculo meo non eri[t]."

33. Soldiers: Dio 80(79).17.1, 19.2–3: συνασελγαινόντων; Herodian 5.8.1, 8; *Historia Augusta, Elagabalus* 15.1–4; note also Tacitus, *Annals* 14.2.1, an insinuation that the soldiers would not support Nero if he had a perverted relationship with his mother. Downfall: Kemezis, "Fall of Elagabalus," is a stimulating article that emphasizes the importance of court politics, though he thinks the sexual stories were circulated by the regime of his successor, Severus Alexander, rather than contributing directly to his downfall (an argument followed by Chrol and Blake, "Sexuality," 370).

34. Heraclius and Martina: Garland, *Byzantine Empresses,* 61–72; Kaegi, *Heraclius,* 106–7; Viermann, *Herakleios,* 171–75. Drawing: Booth, "Images," 397–98. Incest forbidden: *CTh.* 3.12.1. Poem: George of Pisidia, *The Persian Expedition,* 3.410–15 (*PG* 92: 1256); Howard-Johnston, *Witnesses,* 33–34, states the poet usually avoided mention of Martina (Whitby, "Defender of the Cross," 256–57), and therefore argues that the reference was unintentional (this does not, of course, control how it was interpreted by others). Hostility: Nicephorus, *Short History* (ed. de Boor), 14–15 (Sergius and protests); 23 (ἡ ἁμαρτία αὐτοῦ ἐνώπιον αὐτοῦ διὰ παντός, brother's criticism); for the reliability of Nicephorus's Constantinopolitan sources on Heraclius and his family, see Howard-Johnston, *Witnesses,* 252–53; on the Hippodrome protests, Cameron, *Circus Factions,* 339–40.

35. Martina: Nicephorus, *Short History* (ed. de Boor), 27–31; Theophanes AM 6132–34; John of Nikiu 120.1–55; Viermann, *Herakleios,* 318–23, regards the speech as fictional, but see Olster, "Constans II," for its historicity. For resistance against inappropriate marriages in later Byzantium, see Laiou, "Imperial Marriages"; Tougher, *Leo VI,* 133–63.

36. Augustus and Agrippa: Hurlet, *Les collègues,* 25–32; Cooley, *Res Gestae,* 37, 140–41. Agrippa and Marcellus: Velleius Paterculus 2.93.2: "(ut fama loquitur) ob tacitas cum Marcello offensiones praesenti se subduxerat tempori"; Cassius Dio 53.32.1 (legates);

Koenen, "Die *laudatio funebris,*" 269–83. Later versions: Pliny, *Natural History* 7.149; Suetonius, *Augustus* 66.3; *Tiberius* 10.1; Cassius Dio 53.32.1; see also Tacitus, *Annals* 14.53.3, which only says Augustus allowed Agrippa to depart for Mytilene. Modern assessments: Magie, "Mission of Agrippa"; Rich, *Cassius Dio,* 167–68; Hurlet, *Les collègues,* 33–52; Wardle, *Augustus,* 431. Elites: comparative evidence from early modern courts inspired this line of argument (e.g., Coast, *News and Rumour,* 123–28).

37. Tiberius's command: Dio 55.9.4; Levick, *Tiberius,* 22; Swan, *Augustan Succession,* 85. Nemausus: Suetonius, *Tiberius* 13.1: the news need not have taken two years to reach here, since the city was only an eight-day journey by sea from Rome in good weather (calculated using Stanford ORBIS: https://orbis.stanford.edu/); the statue desecration likely had a local catalyst not known to us. Reaction: Suetonius, *Tiberius* 13.1: "exulis"; 59.1: "Non es eques; quare? non sunt tibi milia centum, | omnia si quaeras. et Rhodus exilium est"; Cupaiuolo, *Le pasquinate,* 65; Courtney, *Latin Poets,* 447. Exiles lose citizenship: *Digest* 48.1.2, 48.19.2. Equestrian rank: Davenport, *Equestrian Order,* 214–18.

38. Rhodes: Velleius Paterculus 2.99.1–4, 101.1; Tacitus, *Annals* 1.53.1; Suetonius, *Tiberius* 10.1–13.2; Dio 55.9.1–8: κατεικάζετο πάνθ' ὅσα ἐνεδέχετο; 55.10.19. Gaius and Lucius: Hurlet, *Les collègues,* 113–25.

39. Julian: Ammianus 16.11.13; Julian, *Letter to the Athenians* 274C–D. Stilicho: Priscus 5.2 (ed. Blockley) = Sozomen 9.4.4–8 (Theodosius II); Orosius 7.38; Philostorgius 12.1–2 (Honorius), all of whom are fifth-century sources; McEvoy, *Child Emperor Rule,* 180–86.

40. Virtues: Brown, *Body and Society,* 283; Leppin, "Das Bild," 395–96; McEvoy, "Orations," 118–27. Eudocia: Holum, *Theodosian Empresses,* 176–94; on the Holy Land, see Lenski, "Empresses," 117–18; *CIIP* no. 816 (inscription recording relic deposition). Contemporary discussion: Nestorius, *The Bazaar of Heracleides* 379 (trans. Driver and Hodgson); Cameron, "Empress and the Poet," 258–59; in the sixth century, Evagrius, *Church History* 1.21, expressed skepticism about the official reasons given for Eudocia's presence in Jerusalem. Chrysaphius: Malalas 14.19; Cameron, "Empress and the Poet," 263–70; *Wandering Poets,* 41–64. Cyrus: *Palatine Anthology* 9.136: ὀλοοὶ κηφῆνες.

41. Apple: John Malalas 14.8; Braccini, "Apple," 301–3. Cf. Scharf, "Die 'Apfel-Affäre,'" connecting the events with a court scandal and a putative son, "Arcadius II." Folklore: Holum, *Theodosian Empresses,* 177; Braccini, "Apple." "Husband's Magic Gift Returns to Him": TMI N212.1; gifts in adulterous relationships are very common, see "Lover's Gift Regained" (TMI K1581). "Calumniated Wife": TMI K2110.1. Apple symbolism: Littlewood, "Apple in Byzantine Literature." Historical event: Cameron, *Wandering Poets,* 59, 62.

42. Pulcheria: Burgess, "Accession of Marcian," 50–51; van Esbroeck, "La pomme," discusses a different, Armenian version in which Pulcheria kills her brother; for the conflict over religious orthodoxy in the fifth century, see Scott, "From Propaganda to History"; and Schulz, "*Fragmentum Tusculanum* II," offering different views.

43. Statues and portraits: Hekster, *Caesar Rules,* 45–69; Beard, *Emperor,* 328–31. Megalopsychia mosaic: Matthews, *Journey of Theophanes,* 85. Roman bodies, dress, deportment: Gunderson, *Staging Masculinity;* Gleason, *Making Men;* Masterson, "Late-Ancient Physiognomy"; Olson, *Masculinity.* Deformity and humor: Garland, *Eye of the*

Beholder, 73–86; Plutarch, *Table Talk* 633A–E, discusses which disabilities are appropriate to joke about and which are not. Bodily contrasts: Bakhtin, *Rabelais,* 18–30, 303–436, esp. 317–19; Stallybrass and White, *Politics and Poetics,* 1–26, esp. 21–23. Superiority and incongruity are two of the "big three" reasons for humor (the other is relief): Halliwell, *Greek Laughter,* 10–12; Beard, *Laughter,* 23–24, 37–39 (though with reservations about applicability to all situations).

44. Body and the state: Seneca, *On Clemency* 1.3.5, 1.4.3, 1.5.1; see Meister, *Der Körper,* 163–69, though he is more ambivalent than I am. Suetonius: Gascou, *Suéton historien,* 593–616; Gladhill, "Emperor's No Clothes"; Trimble, "*Corpore enormi*"; similar descriptions are found in other elite works, such as Seneca, *On Firmness* 18.1, on Caligula. Late Antique physical descriptions: Ammianus 21.19.16 (Constantius II), 30.9.6 (Valentinian I), 31.14.7 (Valens). Byzantine chronicles: Head, "Physical Descriptions"; Baldwin, "Physical Descriptions"; Jouanno, "Le corps du prince." Hair: Pliny, *Natural History,* 11.130–31, notes that humans have more hair on their head than other animals; Blanshard, "Naked Apes," 194–98. Baldness and humor: Plutarch, *Table Talk* 633C; Clarke, *Looking at Laughter,* 45–47; Garland, *Eye of the Beholder,* 6; Draycott, "Hair Loss." Sex: Wiseman, *Cinna the Poet,* 148. Caesar: Suetonius, *Caesar* 45.2: "moechum calvom"; Dio 43.43.1; Beard, *Laughter,* 146, and on the triumphal context: Beard, *Roman Triumph,* 247–49. Tiberius: Dio 58.19.1–2; Wiseman, "Games of Flora"; Pasco-Pranger, "Veil Removed." Ritual mockery and social dynamics: Bakhtin, *Rabelais,* esp. 11–12; Davis, *Society and Culture,* esp. 97, 123; see further Critchley, *On Humour,* 82; Halliwell, *Greek Laughter,* 204–5.

45. Domitian: Suetonius, *Domitian* 18; Morgan, "Hair and Heroism." Caligula: Seneca, *On Firmness of Purpose* 18.1; *On Anger* 2.33.3 (showing the contemporary nature of the discussions); Suetonius, *Caligula* 35.2, 50.1. Cilician goat: Pseudo-Diogenianus, *Proverbs* 5.54 (ed. Gaisford). Caligula the goat: Suetonius, *Caligula* 27.4, 50.1; Hurley, *Caligula,* 179–80; see Seneca, *On Firmness* 18.1 for his bald head. Goats have remained a symbol of sexual deviancy used to criticize European monarchs; see, for example, Stratmann, "Golden Rumps," 119, on George II of England. Public bathing: Suetonius, *Titus* 8.2; *Historia Augusta, Hadrian* 17.5–7. Nude statuary: Hallett, *Roman Nude,* 176–83, shows that emperors were depicted nude from Claudius onward. Emperors controlling laughter: Beard, *Laughter,* 132–35; Montlahuc, *Le pouvoir,* Conclusion, explores how emperors reacted to jests in a strategic way.

46. Julian's beard: Ammianus 17.11.1: "in odium venit cum victoriis suis capella, non homo"; 22.14.3; Julian, *Misopogon* 338D: ὑμεῖς δέ φατε δεῖν καὶ σχοινία πλέκειν ἐνθένδε; 335D, 339B, 364B, 365D; see van Hoof and van Nuffelen, "Monarchy," 168, on the chronology; Ephrem the Syrian, *Hymns against Julian* 2.5, 9 (trans. Lieu, *Emperor Julian*). Lions: Julian, *Misopogon* 339B; the idea can be found earlier in Musonius Rufus, *Discourses* 21 (trans. Lutz, *Musonius*); for emperors compared to lions in panegyric, see Claudian, *On the Third Consulship of Honorius* ll. 77–82; Priscian, *In Praise of Anastasius* ll. 67–79.

47. Niketas Choniates, *History* 345; Garland, "And His Bald Head Shone," 16–17.

48. Caracalla: Herodian 4.9.1–3. Julian: Ammianus 22.14.3. Commodus: Dio 74(73).2.2: τὸν κηλήτην. Testicular issues: Clarke, *Looking at Laughter,* 213–15; Watson, "Of

Hernias"; Potamiti, "Hernia Jokes"; Martial, *Epigrams* 12.83. Jokes: *Philogelos* 113, 116–19, 252, 262 (ed. Dawe).

49. Commodus: Dio 74(73).2.2; *Historia Augusta, Commodus* 13.1–2. Reversed acclamations: Aldrete, *Gestures and Acclamations,* 131. Grotesque: Bakhtin, *Rabelais,* esp. 368–436.

50. Claudius: Seneca, *Apocolocyntosis* 1.2, 5.1–3, 6.2; Braund and James, "*Quasi homo.*" Nero's skin: Suetonius, *Nero* 51. Physical features: Makhlaiuk, "Emperors' Nicknames," 222; Corbeill, *Controlling Laughter,* 57–98; Meister, *Der Körper,* 25–26; Rosillo-López, "Nicknames." Cf. Caligula ("Little Boots"), which was not a physical feature, but a name he was given as a child (Suetonius, *Caligula* 9). Anastasius: John Malalas 16.1; Brandes, "Anastasios," 58–61, argues that this was part of the invective portraying the emperor as the Antichrist.

51. Antonius: Cicero, *Philippics* 2.63. Army drinking: *Historia Augusta, Hadrian* 3.2 (Trajan and Hadrian), Ammianus 25.10.15 (Jovian). Tiberius: Suetonius, *Tiberius* 42.1, 59.1: "fastidit uinum, quia iam sitit iste cruorem; tam bibit hunc auide, quam bibit ante merum"; Cupaiuolo, *Le pasquinate,* 65–68. Drunkenness: Plutarch, *Table-Talk* 633A; Edwards, *Politics of Immorality,* 190–92; Humphries, "Lexicon of Abuse"; Morgan, *Popular Morality,* 118. Phocas: Theophanes AM 6101; Maas, "Metrische Akklamationen," 36 no. 2, lists other sources: πάλιν εἰς τὸν καύκον ἔπιες, | πάλιν τον νοῦν ἀπώλεσας (translation adapted from Haldon, "Humour," 64); Cameron, *Circus Factions,* 253–54.

52. Gluttony: Suetonius, *Nero* 27.2; *Galba* 12.3, 22; *Vitellius* 13.1. Vitellius: Suetonius, *Vitellius* 17.1–2; Dio 64(65).20.3 on popular abuse; for constructions of corpulence, see Gourevitch, "L'obésité," 195–98; Bradley, "Obesity." Vomiting: Julian, *Misopogon* 340B–342A.

53. Galba: Suetonius, *Galba* 20.2: "Galba Cupido, fruaris aetate tua"; Galba's quotation is Homer, *Iliad* 5.254: Ἔτι μοι μένος ἔμπεδόν ἐστιν; Power, "Servants' Taunt." Pupienus and Balbinus: Herodian 8.8.6. Heads paraded: Varner, "Execution"; Mawdsley, "Defeat on Display"; Bischoff and Koehler, "Eine illustrierte Ausgabe," 127, 130, for the heads of the three usurpers in Ravenna. Marcus's head: Walker, "Emperors and Deities." Petronius Maximus: Priscus, frag. 30 (ed. Blockley).

54. Emperor's religious role: Hekster, *Caesar Rules,* 133–55. *Pietas: AE* 1952, 165 (shield of Augustus); *Comparison of Mosaic and Roman Law* 6.4.1 (Diocletian's piety); Charlesworth, "*Pietas* and *Victoria*"; Noreña, *Imperial Ideals,* 71–77; Gascou, *Suéton historien,* 727–32. Marcus Aurelius: Ammianus 25.4.17: οἱ βόες οἱ λευκοὶ Μάρκῳ τῷ Καίσαρι χαίρειν. | ἂν πάλι νικήσῃς, ἄμμες ἀπωλόμεθα. Christian piety: Christianity was not above satire (e.g., Magdalino, "Political Satire," 105–7; Maguire, "Parody," 128–31), but the emperor's piety was not itself the subject of lampoons by other Christians.

55. Sacrifices: Julian, *Letters* W 8 [415C–D]; Ammianus 22.12.6, 22.14.3 ("victimarius"); Gregory of Nazianzus, *Orations* 4.7: βουθοίναν . . . Καυσίταυρον; Bernardi, *Grégoire de Nazianze,* 198n1; Elm, *Sons of Hellenism,* 342–43, 362–63; John Chrysostom, *Discourse on Saint Babylas* 19 (*PG* 50: 562): μάγειρον . . . κρειῶν κάπηλον; for the defense against these accusations, see Julian, *Misopogon* 346A–D, 357D, 361B–363D, 365D; Libanius, *Orations* 12.80–82, 18.126–29, 170. *Victimarii:* Lennon, "*Victimarii.*" Sacrifice: Bradbury, "Julian's Pagan Revival."

56. Aeneas and Romulus: Clarke, *Looking at Laughter,* 151–54, 230. Boscotrecase: "Caesaris Augusti femina mater erat" (*CIL* IV 6893). Snake: Suetonius, *Augustus* 94.4, deriving from the works of Asclepiades of Mendes; Dio 45.1.2. Marsus: Hollis, *Fragments,* 304 (frag. 181), with Lebek, "*CIL* IV 6893"; Cupaiuolo, *Le pasquinate,* 87; Beness, "Atia," notes that the interpretation is contentious.

57. Nero: Suetonius, *Nero* 39.2: "dum tendit citharam noster, dum cornua Parthus, | noster erit Paean, ille Hecatebeletes"; the verse was one of those "proscripta aut vulgata sunt"; 45.2: "ascriptum est columnis, etiam Gallos eum cantando excitasse"; for Paetus and the date, see Tacitus, *Annals* 15.10.1–17.3, 15.24.1–25.4; Champlin, "Nero," 276–77 (though I think it is more specific than he allows). Poetic criticism: Nisbet, *Greek Epigram,* 118–23, 131–33; *Palatine Anthology* 11.185, 247.

58. Drusilla: Suetonius, *Caligula* 24.2; Dio 59.11.1–5. Claudius: Seneca, *Apocolocyntosis* 1.2–3, 4.3, 5.3, 8.3, 11.4, 15.2; Price, *Rituals and Power,* 114–17. Gods as humorous figures: Clarke, *Looking at Laughter,* 134–40, 165–89. Saturnalia: Julian, *Caesars* 307B–C.

59. Emperor not God: Tertullian, *Apology* 33.1–34.4; and Theophilus of Antioch, *To Autolycus* 1.11 are but two examples. Herod Agrippa: Josephus, *Jewish Antiquities* 19.343–53; Acts 12: 20–23. Tyrants: Africa, "Worms." Nero: *Martyrdom of Peter* 12 (ed. Lipsius). Titus: Babylonian Talmud, *Tractate Gittin* 56b; *Leviticus Rabbah* 22.3 (just two of many versions): Levinson, "Tragedies"; Boustan, "Immolating Emperors," 227–38; Davenport, "Dying for Justice," 273–74, 282–85.

60. Maurice: John of Antioch, fragment 218c (ed. Müller); Theophanes AM 6093: Εὗρεν τὴν δάμαλιν ἁπαλὴν καὶ τρυφερὰν | καὶ ὡς τὸ καινὸν ἀλεκτόριν οὕτω αὐτὴν ἐπήδηκε | καὶ ἐποίησε παιδία ὡς τὰ ξυλοκούκουδα, | καὶ ουδεὶς τολμᾶ λαλῆσαι, ἀλλ᾽ ὅλους ἐφίμωσεν. Ἅγιέ μου, ἁγιέ, φοβερὲ καὶ δυνατέ, | δός αὐτῷ κατὰ κρανίου ἵνα μὴ ὑπεραίρηται, | κἀγὼ σοι τὸν βοῦν τὸν μέγαν προσαγάγω εἰς εὐχήν (ed. and trans. Alexiou, *After Antiquity,* 81–82); for the context, see Theophylact Simocatta 8.4.11–5.4; on the meaning, see Pfeilschifter, *Der Kaiser,* 258–59. Byzantine chants: Maas, "Metrische Akklamationen"; Jeffreys, "Political Verse," 187–89; Haldon, "Humour," 66–67; Alexiou, *After Antiquity,* 86–87; Bernard, "Laughter," 49–50.

61. Herod Agrippa: Philo, *Against Flaccus* 36–9: for street theater and mimes, see Horsfall, *Roman Plebs,* 98–99; Webb, *Demons and Dancers,* 96–97, 117–19. Funerals: Suetonius, *Vespasian* 19.2; Sumi, "Impersonating." Kalends of January: Asterius of Amasea, *Homilies* 4.7.2 (μεγίστην ἀρχήν) (ed. Datema); Grig, "Kalends of January"; "Looking," 131–33. Emesa: Chapter 1. Usurpers: McCormick, *Eternal Victory,* 134–35; cf. the earlier treatment of defeated foreign enemies in this fashion (McCormick, *Eternal Victory,* 416, on the Column of Arcadius). Kings and clowns: Bakhtin, *Rabelais,* 196–200.

62. Theophanes AM 6094; Whitby, *Emperor Maurice,* 18–19, 24–27; Pfeilschifter, *Der Kaiser,* 252–93.

3. DEATH AND DYNASTY

1. Trajan and Plotina: Bennett, *Trajan,* 24, 54–55; Brennan, *Sabina,* 17–20. Young men: Dio 68.7.4; *Historia Augusta, Hadrian* 2.7.

2. Trajan's last days: Dio 68.33.2–3; Bennett, *Trajan,* 201–4. No senatorial approval: *Historia Augusta, Hadrian* 6.1–2. Coinage: *RIC* II[2] Hadrian 7–11, 2959–60; on the suddenness of the announcement, see Burnett, "Early Coinage"; Roman, Rémy, and Riccardi, "Les intrigues de Plotine."
3. Apronianus: Dio 69.1–4. Plotina: Dio 69.10.3[1]. Executions: Dio 69.2.5–6; *Historia Augusta, Hadrian* 7.1–4, 9.3–4; Birley, *Hadrian,* 87–88.
4. Phaedimus: *CIL* VI 1884; Temporini, *Die Frauen,* 151–59; Constant, "Commentaires et conjectures."
5. Rumor and deaths: Tacitus, *Annals* 4.11.2: "atrociore semper fama erga dominantium exitus"; the same, of course, applied to rumors about leading politicians of the Roman Republic: Beness, "Scipio Aemilianus," on the demise of Scipio the Younger in 129 BCE; Hillard, "Death by Lightning," on the death of Pompeius Strabo in 87 BCE. Peace as benefit of monarchy and empire: Noreña, *Imperial Ideals,* 103–4. Nero: Tacitus, *Annals* 12.69. Justin II: Evagrius, *Church History* 5.1; Cameron, *Corippus,* 130; McEvoy, "Dynastic Dreams," 107–11.
6. Inquiries: Paulus, *Opinions* 5.21.3: "de salute principis uel de summa rei publicae"; *Comparison of Mosaic and Roman Law* 15.2.1; respectable astrologers did not do this: Firmicus Maternus, *Mathesis* 2.30.4; MacMullen, *Enemies,* 128–32; Sünskes, "Astrologie und Aufstand." Decree: Suetonius, *Vitellius* 14.4. Theodosius II: Socrates, *Church History* 7.23: λαθραίως; McEvoy, *Child Emperor Rule,* 228–30; distance and time calculated using the Stanford ORBIS site: https://orbis.stanford.edu. Jovian also tried to manage the flow of news about Julian's death: Sotinel, "Information," 127–28; Drijvers, *Forgotten Reign,* 67. There are also cases of harbors being closed to traffic during crises to prevent the circulation of damaging news from one part of the empire to another: Herodian 8.5.5 (238), *CTh.* 7.16.1 (408), 7.16.2 (410). For other stories of death concealment, see Bauman, "Tanaquil-Livia," 181–84. Diocletian's illness: Lactantius, *On the Deaths of the Persecutors* 17.7–8: "non defuerunt qui suspicarentur celari mortem eius, donec Caesar veniret, ne quid forte a militibus novaretur." Traveling times: Duncan-Jones, *Structure and Scale,* 7–17. Hydatius: Muhlberger, *Fifth-Century Chroniclers,* 210–12; Gillett, *Envoys,* 51–53.
7. Civil war: Horace, *Odes* 1.2. Augustus: Velleius Paterculus 2.123.1: "tempus in quo fuit plurimum metus"; see also 2.124.1 (confusion and anxiety); 2.126.1–4 (blessings of Augustus's peace, a panegyrical sentiment, but that certainly shows relief after civil war). Velleius's value as a contemporary witness: Woodman, *Velleius Paterculus,* 215–16. There is also the story related in Tacitus, *Annals* 1.5, and Dio 56.31.1, of Livia suppressing the news until the time was ripe: see Beard, *Emperor,* 70–71. Bauman, "Tanquil-Livia," 177–78, argues this was a contemporary story that was suppressed by Velleius. Provincial relief: *OGIS* 458, ll. 36–37, a decree of the *koinon* of Asia. Military revolt: Velleius Paterculus 2.125.1–4; Suetonius, *Tiberius* 25.1–2; Tacitus, *Annals* 1.16–35; Dio 57.3.1, 4.1–6.5.
8. Omens: Ripat, "Roman Omens," 166–73; on comets, see Juvenal, *Satires* 6.407–8; on deaths, Manilius, *Astronomica* ll. 874–926, esp. 893–95; see Pseudo-Dionysius of Tel-Mahre, *Chronicle, Part III* s.a. 836 (524/25) (ed. Witakowski), on the panic caused by a comet at the start of the reign of Justin I. Macrinus: Dio 79(78).25.1–5, 30.1; Ramsey,

"Catalogue," 182. Pertinax and Didius Julianus: Dio 74(73).11.1–13.5; Aja Sánchez, "*Vox populi,*" 309–10. Maurice and Phocas: *Teaching of Jacob* 3.12 (ed. Dagron and Dérouche).

9. Claudius: Josephus, *Jewish Antiquities* 19.228; Suetonius, *Claudius* 10.3–4; Flaig, *Den Kaiser herausfordern,* 249–56. Grain shortage: Seneca, *On the Shortness of Life* 18.5–6. Roman privilege: Garnsey, *Famine and Food Supply,* 214–17. Need for bread: Procopius, *Secret History* 26.20. Emperor's role: Tacitus, *Annals* 6.13; Priscian, *In Praise of Anastasius* ll. 206–17. Rome: Purcell, "Rome and Its Development," 794–97; "Populace of Rome," 152–56; Machado, *Urban Space,* 45–60. Wine and pork: *Historia Augusta, Aurelian* 48.1–4; *CTh.* 14.4.4, 10; *Nov. Val.* 36; Durliat, *De la ville antique,* 37–123. Constantinople: Teal, "Grain Supply," esp. 135–37; Durliat, *De la ville antique,* 185–278; Mango, "Commercial Map"; for the impact of the loss of Egypt, see Nicephorus, *Short History* 12 (ed. de Boor).

10. Justinian: Theophanes AM 6053, identified by Jeffreys, Jeffreys and Scott, *Chronicle,* 298, as deriving from John Malalas 18.131 (and therefore contemporary). Grain supply: Josephus, *Jewish War* 4.605–8 (Vespasian takes Alexandria in 69); Kohns, *Versorgungskrisen,* 190–210 (pressure placed on Rome by Gildo's revolt in Africa in 394–398); Zosimus 6.11.1–2 (Heraclianus cuts off grain to usurper Priscus Attalus in 410); Kaegi, *Heraclius,* 43–45 (Heraclian faction secures Egypt in revolt against Phocas in 608–610). Army: *Explanation of the Whole World* 36 (ed. Rougé).

11. Caligula's illness: Philo, *Embassy to Gaius* 14–15, 17–18: ἀνεπόλουν γὰρ ὅσα καὶ ἡλίκα κακὰ ἐξ ἀναρχίας φύεται· λιμόν, πόλεμον, δενδροτομίας, δῃώσεις χωρίων, στερήσεις χρημάτων, ἀπαγωγάς, τοὺς περὶ δουλείας καὶ θανάτου φόβους ἀνηκέστους, ὧν ἰατρὸς ἦν οὐδείς, μίαν ἐχόντων θεραπείαν τὸ ῥωσθῆναι Γάιον. See Smallwood, *Legatio ad Gaium,* 165–66, on the dates; later sources on the anxiety include Suetonius, *Caligula* 14.2, 27.2; Dio 59.8.1–3; see discussion in Christoforou, *Imagining,* 197–98. Provincial recruitment: *P. Mich.* 3.220. Fifth century: Muhlberger, *Fifth-Century Chroniclers,* 89–90, 101–2. Effect of civil wars: Phaedrus 1.30: "humiles laborant ubi potentes dissident."

12. Peasant: "ex quo sum genitus ruri mea vixi colendo | nec ruri pausa nec mihi semper erat" (*CIL* VIII 11824). Edessa: *Chronicle of Pseudo-Joshua the Stylite* 38–44; this is an important passage because the famine required a solution that was outside the governor's control and could only be accomplished by the emperor. Food crisis: Garnsey, *Famine and Food Supply,* esp. 20–21, 224, 228–29 on war. Emperor provides reassurance: Hekster, *Caesar Rules,* 292.

13. Acceptance groups: Flaig, *Den Kaiser herausfordern;* Kaldellis, *Byzantine Republic.* Britannicus: Suetonius, *Nero* 33.2–3; Tacitus, *Annals* 13.15–17; Dio 61(61).1.1–2, 7.4. Jovian's family: John Chrysostom, *Letter to a Young Widow* 4 (*PG* 48:605), *Homilies on Philippians* 15(16).5 (*PG* 62:295); Drijvers, *Forgotten Reign,* 110. Gratian: Symmachus, *Letters* 1.13.2; McEvoy, *Child Emperor Rule,* 54–66; Kelly, "Political Crisis," 377–81, shows that the news of Valentinian II's elevation would have already reached Rome by this time.

14. Gratian: Symmachus, *Orations* 3.2; "noui saeculi spes sperata" (it is difficult to render the alliterative Latin into English without sounding silly, e.g., "the hoped-for hope of a

new hundred years"); McEvoy, *Child Emperor Rule,* 51–52. Debates: Josephus, *Jewish Antiquities* 19.158–61, 189, 248; Herodian 2.12.4–6, 7.10.2–6. Aftermath of Caligula: Josephus, *Jewish Antiquities* 19.167–89; Suetonius, *Caligula* 60; Dio 59.30.3–60.1. Republican ideals in 68–69: *RIC* I² Civil Wars 1, 4–6, 10, 12, 15–22, 24–28; these coins emphasized the state (*res publica*) and freedom (*libertas*) rather than individual generals and their claims to the purple. Winning over army: Josephus, *Jewish War* 1.5. Courtiers: Becker, "Court in Constantinople."

15. Regime change: Kelly, *Ruling,* 193–96. Constantius II's supporters: Libanius, *Letters* B 179; Julian, *Letters* W 13 [389D–390B]; Ammianus 22.3.1–12. Bassianus: Libanius, *Letters* N 79, B 14. Macedonius: Symmachus, *State Letters* 36.2. Phocas's nephew: *Life of Theodore of Sykeon* 152 (ed. Festugière); Kaegi, "New Evidence," 308–11. Priscus Attalus: Paulinus of Pella, *Thanksgiving* 291–327; on the parade of fifth-century usurpers in Gaul, see Sidonius Apollinaris, *Letters* 5.9.1.

16. Astrological text: *P. Oxy.* 31.2554, frag. I col. ii, ll. 4–14. Opportunities: Josephus, *Jewish War* 1.4–5, 7.79; Tacitus, *Histories* 4.54–55; Dyson, "Native Revolts," 264–67.

17. Pupienus: Herodian 7.10.50–6. Bishops: Magalhães de Oliveira, "Communication." Datianus: Libanius, *Letters* N 126–128, B 50; note also the case of Symmachus, who supported the western emperor Magnus Maximus and then had his properties at Ostia occupied by the forces of Valentinian II after Maximus's downfall (Symmachus, *Letters* 2.52, 6.72; Sogno, *Symmachus,* 71–72).

18. Pardons and amnesties: Josephus, *Jewish War* 2.178–81 (Caligula); Ambrose, *On the Death of Theodosius* 5; *CTh.* 15.14.9, 11, 12 (Honorius and Arcadius, issuing the final orders of their father Theodosius I). Exiles: Dio 78(77).3.3 (Caracalla); Dio 79(78).12.1 (Macrinus); *Historia Augusta, Aurelian* 39.4 (Aurelian); Julian, *Letters* W 14 [404B–C], W 17 [426A–C] (Julian); Pseudo-Sebeos, *Armenian History* 42 (Heraclius ordering his son Heraclius Constantine). Rejoicing at clemency: John Chrysostom, *Homilies on Acts* 1 (*PG* 60:26): κἂν μὲν βασιλεὺς πέμψῃ γράμματα, τοὺς ἐν δεσμωτηρίῳ λύων, εὐφροσύνη καὶ χαρά. Caligula's death: Josephus, *Jewish Antiquities* 19.1. Julian's death: Libanius, *Letters* N 120.2; for his policies, see Julian, *Misopogon* 349D–350A. Handouts to the people: Dio 74(73).8.3–4 (Marcus Aurelius and Lucius Verus). Debt remission: Dio 69.8.12; *CIL* VI 967; *RIC* II.3² 262–65 (Hadrian); *Historia Augusta, Marcus* 23.3 (Marcus Aurelius); Victor, *On the Caesars* 35.7, *Historia Augusta, Aurelian* 39.3 (Aurelian); Libanius, *Orations* 18.163 (Julian); Corippus, *In Praise of the Younger Justin Augustus* 2.380–406 (Justin II); Evagrius, *Church History* 5.13 (Tiberius II). Worries about debts: *Oracles of Astrampsychus* questions 25, 26 (trans. Stewart and Morrell, "Oracles"); MacMullen, "Tax-Pressure," 740; Millar, "Fiscus," 32; Morgan, *Popular Morality,* 167.

19. Philip and Decius: Eusebius, *Church History* 6.41.9. Regime change: Libanius, *Orations* 1.118, 120, *Letters* B 179 (Julian's accession), *Orations* 1.136–38, 167, *Letters* N 124, B 141, 154 (death of Julian and accession of Jovian); see Feeney, "Court Construction," 165–70; Drijvers, *Forgotten Reign,* 81–85, on Jovian's own appointments. Julian and Christians: Julian, *Letters* W 14 [404B–C] (restoration of exiles).

20. Valens: Gregory of Nyssa, *Against Eunomius* 1.127–8, *Letters* 3; see also Basil of Caesarea, *Letters* 92, 243 (letters to western bishops about the problems in the East);

Ambrose of Milan, *On Faith* 142 (orthodoxy of the western emperor Gratian compared to the beliefs of the deceased Valens). Theodosius II and Marcian: Leo the Great, *Letters* 24, 83. Chrysaphius: Anonymous Chronicler of 451, *Continuatio codicum Ovetensis et Reichenaviensis* (ed. Mommsen): "fustibus caesus defecit"; Davenport and McEvoy, "Circulation of News," 216–19.

21. Alexandria: Evagrius, *Church History* 2.8; Ps.-Zachariah Rhetor, *Chronicle* 4.1–2 (ed. Greatrex et al., with their observation [132n12] that news of Marcian's death arrived in Alexandria c. February 5, 457, which means the Alexandrians cannot have already known of Leo I's accession, since he was not acclaimed in Constantinople until February 7). Popular interest: Patlagean, *Pauvreté économique,* 217–19; Gregory, *Vox populi.*
22. Palatine Games: Josephus, *Jewish Antiquities* 19.85–96; Suetonius, *Caligula* 57.4. Cluvius Rufus: Josephus, *Jewish Antiquities* 19.92; Mommsen, "Cluvius Rufus," 318–21; Syme, *Tacitus,* 287–88, 293–94; Wiseman, *Death of Caligula,* xiv–xvi, 59, 109–14. Cf. Levick, "Cluvius Rufus," 550–51, 554, who suggests that it was actually the historian's father who was in the audience, but her chronology is not convincing.
23. Caligula's murder: Josephus, *Jewish Antiquities* 19.101–16; see also Suetonius, *Caligula* 58.1–3; Dio 59.29.4–7. Audience: Josephus, *Jewish Antiquities* 19.86. Reaction: Josephus, *Jewish Antiquities* 19.127–57.
24. Josephus, *Jewish Antiquities* 19.217.
25. Suetonius, *Caligula* 60.1.
26. Tiberius: Josephus, *Jewish Antiquities* 18.224–35. Commodus: Dio 74(73).2.5. Constantius II: Libanius, *Orations* 18.118; perhaps Julian's experiences under Constantius rendered this more plausible, e.g., Julian, *Letter to the Athenians* 270D–271A, 273C, 277D–278A. Procopius: Ammianus 27.6.3, Themistius, *Orations* 7.91d: τὰς ἀτόπους φήμας; Lenski, *Valens,* 74–75, emphasizes that control of information was one of the usurper's main tactics.
27. Views: Publilius Syrus, *Sayings* 476: "ni gradus servetur, nulli tutus est summus locus"; Tertullian, *Apology* 35.8–11; Jerome, *Letters* 60.15–16; Peter Chrysologus, *Sermons* 24.1 (ed. Olivar). Astrological text: *P. Oxy.* 31.2554, frag. I, col. ii, l. 9: ἐν ἰδίῳ οἴ[κ]ῳ. Valentinian: Ammianus 30.6.4: "nequis eum necatum suspicaretur." Tiberius: Suetonius, *Tiberius* 73.2; see also Suetonius, *Caligula* 12.2–3; Tacitus, *Annals* 6.50.2–5; Dio 58.28.1–5.
28. Valentinian II: McEvoy, *Child Emperor Rule,* 95–99; see Ambrose, *On the Death of Valentinian* 33, 35, 50, for suggestions of suicide, with Liebeschuetz, *Ambrose of Milan,* 359–60, 380; McLynn, *Ambrose of Milan,* 341 (lack of confirmation). Murder: Jerome, *Letters* 60.15; Scourfield, *Consoling Heliodorus,* 204–5, 230–32; Rufinus, *Church History* 11.31; followed soon after Eunapius, frag. 58 (ed. Blockley); for other sources, see Croke, "Arbogast" (who does not consider Jerome). Suicide: Croke, "Arbogast," 243–44; McLynn, *Ambrose of Milan,* 336–37; McEvoy, *Child Emperor Rule,* 97–98.
29. Jovian: Eutropius, *Short History* 10.18, with Bird, *Eutropius,* xviii–xix; Lenski, *Valens,* 19, 186, on the date and Eutropius's presence; Ammianus 25.10.12–13, with den Boeft et al., *Ammianus Marcellinus XXV,* 308–9, 333–35; Drijvers, *Forgotten Reign,* 109–10, on other sources. Plaster: Quintus Lutatius Catulus (cos. 102 BCE) committed suicide

in 87 BCE by deliberately lighting a fire in a room recently plastered with lime and sand (Velleius Paterculus 2.22.4). Scipio: Kelly, *Ammianus,* 245–46; Beness, "Scipio Aemilianus," 40–42. Jovian's murder: John Chrysostom, *Letter to a Young Widow* 4 (*PG* 48:605), *Homilies on Philippians* 15(16).5 (*PG* 62:295); Eunapius, frag. 29 (ed. Blockley).

30. Domitian: Plutarch, *Aemilius Paullus* 25.5–7; Jones, *Plutarch,* 21–5. Two letters: Socrates, *Church History* 6.2. Rumors: Socrates, *Church History* 5.13 (although a child at the time, Socrates spent his entire life in Constantinople and would likely have been able to discuss incidents with his elders); Sozomen, *Church History* 7.14. Nectarius: Leppin, *Theodosius der Große,* 78–81; Magalhães de Oliveira, "Emperor Is Dead!" 173–74.
31. Heraclius: Whitby, "Defender of the Cross," 258–59; Kaegi, *Heraclius,* 111–12.
32. Julian: Ammianus 25.3.1–23; den Boeft et al., *Ammianus Marcellinus XXV,* xv–xvi; Drijvers, *Forgotten Reign,* 34. Ammianus as participant: den Boeft et al., *Ammianus Marcellinus XXIII,* xii. Rumor: Ammianus 25.6.5–6; den Boeft et al., *Ammianus Marcellinus XXV,* xvii, 206–7.
33. News: Libanius, *Letters* N 111–12, 115, 116, 120, 129. Julian's murder: Libanius, *Letters* N 116, 129 (letter to Alcimus), 133. Persians responsible: *Orations* 17.32; Wiemer, *Libanios und Julian,* 251–55. Christians responsible: *Orations* 18.267–75; Wiemer, *Libanios und Julian,* 260–68; Elm, *Sons of Hellenism,* 443–45; on the war over different versions of Julian's campaign, see Ross, *Ammianus' Julian,* 174–81.
34. Suicide: Ephrem, *Hymns against Julian* 3.16. Versions: Gregory of Nazianzus, *Oration* 5.13; see Elm, *Sons of Hellenism,* 432–33, on the dates, and 445–58, on *Oration* 5 as a response to Libanius, *Oration* 18. Christians as responsible: Sozomen, *Church History* 6.1–2. Different versions: Büttner-Wobst, "Der Tod," esp. 570–73; Wiemer, *Libanios und Julian,* 267–68. Theodosius I: Libanius, *Orations* 24.6–8, 11, 17–30.
35. Valens: Libanius, *Orations* 24.4; Jerome, *Chronicle* s.a. 378; John Chrysostom, *Letter to a Young Widow* 5 (*PG* 48: 606); Ammianus 31.13.12–17; Lenski, "Contemporary Reactions," 152–55; Lenski, *Valens,* 340–41.
36. Nicene reactions: Ambrose, *On Faith* 2.141–2; Lenski, "Contemporary Reactions," 149–54; Lenski, *Valens,* 261–62, for discussion and other sources. Fifth-century version: Rufinus, *Church History* 11.3; Orosius, *History against the Pagans* 7.33.9; Theoderet, *Church History* 3.36.2. Graffito: Headlam, *Ecclesiastical Sites,* 22 no. 1 = Rott, *Kleinasiatische Denkmäler,* 228 no. 1: βασιλεὺς Οὐαλέντη κακῶς ἐποίησας, ὅτι ἀπέδωκας τὴν ἐκ(κ)λ(η)σίαν τοὺ[ς] κακοδόξου[ς] Ἀριανούς.
37. Lollius Bassus: *Palatine Anthology* 7.391: Κλειδοῦχοι νεκύων, πάσας Ἀΐδαο κελεύθους | φράγνυτε· καὶ στομίοις κλεῖθρα δέχοισθε, πύλαι.| αὐτὸς ἐγὼν Ἀΐδας ἐνέπω· Γερμανικὸς ἄστρων,| οὐκ ἐμός· οὐ χωρεῖ νῆα τόσην Ἀχέρων. Astral imagery: Stiles, "*Non potes.*" Accusation: *SCPP* l. 28; Tacitus, *Annals* 2.71.1. Germanicus's body: Suetonius, *Caligula* 1.2; Tacitus, *Annals* 2.73.4–5; Dio 57.18.9. Heart: Pliny, *Natural History* 11.187; the later version of Suetonius, *Caligula* 1.2, gives the same reason. Poisoning: Tacitus, *Annals* 3.14.1–2.
38. News reaches Rome: Tacitus, *Annals* 2.82.1–5; Suetonius, *Caligula* 6.1–2; Woodman and Martin, *Tacitus Book 3,* 69, 78. Chant: Suetonius, *Caligula* 6.1: "salva Roma, salva

patria, salvus est Germanicus"; with Wille, *Musica Romana,* 139; Courtney, *Latin Poets,* 478; Horsfall, *Roman Plebs,* 38, on its meter and authenticity. Popular interest: Courrier, *La plèbe de Rome,* 680–82.

39. Tiberius: Suetonius, *Tiberius* 52.3, and *Caligula* 2.1; Tacitus, *Annals* 2.82.1–2, 3.2.3–3.3, 3.10.1–3; Dio 57.18.10. "Give us back Germanicus": Suetonius, *Tiberius* 52.3 (interestingly, the Latin uses the second-person singular form, *redde,* suggesting it was specifically aimed at one person—perhaps Piso or Tiberius?); see also Tacitus, *Annals* 3.14.4–5, for popular protests. Honors voted by the people: *TS* IIb, ll. 5–11. Desire to punish Piso: *SCPP* ll. 156–58: "cum effusissumis studis ad repraesentandam poenam Cn. Pisonis patris ab semet ipsa accensa esset."

40. Publication: *SCPP* ll. 167–72. Senatorial decree counterbalances rumor: Eck et al., *Das senatus consultum,* 290; Griffin, "Senate's Story," 260; Giua, "Tra storiografia," 263; Eck, "Cheating the Public," 161–62. Piso's crimes: *SCPP* ll. 12–22, 29–71, with Eck et al., *Das senatus consultum,* 146–49, on the charge of treason. Germanicus's claim: *SCPP* l. 28: "cuius mortis fuisse c[aussam Cn.] Pisone patrem ipse testatus sit." Martina's death: Tacitus, *Annals* 3.7.2. Plancina: *SCPP* ll. 109–20, with Eck et al., *Das senatus consultum,* 222–28; Tacitus, *Annals* 3.15.1, 17.1–18.1.

41. Tacitus: Woodman and Martin, *Tacitus Book 3,* 116–18, 196–97, whose views I follow here. Oral traditions: Tacitus, *Annals* 3.16.1; Eck et al., *Das senatus consultum,* 295–96; Woodman and Martin, *Tacitus Book 3,* 169–70. Rumors continue: Tacitus, *Annals* 3.19.2; Giua, "Tra storiografia," 264, 273–74.

42. Clutorius Priscus: Tacitus, *Annals* 3.49.1. Tiberius's lament: *TS* IIb, ll. 11–16. Diana: Eck, "Cheating the Public," 150, 159; Hartmann, "Germanicus und Lady Di"; Baltussen, "How to Console Yourself," 47–48. Tiberius and Drusus: *SCPP* ll. 126–27: "ut omnem curam, quam in duos quondam filios suos partitus erat, ad eum, quem haberet, converteret"; ll. 129–30: "omnem spem futuram paternae pro r(e) p(ublica) stations in uno repos[i]ta<m>." For the language, see Griffin, "Senate's Story," 257. Imperial family: *SCPP* ll. 132–51; Cooley, "Moralizing Message," 207–8; Severy, "Family and State," 27–34. Civil war and peace: *SCPP* ll. 12–16, 45–52: "iam pridem numine divi Aug(usti) virtutibusq(ue) Ti. Caesaris Aug(usti) omnibus civilis belli sepultis malis" (at ll. 45–47).

43. Purple-born heir: Julius Pollux, *Onomasticon* 1.1; see Davenport and Mallan, "Hadrian's Adoption Speech," 657, for a variety of other sources. Faustina: Dio 72(71).22.3–23.1, 29.1, 30.1; see also *Historia Augusta, Marcus Aurelius* 24.6; *Avidius Cassius* 7.1.

44. Accuracy: Priwitzer, *Faustina minor,* 175–207; Levick, *Faustina I and II,* 83–87. No trials: senators were not convicted, but a certain soothsayer named Syrus was exiled for making astrological predictions (*Comparison of Mosaic and Roman Law* 15.2.5). An imperial mother removing her own son from contention was very rare: the classic example is the eighth-century Byzantine empress Irene, who had her son Constantine VI blinded.

45. Faustina: *Historia Augusta, Marcus Aurelius* 19.1–9; Priwitzer, *Faustina minor,* 96–108. Britannicus: Tacitus, *Annals* 12.41–2; Dio 61(60).33.10 has Agrippina cloistering Britannicus away so that people did not even know if he was alive; Ps.-Seneca, *Octavia* ll. 44–46, 115–19, 340–41; Ginsburg, *Representing Agrippina,* 107–12. Cruel

stepmother: TMI S1; Watson, *Ancient Stepmothers,* esp. 92–134, 176–206. Crispus and Fausta: Barnes, *Constantine,* 144–49; Woods, "Empress Fausta," 70–72, 84. Crispus's trial: Victor, *On the Caesars* 41.11. Baths: *Epitome about the Caesars* 41.11–12; Philostorgius, *Ecclesiastical History* 2.4, 4a; Zosimus 2.29.2; Zonaras 13.2.38–41. Folklore: TMI K2111 ("Potiphar's Wife"); TMI S113.2.2 ("Suffocating in Bathroom"); Watson, *Ancient Stepmothers,* 234–35, 265–66, distinguishing between the suicide and execution versions.

46. Poem: Sidonius Apollinaris, *Letters* 5.8.2: "Saturni aurea saecla quis requirat? sunt haec gemmea, sed Neroniana" (trans. Anderson, *Sidonius*). Julian on Fausta: Julian, *Orations* 1.9B–C: κατὰ τοὺς παρ' ἡμῖν νόμους ἀχράντους καὶ καθαρὰς τὰς οἰκειότητας ταύτας φυλάττουσαν; Marasco, "Costantino," 315; see also Hilton, "Cnemon," who notes similarities between the story of Cnemon and his mother-in-law in Helidorus's novel *Aethiopica* (written in Julian's reign) and the rumors about Crispus and Fausta.

47. Wild beasts: John Chrysostom, *Homilies on Philippians* 15(16).5 (*PG* 62:295). Andromeda: Pohlsander, "Crispus," 101. Abortion: Woods, "Empress Fausta," cf. Drijvers, "Flavia Maxima Fausta," 505–6.

48. Hope: Stiles, "Velleius Paterculus"; *RIC* I[2] Claudius 99, 115 (Britannicus; Rawson, *Children,* 37–40); VII Rome 293–94, Ticinum 178, 191, 203–4, Nicomedia 69A, 97, 131, 150 (Fausta; Brubaker and Tober, "Gender of Money," 576); IX Antioch 20A, 20D (Valentinian I and Gratian; McEvoy, *Child Emperor Rule,* 52). Heraclius: *DOC* 2.1: 258, no. (33c).

49. Reflections: Marcus Aurelius, *Meditations* 8.31: ἐπιλογίζεσθαι, πόσα ἐσπάσθησαν οἱ πρὸ αὐτῶν, ἵνα διάδοχόν τινα καταλίπωσιν. Infertility: Scheidel, "Emperors, Aristocrats," 273–79. Reproductive processes: Flemming, "Invention of Fertility," 571–73; Totelin, "Plant Infertility," 58–60; see Flemming, "Fertility Control," 7, on the rare acknowledgment of male fertility problems. No children: *Epitome about the Caesars* 14.8 (Hadrian); Dio 78(77).16.1–2, 4 (Caracalla); Zosimus 5.28.1–3; Philostorgius, *Church History* 12.2 (Honorius). Eudoxia: Holum, *Theodosian Empresses,* 53–54. Constantius II and Eusebia: Julian, *Letter to the Athenians* 270D–271A: ταῦτα ἐθρύλουν οἱ περὶ τὴν αὐλὴν τότε καὶ τὸν μακαρίτην ἀδελφὸν ἐμὸν Γάλλον; 275B–C; McEvoy, "Constantia," 157–58.

50. Treatments: Flemming, "Invention of Infertility," 574, and "Fertility Control," 3–8. Eusebia and Helena: Ammianus 16.10.18–19. Magic and miscarriage: Aubert, "Threatened Wombs."

51. Constantia: McEvoy, "Constantia," esp. 155–59, on the paucity of descendants of Constantine. Helena's death: Ammianus 21.1.5; Hillner, *Helena,* 297. Julian's lack of an heir: Ammianus 25.3.20, 4.2–3; Libanius, *Orations* 17.32, 18.179–81, 18.273. Procopius: Ammianus 26.6.3. Rumor: Libanius, *Orations* 37.1–13. Julian's failure to remarry: Ephrem the Syrian, *Hymns against Julian* 2.9.

52. Galba's childlessness: Plutarch, *Galba* 19.1; Suetonius, *Galba* 17; Tacitus, *Histories* 1.12.2–3, 1.17 (crowd gathers outside palace). Titus: Suetonius, *Titus* 5.1; Tacitus, *Histories* 1.10.3, 2.1.1–3; Ash, *Histories Book II,* 75–76. Cf. Josephus, *Jewish War* 4.497–502, which has the mission but not the adoption story. Nerva's age: estimates vary between sixty and sixty-five, based on Dio 68.4.2; Victor, *On the Caesars* 12.11. Nerva's relatives: Dio 68.4.1; this would seem to be a reference to the descendants of Nerva's

uncle Gaius Octavius Laenas (Grainger, *Nerva,* 67). Rumors: Pliny, *Letters* 9.13.11: "nominat quendam, qui tunc ad orientem amplissimum exercitum non sine magnis dubiisque rumoribus obtinebat"; see Berriman and Todd, "Very Roman Coup," 322, on the date. The man is assumed to be the governor of Syria, either Marcus Cornelius Nigrinus Curiatus Maternus (Alföldy and Hartmann, "M. Cornelius"; Eck, "Emperor Is Made") or Lucius Iavolenus Priscus (Berriman and Todd, "Very Roman Coup"). Adoption of Trajan: Dio 68.4.1–2; Eck, "Emperor Is Made," 222–26; Grainger, *Nerva,* 96–100.

53. Leo's son: *Life of Daniel the Stylite* 38. Horoscope: Pingree, "Political Horoscopes," 146–47; László, "Rhetorius," 341–43. Zeno's unpopularity: Candidus frag. 1 (ed. Blockley). Leo II: Theodore Lector, *Church History,* Epitome 398 (ed. Kosiński et al.); Constantine Porphyrogenitus, *Book of Ceremonies* 1.93; Croke, "Imperial Reigns"; McEvoy, "Leo II." Constantinople: Victor of Tunnuna, *Chronicle* 475.1 (ed. Mommsen); Croke, "Basiliscus."

54. Leo Basiliscus: John Malalas 15.7; Evagrius, *Church History* 3.24. Folkloric motifs: TMI K1847 ("Deception by Substitution of Children"); K1920 ("Substituted Children"); S.252.1 ("Vain Attempt to Save Promised Child by Use of Substitute"). Oral tale: Croke, "Basiliscus," 83–87. Coinage: *RIC* X Leo I (East) 636–38, Leo II 801–2, Leo II and Zeno 803–4.

55. "Wolf Meets the Dog": Babrius, *Fables* 100 = Phaedrus, *Fables* 3.7; also found in international versions, TMI L451.3: "Wolf Prefers Liberty and Hunger to Dog's Servitude and Plenty." Greek origin: van Dijk, *Fables,* 147–48; Rodríguez Adrados, *Graeco-Latin Fable,* 439.

56. Dynastic messages: Hekster, *Emperors and Ancestors.* Antonia: Tacitus, *Annals* 15.53.3. Constantia and Faustina: Ammianus 26.7.10, 9.3.

57. Theodosius: John of Ephesus, *Ecclesiastical History* 5.14; Dagron, "Nés dans la pourpre," 108–12.

4. *RUMORED RETURNS*

1. Suetonius, *Caesar* 83.1–2; Ramsey and Raaflaub, "Chronological Tables," 212–15.

2. Marius: Stevenson, *Julius Caesar,* 35–38, 56–57. Supporters: Cicero, *Letters to Atticus* 12.49 [SB 292]; Nicolaus of Damascus, *Augustus* 31–33 (with Toher, *Nicolaus,* 220–23); Valerius Maximus, 9.15.1.

3. Marius's identity: Cicero, *Philippics* 1.5; Livy, *Epitome* 116; Valerius Maximus, 9.15.1: "ocularius medicus" or "equarius medicus" (the manuscripts have different readings); Appian, *Civil Wars* 3.1.2–3. Modern reconstructions: Pappano, "Pseudo-Marius," 58–59; Meijer, "Marius' Grandson," 113; Stern, "Imposters," 62. Wealth: Yavetz, *Plebs and Princeps,* 60. Cicero's letters: *Letters to Atticus* 12.49 [SB 292], 14.6 [SB 360], 14.7 [SB 361], 14.8 [SB 362]. Not an impostor: Yavetz, *Plebs and Princeps,* 59; Meijer, "Marius' Grandson," 116–19, though I think this is unlikely.

4. Identification: Eliav-Feldon, *Renaissance Impostors,* 194–217; Gottesman, *Politics and the Street,* 156–57. Martin Guerre: Davis, *Return of Martin Guerre,* 42–47, 54–56. Census: for an impostor being refused enrolment, see Valerius Maximus 9.7.1–2. Escaping Italy: Meijer, "Marius' Grandson," 116.

5. Altar: Cicero, *Philippics* 1.5; Appian, *Civil Wars* 3.2; Suetonius, *Caesar* 85 (without mention of Marius). Letters: Cicero, *Letters to Atticus* 12.49 [SB 292], 14.6 [SB 360], 14.7 [SB 361], 14.8 [SB 362]. Marius's death: Appian, *Civil Wars* 3.3. Octavius: Appian, *Civil Wars* 3.16; Toher, "Octavian's arrival," 181–82.
6. Champion: Appian, *Civil Wars* 3.2–3; Yavetz, *Plebs and Princeps,* 70–72. Political impostors: Bercé, *Le roi caché;* Lecuppre, *L'imposture politique;* Hug, *Impostures,* 87–90. Mental illness: Bercé, *Le roi caché,* 339–45. Reasons: Schwinges, *Verfassung,* 182; Lecuppre, *L'imposture politique,* 130–37, 157–77; Hug, *Impostures,* 102–3; see Longworth, "Pretender Phenomenon," 67–69, on economic crises in eighteenth-century Russia. Becoming king: Stern, "Imposters," 56–57 (Smerdis); Ogden, *Polygamy,* 143–46, 187–92; Chrubasik, *Kings and Usurpers,* 162 (Hellenistic cases); Larran, *Le bruit qui vole,* pt. 2, chap. 3, sec. 5–10 (Andriscus); Perrie, *Pretenders,* 84–98 (first false Dmitry's brief reign as tsar in 1605–6).
7. Caesarion: Suetonius, *Caesar* 51.1–3. Antony's declaration: Dio 49.41.1–2. Murder: Plutarch, *Antony* 81.1–82.1: οὐκ ἀγαθὸν πολυκαισαρίη; Suetonius, *Augustus* 17.5; Dio 51.15.5.
8. Bercé, *Le roi caché,* 209–16; Lecuppre, *L'imposture politique,* 88–91, 321–26; Bartlett, *Blood Royal,* 362–65.
9. Perkin Warbeck: Arthurson, *Perkin Warbeck.* False Dmitrys: Perrie, *Pretenders.* Asian examples: Struve, "Southern Ming," 654–55 (China); Flores and Subrahmanyam, "Shadow Sultan" (Mughal India); Rota, "Man Who Would Not Be King" (Safavid Iran). Universal and specific: Davis, *Remaking Impostors,* 8.
10. Evidence: Tacitus, *Annals* 5.10.3: "nos originem finemve eius rei ultra comperimus." Historians' interests: Pekáry, "Unruhen und Revolten," 146; Grünewald, *Bandits,* 5–6. Revolts: MacMullen, *Enemies;* Pekáry, "Unruhen und Revolten." Larger themes: Morgan, "Minor Pretenders"; Ash, *Histories Book II,* 95–96, 243, 279. Confrontation scenes: Grünewald, *Bandits,* 118–19. Boukoloi: Dio 72(71).4.1–2, with brief mentions in *Historia Augusta, Marcus Aurelius* 21.2, *Avidius Cassius* 6.7; see McGing, "Bandits," on the papyrus, *P. Thoumis* 1. Environmental factors: Blouin, *Triangular Landscapes,* 267–97.
11. Doctors: Phaedrus, *Fables* 1.24. Barbers: Lucian, *The Ignorant Book Collector* 28–29. Teachers and Vergil: Aulus Gellius, *Attic Nights* 16.6.1–12. Soothsayers: Juvenal, *Satires* 6.548–91. Exorcists: Acts 19:13–20; Lucian, *The Lover of Lies* 16. Con artists and legacy hunters: Petronius, *The Satyricon* 140; Juvenal, *Satires* 10.319–31; Lucian, *Alexander the False Prophet* 6–7. Philosophers: Epictetus, *Discourses* 4.8; Dio Chrysostom, *Discourses* 13.10–13, 32.9; Lucian, *The Runaways* 14, 16. Sophists: Lucian, *A Professor of Public Speaking* 15, 20. Jews and Christians: Acts 13: 6–12; Josephus, *Jewish War* 6.288; Origen, *Against Celsus* 3.50. Pagan divinity: Tacitus, *Histories* 2.61. Late Antiquity: Leo the Great, *Letters* 42 (deacon), Basil of Caesarea, *Letters* 169–71 (bishop with virgins). Wonder-workers: Philostratus, *Apollonius of Tyana.* Miracle workers: Gregory of Tours, *The History of the Franks* 9.6. Jesus Christ: Matthew 4: 23–25. False holy men: Speyer, "Religiöse Betrüger"; these individuals are connected with "freelance" religious experts, on which I have learned much from Wendt, *At the Temple Gates,* esp. 1–9, 17–30, 62–73, 81–100.

12. Money: Dio Chrysostom, *Discourses* 32.9; Apuleius, *Metamorphoses* 2.12–14, 8.24–28; Lucian, *The Runaways* 20. Christian prophets: Anonymous, *Didache* 11.3–6; see also the teachings of Jesus in Matthew 7: 15–20. Peregrinus: Lucian, *The Passing of Peregrinus* 9–14. John Isthmeos: John Malalas 16.5. Alexander: Lucian, *Alexander the False Prophet,* esp. 26–28, on Severianus. In these sketches, I have freely drawn on evidence from a wide variety of sources, including novels, not as verbatim records of historical events, but as writings that vividly bring Roman society to life (following in particular MacMullen, *Enemies,* and *Roman Social Relations*). For novels as evidence for social history, see Millar, "*Golden Ass*"; Morgan, "History, Romance."
13. Egyptians: *P. Giess.* 40, col. II, ll. 26–29. Documents: Moatti, "Le contrôle de la mobilité," 929–31, 941–44. Citizenship: Reinhold, "Usurpation," 278, 289–90, 292–93; *CIL* V 5050 (Claudius's grant). Equestrian rings: Petronius, *The Satyricon* 57–58; Pliny, *Natural History* 33.32. Equestrian seats: Martial, *Epigrams* 5.8, 5.14, 5.23. Numerianus: Dio 76(75).5.1–3.
14. Soldier or mugger?: Petronius, *The Satyricon* 82. Official dress: *P. Strasb.* 6.560; Lewis, "*Notationes legentis,*" 5–6. Doctors: Phaedrus, *Fables* 1.24; Galen, *On Prognosis* 4.6–11. Philosophers: Dio Chrysostom, *Discourses* 13.10–13. Bandits: Dio 76(75).10.5 (magistrate), Dio 75(75).2.4 (tribune), Ammianus 28.2.13 (treasury official). Croton: Petronius, *The Satyricon* 117. Culture of mistaken identity: Stern, "Imposters," 66.
15. Lookalikes: Valerius Maximus 9.14. Augustus: Macrobius, *Saturnalia* 2.4.20. Syrian: Lucian, *The Ignorant Book Collector* 20–21. Rubria: Valerius Maximus 9.15.ext.1. Scribonianus: Tacitus, *Histories* 2.72.1–2; Ash, *Histories Book II,* 279. Christ: Gregory of Tours, *The History of the Franks* 10.25.
16. Corocotta: Dio 56.43.3. Marcellus: Valerius Maximus 9.15.2. Switched at birth: Bartlett, *Blood Royal,* 364–65.
17. Motives: Speyer, "Religiöse Betrüger," 331; Stern, "Imposters," 71–72. Psychology: Bercé, *Le roi caché,* 339–45; Steiner, "Impostor Revisited," citing earlier medical literature. Modern comparisons: Weisz, *Stolen Valor,* 122, concludes that individuals who pretend to have served in the military are motivated by "financial fraud and attention." False Alexander: Dio 80(79).18.1–3, a "spirit" (δαίμων); Millar, *Cassius Dio,* 214–18. False Christ: Gregory of Tours, *The History of the Franks* 10.25. Peregrinus: Lucian, *The Passing of Peregrinus* 40.
18. Bandits: MacMullen, *Enemies,* 255–68; Shaw, "Bandits." Hideouts: Achilles Tatius, *Leucippe and Clitophon* 4.11–13; Heliodorus, *Aethiopica* 1.5.1–6.2 (Egyptian marshes); Apuleius, *Metamorphoses* 4.6 (Greek mountains). Raiding farms: Herodian 1.10.1–2; Ammianus 28.2.11. Targeting cities: Petronius, *Satyricon* 116; Apuleius, *Metamorphoses* 2.9, 4.13. Equestrians and centurions: Pliny, *Letters* 6.25. Dangerous journeys: Juvenal, *Satires* 10.19–22. Pickpockets: Petronius, *Satyricon* 140. Young men: Apuleius, *Metamorphoses* 2.18.
19. Boukoloi: Blouin, *Triangular Landscapes,* 274–85. Killed by bandits: "interfectus a latronibus" (*CIL* III 1579; other examples in Shaw, "Bandits," 12n26). Disappearance: *P. Tebt.* 2.333. Merchants robbed: *P. Fay.* 108. Concerns of farmers: Schuler, "Inscriptions." "Crop-giving nymphs": *TAM* 5.426. Forces for landowners: Herodian

7.4.3–4. Shepherds: *P. Sarap.* 1 = *BGU* III 759. Rural gangs: *P. Oxy.* 50.3561. Grain shortage: Petronius, *Satyricon* 44; for the connection between poor harvests and banditry, see Josephus, *Jewish Antiquities* 18.274; MacMullen, *Enemies,* 249–54. Moneylenders: *SB* XX 14401; *P. Fouad* I 26 (considering leaving). Environmental changes: Blouin, *Triangular Landscapes,* 297. Tax evasion: McGing, "Bandits," 174–77; Grey, *Constructing Communities,* 216–24. Deserters: Herodian 1.10.1–7; *Historia Augusta, Commodus* 16.2; Alföldy, "*Bellum desertorum.*" Slave revolts: Tacitus, *Annals* 4.27.1. Running away: Dio 76(75).10.5; Libanius, *Orations* 1.51. Resistance: Adas, "Avoidance to Confrontation," on Southeast Asian peasants, inspires this argument.

20. Jesus Christ: Mark 6: 14–16; Luke 9: 7–9. Bandits: Shaw, "Bandits," 36–38 (quotation from 51). As Wolff, "Comment deviant-on brigand?," 403, points out, the Roman state itself never sought to solve issues such as poverty, which led to people taking matters into their own hands. Peasants: Kautsky, *Aristocratic Empires,* 304–6.

21. Ghosts: Apuleius, *Metamorphoses* 4.22. Boukoloi: Dio 72(71).4.1. Mariccus: Tacitus, *Histories* 2.61. Bulla Felix: Dio 76(75).10.1–7. Outlaws: Longworth, "Pretender Phenomenon," 73 (on eighteenth-century Russia, but applicable to many bandits).

22. Adoptions: Velleius Paterculus 2.103.1–104.1; Suetonius, *Augustus* 65.1, *Tiberius* 15.2; Dio 55.13.2 (who does not mention Postumus). Postumus not honored: Dio 55.22.4. Postumus's exile: Velleius Paterculus 2.112.7; Pliny, *Natural History* 7.150; Tacitus, *Annals* 1.3.4, 4.3; Suetonius, *Augustus* 65.1, 65.4; Dio 55.32.1–2. Official story: Wardle, *Augustus,* 419, 423; see further Pettinger, *Republic in Danger,* esp. 93–101, who connects Postumus's exile with the execution of his brother-in-law, L. Aemilius Paullus.

23. Postumus's murder: Tacitus, *Annals* 1.6.1–3; Suetonius, *Tiberius* 22; Dio 57.3.5–6. Audacius and Epicadus: Suetonius, *Augustus* 19.1–2; Pettinger, *Republic in Danger,* 137–41. Augustus's visit: Tacitus, *Annals* 1.5.1–2; Plutarch, *Moralia* 507F–508B; Dio 56.30.1. Julia and Gracchus: Tacitus, *Annals* 1.53.1–6; Dio 57.18.1a.

24. Clemens's plan: Tacitus, *Annals* 2.39.1–2. Backers: Levick, *Tiberius,* 60–61, 151, suggests Julia the Younger for the first, and either of the Julias or Scribonia for the second; Pettinger, *Republic in Danger,* 210–12, conceives of a party opposed to Tiberius. Military revolts: Tacitus, *Annals* 1.16–45; Suetonius, *Tiberius* 25.2–3; Dio 57.4.1–6.5. Cosa: Tacitus, *Annals* 2.39.2–3, cf. Dio 57.16.3–4, who says that Clemens went to Gaul first, which is probably a misunderstanding based on his original intention to go to the armies on the Rhine with Postumus. Bodies: Bercé, *Le roi caché,* 384–85.

25. Pawns: Lecuppre, *L'imposture politique,* 157–66; Hug, *Impostures,* 89, 103; Bartlett, *Blood Royal,* 367–71; Bennett, *Lambert Simnel,* 5–8, 48–54 (Simnel); Perrie, *Pretenders,* 50–58 (Grisha). Clemens's supporters: Suetonius, *Tiberius* 25.1; Dio 57.16.3. Rumor: Tacitus, *Annals* 2.39.3–2.40.1; with Courrier, *La plèbe de Rome,* 688–89, on circulation. Revolt: Tacitus, *Annals* 4.27.1.

26. Elite supporters: Tacitus, *Annals* 2.40.3. Manipulation, rather than belief: Wolff, "Baldwin of Flanders," 294–301, on the false Baldwin, is a good case study of this phenomenon. Libo's pedigree: Tacitus, *Annals* 2.27.2; Pettinger, *Republic in Danger,* 219–32. Libo as a supporter of Clemens: Levick, *Tacitus,* 149–52; Pettinger, *Republic in Danger,* but not all historians are convinced, e.g., Mallan, *Cassius Dio,* 221–22. Libo's conspiracy: *Fasti Amiternini* (*CIL* I² p. 244 = *CIL* IX 4192); Seneca, *Letters* 70.10;

Tacitus, *Annals* 2.27.1–32.3; Suetonius, *Tiberius* 25.2–3; Dio 57.15.4–5. Seriousness of magic: Shotter, "Trial," 91–93. Language of revolution: *Fasti Amiternini;* Velleius Paterculus 2.129.2; Tacitus, *Annals* 2.27.1 (Libo); Tacitus, *Annals* 2.39.1 (Clemens). Atmosphere: Pettinger, *Republic in Danger,* 33–35.

27. Tacitus, *Annals* 2.40.1–3: "quo modo tu Caesar"; Suetonius, *Tiberius* 25.3; Dio 57.16.4.
28. Folklore: Champlin, "Tiberius the Wise," 410–11; Mallan, *Cassius Dio,* 222–23; Christoforou, *Imagining,* 226–28. Motif: TMI U11.2; see also J1280, "Repartee with Ruler (Judge, etc.)."
29. Heirs: Levick, *Tacitus,* 152–79. Nero and Drusus Caesar: Tacitus, *Annals* 4.8.4–5; Suetonius, *Tiberius* 54.1. Exile and death: Tacitus, *Annals* 4.59.3–60.3, 4.67.3–4, 5.3.1–4.2, 6.25.1–3; Suetonius, *Tiberius* 54.1–2. Imprisonment: Tacitus, *Annals* 6.23.2–24.3, 40.3; Suetonius, *Tiberius* 54.2; Dio 58.3.8.
30. False Drusus: Tacitus, *Annals* 5.10.1–3; research emphasized in 5.10.3; Tuplin, "False Drusus," 783–85, on the date of 31; Dio 58.25.1 offers a shorter version with slightly different details, dating it to 34; Mallan, *Cassius Dio,* 340–41. Freedmen: Camia and Rizakis, "Imperial Estates," esp. 84n43, provide examples of imperial freedmen attested in Greece. Bulla Felix: Dio 76(75).10.5. German legions: Woodman, *Tacitus Books 5 and 6,* 77–78. Agrippina and Nero: Tacitus, *Annals* 4.67.4. Poppaeus Sabinus: Tacitus, *Annals* 1.80.1.
31. Rural population: Apuleius's *Metamorphoses,* cited liberally earlier in this chapter, paints a vivid picture of provincial life in the region, including robbers and bandits (on which see also Lucian, *Dialogues of the Dead* 22[27].2). Archaeological evidence suggests decline in the rural landscape of Greece in the early empire, which could result in poverty and despair (Alcock, *Graecia capta,* 33–92). Cities: Dio 58.25.1. Nicopolis: Tacitus, *Annals* 2.54.1.
32. Cyclades: Sweetman, "Networks," 50–51. Silanus: Syme, *Augustan Aristocracy,* 198; Tuplin, "False Drusus," 797–800. Drusus as a scheme: Rogers, "Conspiracy of Agrippina," 165–66 (Agrippina as initiator); Levick, *Tacitus*, 211–13 (Gaius); Tuplin, "False Drusus" (Sejanus). Comparison: Walker, "Rumour, Sedition,"45.
33. Nero's memory: Suetonius, *Nero* 48.1–50.1, 57.1: "quasi viventis et brevi magno inimicorum malo reversuri"; see also Dio 63(64).27.3–29.3. Otho: Plutarch, *Otho* 3.1; Suetonius, *Otho* 7.1; Tacitus, *Histories* 1.78.2. Vitellius: Suetonius, *Vitellius* 11.2; Dio 65(64).7.3. Nero's survival: Tacitus, *Histories* 2.8.1; Suetonius, *Nero* 57.2; Dio Chrysostom 21.9–10; Lucian, *The Ignorant Book Collector* 20. Popularity: Champlin, *Nero,* 6–12.
34. First Nero: Tacitus, *Histories* 2.8.1–9.2; Dio 64(63).9.3 (Xiph.); Zonaras 11.15. Date: Tuplin, "False Neros," 365–68; Morgan, "Minor Pretenders," 792–95. Geographical location: Tacitus's reference to Achaea and Asia in both cases should not cause concern about the historicity of the revolts, given the maritime networks that connected the two (e.g., Acts 16: 11–12, 18: 18–20, 20: 4–6, 13–16); see further Champlin, *Nero,* 273n25; Ash, *Histories Book II,* 96; Malik, *Nero-Antichrist,* 47–48. "Wanderers on the lookout for the next opportunity": a loose, but hopefully faithful, translation of *inopia vagos* (Tacitus, *Histories* 2.8.1). Soldiers and bandits: Shaw, "Bandits," 29–31; "Rebels," 387–88. John of Gischala: Josephus, *Jewish War* 2.585–94. Bandits: *Digest* 48.3.6.1; Robert, *Études anatoliennes,* 90–110; Brélaz, *La sécurité publique,* 52–56.

35. Stories: Tacitus, *Histories* 2.8: "ut alii tradidere" ("as others relate"). Hairstyle: Ash, *Histories Book II,* 98. Imperial figures: Diocletian's wife and daughter, Prisca and Galeria Valeria, were caught in Thessaloniki because people recognized them (Lactantius, *On the Deaths of the Persecutors* 51). Slaves from Asia Minor: Harris, "Roman Slave Trade," 122–23, 126–28; Philostratus, *Life of Apollonius* 8.12.37. Entertainers as outsiders: Shaw, "Rebels," 396–99. Training: Suetonius, *Nero* 20.1. Connections between entertainers and impostors occur in cases of political imposture in France: Lecuppre, *L'imposture politique,* 75–76. Insurrection: only Zonaras 11.15 records an attempt to go to Syria, which is not found in our earliest, and best, account in Tacitus's *Histories.*
36. Name: Tacitus, *Histories* 2.8. Jewish War: Ash, *Histories Book II,* 98. Piracy: Sweetman, "Networks," 59n3. Asprenas: Tuplin, "False Neros," 365–70. Not Nero: Morgan, "Minor Pretenders," 791–92.
37. Second Nero: Zonaras 11.18 = Dio 66(66).19.3b–c; John of Antioch, frag. 131 (ed. Mariev). The precise date is difficult to pin down, especially since the imposture may have lasted for up to a year: see Tuplin, "False Neros," 374–75. Types of followers in Asia: *OGIS* 519 (villagers suffering from imperial soldiers); Aelius Aristides, *Sacred Tales* 4.63–94 (peasant gangs). Rural invocations: Mitchell, *Anatolia,* 187–95; Schuler, "Inscriptions"; note also sacrifices made for the god Men Askenos, the victory of the emperor, and a bountiful harvest in Sardis (*SEG* 49: 1676 = *AE* 1999: 1534). Walking among them: not far-fetched, since after Barnabas and Paul healed a lame man, they were hailed as Zeus and Hermes in human form by the people of Lystra in Asia Minor (Acts 14: 8–18).
38. Tiridates: Champlin, *Nero,* 221–29. Nero and Parthia: Suetonius, *Nero* 47.2, 57.2; Tuplin, "False Neros," 394–95. Parthian politics: Olbrycht, "Vologases." Artabanus: Gallivan, "False Neros," 364; Tuplin, "False Neros," 375. Philip IV: Flores and Subrahmanyam, "Shadow Sultan," 104.
39. Third Nero: Suetonius, *Nero* 57.2; Tacitus, *Histories* 1.2.1: "mota prope etiam Parthorum arma falsi Neronis ludibrio." This event is also briefly alluded to at Tacitus, *Histories* 2.8.1, when he writes of further false Neros to be discussed later in the work. Date: Tuplin, "False Neros," 77–78. Pacorus II: Gallivan, "False Neros," 365. Troop deployment: Jones, "Vettulenus Civica Cerialis," 519–20, *Domitian,* 158–59. Patterns: Lecuppre, *L'imposture politique,* 7–8 (Norway); Bercé, *Le roi caché,* 17–81 (Sebastian I); Perrie, *Pretenders* (false Dmitrys).
40. Reincarnation: Plutarch, *Moralia* 567F: ᾠδικόν . . . ζῷον; Folch, "Nero in Hell," 229–39; Jones, "Chronology," 71.
41. Sibylline Oracles: Collins, "Sibylline Oracles," 317–24. Date of *Fourth Sibylline Oracle:* Collins, "Sibylline Oracles," 381–82; Jones, *Jewish Reactions,* 179–81 (less absolute, favoring a date of 80 or later). Nero's return: *Sibylline Oracles* 4.119–120: ἀπ᾽ Ἰταλίης βασιλεὺς μέγας οἷά τε δράστης φεύξετ᾽ ἄφαντος ἄπυστος ὑπὲρ πόρον Εὐφρήταο (trans. Collins, "Sibylline Oracles"), see fully ll. 119–24, 137–44. Parthia, Jews, and Rome: Jones, *Jewish Reactions.* Date of *Fifth Sibylline Oracle:* Collins, "Sibylline Oracles," 390–91. Nero's return: *Sibylline Oracles* 5.361–70. Supernatural figure: Malik, *Nero-Antichrist,* 90–97. Nero as hero: Champlin, *Nero,* 13–17. Rumor to legend: Zongli, *Early Chinese Empires,* 275 (on China, but the process is the same). Imposture and

direct access: Bercé, *Le roi caché,* 402–12. Prophecies and kings: Thomas, *Religion,* 493–514, on early modern England, is stimulating reading.

42. Choice of Nero: Champlin, *Nero,* chap. 1; Burke, *Popular Culture,* 225–27 (who uses the technical term "crystallize"); Burke, *Varieties,* 51–52. Note the arguments of Gruen, *Sibylline Oracles,* who cautions against interpreting the text as straightforward historical resistance literature; Burke's comments resonate with Gruen's thesis.

43. Different scenarios: Augustine, *City of God* 20.19. Nero *redivivus* ("resurrected") as Antichrist: Malik, *Nero-Antichrist,* 122–26, citing Commodian, *Apologetic Poem* 825–28 and Victorinus, *Commentary on the Apocalypse* 17.16. Malik demonstrates (esp. 50–78) that the Antichrist of the late first-/early second-century Christian texts, such as 1 and 2 John and Revelation, was not intended to be Nero. Nero is not *redivivus* ("resurrected") in the *Sibylline Oracles,* but *rediturus* ("returned"): Collins, "Sibylline Oracles," 391; Van Henten, "*Nero redivivus*"; Malik, *Nero-Antichrist,* 90–97.

44. Nero: Champlin, *Nero,* 21–22. Sleeping king: Bercé, *Le roi caché,* esp. 316 on Zeus; TMI D.1960.2, "King Asleep in Mountain." Examples: Burke, *Popular Culture,* 205–6 (general); Lecuppre, *L'imposture politique,* 357–62; Rader, *Friedrich II,* 509–16 (Fredericks); MacKay, *Baker* (Sebastian I); Thomas, *Religion,* 498–501; Levin, *Heart and Stomach,* 100–120 (Edward VI); Nicol, *Immortal Emperor* (Constantine XI).

45. Sons of Anthemius: John of Antioch, frag. 234 (ed. Mariev); Theodore Lector, *Church History* Epitome 420 (ed. Kosiński et al.); Theophanes AM 5971. Procopius and his impostor: *PLRE* II Procopius Anthemius 9; Theosebius 2; John of Antioch, frag. 235 (ed. Mariev), who incorrectly calls Procopius the son, rather than the brother, of Marcianus (whose children were all daughters).

46. Maurice and family: *PLRE* III Mauricius 4, Theodosius 13. Downfall: Whitby, *Emperor Maurice,* 26–27; Theophylact Simocatta 8.11.1–6; *Chronicon Paschale* s.a. 602. Maurice as a saint: Whitby, "Theophanes' Chronicle Sources," 337–44. Folkloric motif: TMI S.252.1, "Vain Attempt to Save Promised Child by Use of Substitute"; on such stories in medieval Europe, see Bartlett, *Blood Royal,* 364–65. Theodosius: Theophylact Simocatta 8.9.11–12, 8.11.1–2, 8.13.3.

47. Rumor: Theophylact Simocatta 8.13.4–6, 8.15.8–9; Pseudo-Sebeos, *Armenian History* 31; Theophanes AM 6095 (who also notes the severed heads of his family members on display). Constantina: *Chronicon Paschale* s.a. 605; Theophanes AM 6098–99.

48. Other traditions: Booth, "Ghost of Maurice," 798–807. Narses: *PLRE* III Narses 10. My reconstruction of events, including the coronation, follows Thomson and Howard-Johnston, *Armenian History,* II, 197–98; Howard-Johnston, *Witnesses,* 132–33. Theodosiopolis: Pseudo-Sebeos, *Armenian History* 33. Not an impostor: Booth, "Ghost of Maurice," 803–7; see also Howard-Johnston, *Witnesses,* 437, who considers it a strong possibility. Foreign powers: Bartlett, *Blood Royal,* 367–71; Perrie, *Pretenders,* 50–58, 243–44.

49. John IV Laskaris: Shawcross, "Politics of Resistance"; Angelov, *Byzantine Hellene,* 217–22. First impostor: George Pachymeres, *History* 3.12–13 (ed. Failler and Laurent); Angelov, *Byzantine Hellene,* 16–18, 37–42, 53–56 (the region). Third impostor: Failler, "Le complot antidynastique." Sainthood: Shawcross, "Politics of Resistance," 218–21; with Majeska, *Russian Travellers,* 38, 267–68, for a visit to his shrine by the Russian pilgrim Stephen of Novgorod.

50. George Pachymeres, *History* 3.12–13 (ed. Failler and Laurent).
51. Predictions: *P. Oxy.* 31.2554, frag. I, col. II, ll. 4–14, as interpreted by J. Rea *ad loc.* Imagination: I am influenced here by Thomas, *Religion,* 502–6; Burke, *Popular Culture,* 230–35. Liberation: Scott, *Arts of Resistance,* 147. Roman worldview: Cf. Christoforou, *Imagining,* 230–31, who argues provincials "could not think of themselves outside of Roman power," on which note my important caveats below. Not universally shared: I have concentrated on Simeon bar Kosiba and the Jewish revolt of 132–135 because of the existence of a Jewish oral tradition and the coinage that gives us insights into the rebels' own views and motivations. We could also mention the revolt of the Iceni under Nero and the Batavians of the "Year of the Four Emperors" in this context, but the lack of sources preserving their perspective makes this discussion difficult (for these rebellions, see Dyson, "Native Revolt"; Gambash, *Provincial Resistance*).
52. Crusades: Lecuppre, *L'imposture politique,* 88–91. Louis XVII: Bercé, *Le roi caché,* 328–39. Russia: Longworth, "Pretender Phenomenon." Equitius: Beness and Hillard, "Death," and "Wronging Sempronia," 93–99.
53. Dynastic crisis: Lecuppre, *L'imposture politique,* 256–61, 275–76; Hug, *Impostures,* 89–91; Bartlett, *Blood Royal,* 364–65. Female impostors: Bartlett, *Blood Royal,* 365–66; cf. examples of women masquerading as Mary I in Tudor England (Hug, *Impostures,* 94–95; Levin, *Heart and Stomach,* 95).
54. Byzantine dynasties: Dagron, *Emperor and Priest,* 14. Condianus: Dio 73(72).6.1–7.2. Valerianus: *Nov. Theod.* 15.2.1.
55. Julian still lives: Ammianus 25.10.7: "quendam medium." Procopius: *PLRE* I Procopius 4; Lenski, *Valens,* 68–115.
56. False sons: Speyer, "Religiöse Betrüger," 327–28 (Greek and Hellenistic kings); Lecuppre, *L'imposture politique,* 69–70 (medieval Europe); Perrie, *Pretenders,* 240 (Russia).
57. Uranius Antoninus: Baldus, *Uranius Antoninus,* 229–69. Constantine III: *PLRE* II Constantinus 21; Constans 1; Iulianus 7; Drinkwater, "Usurpers," 272. Invented ancestry: Hekster, *Emperors and Ancestors,* 206–33. Galba: *RIC* I[2] Galba 13–14, 36, 52, 55, 65–67, all minted in Spain at the beginning of his rebellion; other examples were minted at Rome (e.g., 142–43, 184–89). False Antoninus: Dio 80(79).1.1.
58. Army: Flaig, *Den Kaiser herausfordern,* esp. 169–97. Secret: Tacitus, *Histories* 1.4.2: "evulgato imperii arcano posse principem alibi quam Romae fieri."
59. Usurpation: Dagron, *Emperor and Priest,* 14–15. Factions: Becker, "Court in Constantinople." Third century: Hartmann, *Herrscherwechsel und Reichskrise.* Brigandage: Anonymous, *On Matters of War* 2.1–3: "et per gradus criminum fovit tyrannos" (at 2.3); as Grig, *Popular Culture,* 74, has written: "peasants could exercise agency." Medieval Europe: Bartlett, *Blood Royal,* 360–78 (quotation at 360). Election: Kaldellis, *Byzantine Republic.*

5. *PATTERNS OF THE PAST*

1. Palatine: Martial, *Epigrams* 8.36.12: "par domus est caelo." Fronto's apologies: *Letters to Marcus as Caesar* 5.45, 5.57, *Letters to Antoninus Pius* 5 (ed. van den Hout).

2. Time: Christoforou, *Imagining,* 182–83. Festivals: Hopkins, *Conquerors and Slaves,* 206–9. Accession: *SEG* 41, 328 (Tiberius), *P. Oxy.* 55.3781 (Hadrian). Anniversaries: Laffi, "Le iscrizioni"; Price, *Rituals and Power,* 54–55, 106–7 (Asia Minor); *Babylonian Talmud, Avodah Zarah* 1, *Mishnah* 3 (trans. Rodkinson, *Babylonian Talmud,* XVIII); in general, see Graf, *Roman Festivals,* 66, 70–77 (eastern provinces); Kantirea, "Imperial Birthday Rituals" (birthdays). Villages: Price, *Rituals and Power,* 84–85 (village cults in Asia Minor); de Jong, *Emperors in Egypt,* 63–67 (villages in Egypt); Rogers, "Demosthenes," 97–98 (Oenoanda); Thonemann, *Lives of Ancient Villages,* 327–28 (other village *agones*). Ancient evidence for rituals: *P. Dura* 54, ll. 12–13 (sacrifices to Germanicus); *P. Oxy.* 12.1449, frag. 1–2, ll. 8–9 (portraits); *P. Oxy.* 61.4125, ll. 13–15 (priest and carrier of imperial portrait busts); *BGU* 2.362, p. xi, l. 13 (carrying statues). Theodosius II: Kelly, "Stooping to Conquer," 239–40.
3. Burke, *Popular Culture*; Davis, *Society and Culture.* Throughout this chapter, references to ancient sources are only given for events or concepts not discussed in the previous chapters.
4. License: Tertullian, *Apology* 35.5–7: "an alicui Caesari suo parcat illa lingua Romana?" Rome as capital: Millar, *Emperor,* 15–53; Davenport, "Rome"; and on the fifth century: Gillett, "Rome, Ravenna"; McEvoy, "Rome," and "Shadow Emperors." Constantinople: Croke, "Reinventing Constantinople"; Grig and Kelly, "Introduction"; Pfeilschifter, *Der Kaiser;* see Hekster, *Caesar Rules,* 263–85, on both cities. Urban centers: Fargette, "Rumeurs, propaganda," 316–17 (medieval France); Cust, "News and Politics," 70–71; Fox, *Oral and Literate Culture,* 346–49 (early modern England). Courts and cities: Magdalino, "Court and Capital" (Byzantium); Shoshan, *Popular Culture,* 52–66 (medieval Cairo); Hartmann, "Das Gerücht," 343–44 (medieval Europe); Fleet and Boyar, *Ottoman Istanbul,* 45 (Istanbul); Duindam, *Dynasties,* 173–76, 261–73 (early modern world); Gestrich, *Absolutismus und Öffentlichkeit,* 137 (early modern Germany).
5. Rome: Lo Cascio, "Population"; Purcell, "Populace of Rome," 137–40; Lançon, *Rome in Late Antiquity,* 14–15. Constantinople: Jacoby, "La population de Constantinople"; Durliat, *De la ville antique,* 260–61. European cities: Blanning, *Culture of Power,* 124–25, 154–61. Reading aloud: Libanius, *Letters* N 16.
6. Fourth-century capitals: *Explanation of the Whole World* 23, 32, 57, 58 (ed. Rougé). Tarsus: Libanius, *Orations* 15.77, 86, 16.53–55, *Letters* B 75; Ammianus 23.2.5. Continuity in expression of popular opinion: Aja Sánchez, "*Vox populi,*" 324.
7. Lucius Verus: Lucian, *Images* 2 (Panthea's retinue), 10 (their relationship); Marcus Aurelius, *Meditations* 8.37 contains a brief allusion to the relationship; Vout, *Power and Eroticism,* 213–39. Caracalla: Dio 78(77).20.1–2. Trier: Sulpicius Severus, *Life of Saint Martin* 18.1–2, describes the panic caused by rumors of a barbarian invasion. Felix: Marcellinus *comes* s.a. 430; Prosper, *Chronicle,* s.a. 430; Agnellus, *Book of the Bishops of the Church of Ravenna* 31 (ed. Holder-Egger), shows that the incident lived long in local memory, despite Agnellus's misdating of events. Ravenna: the imperial family was visible, for example at church services (Peter Chrysologus, *Sermons* 85bis.3, 130.3 [ed. Olivar]); further glimpses into the life of the city come in Constantius, *Life of Germanus* 35–44 (ed. Levison), which vividly portrays oral discourse in Ravenna.

8. Arles as prefectural capital from c. 395: Palanque, "La date du transfert," cf. Chastagnol, "Le repli sur Arles," arguing for the much too late 407; see also *Explanation of the Whole World* 58 (ed. Rougé) (previously second to Trier); Honorius and Theodosius II to Agricola, prefect of Gaul, *Authentic Letters from Arles* 8 (ed. Gundlach) (melting pot and major trading center). Majorian never visited Rome: McEvoy, "Shadow Emperors," 99. Verses in Arles: Sidonius Apollinaris, *Letters* 1.11.2–17; Harries, *Sidonius Apollinaris,* 84–85, 92–95.
9. Germanicus: *P. Oxy.* 25.2435 recto. Vespasian: *P. Fouad* 8. Alexandria: Philo, *Against Flaccus* 29, 32–33; Dio Chrysostom, *Oration* 32, esp. 24–34, 95–96; Herodian 4.8.7, 9.2; *Explanation of the Whole World* 37 (ed. Rougé). Caesarea Philippi: Ma'oz, "Civil Reform," 108–9, 117–19.
10. Verus: Fronto, *Beginnings of a History* 14, 16–18, 20 (ed. van den Hout); Davenport and Manley, *Fronto,* 154–57, 189–90. Gavius Clarus: Fronto, *Letters to Verus* 1.6 (ed. van den Hout). Caracalla in Alexandria: Dio 78(77).22.1–3; Herodian 4.9.1–3. Constantine: *CTh.* 1.16.6; Roueché, "Acclamations," 184–87.
11. Newspapers: Cust, "News and Politics," 69 (England); Fujitani, *Splendid Monarchy,* 205–6 (Japan). Jovian: Ammianus 25.8.7–12; see also Zosimus 3.33.1 (messengers); Ammianus 25.8.13–17 (Nisibis); Chauvot, *Les "barbares" des Romains,* 359–62; the chronology comes from den Boeft et al., *Ammianus Marcellinus XXV,* xxi–xxii, 261, 269–70, 308, 316–17; Drijvers, *Forgotten Reign,* 193–99. Demophilus: Basil of Caesarea, *Letters* 48. Mechanics of circulation: Gillett, *Envoys,* 54. Distances: calculated using the Stanford ORBIS website: https://orbis.stanford.edu. In the cases of Nemausus, Caralis, and Carthage, I am not arguing that the news came to them directly from Rome; the distances from the capital are used to give a sense of scale.
12. Skaptopara: *CIL* III 12336 = *SEG* 44, 610. Lollianus: *P. Oxy.* 46.3366; Parsons, "Grammarian's Complaint."
13. Harpocration's death: *P. Ammon.* 7, ll. 23–26; 9, ll. 12–14; 13, ll. 37–39; Willis and Maresch, *Archive of Ammon Scholasticus,* 139; Kelly, *Ruling,* 200–203. Suevic envoys: Hydatius, *Chronicle* 241 [247] (ed. Burgess). Aspar: Davenport and McEvoy, "Circulation of News," 223–26.
14. Agamemnon: Synesius, *Letters* 148.16. We should note that this kind of *aporia* about the emperor existed in villages in nineteenth-century Japan whose residents thought of him as a folk deity (Fujitani, *Splendid Monarchy,* 6–9). But the Japanese empire did not as yet have the kind of extensive festival and commemorative culture surrounding the emperors and the state as Rome did; this would only be introduced, as Fujitani's book shows, with the Meiji emperors. Caranis: *P. Haun.* 3.58; Rea, "Caranis in the Fifth Century." Skaptopara: *IG Bulg.* IV. 2236 col. b., ll. 8–18. Connections to rural areas: *P. Oxy.* 60.4087 records imperial officials and military officers at the *mansio* in the village of Tacona in the Oxyrhynchite nome in Egypt, including two high-ranking courtiers: a *praepositus sacri cubiculi* and a *comes* with the rank of *vir clarissimus.*
15. High interest: Shibutani, *Improvised News,* 41; Scott, *Arts of Resistance,* 142. Heraclius: John of Nikiu 116.3 (ed. Charles).
16. Edicts: Duncan-Jones, *Structure and Scale,* 17–23, esp. 21. For the sort of discussions these decisions could generate, see *PSI* 8.965 and *P. Ryl.* 4.607, on fourth-century

imperial economic policies in Egypt (the first specifically citing Diocletian's Edict of Maximum Prices).

17. Domitian: Dio Chrysostom, *Orations* 13.1–2, 45.1. Nero: *Fourth Sibylline Oracle* l. 158; *Fifth Sibylline Oracle* ll. 39–46, 490. Plotina: Davenport, "Envisioning Audiences," 301.
18. Ruffini, *Aphrodito,* 210, on this village in the sixth century.
19. Japanese court: Butler, *Emperor and Aristocracy,* 169–97. Elizabeth and Dudley: Fox, *Oral and Literate Culture,* 361–63. French kings: Darnton, *Literary Underground.*
20. Pompeii: *CIL* IV 2333–35, 2338, as discussed by Loar, "Sexual Graffiti," 413–20, whose interpretation I follow here. Doryphorus and gossip: *Suetonius*, Nero, 29: "ex nonnullis comperi persuasissimum habuisse eum neminem hominem pudicum aut ulla corporis parte purum esse." Egypt: *P. Oxy.* 46.3298: Ἀντωνείνου τοῦ κορύφ(ου); see J. Rea *ad loc,* citing LSJ s.v. κορύφος 3; Łukaszewicz, "Antoninus," and "Ergänzende Bemerkungen"; *P. Oxy.* 46.3299: ἀνόσιου Ἀντωνίνου μικροῦ; as Rea points out, *ad loc,* "little" distinguishes Elagabalus from the "great" Antoninus (Caracalla), but the addition of "sacrilegious" makes this a pejorative term (see also *P. Ryl.* 1.27). Astrologers: *P. Oxy.* 61.4126 refers to a "one eyed-astrologer" known to the recipient and sender of a private letter.
21. Peace: Ennodius, *Life of Epiphanius of Pavia* 73–75; the hagiographer's flattering language does not invalidate the basic point, for the later sack of Ticinum (95–100) shows the importance of peace and stable government to the people of Italy.
22. Augustine, *Confessions* 9.7.15.
23. *Circuli:* Seneca, *On Providence* 1.5.4*:* "optimos ... tempus in aliquo circulo terat"; O'Neill, "Going Round in Circles." Domitian: Tacitus, *Agricola* 43.1: "per fora et circulos ... constans rumor"; Hartnett, *Roman Street,* 52–53.
24. Senatorial snobs: Seneca, *Letters* 80; Pliny, *Letters* 9.6. Rome: Ammianus 28.4.30: "rem publicam stare non posse"; on the language this passage mocks, see den Boeft et al., *Ammianus Marcellinus XXVIII,* 220. Tiberius: Pliny *Natural History* 34.62. Constantinople: Cameron, *Circus Factions;* as he argues (161–62), the theater declined in importance in Constantinople; see 251–53 on Phocas and Maurice.
25. Antioch: Eunapius, frag. 29.1 (ed. Blockley): ἤλυθες ἐκ πολέμου, ὡς ὤφελες αὐτόθ᾽ ὀλέσθαι (Homer, *Iliad* 3.428); Δύσπαρι, εἶδος ἄριστε (Homer, *Iliad* 3.39, 13.769); see also Homer, *Iliad* 2.261–3; Drijvers, *Forgotten Reign,* 62–63. Paris's epithets: Suter, "Paris and Dionysos," 1–5. Pamphlets: Angius, "Graffiti e pamphlet," 270–71. Fear: John of Antioch frag. 206, ll. 15–20 (ed. Mariev); Lenski, *Valens,* 17–18; Turcan, "L'abandon de Nisibe."
26. Dio Chrysostom, *Orations* 40.8–15, 45.2–3, see also 46.3–4, which emphasizes his grandfather's relationship with the emperors; Jones, *Dio Chrysostom,* 100, 111–14; Krause, *Strategie der Selbstinszenierung,* 123–25.
27. Thonemann, *Lives of Ancient Villages,* 355.
28. Enslaved people: Seneca, *On Clemency* 1.18; see Hopkins, *Conquerors and Slaves,* 222–23, for this and other legal evidence. Provincial divisions: Basil of Caesarea, *Letters* 74–76; Lactantius, *On the Deaths of the Persecutors* 7.4: "provinciae in frusta concisae." Recruitment tax: *P. Oxy.* 48.3401: ἐ[πεί]περ γέγονεν φήμη περὶ [το]ῦ χρυσοῦ τῶν τιρόνων κα[ὶ] [π]άντες ζητι νομισμ[ά]τια καὶ καθ' ἥμερα ἀναβένι ἡ [τι]μή (translation adapted

from that provided by John Shelton, *ad loc*); Lenski, *Valens*, 312–19, suggests a connection with Valens's troop recruitments. India: Yang, "Conversation of Rumors," 488–91. There are similar connections between the census and rumors of taxation by the British government in Nigeria in 1921 (van den Bersselaar, "Establishing the Facts," 87) and by Soviet Russia in the 1930s, when Christians believed the state might target them with new taxes or deportation (Corley, "Believers' Responses," 406). Note also the role played by rumors of new taxes in peasant rebellion, for example in early modern England (Bush, "Tax Reform," 392; Shagan, "Rumours and Popular Politics," 44) and France (Bonney, *Society and Government*, 205). Protector and punishment: this dual image is attested in the popular culture around many kings, such as Ivan the Terrible (Perrie, *Image of Ivan*, 109).

29. Local issues: Gleason, "Visiting and News," on monks; Grey, *Constructing Communities*, 84–90, on the countryside; and for Aphrodito, see Ruffini, *Aphrodito*, esp. 59, 125, on the prominence of community jurisdictions and concerns, and 171–72 on slander. Gossip not about emperors: Ruffini, *Aphrodito*, 210; Malik, *Nero-Antichrist*, 34–36; see further Davenport, "Sexual Habits," distinguishing the generation of popular rumor from circulation of gossip at court. Peasant networks: Bowes and Grey, "Conclusions," 628–30. Local concerns: The different sources I have drawn upon in this sketch, some of which directly attest gossip, others which concern topics which plausibly generated gossip, are: 1 Timothy 5: 13–14; Galatians 2: 11–14; Petronius, *Satyricon* 37–38; Apuleius, *Metamorphoses* 8.30; Lucian, *Slander Should Not Be Believed* 1; Augustine, *Confessions* 9.2.3, 9.9.19–20; *CIL* IV 8259, 5251; *BGU* 4.1097; *P. Abinn.* 19, 28; *P. Cair. Masp.* 1.67004, line 17; *P. Lips.* 29; *P. Mich.* 7.434, 8.514; *P. Oxy.* 7.1067, 46.3313; *P. Ryl.* 2.124; *SB* 3.6264, 16.12326. Harvester: "nullo lingua crimine laedit atrox" (*CIL* VIII, 11824); see also Bailey, "Preaching," 256–57, 265–66, on Late Antique priests warning their congregations against speaking ill of one another. Azitta: *TAM* V.1 318; Thonemann, *Lives of Ancient Villages*, 311–13. Tuvalu: Besnier, *Gossip*.

30. *Maiestas:* Suetonius, *Augustus* 55; Tacitus, *Annals* 1.72.4; Bauman, *Impietas in principem*, 25–51, 143–53. Granius: Tacitus, *Annals* 1.74.3: "ex moribus principis foedissima quaeque." Patavinus: Suetonius, *Augustus* 51.1 ("e plebe"); see also the Cyrene edicts (*SEG* 9, 8, ll. 40–55 [no. II]; Peachin, "Judicial Powers," 541–49), which suggest that people in Cyrenaica knew that talk about the emperor mattered. However, this case more likely refers to accusations about conspiracy rather than loose lips at dinner. Paul: Ammianus 14.5.6–9, 19.12.1–19; Harries, *Law and Crime*, 81–83, on treason in Late Antiquity. Critical speech: *C.Th.* 9.4.1 = *CJ* 9.7.1.

31. England: Freist, *Governed by Opinion*, 177–238, esp. 185–91; Fox, *Oral and Literate Culture*, 337–63; Shagan, "Rumours and Popular Politics." Christians: Pliny, *Letters* 10.96–7; Tertullian, *To the Nations* 1.7.15; Harries, *Law and Crime*, 39–41. Unorthodox: Humfress, *Orthodoxy and the Courts*, 256–59. Gossip and religion: see Wickham, "Gossip and Resistance," 8–9, for medieval evidence. Other topics for denouncement include a failure to pay taxes, as shown in a complaint from a fifth-century tax collector who was met with opposition by a village mob (*P. Col.* 8.242).

32. *Delatores:* Rutledge, *Imperial Inquisitions;* Williamson, "Crimes against the State." Enslaved people: *Digest* 37.14.1, 49.14.2.6; with the prejudicial comments of Jerome,

Letters 117.8; for the idea of enslaved people as eavesdroppers, see Plautus, *Epidicus,* ll. 236–40. Experiencing fear: Epictetus, *Discourses* 4.13.1–4. Censorship and slander: Kaplan, *Culture of Slander;* Hanrahan, "Defamation," dealing with medieval and early modern England, have been helpful to my thinking here. Rome and other states: Rosenblitt, "Rome and North Korea," 211–13; Watts, "Introduction," 158–59.

33. Henry VIII: Cressy, *Dangerous Talk,* esp. 48–54. Duke: Gestrich, *Absolutismus und Öffentlichkeit,* 140. Ottomans: Kırlı, "Surveillance." France: Farge, *Subversive Words,* 161–66; Streckfuss, "Kings in the Age of Nations," 446–48, who emphasizes a similar extension in the policing of speech in modern-day Thailand. China: Zongli, *Early Chinese Empires,* 154–68.

34. Augustus: Suetonius, *Augustus* 85.1; Powell, "Augustus' Age of Apology." Campaigns: Suetonius, *Caligula* 50.1 (Caligula's pale skin is a sign of cowardice); Tacitus, *Germania* 37 (snide remarks about Domitian's German campaigns); Dio 60.2.6, 73(72).1.1, 78(77).13.3 (cowardice of emperors). Emperor's military role: Hekster, *Caesar Rules,* 109–33.

35. Soldiers' sentiments: we know most about soldiers' humor, on which see Montalhuc, *Le pouvoir,* chap. 2.IV, but these often focus on other personal qualities (e.g., drinking) rather than military competency. Inscribed slingshots from Sertorius's civil war in Spain in the 70s BCE contain political slogans such as *pietas, fides, ius,* and perhaps also *libertas,* suggesting the qualities their general would defend if victorious (Díaz Ariño, *Glandes inscriptae,* 226–27). Alexander: Herodian 6.9.4–5. Otho: Suetonius, *Otho* 10.1–3: "referre crebro solebat Othonem etiam privatum usque adeo detestatum civilia arma"; "hoc viso proclamasse eum aiebat, non amplius se in periculum talis tamque bene meritos coniecturum."

36. Jovian and Julian: Ammianus 25.7.11; Ephrem the Syrian, *Hymns against Julian* 15–18 (trans. J. Lieu, *Emperor Julian*).

37. Gauls: Suetonius, *Caesar* 76.3, 80.2: "bonum factum: ne quis senatori novo curiam monstrare velit" (with Meyer, *Legitimacy and Law,* 66–67); "Gallos Caesar in triumphum ducit, idem in curiam | Galli bracas deposuerunt, latum clavum sumpserunt"; Syme, "Caesar," 15. Claudius: Tacitus, *Annals* 11.23–25, esp. 23.1; Malloch, *Tabula Lugdunensis,* 28–29, 60–61. Note, however, aristocratic criticism about Claudius's citizenship grants: Seneca, *Apocolocyntosis* 3.3.

38. Limitations: White, "Between Gluckman and Foucault," 82; Coast and Fox, "Rumour and Politics," 231. Transactions: Wickham, "Gossip and Resistance," 10; Epictetus, *Discourses* 4.13.1–24. Speeches: Gregory of Nazianus, *Orations* 4.52, 96.

39. Libanius, *Orations* 37.1–3.

40. Horace, *Satires* 2.6.50–58.

41. Antonius: Cicero, *Letters to Atticus* 14.3.1 [SB 357.1]. Seismos: *Chronicon Paschale* s.a. 618, 626 (ed. Whitby and Whitby); for the anxiety at Heraclius's absence, see Whitby, "Defender of the Cross," 250–52, 258, 261–64.

42. Alexander: Bosworth, "Death of Alexander," 113–16. Assyria: Pečírková, "Divination and Politics," 165. Popes: Hunt, "Rumour, Newsletters"; Pattenden, *Electing the Pope,* 147–49. Ottomans: Boyar and Fleet, *Ottoman Istanbul,* 44–45. Medieval Europe: Depreux, "Rumeur"; Hartmann, "Das Gerücht," 351–54. Henry VIII: Shagan, "Rumours

and Popular Politics," 43–45. Dynastic grief: Larran, *Le bruit qui vole,* pt. I, chap. 2, sec. 48 (mourning at the death of Arsinoe of Egypt in 204 BCE). Abdications: Shoshan, *Popular Culture,* 52 (medieval Cairo).

43. Caesar: Stevenson, *Julius Caesar,* 153–60; Morstein-Marx, *Julius Caesar,* 499–544, 573–79, esp. 523 on popular opposition.

44. Caesar's triumph: Dio 43.20.3: ἂν μὲν καλῶς ποιήσῃς, κολασθήσῃ, ἂν δὲ κακῶς, βασιλεύσεις; Corbeill, *Controlling Laughter,* 205; Montlahuc, *Le pouvoir,* chap. IV, sec. I.B.2. Advisors: Burke, *Popular Culture,* 208; Duindam, *Dynasties,* 166, 195–96, 277. Women: van Leeuwen, *Narratives of Kingship,* 49–50, 166–67. Tales of love and sex: Sharma, "Forbidden Love" (homosexual and heterosexual love affairs at the Mughal court). Greedy Chinese emperors: Zongli, *Early Chinese Empires,* 131–32.

45. Cultural contexts: White, *Speaking with Vampires,* 58–59. China: Barrett, "Emperor Wuzong." Paris: Farge and Revel, *Vanishing Children,* esp. 105, 108, 112, 128, with the story of Herod in Matthew 2: 1–18. Constantine: *Edict of Constantine to Pope Sylvester* 6 (trans. Edwards, *Constantine and Christendom,* 99–100, who points to the biblical story of Naaman being cured of leprosy by bathing in the River Jordan in 2 Kings 5: 10–14); for the date, see Liverani, "Saint Peter's," who argues the story of Constantine's leprosy was known in Rome in the fifth century. Magical practices: Rives, "Human Sacrifice," 78–80.

46. Zhengde emperor: ter Haar, *Telling Stories,* 1–3, 299–318. Louis XV's deer park: Blanning, *Culture of Power,* 390–91.

47. Criticism and discussion: attacks on the Japanese emperor's morals and character have long been regarded as both unwarranted and undistinguished, and although recent emperors have appeared more accessible, this sense of reservation about the emperor's private life remains (Spellman, *Monarchies,* 55–69; Oakley, *Kingship,* 19–23). Sex: Lo and Barrett, "Other Pleasures?" 38 (Ming China); McLaughlin, "Disgusting Acts" (Henry IV of Germany and the Church). Baybars al-Jashnikīr: Shoshan, *Popular Culture,* 53; Guo, "Protest Songs," 18, 23–24.

48. China: Pirazzoli-t'Serstevens, "Imperial Aura," 302, 308–9. Ottoman Empire: Kırlı, "Surveillance," 294. Satanic fairyland: Darnton, *Art of Slander,* 6; for Roman parallels, see Beard, *Emperor,* 194–96.

49. Parody medals: Wellington, *Antiquarianism,* 131–35. Nero graffito: Castrén and Lilius, *Graffiti,* 121. Pannonia: Vágó and Bóna, *Der spätrömische Südostfriedhof,* 185; Bruun, "Roman Emperors," 78–79, reviews different interpretations.

50. Statue modification as commentary: Rosso, "Les 'statues parlantes.'" Maximinus's head: Herodian 8.5.9, 8.6.5, 8.6.7; Wienand, "Impaled King," who suggests it may have been reworked by a soldier.

51. Farce: Suetonius, *Nero* 39.3. Mummery and *charivari:* the festival culture evoked by Bakhtin, *Rabelais,* and Davis, *Society and Culture,* was not limited to the European West—e.g., in Mamluk Egypt, the Coptic New Year festival featured a "lord of misrule," the *amir Nawrūz* (Molan, "Charivari"; Shoshan, *Popular Culture,* 40–51).

52. Charles II: Zaller, "Breaking the Vessels," 775–78. Bodily discourse: Stratmann, "Golden Rumps." Romanovs: Figes and Kolonitskii, *Russian Revolution,* 9–29; Rowley, "Monarchy and the Mundane." Imperial house: Corbier, "La maison"; Moreau, "La *domus Augusta*"; *AE* 1988, 553 (*domus divina*).

53. Imperial responses: Suetonius, *Augustus* 55–56.1; Suetonius, *Claudius* 38.1; Suetonius, *Vespasian* 23.1; Dio 66(65).11.1–2; *Historia Augusta, Marcus Aurelius* 22.5–6. Byzantine popular criticism: Jeffreys, "Political Verse," 188–89; Haldon, "Humour," 64–67; Kaldellis, *Byzantine Republic,* 146–47. Orthodoxy: Basiliscus, as described in *The Life of Daniel the Stylite* 73, 83–84; McEvoy, "Emperors, Aristocrats, and Columns," 448–49. This paragraph summarizes the argument of my forthcoming paper, "The Emperor Writes Back."
54. Manuel Komnenos: Magdalino, "Eros," esp. 202: "Manuel positively relished his sexual reputation"; *Manuel I Komnenos,* 420–21, 449, 453–54; Bourbouhakis, "Devices of Ares," 222.

Bibliography

Adas, Michael. "From Avoidance to Confrontation: Peasant Protest in Precolonial and Colonial Southeast Asia." *Comparative Studies in Society and History* 23 (1981): 217–47.

Africa, Thomas. "Worms and the Death of Kings: A Cautionary Note on Disease and History." *Classical Antiquity* 1 (1982): 1–17.

Ahl, Frederick M. "Lucan's *De Incendio Urbis, Epistulae ex Campania* and Nero's Ban." *TAPA* 102 (1971): 1–27.

Airlie, Stuart. "Private Bodies and the Body Politic in the Divorce Case of Lothar II." *Past and Present* 161 (1998): 3–38.

Aja Sánchez, José Ramón. "*Vox populi et princeps:* El impacto de la opinión pública sobre el comportamiento político de los emperadores romanos." *Latomus* 55 (1996): 295–328.

Aksenov, Vladislav Benovich. "The War and the Regime in Peasant Popular Consciousness, 1914–1917: Archetypes, Rumours, Interpretations." *Russian Studies in History* 56 (2017): 126–40.

Alcock, Susan E. Graecia capta: *The Landscapes of Roman Greece.* Cambridge: Cambridge University Press, 1993.

Aldrete, Gregory S. *Gestures and Acclamations in Ancient Rome.* Baltimore: Johns Hopkins University Press, 1999.

Alexander, Paul J. *The Byzantine Apocalyptic Tradition.* Berkeley: University of California Press, 1985.

Alexiou, Margaret. *After Antiquity: Greek Language, Myth, and Metaphor.* Ithaca, NY: Cornell University Press, 2011.

Alföldy, Géza. "*Bellum desertorum.*" *Bonner Jahrbücher* 171 (1971): 367–76.

Alföldy, Géza, and Helmut Hartmann. "M. Cornelius Nigrinus Curiatius Maternus: General Domitians and Rivale Trajans." *Chiron* 3 (1973): 331–73.

Allemeyer, Marie Luisa. "Profane Hazard or Divine Judgement? Coping with Urban Fire in the 17th Century." *Historical Social Research* 32 (2007): 145–68.

Allen, Pauline, ed. *John Chrysostom, Homilies on Philippians.* Atlanta: Society of Biblical Literature, 2013.

Allen, Pauline, and Wendy Mayer. "Chrysostom and the Preaching of Homilies in Series: A New Approach to the Twelve Homilies *In epistulam ad Colossenses* (*CPG* 4433)." *Orientalia Christiana Periodica* 60 (1994): 21–39.

———. "Chrysostom and the Preaching of Homilies in Series: A Re-Examination of the Fifteen Homilies *In epistulam ad Philippenses* (*CPG* 4432)." *Vigiliae Christianae* 49 (1995): 270–89.

Allport, Gordon W., and Leo Postman. *The Psychology of Rumor.* New York: Henry Holt, 1947.

Althoff, Gerd. "Vom Lächeln zum Verlachen." In *Lachgemeinschaften: Kulturelle Inszenierungen und soziale Wirkungen von Gelächter im Mittelalter und in der Frühen Neuzeit,* edited by Werner Röcke and Hans Rudolf Velten, 3–16. Berlin: De Gruyter, 2005.

Anderson, Benjamin. "The Disappearing Imperial Statue: Toward a Social Approach." In *The Afterlife of Greek and Roman Sculpture,* edited by Troels Myrup Kristensen and Lea Stirling, 290–309. Ann Arbor: University of Michigan Press, 2016.

Anderson, Graham. *Ancient Fairy and Folk Tales: An Anthology.* London: Routledge, 2019.

Anderson, W. B., ed. *Sidonius Apollinaris. Poems. Letters.* 2 vols. Cambridge, MA: Harvard University Press, 1936–65.

Ando, Clifford. *Imperial Ideology and Provincial Loyalty.* Berkeley: University of California Press, 2000.

Angelov, Dimiter. *The Byzantine Hellene: The Life of Emperor Theodore Laskaris and Byzantium in the Thirteenth Century.* Cambridge: Cambridge University Press, 2019.

Angius, Andrea. "Graffiti e pamphlet: Lessico e sociologia di un fenomeno politico." *Bullettino dell'Istituto di Diritto Romano* 109 (2015): 247–77.

Angkasa, William. "Synchronous Chanting in Indonesian Social Movement Repertoires: A Tool for Emoting and for Manipulating Emoters." *Human Arenas* (September 2023): https://doi.org/10.1007/s42087-023-00360-8.

Arthurson, Ian. *The Perkin Warbeck Conspiracy, 1491–1499.* Stroud: History Press, 2009.

Ash, Rhiannon, ed. *Tacitus: Histories Book II.* Cambridge: Cambridge University Press, 2007.

———, ed. *Tacitus: Annals Book XV.* Cambridge: Cambridge University Press, 2018.

———. "Tiberius in Space." In *Representing Rome's Emperors,* edited by Caillan Davenport and Shushma Malik, 40–62. Oxford: Oxford University Press, 2024.

Aubert, Jean-Jacques. "Threatened Wombs: Aspects of Ancient Uterine Magic." *Greek, Roman, and Byzantine Studies* 30 (1989): 421–49.

Augoustakis, Antony. "Castrate the He-Goat! Overpowering the *Paterfamilias* in Plautus' *Mercator.*" *Scholia* 17 (2008): 37–48.

Bai, Matt. *All the Truth Is Out: The Week Politics Went Tabloid.* New York: Knopf, 2015.

Bailey, Lisa. " 'No Use Crying over Spilt Milk': The Challenge of Preaching God's Justice in Fifth-and Sixth-Century Gaul." *Journal of the Australian Early Medieval Association* 4 (2008): 19–31.

———. "Preaching in Fifth-Century Gaul: Valerian of Cimiez and the Eusebius Gallicanus Collection." In *Preaching in the Patristic Era: Sermons, Preachers, and Audiences in the Latin West,* edited by Anthony Dupont, Shari Boodts, Gert Partoens, and Johan Leemans, 253–73. Leiden: Brill, 2018.

Baker-Brian, Nicholas. *The Reign of Constantius II.* London: Routledge, 2022.

Baker-Brian, Nicholas, and Shaun Tougher, eds. *The Sons of Constantine, AD 337–361: In the Shadows of Constantine and Julian.* Cham: Palgrave, 2020.

Bakhtin, Mikhail. *Rabelais and His World.* Translated by Hélène Iswolsky. Cambridge, MA: MIT Press, 1968.

Baldus, Hans Roland. *Uranius Antoninus: Münzprägung und Geschichte.* Bonn: R. Habelt, 1971.

Baldwin, Barry. "Physical Descriptions of Byzantine Emperors." *Byzantion* 51 (1981): 8–21.

Baldwin, Peter. "Comparing and Generalizing: Why All History Is Comparative, Yet No History Is Sociology." In *Comparison and History,* edited by Deborah Cohen and Maura O'Connor, 1–22. London: Routledge, 2004.

Baltussen, Han. "How to Console Yourself and Others: Ancient and Modern Perspectives on Managing Grief." *Humanities Australia* 7 (2017): 45–55.

Barnes, T. D. "The Career of Abinnaeus." *Phoenix* 39 (1985): 368–74.

Barnes, Timothy. *Constantine: Dynasty, Religion, and Power in the Later Roman Empire.* Oxford: Blackwell, 2011.

Barnes, Timothy D., and George Bevan, eds. *The Funerary Speech for John Chrysostom.* Translated Texts for Historians 60. Liverpool: Liverpool University Press, 2013.

Barrett, Anthony A. *Caligula: The Corruption of Power.* 2nd ed. London: Routledge, 2015.

———. *Rome Is Burning.* Princeton, NJ: Princeton University Press, 2020.

Barrett, Timothy H. "The Madness of Emperor Wuzong." *Cahiers d'Extrême-Asie* 14 (2004): 173–86.

Bartlett, Robert. *Blood Royal: Dynastic Politics in Medieval Europe.* Cambridge: Cambridge University Press, 2020.

Bartsch, Shadi. *Actors in the Audience: Theatricality and Doublespeak from Nero to Hadrian.* Cambridge, MA: Harvard University Press, 1994.

Bauer, Michael. *Asterios Bischof von Amaseia: Sein Leben und seine Werke.* Würzburg: Franz Staudenraus, 2011.

Bauman, Richard A. Impietas in principem: *A Study of Treason against the Roman Emperor with Special Reference to the First Century AD.* Munich: C. H. Beck, 1974.

———. "Tanaquil-Livia and the Death of Augustus." *Historia* 43 (1994): 177–88.

Baumkamp, Eva. *Kommunikation in der Kirche des 3. Jahrhunderts.* Tübingen: Mohr Siebeck, 2014.

Bayly, C. A. *Empire and Information: Intelligence Gathering and Social Communication in India, 1780–1870.* Cambridge: Cambridge University Press, 1996.

Beagon, Mary. "Situating Nature's Wonders in Pliny's *Natural History.*" In Vita Vigilia Est: *Essays in Honour of Barbara Levick,* edited by Edward Bispham and Greg Rowe, 19–40. London: Institute of Classical Studies, 2007.

Beard, Mary. *Emperor of Rome: Ruling the Ancient Roman World.* London: Profile, 2023.

———. *Laughter in Ancient Rome: On Joking, Tickling, and Cracking Up.* Berkeley: University of California Press, 2014.

———. *The Roman Triumph.* Cambridge, MA: Harvard University Press, 2007.

Becker, Audrey. "The Court in Constantinople Facing the Death of the Emperor." In *The Roman Imperial Court in the Principate and Late Antiquity,* edited by Caillan Davenport and Meaghan McEvoy, 105–18. Oxford: Oxford University Press, 2023.

Bell, H. I. "An Egyptian Village in the Age of Justinian." *Journal of Hellenic Studies* 64 (1994): 21–36.

Ben Zeev, Miriam Pucci. *Diaspora Judaism in Turmoil, 116/117 BC.* Leuven: Peeters, 2005.

Benefiel, Rebecca. "Rome in Pompeii: Wall Inscriptions and GIS." In *Latin on Stone: Epigraphic Research and Electronic Archives,* edited by Francisca Feraudi-Gruénais, 45–75. Lexington: Rowman and Littlefield, 2020.

Beness, J. Lea. "Atia." In *The Encyclopedia of Ancient History,* 2nd ed., edited by A. Erskine, D. Hollander, and A. Papaconstantinou. Oxford: Blackwell, 2023. https://doi.org/10.1002/9781444338386.wbeah10099.pub2.

———. "Scipio Aemilianus and the Crisis of 129 B.C." *Historia* 54 (2005): 37–48.

Beness, J. Lea, and T. W. Hillard. "The Death of Lucius Equitius on 10 December 100 BC." *Classical Quarterly* 40 (1990): 269–72.

Beness, J. Lea, and Tom Hillard. "Wronging Sempronia." *Antichthon* 50 (2016): 80–106.

Benner, Margareta. *The Emperor Says: Studies in the Rhetorical Style in Edicts of the Early Empire.* Göteborg: Acta Universitatis Gothoburgensis, 1975.

Bennett, Julian. *Trajan:* Optimus Princeps. London: Routledge, 1997.

Bennett, Michael. *Lambert Simnel and the Battle of Stoke.* Stroud: History Press, 1987.

Bercé, Yves-Marie. *Le roi caché. Sauveurs et imposteurs. Mythes politiques populaires dans l'Europe moderne.* Paris: Fayard, 1990.

Berg, Christopher ven den. "The *Pulvinar* in Roman Culture." *TAPA* 138 (2008): 239–73.

Bergmann, Jörg R. *Discreet Indiscretions: The Social Organization of Gossip.* Translated by John Bednarz, Jr. New York: Transaction, 1993.

Bernard, Floris. "Laughter, Derision, and Abuse in Byzantine Verse." In *Satire in the Middle Byzantine Period: The Golden Age of Laughter?,* edited by Przemysław Marciniak and Ingela Nilsson, 39–61. Leiden: Brill, 2021.

Bernardi, Jean, ed. *Grégoire de Nazianze. Discours 4–5. Contre Julien.* Paris: Les éditions du Cerf, 1984.

Berriman, Andrew, and Malcolm Todd. "A Very Roman Coup: The Hidden War of Imperial Succession, AD 96–8." *Historia* 50 (2001): 312–31.

Berrouard, Marie-François. "Un tournant dans la vie de l'Église d'Afrique: Les deux missions d'Alypius en Italie à la lumière des *Lettres* 10*, 15*, 16*, 22* et 23*A de saint Augustin." *Revue des études Augustiniennes* 31 (1985): 46–70.

Bersselaar, Dmitri van den. "Establishing the Facts: P. A. Talbot and the 1921 Census of Nigeria." *History in Africa* 31 (2004): 69–102.

Besnier, Niko. *Gossip and the Everyday Production of Politics.* Honolulu: University of Hawai'i Press, 2009.

Bhabha, Homi L. "In a Spirt of Calm Violence." In *After Colonialism: Imperial Histories and Postcolonial Displacements,* edited by Gyan Prakash, 326–43. Princeton, NJ: Princeton University Press, 1995.

Bird, Donald Allport. *Rumor as Folklore: An Interpretation and Inventory.* PhD diss., Indiana University, 1979.

Bird, H. W., ed. *The* Breviarium ab Urbe Condita *of Eutropius.* Translated Texts for Historians 14. Liverpool: Liverpool University Press, 1993.

Birley, Anthony R. *Hadrian: The Restless Emperor.* London: Routledge, 1997.

Bischoff, Bernhard, and Wilhelm Koehler. "Eine illustrierte Ausgabe der Spätantiken Ravennater Annalen." In *Medieval Studies in Memory of A. Kingsley Porter,* vol. 1, edited by Wilhelm Koehler, 125–64. Cambridge, MA: Harvard University Press, 1939.

Blanning, T. C. W. *The Culture of Power and the Power of Culture: Old Regime Europe 1660–1789.* Oxford: Oxford University Press, 2002.

Blanshard, Alastair J. L. "Naked Apes, Featherless Chickens, and Talking Pigs: Adventures in the Platonic History of Body-Hair and Other Human Attributes." In *Reception in the Greco-Roman World: Literary Studies in Theory and Practice,* edited by Marco Fantuzzi, Helen Morales, and Tim Whitmarsh, 194–216. Cambridge: Cambridge University Press, 2021.

———. *Sex: Vice and Love from Antiquity to Modernity.* Oxford: Blackwell, 2010.

Bloch, Marc. *The Royal Touch: Monarchy and Miracles in France and England.* Translated by J. E. Anderson. New York: Dorset, 1989.

Blockley, R. C. *The Fragmentary Classicizing Historians of the Later Roman Empire.* Leeds: Francis Cairns, 1981.

Blouin, Katherine. *Triangular Landscapes: Environment, Society, and the State in the Nile Delta under Roman Rule.* Oxford: Oxford University Press, 2014.

Boeft, J. den, J. W. Drijvers, D. den Hengst, and H. C. Teitler. *Philological and Historical Commentary on Ammianus Marcellinus XXIII.* Leiden: Brill, 1998.

———. *Philological and Historical Commentary on Ammianus Marcellinus XXV.* Leiden: Brill, 2005.

———. *Philological and Historical Commentary on Ammianus Marcellinus XXVIII.* Leiden: Brill, 2011.

———. *Philological and Historical Commentary on Ammianus Marcellinus XXXI.* Leiden: Brill, 2018.

Bond, Sarah E. *Trade and Taboo: Disreputable Professions in the Ancient Mediterranean.* Ann Arbor: University of Michigan Press, 2016.

Bonney, Richard. *Society and Government in France under Richelieu and Mazarin, 1624–61.* London: Palgrave Macmillan, 1988.

Boon, George C. "A Roman Pastrycook's Mould from Silchester." *Antiquaries Journal* 38 (1958): 237–40.

Boor, Carl de, ed. *Nicephori Archiepiscopi Constantinopolitani: Opuscula Historica.* Leipzig: Teubner, 1880.

Booth, Phil. "The Ghost of Maurice at the Court of Heraclius." *Byzantinische Zeitschrift* 112 (2019): 781–826.

———. "Images of Emperors and Emirs in Early Islamic Egypt." In *The Good Christian Ruler in the First Millennium: Views from the Wider Mediterranean World in Conversation,* edited by Philip Michael Forness, Alexandra Hasse-Ungeheuer, and Hartmut Leppin, 397–420. Berlin: De Gruyter, 2021.

Bosworth, A. B. "The Death of Alexander the Great: Rumour and Propaganda." *Classical Quarterly* 21 (1971): 113–36.

Boucheron, Patrick, and Nicholas Offenstadt, eds. *L'espace public au Moyen Âge: Débats autour de Jürgen Habermas.* Paris: Presses universitaires de France, 2011.

Bourbouhakis, Emmanuel C. "Exchanging the Devices of Ares for the Delights of the Erotes: Erotic Misadventures and the *History* of Niketas Choniates." In *Plotting with Eros: Essays on the Poetics of Love and the Erotics of Reading,* edited by Inga Nilsson, 213–34. Copenhagen: Museum Tusculanum, 2009.

Boustan, Ra'anan S. "Immolating Emperors: Spectacles of Imperial Suffering and the Making of a Jewish Minority Culture in Late Antiquity." In *Violence, Scripture, and Textual Practice in Early Judaism and Christianity,* edited by Ra'anan S. Boustan, Alex P. Jassen, and Calvin J. Roetzel, 207–38. Leiden: Brill, 2009.

Bowes, K., and Cam Grey. "Conclusions: The Roman Peasant Reframed." In *The Roman Peasant Project 2009–2014,* edited by Kim Bowes, 617–39. Philadelphia: University of Pennsylvania Museum of Archaeology and Anthropology, 2020.

Boyar, Ebru, and Kate Fleet. *A Social History of Ottoman Istanbul.* Cambridge: Cambridge University Press, 2010.

Boyle, A. J., ed. *Octavia: Attributed to Seneca.* Oxford: Oxford University Press, 2008.

Braccini, Tomasso. "An Apple between Folktales, Rumors, and Novellas: Malalas 14.8 and Its Oriental Parallels." *Greek, Roman, and Byzantine Studies* 58 (2018): 299–323.

Bradbury, Scott. "Julian's Pagan Revival and the Decline of Blood Sacrifice." *Phoenix* 49 (1995): 331–56.

———. ed. *Selected Letters of Libanius from the Age of Constantius and Julian.* Translated Texts for Historians 41. Liverpool: Liverpool University Press, 2004.

Bradley, K. R., ed. *Suetonius'* Life of Nero: *An Historical Commentary.* Brussels: Collection Latomus, 1978.

Bradley, Mark. "Obesity, Corpulence and Emaciation in Roman Art." *Papers of the British School at Rome* 79 (2011): 1–41.

Brake, Wayne te. *Shaping History: Ordinary People in European Politics, 1500–1700.* Berkeley: University of California Press, 1988.

Brandes, Wolfram. "Anastasios ὁ Δίκορος: Endzeiterwartung und Kaiserkritik in Byzanz um 500 n. Chr." *Byzantinische Zeitschrift* 90 (1997): 24–63.

Braund, David C. *Rome and the Friendly King.* London: Croom Helm, 1984.

Braund, Susanna Morton, ed. *Juvenal:* Satires *Book 1.* Cambridge: Cambridge University Press, 1996.

Braund, Susanna Morton, and Paula James. "*Quasi homo:* Distortion and Contortion in Seneca's *Apocolocyntosis.*" *Arethusa* 31 (1998): 285–311.

Brélaz, Cédric. *La sécurité publique en Asie Mineure sous le Principat (Ier–IIIème s. ap. J.-C.).* Basel: Schwabe, 2005.

Brennan, T. Corey. *Sabina Augusta: An Imperial Journey.* Oxford: Oxford University Press, 2018.

Bronner, Simon J. *Folklore: The Basics.* London: Routledge, 2017.

Brown, Peter. *Augustine of Hippo: A Biography.* 2nd ed. Berkeley: University of California Press, 2000.

———. *The Body and Society: Men, Women and Sexual Renunciation in Early Christianity.* 20th anniv. ed. New York: Columbia University Press, 2008.

———. *Poverty and Leadership in the Later Roman Empire.* Hanover, NH: University Press of New England for Brandeis University Press, 2001.

———. "The Rise and Function of the Holy Man in Late Antiquity." *Journal of Roman Studies* 61 (1971): 80–101.

Browning, Robert. "The Riot of AD 387 in Antioch: The Role of the Theatrical Claques in the Later Roman Empire." *Journal of Roman Studies* 42 (1952): 13–20.

Brubaker, Leslie, and Helen Tober. "The Gender of Money: Byzantine Empresses on Coins (324–802)." *Gender and History* 12 (2000): 572–94.

Bruun, Christer. "Roman Emperors in Popular Jargon: Searching for Contemporary Nicknames (I)." In *The Representation and Perception of Roman Imperial Power,* edited by Lukas de Blois, Paul Erdkamp, Olivier Hekster, Gerda de Kleijn, and Stephan Mols, 69–98. Leiden: Brill, 2003.

Bryen, Ari. "Histories of Violence: Notes from the Roman Empire." In *Violence and Civilization,* edited by Roderick Campbell, 125–51. Providence, RI: Joukowsky Institute, 2014.

Burgess, Richard W. "The Accession of Marcian in the Light of Chalcedonian Apologetic and Monophysite Polemic." *Byzantinische Zeitschrift* 86–87 (1993–94): 47–68.

———. ed. *The* Chronicle *of Hydatius and the* Consularia Constantinopolitana: *Two Contemporary Accounts of the Final Years of the Roman Empire.* Oxford: Oxford University Press, 1993.

Burke, Peter. *Popular Culture in Early Modern Europe.* 3rd ed. London: Routledge, 2009.

———. *Varieties of Cultural History.* Ithaca, NY: Cornell University Press, 1997.

Burnett, Andrew. "The Early Coinage of Hadrian and the Deified Trajan at Rome and Alexandria." *American Journal of Numismatics* 20 (2008): 459–77.

Bush, Michael. "Tax Reform and Rebellion in Early Tudor England." *History* 76 (1991): 379–400.

Butler, Lee. *Emperor and Aristocracy in Japan, 1467–1680: Resilience and Renewal.* Leiden: Brill, 2002.

Butterworth, Emily. *The Unbridled Tongue: Babble and Gossip in Renaissance France.* Oxford: Oxford University Press, 2016.

Büttner-Wobst, Theodor. "Der Tod des Kaisers Julian: Eine Quellenstudie." *Philologus* 51 (1892): 561–80.

Cameron, Alan. *Circus Factions: Blues and Greens at Rome and Byzantium.* Oxford: Oxford University Press, 1976.

———. "The Empress and the Poet: Paganism and Politics at the Court of Theodosius II." *Yale Classical Studies* 27 (1982): 217–89.

———. *The Last Pagans of Rome.* New York: Oxford University Press, 2011.

———. *Wandering Poets and Other Essays on Late Greek Literature and Philosophy.* New York: Oxford University Press, 2016.

Cameron, Averil, ed. *Flavius Cresconius Corippus:* In laudem Iustini Augusti minoris. Libri IV. London: Athlone, 1976.

———. *Procopius and the Sixth Century.* London: Routledge, 2015.

Camia, Francesco, and Athanasios Rizakis. "Notes on the Imperial Estates and Valorisation of Public Land in the Province of Achaia." In *Villae Rusticae: Family and Market-Oriented Farms in Greece under Roman Rule,* edited by A. D. Rizakis and I. P. Touratsoglou, 74–86. Athens: National Hellenic Research Foundation, 2013.

Castrén, Paavo, and Henrik Lilius. *Graffiti del Palatino. II: Domus Tiberiana.* Helskini: Akateeminen Kirjakauppa, 1970.

Chadwick, Henry. "New Letters of St. Augustine." *Journal of Theological Studies* 34 (1983): 425–52.

Champlin, Edward. "Mallonia." *Histos* 9 (2015): 220–30.

———. *Nero.* Cambridge, MA: Harvard University Press, 2003.

———. "Nero, Apollo, and the Poets." *Phoenix* 57 (2003): 276–83.

———. "Sex on Capri." *TAPA* 141 (2011): 315–32.

———. "Tiberius and Pan." In *Ahoros: Gedenkschrift für Hugo Meyer von Weggefährten, Kollegen und Freunden,* edited by Michaela Fuchs, 157–66. Vienna: Phoibos, 2018.

———. "Tiberius the Wise." *Historia* 57 (2008): 408–25.

Chaniotis, Angelos. "Listening to Stones: Orality and Emotions in Ancient Inscriptions." In *Epigraphy and the Historical Sciences,* edited by John Davies and John Wilkes, 299–328. Oxford: Oxford University Press, 2012.

Charles, R. H., ed. *The Chronicle of John, Bishop of Nikiu.* London: Williams and Norgate, 1916.

Charlesworth, M. P. "*Pietas* and *Victoria:* The Emperor and the Citizen." *Journal of Roman Studies* 33 (1943): 1–10.

Chastagnol, André. "Le repli sur Arles des services administratifs gaulois en l'an 407 de notre ère." *Revue Historique* 249 (1973): 23–40.

Chauvot, Alain. *Les "barbares" des Romains: Représentations et confrontations.* Edited by A. Becker and H. Huntzinger. Metz: Université de Lorraine, 2016.

Chong-Gossard, James H. Kim On. "Who Slept with Whom in the Roman Empire? Women, Sex, and Scandal in Suetonius' *Caesares.*" In *Private and Public Lies: The Discourse of Despotism and Deceit in the Graeco-Roman World,* edited by Andrew Turner, James. H. Kim On Chong-Gossard, and Frederik Vervaet, 295–327. Leiden: Brill, 2010.

Christoforou, Panayiotis. *Imagining the Roman Emperor: Perceptions of Rulers in the High Empire.* Cambridge: Cambridge University Press, 2023.

Chrol, E. Del, and Sarah Blake. "Sexuality and the Court." In *The Roman Emperor and His Court, c. 30 BC–AD 300,* vol. 1, edited by Benjamin Kelly and Angela Hug, 349–70. Cambridge: Cambridge University Press, 2022.

Chrubasik, Boris. *Kings and Usurpers in the Seleucid Empire: The Men Who Would Be King.* Oxford: Oxford University Press, 2016.

Clark, Anna. *Scandal: The Sexual Politics of the British Constitution.* Princeton, NJ: Princeton University Press, 2004.

Clarke, G. W. "Prosopographical Notes on the Epistles of Cyprian—III: Rome in August, 258." *Latomus* 34 (1975): 437–48.

Clarke, John R. *Looking at Laughter: Humor, Power, and Transgression in Roman Visual Culture, 100 B.C.–A.D. 250.* Berkeley: University of California Press, 2007.

Clauss, Manfred. "*Deus praesens:* Der römische Kaiser als Gott." *Klio* 78 (1996): 400–433.

———. *Kaiser und Gott.* Berlin: De Gruyter, 1999.

Coast, David. *News and Rumour in Jacobean England: Information, Court Politics, and Diplomacy 1618–25.* Manchester: Manchester University Press, 2014.

Coast, David, and Jo Fox. "Rumour and Politics." *History Compass* 13 (2015): 222–34.

Cohn, Samuel K., Jr. *Lust for Liberty: The Politics of Social Revolt in Medieval Europe, 1200–1425.* Cambridge, MA: Harvard University Press, 2008.

———. *Popular Protest in Late Medieval English Towns.* Cambridge: Cambridge University Press, 2012.

Coleman, K. M. "Fatal Charades: Roman Executions Staged as Mythological Enactments." *Journal of Roman Studies* 80 (1990): 44–73.

Coleman, Kathleen M. "Epigram, Society and Political Power." In *A Companion to Ancient Epigram,* edited by Christer Henriksén, 59–75. Oxford: Blackwell, 2019.

———. ed. *M. Valerii Martialis Liber Spectaculorum.* Oxford: Oxford University Press, 2006.

Collins, J. J. "Sibylline Oracles (Second Century B.C.–Seventh Century A.D.)." In *The Old Testament Pseudepigrapha,* vol. 1, edited by James H. Charlesworth, 317–472. New York: Doubleday, 1983.

Connolly, Serena. *Lives behind the Laws: The World of the* Codex Hermogenianus. Bloomington: Indiana University Press, 2010.

Constant, Marice-Luce. "Commentaires et conjectures sur la carrière et la mort d'un affranchide Trajan: Marcus Ulpius Phaedimus." *Cahiers des études anciennes* 37 (2001): 65–74.

Cook, Genevive Marie. *The Life of Saint Epiphanius by Ennodius: A Translation with an Introduction and Commentary.* Washington, DC: Catholic University of America Press, 1942.

Cooley, Alison. "The Moralizing Message of the *Senatus Consultum de Cn. Pisone patre.*" *Greece and Rome* 45 (1998): 199–212.

———. ed. Res Gestae Divi Augusti: *Text, Translation, and Commentary.* Cambridge: Cambridge University Press, 2009.

Corbeill, Anthony. *Controlling Laughter: Political Humor in the Late Roman Republic.* Princeton, NJ: Princeton University Press, 1996.

Corbier, Mireille. *Donner à voir, donner à lire: Mémoire et communication dans la Rome ancienne.* Paris: CNRS, 2006.

———. "L'ecriture dans l'space public romain." In *L'urbs: Espace urbain et histoire,* edited by Charles Pietri, 27–60. Rome: École française de Rome, 1987.

———. "La maison des Césars." In *Épouser au plus proche: Inceste, prohibitions et stratégies matrimoniales autour de la Méditerranée,* edited by Pierre Bonte, 243–91. Paris: Éditions de l'École des hautes études en sciences sociales, 1994.

Corley, Felix. "Believers' Responses to the 1937 and 1939 Soviet Censuses." *Religion, State and Society* 22 (1994): 403–17.

Cornell, T. J. *The Beginnings of Rome: Italy and Rome from the Bronze Age to the Punic Wars (c. 1000–264 BC).* London: Routledge, 1995.

Corte, M. della. "Publius Paquius Proculus." *Journal of Roman Studies* 16 (1926): 145–54.

Courrier, Cyril. "'Une' culture populaire dans l'Antiquité Romaine? Quelques remarques sur l'ouvrage de J. Toner, *Popular Culture in Ancient Rome.*" *Antiquité tardive* 19 (2011): 333–38.

———. *La plèbe de Rome et sa culture (fin du IIe siècle av. J.-C.–fin du Ier siècle ap. J.-C.).* Rome: École française de Rome, 2014.

———. "The Roman Plebs and Rumour: Social Interactions and Political Communication in the Early Principate." In *Political Communication in the Roman World,* edited by Cristina Rosillo-López, 137–64. Leiden: Brill, 2017.

Courtney, Edward, ed. *The Fragmentary Latin Poets.* Oxford: Oxford University Press, 1993.

Cressy, David. *Dangerous Talk: Scandalous, Seditious, and Treasonable Speech in Pre-Modern England.* Oxford: Oxford University Press, 2010.

Cribiore, Raffaella, ed. *Between City and School: Selected Orations of Libanius.* Translated Texts for Historians 65. Liverpool: Liverpool University Press, 2015.

Critchley, Simon. *On Humour.* London: Routledge, 2002.

Croke, Brian. "Arbogast and the Death of Valentinian II." *Historia* 25 (1976): 235–44.

———. "Ariadne Augusta: Shaping the Identity of the Early Byzantine Empress." In *Christians Shaping Identity from the Roman Empire to Byzantium,* edited by Geoffrey D. Dunn and Wendy Mayer, 291–320. Leiden: Brill, 2015.

———. "Basiliscus the Boy Emperor." *Greek, Roman, and Byzantine Studies* 24 (1983): 81–91.

———. "The Imperial Reigns of Leo II." *Byzantinische Zeitschrift* 96 (2003): 559–75.

———. "Justinian: The Sleepless Emperor." In *Basileia: Essays on Imperium and Culture in Honour of E. M. and M. J. Jeffreys,* edited by Geoffrey Nathan and Lynda Garland, 103–8. Canberra: Australian Association for Byzantine Studies, 2011.

———. "Reinventing Constantinople: Theodosius I's Imprint on the Imperial City." In *From the Tetrarchs to the Theodosians: Later Roman History and Culture, 284–250 CE,* edited by Scott McGill, Cristiana Sogno, and Edward Watts, 241–64. Cambridge: Cambridge University Press, 2010.

Crone, Patricia. *Pre-Industrial Societies: Anatomy of the Pre-Modern World.* London: Oneworld, 2015.

Cupaiuolo, Giovanni. *Tra poesia e politica: Le pasquinate nell'antica Roma.* Naples: Loffredi, 1993.

Cust, Richard. "News and Politics in Early Seventeenth-Century England." *Past and Present* 112 (1986): 60–90.

Dagron, Gilbert. *Emperor and Priest: The Imperial Office in Byzantium.* Translated by Jean Birrell. Cambridge: Cambridge University Press, 2003.

———. "Nés dans la pourpre." *Travaux et mémoires du Centre de recherche d'histoire et civilisation de Byzance* 12 (1994): 105–42.

Dagron, Gilbert, and Vincent Dérouche. *Juifs et chrétiens dans l'Orient du VIIe siècle.* Paris: Association des amis du Centre d'histoire et civilisation de Byzance, 1991.

Darnton, Robert. *The Devil in the Holy Water, or the Art of Slander from Louis XIV to Napoleon.* Philadelphia: University of Pennsylvania Press, 2011.

———. *The Literary Underground of the Old Regime.* Cambridge, MA: Harvard University Press, 1982.

Datema, C., ed. *Asterius of Amasea: Homilies I–XIV: Text, Introduction and Notes.* Leiden: Brill, 1970.

Davenport, Caillan. "Dying for Justice: Narratives of Roman Judicial Authority in the High Empire." In *Literary and Cultural Interactions in the Roman Empire: 96–235,* edited by Alice König, Rebecca Langlands, and James Uden, 269–88. Cambridge: Cambridge University Press, 2020.

———. "Envisioning Audiences at the Roman Imperial Court." In *The Roman Imperial Court in the Principate and Late Antiquity,* edited by Caillan Davenport and Meaghan McEvoy, 278–306. Oxford: Oxford University Press, 2023.

———. *A History of the Roman Equestrian Order.* Cambridge: Cambridge University Press, 2019.

———. "News, Rumour, and the Political Culture of the Roman Imperial Monarchy in the *Roman History.*" In *Emperors and Political Culture in Cassius Dio's* Roman History, edited by Caillan Davenport and Christopher Mallan, 52–73. Cambridge: Cambridge University Press, 2021.

———. "Roman Emperors, Conquest, and Violence: Images from the Eastern Provinces." In *The Social Dynamics of Roman Imperial Imagery,* edited by Amy Russell and Monica Hellström, 100–127. Cambridge: Cambridge University Press, 2020.

———. "Rome and the Rhythms of Imperial Life from the Antonines to Constantine." *Antiquité tardive* 25 (2017): 23–39.

———. "The Sexual Habits of Caracalla: Rumour, Gossip, and Historiography." *Histos* 11 (2017): 75–100.

Davenport, Caillan, and Christopher Mallan. "Hadrian's Adoption Speech in Cassius Dio's *Roman History* and the Problems of Imperial Succession." *American Journal of Philology* 135 (2014): 637–68.

Davenport, Caillan, and Jennifer Manley, eds. *Fronto: Selected Letters.* London: Bloomsbury Academic, 2014.

Davenport, Caillan, and Meaghan McEvoy. "The Circulation of News and Rumour from the Imperial Courts at Rome and Constantinople in the Fifth Century AD." In *From East to West in Late Antiquity: Studies in Honour of Jan Willem Drijvers,* edited by Noel Lenski, Roger Rees, and Onno van Nijf, 211–30. Bari: Edipuglia, 2024.

———. "Introduction: Connecting Courts." In *The Roman Imperial Court in the Principate and Late Antiquity,* edited by Caillan Davenport and Meaghan McEvoy, 1–38. Oxford: Oxford University Press, 2023.

———. eds. *The Roman Imperial Court in the Principate and Late Antiquity.* Oxford: Oxford University Press, 2023.

Davis, Godfrey. "English Political Sermons, 1603–1640." *Huntington Library Quarterly* 3 (1939): 1–22.

Davis, Natalie Zemon. *Remaking Impostors: From Martin Guerre to Sommersby.* Hayes Robinson Lecture Series 1. London: Royal Holloway, 1997.

———. *The Return of Martin Guerre.* Cambridge, MA: Harvard University Press, 1983.

———. *Society and Culture in Early Modern France.* Stanford: Stanford University Press, 1975.

Dawe, Roger D., ed. *Philogelos.* Leipzig: Teubner, 2000.

Depreux, Philippe. "Rumeur, circulation des nouvelles et gouvernement aux temps carolingiens." In *La rumeur au Moyen Âge,* edited by Myriam Soria and Maïté Billoré, 133–47. Rennes: Presses universitaires de Rennes, 2011.

Derby, Lauren. "Beyond Fugitive Speech: Rumor and Affect in Caribbean History." *Small Axe* 18 (2014): 123–40.

Devillers, Olivier. "L'*Octavie* et les *Annales* de Tacite." *Vita Latina* 159 (2000): 51–66.

Díaz Ariño, Borja. "*Glandes inscriptae* de la Península Ibérica." *Zeitschrift für Papyrologie und Epigraphik* 153 (2005): 219–36.

Dickey, Eleanor. *Stories of Daily Life from the Roman World: Extracts from the Ancient Colloquia.* Cambridge: Cambridge University Press, 2017.

Dieten, Jan-Louis A. van, ed. *Nicetae Choniatae Historia.* Berlin: De Gruyter, 1975.

DiFonzo, Nicholas, and Prashant Bordia. *Rumor Psychology: Social and Organizational Approaches.* Washington, DC: American Psychological Association, 2006.

Dijk, Gert-Jan van. *ΑΙΝΟΙ, ΛΟΓΟΙ, ΜΥΘΟΙ: Fables in Archaic, Classical, and Hellenistic Greek Literature.* Leiden: Brill, 1997.

Dilke, O. A. W. "Horace and the Verse Letter." In *Horace,* edited by C. D. N. Costa, 94–112. London: Routledge, 1973.

Dillon, John Noël. *The Justice of Constantine: Law, Communication, and Control.* Ann Arbor: University of Michigan Press, 2012.

Dindorf, Ludwig, ed. *Chronicon Paschale.* Vol. 1. Bonn: De Gruyter, 1832.

Donderer, Michael. "Zu den Häusern des Kaisers Augustus." *Mélanges de l'école française de Rome* 107 (1995): 621–60.

Draycott, Jane. "Hair Loss as Facial Disfigurement in Ancient Rome?" In *Approaching Facial Difference, Past and Present,* edited by Patricia Skinner and Emily Cock, 65–83. London: Bloomsbury Academic, 2018.

Drijvers, Jan Willem. "Flavia Maxima Fausta: Some Remarks." *Historia* 41 (1992): 500–506.

———. *The Forgotten Reign of the Emperor Jovian (363–364): History and Fiction.* Oxford: Oxford University Press, 2022.

———. "Helena Augusta, the Cross and the Myth: Some New Reflections." *Millennium* 8 (2011): 125–74.

———. *Helena Augusta: The Mother of Constantine the Great and the Legend of Her Finding of the True Cross.* Leiden: Brill, 1992.

Drinkwater, J. F. "The Usurpers Constantine III (407–411) and Jovinus (411–413)." *Britannia* 29 (1998): 269–98.

Driver, G. R., and Leonard Hodgson, eds. *Nestorius: The Bazaar of Heracleides.* Oxford: Clarendon, 1925.

Dufallo, Basil. "Appius' Indignation: Gossip, Tradition, and Performance in Republican Rome." *TAPA* 131 (2001): 119–42.

Dugan, John. "Preventing Ciceronianism: C. Licinius Calvus' Regimens for Sexual and Oratorical Self-Mastery." *Classical Philology* 96 (2001): 400–428.

Duindam, Jeroen. *Dynasties: A Global History of Power.* Cambridge: Cambridge University Press, 2016.

Duncan-Jones, Richard. *Structure and Scale in the Roman Economy.* Cambridge: Cambridge University Press, 1990.

Dunkle, J. Roger. "The Greek Tyrant and Roman Political Invective of the Late Republic." *TAPA* 98 (1967): 151–71.

Durliat, Jean. *De la ville antique à la ville byzantine: Le problème des subsistances.* Rome: École française de Rome, 1990.

Dyson, Stephen, L. "Native Revolts in the Roman Empire." *Historia* 20 (1971): 239–74.

Eck, Werner. "Cheating the Public, or: Tacitus Vindicated." *Scripta Classica Israelica* 21 (2002): 149–64.

———. "An Emperor Is Made: Senatorial Politics and Trajan's Adoption by Nerva in 97." In *Philosophy and Power in the Graeco-Roman World,* edited by Gillian Clark and Tessa Rajak, 211–26. Oxford: Oxford University Press, 2002.

———. "I sistemi di trasmissione delle comunicazioni d'ufficio in èta altoimperiale." In *Epigrafia e territorio. Politica e società. Temi di antichità romane IV,* edited by Mario Pani, 331–52. Bari: Edipuglia, 1996.

Eck, Werner, Antonio Caballos, and Fernando Fernández, eds. *Das senatus consultum de Cn. Pisone patre.* Munich: C. H. Beck, 1996.

Eden, P. T., ed. *Seneca: Apocolocyntosis.* Cambridge: Cambridge University Press, 1984.

Edwards, Catharine. *The Politics of Immorality in Ancient Rome.* Cambridge: Cambridge University Press, 1993.

Edwards, Mark, ed. *Constantine and Christendom: The Oration to the Saints: The Greek and Latin Accounts of the Discovery of the Cross: The Edict of Constantine to Pope*

Sylvester. Translated Texts for Historians 39. Liverpool: Liverpool University Press, 2003.

Eich, Armin. *Politische Literatur in der römischen Gesellschaft.* Cologne: Böhlau, 2000.

Eidinow, Esther. "Gossip, Slander, Hearsay, Truth: Oral Evidence in Athenian Courts." In *The Discovery of the Fact,* edited by Clifford Ando and William P. Sullivan, 112–37. Ann Arbor: University of Michigan Press, 2020.

Eliav-Feldon, Miriam. *Renaissance Impostors and Proofs of Identity.* Basingstoke: Palgrave, 2012.

Elm, Susanna. *Sons of Hellenism, Fathers of the Church: Emperor Julian, Gregory of Nazianzus, and the Vision of Rome.* Berkeley: University of California Press, 2012.

Eltester, Walther. "Die Kirchen Antiochias im IV. Jahrhundert." *Zeitschrift für die neutestamentliche Wissenschaft* 36 (1937): 251–86.

Engster, Dorit. "Der Kaiser als Wundertäter: Kaiserheil als neue Form der Legitimation." In *Tradition und Erneuerung: Mediale Strategien in der Zeit der Flavier,* edited by Norbert Kramer and Christiane Reitz, 289–310. Berlin: De Gruyter, 2010.

Erdkamp, Paul. "'A Starving Mob Has No Respect': Urban Markets and Food Riots in the Roman World, 100 B.C.–400 AD." In *The Transformation of Economic Life under the Roman Empire,* edited by Lukas de Blois and John Rich, 93–115. Leiden: Brill, 2002.

Esbroeck Michel van. "La pomme de Théodose II et sa réplique arménienne." In *Novum Millennium,* edited by Clauda Sode and Sarolta Takács, 109–12. Aldershot: Ashgate, 2001.

Failler, Albert. "Le complot antidynastique de Jean Drimys." *Revue des études byzantines* 54 (1996): 235–44.

Failler, Albert, and Vitalien Laurent, eds. *Georges Pachymérès: Relations historiques.* 2 vols. Paris: Les Belles Lettres, 1984.

Färber, Roland. *Römische Gerichtsorte: Räumliche Dynamkien von Jurisdiction im Imperium Romanum.* Munich: C. H. Beck, 2014.

Farge, Arlette. *Subversive Words: Public Opinion in Eighteenth-Century France.* Translated by Rosemary Morris. University Park: Pennsylvania State University Press, 1995.

Farge, Arlette, and Jacques Revel. *The Vanishing Children of Paris: Rumor and Politics before the French Revolution.* Translated by Claudia Miéville. Cambridge, MA: Harvard University Press, 1993.

Fargette, Séverine. "Rumeurs, propagande et opinion publique au temps de la guerre civile (1407–1420)." *Le Moyen Âge* 113 (2007): 308–34.

Feeney, Kevin. "Court Construction and Regime Change in the Mid-Fourth Century." In *The Roman Imperial Court in the Principate and Late Antiquity,* edited by Caillan Davenport and Meaghan McEvoy, 156–71. Oxford: Oxford University Press, 2023.

Feldherr, Andrew. "The Poisoned Chalice: Rumor and Historiography in Tacitus' Account of the Death of Drusus." *Materiali e discussioni per l'analisi dei testi classici* 61 (2009): 175–89.

Feldman, Louis H. "Some Observations on Rabbinic Reaction to Roman Rule." *Hebrew Union College Annual* 63 (1992): 39–81.

Felton, D. "Advice to Tyrants: The Motif of 'Enigmatic Counsel' in Greek and Roman Texts." *Phoenix* 52 (1998): 42–54.

Ferri, Rolando, ed. *Octavia: A Play Attributed to Seneca.* Cambridge: Cambridge University Press, 2003.

Festugière, André-John, ed. *Vie de Théodore de Sykeôn.* 2 vols. Brussels: Société des Bollandistes, 1970.

Figes, Orlando, and Boris Kolonitskii. *Interpreting the Russian Revolution: The Language and Symbols of 1917.* New Haven: Yale University Press, 1999.

Fishwick, D. "Votive Offerings to the Emperor?" *Zeitschrift für Papyrologie und Epigraphik* 80 (1990): 121–30.

Flaig, Egon. *Den Kaiser herausfordern: Die Usurpation im Römischen Reich.* 2nd ed. Frankfurt: Campus, 2019.

———. "Wie Kaiser Nero die Akzeptanz bei der *Plebs urbana* verlor: Eine Fallstudie zum politischen Gerücht im Prinzipat." *Historia* 52 (2003): 351–72.

Flemming, Rebecca. "Fertility Control in Ancient Rome." *Women's History Review* 30 (2021): 896–914.

———. "The Invention of Infertility in the Classical Greek World." *Bulletin of the History of Medicine* 87 (2013): 565–90.

Flores, Jorge, and Sanjay Subrahmanyam. "The Shadow Sultan: Succession and Imposture in the Mughal Empire, 1628–1640." *Journal of the Economic and Social History of the Orient* 47 (2004): 80–121.

Floridi, Lucia, ed. *Lucillio, Epigrammi: Introduzione, testo critico, traduzione e commento.* Berlin: De Gruyter, 2014.

Folch, Marcus. "Nero in Hell: Plutarch's *De Sera Numinis Vindicta.*" In *Pain and Pleasure in Classical Times,* edited by W. V. Harris, 213–39. Leiden: Brill, 2018.

Forness, Philip Michael. "Faithful Rulers and Theological Deviance: Ephrem the Syrian and Jacob of Serugh on the Roman Emperor." In *The Good Christian Ruler in the First Millennium: Views from the Wider Mediterranean World in Conversation,* edited by Philip Michael Forness, Alexandra Hasse-Ungeheuer, and Hartmut Leppin, 141–67. Berlin: De Gruyter, 2021.

Forsdyke, Sara. *Slaves Tell Tales: And Other Episodes in the Politics of Popular Culture in Ancient Greece.* Princeton, NJ: Princeton University Press, 2012.

Foucault, Michel. *Discipline and Punish: The Birth of the Prison.* Translated by Alan Sheridan. New York: Vintage, 1977.

Fowler, Rebecca J. "Anastasia: The Mystery Resolved." *Washington Post,* October 6, 1994. https://www.washingtonpost.com/archive/lifestyle/1994/10/06/anastasia-the-mystery-resolved/f208f264-a141-4f54-8354-934a3005f091/.

Fox, Adam. "Ballads, Libels and Popular Ridicule in Jacobean England." *Past and Present* 145 (1994): 47–83.

———. *Oral and Literate Culture in England 1500–1700*. Oxford: Oxford University Press, 2000.

———. "Rumour, News, and Popular Political Opinion in Elizabethan and Stuart England." *Historical Journal* 40 (1997): 597–620.

Fraenkel, Eduard. "Die Vorgeschichte des *versus quadratus*." *Hermes* 62 (1927): 357–70.

Franklin, James L., Jr. Pompeis Difficile Est: *Studies in the Political Life of Imperial Pompeii*. Ann Arbor: University of Michigan Press, 2001.

Fraser, Trudie E. "Domitia Longina: An Underestimated Augusta (c. 53–126/8)." *Ancient Society* 45 (2015): 205–66.

Freedman, H., and Maurice Simon, eds. *Midrash Rabbah: Deuteronomy; Lamentations*. London: Soncino, 1939.

Freist, Dagmar. *Governed by Opinion: Politics, Religion and the Dynamics of Communication in Stuart London 1637–1645*. London: Bloomsbury Academic, 1997.

Fujitani, T. *Splendid Monarchy: Power and Pageantry in Modern Japan*. Berkeley: University of California Press, 1996.

Gagé, J. "L'empereur romain et les rois: Politique et protocole." *Revue historique* 22 (1959): 221–60.

Gaisford, Thomas, ed. *Paroemiographi Graeci quorum pars nunc ex codicibus manuscriptis vulgatur*. Oxford: Clarendon, 1836.

Gallivan, Paul A. "The False Neros: A Re-Examination." *Historia* 22 (1973): 364–65.

Gambash, Gil. *Rome and Provincial Resistance*. London: Routledge, 2015.

Gantar, K. "Kaiser Justinian als kopfloser Dämon." *Byzantinische Zeitschrift* 54 (1961): 1–3.

Garland, Lynda. "'And His Bald Head Shone Like a Full Moon . . .': An Appreciation of the Byzantine Sense of Humour as Recorded in the Historical Sources of the Eleventh and Twelfth Centuries." *Parergon* 8 (1990): 1–31.

———. *Byzantine Empresses: Women and Power in Byzantium AD 527–1204*. London: Routledge, 1999.

Garland, Robert. *The Eye of the Beholder: Deformity and Disability in the Graeco-Roman World*. London: Bloomsbury Academic, 2010.

Garnsey, Peter. *Famine and Food Supply in the Graeco-Roman World*. Cambridge: Cambridge University Press, 1988.

Garry, Jane, and Hasan El-Shamy, eds. *Archetypes and Motifs in Folklore and Literature: A Handbook*. London: Routledge, 2005.

Gascou, Jacques. *Suéton historien*. Rome: École française de Rome, 1984.

Gauvard, Claude. "Rumeur et stéréotypes à la fine due Moyen Âge." *Actes des congrès de la Société des historiens médiévistes de l'enseignement supérieur public* 24 (1993): 157–77.

Geertz, Clifford. *The Interpretation of Cultures: Selected Essays.* 1973. Reprint, New York: Basic, 2000.

Gestrich, Andreas. *Absolutismus und Öffentlichkeit. Politische Kommunikation in Deutschland zu Beginn des 18. Jahrhunderts.* Göttingen: Vandenhoeck und Ruprecht, 1994.

Geue, Tom. *Author Unknown: The Power of Anonymity in Ancient Rome.* Cambridge, MA: Harvard University Press, 2019.

———. "Keeping/Losing Records, Keeping/Losing Faith: Suetonius and Justin Do the Document." In *Literature and Culture in the Roman Empire, 96–235,* edited by Alice König, Rebecca Langlands, and James Uden, 203–22. Cambridge: Cambridge University Press, 2020.

Gibson, B. J. "Rumours as Causes of Events in Tacitus." *Materiali e discussioni per l'analisi dei testi classici* 40 (1998): 111–29.

Gillett, Andrew. "Communication in Late Antiquity: Use and Reuse." In *The Oxford Handbook of Late Antiquity,* edited by Scott Fitzgerald Johnson, 815–46. Oxford: Oxford University Press, 2012.

———. *Envoys and Political Communication in the Late Antique West, 411–533.* Cambridge: Cambridge University Press, 2003.

———. "Rome, Ravenna, and the Last Western Emperors." *Papers of the British School at Rome* 69 (2001): 131–67.

Ginsberg, Lauren Donovan. *Staging Memory, Staging Strife: Empire and Civil War in the* Octavia. Oxford: Oxford University Press, 2017.

Ginsburg, Judith. *Representing Agrippina: Constructions of Female Power in the Early Roman Empire.* Oxford: Oxford University Press, 2006.

Giua, Maria Antonietta. "Sul significato dei rumores nella storiografia di Tacito." *Rivista Storica Italiana* 110 (1998): 38–59.

———. "Tra storiografia e comunicazione ufficiale." *Athenaeum* 88 (2000): 253–75.

Gladhill, Bill. "The Emperor's No Clothes: Suetonius and the Dynamics of Corporeal Ecphrasis." *Classical Antiquity* 31 (2012): 315–48.

Gleason, Maud W. "Festive Satire: Julian's Misopogon and the New Year at Antioch." *Journal of Roman Studies* 76 (1986): 106–19.

———. *Making Men: Sophists and Self-Presentation in Ancient Rome.* Princeton, NJ: Princeton University Press, 1995.

———. "Mutilated Messengers: Body Language in Josephus." In *Being Greek under Rome: Cultural Identity, the Second Sophistic and the Development of Empire,* edited by Simon Goldhill, 50–85. Cambridge University Press, 2001.

———. "Visiting and News: Gossip and Reputation Management in the Desert." *Journal of Early Christian Studies* 6 (1998): 501–21.

Glinister, Fay. "Kingship and Tyranny in Archaic Rome." In *Ancient Tyranny,* edited by Sian Lewis, 17–32. Edinburgh: Edinburgh University Press, 2006.

Gluckman, Max. "Gossip and Scandal." *Current Anthropology* 4 (1963): 307–16.

Goldin, Judah., ed. *The Fathers according to Rabbi Nathan.* New Haven: Yale University Press, 1955.

Goodman, Martin. "Coinage and Identity: The Jewish Evidence." In *Coinage and Identity in the Roman Provinces,* edited by Christopher Howgego, Volker Heuchert, and Andrew Burnett, 163–66. Oxford: Oxford University Press, 2005.

———. *The Ruling Class of Judaea: The Origins of the Jewish Revolt against Rome, AD 66–70.* Cambridge: Cambridge University Press, 1987.

———. *State and Society in Roman Galilee, A.D. 132–212.* Totowa, NJ: Rowman and Allenheld, 1983.

———. "Trajan and the Origins of Roman Hostility to the Jews." *Past and Present* 182 (2004): 3–29.

Gorshkov, Boris B. "Democratizing Habermas: Peasant Public Sphere in Pre-Reform Russia." *Russian History* 31 (2004): 373–85.

Gottesman, Alex. *Politics and the Street in Democratic Athens.* Cambridge: Cambridge University Press, 2014.

Gourevitch, Danielle. "L'obésité et son traitement dans le monde romain." *History and Philosophy of the Life Sciences* 7 (1985): 195–215.

Graeber, David, and Marshall Sahlins. *On Kings.* Chicago: HAU, 2017.

Graf, Fritz. *Roman Festivals in the Greek East: From the Early Empire to the Middle Byzantine Era.* Cambridge: Cambridge University Press, 2015.

Grainger, John D. *Nerva and the Roman Succession Crisis of AD 96–99.* London: Routledge, 2003.

Granovetter, Mark S. "The Strength of Weak Ties." *American Journal of Sociology* 78 (1973): 1360–80.

Greatrex, Geoffrey, ed. *The Chronicle of Pseudo-Zachariah Rhetor: Church and War in Late Antiquity.* Translated Texts for Historians 55. Liverpool: Liverpool University Press, 2011.

Greenwood, David Neal. "Julian's Use of Asclepius against the Christians." *Harvard Studies in Classical Philology* 109 (2014): 491–509.

Greenwood, M. A. P. "Martial, Gossip, and the Language of Rumour." In *Toto notus in orbe: Perspektiven der Martial-Interpretation,* edited by Farouk Grewing, 278–314. Stuttgart: Franz Steiner, 1998.

Gregory, Timothy E. Vox populi: *Popular Opinion and Violence in the Religious Controversies of the Fifth Century AD.* Columbus: Ohio State University Press, 1979.

Grey, Cam. *Constructing Communities in the Late Roman Countryside.* Cambridge: Cambridge University Press, 2011.

Griffin, Miriam T. *Nero: The End of a Dynasty.* London: Routledge, 1984.

———. "The Senate's Story." *Journal of Roman Studies* 87 (1997): 249–63.

Griffith, Sidney H. "Ephraem the Syrian's Hymns 'against Julian': Meditations on History and Imperial Power." *Vigiliae Christianae* 41 (1987): 238–66.

Grig, Lucy. "Interpreting the Kalends of January: A Case Study for Late Antique Popular Culture." In *Popular Culture in the Ancient World,* edited by Lucy Grig, 237–56. Cambridge: Cambridge University Press, 2017.

———. "Introduction: Approaching Popular Culture in the Ancient World." In *Popular Culture in the Ancient World,* edited by Lucy Grig, 1–36. Cambridge: Cambridge University Press, 2017.

———. "Looking for Representations of Emperors in Late Antique Popular Culture." In *Representing Rome's Emperors: Historical and Cultural Perspectives through Tim*e, edited by Caillan Davenport and Shushma Malik, 115–43. Oxford: Oxford University Press, 2024.

———. *Popular Culture and the End of Antiquity in Southern Gaul, c. 400–550.* Cambridge: Cambridge University Press, 2024.

Grig, Lucy, and Gavin Kelly. "Introduction: From Rome to Constantinople." In *Two Romes: Rome and Constantinople in Late Antiquity,* edited by Lucy Grig and Gavin Kelly, 3–30. New York: Oxford University Press, 2012.

Gruen, Erich S. "The Sibylline Oracles and Resistance to Rome." In *The Future of Rome: Roman, Greek, Jewish and Christian Visions,* edited by Jonathan J. Price and Katell Berthelot, 189–205. Cambridge: Cambridge University Press, 2020.

Grünewald, Thomas. *Bandits in the Roman Empire: Myth and Reality.* Translated by John Drinkwater. London: Routledge, 2004.

Guggenheimer, Heinrich W., ed. *The Jerusalem Talmud. First Order: Zeraïm. Tractates Kilaim and Ševiït.* Berlin: De Gruyter, 2001.

———. *The Jerusalem Talmud. First Order: Zeraïm. Tractates Terumot and Ma'serot.* Berlin: De Gruyter, 2002.

———. *The Jerusalem Talmud. Fourth Order: Neziqin. Tractates Ševu'ot and 'Avodah Zarah.* Berlin: De Gruyter, 2011.

———. *The Jerusalem Talmud. Tractates Šeqalim, Sukkah, Roš Haššanah, and Yom Tov (Besah).* Berlin: De Gruyter, 2014.

———. *The Jerusalem Talmud. Tractates Ta'aniot, Megillah, Hagigah and Mo'ed Qatana (Mašqin).* Berlin: De Gruyter, 2015.

Guha, Ranajit. *Elementary Aspects of Peasant Insurgency in Colonial India.* Delhi: Oxford University Press, 1983.

Gunderson, Eric. *Staging Masculinity: The Rhetoric of Performance in the Roman World.* Ann Arbor: University of Michigan Press, 2000.

Gundlach, W. "*Epistolae Arelateneses genuinae.*" In *MGH Epistolae,* vol. 3, *Epistolae Merowingici et Karolini Aevi Tomus I,* 1–83. Berlin: Weidmann, 1892.

Guo, Li. "Protest Songs from the Streets of Mamluk Cities." In *Egypt and Syria under Mamluk Rule,* edited by Amalia Levanoni, 17–24. Leiden: Brill, 2021.

Haar, Barend ter. *Telling Stories: Witchcraft and Scapegoating in Chinese History.* Leiden: Brill, 2006.

Haarer, F. K. *Anastasius I: Politics and Empire in the Late Roman World.* Leeds: Francis Cairns, 2006.

Habermas, Jürgen. *Communication and the Evolution of Society.* Translated by Thomas McCarthy. Boston: Beacon, 1979.

———. "Concluding Remarks." In *Habermas and the Public Sphere,* edited by Craig Calhoun, 462–79. Cambridge, MA: MIT Press, 1993.

———. "Further Reflections on the Public Sphere." In *Habermas and the Public Sphere,* edited by Craig Calhoun, 421–61. Cambridge, MA: MIT Press, 1993.

———. *The Structural Transformation of the Public Sphere.* Translated by Thomas Burger with Frederick Lawrence. Cambridge, MA: MIT Press, 1991.

———. *The Theory of Communicative Action: Reason and the Rationalization of Society.* Translated by Thomas McCarthy. Cambridge: Polity, 1986.

Hadas, Moses. "Roman Allusions in Rabbinic Literature." *Philological Quarterly* 8 (1929): 369–87.

Hadas-Lebel, Mireille. "La fiscalité romaine dans la littérature rabbinique jusqu'à la fin du IIIe siècle." *Revue des études juives* 143 (1984): 5–29.

Hague, Rod, and Martin Harrop. *Comparative Government and Politics.* 6th ed. Basingstoke: Palgrave Macmillan, 2004.

Haldon, John. "Humour and the Everyday in Byzantium." In *Humour, History, and Politics in Late Antiquity and the Early Middle Ages,* edited by Guy Halsall, 48–72. Cambridge: Cambridge University Press, 2002.

Hall, Stuart. "Encoding/Decoding." In *Culture, Media, Language: Working Papers in Cultural Studies, 1972–1979,* edited by Stuart Hall, Dorothy Hobson, Andrew Lowe, and Paul Willis, 128–38. London: Routledge, 1980.

Hall, Stuart George. "Gregory of Nyssa: *Contra Eunomium* I." In *Gregory of Nyssa,* Contra Eunomium I: *An English Translation with Supporting Studies,* edited by Miguel Brugarolas, 73–195. Leiden: Brill, 2018.

Hallett, Christopher H. *The Roman Nude: Heroic Portrait Statuary 200 BC–AD 300.* Oxford: Oxford University Press, 2005.

Hallett, Judith P. "*Perusinae glandes* and the Changing Image of Augustus." *American Journal of Ancient History* 2 (1977): 151–71.

Halliwell, Stephen. *Greek Laughter: A Study of Cultural Psychology from Homer to Early Christianity.* Cambridge: Cambridge University Press, 2008.

Hanrahan, Michael. "Defamation as Political Contest during the Reign of Richard II." *Medium Aevum* 72 (2003): 259–76.

Hansen, William. *Ariadne's Thread: A Guide to International Tales Found in Classical Literature.* Ithaca, NY: Cornell University Press, 2002.

Harbus, Antonina. *Helena of Britain in Medieval Legend.* Cambridge: D. S. Brewer, 2002.

Hardie, Philip. *Rumour and Renown: Representations of* Fama *in Western Literature.* Cambridge: Cambridge University Press, 2012.

Harding, Philip. "All Pigs Are Animals, but Are All Animals Pigs?" *Ancient History Bulletin* 5 (1991): 145–48.

Harries, Jill. *Law and Crime in the Roman World.* Cambridge: Cambridge University Press, 2007.

———. *Sidonius Apollinaris and the Fall of Rome.* Oxford: Oxford University Press, 1994.

Harris, Joseph. "The King in Disguise: An International Popular Tale in Two Old Icelandic Adaptations." *Arkiv för nordisk filologi* 94 (1979): 57–81.

Harris, William V. *Ancient Literacy.* Cambridge, MA: Harvard University Press, 1989.

———. *Restraining Rage: The Ideology of Anger Control in Classical Antiquity.* Cambridge, MA: Harvard University Press, 2001.

———. "Towards a Study of the Roman Slave Trade." *Memoirs of the American Academy in Rome* 36 (1980): 117–40.

Harrison, Carol. *The Art of Listening in the Early Church.* Oxford: Oxford University Press, 2023.

Hartmann, Andreas. "Germanicus und Lady Di: Zur öffentlichen Verarbeitung zweier Todesfälle." In *Der Vergleich—eine Methode zur Förderung historischer Kompetenzen. Ausgewählte Beispiele,* edited by Waltraud Schreiber, 61–126. Neuried: ars una, 2005.

Hartmann, Felix. *Herrscherwechsel und Reichskrise: Untersuchungen zu den Ursachen und Konsequenzen der Herrscherwechsel im Imperium Romanum der Soldatenkaiserzeit (3. Jahrhundert n. Chr.).* Frankfurt: Peter Lang, 1982.

Hartmann, Florian. "Das Gerücht vom Tod des Herrschers im frühen und hohen Mittelalter." *Historische Zeitschrift* 302 (2016): 340–62.

Hartnett, Jeremy. *The Roman Street: Urban Life and Society in Pompeii, Herculaneum and Rome.* Cambridge: Cambridge University Press, 2016.

Hasan-Rokem, Galit. *Tales of the Neighborhood: Jewish Narrative Dialogues in Late Antiquity.* Berkeley: University of California Press, 2003.

Hauken, Tor. *Petition and Response: An Epigraphic Study of Petitions to Roman Emperors, 181–249.* Bergen: Norwegian Institute at Athens, 1998.

Hawkins, Tom. "Pollio's Paradox: Popular Invective and the Transition to Empire." In *Popular Culture in the Ancient World,* edited by Lucy Grig, 129–48. Cambridge: Cambridge University Press, 2017.

Head, Constance. "Physical Descriptions of the Emperors in Byzantine Historical Writing." *Byzantion* 50 (1980): 226–40.

Headlam, Arthur C. *Ecclesiastical Sites of Isauria (Cilicia Trachea).* London: Society for the Promotion of Hellenic Studies, 1892.

Hekster, Olivier. *Caesar Rules: The Emperor in the Changing Roman World (c. 50 BC–AD 565).* Cambridge: Cambridge University Press, 2023.

———. *Commodus: An Emperor at the Crossroads.* Leiden: Brill, 2002.

———. *Emperors and Ancestors: Roman Rulers and the Constraints of Tradition.* Oxford: Oxford University Press, 2015.

———. "Imperial Justice? The Absence of Images of Roman Emperors in a Legal Role." *Classical Quarterly* 70 (2020): 247–60.

Henderson, John. *Telling Tales on Caesar: Roman Stories from Phaedrus.* Oxford: Oxford University Press, 2001.

Henrichs, Albert. "Vespasian's Visit to Alexandria." *Zeitschrift für Papyrologie und Epigraphik* 3 (1968): 51–80.

Henriksén, C. "Earinus: An Imperial Eunuch in the Light of the Poems of Martial and Statius." *Mnemosyne* 50 (1997): 281–94.

Henten, Jan Willem van. "*Nero redivivus* Demolished: The Coherence of the Nero Traditions in the Sibylline Oracles." *Journal for the Study of the Pseudepigrapha* 21 (2000): 3–17.

Hillard, T. W. "Death by Lightning, Pompeius Strabo and the People." *Rheinisches Museum* 139 (1996): 135–45.

———. "*Res publica* in Theory and Practice." In *Roman Crossings: Theory and Practice in the Roman Republic,* edited by Kathryn Welch and T. W. Hillard, 1–48. Swansea: Classical Press of Wales, 2005.

Hillard, Tom. "Graffiti's Engagement: The Political Graffiti of the Late Roman Republic." In *Written Space in the Latin West, 200 BC–AD 300,* edited by Gareth Sears, Peter Keegan, and Ray Laurence, 105–22. London: Bloomsbury Academic, 2013.

———. "The Popular Reception of Augustus and the Self-Infantilization of Rome's Citizenry." In *The Alternative Augustan Age,* edited by Kit Morrell, Josiah Osgood, and Kathryn Welch, 305–24. Oxford: Oxford University Press, 2019.

Hillner, Julia. *Helena Augusta: Mother of the Empire.* Oxford: Oxford University Press, 2022.

Hilton, John L. "Cnemon, Crispus, and the Marriage Laws of Constantine in the *Aethiopica* of Heliodorus." *Greek, Roman, and Byzantine Studies* 59 (2019): 427–59.

Hoffmann, Gustav. *Schimpfwörter der Griechen und Römer.* Berlin: Gaertner, 1892.

Holder-Egger, Oswald. "*Agnelli qui et Andreas liber pontificalis ecclesiae Ravennatis.*" In *MGH Scriptores rerum Langobardicarum et Italicarum Saec. VI–IX,* 265–391. Berlin: Weidmann, 1878.

Hollis, A. S. "Statius' Young Parthian King (*Thebaid* 8.286–93)." *Greece and Rome* 41 (1994): 205–12.

Hollis, Adrian S. *Fragments of Roman Poetry, c. 60 BC–AD 20.* Oxford: Oxford University Press, 2007.

Holton, Robert J. "The Crowd in History: Some Problems in Theory and Method." *Social History* 3 (1978): 219–33.

Holum, Kenneth G. *Theodosian Empresses: Women and Imperial Domination in Late Antiquity.* Berkeley: University of California Press, 1982.

Hoof, Lieve, and Peter van Nuffelen. "Monarchy and Mass Communication: Antioch AD 362/3 Revisited." *Journal of Roman Studies* 101 (2011): 166–84.

Hopkins, Keith. *Conquerors and Slaves.* Cambridge: Cambridge University Press, 1981.

———. "Rules of Evidence." *Journal of Roman Studies* 68 (1978): 178–86.

Horbury, William. *Jewish War under Trajan and Hadrian.* Cambridge: Cambridge University Press, 2014.

Horodowich, Elizabeth. "The Gossiping Tongue: Oral Networks, Public Life and Political Culture in Early Modern Venice." *Renaissance Studies* 19 (2005): 22–45.

Horsfall, Nicholas. "The Cultural Horizons of the *Plebs Romana*." *Memoirs of the American Academy in Rome* 44 (1996): 101–19.

———. *The Culture of the Roman Plebs.* London: Bloomsbury Academic, 2003.

Höschele, Regina. "Two Lovers and a Lion: Pankrates' Poem on Hadrian's Royal Hunt." *Philologus* 163 (2019): 214–36.

Hosius, Carl, ed. *M. Annaei Lucani Belli civilis libri decem.* Leipzig: Teubner, 1913.

Hout, Michael P. J. van den, ed. *M. Cornelii Frontonis epistulae.* 2nd ed. Leipzig: Teubner, 1988.

Howard-Johnston, James. *The Last Great War of Antiquity.* Oxford: Oxford University Press, 2021.

———. *Witnesses to a World Crisis. Historians and Histories of the Middle East in the Seventh Century.* Oxford: Oxford University Press, 2010.

Hug, Angela. *Fertility, Ideology, and the Cultural Politics of Reproduction at Rome.* Leiden: Brill, 2023.

Hug, Tobias B. *Impostures in Early Modern England: Representations and Perceptions of Fraudulent Identities.* Manchester: Manchester University Press, 2009.

Hülsen, C. "Miscellanea epigrafica. XXI. Tessere lusorie." *Mitteilungen des Deutschen archäologischen Instituts (Röm. Abt.)* 11 (1896): 227–52.

Humfress, Caroline. *Orthodoxy and the Courts in Late Antiquity.* Oxford: Oxford University Press, 2007.

Humphries, Mark. "The Lexicon of Abuse: Drunkenness and Political Illegitimacy in the Late Roman World." In *Humour, History, and Politics in Late Antiquity and Byzantium,* edited by Guy Halsall, 75–88. Cambridge: Cambridge University Press, 2002.

Hunt, Arnold. "The Succession in Sermons, News and Rumour." In *Doubtful and Dangerous: The Question of Succession in Late Elizabethan England,* edited by Susan Doran and Paulina Kewes, 155–72. Manchester: Manchester University Press, 2014.

Hunt, John M. "Rumour, Newsletters and the Pope's Death in Early Modern Rome." In *News in Early Modern Europe: Currents and Connections,* edited by Simon Davies and Puck Fletcher, 141–58. Leiden: Brill, 2014.

Hunt, Lynn. "The Many Bodies of Marie Antoinette: Political Pornography and the Problem of the Feminine in the French Revolution." In *Eroticism and the Body Politic,* edited by Linda Hunt, 108–30. Baltimore: Johns Hopkins University Press, 1990.

Hunt, Tamara L. "Morality and Monarchy in the Queen Caroline Affair." *Albion* 23 (1991): 697–722.

Hunter, Virginia. "Gossip and the Politics of Reputation in Classical Athens." *Phoenix* 44 (1990): 299–325.

Hurlet, Frédéric. *Les collègues du prince sous Auguste et Tibère: De la légalité républicaine à la légitimité dynastique.* Rome: École française de Rome, 1997.

Hurley, Donna W. *An Historical and Historiographical Commentary on Suetonius'* Life of Caligula. Atlanta: American Philological Association, 1993.

———. ed. *Suetonius:* Divus Claudius. Cambridge: Cambridge University Press, 2001.

Isele, Bernd. "Moses oder Pharao? Die ersten christlichen Kaiser und das Argument der Bibel." In *Die Bibel als politisches Argument,* edited by Andreas Pečar and Kai Trampedach, 103–18. Munich: Oldenbourg, 2007.

Jackson, Nigel A., and Stephen D. Tansey. *Politics: The Basics.* London: Routledge, 2014.

Jacobson, David M. "Insights on the Bar Kokhba Revolt from the Coins." *Electrum* 29 (2003): 171–96.

Jacoby, David. "La population de Constantinople à l'époque byzantine: Un problème de démographie urbaine." *Byzantion* 31 (1961): 81–109.

Jal, Paul. *La guerre civile à Rome: Étude littéraire et morale.* Paris: Presses universitaires de France, 1963.

Jasnow, Benjamin. "Germanicus, Nero and the Incognito King in Tacitus' *Annals* 2.13 and 13.25." *Classical Journal* 110 (2015): 313–31.

Jauss, Hans Robert. *Toward an Aesthetic of Reception.* Translated by Timothy Bahti. Minneapolis: University of Minnesota Press, 1982.

Jeffreys, Elizabeth, Michael Jeffreys, and Roger Scott, eds. *The Chronicle of John Malalas.* Canberra: Australasian Society for Byzantine Studies, 1986.

Jeffreys, Michael J. "The Nature and Origins of the Political Verse." *Dumbarton Oaks Papers* 28 (1974): 141–95.

Jennings, Victoria. "Divination and Popular Culture." In *Popular Culture in the Ancient World,* edited by Lucy Grig, 189–207. Cambridge: Cambridge University Press, 2017.

Johnson, Scott Fitzgerald. "Miracles of Saint Thekla." In *Miracle Tales from Byzantium,* edited by Alice-Mary Talbot and Scott Fitzgerald Johnson, 1–201. Cambridge, MA: Harvard University Press, 2012.

Johnson, Tom, and Claire Judde de Larivière. "Ordinary Politics in Late Medieval Europe." *Past and Present* Advance Access 15 October, 2024: https://doi.org/10.1093/pastj/gtae036.

Johnston, Timothy. *Being Soviet: Identity, Rumour, and Everyday Life under Stalin 1939–1953.* Oxford: Oxford University Press, 2011.

Jones, B. W. "C. Vettulenus Civica Cerialis and the 'False Nero' of AD 88." *Athenaeum* 61 (1983): 516–21.

Jones, Brian W. *The Emperor Domitian.* London: Routledge, 1992.

Jones, C. P. *Plutarch and Rome.* Oxford: Oxford University Press, 1971.

———. *The Roman World of Dio Chrysostom.* Cambridge, MA: Harvard University Press, 1978.

———. "Towards a Chronology of Plutarch's Works." *Journal of Roman Studies* 56 (1966): 61–74.

Jones, Christopher P. "Three Temples in Libanius and the Theodosian Code." *Classical Quarterly* 63 (2013): 860–65.

Jones, Kenneth R. *Jewish Reactions to the Destruction of Jerusalem in AD 70: Apocalypses and Related Pseudepigrapha.* Leiden: Brill, 2011.

Jones, Linda G. "A Case of Medieval Political 'Flip-Flopping'? Shifting Allegiances in the Sermons of Al-Qadi 'Iyad." In *Preaching and Political Society: From Late Antiquity to the End of the Middle Ages,* edited by Franco Morenzoni, 65–110. Turnhout: Brepols, 2013.

Jong, Janneke de. *Emperors in Egypt: The Representation and Perception of Roman Imperial Power in Greek Papyrus Texts from Egypt.* PhD diss., University of Nijmegen, 2006.

Jongman, Willem. "Beneficial Symbols: *Alimenta* and the Infantilization of the Roman Citizen." In *Essays in Ancient History in Honour of H. W. Pleket,* edited by Willem Jongman and Marc Kleijwegt, 47–80. Leiden: Brill, 2002.

Joshel, Sandra R., and Lauren Hackworth Petersen. "Introduction." In *The Material Life of Roman Slaves,* edited by Sandra R. Joshel and Lauren Hackworth Petersen, 1–23. Cambridge: Cambridge University Press, 2014.

Jouanno, Corinne. "Le corps du prince dans la *Chronographie* de Michel Psellos." *Kentron* 19 (2023): 205–21.

Judge, E. A. *The Failure of Augustus: Essays on the Interpretation of a Paradox.* Newcastle upon Tyne: Cambridge Scholars Press, 2019.

Kaegi, W. E. "New Evidence on the Early Reign of Heraclius." *Byzantinische Zeitschrift* 66 (1978): 308–30.

Kaegi, Walter E. *Heraclius, Emperor of Byzantium.* Cambridge: Cambridge University Press, 2003.

Kaicker, Abhishek. *The King and the People: Sovereignty and Popular Politics in Mughal Delhi.* Oxford: Oxford University Press, 2020.

Kaldellis, Anthony. *The Byzantine Republic: People and Power in New Rome.* Cambridge, MA: Harvard University Press, 2015.

———. "Identifying Dissident Circles in Sixth-Century Byzantium: The Friendship of Prokopios and Ioannes Lydos." *Florilegium* 21 (2004): 1–17.

Kantirea, Maria. "Imperial Birthday Rituals in Late Antiquity." In *Court Ceremonies and Rituals of Power in Byzantium and the Medieval Mediterranean,* edited by Alexander Beihammer, Stavroula Constantinou, and Maria G. Parani, 35–50. Leiden: Brill, 2013.

Kapferer, Jean-Noël. *Rumors: Uses, Interpretations, and Images.* New Brunswick, NJ: Transaction, 1990.

Kaplan, M. Lindsay. *The Culture of Slander in Early Modern England.* Cambridge: Cambridge University Press, 1997.

Kautsky, John H. *The Politics of Aristocratic Empires*. Chapel Hill: University of North Carolina Press, 1982.

Keddie, Anthony. *Class and Power in Roman Palestine: The Socio-Economic Setting of Judaism and Christian Origins.* Cambridge: Cambridge University Press, 2019.

Keller, Otto. *Die antike Tierwelt. Erster Band: Säugetiere.* Leipzig: Wilhelm Engelmann, 1909.

Kelly, Benjamin. "Introduction." In *The Roman Emperor and His Court, c. 300 BC–AD 300,* vol. 1, edited by Benjamin Kelly and Angela Hug, 1–15. Cambridge: Cambridge University Press, 2022.

———. *Petitions, Litigation, and Social Control in Roman Egypt.* Oxford: Oxford University Press, 2011.

———. "Riot Control and Imperial Ideology in the Roman Empire." *Phoenix* 61 (2007): 150–76.

Kelly, Benjamin, and Angela Hug, eds. *The Roman Emperor and His Court, c. 300 BC–AD 300.* 2 vols. Cambridge: Cambridge University Press, 2022.

Kelly, Christopher. "Emperors, Government and Bureaucracy." In *The Cambridge Ancient History,* vol. 13, *The Late Empire, AD. 337–425,* edited by Averil Cameron and Peter Garnsey, 138–83. Cambridge: Cambridge University Press, 1998.

———. *Ruling the Later Roman Empire.* Cambridge, MA: Harvard University Press, 2004.

———. "Stooping to Conquer: The Power of Imperial Humility." In *Theodosius II: Rethinking the Roman Empire in Late Antiquity,* edited by Christopher Kelly, 221–43. Cambridge: Cambridge University Press, 2013.

Kelly, Doug. "An Unforgotten Episode in the Life of Caesar." *Ancient History: Resources for Teachers* 41–44 (2011–14): 66–76.

Kelly, Gavin. *Ammianus Marcellinus: The Allusive Historian.* Cambridge: Cambridge University Press, 2008.

———. "The Political Crisis of AD 375–6." *Chiron* 43 (2013): 357–408.

Kelly, J. N. D. *Golden Mouth. The Story of John Chrysostom—Ascetic, Preacher, Bishop.* Ithaca, NY: Cornell University Press, 1995.

Kemezis, Adam. "The Fall of Elagabalus as Literary Narrative and Political Reality." *Historia* 65 (2016): 348–90.

Kierdorf, Wilhelm. *Sueton: Leben des Claudius und Nero.* Paderborn: Schöningh, 1992.

Kim, Lawrence. "Orality, Folktales and the Cross-Cultural Transmission of Narrative." In *The Romance between Greece and the East,* edited by Tim Whitmarsh and Stuart Thomson, 300–321. Cambridge: Cambridge University Press, 2013.

Kırlı, Cengiz. "Surveillance and Constituting the Public in the Ottoman Empire." In *Publics, Politics, and Participation: Locating the Public Sphere in the Middle East and North Africa,* edited by Seteney Shami, 282–305. New York: Columbia University Press, 2009.

Klein, Annika, and Muriel Moser. "Modern Scandal Theory and the Case of Clodia and Cicero in Ancient Rome." In *Scandalogy 2: Cultures of Scandals—Scandals in Culture,* edited by André Haller and Hendrik Michael, 82–103. Cologne: Herber von Halem, 2020.

Kniffin, Kevin M., and David Sloan Wilson. "Utilities of Gossip across Organizational Levels: Multilevel Selection, Free-Riders, and Teams." *Human Nature* 16 (2005): 278–92.

Kocka, Jürgen. "Asymmetrical Historical Comparison: The Case of the German *Sonderweg.*" *History and Theory* 38 (1999): 40–50.

Koenen, L. "Die *laudatio funebris* des Augustus für Agrippa auf einem neuen Papyrus (*P. Colon.* inv. nr. 4701)." *Zeitschrift für Papyrologie und Epigraphik* 5 (1970): 217–83.

Kohns, Hans Peter. *Versorgungskrisen und Hungerrevolten im spätantiken Rom.* Bonn: R. Habelt, 1961.

Kolb, Frank. "Der Bußakt von Mailand: Zum Verhältnis von Staat und Kirche in der Spätantike." In *Geschichte und Gegenwart: Festschrift für Karl Dietrich Erdmann,* edited by Harmut Boockmann, Kurt Jürgensen, and Gerhard Stoltenberg, 41–74. Neumünster: Wachholtz, 1980.

Kolchin, Peter. *A Sphinx on the American Land: The Nineteenth-Century South in Comparative Perspective.* Baton Rouge: Louisiana State University Press, 2003.

Kosiński, Rafał, Kamilla Twardowksa, Aneta Zabrocka, and Andrian Szopa, eds. *The Church Histories of Theodore Lector and John Diakrinomenos.* Frankfurt am Main: Peter Lang, 2021.

Kouli, Maria. "Life of St. Mary of Egypt." In *Holy Women of Byzantium,* edited by Alice-Mary Talbot, 65–93. Cambridge, MA: Harvard University Press, 1996.

Kraemer, David. "The Mishnah." In *The Cambridge History of Judaism,* vol. 4, edited by Steven T. Katz, 299–315. Cambridge: Cambridge University Press, 2006.

Kraft, András. "The 'Last Roman Emperor' *Topos* in the Byzantine Apocalyptic Tradition." *Byzantion* 82 (2012): 213–57.

———. "Miracles and Pseudo-Miracles in Byzantine Apocalypses." In *Recognizing Miracles in Antiquity and Beyond,* edited by Maria Gerolemou, 111–30. Berlin: De Gruyter, 2018.

Kragelund, Patrick. *Roman Historical Drama: The* Octavia *in Antiquity and Beyond.* Oxford: Oxford University Press, 2015.

Krause, Christiane. *Strategie der Selbstinszenierung: Das rhetorische Ich in den Reden Dions von Prusa.* Wiesbaden: Reichert, 2003.

Kröss, Katja. *Die politische Rolle der stadtrömischen Plebs in der Kaiserzeit.* Leiden: Brill, 2017.

Kuhn, Christina. "Politische Kommunikation und öffentliche Meinung in der antiken Welt: Einleitende Bemerkungen." In *Politische Kommunikation und öffentliche Meinung in der antiken Welt,* edited by Christina Kuhn, 11–30. Stuttgart: Franz Steiner, 2012.

Kunderewicz, C. "Quelques remarques sur le role des καισαρεῖα dans la vie juridique de l'Égypte romaine." *Journal of Juristic Papyrology* 13 (1961): 123–29.

Kurke, Leslie. *Aesopic Conversations: Popular Tradition, Cultural Dialogue, and the Invention of Greek Prose.* Princeton, NJ: Princeton University Press, 2011.

Laes, Christian, and Johan Strubbe. *Youth in the Roman Empire: The Young and the Restless Years?* Cambridge: Cambridge University Press, 2014.

Laffi, Umberto. "Le iscrizioni relative all'introduzione nel 9 a. C. del nuovo calendario della provincial d'Asia." *Studi Classici e Orientali* 16 (1967): 5–98.

Laiou, Angeliki E. "Imperial Marriages and Their Critics in the Eleventh Century: The Case of Skylitzes." *Dumbarton Oaks Papers* 46 (1992): 165–76.

Lançon, Bertrand. *Rome in Late Antiquity: Everyday Life and Urban Change, AD 312–609.* Translated by Antonina Nevill. Edinburgh: Edinburgh University Press, 2000.

Langlands, Rebecca. *Exemplary Ethics in Ancient Rome.* Cambridge: Cambridge University Press, 2018.

———. "Extratextuality." In *Roman Literature under Nerva, Trajan and Hadrian,* edited by Alice König and Christopher Whitton, 330–46. Cambridge: Cambridge University Press, 2018.

———. *Sexual Morality in Ancient Rome.* Cambridge: Cambridge University Press, 2006.

Larran, Francis. *Le bruit qui vole: Histoire de la rumeur et de la renommée en Gréce ancienne.* Toulouse: Presses universitaires du Mirail, 2011.

László, Levente. "Rhetorius, Zeno's Astrologer, and a Sixth-Century Astrological Compendium." *Dumbarton Oaks Papers* 74 (2020): 329–50.

Laurence, Ray. "Rumour and Communication in Roman Politics." *Greece and Rome* 41 (1994): 62–74.

Laurence, Ray, and Jeremy Paterson. "Power and Laughter: Imperial Dicta." *Papers of the British School at Rome* 67 (1999): 183–97.

Lauterbach, Jacob Z., ed. *Mekhilta De-Rabbi Ishmael.* 2nd ed. 2 vols. Philadelphia: Jewish Publication Society, 2020.

Lawlor, Hugh Jackson, and John Ernest Leonard Oulton, eds. *Eusebius, Bishop of Caesarea: The Ecclesiastical History and the Martyrs of Palestine.* London: Society for Promoting Christian Knowledge, 1927.

Layton, Bentley. *The Canons of Our Fathers: Monastic Rules of Shenoute.* Oxford: Oxford University Press, 2014.

Lebek, W. D. "*CIL* IV 6893 (=*CE* 2050)—ein Vers auf Augustus' Mutter Atia?" *Zeitschrift für Papyrologie und Epigraphik* 24 (1977): 25–31.

Lecuppre, Gilles. *L'imposture politique au Moyen Âge.* Paris: Presses universitaires de France, 2005.

Lecuppre-Desjardin, Élodie. "Des portes qui parlent: Placards, feuilles volantes et communication politique dans les villes des Pays-Bas à la fin du Moyen Âge." *Bibliothèque de l'École des chartes* 168 (2010): 151–72.

Leeuwen, Richard van. *Narratives of Kingship in Eurasian Empires, 1300–1800.* Leiden: Brill, 2017.

Leftwich, Adrian. "The Political Approach to Human Behaviour: People, Resources and Power." In *What Is Politics? The Activity and Its Study,* edited by Adrian Leftwich, 100–118. Cambridge: Polity, 2004.

———. "Thinking Politically: On the Politics of Politics." In *What Is Politics? The Activity and Its Study,* edited by Adrian Leftwich, 1–22. Cambridge: Polity, 2004.

Lehnen, Joachim. Adventus principis: *Untersuchungen zu Sinngehalt und Zeremoniell der Kaiserankunft in den Städten des* Imperium Romanum. Frankfurt am Main: Peter Lang, 1997.

Lendon, J. E. *Empire of Honour: The Art of Government in the Roman World.* Oxford: Oxford University Press, 1997.

Lennon, Jack J. "*Victimarii* in Roman Religion and Society." *Papers of the British School at Rome* 83 (2015): 65–89.

Lenski, Noel. "Assimilation and Revolt in the Territory of Isauria, from the 1st Century BC to the 6th Century AD." *Journal of the Economic and Social History of the Orient* 42 (1999): 413–65.

———. "Empresses in the Holy Land: The Creation of a Christian Utopia in Late Antique Palestine." In *Communication and Geography in Late Antiquity,* edited by Linda Ellis and Frank L. Kidner, 113–24. Aldershot: Ashgate, 2004.

———. *Failure of Empire: Valens and the Roman State in the Fourth Century A.D.* Berkeley: University of California Press, 2002.

———. "Imperial Legislation and the Donatist Controversy: From Constantine to Honorius." In *The Donatist Schism: Controversy and Contexts,* edited by Richard Miles, 166–219. Liverpool: Liverpool University Press, 2019.

———. "*Initium mali Romano imperio:* Contemporary Reactions to the Battle of Adrianople." *TAPA* 127 (1997): 129–68.

———. "Moving the Mail: The Status and Operations of Letter Carriers in the *Collectio Avellana.*" In *The Collection Avellana and the Development of Notarial Practices in Late Antiquity,* edited by Rita Lizzi Testa and Giulia Marconi, 507–63. Turnhout: Brepols, 2023.

Leppin, Hartmut. "Das Alte Testament und der Erfahrungsraum der Christen: Davids Buße in den Apologien des Ambrosius." In *Die Bibel als politisches Argument,* edited by Andreas Pečar and Kai Trampedach, 119–33. Munich: Oldenbourg, 2007.

———. "Das Bild der kaiserlichen Frauen bei Gregor von Nyssa." In *Gregory of Nyssa: Homilies on the Beatitudes,* edited by Hubertus R. Drobner and Albert Viciano, 487–506. Leiden: Brill, 2000.

———. "Imperial Miracles and Elitist Discourses." In *Miracles Revisited: New Testament Miracle Stories and Their Concepts of Reality,* edited by Stefan Alkier and Annette Weissenrieder, 233–48. Berlin: De Gruyter, 2013.

———. *Justinian: Das Christliche Experiment.* Stuttgart: Klett Cotta, 2011.

———. *Paradoxe der Parrhesie: Eine antike Wortgeschichte.* Tübingen: Mohr Siebeck, 2022.

———. "Pastoral und Politik: Politische Ordnungsvorstellungen im frühen Christentum." In *Die Anfänge des Christentums,* edited by Friedrich Wilhelm Graf and Klaus Wiegandt, 308–38. Frankfurt: Fischer Taschenbuch, 2009.

———. "Steuern, Aufstand und Rhetoren: Der Antiocher Steueraufstand von 387 in christlicher und heidnischer Deutung." In *Gedeutete Realität: Krisen, Wirklichkeiten, Interpretation (3.–6. Jh. n. Chr.),* edited by Hartwin Brandt, 103–23. Stuttgart: Franz Steiner, 1999.

———. *Theodosius der Große.* Darmstadt: Primus, 2003.

Levick, Barbara M. "Cluvius Rufus (no. 84)." In *The Fragments of the Roman Historians,* edited by T. J. Cornell, 3 vols., vol. 1, 549–60; vol. 2, 1036–41; vol. 3, 617–19. Oxford: Oxford University Press, 2013.

———. "Fabius Rusticus (no. 87)." In *The Fragments of the Roman Historians,* edited by T. J. Cornell, 3 vols., vol. 1, 568–72; vol. 2, 1052–57; vol. 3, 622–23. Oxford: Oxford University Press, 2013.

———. *Faustina I and II: Imperial Women of the Golden Age.* New York: Oxford University Press, 2014.

———. *Tiberius the Politician.* Rev. ed. London: Routledge, 1999.

Levin, Carole. *The Heart and Stomach of a King: Elizabeth I and the Politics of Sex and Power.* Philadelphia: University of Pennsylvania Press, 2013.

Levinson, Joshua. "Tragedies Naturally Performed: Fatal Charades, *Parodia Sacra,* and the Death of Titus." In *Jewish Culture and Society under the Christian Roman Empire,* edited by Richard Kalmin and Seth Schwartz, 349–82. Leuven: Peeters, 2003.

Levison, Wilhelm. "*Vita Germani episcopi Autissiodorensis auctore Constantio.*" In *MGH Scriptores rerum Merovingicarum,* vol. 7, *Passiones Vitaeque Sanctorum Aevi Merovingici Tomus V,* 225–83. Berlin: Weidmann, 1920.

Lewis, Naphtali. "*Notationes legentis.*" *Bulletin of the American Society of Papyrologists* 13 (1976): 5–14.

Lieberman, Saul. "Palestine in the Third and Fourth Centuries." *Jewish Quarterly Review* 36 (1946): 329–70.

———. "Roman Legal Institutions in Early Rabbinics and in the *Acta Martyrum.*" *Jewish Quarterly Review* 35 (1944): 1–57.

Liebeschuetz, J. H. W. G., ed. *Ambrose of Milan: Political Letters and Speeches.* Translated Texts for Historians 43. Liverpool: Liverpool University Press, 2005.

Lieu, Samuel N. C. *The Emperor Julian: Panegyric and Polemic.* 2nd ed. Translated Texts for Historians 2. Liverpool: Liverpool University Press, 1989.

Lim, Richard. "Religious Disputation and Social Disorder in Late Antiquity." *Historia* 44 (1995): 204–31.

Lipsius, Richard Adelbert, ed. *Acta Apostolorum Apocrypha: Pars Prior.* Leipzig: Hermann Mendelssohn, 1891.

Lisle, Christopher de. *Agathokles of Syracuse: Sicilian Tyrant and Hellenistic King.* Oxford: Oxford University Press, 2021.

Littlewood, Antony Robert. "The Symbolism of the Apple in Byzantine Literature." *Jahrbuch der österreichischen Byzantinistik* 23 (1974): 33–69.

Liverani, Paolo. "Saint Peter's, Leo the Great and the Leprosy of Constantine." *Papers of the British School at Rome* 76 (2008): 155–72.

Livrea, Enrico. "Chi e' l'autore di *P. Oxy.* 4352?" *Zeitschrift für Papyrologie und Epigraphik* 125 (1999): 69–73.

Lo, Vivienne, and Penelope Barrett. "Other Pleasures? Anal Sex and Medical Discourse in Pre-Modern China." In *Sexual Diversity in Asia, c. 600–1950,* edited by Raquel A. G. Reyes and William G. Clarence-Smith, 25–46. London: Routledge, 2012.

Lo Cascio, Elio. "The Population." In *A Companion to the City of Rome,* edited by Claire Holleran and Amanda Claridge, 137–53. Oxford: Blackwell, 2018.

Loar, Matthew P. "Sexual Graffiti in the House of Marcus Lucretius in Pompeii (IX.3.5, 24)." *Classical World* 111 (2018): 405–31.

Lohmann, Polly. *Graffiti als Interaktionsform: Geritzte Inschriften in den Wohnhäusern Pompejis.* Berlin: De Gruyter, 2018.

Long, Jacqueline. "Julia-Jokes at Macrobius' Saturnalia: Subversive Decorum in Late Antique Reception of Augustan Political Humour." *International Journal of the Classical Tradition* 6 (2000): 337–55.

Longworth, Philip. "The Pretender Phenomenon in Eighteenth Century Russia." *Past and Present* 66 (1975): 61–83.

Luhmann, Niklas. "Der neue Chef." *Verwaltungs Archiv* 53 (1962): 11–24.

Łukaszewicz, Adam. "Antoninus the κόρυφος (note on *P. Oxy.* XLVI 3298.2)." *Journal of Juristic Papyrology* 22 (1992): 43–46.

———. "Ergänzende Bemerkungen zu *P. Oxy.* XLVI 3298.2." *Journal of Juristic Papyrology* 23 (1993): 115–18.

Lutz, Cora E., ed. *Musonius Rufus: That One Should Disdain Hardships: The Teachings of a Roman Stoic.* New Haven: Yale University Press, 2020.

Ma, John. "Kings." In *A Companion to the Hellenistic World,* edited by Andrew Erskine, 177–95. Oxford: Blackwell, 2003.

Maas, Paul. "Metrische Akklamationen der Byzantiner." *Byzantinische Zeitschrift* 34 (1912): 28–51.

MacCoull, Leslie S. B. *Dioscorus of Aphrodito.* Berkeley: University of California Press, 1988.

Machado, Carlos. *Urban Space and Aristocratic Power in Late Antique Rome.* Oxford: Oxford University Press, 2019.

MacKay, Ruth. *The Baker Who Pretended to Be King of Portugal.* Chicago: University of Chicago Press, 2012.

MacMullen, Ramsay. "Constantine and the Miraculous." *Greek, Roman, and Byzantine Studies* 6 (1968): 81–96.

———. *Enemies of the Roman Order.* Cambridge, MA: Harvard University Press, 1966.

———. "The Preacher's Audience." *Journal of Theological Studies* 40 (1989): 503–11.

———. *Roman Social Relations.* New Haven: Yale University Press, 1974.

———. "Tax-Pressure in the Roman Empire." *Latomus* 46 (1987): 737–54.

Magaldi, Emilio. "Echi di Roma a Pompei." *Rivista di Studi Pompeiani* 2 (1936): 25–100.

Magalhães de Oliveira, Julio Cesar. "Communication and Plebeian Sociability in Late Antiquity: The View from North Africa in the Age of Augustine." In *Popular Culture in the Ancient World,* edited by Lucy Grig, 296–317. Cambridge: Cambridge University Press, 2017.

———. "The Emperor Is Dead! Rumours, Protests, and Political Opportunities in Late Antiquity." In *Political Communication in the Roman World,* edited by Cristina Rosillo-López, 165–78. Leiden: Brill, 2017.

———. "Late Antiquity: The Age of Crowds?" *Past and Present* 249 (2020): 3–52.

———. Potestas populi: *Participation populaire et action collective dans les villes de l'Afrique romaine tardive (vers 300–430 apr. J.-C.).* Turnhout: Brepols, 2017.

Magdalino, Paul. "Court and Capital in Byzantium." In *Royal Courts in Dynastic States and Empires: A Global Perspective,* edited by Jeroen Duindam, Tülay Artan, and Metin Kunt, 129–44. Leiden: Brill, 2011.

———. *The Empire of Manuel I Komnenos, 1143–1180.* Cambridge: Cambridge University Press, 1993.

———. "Eros the King and the King of *Amours:* Some Observations on *Hysmine and Hysminias.*" *Dumbarton Oaks Papers* 46 (1992): 197–204.

———. "Generic Subversion? The Political Ideology of Urban Myth and Apocalyptic Prophecy." In *Power and Subversion in Byzantium,* edited by Dimiter Angelov and Michael Saxby, 207–19. London: Routledge, 2013.

———. "Political Satire." In *Satire in the Middle Byzantine Period: The Golden Age of Laughter?,* edited by Przemysław Marciniak and Ingela Nilsson, 127–51. Leiden: Brill, 2011.

Magie, David. "The Mission of Agrippa to the Orient in 23 B.C." *Classical Philology* 3 (1908): 145–52.

Maguire, Henry. "Gardens and Parks in Constantinople." *Dumbarton Oaks Papers* 54 (2000): 251–64.

———. "Parody in Byzantine Art." In *Satire in the Middle Byzantine Period: The Golden Age of Laughter?*, edited by Przemysław Marciniak and Ingela Nilsson, 104–26. Leiden: Brill, 2021.

Mahoney, James, and Dietrich Rueschemeyer. "Comparative Historical Analysis: Achievements and Agendas." In *Comparative Historical Analysis in the Social Sciences,* edited by James Mahoney and Dietrich Rueschemeyer, 3–38. Cambridge: Cambridge University Press, 2003.

Majeska, George P. *Russian Travelers to Constantinople in the Fourteenth and Fifteenth Centuries.* Dumbarton Oaks Studies XIX. Washington, DC: Dumbarton Oaks, 1984.

Makhlaiuk, Alexander V. "Emperors' Nicknames and Roman Political Humour." *Klio* 102 (2020): 202–35.

Malik, Shushma. "*Cucuta ab rationibus Neronis Augusti:* A Joke at Nero's Expense?" *Classical Quarterly* 69 (2019): 783–92.

———. *The Nero-Antichrist: Founding and Fashioning a Paradigm.* Cambridge: Cambridge University Press, 2020.

Mallan, C. T. *Cassius Dio:* Roman History *Books 57 and 58 (The Reign of Tiberius).* Oxford: Oxford University Press, 2020.

———. "Tiberius the Goat: An Addition to Champlin's 'Mallonia.' " *Histos* 10 (2016): 15–16.

Malloch, S. J. V. *The* Tabula Lugdunensis: *A Critical Edition with Translation and Commentary.* Cambridge: Cambridge University Press, 2020.

Manabe, Noriko. "Chants of the Resistance: Flow, Memory, and Inclusivity." *Music and Politics* 13 (2019): http://dx.doi.org/10.3998/mp.9460447.0013.105.

Mango, Cyril. "Constantine's Porphyry Column and the Chapel of St Constantine." Δελτίον Χριστιανικής Αρζαιολογικής Εταιρείας 10 (1993): 103–10.

Mango, Cyril, and Roger Scott. *The Chronicle of Theophanes Confessor: Byzantine and Near Eastern History AD 284–813.* Oxford: Clarendon, 1997.

Mango, Marlia Mundell. "The Commercial Map of Constantinople." *Dumbarton Oaks Papers* 54 (2000): 189–207.

Ma'oz, Zvi Uri. "The Civil Reform of Diocletian in the Southern Levant." *Scripta Classica Israelica* 25 (2006): 105–19.

Marasco, Gabriele. "Costantino e le uccisioni di Crispo e Fausta (326 d. C.)." *Rivista di Filologia e di Istruzione Classica* 121 (1993): 297–317.

Mariev, Sergei, ed. *Ioannis Antiocheni fragmenta quae supersunt omnia.* Berlin: De Gruyter, 2008.

Marx, F. A. "Tacitus und die Literatur der *exitus illustrium virorum.*" *Philologus* 92 (1937): 83–103.

Masterson, Mark. "Toward a Late-Ancient Physiognomy." In *Sex in Antiquity: Exploring Gender and Sexuality in the Ancient World,* edited by Mark Masterson, Nancy Sorkin Rabinowitz, and James Robson, 536–51. London: Routledge, 2014.

Matthews, J. F. "The Origin of Ammianus." *Classical Quarterly* 44 (1994): 252–69.

Matthews, John. *The Journey of Theophanes: Travel, Business, and Daily Life in the Roman East.* New Haven: Yale University Press, 2006.

———. *Laying down the Law: A Study of the Theodosian Code.* New Haven: Yale University Press, 2000.

———. *The Roman Empire of Ammianus.* London: Duckworth, 1989.

———. "The Roman Empire and the Proliferation of Elites." *Arethusa* 33 (2000): 429–46.

Mawdsley, Harry. "Defeat on Display: The Public Abuse of Usurpers and Rebels in Late Antiquity." *Journal of Late Antiquity* 17 (2024): 35–69.

Maxwell, Jacyln L. *Christianization and Communication in Late Antiquity.* Cambridge: Cambridge University Press, 2006.

Mayer, Wendy. "The Dynamics of Liturgical Space: Aspects of Interaction between St John Chrysostom and His Audiences." *Ephemerides Liturgicae* 111 (1997): 104–15.

———. "John Chrysostom and His Audiences: Distinguishing Different Congregations at Antioch and Constantinople." *Studia Patristica* 31 (1997): 70–75.

———. "Who Came to Hear John Chrysostom Preach?: Recovering a Late Fourth-Century Preacher's Audience." *Ephemerides Theologicae Lovanienses* 76 (2000): 73–87.

Maza, Sara. "The Diamond Necklace Affair Revisited (1785–1786): The Case of the Missing Queen." In *Eroticism and the Body Politic,* edited by Linda Hunt, 63–89. Baltimore: Johns Hopkins University Press, 1990.

McAndrew, Francis T. "Gossip as a Social Skill." In *The Oxford Handbook of Gossip and Reputation,* edited by Francesca Giardini and Rafael Wittek, 172–92. Oxford: Oxford University Press, 2019.

———. "How 'The Gossip' Became a Woman and How 'Gossip' Became Her Weapon of Choice." In *The Oxford Handbook of Women and Competition,* edited by Maryanne L. Fisher, 191–206. Oxford: Oxford University Press, 2014.

McCormick, Michael. *Eternal Victory: Triumphal Rulership in Late Antiquity, Byzantium, and the Early Medieval West.* Cambridge: Cambridge University Press, 1986.

McEvoy, Meaghan. "Becoming Roman?: The Not-So-Curious Case of Aspar and the Ardaburii." *Journal of Late Antiquity* 9 (2016): 483–511.

———. *Child Emperor Rule in the Late Roman West, AD 367–455.* Oxford: Oxford University Press, 2013.

———. "Constantia: The Last Constantinian." *Antichthon* 50 (2016): 154–79.

———. "Dynastic Dreams and Visions of Early Byzantine Emperors." In *Dreams, Memory and Imagination in Byzantium,* edited by Eva Anagnostou-Laoutides and Bronwen Neil, 99–117. Leiden: Brill, 2018.

———. "Leo II, Zeno, and the Transfer of Power from a Son to His Father in 474 AD." In *Shifting Frontiers: The Fifth Century—Age of Transformation,* edited by Jan Willem Drijvers and Noel Lenski, 197–208. Bari: Edipuglia, 2019.

———. "Orations for the First Generation of Theodosian Imperial Women." *Journal of Late Antiquity* 14 (2021): 117–41.

———. "Rome and the Transformation of the Imperial Office in the Late Fourth–Mid-Fifth Centuries." *Papers of the British School at Rome* 78 (2010): 151–92.

———. "Shadow Emperors and the Choice of Rome, AD 455–476." *Antiquité tardive* 25 (2017): 95–112.

McGing, B. C. "Bandits, Real and Imagined, in Greco-Roman Egypt." *Bulletin of the American Society of Papyrologists* 35 (1998): 159–83.

McIlvenna, Una. "Poison, Pregnancy, and Protestants: Gossip and Scandal at the Early Modern French Court." In *"Fama" and Her Sisters: Gossip and Rumour in Early Modern Europe,* edited by Claire Walker and Heather Kerr, 137–60. Turnhout: Brepols, 2015.

McLaughlin, Megan. "'Disgusting Acts of Shamelessness': Sexual Misconduct and the Deconstruction of Royal Authority in the Eleventh Century." *Early Medieval Europe* 19 (2011): 312–31.

McLynn, Neil B. *Ambrose of Milan: Church and Court in a Christian Capital.* Berkeley: University of California Press, 1994.

Meier, Mischa. *Anastasios I: Die Entstehung des Byzantinischen Reiches.* Stuttgart: Klett-Cotta, 2009.

———. *Das andere Zeitalter Justinians.* Göttingen: Vandenhoeck und Ruprecht, 2004.

Meijer, F. J. "Marius' Grandson." *Mnemosyne* 39 (1986): 112–21.

Meister, Jan Bernhard. *Der Körper des Princeps: Zur Problematik eines monarchischen Körpers ohne Monarchie.* Stuttgart: Franz Steiner, 2012.

———. "Klatsch, Gerüchte und *fama* also moralisches Kapital im spätrepublikanischen und frühkaiserzeitlichen Rom." In *Moral als Kapital im antiken Athen und Rom,* edited by Elke Hartmann, Sven Page, and Anabelle Thurn, 95–116. Stuttgart: Franz Steiner, 2018.

———. "Lachen und Politik: Zur Funktion von Humor in der politischen Kommunikation des römischen Principats." *Klio* 96 (2014): 26–48.

———. "Pisos Augenbrauen: Zur Lesbarkeit aristokratischer Körper in der späten römischen Republik." *Historia* 58 (2009): 71–95.

Merry, Sally Engle. "Rethinking Gossip and Scandal." In *Toward a General Theory of Social Control,* edited by Donald Black, 271–302. Orlando: Academic, 1984.

Meyer, Elizabeth A. *Legitimacy and Law in the Roman World:* Tabulae *in Roman Belief and Practice.* Cambridge: Cambridge University Press, 2004.

Millar, Fergus. *The Crowd in Rome in the Late Republic.* Ann Arbor: University of Michigan Press, 1998.

———. *The Emperor in the Roman World.* 2nd ed. London: Duckworth, 1992.

———. "Emperors at Work." *Journal of Roman Studies* 57 (1967): 9–19.

———. "The *Fiscus* in the First Two Centuries." *Journal of Roman Studies* 53 (1963): 29–42.

———. *A Greek Roman Empire: Power and Belief under Theodosius II (408–450).* Berkeley: University of California Press, 2006.

———. *A Study of Cassius Dio.* Oxford: Clarendon, 1964.

———. "The World of the *Golden Ass.*" *Journal of Roman Studies* 71 (1981): 63–75.

Milnor, Kristina. *Gender, Domesticity, and the Age of Augustus: Inventing Private Life.* Oxford: Oxford University Press, 2005.

Milns, R. D. "Suetonius and Vespasian's Humour." *Acta Classica* 53 (2010): 117–23.

Mitchell, Lynette, and Charles Melville. "'Every Inch a King': Kings and Kingship in the Ancient and Medieval Worlds." In *Every Inch a King: Comparative Studies on Kings and Kingship in the Ancient and Medieval Worlds,* edited by Lynette Mitchell and Charles Melville, 1–21. Leiden: Brill, 2013.

Mitchell, Stephen. *Anatolia. Land, Men, and Gods in Asia Minor.* Vol. 1, *The Celts and the Impact of Roman Rule.* Oxford: Oxford University Press, 1993.

Moatti, Claudia. "La communication publique écrite à Rome, sous la République et le Haut Empire." In *Rome et l'État moderne européen,* edited by Jean-Philippe Genet, 217–50. Rome: École française de Rome, 2007.

———. "Le contrôle de la mobilité des personnes dans l'Empire romain." *Mélanges de l'école française de Rome* 112 (2000): 925–58.

Moffatt, Nicole. *A World Both Small and Wide: The Letter-Bearer's Journey from Cicero to Jerome.* PhD diss., Macquarie University, 2021.

Moin, A. Azfar, and Alan Strathern. "Sacred Kingship in World History: Between Immanence and Transcendence." In *Sacred Kingship in World History: Between Immanence and Transcendence,* edited by A. Azfar Moin and Alan Strathern, 1–30. New York: Columbia University Press, 2022.

Molan, Peter D. "Charivari in a Medieval Egyptian Shadow Play." *Al-Masāq* 1 (1988): 5–24.

Mommsen, Theodor. "*Additamenta altera a. 446–457.*" In *MGH Auctores antiquissimi,* vol. 9, *Chronica Minora saec. IV. V. VI. VII,* vol. 1, 488–90. Berlin: Wiedmann, 1892.

———. "Cornelius Tacitus und Cluvius Rufus." *Hermes* 4 (1870): 295–325.

———. "*Hydatii Lemici continuatio chronicorum Hieronymianorum.*" In *MGH Auctores antiquissimi,* vol. 11, *Chronica Minora saec. IV. V. VI. VII.,* vol. 1, 1–36. Berlin: Wiedmann, 1894.

———. "*Prosperi Tironis epitome chronicon ed. primum a. CCCCXXXIII, continuata ad a. CCCCLV.*" In *MGH Auctores antiquissimi,* vol. 9, *Chronica Minora saec. IV. V. VI. VII.,* vol. 1, 341–485. Berlin: Wiedmann, 1892.

———. "*Victoris Tonnennensis episcopi chronica.*" In *MGH Auctores antiquissimi,* vol. 11, *Chronica Minora saec. IV. V. VI. VII.,* vol. 1, 184–206. Berlin: Wiedmann, 1894.

Montlahuc, Pascal. *Le pouvoir des bons mots. «Faire rire» et politique à Rome du milieu du IIIe siècle a.C. à l'avènement des Antonins.* Rome: École française de Rome, 2019. https://books.openedition.org/efr/31670.

Moreau, Philippe. "La *domus Augusta* et les formations de parenté à Rome." *Cahiers du Centre Gustave Glotz* 16 (2005): 7–23.

Morgan, J. R. "History, Romance, and Realism in the *Aithiopika* of Heliodorus." *Classical Antiquity* 1 (1981): 221–65.

Morgan, Llewelyn. "*Achilleae Comae:* Hair and Heroism According to Domitian." *Classical Quarterly* 47 (1997): 209–14.

Morgan, M. Gwyn. "Three Minor Pretenders in Tacitus, *Histories* II." *Latomus* 52 (1993): 769–96.

Morgan, Teresa. *Popular Morality in the Early Roman Empire.* Cambridge: Cambridge University Press, 2007.

Morstein-Marx, Robert. *Julius Caesar and the Roman People.* Cambridge: Cambridge University Press, 2021.

———. "Political Graffiti in the Late Roman Republic: 'Hidden Transcripts' and 'Common Knowledge.'" In *Politische Kommunikation und öffentliche Meinung in der antiken Welt,* edited by Christina Kuhn, 191–217. Stuttgart: Franz Steiner, 2012.

Mort, Frank. "Love in a Cold Climate: Letters, Public Opinion and Monarchy in the 1936 Abdication Crisis." *Twentieth Century British History* 25 (2014): 30–62.

Mouritsen, Henrik, and Ittai Gradel. "Nero in Pompeian Politics: *Edicta Munerum* and Imperial Flaminates in Late Pompeii." *Zeitschrift für Papyrologie und Epigraphik* 87 (1991): 145–55.

Muhlberger, Steven. *The Fifth-Century Chroniclers: Prosper, Hydatius, and the Gallic Chronicler of 452.* Leeds: Francis Cairns, 1990.

Mukhia, Harbans. *The Mughals of India.* Oxford: Blackwell, 2008.

Müller, Karl, ed. *Fragmenta Historicorum Graecorum.* Vol. 5, *Pars Prior.* Paris: Firmin Didot, 1883.

Münscher, Karl. *Senecas Werke. Untersuchungen zur Abfassungszeit und Echtheit.* Philologus Supplementband 16. Leipzig: Dieterich'sche Verlagsbuchhandlung, 1922.

Nasrallah, Laura Salah. *Christian Responses to Roman Art and Architecture.* Cambridge: Cambridge University Press, 2010.

Nau, François. "Histoires des solitaires égyptiens." *Revue de l'Orient chrétien* 13 (1908): 266–97.

Nauta, R. R. "Seneca's *Apocolocyntosis* as Saturnalian Literature." *Mnemosyne* 40 (1987): 69–96.

Neureuter, H.-P. "Zur Theorie der Anekdote." *Jahrbuch des Freien Deutschen Hochstifts* (1973): 458–80.

Nicol, Donald M. *The Immortal Emperor: The Life and Legend of Constantine Palaiologos, Last Emperor of the Romans.* Cambridge: Cambridge University Press, 2002.

Nisbet, Gideon. *Greek Epigram in the Roman Empire: Martial's Forgotten Rivals.* Oxford: Oxford University Press, 2003.

Nixon, C. E. V., and Barbara Saylor Rodgers, eds. *In Praise of Later Roman Emperors: The* Panegyrici Latini. Berkeley: University of California Press, 1994.

Noelle-Neumann, Elisabeth. *The Spiral of Silence. Public Opinion—Our Social Skin.* Chicago: University of Chicago Press, 1984.

Noreña, Carlos F. "The Ethics of Autocracy in the Roman World." In *A Companion to Greek and Roman Political Thought,* edited by Ryan K. Balot, 266–79. Oxford: Blackwell, 2009.

———. "Hadrian's Chastity." *Phoenix* 61 (2007): 296–317.

———. *Imperial Ideals in the Roman West: Representation, Circulation, Power.* Cambridge: Cambridge University Press, 2011.

Nuyts, Linde. "From Siege to Songbook: Late Medieval Folk Song as Political Memory." In *Old Songs, New Discoveries,* edited by Steve Roud and David Atkinson, 131–45. London: Ballad Partners, 2018.

Oakley, Francis. *Kingship: The Politics of Enchantment.* Oxford: Blackwell, 2006.

Ogden, Daniel. "The Apprentice's Sorcerer: Pancrates and His Powers in Context (Lucian, *Philopseudes* 33–36)." *Acta Classica* 47 (2004): 101–26.

———. *Polygamy, Prostitutes and Death: The Hellenistic Dynasties.* Swansea: Classical Press of Wales, 1999.

Olbrycht, Marek Jan. "Vologases I, Pakoros II and Artabanos III: Coins and Parthian History." *Iranica Antiqua* 51 (2016): 215–33.

Olivar, Alexander, ed. *Sancti Petri Chrysologi collectio sermonum a Felice episcopo parata sermonibus extravagantibus adieticis. Pars I. CCSL XXIV.* Turnholt: Brepols, 1975.

———. *Sancti Petri Chrysologi collectio sermonum a Felice episcopo parata sermonibus extravagantibus adieticis. Pars II. CCSL XXIVA.* Turnholt: Brepols, 1981.

———. *Sancti Petri Chrysologi collectio sermonum a Felice episcopo parata sermonibus extravagantibus adieticis. Pars III. CCSL XXIVB.* Turnholt: Brepols, 1982.

Olson, Kelly. *Masculinity and Dress in Roman Antiquity.* London: Routledge, 2017.

Olster, David. "Constans II's Odd Speech." In *Radical Traditionalism: The Influence of Walter Kaegi in Late Antique, Byzantine, and Medieval Studies,* edited by Christian Raffensperger and David Olster, 57–73. Lanham: Lexington, 2019.

O'Neill, Peter. *A Culture of Sociability: Popular Speech in Ancient Rome.* PhD diss., University of Southern California, 2001.

———. "Going Round in Circles: Popular Speech in Ancient Rome." *Classical Antiquity* 22 (2003): 135–76.

Osgood, Josiah. "Caesar and Nicomedes." *Classical Quarterly* 58 (2008): 687–91.

———. "Cassius Dio's Secret History of Elagabalus." In *Cassius Dio: Greek Intellectual and Roman Politician,* edited by Cartsen Hjort Lange and Jesper Majbom Madsen, 177–90. Leiden: Brill, 2016.

Overwien, Oliver. "Secundus the Silent Philosopher in the Ancient and Eastern Tradition." In *Fictional Storytelling in the Medieval Eastern Mediterranean and Beyond,* edited by Carolina Cupane and Bettina Krönung, 338–64. Leiden: Brill, 2016.

Padilla Peralta, Dan-El. "Slave Religiosity in the Roman Middle Republic." *Classical Antiquity* 36 (2017): 317–69.

Paillard, Bernard. "L'écho de la rumeur." *Communications* 52 (1990): 125–39.

Paine, Robert. "What Is Gossip About? An Alternative Hypothesis." *Man* 2 (1967): 278–85.

Palanque, Jean-Rémy. "La date du transfert de la prefecture des Gaules de Trèves à Arles." *Revue des études anciennes* 36 (1935): 358–62.

Pappano, Albert Earl. "The Pseudo-Marius." *Classical Philology* 30 (1935): 58–65.

Parker, Holt N. "The Teratogenic Grid." In *Roman Sexualities,* edited by Judith P. Hallett and Marilyn B. Skinner, 47–65. Princeton, NJ: Princeton University Press, 1998.

———. "Toward a Definition of Popular Culture." *History and Theory* 50 (2011): 147–70.

Parsons, Peter J. "The Grammarian's Complaint." In *Collectanea Papyrologica: Texts Published in Honor of H.C. Youtie,* vol. 2, edited by Ann Ellis Hansen, 409–46. Bonn: Habelt, 1976.

Paschoud, F. "Valentinian travesti, ou: De la malignité d'Ammien." In *Cognitio Gestorum: The Historiographic Art of Ammianus Marcellinus,* edited by J. den Boeft, D. den Hengst, and H. C. Teitler, 67–84. Amsterdam: Royal Netherlands Academy of Science, 1992.

Pasco-Pranger, Molly. "With the Veil Removed: Women's Public Nudity in the Early Roman Empire." *Classical Antiquity* 38 (2019): 217–49.

Patlagean, Evelyne. *Pauvreté économique et pauvreté sociale à Byzance, 4e–7e siècles.* Paris: Mouton, 1977.

Pattenden, Miles. *Electing the Pope in Early Modern Italy, 1450–1700.* Oxford: Oxford University Press, 2017.

Patterson, John R. "Crisis: What Crisis? Rural Change and Urban Development in Imperial Apennine Italy." *Papers of the British School at Rome* 55 (1987): 115–46.

———. *Landscapes and Cities: Rural Settlement and Civic Transformation in Early Imperial Italy.* Oxford: Oxford University Press, 2006.

Paverd, Frans van de. *St. John Chrysostom, The Homilies on the Statues: An Introduction.* Rome: Pontifical Oriental Institute, 1991.

Peachin, Michael. "Augustus' Emergent Judicial Powers, the 'Crimen Maiestatis,' and the Second Cyrene Edict." In *Il princeps romano: Autocrate o magistrato? Fattori giuridici e fattori sociali del potere imperiale da Augusto a Commodo,* edited by J.-L. Ferrary and J. Scheid, 3–59. Pavia: Pavia University Press, 2015.

Pečírková, Jana. "Divination and Politics in the Late Assyrian Empire." *Archív Orientální* 53 (1985): 155–68.

Pekáry, Thomas. "*Seditio:* Unruhen und Revolten im römischen Reich von Augustus bis Commodus." *Ancient Society* 18 (1987): 133–50.

Perrie, Maureen. *The Image of Ivan the Terrible in Russian Folklore.* Cambridge: Cambridge University Press, 1987.

———. *Pretenders and Popular Monarchism in Early Modern Russia: The False Tsars of the Time of Troubles.* Cambridge: Cambridge University Press, 1995.

Perry, Ben Edwin. *Secundus the Silent Philosopher: The Greek Life of Secundus.* New York: American Philological Association, 1964.

Peters, B. Guy. "Politics Is about Governing." In *What Is Politics? The Activity and Its Study,* edited by Adrian Leftwich, 23–40. Cambridge: Blackwell, 2004.

Petit, Paul. *Libanius et la vie municipale à Antioche au IVe siècle après J.-C.* Paris: P. Geuthner, 1955.

Pettinger, Andrew. *The Republic in Danger: Drusus Libo and the Succession of Tiberius.* Oxford: Oxford University Press, 2012.

Pfeilschifter, Rene. *Der Kaiser und Konstantinopel. Kommunikation und Konfliktaustrag in einer spätantiken Metropole.* Berlin: De Gruyter, 2013.

Pingree, David. "Political Horoscopes from the Reign of Zeno." *Dumbarton Oaks Papers* 30 (1976): 135–50.

Pirazzoli-t'Serstevens, Michele. "Imperial Aura and the Image of the Other in Han Art." In *Conceiving the Empire: China and Rome Compared,* edited by Fritz-Heiner Mutschler and Achim Mittag, 299–317. Oxford: Oxford University Press, 2009.

Pohlsander, Hans A. "Crispus: Brilliant Career and Tragic End." *Historia* 33 (1984): 79–106.

Pond Rothman, Margaret S. "The Thematic Organisation of the Panel Reliefs on the Arch of Galerius." *American Journal of Archaeology* 81 (1977): 427–54.

Potamiti, Anna. "Hernia Jokes in Graeco-Roman Antiquity." *Illinois Classical Studies* 43 (2018): 388–403.

Pottenger, A. J. *Power and Rhetoric in the Ecclesiastical Correspondence of Constantine the Great.* London: Routledge, 2022.

Potter, David. *Prophets and Emperors: Human and Divine Authority from Augustus to Theodosius.* Cambridge, MA: Harvard University Press, 1994.

Powell, Anton. "Augustus' Age of Apology: An Analysis of the Memoirs—and an Argument for Two Further Fragments." In *The Lost Memoirs of Augustus and the Development of Roman Autobiography,* edited by Christopher Smith and Anton Powell, 173–94. Swansea: Classical Press of Wales, 2009.

Power, Tristan J. "Galba, Onesimus, and Servitude." *Eranos* 107 (2012–13): 38–40.

———. "The Servants' Taunt: Homer and Suetonius' *Galba*." *Historia* 58 (2009): 242–45.

Price, Richard, and Mary Whitby, eds. *Chalcedon in Context: Church Councils 400–700*. Liverpool: Liverpool University Press, 2009.

Price, S. R. F. *Rituals and Power: The Roman Imperial Cult in Asia Minor*. Cambridge: Cambridge University Press, 1984.

Priwitzer, Stefan. *Faustina minor: Ehefrau eines Idealkaisers und Mutter eines Tyrannen*. Bonn: Rudolf Habelt, 2009.

Purcell, Nicholas. "The Populace of Rome in Late Antiquity." In *The Transformation of Urbs Roma in Late Antiquity*, edited by William V. Harris, 135–61. Portsmouth, RI: Journal of Roman Archaeology, 1999.

———. "Rome and Its Development under Augustus and His Successors." In *The Cambridge Ancient History*. 2nd ed. Vol. 10, *The Augustan Empire, 43 BC–AD 69*, edited by Alan K. Bowman, Edward Champlin, and Andrew Lintott, 782–811. Cambridge: Cambridge University Press, 1996.

Quigley, Declan. "Introduction: The Character of Kingship." In *The Character of Kingship*, edited by Declan Quigley, 1–23. London: Routledge, 2005.

Rader, Olaf B. *Friedrich II. Der Sizilianer auf dem Kaiserthron*. Munich: C. H. Beck, 2019.

Ramsey, John T. "A Catalogue of Greco-Roman Comets from 500 B.C. to A.D. 400." *Journal for the History of Astronomy* 38 (2007): 175–97.

Ramsey, John T., and Kurt A. Raaflaub. "Chronological Tables for Caesar's Wars (58–45 BC)." *Histos* 11 (2017): 162–217.

Raschle, Christian R. "Jean Chrysostome et les *exempla* tirés de l'histoire impériale récente." *Dialogues d'histoire ancienne*, supp. 8 (2013): 355–77.

Rawson, Beryl. *Children and Childhood in Roman Italy*. Oxford: Oxford University Press, 2003.

Rawson, Elizabeth. "Caesar's Heritage: Hellenistic Kings and Their Roman Equals." *Journal of Roman Studies* 65 (1975): 148–59.

Rea, John. "A Letter of the Emperor Elagabalus." *Zeitschrift für Papyrologie und Epigraphik* 96 (1993): 127–32.

———. "Österreichische Nationalbibliothek GWT 2." *Zeitschrift für Papyrologie und Epigraphik* 56 (1984): 89–92.

———. "*P. Haun.* III 58: Caranis in the Fifth Century." *Zeitschrift für Papyrologie und Epigraphik* 99 (1993): 89–95.

Reinhold, Meyer. "Usurpation of Status and Status Symbols in the Roman Empire." *Historia* 20 (1971): 275–302.

Rich, J. W. *Cassius Dio: The Augustan Settlement,* Roman History *53.1–55.9*. Liverpool: Liverpool University Press, 1990.

Richlin, Amy. *Arguments with Silence: Writing the History of Roman Women*. Ann Arbor: University of Michigan Press, 2014.

———. *The Garden of Priapus: Sexuality and Aggression in Roman Humor.* Rev. ed. New York: Oxford University Press, 1992.

———. "Not before Homosexuality: The Materiality of the *Cinaedus* and the Roman Law against Love between Men." *Journal of the History of Sexuality* 3 (1993): 523–73.

———. *Slave Theater in the Roman Republic: Plautus and Popular Comedy.* Cambridge: Cambridge University Press, 2017.

Riemer, Ulrike. "Wundergeschichten und ihre Erzählabsicht im Kontext antiker Herrscherverehrung." *Klio* 86 (2004): 218–34.

Ries, Wolfgang. *Gerücht, Gerede, öffentliche Meinung: Interpretation zur Psychologie und Darstellungskunst des Tacitus.* PhD diss., Heidelberg, 1969.

Ripat, Pauline. "Roman Omens, Roman Audiences, and Roman History." *Greece and Rome* 52 (2006): 155–74.

Rives, J. "Human Sacrifice among Pagans and Christians." *Journal of Roman Studies* 85 (1995): 65–85.

Rizzi, Andrea. "Violent Language in Early Fifteenth-Century Italy: The Emotions of Invectives." In *Violence and Emotions in Early Modern Europe,* edited by Susan Broomhall and Sarah Finn, 145–58. London: Routledge, 2016.

Robert, Louis. *Études anatoliennes: Recherches sur les inscriptions grecques de l'Asie Mineure.* Paris: de Boccard, 1937.

Roberts, Penny. "Arson, Conspiracy and Rumour in Early Modern Europe." *Continuity and Change* 12 (1997): 9–29.

Röcke, Werner, and Hans Rudolf Velten. "Einleitung." In *Lachgemeinschaften: Kulturelle Inszenierungen und soziale Wirkungen von Gelächter im Mittelalter und in der Frühen Neuzeit,* edited by Werner Röcke and Hans Rudolf Velten, ix–xxxi. Berlin: De Gruyter, 2005.

Rodkinson, Michael L., ed. *The Babylonian Talmud.* 19 vols. Boston: Talmud Society, 1918.

Rodríguez Adrados, Francisco. *History of the Graeco-Latin Fable.* Vol. 1. Leiden: Brill, 1999.

Rogers, Guy M. "Demosthenes of Oenoanda and Models of Euergetism." *Journal of Roman Studies* 81 (1991): 91–100.

Rogers, John D. "The 1866 Grain Riots in Sri Lanka." *Comparative Studies in Society and History* 29 (1987): 495–513.

Rogers, Robert Samuel. "The Conspiracy of Agrippina." *TAPA* 62 (1931): 141–68.

Röhrich, Lutz. "König, Königin." In *Enzyklopädie des Märchens Online,* edited by Kurt Ranke et al., 134–46. Berlin: De Gruyter, 2016.

Roman, Yves, Bernard Rémy, and Laurent Riccardi. "Les intrigues de Plotine et la succession de Trajan à propos d'un *aureus* au nom d'Hadrien César." *Revue des études anciennes* 111 (2009): 508–17.

Rosenblitt, Alison. "Rome and North Korea: Totalitarian Questions." *Greece and Rome* 59 (2012): 202–13.

Rosillo-López, Cristina. "Introduction." In *Communicating Public Opinion in the Roman Republic,* edited by Cristina Rosillo-López, 7–19. Stuttgart: Franz Steiner, 2019.

———. "Political Participation and the Identification of Politicians in the Late Roman Republic." In *Institutions and Ideology in Republican Rome,* edited by Henriette van der Blom, Christa Gray, and Catherine Steel, 69–87. Cambridge: Cambridge University Press, 2018.

———. "Popular Public Opinion in a Nutshell: Nicknames and Non-Elite Political Culture in the Late Republic." In *Popular Culture in the Ancient World,* edited by Lucy Grig, 91–106. Cambridge: Cambridge University Press, 2017.

———. *Public Opinion and Politics in the Late Roman Republic.* Cambridge: Cambridge University Press, 2017.

Ross, Alan J. *Ammianus' Julian: Narrative and Genre in the* Res Gestae. Oxford: Oxford University Press, 2016.

Rosso, Emmanuelle. "Les 'statues parlantes' de César et Brutus à Rome: Paroles de pierre et identités usurpées." In *Faire parler et faire taire les statues,* edited by Caroline Michel d'Annoville and Yann Rivière, 245–95. Rome: École française de Rome, 2016.

Rostagni, Augusto. *Svetonio.* De poetis *e biografi minori.* Torino: Loescher, 1944.

Rota, Giorgio. "The Man Who Would Not Be King: Abu'l Fath Sultan Muhammad Mirza Safavi in India." *Iranian Studies* 32 (1999): 513–15.

Rott, Hans. *Kleinasiatische Denkmäler aus Pisidien, Pamphylien, Kappadokien und Lykien.* Leipzig: Dieterich, 1908.

Roueché, Charlotte. "Acclamations in the Later Roman Empire: New Evidence from Aphrodisias." *Journal of Roman Studies* 74 (1984): 181–99.

Rougé, J., ed. Expositio totius mundi et gentium: *Introduction, texte critique, traduction, notes et commentaire.* Paris: Éditions du Cerf, 1966.

Rowan, Clare. *Tokens and Social Life in Roman Imperial Italy.* Cambridge: Cambridge University Press, 2003.

Rowley, Alison. "Monarchy and the Mundane: Picture Postcards and Images of the Romanovs, 1890–1917." *Revolutionary Russia* 22 (2009): 125–52.

Rudé, George. *The Crowd in History: A Study of Popular Disturbances in France and England, 1730–1848.* New York: John Wiley, 1964.

Ruffell, I. A. "Beyond Satire: Horace, Popular Invective and the Segregation of Literature." *Journal of Roman Studies* 93 (2003): 35–65.

Ruffini, Giovanni R. *Life in an Egyptian Village in Late Antiquity: Aphrodito before and after the Islamic Conquest.* Cambridge: Cambridge University Press, 2018.

Ruggini, Lellia Cracco. "The Ecclesiastical Histories and the Pagan Historiography: Providence and Miracles." *Athenaeum* 55 (1977): 107–26.

———. *Economia e società nell'Italia Annonaria: Rapporti fra agricoltura e commercio dal IV al VI secolo d. C.* Milan: A Giuffré, 1961.

Ruscu, Dan. "The Revolt of Vitalianus and the 'Scythian controversy.'" *Byzantinische Zeitschrift* 101 (2008): 773–85.

Russell, Amy. *The Politics of Public Space in Republican Rome.* Cambridge: Cambridge University Press, 2015.

Rutledge, Steven H. *Imperial Inquisitions: Prosecutors and Informants from Tiberius to Domitian.* London: Routledge, 2001.

Sabbah, Guy. *La methode d'Ammien Marcellin.* Paris: Les Belles Lettres, 1978.

Sahlins, Marshall. "Kings before Kingship: The Politics of the Enchanted Universe." In *Sacred Kingship in World History: Between Immanence and Transcendence,* edited by A. Azfar Moin and Alan Strathern, 31–52. New York: Columbia University Press, 2022.

Saller, Richard. "Anecdotes as Historical Evidence for the Principate." *Greece and Rome* 27 (1980): 69–83.

Sarmiento-Mirwaldt, Katja, Nicholas Allen, and Sarah Birch. "No Sex Scandals Please, We're French: French Attitudes towards Politicians' Public and Private Conduct." *West European Politics* 37 (2014): 867–85.

Schaberg, David. "Word of Mouth and the Sources of Western Han History." In *Idle Talk: Gossip and Anecdote in Traditional China,* edited by Jack W. Chen and David Schaberg, 17–37. Berkeley: University of California Press, 2014.

Schäfer, Peter. *Der Bar Kokhba-Aufstand.* Tübingen: Mohr Siebeck, 1981.

Scharf, R. "Die 'Apfel-Affäre' oder gab es einem Kaiser Arcadius II?" *Byzantinische Zeitschrift* 83 (1990): 435–50.

Schatkin, Margaret A. "Discourse on Blessed Babylas and against the Greeks." In *Saint John Chrysostom: Apologist,* edited by Margaret A. Schatkin and Paul W. Harkins, 1–152. Washington, DC: Catholic University of America Press, 1985.

Scheidel, Walter. "Emperors, Aristocrats, and the Grim Reaper: Towards a Demographic Profile of the Roman Élite." *Classical Quarterly* 49 (1999): 254–81.

———. "Introduction." In *Rome and China: Comparative Perspectives on Ancient World Empires,* edited by Walter Scheidel, 1–10. Oxford: Oxford University Press, 2009.

Schuler, Christof. "Inscriptions and Identities of Rural Population Groups in Roman Asia Minor." In *Epigraphy and the Historical Sciences,* edited by John Davies and John Wilkes, 63–100. Oxford: Oxford University Press, 2012.

Schulz, Fabian. "*Fragmentum Tusculanum* II und die Geschichte eines Zankapfels." In *Die Weltchronik des Johannes Malalas. Autor—Werk—Überlieferung,* edited by Mischa Meier, Christine Radtki, and Fabian Schulz, 153–66. Stuttgart: Franz Steiner, 2016.

Schwinges, Rainer Christoph. "Verfassung und kollektives Verhalten. Zur Mentalität des Erfolges falscher Herrscher im Reich des 13. und 14. Jahrhunderts." In

Mentalitäten im Mittelalter, edited by František Graus, 177–202. Sigmaringen: Jan Thorbecke, 1987.

Scobie, Alex. "Storytellers, Storytelling and the Novel in Graeco-Roman Antiquity." *Rheinisches Museum* 122 (1979): 229–59.

Scott, James C. *Domination and the Arts of Resistance: Hidden Transcripts.* New Haven: Yale University Press, 1992.

Scott, Kenneth. "The Political Propaganda of 44–30 BC." *Memoirs of the American Academy in Rome* 11 (1933): 7–49.

Scott, R. "Malalas, *The Secret History,* and Justinian's Propaganda." *Dumbarton Oaks Papers* 39 (1985): 99–109.

Scott, Roger. "From Propaganda to History to Literature: The Byzantine Stories of Theodosius' Apple and Marcian's Eagles." In *History as Literature in Byzantium,* edited by Ruth Macrides, 115–31. Basingstoke: Ashgate, 2010.

Scourfield, J. H. D. *Consoling Heliodorus: A Commentary on Jerome, Letter 60.* Oxford: Oxford University Press, 1992.

Seeck, Otto. "Libanius gegen Lucianus." *Rheinisches Museum* 73 (1920): 84–101.

Severy, Beth. *Augustus and the Family at the Birth of the Roman Empire.* London: Routledge, 2003.

———. "Family and State in the Early Imperial Monarchy: The *Senatus Consultum de Pisone Patre,* the Tabula Siarensis, and Tabula Hebana." *Classical Philology* 95 (2000): 318–37.

Shagan, Ethan H. "Rumours and Popular Politics in the Reign of Henry VIII." In *The Politics of the Excluded, c. 1500–1850,* edited by Tim Harris, 30–66. Basingstoke: Ashgate, 2010.

Shanzer, Danuta. "Augustine's *Epp.* 77–78 (a Scandal in Hippo): Microhistory and Ordeal by Oath." *Reading Medieval Studies* 40 (2014): 11–33.

———. "Some Treatments of Sexual Scandal in (Primarily) Later Latin Epistolography." In *In Pursuit of Wissenschaft: Festschrift für William M. Calder III zum 75. Geburtstag,* edited by Stephan Heilen et al., 393–410. Hildesheim: Georg Olms, 2008.

Sharma, Sunil. "Forbidden Love, Persianate Style: Re-Reading Tales of Iranian Poets and Mughal Patrons." *Iranian Studies* 42 (2009): 765–79.

Shatzman, I. "Tacitean Rumours." *Latomus* 33 (1974): 549–78.

Shaw, Brent D. "Bandits in the Roman Empire." *Past and Present* 105 (1984): 3–52.

———. "Rebels and Outsiders." In *The Cambridge Ancient History.* 2nd ed. Vol. 11, *The High Empire,* edited by Alan K. Bowman, Peter Garnsey, and Dominic Rathbone, 361–403. Cambridge: Cambridge University Press, 2000.

———. *Sacred Violence: African Christians and Sectarian Hatred in the Age of Augustine.* Cambridge: Cambridge University Press, 2011.

Shawcross, Teresa. "In the Name of the True Emperor: Politics of Resistance after the Palaiologan Usurpation." *Byzantinoslavica* 66 (2008): 203–27.

Shibutani, Tamotsu. *Improvised News: A Sociological Study of Rumor.* Indianapolis: Bobbs-Merrill, 1966.

Shillony, Ben-Ami. *Enigma of the Emperors: Sacred Subservience in Japanese History.* Leiden: Brill, 2005.

Shoshan, Boaz. *Popular Culture in Medieval Cairo.* Cambridge: Cambridge University Press, 2002.

Shotter, D. C. A. "The Trial of M. Scribonius Libo Drusus." *Historia* 21 (1972): 88–98.

Siebert, Fred S. "The Press and the British Constitutional Crisis." *Public Opinion Quarterly* 1 (1937): 120–25.

Skinner, Alexander. "Violence at Constantinople in AD 341–2 and Themistius, *Oration* I." *Journal of Roman Studies* 105 (2015): 234–49.

Slater, Laura. "Rumour and Reputation Management in Fourteenth-Century England: Isabella of France in Text and Image." *Journal of Medieval History* 47 (2021): 257–92.

Slater, Niall W. "Speaking Verse to Power: Circulation of Oral and Written Critique in the *Lives of the Caesars.*" In *Between Orality and Literacy: Communication and Adaptation in Antiquity*, edited by Ruth Scodel, 289–308. Leiden: Brill, 2014.

Smallwood, E. Mary, ed. *Philonis Alexandrini Legatio ad Gaium.* Leiden: Brill, 1970.

Smith, Christopher. "*Adfectatio regni* in the Roman Republic." In *Ancient Tyranny,* edited by Sian Lewis, 49–64. Edinburgh: Edinburgh University Press, 2006.

Smith, Steven D. "Art, Nature, Power: Garden Epigrams from Nero to Heraclius." In *Greek Epigram from the Hellenistic to the Early Byzantine Era,* edited by Maria Kanellou, Ivana Petrovic, and Chris Carey, 339–53. Oxford: Oxford University Press, 2019.

———. *Man and Animal in Severan Rome: The Literary Imagination of Claudius Aelianus.* Cambridge: Cambridge University Press, 2014.

Sogno, Cristiana. *Q. Aurelius Symmachus: A Political Biography.* Ann Arbor: University of Michigan, 2006.

Solovyova, Sophia. *The National Monarchy and Its Brokers: A Study of Advisers to Nicholas II.* PhD diss., City University of New York, 2005.

Sotinel, C. "How Were Bishops Informed? Information Transmission across the Adriatic Sea in Late Antiquity." In *Travel, Communication and Geography in Late Antiquity,* edited by Linda Ellis and Frank L. Kidner, 54–63. Basingstoke: Ashgate, 2004.

Sotinel, Claire. "La circulation de l'information dans les Églises." In *La circulation de l'information dans les États antique,* edited by L. Capdetery and J. Nelis-Clément, 177–94. Bordeaux: Ausonius, 2006.

———. "Information and Political Power." In *A Companion to Late Antiquity,* edited by Philip Rousseau, 125–38. Oxford: Blackwell, 2009.

———. “L’utilisation des ports dans l’arc adriatique à l’époque tardive (IVe–VIe siècles).” *Antichità Altoadriatiche* 46 (2001): 55–71.

Spacks, Patricia Meyer. *Gossip.* New York: Knopf, 1985.

Spahlinger, Lothar. “Sueton-Studien II: Der wundertätige Kaiser Vespasian (Sueton, *Vesp.* 2,2–3).” *Philologus* 148 (2004): 325–46.

Spellman, W. M. *Monarchies, 1000–2000.* London: Reaktion, 2011.

Speyer, Wolfgang. “Religiöse Betrüger: Falsche göttiche Menschen und Heilige in Antike und Christentum.” In *Fälschung im Mittelalter. Teil V,* edited by Detlev Jasper, 321–43. Hanover: Hahn, 1988.

Spingou, Fonteini. “Snapshots from the Eleventh Century: The Lombards from Bari, a *Chartoularios* from ‘Petra,’ and the Complex of Mangana.” *Byzantine and Modern Greek Studies* 39 (2015): 50–65.

Stallybrass, Peter, and Allon White. *The Politics and Poetics of Transgression.* Ithaca, NY: Cornell University Press, 1986.

Steiner, John. “The Impostor Revisited.” *Psychoanalytic Quarterly* 80, no. 4 (2011): 1061–71.

Stemberger, Günter. *Die römische Herrschaft im Urteil der Juden.* Darmstadt: Wissenschaftliche Buchgesellschft, 1983.

Stenger, Jan. “Libanios und die öffentliche Meinung in Antiochia.” In *Politische Kommunikation und öffentliche Meinung in der antiken Welt,* edited by Christina Kuhn, 231–54. Stuttgart: Franz Steiner, 2012.

Stern, G. C. “Imposters in Ancient Persia, Greece, and Rome.” In *Splendide Mendax: Rethinking Fakes and Forgeries in Classical, Late Antique, and Early Christian Literature,* edited by Edmund P. Cueva and Javier Martínez, 55–72. Groningen: Barkhuis, 2016.

Stevenson, Tom. *Julius Caesar and the Transformation of the Roman Republic.* London: Routledge, 2015.

———. “The Succession Planning of Augustus.” *Antichthon* 47 (2013): 118–39.

Stewart, Peter. *Statues in Roman Society: Representation and Response.* Oxford: Oxford University Press, 2004.

Stewart, Randall, and Kenneth Morrell. “The Oracles of Astrampsychus.” In *Anthology of Ancient Greek Popular Literature,* edited by William Hansen, 285–324. Bloomington: Indiana University Press, 1998.

Stiles, Andrew. “*Non potes officium vatis contemnere vates:* Germanicus, Ovid’s *Fasti,* and the *Aratea.*” *Mnemosyne* 70 (2017): 878–88.

———. “Velleius Paterculus, the Adoptions of 4 CE, and the *Spes* Race.” In *Hope in Ancient Literature, History, and Art,* edited by George Kazantzidis and Dimos Spatharas, 259–74. Berlin: De Gruyter, 2018.

Stone, Rachel, and Charles West. *The Divorce of King Lothar and Queen Theutberga: Hincmar of Rheims’* De divortio. Manchester: Manchester University Press, 2016.

Stoneman, Richard. "Naked Philosophers: The Brahmans in the Alexander Historians and the *Alexander Romance.*" *Journal of Hellenic Studies* 115 (1995): 99–114.

Strathern, Alan. *Unearthly Powers: Religious and Political Change in World History.* Cambridge: Cambridge University Press, 2019.

Stratmann, Gerd. "Golden Rumps and Royal Vaginas: The Body Language of Anti-Monarchical Satire." In *(Un)Making the Monarchy,* edited by Anette Pankratz and Claus-Ulrich Viol, 111–28. Heidelberg: Universitätsverlag Winter, 2017.

Streckfuss, David. "Kings in the Age of Nations: The Paradox of Lèse-Majesté as Political Crime in Thailand." *Comparative Studies in Society and History* 37 (1995): 445–75.

Struve, Lynn A. "The Southern Ming, 1644–1662." In *The Cambridge History of China,* vol. 7, *The Ming Dynasty, 1368–1644,* pt. 1, edited by Denis C. Twitchett and Frederick W. Mote, 471–525. Cambridge: Cambridge University Press, 1998.

Studer, Basil. "Der geschichtliche Hintergrund des ersten Buches *Contra Eunomium* Gregors von Nyssa." In *Gregory of Nyssa,* Contra Eunomium I: *An English Translation with Supporting Studies,* edited by Miguel Brugarolas, 3–39. Leiden: Brill, 2018.

Sumi, Geoffrey S. "Impersonating the Dead: Mimes at Roman Funerals." *American Journal of Philology* 123 (2002): 559–85.

Summers, John H. "What Happened to Sex Scandals? Politics and Peccadilloes, Jefferson to Kennedy." *Journal of American History* 87 (2000): 825–54.

Sünskes, Julia. "Astrologie und Aufstand: Die Angst der römischen Kaiser vor Machtverlust." In Migratio et commutatio. *Studien zur Alten Geschichte und deren Nachleben,* edited by Hans J. Drexhage and Julia Sünskes, 60–67. St. Katharinen: Scripta Mercaturae, 1989.

Suter, Ann. "Paris and Dionysos: *Iambos* in the *Iliad.*" *Arethusa* 26 (1993): 1–18.

Swan, Peter Michael. *The Augustan Succession: A Commentary on Cassius Dio's* Roman History *Books 55–56 (9 BC–AD 14).* New York: Oxford University Press, 2004.

Sweetman, Rebecca. "Networks: Exile and Tourism in the Roman Cyclades." In *Beyond Boundaries: Connecting Visual Cultures in the Provinces of Ancient Rome,* edited by Susan E. Alcock, Mariana Egri, and James F. D. Frankes, 46–61. Los Angeles: Getty, 2016.

Syme, Ronald. *The Augustan Aristocracy.* Oxford: Clarendon, 1986.

———. "Caesar, the Senate and Italy." *Papers of the British School at Rome* 14 (1938): 1–31.

———. *Tacitus.* 2 vols. Oxford: Clarendon, 1958.

Symes, Carol. *A Common Stage: Theater and Public Life in Medieval Arras.* Ithaca, NY: Cornell University Press, 2007.

Talbot, Alice-Mary. "Pilgrimage to Healing Shrines: The Evidence of Miracle Accounts." *Dumbarton Oaks Papers* 56 (2002): 154–73.

Teall, John L. "The Grain Supply of the Byzantine Empire, 330–1025." *Dumbarton Oaks Papers* 13 (1959): 87–139.

Temporini, Hildegard. *Die Frauen am Hofe Trajans.* Berlin: De Gruyter, 1979.

Thomas, Keith. *Religion and the Decline of Magic.* London: Penguin, 1971.

Thomas, Rosalind. *Literacy and Orality in Ancient Greece.* Cambridge: Cambridge University Press, 1992.

Thompson, E. A. *Romans and Barbarians: The Decline of the Western Empire.* Madison: University of Wisconsin Press, 1982.

Thompson, E. P. "The Moral Economy of the English Crowd in the Eighteenth Century." *Past and Present* 50 (1971): 76–136.

Thompson, John B. *Political Scandal.* Cambridge: Polity, 2000.

Thompson, Stith. *The Folktale.* Berkeley: University of California Press, 1977.

———, ed. *Motif-Index of Folk-Literature.* Copenhagen: Rosenkilde and Bagger, 1955–58.

Thomson, R. W., and James Howard-Johnston, eds. *The Armenian History Attributed to Sebeos.* 2 vols. Translated Texts for Historians 31. Liverpool: Liverpool University Press, 1999.

Thonemann, Peter. *The Lives of Ancient Villages: Rural Society in Roman Anatolia.* Cambridge: Cambridge University Press, 2022.

Toher, Mark, ed. *Nicolaus of Damascus.* The Life of Augustus *and* The Autobiography. Cambridge: Cambridge University Press, 2007.

———. "Octavian's Arrival in Rome, 44 BC." *Classical Quarterly* 54 (2004): 174–84.

Tomkowiak, I. "Herrschaft, Herrscher." In *Enzyklopädie des Märchens Online,* edited by Kurt Ranke et al., 894–909. Berlin: De Gruyter, 2016.

Toner, Jerry. "Barbers, Barbershops and Searching for Roman Popular Culture." *Papers of the British School at Rome* 83 (2015): 91–109.

———. *Popular Culture in Ancient Rome.* Cambridge: Blackwell, 2009.

Totelin, Laurence M. V. "Whose Fault Is It Anyway? Plant Infertility in Antiquity." In *The Palgrave Handbook of Infertility in History,* edited by Gayle Davis and Tracey Loughran, 57–75. London: Palgrave MacMillan, 2017.

Tougher, Shaun. *The Reign of Leo VI (886–912): Politics and People.* Leiden: Brill, 1997.

Treggiari, Susan. *Roman Marriage:* Iusti Coniuges *from the Time of Cicero to the Time of Ulpian.* Oxford: Oxford University Press, 1991.

Trimble, Jennifer. "*Corpore enormi:* The Rhetoric of Physical Appearance in Suetonius and Imperial Portrait Statuary." In *Art and Rhetoric in Roman Culture,* edited by Jaś Elsner and Michel Meyer, 115–54. Cambridge: Cambridge University Press, 2014.

Tuori, Kaius. *The Emperor of Law: The Emergence of Roman Imperial Adjudication.* Oxford: Oxford University Press, 2016.

Tuplin, Christopher J. "The False Drusus of A.D. 31 and the Fall of Sejanus." *Latomus* 46 (1987): 781–805.

———. "The False Neros of the First Century A.D." In *Studies in Latin Literature and Roman History V,* edited by Carl Deroux, 364–404. Brussels: Collection Latomus, 1989.

Turcan, Robert. "L'abandon de Nisibe et l'opinion publique (363 ap. J.C.)." In *Mélanges d'archéologie et d'histoire offerts à André Piganiol,* edited by Raymond Chevallier, 875–90. Paris: École pratique des hautes études, 1966.

Turpin, William. "Imperial Subscriptions and the Administration of Justice." *Journal of Roman Studies* 81 (1991): 101–18.

Uther, K.-J. "König und Soldat (AaTh 952)." In *Enzyklopädie des Märchens Online,* edited by Kurt Ranke et al., 175–77. Berlin: De Gruyter, 2016.

Vágó, Eszter B., and István Bóna. *Der spätrömische Südostfriedhof: Die Gräberfelder von Intercisa I.* Budapest: Akadémiai Kiadó, 1976.

Vansina, Jan. *Oral Tradition: A Study in Historical Methodology.* Translated by H. M. Wright. London: Routledge, 2017.

Varner, Eric R. "Execution in Effigy: Severed Heads and Decapitated Statues in Imperial Rome." In *Roman Bodies,* edited by Andrew Hopkins and Maria Wyke, 66–81. London: British School at Rome, 2005.

Veyne, Paul. *Bread and Circuses: Historical Sociology and Political Pluralism.* Translated by Oswyn Murray. London: Allen Lane, 1990.

———. "Le folklore à Rome et les droits de la conscience publique sur la conduit individuelle." *Latomus* 42 (1983): 3–30.

Viermann, Nadine. *Herakleios, der schwitzende Kaiser.* Berlin: De Gruyter, 2021.

Vigourt, Annie. *Les présages impériaux d'Auguste à Domitien.* Paris: Boccard, 2001.

Villard, Renaud. "Incarnare una voce: Il caso della sede vacante (Roma, XIV secolo)." *Quaderni Storici* 121 (2006): 39–68.

Vinson, Martha P. "Domitia Longina, Julia Titi, and the literary tradition." *Historia* 38 (1989): 431–50.

Vivo, Filippo de. *Information and Communication in Venice: Rethinking Early Modern Politics.* Oxford: Oxford University Press, 2007.

Vout, Caroline. *Power and Eroticism in Imperial Rome.* Cambridge: Cambridge University Press, 2007.

Walker, Simon. "Rumour, Sedition and Popular Protest in the Reign of Henry IV." *Past and Present* 166 (2000): 31–65.

Walker, Susan. "Emperors and Deities in Rural Britain: A Copper-Alloy Head of Marcus Aurelius from Steane, near Brackley (Northants.)." *Britannia* 45 (2014): 223–42.

Wallace-Hadrill, Andrew. "*Civilis princeps:* Between Citizen and King." *Journal of Roman Studies* 72 (1982): 32–48.

———. "The Emperor and His Virtues." *Historia* 30 (1981): 298–323.

———. "The Imperial Court." In *The Cambridge Ancient History*. 2nd ed., vol. 10, *The Augustan Empire, 43 BC–AD 69*, edited by Alan K. Bowman, Edward Champlin, and Andrew Lintott, 283–308. Cambridge: Cambridge University Press, 1996.

———. *Suetonius*. 2nd ed. Bristol: Bristol Classical, 1995.

Walquist, Emma M., Christina Byrd, Domenic P. Roberto, and Melissa M. McDonald. "Sexual Assault Gossip: Who Do We Share with and Why?" *Archives of Sexual Behaviour* (2024): 1–17. https://doi.org/10.1007/s10508-024-03045-7.

Walsh, Elizabeth. "The King in Disguise." *Folklore* 86 (1975): 3–24.

Wardle, D., ed. *Suetonius: Life of Augustus*. Oxford: Oxford University Press, 2014.

———. *Suetonius' Life of Caligula: A Commentary*. Brussels: Collection Latomus 1994.

Watson, Lindsay C. "Of Hernias and Wine-Jugs: *Catalepton* 12." *Mnemosyne* 61 (2008): 245–56.

Watson, Patricia A. *Ancient Stepmothers: Myth, Misogyny and Reality*. Leiden: Brill, 1995.

Watts, Edward. "Introduction: Freedom of Speech and Self-Censorship in the Roman Empire." *Revue belge de Philologie et d'Histoire* 92 (2014): 157–66.

Webb, Ruth. *Demons and Dancers: Performance in Late Antiquity*. Cambridge, MA: Harvard University Press, 2008.

Weber, M. *Economy and Society: An Outline of Interpretive Sociology*. Edited by Guenther Roth and Claus Wittich. Berkeley: University of California Press, 1978.

Webster, Jane. "Less Beloved: Roman Archaeology, Slavery and the Failure to Compare." *Archaeological Dialogues* 15 (2008): 103–23.

Wehrli, Fritz. "Gnome, Anekdote und Biographie." *Museum Helveticum* 30 (1973): 193–208.

Weingarten, Susan. "The Rabbi and the Emperors: Artichokes and Cucumbers as Symbols of Status in Talmudic Literature." In *When West Met East: The Encounter of Greece and Rome with the Jews, Egyptians, and Others*, edited by David M Schaps, Uri Yiftach, and Daniela Dueck, 51–65. Trieste: Edizioni Università di Trieste, 2016.

Weisz, Elishewah Rosa. *Stolen Valor: The People Who Commit Military Impersonation*. PhD diss., Sam Houston State University, 2016.

Welch, Kathryn. "*Lux* and *lumina* in Cicero's Rome: A Metaphor for the *Res Publica* and Her Leaders." In *Roman Crossings: Theory and Practice in the Roman Republic*, edited by Kathryn Welch and T. W. Hillard, 313–37. Swansea: Classical Press of Wales, 2005.

Welch, Michael Thomas James. *Tales of Philip II under the Roman Empire*. PhD diss., University of Queensland, 2016.

Wellington, Robert. *Antiquarianism and the Visual Histories of Louis XIV: Artifacts for a Future Past*. London: Routledge, 2015.

Wendt, Heidi. *At the Temple Gates: The Religion of Freelance Experts in the Roman Empire*. Oxford: Oxford University Press, 2016.

West, M. L. *Indo-European Poetry and Myth.* Oxford: Oxford University Press, 2007.

———. "The Metre of Arius' *Thalia.*" *Journal of Theological Studies* 33 (1982): 98–105.

Whitby, L. Michael. "Theophanes' Chronicle Source for the Reigns of Justin II, Tiberius, and Maurice (A.D. 565–602)." *Byzantion* 53 (1983): 312–45.

Whitby, Mary. "Defender of the Cross: George of Pisidia on the Emperor Heraclius and His Deputies." In *The Propaganda of Power: The Role of Panegyric in Late Antiquity,* edited by Mary Whitby, 247–73. Leiden: Brill, 1998.

Whitby, Michael. *The Emperor Maurice and His Historian: Theophylact Simocatta on Persian and Balkan Warfare.* Oxford: Oxford University Press, 1988.

———. "Evagrius on Patriarchs and Emperors." In *The Propaganda of Power: The Role of Panegyric in Late Antiquity,* edited by Mary Whitby, 321–44. Leiden: Brill, 1998.

White, Luise. "Between Gluckman and Foucault: Historicizing Rumour and Gossip." *Social Dynamics* 20 (1994): 75–92.

———. *Speaking with Vampires: Rumor and History in Colonial Africa.* Berkeley: University of California Press, 2000.

Wickham, Chris. "Gossip and Resistance among the Medieval Peasantry." *Past and Present* 160 (1998): 3–24.

Wiemer, Hans-Ulrich. "Akklamationen im spätrömischen Reich. Zur Typologie und Funktion eines Kommunikationsrituals." *Archiv für Kulturgeschichte* 86 (2004): 27–73.

———. *Libanios und Julian: Studien zum Verhältnis von Rhetorik und Politik im vierten Jahrhundert n. Chr.* Munich: C. H. Beck, 1995.

———. "*Voces populi:* Akklamation als Surrogat politischer Partizipation." In *Genesis and Dynamiken der Mehrheitsentscheidung,* edited by Egon Flaig, 173–202. Oldenbourg: De Gruyter, 2013.

Wienand, Johannes. "The Impaled King: A Head and Its Context." In *Civil War in Ancient Greece and Rome: Contexts of Disintegration and Reintegration,* edited by Henning Börm, Marco Mattheis, and Johannes Wienand, 417–32. Stuttgart: Franz Steiner, 2016.

Wilkinson, Kevin W. "The Sarmatian and the Indians: A New Satirical Epigram on the Victory Titles of Galerius." *Zeitschrift für Papyrologie und Epigraphik* 183 (2012): 39–52.

Wille, Günther. Musica Romana: *Die Bedeutung der Musik im Leben der Römer.* Amsterdam: P. Schippers, 1967.

Williamson, Callie. "Crimes against the State." In *The Oxford Handbook of Roman Law and Society,* edited by Paul J. du Plessis, Clifford Ano, and Kaius Tuori, 333–44. Oxford: Oxford University Press, 2016.

Willis, William H., and Klaus Maresch, eds. *The Archive of Ammon Scholasticus of Panopolis.* Vol. 1, *The Legacy of Harpocration.* Opladen: Westdeutscher, 1997.

Wilson, Peter J. "Filcher of Good Names: An Enquiry into Anthropology and Gossip." *Man* 9 (1974): 93–102.

Wiseman, T. P. *Cinna the Poet and Other Roman Essays.* Leicester: Leicester University Press, 1974.

———. *The Death of Caligula.* Liverpool: Liverpool University Press, 2013.

———. "The Games of Flora." *Studies in the History of Art* 56 (1999): 193–203.

———. "Popular Memory." In *Memoria Romana: Memory in Rome and Rome in Memory,* edited by Karl Galinsky, 43–62. Ann Arbor: University of Michigan Press, 2016.

———. *The Roman Audience: Classical Literature as Social History.* Oxford: Oxford University Press, 2015.

Witakowski, Witold, ed. *Pseudo-Dionysius of Tel-Mahre, Chronicle, Part III.* Liverpool: Liverpool University Press, 1996.

Wolff, Catherine. "Comment devient-on brigand?" *Revue des études anciennes* 101 (1999): 393–403.

Wolff, Robert Lee. "Baldwin of Flanders and Hainaut, First Latin Emperor of Constantinople: His Life, Death, and Resurrection, 1172–1225." *Speculum* 27 (1952): 281–322.

Wong, R. Bin. "Les émeutes de subsistances en Chine et en Europe occidentale." *Annales* 38 (1983): 234–58.

———. "Food Riots in the Qing Dynasty." *Journal of Asian Studies* 41 (1982): 767–88.

Woodman, A. J., ed. *The Annals of Tacitus Books 5 and 6.* Cambridge: Cambridge University Press, 2016.

———. *Velleius Paterculus: The Tiberian Narrative (2.94–131).* Cambridge: Cambridge University Press, 1977.

Woodman, A. J., and R. H. Martin, eds. *The Annals of Tacitus Book 3.* Cambridge: Cambridge University Press, 1996.

Woods, David. "On the Death of the Empress Fausta." *Greece and Rome* 45 (1998): 70–86.

Worley, John. *The Anonymous Sayings of the Desert Fathers.* Cambridge: Cambridge University Press, 2013.

———. "The 'Sacred Remains' of Constantine and Helena." In *Byzantine Narrative: Papers in Honour of Roger Scott,* edited by John Burke, 351–67. Canberra: Australian Association for Byzantine Studies, 2006.

Yang, Anand A. "A Conversation of Rumors: The Language of Popular *Mentalitès* in Nineteenth-Century Colonial India." *Journal of Social History* 20 (1987): 485–505.

Yavetz, Z. *Plebs and Princeps.* Oxford: Clarendon, 1969.

Zadorojnyi, Alexei V. "Transcripts of Dissent? Political Graffiti and Elite Ideology under the Principate." In *Ancient Graffiti in Context,* edited by J. A. Baird and Claire Taylor, 110–33. London: Routledge, 2011.

Zaller, Robert. "Breaking the Vessels: The Sesacralization of Monarchy in Early Modern England." *Sixteenth Century Journal* 29 (1998): 757–78.

Ziegler, Ignaz. *Die Königsgleichnisse des Midrasch beleuchtet durch die römische Kaiserzeit.* Breslau: Schlesische, 1903.

Zongli, Lu. *Rumor in the Early Chinese Empires.* Translated by Wee Kek Koon. Cambridge: Cambridge University Press, 2021.

Index